The Hirsch Chumash

חמשה חומשי תורה

מתורגם ומבואר

מאת

הגאון כמוהר״ר **שמשון**

בן כמוהר״ר **רפאל הירש** פ״פ זללה״ה

שומר משמרת הקודש בק״ק עדת ישורון בפפד״ם

ספר ויקרא חלק א׳

תורגם לאנגלית

ע״י

דניאל הברמן

הוצאת פלדהיים ~ יודאיקא פרעסס

ירושלים - ניו יארק, תשס״ח לפ״ק

The Hirsch Chumash

THE FIVE BOOKS OF THE TORAH

Sefer Vayikra - Part 1

Translation and Commentary by

RAV SAMSON RAPHAEL HIRSCH

English Translation
by
Daniel Haberman

FELDHEIM PUBLISHERS ~ JUDAICA PRESS

Jerusalem - New York

Sefer Vayikra 2-volume set
ISBN 1–58330–196–8

First printing, 2000
Second printing, 2008

FELDHEIM PUBLISHERS
POB 43163, Jerusalem, Israel 91350
208 Airport Executive Park, Nanuet, N.Y. 10954

www.feldheim.com

Typography by:
Simcha Graphic, Brooklyn, N.Y.

Printed in Israel

10 9 8 7 6 5 4 3 2

Editors' Foreword

A new English translation of the Hirsch Chumash, ספר ויקרא, marks an important milestone in the dissemination of the works of Rav Samson Raphael Hirsch זצ״ל. The original Hirsch Chumash, with German translation and commentary, was published between 1867 and 1878. It was almost a century later (1956-1962) that a translation of the Hirsch Chumash into English, prepared by Dr. Isaac Levy ז״ל, was published. This major work introduced the English-speaking public to the magnum opus that is Hirsch's Commentary. Due in large measure to Dr. Levy's translation, learning of the Hirsch Chumash has become an integral part of Torah study. A one-volume English edition containing translation of the Scriptural text and excerpts from the Commentary, prepared by Gertrude Hirschler ע״ה and edited by Rabbi Ephraim Oratz, was published in 1986.

The initial English translation was followed shortly by a Hebrew version, translated from the German by Rabbi Mordechai (ben Shamshon) Breuer and edited by Prof. Mordechai (ben Yitzchak) Breuer, which was published between 1966 and 1990. The Hebrew edition has similarly gained a wide following, especially in ארץ ישראל.

In 1995, the Rabbi Dr. Joseph Breuer Foundation undertook the publication of a new English version of the Hirsch Chumash. Rav Breuer זצ״ל had urged that a new English edition of the Hirsch Chumash be prepared which would accommodate modern English usage. It was felt that, despite the enormous contribution that the Levy translation had made to the world of Torah learning, the style of English used was a demanding one for the current and future generations. As Dr. Levy wrote in his introduction to the first volume published (which was ספר שמות), his work was intended as a literal translation of the German. Rav Hirsch's style of writing presents a formidable challenge for translation into an English format that is easily read. Additionally, as Dr. Levy stated in his introduction, certain etymological derivations and other difficult passages were omitted, and there was concern that these would be lost to posterity.

In the current edition, the Foundation has sought to present to the English-speaking public a new work that is a faithful rendering of Rav

Hirsch's translation of and commentary on חמשה חומשי תורה. The translation of the Scriptural verse is essentially that of Gertrude Hirschler, with revisions that take into account modern usage and interpretation in the Commentary. The Commentary is a translation of the Hebrew edition, with consultation of the German edition. Where the language flow of the Commentary permitted, a literal translation was preserved; otherwise, the clearest language was used to most accurately convey the meaning of the German original.

Several points should be noted:

Unless specified, the word "Commentary" in the text refers to the Hirsch Commentary.

In accordance with Rav Hirsch's Commentary to Bereshis, 2:4, translation of the Divine Name in the Scriptural verse is distinguished with regular type when referring to the שם הוי', as opposed to italicized type when referring to אלקים.

Transliterated Hebrew words in the Commentary are italicized if the words are not common to English usage. For example, "mitzvos" is italicized; "mitzvah" is not italicized.

Differentiation is made between the "Halachah" as the corpus of the Law, and the "halachah" referring to a specific law in a particular case.

References to ספר ויקרא are referred to as being "above" or "below" the verse under discussion.

To facilitate learning of the Commentary, the first occurrence of a word or phrase in a פסוק for which Rav Hirsch writes commentary is printed in bold. This should encourage the reader to refer back to the לשון הקרא, which is so crucial to Rav Hirsch's approach. Punctuation has been added for פסוקים from נביאים and כתובים. In a few places, brief explanatory remarks have been inserted in square brackets to clarify Rav Hirsch's words.

The editors appreciate the remarkable work of Rabbi Daniel Haberman, the translator. Only a תלמיד חכם with outstanding proficiency in the English language could have accomplished the goal of preserving Rav Hirsch's style, his interweaving of תורה שבכתב and תורה שבעל פה, his etymological derivations, and his impassioned expression — all in a modern English usage.

The editors wish to acknowledge:

The members of the Schwalbe family for their support of the Hirschian publications, in the tradition of their parents ז"ל;

Mossad Yitzchak Breuer for permission to use the Hebrew edition, and to the family of Hermann Merkin ז"ל for its support;

Yaakov and Yitzchak Feldheim, of Feldheim Publishers, for their personal dedication to this publication, in the spirit of their father Philipp Feldheim ז"ל;

The family of Jack Goldman ז"ל, of Judaica Press, for its cooperation in publishing this new edition;

Nochum Kornfeld and Avrohom Walzer, of Simcha Graphic Associates, for their professional expertise.

May the סייעתא דשמיא that made possible this volume enable the publication of the remaining volumes of the Hirsch Chumash. It is our hope that this work should find favor in the eyes of all those who come to be inspired by the teachings of Rav Hirsch.

Elliott Bondi
David Bechhofer

לז״נ

ר׳ יעקב בן ר׳ יצחק שוואלבע
ואשתו מ׳ חנה בת מוה״ר ר׳ לוי יוסף ברייער
זכרונם לברכה

מאת בניהם ובנותיהם

The Hirsch Chumash

1 1 *And He called to Moshe, and* God *spoke to him from the Tent of Appointed Meeting, saying:*

א א וַיִּקְרָ֖א אֶל־מֹשֶׁ֑ה וַיְדַבֵּ֤ר יְהֹוָה֙ אֵלָ֔יו מֵאֹ֥הֶל מוֹעֵ֖ד לֵאמֹֽר׃
אֹלף זעירא

ויקרא

CHAPTER 1

1 **ויקרא אל משה וגו׳**. If it had said ויקרא ה׳ אל משה וידבר אליו (with the subject, ה׳, separating the two predicates, ויקרא and וידבר), the call would have been construed as an independent act, separate from the speaking — i.e., God called him, in order to speak with him. Scripture, however, says ויקרא אל משה וידבר ה׳ אליו. Worded this way, God's call (ויקרא) is connected to His speaking (וידבר) and serves to define its character: God called and spoke to Moshe, i.e., the speech was initiated by a call to Moshe.

In this way, Scripture teaches us that God's Word to Moshe was addressed *to* Moshe. Scripture thus refutes those who would misrepresent and distort God's revelation to Moshe, as though it were a revelation arising from within Moshe's own heart; as though it were comparable to artificially induced ecstatic states; as though it were merely the inspiration of a man's spirit, which takes place within man; as though "the Jewish religion" were like all other religious phenomena in the world — it, too, being merely a phase in the development of the human spirit.

But this is not the case. Rather, כאשר ידבר איש אל רעהו, "As the word of one man comes to another" (*Shemos* 33:11); as the word spoken by one man to another derives solely from the mind of the speaker and is in no way the product of the thought of the listener — for the word that is heard is not produced inside the listener; he contributes nothing to its creation — so God's Word to Moshe was His Word alone. It did not derive from within Moshe but came to him from without, calling him, interrupting and rousing him from his own thoughts, so that he would concentrate on listening to what God wished to say to him.

This call, which came before God spoke to Moshe, precludes the idea that His Word was preceded by some process taking place within

Moshe. It distinguishes God alone as speaker, and Moshe merely as listener. Moshe did not bring it about that God would speak to him, nor did he have any idea beforehand what God would say to him. The Word came to him from without as a purely historical event — something that simply happened to him.

Perhaps this is the meaning of what our Sages said of the difference between the prophecy of Moshe and that of Bil'am: משה לא היה יודע מתי מדבר עמו עד שנדבר עמו ובלעם היה יודע אימתי מדבר עמו, "Moshe did not know when God would speak to him, until He spoke to him; but Bil'am knew when God would speak to him" (*Sifre, Devarim* 34:10). Their point may have been that Bil'am's prophecy was always preceded by a self-induced state of ecstasy, which was not the case with Moshe's prophecy.

Perhaps for this reason it says of Bil'am's prophecy וַיִּקָּר ה׳ אל בלעם (*Bemidbar* 23). The advent of God's Word to Bil'am is portrayed as something passive, as it were; for Bil'am would bring it about that God's Word would come to him — perhaps by means of a spiritual ascent that he himself would induce. Bil'am would seek out God's Word. Moshe, on the other hand, merited God's Word without preparing for it or anticipating it.

Perhaps also for this reason there is a small א (א זעירא) in the word ויקרא — to allude to the lack of preparation which distinguished the prophecy of Moshe. Of Moshe's prophecy it may be said וַיִּקָּר אל משה (in the *kal*) — God's Word came to Moshe as something that *happened* to him, unforeseen from the start.

A call preceding God's Word is indeed characteristic of Moshe's prophecy. Thus, it says in the ספרא that on every occasion that God spoke to Moshe, a call preceded His Word. Scripture explicitly mentions this, however, in only three places — (1) when God first spoke to him from the אהל מועד (here); (2) when God spoke to him for the first time, viz., at the thorn bush (*Shemos* 3:4); and (3) when God first spoke to him at Mount Sinai (ibid. 19:3) — in order to teach us that in all circumstances and in every place, whether from an isolated thorn bush, from a flaming mountaintop in the sight of the entire people, or in the privacy of the Tent of Meeting, whenever God's Word came to Moshe, a call preceded His Word.

מאהל מועד לאמר. The אהל מועד represents the acceptance of the Torah as a center for the nation's soul. It also signifies that the nation's material

ב דַּבֵּ֞ר אֶל־בְּנֵ֤י יִשְׂרָאֵל֙ וְאָמַרְתָּ֣
אֲלֵהֶ֔ם אָדָ֗ם כִּֽי־יַקְרִ֥יב מִכֶּ֛ם
קָרְבָּ֖ן לַֽיהוָ֑ה מִן־הַבְּהֵמָ֗ה מִן־
הַבָּקָר֙ וּמִן־הַצֹּ֔אן תַּקְרִ֖יבוּ אֶת־
קָרְבַּנְכֶֽם׃

2 *Speak to the Children of Israel and explain it to them: If any man among you would bring near an offering to* God, *from animals — from cattle or from flocks — shall you bring near your offering.*

and spiritual welfare depend on the Torah and are dedicated to the fulfillment of its commandments. It is by virtue of a national life conducted according to the Torah that His Presence will dwell in Israel. All this came to expression in the אהל מועד — as a vision for the future. The ways to the realization of this vision are outlined in the commandments of this book, תורת כהנים. Not only were these commandments revealed in the אהל מועד, but they are essentially its logical consequences: their spiritual source is in the אהל מועד.

2 **דבר אל בני ישראל ואמרת אלהם**. דבר — say it in concise and compact words: תורה שבכתב. ואמרת אלהם — and explain it to them: תורה שבעל פה. (See Commentary to *Bereshis* 1:22.) "אלהם" written חסר: make sure that the Oral Law reaches them in a uniform version. Indeed, despite the destruction of the State and recurring troubles, no controversies developed in the Oral Law until the early years of the Second Temple. Only then did a controversy erupt in regard to the law of סמיכה, which is mentioned just below (in v. 4) and is closely connected to בני ישראל of this verse (see below). Yet even this controversy, according to ר׳ יוחנן (*Chagigah* 16b), did not touch upon a דין דאורייתא, but merely upon a שבות דרבנן.

דבר אל בני ישראל וגו׳ אדם כי יקריב מכם וגו׳ מן הבהמה מן הבקר ומן הצאן תקריבו את קרבנכם. If the explanation of the verse were only according to its plain sense, it would have been sufficient for it to say simply: כי תקריבו קרבן להי בקר וצאן תקריבוהו (cf. וזבחת פסח לה׳ אלקיך צאן ובקר — *Devarim* 16:2), or, according to ר׳ יאשיה (*Sanhedrin* 85b): בקר או צאן. But Scripture does not say this. Instead, the subject, already alluded to by the words בני ישראל, is first extended by a general term, אדם, and then limited by a specification, מכם. The same is done to the object, בקר וצאן:

Scripture first extends it by a general term, בהמה, and then limits it by a partitive preposition, מן. Moreover, in the first clause, Scripture uses the singular, כי יקריב, and in the final clause switches to the plural, תקריבו את קרבנכם. All these are variations in style which are explained by the *halachos* to which they allude.

First, Scripture extends the subject, בני ישראל, by a general term, אדם. Thus, at the very beginning of the laws of the offerings, Scripture opens the gates to all men, whoever they may be — not just to Jews. Any man is entitled to bring near an offering in the Sanctuary.

From the conditional clause כי יקריב we infer that the discussion here is primarily of free-will offerings, נדרים ונדבות; and in the Oral Law it is explicitly stated: נכרים נודרים נדרים ונדבות כישראל (*Chullin* 13b). רש״י, too (ibid. 5a, ד״ה מכם בכם חלקתי), takes the word אדם here in its broad sense — i.e., to include all of mankind and not just Jews. One may say that this is even according to רבי שמעון בר יוחאי (*Bava Metzia* 114b), who sometimes interprets אדם in a limited sense. For אדם is used here in contrast to the term בני ישראל, which preceded it; hence, all would agree that in this context אדם should be interpreted as a general term, in its broad sense (cf. *Yevamos* 61a for a similar interpretation, based on the contrast between אדם and בהמה).

One concludes, then, that it was not the "progressiveness of Shlomo's enlightened spirit" that broadened the "narrow horizons of Mosaic law," enriching the "concept of God and the Sanctuary" with a broad, cosmopolitan outlook. For the very opening of the "Mosaic" laws of the offerings already invests the Sanctuary with its universal mission. In one word it expresses what was said by Yeshayahu of the people of other nations: וַהֲבִיאוֹתִים אֶל־הַר קָדְשִׁי וְשִׂמַּחְתִּים בְּבֵית תְּפִלָּתִי עוֹלֹתֵיהֶם וְזִבְחֵיהֶם לְרָצוֹן עַל־מִזְבְּחִי כִּי בֵיתִי בֵּית־תְּפִלָּה יִקָּרֵא לְכָל־הָעַמִּים, "I will bring them to the Mount of My Sanctuary; I will make them happy in My House of Prayer; their ascent offerings and their meal offerings will find favor on My altar; for My House will be called a House of Prayer for all the nations" (*Yeshayahu* 56:7).

Although the term אדם extends the subject, the added term מכם limits it. This limitation, however, applies only to בני ישראל, who were directly charged with this precept: מכם ולא כולכם – להוציא את המומר. A מומר is excluded because he has turned into "another" and become "un-Jewish." Non-Jews are included without exception; whoever has the calling of "אדם" is entitled to bring an offering to the altar. For a Jew, on the other hand, it is not sufficient to be a human being merely by virtue of such a calling if he is totally at odds with his calling as a human being as defined in the Torah of Israel: בכם חלקתי ולא באומות (*Chullin* 5a). This does not, however, exclude every Jew who has not yet reached moral perfection, for Scripture immediately adds: מן הבהמה – להביא בני אדם שדומין לבהמה. Indeed, this is the very essence of an offering: the one who brings it offers the "animal" side within himself, that which still needs to be refined. He sanctifies and purifies his sensory drives by bringing near the "animal" within himself. מכאן אמרו מקבלין קרבנות מפושעי ישראל כדי שיחזרו בהן בתשובה, "We accept offerings from transgressors in Israel, so that as a result they be moved to repent," חוץ ממומר, but not from a מומר — viz., one who has cut himself off entirely, his whole being, from Judaism; or one who is a מומר with respect to עבודה זרה; or the equivalent, a מומר with respect to חלול שבת בפרהסיא (see *Chullin* 5a).

Perhaps the reason for this halachah, which excludes Jews who have become like gentiles but includes gentiles who were born as gentiles, is as follows. An altar established by Jewish hands would forfeit its mission if an offering of apostate Jews were to be offered upon it. For the mission of the altar is bound up with the spirit of the Jew; hence, when this spirit is heathenized, so is the altar. On the other hand, an altar established by Jews cannot be desecrated by non-Jews. The very reason it was built by the people of Israel was to ultimately draw all the other peoples closer to Hashem, the God of Israel.

קָרְבָּן. We have no word in Western languages that adequately conveys the concept inherent in the Hebrew term קָרְבָּן. The common German translation *Opfer*, deriving from the Latin *offero*, is related to "offering" in meaning; but unfortunately, in the sense of "sacrifice," it has taken on the connotation of destruction, annihilation, and loss — a connotation that is foreign and antithetical to the Hebrew concept of קָרְבָּן.

Even the original meaning of the term *offero*, in the sense of "offering," does not correspond to קָרְבָּן in its full sense. For the idea of an offering implies a prior request or need on the part of the one to whom the object is offered; the purpose of the offering is to meet his request or to satisfy his needs. There is no distinction between an offering and a gift, a present. The concept of קָרְבָּן, however, is far removed from all of these; it is never to be understood as a gift or a present. It is found solely in the context of man's relationship to God, and can only be understood on the basis of the meaning of the root קרב.

The meaning of קרב is in accord with its plain sense: to draw closer, to arrive at a close relationship with someone. It follows, then, that the purpose and the result of הקרבה is a positive attainment, the realization of a more noble existence, and that the opposite — destruction, annihilation, and loss — should not be ascribed to it. It also follows that a קרבן serves to meet the needs of the מקריב, and not the needs of the One to Whom the קרבן is brought near. The will of the מקריב is that something of his own should come into closer relationship with God. This is the very essence of a קרבן; and the act that is designed to bring this about is called הקרבה.

The purpose of a קרבן is to seek God's nearness. קִרְבַת אֱלֹקִים יֶחְפָּצוּן (*Yeshayahu* 58:2); קִרְבַת אֱלֹקִים, which for a Jew is the sole good (*Tehillim* 73:28), without which he feels "בְּהֵמוֹת," beast-like, stripped of the true calling of a human being (ibid. 73:22).

In God's Sanctuary a man will understand that closeness to God is the sole criterion for shaping his outlook on life and for evaluating his true happiness: עַד־אָבוֹא אֶל־מִקְדְּשֵׁי־אֵל אָבִינָה לְאַחֲרִיתָם (ibid. 73:17). There, in the דביר and the היכל, he will see clearly that his spiritual and material happiness will flourish only through closeness to God and the rule of His Law, and that this is his ultimate calling. There, in the חצר, he will learn that the only way to attain God's nearness is total dedication to the illuminating, purifying, life-giving fire of the Torah. There, life's riddles are solved. There, the measure of one's happiness is determined by the measure of one's closeness to God. There, כָּלָה שְׁאֵרִי וּלְבָבִי (ibid. 73:26): body and spirit yearn for the living God and learn to know Him. There, any distancing from God brings ruin — רְחֵקֶיךָ יֹאבֵדוּ (ibid. 73:27). There, the good is found only in closeness to God; moreover, only closeness to God is good for man — קִרְבַת אֱלֹקִים לִי טוֹב (ibid. 73:28). Hence, "happiness" loses its appeal if found far from God, while in God's nearness suffering is sweetened and is even transformed into good. For in God's Sanctuary every spirit, every soul, is refined — to understand and feel what is truly good for man: אַךְ טוֹב לְיִשְׂרָאֵל אֱלֹקִים לְבָרֵי לֵבָב (ibid. 73:1).

קרבן לה׳. ר׳ יוסי אומר: כל מקום שנאמר קרבן אמור ביו״ד ה״א, שלא ליתן פתחון פה לאפיקורסים לרדות, "R. Yosei says: Wherever [Scripture] speaks of offerings, [the Divine Name that begins with] *yud hey* is used, so as not to give *apikorsim* opportunity to degrade the truths of Judaism to the level of pagan delusion" (*Toras Kohanim*, our verse; see Commentary, *Bereshis* 8:20). The Name אלקים is not associated with offerings. In such a context, God does not refer to Himself by the attribute of strict, unrelenting justice, that of God of retribution. God does not demand to be appeased through an offering, in accord with the blasphemous pagan delusion. He does not seek vengeance and thirst for blood and accept the dying animal as a substitute for the man who deserves to die.

Rather, the Name ה׳ is associated with offerings; God refers to Himself by the attribute of mercy. He appears in the full force of His liberating love, which brings into being all of life, sustains its existence anew, and grants it a renewed future. The essence of an offering is not killing, but rebirth and renewal of existence. Spiritual and moral awakening and revival; entering into a life more noble and pure; renewing strength for such a life from the never-failing source of God's love — that is the Jewish concept of an offering. What dies there has died long before — namely, the part that is dead in the person. What is lost there is a mere fleeting thing — but only so long as it remains far from God. But when brought closer to God, it takes its share of eternal life, finding favor before Him.

The Name ה׳, associated with the offerings, also silences the chatter — of today's אפיקורסים — about the "bloody sacrificial cult." Their intention, too, is לרדות, to lower "Mosaic" Judaism from its ideal eternal heights, in order to recast the truth of God's Torah as paganistic drivel, now obsolete.

מן הבהמה מן הבקר ומן הצאן. Scripture first mentions בהמה, a term which, in its broader sense, includes the whole order of mammals: חיה בכלל בהמה (as in *Devarim* 14:4–5). Then it restricts the general term, reducing it to בקר וצאן. Here we have an application of the hermeneutic rule כלל ופרט אין בכלל אלא מה שבפרט; the general term בהמה is limited by the specification בקר וצאן.

בהמה is to be taken, then, in its narrow sense: it includes only animals that, by their nature, submit to man, and excludes חיה, animals of the wild (*Zevachim* 34a). Below (vv. 3 and 10), Scripture again excludes animals of the wild, deeming only cattle and the flock as fit for an offering. From this we derive that a wild animal is unfit even בדיעבד:

בקר וצאן אמרתי לך ולא חיה (*Zevachim* 34a). Thus, only those animals that are by nature capable of cooperation with man are fit to represent his personality in the offering that he brings.

מן הבהמה להוציא את הרובע ונרבע, מן הבקר להוציא את הנעבד, מן הצאן להוציא את המוקצה, ומן הצאן להוציא את הנוגח (*Temurah* 28a–b). The preposition מן indicates a selection and serves to exclude. So does the conjunctive ו, as this letter refers back to the preceding two uses of the word מן and relates them also to the word צאן. Thus, רובע ונרבע (an animal used for sexual immorality), מוקצה ונעבד (an animal set aside for idolatry or one that was worshipped), and נוגח (an animal that killed a person) are all excluded. These represent the ultimate human sins — עבודה זרה גילוי עריות ושפיכות דמים; obviously, then, they are unfit to be brought as offerings. For an offering symbolizes man's sanctification in his approach to God and in the moral and social spheres; hence, in an offering's past there should be nothing related to desecration of sanctity in these three spheres.

The Gemara's question ואיפוך אנא (ibid.) is explained by קרבן אהרן (to our verse) as follows. The first מן excludes רובע ונרבע, and the second excludes עבודה זרה — yet it stands to reason that עבודה זרה should be the very first to be excluded. The Gemara answers that the term בהמה is mentioned in connection with the sin of רובע ונרבע: ואיש אשר יתן שכבתו בבהמה (below, 20:15), while עבודה זרה is called בקר: וַיָּמִירוּ אֶת־כְּבוֹדָם בְּתַבְנִית שׁוֹר אֹכֵל עֵשֶׂב (*Tehillim* 106:20).

Our interpretation of the words בהמה, בקר, צאן (Commentary, *Bereshis* 1:24–25 and *Shemos* 21:37) points to an inherent connection between the terms limited by the word "מן" (בהמה, בקר, צאן) and the characteristics of the animals that are excluded (רובע ונרבע, נעבד, מוקצה, נוגח).

We interpreted בהמה (from the root בהם = בום, which is the root of במה; cf. also פעם: to tread) as an animal that, by its nature, submits to man. This cooperation should not, however, lead to an offense. Thus, מן הבהמה להוציא את הרובע ונרבע.

We interpreted בקר (related to בכר, פקר) as an animal that is independent and self-sufficient. This independence should not, however, lead to deification. Thus, מן הבקר להוציא את הנעבד.

We interpreted צאן (from שאן, with the letter צ indicating effort) as an animal that is maintained through an artificial effort. Only man, however, should see to its proper care; one should not place it in the care of the gods by consecrating it, so to speak, to the gods. Thus, מן

ג אִם־עֹלָה קָרְבָּנוֹ מִן־הַבָּקָר זָכָר תָּמִים יַקְרִיבֶנּוּ אֶל־פֶּתַח אֹהֶל מוֹעֵד יַקְרִיב אֹתוֹ לִרְצֹנוֹ לִפְנֵי יְהוָה׃

3 *If his offering is an ascent offering from cattle, then he shall bring it male and whole, to the entrance of the Tent of Appointed Meeting shall he bring it near, to express his striving before* God.

הצאן להוציא את המוקצה. It also becomes unfit for an offering if it loses the natural mildness of its disposition and no longer is deserving of man's protective care. Thus, ומן הצאן להוציא את הנוגח.

תקריבו את קרבנכם. Scripture starts with the singular, אדם כי יקריב, and finishes with the plural. תורת כהנים derives from here that an עולת בהמה may be brought as נדבת שנים, the joint offering of two (or more) individuals, or as נדבת צבור, the free-will offering of the entire community. In this it differs from עולת עוף, which may be brought jointly by two (or more) but is never brought on behalf of the entire community; and differs also from מנחה, which, as a free-will offering, is brought only by the individual. When we come to consider the meaning of עולת עוף and מנחת נדבה, we will have to address these *halachos*.

3 The previous verse established the classes, and the particular types, of animals relevant to free-will offerings. Now, Scripture begins to discuss קרבן עולה, which is one of the types of offerings.

The opening of this verse in the conditional (אם) teaches us that the restrictions stated in the previous verse apply also to קרבן שלמים — which is the other type of free-will offering; for the meaning of this opening is as follows: "If the קרבן discussed in the previous verse is an עולה..." — implying that it could also have been a שלמים: אם עולה קרבנו – לרבות את השלמים.

Furthermore, Scripture places the predicate, עולה, before the subject, קרבנו, to imply that these restrictions apply as long as there is an עולה — even if it is not קרבנו, his original offering: אם עולה – לרבות את התמורה (*Toras Kohanim*; see also קרבן אהרן, our verse).

עלה. The common translation of עולה is "wholly burned" — i.e., an offering that is entirely consumed by fire. Yet there is almost no basis for this in the root, עלה. The meaning of תָּבוֹא בְכֶלַח אֱלֵי־קָבֶר כַּעֲלוֹת גָּדִישׁ בְּעִתּוֹ (*Iyov* 5:26) is as follows: You will come to the grave in full maturity (כלח = כלה), as the ripe grain rises to fullest perfection. There is certainly no mention of annihilation here. The whole context belies such an interpretation. עלה in the sense of "rising" is also the apparent meaning of the word in the verse אַל־תַּעֲלֵנִי בַּחֲצִי יָמָי (*Tehillim* 102:25): Do not take me upwards; do not take me up from this world. אל תעלני may, however, mean: Do not take me away from here; do not remove me from the world.

Let us compare the names of the other offerings: חטאת, אשם, שלמים, תודה, מנחה. They all point to the reason for the offering and its purpose. None of them is named after a special action that is performed with the offering. It therefore seems to us that the name עולה derives from the need and aspiration לעלות, to ascend and advance.

Elsewhere (Commentary to *Bereshis* 22:2), we have pointed out that since all non-living matter submits to the force of gravity, the Hebrew language therefore depicts all development toward growth and life, toward the spiritual and the good, not as mere progress, but as an ascent and an uplifting (cf. עלה, leaf; תעלה, healing). One who brings an עולה is aware that he must make strides toward goodness and godliness and that he is capable of doing so. Indeed, an עולה is מכפר על עשה ועל לא תעשה הניתק לעשה (*Yoma* 36a), or in the words of *Toras Kohanim* to verse 4: לא תעשה שיש בו קום עשה. The Mishnah, too, in *Makkos* 17a, uses the expression לא תעשה שיש בו קום עשה, meaning: לאו הניתק לעשה.

(The above would also explain what is said in the וידוי of יום כיפור: בין שיש בו קום עשה ובין שאין בו קום עשה. These words refer back to the preceding לא תעשה; thus, their meaning is: whether a לאו הניתק לעשה or a לאו שאינו ניתק לעשה.)

In any case, one who brings an עולה is aware that he has failed to carry out his duty; the purpose of the עולה is to caution against any such failure in the future. Surely, any fulfillment of duty is a positive step forward, an ascent in moral perfection, another step toward the moral heights which lead to closeness to God.

Thus, the עולה is an offering of ascent and advancement; its name gives expression to the very essence of the offering, to its reason and purpose. Viewing עולה conceptually, the phrase אם עלה קרבנו מן הבקר means: If, by advancing, he seeks to draw closer to God, and he wishes to express this by means of an animal from the herd ...

In our essay "Basic Guidelines for a Jewish Symbolism" (*Collected Writings*, vol. III; see also Commentary to *Bereshis* 15:9-21) we have shown that animals appear in Scripture as symbols of human traits. בקר (פר and עגל) represent man who is dynamic, who works in the service of his Master. צאן (כבש and איל, עז and שעיר), on the other hand, represent man whose vital needs are provided for by his Shepherd. בקר and צאן, then, represent the two aspects which, together, comprise the essence of a person's life: his work and his lot.

Here and in verse 10 we are given the option of bringing an עולה from either בקר or צאן. There are times when we admit that we have not fulfilled our duty in the past, and we commit ourselves to discharging it from now onward. We recognize that God has given us a task, to which we must devote all our energies. If this recognition is what underlies our admission and new commitment, we bring an עולה from בקר; we approach God as a פר — or as an עגל which will become a פר — in order to do the work that has been entrusted to us.

Yet there are times when our admission about the past and our commitment for the future stem from the recognition of our indebtedness to God, our Shepherd. We sense that all that we have comes from His hand and is sustained by His providence. We ardently desire to devote to His service our lives, which are in His hands, and resolve to live according to His will with all the strength that He has given us. If this is what informs our awareness, then we bring an עולה from צאן: We approach the Shepherd of Israel as a כבש; or, at the height of feeling our debt of gratitude, we approach Him as an איל, as one of the flock who has been graced with special blessing; or we approach Him as an עז or שעיר, firm in our resolve to resist any temptation that would remove us from Divine guidance.

In this verse, Scripture begins to discuss the law of an עולה from בקר: **אם עולה קרבנו מן הבקר — זכר תמים יקריבנו**. An עולה is brought only מן הזכרים. God expects a person to fulfill his responsibilities with manly independence. The very responsibility with which one is charged makes a "man" of the person, irrespective of that person's gender or status: אם עולה קרבנו – זכר יקריבנו. All of a person's manly strength and independence should be dedicated to serving God. Not with feminine passivity but by manly action does one seek closeness to God through the עולה.

And תמים יקריבנו, whole must be the animal by which one draws closer to God in one's deeds and aspirations. Elsewhere (below,

22:17–25; *Devarim* 15:21), Scripture explains what is termed תמים with respect to the laws of the offerings. The examples specified there amount to a principle: מום שבגלוי ואינו חוזר (a defect that is external and will not naturally become sound again) is considered a מום and disqualifies an animal for use as an offering (*Bechoros* 37a).

מום is to be distinguished from טריפה (a terminal ailment in or injury to the organs), חולה (illness), זקן (old age), and מזוהם (an offensive odor). These, too, disqualify an animal for use as an offering. We derive these disqualifications from the repetition of the word מן. מן הבקר (v. 3) — להוציא את הטריפה (*Menachos* 5b): בקר are left in the fields to fend for themselves; such an animal is disqualified, however, if, as a result of this independence, its condition becomes terminal. מן הצאן, מן הכבשים, מן העזים (v. 10) — להוציא חולה זקן ומזוהם (*Temurah* 28b): צאן require artificial care and protection; such an animal is disqualified, however, if this need derives from a sickly condition of weakness.

A בעל מום may be healthy and hearty, only that it has some external defect that will never right itself, even if only a tiny defect, such as if its ear had become defective in the cartilage (נפגמה אזנו מן הסחוס), or its eyelid was pierced (ריס של עין שניקב), etc., or if one of its limbs was abnormal — for example, a high hip (שרוע), a clubfoot (קלוט), etc.

Malachi condemns the offering up of blind, lame and sick animals, calling this a desecration of God's Name and the altar. He censures the priests for having caused this desecration by their teachings: וְאַתֶּם מְחַלְּלִים אוֹתוֹ בֶּאֱמָרְכֶם שֻׁלְחַן ה׳ מְגֹאָל הוּא וְנִיבוֹ נִבְזֶה אָכְלוֹ. "You desecrate [God's Name]; in your speeches you represent the table of God as detestable and God's harvest as something of which no one would wish to partake" (*Malachi* 1:12). The prophet's censure of the priests is this: In their eyes, God's Sanctuary is not supreme over all; it does not deserve to receive the best and freshest, all the strength and vitality that a man has to offer. For they have degraded it to the level of a hospital, a home for the crippled, founded solely for those whose lives have been shipwrecked. It is a shelter for life's castoffs, who can find no other place. Only the dregs, needed nowhere else, are to be brought to God's House. As it were, only the maimed, who gather crumbs from the table of humanity, are to be brought there. הַקְרִיבֵהוּ נָא לְפֶחָתֶךָ, "Try presenting it to your governor," cries the prophet angrily, "and see whether he will be pleased with you or receive you graciously!" (ibid. 1:8).

This is the same rebuke hurled by Hoshea at the priests of the Kingdom of Israel: כִּי־אָבַל עָלָיו עַמּוֹ וּכְמָרָיו עָלָיו יָגִילוּ, "When the people mourn over themselves, their priests are delighted" (*Hoshea* 10:5). The priests, with their sanctuaries, await the misfortune and grief of their "believers." For it is not the joyous and happy ones who go up to their halls; it is, rather, the blind, the lame, the sick, and the weak, who go on pilgrimages to their altars. Religion, to them, is a consolation for the suffering and the disadvantaged; religion does not hold sway in life that is vibrant and effervescent with the joy of action.

Not so is God's altar, through which Israel calls in the Name of God of the World. For the Sanctuary demands the whole of a person's life — unlimited and total commitment. In return, it grants life that is worthy of the name "life," in which even death and pain lose their force.

Therefore, just as *Kohanim*, to approach and serve at the altar, must be without blemish, so too — and to a greater extent — must the offerings be whole, without blemish. For by offering them, man advances toward and draws near to the Divine Presence.

The Torah prohibits offering a בעל מום in four separate expressions — לא תקריבו, לא תקריבו, לא תקריבו, ואשה לא תתנו מהם — (below, 22:20, 22, 24) — to teach us that a בעל מום is prohibited at each of the stages of הקרבה; thus, המקדיש or השוחט or הזורק or המקטיר בעל מום is liable to the penalty of מלקות (*Temurah* 6b). The פסול of בעל מום is stressed over the other פסולי המוקדשים; for the Torah not only prohibits offering a בעל מום, but prescribes the wholeness of the offering: תמים יקריבנו (our verse); תמים יהיה לרצון (below, 22:21). And the positive command of תמימות goes beyond the negative prohibition of בעל מום. For the concept of בעל מום relates only to visible external defects, whereas תמימות entails internal wholeness as well; hence, if one of an animal's inner organs was found to be missing (מחוסר אבר מבפנים), the animal is פסול for an offering (*Bechoros* 39a).

An offering embodies the nature of our relationship with God; "wholeness" is a primary condition of this relationship. Wholeness with God entails no less than the absolute surrender of one's entire being to Him. It is the essence of בכל לבבך ובכל נפשך ובכל מאדך (*Devarim* 6:5). It is a duty that follows directly from the very first demand made of us: והייתם לי סגלה (*Shemos* 19:5; see Commentary, ad loc.). For this command lays the foundation-stone for our entire mission: our relationship to God must be all-encompassing, without reserve or limit.

Thus, a blemish in the animal to be offered would represent a defect in the *person* seeking to draw near. A defective limb in the animal would represent an aspect of the person's personality, an aspect that he has excluded from total commitment to God. The person offering a defective animal does not attach himself completely to God, with his whole being and in all his relationships; rather, he holds something back and keeps it for himself. But the direct result of the belief in **אחדות** (God's oneness) is total commitment to God. The direct result of **שמע ישראל ה׳ אלקינו ה׳ אחד** is **ואהבת את ה׳ אלקיך בכל לבבך ובכל נפשך ובכל מאדך**. So, too, whoever holds back part of himself, removing it from the domain of his relationship with God, denies God's oneness. Elsewhere (*Bereshis* 17:10), we pointed out that **תמם**, which is the root of **תמים**, not only indicates the most perfect state of being but also rules out any other state of being.

Toras Kohanim on our verse states as follows: **תמים – כשם שאם אינו תמים אינו לרצון כך אם אינו כענין הזה אינו לרצון**. The meaning of this statement is not definite (see **קרבן אהרן**, ad loc.), but perhaps it means as follows: Just as the animal to be offered must be **תמים**, so must the act of **הקרבה** be carried out perfectly **כענין הזה** — in accordance with the procedure outlined in this section. According to this reading of the statement in *Toras Kohanim*, **תמים** functions in the verse not as an adjective modifying the pronominal object "it," but as an adverb modifying **יקריבנו**.

קרבן אהרן, however, cites from **פסיקתא זוטרתא** a different version: **תמים – כשם שהקרבן אם אינו תמים אינו לרצון כך האיש אם אינו תמים אינו לרצון**. In light of this citation, the statement in *Toras Kohanim* can be interpreted as follows: The **אינו** in the statement's second part refers not to the offering, but to the person who brings it. Here, too, in this interpretation we find the same conception as presented above. The offering is an expression of the one who brings it, and the qualities that the offering must have in order to be valid signify human character traits without which the one who brings the offering will not be accepted favorably. **זכר תמים** would then characterize both the subject and the object: his offering should be male and whole, and with manliness and wholeness should he offer it.

יקריבנו. This is the first act that one who brings an offering performs: the **הקדשה**. He consecrates the animal, designating it for use as an offering. In this way, he "brings it near" to God. Bringing the animal spatially near is referred to only in the second half of the verse (קרבן אהרן).

אל פתח אהל מועד יקריב אותו. One who wishes to draw near to God should draw near to His Torah. One who wishes לעלות, to ascend and progress, should progress through the performance of *mitzvos*. For this reason, an offering that is consecrated to God is to be brought to the entrance of the Tent of Appointed Meeting; because one who seeks God must seek out His Torah, the testimony to which rests in the ארון. And God previously said: ונועדתי לך שם (*Shemos* 25:22) — that is the place that I have appointed for Myself to meet you. Where the testimony to My Torah rests, there will you find me.

יקריב אותו לרצונו. יקריב אותו, it is obligatory upon him to bring the offering, but לרצונו, the offering should be an expression of his own inner will. From here we learn that he must direct his will in a certain way. On the one hand, the very bringing of the offering is no longer dependent upon his will, as he has already consecrated the animal for use as an עולה, as it says beforehand: יקריבנו. This consecration has the force of a vow to God, and he must fulfill what he has uttered with his lips. The court may even pressure him in this regard, if need be, in the same way that they are to resort to coercion vis-à-vis all *mitzvos*. יקריב אותו implies כופין אותו.

On the other hand, it is incumbent upon him to bring the offering לרצונו — as an expression of his own will before God. Only if he offers it as such does he fulfill his vow. For this reason it is not sufficient for the court to compel him to bring the offering; rather, כופין אותו עד שיאמר רוצה אני, "they pressure him until he says, 'I wish (to bring it).'" We assume that one who says רוצה אני truly wishes to carry out the act — even if he was coerced to say the words.

This assumption applies to a case where they pressure him to fulfill a mitzvah or to perform an act that brings him no actual loss. Hence, the Mishnah says: חייבי עולות ושלמים ממשכנין אותן אף על פי שאין מתכפר לו עד שיתרצה שנאמר לרצונו, כופין אותו עד שיאמר רוצה אני. Similarly, if he is obligated by law to divorce his wife כופין אותו עד שיאמר רוצה אני (*Arachin* 21a). The rationale of the Mishnah is elucidated in *Kiddushin* (50a) and *Bava Basra* (48a): דאנן סהדי דניחא ליה בכפרה and משום דמצוה לשמוע דברי חכמים. Hence, if they force him to fulfill a mitzvah, it is enough that he says רוצה אני; we pay no heed to the circumstances that led him to make this

4 *He shall lean his hand upon the head of the ascent offering; thus it will be accepted as being in accordance with the Divine Will, to effect atonement for him.*	ד וְסָמַךְ יָדוֹ עַל רֹאשׁ הָעֹלָה וְנִרְצָה לוֹ לְכַפֵּר עָלָיו׃

statement. We assume that he has agreed to perform the mitzvah because he is truly repentant. Similarly, תליוהו וזבין זביניה זביני: If he is compelled to express agreement to a sale and then peacefully goes through with the sale, we assume that אגב אונסיה גמר ומקני (ibid.) — since he is forced to agree, he then sells of his own free will.

The law is different, however, where he is forced to carry out an act that is not obligatory upon him (גט מעושה שלא כדין) or he is coerced to give away something without receiving payment (תליוהו ויהיב). In such a case, we pay no heed to his verbal agreement; we do not assume that he carried out the act willingly. Hence, an act carried out under such circumstances has no legal force (see תוספות, ad loc.).

4 **וסמך ידו על** is not merely the laying-on of one's hand. The principal meaning of סמך is to support or to lean upon. In only a few cases is this not its meaning; but even in those cases, it is always indicative of intense contact, in terms of nearness in place or length of time. For example: סָמַךְ מֶלֶךְ־בָּבֶל (*Yechezkel* 24:2) — the king drew exceedingly close; עָלַי סָמְכָה חֲמָתֶךָ (*Tehillim* 88:8) — for a long time Your wrath has assailed me. Similarly, the halachah states: סמיכה בכל כחו בעינן, "סמיכה must be with all one's strength" (*Chagigah* 16b) and with both one's hands (*Menachos* 93a).

סמיכת יד על is found further (1) at the inauguration of the *Levi'im*: וסמכו בני ישראל את ידיהם על הלוים (*Bemidbar* 8:10); (2) at the appointment of Yehoshua: וסמכת את ידך עליו (ibid. 27:18), ויסמך את ידו עליו ויצוהו (ibid. 27:23), ויהושע בן נון מלא רוח חכמה כי סמך משה את ידיו עליו (*Devarim* 34:9); and (3) at the execution of the blasphemer: וסמכו כל השמעים את ידיהם על ראשו (below, 24:14). Let us attempt to find the common concept that is expressed in these three סמיכות (rites of leaning).

The common denominator in the first two cases is clear. In both, the one who performs the leaning grants authority to another, this authority being intrinsically related to the personality of the one who leans. The community authorizes the *Levi'im* to substitute for it in the Service of the Sanctuary. Moshe appoints Yehoshua as his successor to lead the nation. This rite of leaning, then, incorporates two ideas: granting and gaining, as one who grants authority gains a representative, thus increasing the grantor's power in terms of place or time. The obligation of the community is fulfilled through the Service of the *Levi'im*, whereas the community itself is exempted from Service. Through Yehoshua, Moshe's life and work are continued. Thus, the hand of the one who leans represents his duty and his authority to act. This "hand" is transferred to the one who is leaned upon, the "hand" itself thereby gaining him as a support.

How does the third case, the leaning upon the head of the blasphemer performed by the witnesses and judges, fit in? *Toras Kohanim* (below, 24:14) explains as follows: אומרים לו דמך בראשך שאתה גרמת לכך, "They say to him, 'Your blood is on your own head, as you have brought it about yourself.'" They place upon him the responsibility for his own death. Their "hand," which acts against him, is none other than his own hand, supported by himself. He and his own actions have obligated and authorized them to act. Here, we observe, the relation has been reversed. The essence of this rite of leaning is to receive support: the one who leans is supported, i.e., empowered to act, by the one who is leaned upon. Nevertheless, even here, there is giving and gaining. The sinner himself, as it were, carries out the act that is executed upon him; he bears the burden of the act, while the judges and witnesses are freed of responsibility.

Now let us ask: what is the meaning of סמיכת יד on the head of an offering?

We would explain simply as follows. The "hand" of the one who brings an offering had been weak and had violated a positive or negative commandment. Now, he "supports" this "hand" with a decision of the heart, which is expressed in the offering. From now onward, his hand will be steady in remaining faithful to the commandments.

According to this explanation, the rite of leaning, here, too, is essentially for the sake of receiving support. Yet it also contains an element of "giving," in that the leaning of the "hand" invests the offering with its special relation to the deeds of the one who leans. Proof to this idea may be adduced from the fact that סמיכה is performed only at those offerings which are related to active man and to his actions, such as

אשם, עולה, חטאת, and שלמים; it is not performed at בכור, מעשר, and פסח, since these derive essentially from relations of property and lot in life (see *Menachos* 92b).

This connection between סמיכה and atonement for one's actions would explain the halachah that an agent cannot perform סמיכה: ידו ולא יד שלוחו (ibid. 93b). The "hand" that seeks atonement through an offering must itself perform the סמיכה. This is also the law when an offering is brought jointly by two or more people: קרבנו – לרבות כל בעלי קרבן לסמיכה (ibid. 94a). Every one who wishes to bring his deeds closer to God by means of an offering must lean his hand on it.

Perhaps this is the reason why סמיכה is generally not performed at קרבנות צבור, as in their case it would be impossible for all the בעלים to perform סמיכה. Thus, the absence of סמיכה at an offering, because it lacks definite בעלים, is a sure sign of it being a קרבן צבור.

סמיכה is performed at only two קרבנות צבור: (1) פר העלם דבר של צבור, where three elders of the בית דין perform סמיכה (the Mishnah in *Menachos* [92a] refers to this קרבן as "פר הבא על כל המצות," but as a rule this term refers to פר כהן המשיח), and (2) שעיר המשתלח, where the כהן גדול performs סמיכה.

The performance of סמיכה at these two קרבנות צבור could be explained as follows. The פר העלם דבר של צבור is brought first and foremost for an error of בית דין. The special relationship between this קרבן and בית דין is therefore expressed by the סמיכה performed by the elders. Similarly, in the case of שעיר המשתלח, the סמיכה performed by the כהן גדול proclaims that the כפרה includes *Kohanim* as well. They, too, live among their people and need atonement like the rest of the community. This is in accordance with R. Yehudah's view (ibid.), which is accepted as the halachah.

According to the explanation outlined above, however, סמיכה derives entirely from the intrinsic relation between the offering and the one who seeks closeness to God through the offering; it derives from the purely individualistic and personal standpoint. Hence, we would expect סמיכה to apply to all persons and to be indispensable to the atonement. Yet the halachah does not confirm this, as we learn in *Menachos* (93a): הכל סומכין חוץ מחרש שוטה וקטן וסומא ונכרי והעבד והשליח והאשה, and in the immediately following statement וסמיכה שירי מצוה, which is explained there as follows: שאם עשאה לסמיכה שירי מצוה מעלה עליו הכתוב כאלו לא כיפר וכיפר (ibid. 93b). That is to say, סמיכה merely completes the mitzvah; like שירים, it is not the essential part. Even if one does not perform

סמיכה, he still attains the basic atonement; it is only that Scripture regards it as though he had not attained atonement: וסמך ידו ... ונרצה לו לכפר עליו (see below). We must therefore say that סמיכת קרבנות includes an additional concept which would explain these *halachos*.

An examination of the list of those who are exempted from סמיכה reveals that, except for the שליח, their common denominator is that their disqualification lies not in the personal but in the national realm. They do not represent the national mission of fulfilling the Torah, at least not on the front line. Even סומא, a blind person, is exempt from סמיכה, as he is also exempt from the national mitzvah of ראיה, the duty to appear before the Presence of God three times a year. A סומא is also disqualified from being a judge; he cannot be one of the זקני העדה (ibid. 93a).

We pointed out above (v. 2) that the laws of the offerings elaborated here apply to all men, to every אדם, whereas the specification בני ישראל applies only to the law of סמיכה, a law that can be fulfilled only by the בעלים and whose content is linked to the personality of the one bringing the offering. Both נכרי and אשה are therefore exempt from סמיכה.

Thus, in סמיכה at an offering, the סומך appears not only as an individual but as one of the sons of the national Jewish community. סמיכת הקרבן, then, resembles סמיכת הלויים and סמיכת יהושע; it entails not only gaining and receiving support, but also granting.

This is how we would explain the meaning of סמיכה: The סומך appears as a representative of the Torah vis-à-vis himself. In this way he expresses the idea that the demands of the Torah represented by this offering are made in *his* name. He addresses the demands of the Sanctuary to himself. Were it not for the סמיכה, the address would issue from the Sanctuary; it would be the Sanctuary which demands of him to progress or to remain within the bounds of the good. Through סמיכה, however, he addresses himself in the name of the Sanctuary; he is one of בני ישראל, who as a nation bear the yoke of the Torah; he gives the order, in the name of the Torah and for the sake of the fulfillment of its commandments, לשחוט ולהקריב (for this reason תיכף לסמיכה שחיטה, the שחיטה should follow immediately after the סמיכה [*Zevachim* 33a]). This constitutes atonement of the highest order for his negligence or folly, for now he remembers his standing as a "Man of Israel." As a member of the national community it is his responsibility that others fulfill the Torah, and how much more so is it his responsibility to keep himself from negligence and folly.

ה וְשָׁחַט אֶת־בֶּן הַבָּקָר לִפְנֵי יְהוָה וְהִקְרִיבוּ בְּנֵי אַהֲרֹן הַכֹּהֲנִים אֶת־הַדָּם וְזָרְקוּ אֶת־הַדָּם עַל־הַמִּזְבֵּחַ סָבִיב אֲשֶׁר־פֶּתַח אֹהֶל מוֹעֵד׃

5 *He shall then slaughter the animal of the cattle species before* God; *and Aharon's sons, the priests, shall bring the blood near and dash the blood against the altar that is at the entrance to the Tent of Appointed Meeting, all around.*

In light of the above we can understand that סמיכה is not מעכבת כפרה, but without סמיכה his כפרה is incomplete. In *Zevachim* (6a–b) this is stated as follows: כיפר גברא, לא כיפר קמי שמיא. The meaning of this statement is perhaps: without סמיכה he can achieve atonement as a גברא, as an individual — no less than all those who by law are exempt from סמיכה — but he does not yet complete his atonement קמי שמיא, in his standing before God as a "Man of Israel." We also now understand the halachah that סמיכה is observed only לפני ה׳ — in the משכן and in the מקדש; for the relation of the offering to God is there portrayed as a relation to the Torah. At a במה, however, סמיכה is not observed, for there is no expression there whatsoever of such a relation (ibid. 119b).

על ראש העולה. Only סמיכה on the head of the offering relates to the animal as a whole; סמיכה on any other part would relate only partially.

העולה. Any עולה requires סמיכה, whether an עולת חובה or an עולת נדבה. However, the definite article ה (in העולה) serves to exclude. Thus, סמיכה is observed only at עולת בהמה which is under discussion here, but not at עולת העוף (see Commentary to v. 14).

לכפר עליו. The כפרה is dependent not on the סמיכה but on the זריקת הדם, as only the latter expresses the devotion of the נפש, the whole personality, to the task required of us by the Torah. סמיכת ידים על ראש העולה, rather, commits all the strength of the Man of Israel to the devotion of self which is expressed by the זריקה. This constitutes complete preparation for כפרה, as explained above.

5 **ושחט וגו׳ והקריבו בני אהרן וגו׳**. The כהנים are mentioned only with the הקרבה. From this we see that שחיטה כשרה בזר — the act of שחיטה may be

performed by anyone — and that only מקבלה ואילך מצות כהונה. Receiving the blood in a Service vessel is the third הקרבה, the third "bringing near" of the קרבן. The first is consecrating the animal for use as an offering, the הקדשה (v. 2); the second is bringing the animal into the עזרה (v. 3). With the third begins the Service of the כהנים (*Zevachim* 32a).

שחיטה is a prerequisite for entrance into the sphere of the Sanctuary. It represents the cessation of all existence that is merely physical and selfish.

Indeed, this is the source of all negligence and foolishness: the human being — whose נפש is present in the דם — still serves himself; in some respect he still concerns himself only with his purely physical existence; he has not yet ceased to live for himself; he has not yet completely subordinated himself to God's kingship.

But one who seeks to draw near to God by means of an offering will desist from such a selfish existence. He dedicates an animal as an offering as a means of self-expression. Since it is clear to him that one who seeks God must seek Him by way of His Law, he brings to the entrance of the Sanctuary the animal he has dedicated. There, he fulfills the law of סמיכה; as a Man of Israel he demands of himself to fulfill the prerequisites for attaining closeness to God, and devotes toward this end his whole future life of endeavor. Having done all this, he then slaughters his offering (either by himself or through the service of his agent). In this way he becomes conscious of the first of these prerequisites: the nullification of his egocentric being. This prerequisite can be met only לפני ה׳, before God and His Torah. But it is not the Sanctuary that should effect this nullification of a person's being; rather, the person himself should nullify himself before God. Only then can he move from negation to affirmation; for the Sanctuary will teach him of God's ways, and he will walk in His paths.

This idea would explain the halachah mentioned above: שחיטה כשרה בזרים ובנשים ובעבדים ובטמאים ואפילו בקדשי קדשים וכו׳ (ibid. 31b); it would also explain the halachah that the שחיטה must be לפני ה׳ — "ולא השוחט לפני ה׳" (ibid. 32b), that is to say: the act of שחיטה is valid only inside the עזרה, but the שוחט, the one who performs the act, may stand outside; and it would explain why generally שחיטה לאו עבודה היא (ibid. 14b) — שחיטה is not an עבודה (an act of Service). This is most characteristic of the Jewish concept of offerings. The common notion is that שחיטה is the central part of the offering, but the truth of the matter is that שחיטה is not part of the "cult"; even in its symbolic meaning, it is merely a necessary precondition. Not by killing and not by self-destruction does man serve God. שחיטה is merely a prerequisite for קבלה and the rest of the עבודות; it merely affords entry to a higher stage of life and activity. Only when one has attained a higher and holier existence does he begin to serve God!

That is why Scripture here, regarding שחיטה, speaks of בן הבקר, whereas regarding סמיכה (in the preceding verse) it calls the animal עולה, and also below (v. 6) the animal is called עולה. For this is the whole essence of שחיטה: it serves to nullify the בן הבקר existence that is not ruled by the Law; only then does the animal become fit to be an עולה.

In spite of this — or precisely because of this — שחיטה must be carried out with full awareness; the שוחט must direct his mind to the animal standing before God: מנין למתעסק בקדשים שהוא פסול שנאמר ושחט את בן הבקר לפני ה׳ עד שתהא שחיטה לשם בקר. Moreover, if the שחיטה is performed with one's mind on something else (מתעסק בדבר אחר) — e.g., if one thought one was slaughtering an unconsecrated animal (שחט משום חולין) — the offering is invalidated. That such an offering is invalidated is derived from the fact that Scripture states in another place as well that שחיטת קדשים requires כוונה: לרצונכם תזבחהו (below, 19:8) — i.e., לדעתכם תזבחהו. Scripture reiterates the requirement of כוונה to teach us that כוונה is indispensable: שנה עליו הכתוב לעכב (*Zevachim* 47a). Any rule concerning offerings which is repeated becomes an indispensable condition.

בן הבקר. In *Rosh Hashanah* (10a) it says: כל מקום שנאמר עגל בתורה סתם בן שנה בן בקר בן שתים פר בן שלש. רש״י and תוספות explain — and it is also evident from the word סתם — that the statement of the Gemara בן בקר בן שתים refers to the use of the term בן בקר in conjunction with עגל: an עגל בן בקר is two years old, as a פר בן בקר is three years old (see below, 4:3). The inference is that בן בקר serves to indicate age only when attached to עגל or to פר; בן בקר alone, however, indicates only the type of the animal and includes both עגל and פר. This suits our verse well, as an עולת נדבה can be either an עגל or a פר, and there is no reason why our verse should speak only of a *young* bull (compare, however משנה למלך הל׳ פרה אדומה פ״א הלכה א׳ בסוף דבריו).

והקריבו. This "bringing near" includes קבלה and הולכה: the כהן receives the blood in a כלי שרת, a Service vessel, and conveys it to the place from which the blood is to be dashed upon the altar.

As we have pointed out (*Shemos* 29:37; 30:29), a כלי שרת sanctifies all of its contents and includes them within the sphere of the Sanctuary. The שחיטה arrested the דם הנפש and nullified the selfishness that had distinguished it previously. Now the blood is received in a כלי שרת, and in this way is elevated and comes to belong to the Sanctuary. The הולכה, the conveying of the blood into the spatial proximity of the altar, is a physical representation of the conceptual הקרבה ("bringing near") that had been realized already at the time of קבלת הדם. For this reason הולכה is termed an עבודה שאפשר לבטלה: if the blood is received near the altar, so that זריקה can be performed from that very place, then הולכה is not done (*Zevachim* 4a; but see משנה למלך הלכות פסולי המוקדשין, 1:23).

בני אהרן הכהנים. בני אהרן הכהנים – שתהא בכהן כשר ובכלי שרת (*Zevachim* 13a). "בני אהרן" denotes personal כשרות: unblemished lineage and wholeness in body — i.e., not חללים and not בעלי מומין. "הכהנים" denotes priestly character, which is expressed through external appearance — i.e., כהנים dressed in the priestly garments (see Commentary to *Shemos* 28:43). It is worth noting that, in this citation from *Zevachim*, the בגדי כהונה are called כלי שרת (literally, service vessels). As a service vessel receives an article for the needs of the Sanctuary, so, too, a כהן assumes the Service of the Sanctuary by donning the priestly garments. And only so long as he wears the garments does he appear as one who serves in the Sanctuary; only if he is wearing sacred garments does he represent the symbolic meaning of his office.

Furthermore, כל מקום שנאמרה כהונה (wherever the Torah identifies the performer as a כהן) in a דבר המעכב כפרה (an act of Service that is indispensable to כפרה), אינה אלא ימין (the act may only be performed with the right hand) (*Menachos* 10a). That is the case here: the כהן must execute the קבלה with his right hand; and if he does it with his left hand, it is invalid. Indeed, with force and power (signified by the mighty right hand) should he carry out this act which teaches us how to draw closer to God.

וזרקו וגו' סביב. In *Zevachim* (53b) the nature of this *avodah* is explained as follows: יכול יזרקנו זריקה אחת תלמוד לומר סביב אי סביב יכול יקיפנו בחוט תלמוד לומר וזרקו (פירש"י: ואין זריקה אלא מרחוק ובחוט אי אפשר להקיף אלא באצבע ובנגיעה) הא כיצד כמין גמא ודמה טעון שתי מתנות שהן ארבע. In other words, זריקה and סביב are the two defining features of this *avodah*. The blood is thrown from a distance and reaches "all around," on all four sides of the altar.

For it is dashed in two זריקות, against two diagonally opposite corners of the altar, and each one of these two זריקות constitutes a זריקה סביב. How so? When the blood dashes against one of the corners, it spreads to both sides of that corner. Hence, when this is repeated on the diagonally opposite corner, the blood — via these two dashings — will have reached the four sides of the altar: שתי מתנות שהן ארבע.

The blood is dashed against the northeast corner and against the southwest corner, the מזרחית צפונית and מערבית דרומית. Only these two corners are fit for זריקה — not the southeast or northwest corners. The reason for this is explained in *Yoma* (15b): עולה טעונה יסוד וקרן דרומית מזרחית לא הוה ליה יסוד. This is also the case with the other offerings whose blood is dashed against the lower half of the altar, namely אשם and שלמים. In all these offerings, the blood must be dashed above the יסוד (the base) of the altar — and the southeast corner has no base.

In our Commentary to *Shemos* (27:8) we explained the ideas that are expressed in the structure of the altar. We also explained there the differences between the national altar in the Sanctuary and a *bamah*. This is how it seems to us: The term הראל expresses the notion of elevation of the earth to God; it alludes to the elevation of all earthly powers, the elevation of man with all his earthly powers — over the earth and from the earth — to God.

A further development of this idea is that the altar in the Sanctuary must have a יסוד. This teaches us the course that a person should choose for himself in order to elevate all earthly powers to God. He should fulfill God's Will with all his earthly powers; that is, he must stand firmly on the ground of the national Sanctuary of the Torah, where the יסוד of the altar of ascent was established.

This is the law for one who brings his offering to this altar: Through the *avodos* of the דם, his נפש will learn the way to ascend to God. He should base his deeds on the foundation of the Torah, which was passed on to him by the nation, and only on this foundation will he find the way that ascends to God.

This is also the rule for the non-Jew who brings his offering to this altar: He should learn to know God, as revealed in Israel. He, too, should fulfill the general commandments that were revealed in the Torah of Israel for all mankind (the Noachide laws).

We can understand that this relation to the "base" is emphasized primarily at דמים תחתונים — at the עולה and the like. For these teach only of the beginning of the ascent; they bring a person to the עזרה, which leads to the heights of the altar (the lower half of the altar is called עזרה; see our Commentary, ibid.).

We also explained there (ibid.) the significance of the square shape that is characteristic of the altar in the Sanctuary. We observed that the altar loses all its meaning if the doors of the Sanctuary, פתח אהל מועד, are shut. These two *halachos* are emphasized here by the words המזבח סביב אשר פתח אהל מועד (see *Toras Kohanim* on our verse, and *Zevachim* 62b).

It seems, then, that the altar is a means to the higher purpose of which the Sanctuary teaches; the altar derives all its meaning from the Sanctuary. Furthermore, the Sanctuary courtyard and halls are of differing levels of sanctity. What these represent in a horizontal sequence, the altar represents through upward projection. Consequently, once the doors of the Sanctuary are opened, the sides of the altar take on the meaning of the sides of the Sanctuary: The west side, through the ארון, represents the Torah. The south side, through the מנורה, represents the spiritual. The north side, through the שולחן, represents material prosperity. On the east side is situated the gate through which the people may enter the Sanctuary; the east, then, represents the people on its way to the Sanctuary, a people whose sources are שולחן ,תורה and מנורה, and whose ultimate perfection is represented by the מזבח הקטרת.

These sides converge at corners, whose significance is as follows. The southwest corner represents a spiritual life that flows from the Torah. The southeast corner represents a nation whose source is in the spiritual life and whose direction is to the Torah. The northeast corner represents material prosperity that is developed through the powers of the nation. The northwest corner represents material plenty that is dedicated to the Torah and whose source is the nation uplifted by the spirit of the Torah. To summarize: southwest = the spiritual whose source is the Torah; southeast = the nation whose source is in the spiritual life and whose direction is to the Torah; northeast = material plenty produced by the nation; northwest = Torah fulfilled out of prosperity.

Any progress toward perfection (as embodied by the עולה offering), any cleaving to heights already attained, can be achieved only by the combination of all these aspects. The Torah must be the source of the spiritual; the spiritual must awaken the consciousness of Israel as to its national mission in Torah; only in the spirit of such consciousness are material property and life to be pursued; and all property and material life must be dedicated to the fulfillment of the Torah.

These four fundamentals are alluded to in the mitzvah of תפלין. In תפלין של ראש these fundamentals address the consciousness, each one by itself; in תפלין של יד they are put into practice, combined. קדש is the consecration of the nation through the Torah — east. והיה כי יביאך is the material prosperity granted to the nation — north. שמע is the spiritual life awakened by the Torah — south. והיה אם שמוע is the fulfillment of the Torah out of prosperity — west. Or, better: קדש — southeast; והיה כי יביאך — northeast; שמע — southwest; והיה אם שמוע — northwest.

We have already pointed out in our essay on the שמונה עשרה (*Collected Writings*, vol. III) that it is emblematic of the entire Jewish concept of history that the קרן דרומית מזרחית, the southeast corner of the altar, had no יסוד. Only on the northern and western sides was there a complete base; on the eastern and southern sides, however, there was only the beginning of a base: one cubit at the northeast corner and one cubit at the southwest corner. The length of the base of the altar was thirty-two cubits, but on the eastern and southern sides thirty-one cubits were missing. The meaning of this is as follows:

We received from God תורה and ארץ ישראל, a good and desirable land. These are represented by west and north, and their basis was firm and complete. However, these gifts given to us by God demand of us dedication and action, a spiritual life whose source is the Torah, and a national life deriving solely from the Torah. These are represented by south and east, and only a beginning has been made in them. Perhaps it is not too bold to say that the lack of the southeastern basis has been the cause of all the adversity in Jewish history, whereas the completion of the southeastern corner is the goal and hope of Israel's entire future.

Such an historical outlook receives added weight in light of what is stated in *Zevachim* (53b) to explain the lack of a base at the southeast corner: לפי שלא היתה בחלקו של טורף — that is, the ground needed for the completion of the base was not in the territorial portion of Binyamin. For, according to the view that ירושלים נתחלקה לשבטים (*Yoma* 12a; *Megillah* 26a), the border between Binyamin and Yehudah passed through the Temple Mount. In the territory of Yehudah were the whole eastern approach, the לשכות (chambers) — including the לשכת הגזית, the seat of the Great Sanhedrin — and the three courts: the עזרת נשים, the עזרת

ישראל, and the עזרת כהנים, up to the altar. The area of the altar and everything west of it — i.e., the altar, the Sanctuary, and the Holy of Holies — were all in the territory of Binyamin.

מהרש״א (in his חדושי אגדות to *Zevachim*, ad loc.) points out that from *Shoftim* (1:8, 21) it is also clear that Yehudah and Binyamin both had a share in Yerushalayim, and so it seems from the delineation of the boundaries in *Yehoshua* (15:8; 18:28). Also, in the blessing of Moshe, Binyamin is mentioned after Yehudah; the two are separated only by Levi, who was associated with both. Yehudah was granted kingship (*Devarim* 33:7), Binyamin was endowed with the Shechinah (ibid. 33:12), and Levi took his share of both (ibid. 33:10). Levi was a partner to the Sanhedrin (which was in Yehudah), as it says: יורו משפטיך ליעקב, and he had a share in the altar (which was in Binyamin), as its says: ישימו קטורה וגו׳.

According to this tradition the Sanctuary stood not in the territory of the ruling tribe, the young lion, Yehudah, but in that of the humblest and youngest of the tribes, Binyamin. Where the base of the altar touched the territory of Yehudah, it was not completed.

We have here a profound truth that contains the essence of the whole goal of Jewish history: Kingship in Israel *should* be permeated with the spirit of the Torah and *should* be only a means of directing the nation to the Torah; the southern and eastern base of the altar *should* rest in kingship's realm. This union of power and spirit, however, is a vision for the future. A twig will sprout from the stem of Yehudah, and he will combine power and valor with a spirit from on high. Only when this spirit rests upon him will he clothe himself in majesty and strength (see *Yeshayahu* 11:1, et seq.); he alone will be "a priest on his throne" (*Zecharyah* 6:13). But in most periods of Jewish history we did not have a "kingdom of priests." The spirit of the Torah and the nation of the Torah found no basis in the realm of kingship; the southern and eastern base of the altar was not completed where it touched upon the province of Yehudah.

Since there was no יסוד at the southeast corner, the two dashings against diagonally opposite corners of the altar (שתים שהן ארבע) could only be executed against the northeast corner and the southwest corner. The first זריקה was against the northeast corner and the second against the southwest corner. The reason for this order is the following:

In verse 11 it is said of the עולה: ושחט אותו על ירך המזבח צפנה לפני ה׳

וזרקו וגו׳, from which we learn two things: (1) שחיטת עולה (as well as that of all קדשי קדשים) was performed בצפון, on the north side; (2) ירך המזבח, the back of the altar, was the north side. The front of the altar was on the south side, which was also the site of the כבש, the ascent, which had no steps (*Shemos* 20:23) but, rather, a ramp (see *Zevachim* 62b). The כהן would ascend this ramp when offering the חטאת, as its blood requires four applications on the four horns of the altar, which was ten cubits high.

The order of עבודת החטאת was as follows: שחיטה and קבלת הדם were performed on the north side. The כהן would then convey the blood to the south, where he would ascend the ramp and apply blood to the southeastern horn, the northeastern horn, the northwestern horn, and the southwestern horn. The applications were made in this order because כל פנות שאתה פונה לא יהו אלא דרך ימין, all turns in the Sanctuary were to be made to the right, and turning right, after ascending the ramp at the south, one arrived first at the southeast corner.

The procedure in the case of עולה was similar, even though its blood was not applied to the horns, up above, but was thrown from a distance against the corners, on the lower half of the altar. The כהן would not ascend the ramp at all. Nevertheless, he would convey the blood from the site of the שחיטה to the ramp — i.e., from the back of the altar to the front; facing the ramp, he would turn right and make his way around the altar. Since there was no יסוד at the southeast corner, he could not dash the blood there. Thus, the first suitable corner he arrived at was the northeastern one (see *Yoma* 15b; רש״י, ad loc.).

As stated, the front of the altar was on the south side, which was also the site of the כבש. The reason for this is alluded to by רש״י (ibid., ד״ה ברישא בההוא פגע): מתחיל להקיף מדרך הדרום שהוא פניו של מזבח בפתח כניסת הבית ומשם פונה לימין — that is, the south side of the altar was the side closest to the entrance of the Sanctuary courtyard; one who entered the courtyard would arrive first at this side. This rationale works out only according to the opinion that כוליה מזבח בצפון קאי (*Zevachim* 53a; 58a, et seq.), the entire altar stood in the northern half of the courtyard. (This opinion is identical to the second version cited in *Zevachim* 53a: כוליה פתח בדרום קאי.) For the entrance to the courtyard was located midway between the northern and southern walls of the courtyard; hence, one who entered the courtyard would arrive first at the ramp, at the south of the altar.

A different opinion, however, is stated in *Middos* (5:2) and accepted as the halachah by the רמב"ם (הל' בית הבחירה, 5:13–15). According to this opinion, the entire altar — or most of it (27 or 25 out of its 32 cubits; see תוספות יום טוב, *Middos* 5:2) — stood in the southern half of the courtyard. Accordingly, the north side of the altar was the side closest to the entrance of the Sanctuary courtyard, and the ramp at the south of altar was furthest from the entrance. We must therefore seek an inner reason why the front of the altar was on the south side.

We stated above that the south side, on which the מנורה is located, is the side of light and spirit. Now, the altar — particularly the front and the ramp leading up to it — are in the south (even according to the opinion that כוליה מזבח בצפון, the כבש was בדרום). If we are not mistaken in our approach, the following idea is self-evident: The "drawing near to God" that is learned from the altar — particularly the ascent to such heights — are matters of spirit and consciousness. Judaism is not interested in the bliss that comes from nebulous emotions; it does not subordinate the intellect to the vagueness of emotion, as if the latter were the essence of religion. For Judaism does not turn to the emotions as a means of influencing the intellect but, rather, turns to the spirit and to the intellect in order to refine the soul through clear thinking. The ascent to the altar is found only beside the light. Only there will all ascent and all maintaining of standards begin. Only from there can man draw closer to God, by advancing in and cleaving to the good.

Though the front of the altar is in the south, the back of the altar faces north, the side of the שולחן and material wealth. All קדשי קדשים — such as עולה חטאת ואשם — require שחיטתן בצפון וקיבול דמן בכלי שרת בצפון (*Zevachim* 5:1–5); what they all have in common is that they are brought for some failing in one's active life. For this reason the animal to be offered must first be placed on the north side, which symbolizes the material and the sensual. There, its selfish existence will be ended by שחיטה. There, it will enter the higher existence of the Sanctuary through the קבלת הדם. Indeed, any lack of moral progress or moral stability has its roots in the material and the sensual.

Milah — the subordination and sanctification of the material and the sensual — is a prerequisite for the moral existence of the Jewish community and individual (see Commentary, *Bereshis* 17:10). שחיטה בצפון וקיבול דם בכלי שרת בצפון — cessation of uncontrolled sensual existence, and entrance into the sphere of the Sanctuary — are prerequisites for repairing any moral deficiency. Once sensuality (embodied by the animal) is "slaughtered," it awaits moral resurrection. Toward this end it is brought to the south, to be enlightened by the light of the spirit. By being conveyed from south to east, it learns that the individual is a part of the "Nation of the Torah." In being dashed against the northeast corner, it is assigned its first active task: the utilization of material and sensory powers in relating to the national community. In this way, the material and the sensory attain their first sanctification. The liberation of the material and of the senses starts with this: they are released from the bonds of bodily drives and begin to ascend in moral freedom — provided that they are stripped of selfish purpose and put at the service of human fellowship and communal goals. Money that is earned to benefit oneself alone is no higher than the food that an animal takes to eat. But if earned in order to support others, or to support oneself in order to help others, then it belongs to the realm of moral freedom, the realm of duty, love, and holiness. It is not enough that an individual regard himself as part of the community; rather, he must be aware that the mission of the Jewish nation is in the Torah. And this Torah does not call for the elimination of material and sensory powers, but teaches one to utilize the material and the senses for the realization of Divine ends. It seeks to join heaven and earth, "to plant the heavens in the earth and to uplift the earth to the highest heavens," as the prophet says: לִנְטוֹעַ שָׁמַיִם וְלִיסֹד אָרֶץ (*Yeshayahu* 51:16). This is the whole mission of the Jewish national community. The sensory life that is slaughtered in the north attains enlightenment in the south and rises in a godly-human resurrection in the elevating northeast corner.

This human being, a combination of the material and the spiritual, continues to circle to the right. On his passage from north to west he learns to consecrate all the powers in his possession to God. All that has been set before him on the table of his life is to be dedicated to the fulfillment of the Torah, which rests beneath the wings of the cherubim. This is his whole life's purpose. And with the dashing of the blood against the southwest corner he is assigned a second task: to enlighten his spirit with the Torah, and meditate on it day and night (והגית בו יומם ולילה), as this is a condition for any ascent to moral heights.

These are the two tasks alluded to by the שתי מתנות שהן ארבע בקרן מזרחית צפונית ומערבית דרומית: (1) unselfish cultivation of the material and (2) enlightenment of the spirit through the Torah. One may have been negligent in these duties in the past, but from now onward will be diligent in performing them. Only in this way will he atone for his negligence and merit to draw closer to God.

All of the blood applications conclude with שפיכת שיריים ליסוד: the blood remaining in the כלי שרת is poured on the base of the altar. שפיכה differs from זריקה. In the case of זריקה the כהן stands at a distance from the altar, whereas in the case of שפיכה he stands beside the base and pours the blood onto it. שפיכת שיריים ליסוד is mentioned explicitly in connection with חטאת: ואת כל דם הפר ישפך אל יסוד מזבח העלה (below, 4:7) and similarly in connection with other חטאות פנימיות וחיצוניות (ibid. 4:18, 25, 30, 34). As for other offerings, it is mentioned in the verse: ודם זבחיך ישפך (*Devarim* 12:27), or alluded to by the seemingly superfluous wording in the verse: והנשאר בדם ימצה אל יסוד המזבח (below, 5:9; see *Zevachim* 37a). The remainder of the blood of חטאות הפנימיות was poured onto the יסוד מערבי; that of other קרבנות was poured onto the יסוד דרומי. In all cases, the כהן poured it בסמוך לו, that is to say, on the side nearest to the place where he stood upon completing the מתנות. In the case of חטאות פנימיות, upon exiting the היכל he was closest to the western base; in the case of חטאות חיצוניות, upon descending the ramp he was closest to the southern base (ibid. 53a). The law of שפיכת שיריים is like that of סמיכה, in that it applies למצוה but not לעכב (ibid. 52a).

Let us try to understand the meaning of שפיכת שיריים, which concludes the blood applications. First, let us note the difference between שפיכה and נתינה or זריקה. זריקה and נתינה symbolize devotion of self to aims represented by the altar. שפיכה אל היסוד, on the other hand, does not symbolize action but a quality that is found in the נפש of the one who is bringing the offering. זריקה and נתינה represent deeds that are expected of the נפש. שפיכה points to the base in which the whole personality is rooted: it is rooted לפני ה׳, in the base of Torah (שפיכת שיריים במערב); or it is rooted in the base of spiritual light that radiates from the Torah (שפיכת שיריים בדרום). שפיכת שיריים comes as a consequence of the מתנות. One is no longer remembered for past deeds, for he has already undertaken (as expressed through the מתנות) to perform the actions that are necessary in order to progress and hold fast to the good. From now onward he is assured that כל הדם, the whole נפש, which is represented by the offering, will be rooted in the base of Torah, לפני ה׳.

6 *He shall skin the ascent offering and cut it up into its parts.*

ו וְהִפְשִׁיט אֶת־הָעֹלָה וְנִתַּח אֹתָהּ לִנְתָחֶיהָ:

Perhaps it may be said that שפיכת כל הדם אל היסוד is the antithesis of הכרת נפש מלפני and הכרת הנפש מישראל, הכרת הנפש מעמיה (as in below, 22:3). הכרת should be understood according to its plain sense: to be cut off from the base through which the נפש has its roots in its people, in Israel, before God. Indeed, most of those seeking atonement through the מתנות דם הנפש had committed transgressions (חיובי חטאת) for whose willful violation one is liable to כרת. Due to negligence and indiscretion, the נפש is liable להכרת מיסודה בקרב עמיה לפני ה׳. Through נתינת הנפש על המזבח, the נפש undertakes to fulfill its duty faithfully; it then, once again, becomes rooted ביסוד ישראל לפני ה׳.

והקריבו וגו׳ את הדם וזרקו את הדם. The object of the קבלה and the זריקה (namely, the דם) is obvious, and yet Scripture repeats it. From this repetition the Gemara (*Zevachim* 81a–b) derives that the זריקה should be carried out even if the link between the blood and the specific offering was lost, e.g., if the blood of an עולה became mixed with the blood of another offering or with ordinary blood: נתערב דם עולה בדם עולה, בדם תמורה, בדם חולין, ובדם תודה, שלמים, אשם.

6 הפשט וניתוח are alike in that both may be performed by a זר (*Yoma* 26b); that is why nonspecific language is employed here (והפשיט, ונתח) as well as above (ושחט), whereas in the next verse the agent is again specified (בני אהרן).

Scripture spells out that the object of הפשט וניתוח is עלה; from this we learn that הפשט וניתוח are applicable to all kinds of עולות. On the other hand, the definite article ה־ (in העולה) and the specifying word אותה limit הפשט וניתוח to עולות כשרות. In the case of פסולין, however, הפשט וניתוח are inapplicable — even if עלו על המזבח and hence לא ירדו (see Commentary, *Shemos* 29:37; see *Zevachim* 85a).

It does not say ונתח אותה לנתחים but לנתחיה. The parts are not to be cut as one sees fit; rather, they are to be cut into *its* parts, i.e., its natural parts. Furthermore, one should not cut נתחיה לנתחים — an organic unit should not be cut into smaller parts (see Commentary below, v. 8).

7 *And the sons of Aharon the priest shall put fire upon the altar and arrange [logs of] wood upon the fire.*

ז וְנָתְנוּ בְּנֵי אַהֲרֹן הַכֹּהֵן אֵשׁ עַל־הַמִּזְבֵּחַ וְעָרְכוּ עֵצִים עַל־הָאֵשׁ׃

7 נתינת האש ועריכת העצים, putting fire upon the altar and arranging the wood, are not procedures that are repeated at every offering; they are not part of the order of procedures for offerings, as are שחיטה הפשט וניתוח. For "a fire is to be kept continually burning on the altar, where it must never go out" (below, 6:6). In accordance with this command several מערכות were arranged each morning for various purposes. In particular they would arrange and kindle *the* מערכה גדולה, *the* altar fire, on which the offering parts were burned. The altar fire, which was kept continually burning, was ever present; there was no need to rekindle it whenever an offering was to be offered up in flames. Nevertheless, Scripture here, between ניתוח and הקטרת איברים, interrupts with the law of the fire and the wood. The intention, apparently, is to mention the precept of the אש תמיד (which is commanded explicitly only later — below, ibid.) in conjunction with הקטרת האיברים of the עולה; thereby Scripture establishes the אש תמיד as the site of הקטרת האיברים for all offerings (see רש״י, *Yoma* 27b, ד״ה הוי אומר זה טלה).

From ונתנו בני אהרן הכהן אש על המזבח, stated here, we learn (*Yoma* 21b; 45a, תוספות ד״ה וכי): אף על פי שאש יורדת מן השמים מצוה להביא מן ההדיוט, although fire descends from heaven, it is a duty to provide man-made fire as well. (*Toras Kohanim*, here, adds: "The fire that descended in the time of Moshe did not depart from the copper altar until they came to the eternal House; the fire that descended in the time of Shlomo did not depart from the עולה altar until it departed in the time of Menashe.") These words (ונתנו וגו׳ אש וגו׳) also refer to הצתת אליתא, the igniting of kindling wood through which they would ignite the מערכה הגדולה, the large wood pyre. These two duties are to be performed only בראשו של מזבח, on the top of the altar, and בכהן כשר ובכלי שרת, by a valid כהן wearing the priestly garments.

From וערכו עצים על האש, stated here, we learn that two כהנים would bring שני גזרי עצים (two logs) up to the altar before the תמיד של בין הערבים, the afternoon daily offering; and from ובער עליה הכהן עצים בבקר בבקר (below, 6:5) we learn that one כהן would add two logs before the morning daily offering (*Yoma* 26b).

We have explained that the fire on the altar symbolizes the Torah, for the Torah is an אשדת, giving light and warmth, and it refines and revives our very being. Torah is also portrayed as אריאל and אש אוכלה, for with the strength of a lion and the power of fire it will absorb us and all that is ours, so that we become its "food of the fire," i.e., that we perpetuate the holy and sustain it on earth. For this reason we add אש הדיוט to the אש מן השמים — for the fire flames upon the altar in the name of God and in the name of the nation as well. Both God and Israel portray the Torah as אש. The אש מן השמים demands, in the name of God, that the "power of fire" be used for the Torah; the כהנים, who in the Sanctuary represent the nation, add אש הדיוט, thus declaring the national recognition of this demand.

The continual nurturing of this fire, effected by means of שני גזרי עצים בבוקר and שני גזרי עצים בין הערבים, teaches us that a one-time recognition, in principle, that the Torah rules with the force of fire is insufficient; rather, this recognition must be maintained continually and must be renewed in the consciousness of Israel.

The meaning of the שני גזרי עצים that are brought up to the altar by one כהן in the morning and by two כהנים in the afternoon is this: Perpetuating this conception of the Torah is the responsibility of both the community as a whole (one כהן with two logs) and its various individuals (two כהנים with two logs). Alternatively, it is the responsibility of the individual to the full extent of his powers (one כהן with two logs) and of the community with its combined powers (two כהנים with two logs). But above all, one who would maintain the fire of the Torah and make pronouncements about the force of its commandments must first himself stand בראש המזבח. Woe unto one who, in the words of the Gemara, קאי ארעא ועביד במפוחא (*Yoma* 45a), thinks that he can ignite the fire for others while he himself remains below on the ground!

This meaning of the altar fire is impressed here upon the one bringing his ascent offering. He has dedicated his whole being to the aspiration of ascending to the heights of Torah. He now turns over to the *Kohanim* נתחי קרבנו (איברים), to be offered up in the altar fire; by so doing he commits all the powers in his possession to the fire of Torah, to realize his aspiration to ascend. At this moment it is brought home to him that the fire that flames in the name of the community has been

8 *Sons of Aharon, the priests, shall arrange the parts, the head and the loose fat upon the [logs of] wood that are upon the fire that is upon the altar.*	ח וְעָרְכוּ בְּנֵי אַהֲרֹן הַכֹּהֲנִים אֵת הַנְּתָחִים אֶת־הָרֹאשׁ וְאֶת־הַפָּדֶר עַל־הָעֵצִים אֲשֶׁר עַל־הָאֵשׁ אֲשֶׁר עַל־הַמִּזְבֵּחַ׃

prepared for him also. The Torah's universal call to duty is addressed to him also, and it awaits his individual devotion in response. For the national Jewish mission is the responsibility of each Jewish individual, and only by contributing to the fulfillment of the national mission will the individual realize his own calling.

Verses 6 and 7 should be interpreted according to their context as follows. The שחיטה, symbolizing the surrender of independent existence, is not to be performed by an agent of the Sanctuary but by the one bringing the offering or by his agent. The same applies to הפשט וניתוח. He, and not an agent of the Sanctuary, should section the offering into its parts; he himself should prepare his offering to be given over to the Torah fire upon the altar. But the altar fire itself is to be kindled and perpetuated solely by the servants of the Sanctuary, for it symbolizes what the Torah demands of us: all the will and energy of one seeking closeness to God is to be given over to it. The altar fire, then, is the objective factor. The one bringing the offering must prepare his heart, so as to respond with homage and self-surrender to the Torah's call. This alone constitutes the subjective service and self-development incumbent upon the individual.

8 **את הנתחים**. From *Tamid* (chapters 3 and 4) and *Yoma* (25a–b) we learn that an עולה comprised of a sheep was sectioned into ten parts, besides the intestines and lower legs. These ten parts were divided into five groups of two and each group was brought to the altar by one כהן. Before it was given over to the fire, it was placed on the lower half of the ramp: הולכת איברים לכבש.

The parts were as follows: 1. (a) הראש עם הפדר, the head together with the fat (the fat was used to cover the cut where the animal was slaughtered); (b) רגל הימנית וב׳ ביצים עמה, the right leg together with the testicles. 2. שתי ידים, the two forelegs. 3. (a) העוקץ עם שתי צלעות מכאן ומכאן והאליה ואצבע הכבד וב׳ כליות עמו, the lower part of the spine with two ribs on either side, the tail, the finger of the liver and the two kidneys; (b) הרגל השמאלית, the left hindleg. 4. (a) החזה, the breast; (b) והגרה, the neck, עם שתי צלעות מכאן ומכאן ובה הקנה הלב והריאה, with two ribs on either side and with the windpipe (and esophagus), the heart, and lung attached to it. 5. שתי דפנות, the two flanks: (a) דופן הימנית עם צלעות והכבד תלויה בה, the right flank with the ribs, and the liver attached to it; (b) ודופן השמאלית עם צלעות והשדרה עמו והטחול תלוי בה, the left flank with the ribs and the backbone, and the spleen attached to it. 6. הקרביים וכרעיים על גביהן, the intestines and stomach, with the lower legs placed on top of them.

Thus, the conveyance of the parts of a כבש to the altar was entrusted to six כהנים. We learn from *Yoma* (26b), however, that the conveyance of the parts of a פר was entrusted to eighteen כהנים. In addition to those carrying the parts of the פר, another six would carry the סולת and יין, and so their number reached twenty-four. The ראב״ד and קרבן אהרן (on *Toras Kohanim* to our verse) conclude from this that, in striking contrast to the rule ולא נתחיה לנתחים, the parts of a פר were sectioned into yet further parts, hence the need for more כהנים. תוספות י״ט, however, based on the רמב״ם (הל׳ מעשה קרבנות, 6:19), asserts that the limbs of a פר are large and heavy and for this reason were carried by a greater number of כהנים. For example, the head and leg of a כבש were carried together by one כהן; in the case of a פר, on the other hand, its head alone was carried by one כהן, and its leg by two כהנים, and so with the other limbs.

From the Mishnah (*Yoma* 26b) we see that the groups of parts in the case of a פר resembled those of a כבש: הראש והרגל, העוקץ והרגל, החזה והגרה, שתי ידים, שתי דפנות, הקרביים. These are the same six groups of which we learned in the case of עולת הכבש, except that they are listed in a different order (see תוספות, ad loc.).

The conclusion we reach is that the הולכת איברים of a פר was patterned after the groupings of parts in the case of a כבש. This would explain why ר׳ עקיבא (*Toras Kohanim* to our verse) and the Gemara (*Yoma* 27a) find in our verse an allusion to the number of *Kohanim* needed to convey the parts of a כבש, even though the verse deals with the parts of a פר. The very concept of arrangement according to groups is alluded to by the change in wording in verses 8 and 12: וערכו בני אהרן הכהנים vs. וערך הכהן אותם. וערכו implies that a number of כהנים are to participate in הולכת איברים, while וערך הכהן אותם implies that one כהן is to convey more than one part. Thus, a number of כהנים are to participate in the conveyance, and each one is to convey at least two parts (*Toras Kohanim* to our verse). (For the significance of these groups, see our essay on the שמונה עשרה in *Collected Writings*, vol. III.)

את הנתחים את הראש ואת הפדר. The head is mentioned here beside the נתחים and is not included with them. Clearly, then, it had already been severed from the body, before the ניתוח described in verse 6. Indeed, in *Chullin* (27a) the Gemara states that the halachah שחיטה מן הצואר, which we know from tradition, lies at the root of this verse.

פדר is apparently related to פטר. The primary meaning of פטר is natural separation; similarly, פטר רחם (*Shemos* 13:2), פְּטוּרֵי צִצִּים (*Melachim* I, 6:18), and also פּוֹטֵר מַיִם (*Mishlei* 17:14), which refers to the gushing forth of waters from a place of previous confinement. Hence the general meaning of פטר is to be released. פדר is also related to בתר (sever), except that the latter denotes mechanical separation whereas פטר denotes natural separation.

According to the רמב״ן, the פדר is the layer of fat that covers the intestines like a cloth; in other places in Scripture it is called חלב המכסה את הקרב. It is fat that has been set apart by the body; it comprises a naturally independent unit. For this reason the פדר, like the ראש, is not included in the נתחים, as the נתחים are created only through mechanical separation.

הראש והפדר comprise the two extremes of the living organism: The head is the life of the individual concentrated to its highest spiritual potential; it is therefore that which governs animal existence. The reverse is true of the פדר; it is fat which the body has separated for the time being, setting it aside in reserve for use when the need should arise.

על העצים אשר על האש אשר על המזבח. In this phrasing, the meaning of העצים is amplified by האש, and the meaning of האש is amplified by המזבח. Thus, the halachah: על העצים אשר על האש – עצים הנתוכים להיות אש (*Tamid* 29b), i.e., wood that "melts" easily and turns quickly into fire. Further: על המזבח וגו׳ – שלא יהיו עצים יוצאין מן המזבח כלום, "wood should not protrude over the edges of the altar" (*Zevachim* 62b): the offering is not to be offered up in just any fire but only in fire of the altar. And finally: על העצים וגו׳ – מה מזבח משל ציבור אף עצים ואש משל ציבור. מה מזבח שלא נשתמש בו הדיוט אף עצים ואש שלא נשתמש בהן הדיוט (*Menachos* 22a). The altar fire becomes, as it were, the living embodiment of the altar, summoning and calling upon the earth to rise up from the soil of Israel, before the Sanctuary, toward God. Therefore, the fire and that which will become fire (the wood) must conform to the character of the altar.

A further note: In the command to put fire upon the altar (v. 7) it says: בני אהרן הכהן. This expression is found nowhere else in the Torah. Elsewhere — as well as here, in our verse, regarding הולכת איברים לכבש — it always says בני אהרן הכהנים. We pointed out in our Commentary to *Shemos* (28:1) that the priestly service is attributed primarily to Aharon, the כהן גדול, whereas the כהנים הדיוטות, in relation to him, are as sons to their father — they assist him and carry out part of the service in his stead. The כהן גדול is attired in the שמונה בגדים, and only so long as he is wearing these garments is he the כהן גדול of the Sanctuary. It is he who represents the ideal that is to be realized in the life of the individual and that of the community, according to the dictates of the Torah which rests in the Sanctuary. This is the very ideal to be attained through the altar fire, which transforms and refines the individual and the community. The כהן הדיוט, however, represents a level that is merely preparation for this higher ideal. For this reason it does not say (in v. 7) בני אהרן הכהנים but, rather, בני אהרן הכהן; for it is in the service of the highest Jewish ideal — represented by אהרן הכהן — that the כהנים הדיוטות are to light the fire upon the altar. Indeed, the level of the מזבח החיצון is merely preparation for the level of the מזבח הפנימי; the הקטרה על מזבח החיצון is merely preparatory to the קטורת על מזבח הפנימי. Understanding this relationship is essential for an understanding of the idea of the מקדש, and especially so for an understanding of the idea of the עזרה and of the offerings to be rendered there. Scripture therefore emphasizes this relationship by using the appellation בני אהרן הכהן at the first mention of the mitzvah of kindling the fire upon the altar, by which the full magnitude of the level of the עזרה is expressed.

Thus, the Gemara (*Zevachim* 18a) also derives from verses 7 and 8 the following *halachos*: ונתנו בני אהרן הכהן – בכיהונו, לימד על כהן גדול שלבש בגדי הדיוט ועבד עבודתו פסולה. וערכו בני אהרן הכהנים וגו׳ – הכהנים בכיהונן, מכאן לכהן הדיוט שלבש בגדי כהן גדול ועבד עבודתו פסולה. Both the כה״ג and the כהן הדיוט must officiate in the garments that characterize the relative nature of their service. Every עבודה performed either by the כה״ג in the garments of a כהן הדיוט or by a כהן הדיוט in the garments of a כה״ג is פסולה.

It still remains for us to explain the nature of the procedure referred to by the words וערכו וגו׳ את הנתחים וגו׳ על העצים וגו׳.

From the meaning of the words it would appear at first glance

9 *He shall wash its intestines and its feet in water, and the priest shall turn all of it into smoke upon the altar as an ascent offering, an offering made by fire as an expression of compliance, to* God.

ט וְקִרְבּ֥וֹ וּכְרָעָ֖יו יִרְחַ֣ץ בַּמָּ֑יִם וְהִקְטִ֨יר הַכֹּהֵ֤ן אֶת־הַכֹּל֙ הַמִּזְבֵּ֔חָה עֹלָ֛ה אִשֵּׁ֥ה רֵֽיחַ־נִיח֖וֹחַ לַיהוָֽה׃ ס

that the reference is to הקטרת האיברים על גבי המזבח, i.e., to הולכת האיברים מן הכבש למזבח. But the next verse still speaks of the washing of the intestines and lower legs, and only afterwards does it say: והקטיר הכהן וגו׳. Moreover, we have already pointed out above that the expressions וערכו בני אהרן הכהנים (v. 8) and וערך הכהן אתם (v. 12) allude to the arrangement of the parts according to groups; they also allude to the fact that the conveyance of the parts of a כבש is to be performed by six כהנים, and that, accordingly, the conveyance of the parts of a פר is to be performed also in six groups. All these laws, however, apply only to הולכת איברים לכבש, to the conveyance of parts to the ramp, whereas the conveyance of parts from the ramp to the altar — the essence of the הקטרה — is to be carried out, according to most authorities, by only one כהן. (See *Yoma* 26b, רש״י ד״ה ה״ג והא תניא; תוספות ד״ה ההוא ;רמב״ם הל׳ תמידין ומוספין, 4:8; רמב״ן and בעל שבעה עשר, and המאור, *Yoma* 26b. Only תוספות ישנים [ibid.] disagree. In their opinion, the הולכה מן הכבש למזבח is carried out by the same number of כהנים as required for conveyance to the ramp. According to ר׳ אליעזר בן יעקב, this is indeed the law: המעלה איברים לכבש הוא המעלה אותן למזבח [ibid. 26a]; this opinion, however, is not accepted as the halachah.) In this light it would appear, then, that the words וערכו וגו׳ את הנתחים וגו׳ על העצים וגו׳ (with the plural וערכו) refer only to הולכת איברים לכבש. The meaning of על העצים, then, would be: "beside, toward, the עצים," as in: וזבחת עליו (*Shemos* 20:21); ונתת על המערכת (below, 24:7). Even if we understand (as the Gemara does) that וערכו וגו׳ refers to סידור האיברים על גבי המזבח, we find that the Gemara (*Menachos* 26b–27a) is undecided as to the meaning of the word על — whether it means על העצים ממש or should be understood in the sense of בסמוך לעצים. וצ״ע.

9 **וכרעיו**. כרעיים, apparently, are the lower parts of the legs; when the animal kneels, the כרעיים rest on the ground. The intestines and lower legs

require washing in order to be cleared of any foreign matter that is not a part of the offering.

והקטיר וגו׳ המזבחה. See our Commentary to *Shemos* 29:13. The delivery of the parts to the fire upon the altar is the second act to be performed with the offering, as זריקת הדם and הקטרת האיברים are the two major acts in the offering of an עולה. Scripture says: ועשית עלתיך הבשר והדם על מזבח ה׳ אלהיך, "And you shall offer your ascent offerings, the flesh and the blood, upon the altar of Hashem your God" (*Devarim* 12:27), and the Gemara (*Zevachim* 104a) derives from this the close connection between these two acts, זריקת הדם and הקטרת איברים: they are similar in their external form, and they are connected in meaning, each essential to the other.

With regard to the form of the two acts, the Gemara says: מה דם בזריקה אף בשר בזריקה — i.e., just as the blood is thrown to the altar from a distance, so are the parts thrown to the altar fire; ריוח יש בין כבש למזבח, there was a space between the top of the ramp and the altar, in order to emphasize the importance of this throwing to the fire (see לחם משנה to הל׳ מעשה הקרבנות, 6:4).

And, similarly, with regard to the meaning of these acts, both זריקת הדם and זריקת הבשר are indicative of resolve to ascend and advance; they both represent a call for the exercise of moral will. They are connected by their nature and are interdependent: The דם represents the נפש, the inner individual personality; the בשר represents the איברים, the complex of activities through which the will of the personality is expressed. בשר is just what the word says, an agent that heralds (מבשר) and implements the will of the נפש (see Commentary to *Bereshis* 2:21). זריקת הדם demands of the נפש to rivet the will to its solemn task: all of one's inner will should be concentrated on the aspiration to ascend to moral heights. זריקת האיברים calls for actualizing one's will: all actions at the disposal of the נפש should be dedicated to the goal of becoming "fuel of the fire unto God," i.e., sustaining the holy on earth by doing the Will of God.

Now, these two acts (זריקת הדם and זריקת האיברים) are interdependent, as it says: אם אין דם אין בשר, אם אין בשר אין דם (*Zevachim* 104a). זריקת איברים without זריקת דם amounts to outward correctness (perfunctory performance) without inward consecration; זריקת דם without זריקת איברים amounts to an inner consecration that, content with such inwardness, has no impact on life itself and does not shape one's deeds. The closeness to God that is sought through an offering can be found only in the harmony of one's inner life and outer life. Neither outward correctness without inward devotion, nor inner feeling without outward obedience to the Torah, is the way that leads to God. Only the observance of *mitzvos* that springs from the depths of the heart, only the inner devotion that comes to expression in the observance of *mitzvos*, is the way that leads one up high. Thus, "Only with the בשר and the דם is our ascent offering rendered upon the altar of our God" (cf. *Devarim* 12:27).

The connection between these two acts comes to expression, according to the ריטב״א, in another halachah. In his opinion, the כהן who performs the זריקת דם must be the one who performs the הקטרת איברים (see משנה למלך הל׳ תמידין ומוספין, 4:6).

Since here it says והקטיר הכהן את הכל, implying that the whole animal with all its parts is to be given over to the fire, whereas in the verse cited above (*Devarim* 12:27) it says ועשית עלתיך הבשר והדם, implying that only the בשר, the flesh and nerve tissue, is to be given over to the fire, the Mishnah (*Zevachim* 85b) concludes: העצמות והגידים והקרנים והטלפים בזמן שהן מחוברין יעלו פירשו לא יעלו, "Bones, tendons, horns, and hooves are to be brought up to the altar only if they are attached to the flesh of the offering; if they become detached, they are not to be brought up." Only the בשר, representing the activities of life, is fit to fuel the fire of God; עצמות are merely passive instruments of these activities and are fit for the fire only while connected to the בשר.

עלה אשה ריח ניחוח לה׳ is in apposition with הכל: he must turn all of it into smoke upon the altar as an עולה אשה ריח ניחוח לה׳. The Mishnah (ibid. 46b) derives from here that in making an offering one should have in mind six specific intentions: לשם ששה דברים הזבח נזבח לשם זבח לשם זובח לשם השם לשם אישים לשם ריח לשם ניחוח. All these are derived from our verse (with the exception of לשם זובח, which is explained elsewhere [ibid. 4a]; it cannot be derived from our verse, as our verse deals with הקטרה, whereas intent for the sake of the offerer is essential only to the four עבודות הדם [דם represents the נפש, the personality]; see תוספות, *Zevachim* 2a, ד״ה כל הזבחים and משנה למלך הל׳ מעשה הקרבנות, 4:11). The Gemara (*Zevachim* 46b) explains their derivation from our verse as follows: עולה לאפוקי לשם שלמים דלא, אשה לשם אשה לאפוקי כבבא (על מנת לעשותו חתיכות צלויות בגחלים – רש״י) דלא, ריח לשם ריח לאפוקי איברים שצלאן והעלן דלא, ניחוח לשם הנחת

רוח, לה׳ לשם מי שאמר והיה העולם. (For explanation of these *halachos*, see below; for more on אשה, see Commentary below, 3:11.)

Note that the Gemara's formulation of these *halachos* is not אשה לאפוקי כבבא דלא, ריח לאפוקי איברים שצלאן והעלן דלא but, rather, אשה לשם אשה לאפוקי וכו׳, ריח לשם ריח לאפוקי וכו׳. This not only rules out the actual bringing of the offering as כבבא or as איברים שצלאן, but also prohibits any such intention: when bringing a קרבן, it is forbidden to plan to offer it with such an intention. (According to one opinion cited in תוספות [*Zevachim* 2a], such an intention is prohibited in all procedures of the offering — and not only in the procedure to which the specific intention relates; for example: even at the שחיטה it is forbidden to intend להקטיר כבבא, and so on. See משנה למלך הל׳ מעשה הקרבנות, 4:11).

It must be, then, that these *halachos* are intimately connected with the very concept of an offering, and any infringement of them detracts from the offering's perfection. This is clearly so with respect to the halachah of עולה לשם עולה לאפוקי לשם שלמים דלא. It is self-evident that one should have the offering in mind when rendering it; in any case, one should not have in mind — and certainly not pronounce it to be — some other offering (see תוספות, *Zevachim* 2a and *Bava Metzia* 43b, ד״ה החושב). Let us now analyze the other *halachos*.

אשה לשם אשה לאפוקי כבבא דלא: Roasting the parts of the offering — rather than having them consumed — on the altar fire (as might conceivably be done in the case of קרבן פסח, which is supposed to be eaten by the בעלים) is antithetical to the very purpose of an offering. The purpose of an offering is אכילת מזבח; as Scripture says, an offering is meant to be לחם אשה לה׳ (below, 3:11) and to fuel the fire of God. Roasting (כבבא) would make it seem as though the offering itself were the end and the fire only a means to its preparation, while the very opposite is intended. The אשדת is to be kept burning on the altar, as אריאל atop הראל (see Commentary to *Shemos* 27:8); the fire of Torah is to be perpetuated in this world which yearns to rise upward to God. This fire is to rule over all, and all is to be absorbed in it; one who brings an offering should devote to this fire all the activities of life and thus sustain it on earth. The idea of אשה, then, is diametrically opposed to that of כבבא.

ריח לשם ריח לאפוקי אברים שצלאן והעלן דלא (one should not intend to roast the parts before bringing them onto the altar): Something happening in a distant place can be sensed via ריח. In our Commentary to

Bereshis (8:21) we explained that ריח denotes the reception of a subtle impression that comes from afar. We also showed there that ניחוח — or, rather, the root נוח in its active form — nowhere denotes sensory gratification.

Here, the halachah states that the one bringing the offering should intend that his offering be discernible from afar via ריח. This very intention ensures the symbolic character of the offering: what is happening up there on the altar must be noticed. From this we see that the objective is not the burning per se, but the idea that is expressed thereby. From the added word, לה׳, we learn that the objective is to direct the expression of the idea of the offering toward God. להעלות איברים שצלאן (to offer up parts that have already been roasted) would produce no ריח (*Zevachim* 46b); the objective of the offering would then be the physical process of burning, per se.

ניחוח לשם הנחת רוח — to give spiritual satisfaction: This disproves the erroneous conception that an offering is intended to provide God with tangible, sensory pleasure. Rather, one who seeks closeness to God by means of an offering undertakes to fulfill the Divine Will and so directs toward God the aspiration to give spiritual satisfaction.

לה׳ לשם מי שאמר והיה העולם — or, in the words of the ספרא, לשם מי שעשה את העולם: Here we see again what we have already shown in our Commentary to *Bereshis* (2:4). The erroneous conception of the meaning of God's Name — as though it were an expression of the transcendental concept of eternity — was far from the view of our Sages. ה׳ is, rather, an active form: it does not denote "the One Who exists for all time" but "the One Who creates all that exists."

It is not required of one who performs the various procedures of the offering to verbalize these six intentions; it is sufficient that he expresses no opposite intention. For the halachah is that סתמא לשמן: we assume — in the absence of intent — that the one bringing the offering intended to fulfill its *halachos*. It is not even desirable that he verbalize his intention, lest he erringly express a contradictory intention: אתנו בית דין דלא לימא לשמו דלמא אתי למימר שלא לשמו (*Zevachim* 2b; 46b).

Regarding the six specific intentions in making an offering, the effect of an expressed contradictory intention (שלא לשמו) varies. In the case of שינוי קודש (עולה לשם שלמים) or שינוי בעלים (עולת ראובן לשם שמעון) the קרבן is כשר, but the one who brought it has not fulfilled his obligation and must bring another offering: כל הזבחים שנזבחו שלא לשמן כשרים אלא שלא

10 *And if his offering is from the flock, from the sheep or from the goats, as an ascent offering, then he shall bring it male and whole.*

11 *He shall slaughter it at the back of the altar, northward, before* God, *and the sons of Aharon, the priests, shall dash its blood against the altar, all around.*

י וְאִם־מִן־הַצֹּאן קׇרְבָּנוֹ מִן־
הַכְּשָׂבִים אוֹ מִן־הָעִזִּים לְעֹלָה
זָכָר תָּמִים יַקְרִיבֶנּוּ׃

יא וְשָׁחַט אֹתוֹ עַל יֶרֶךְ הַמִּזְבֵּחַ צָפֹנָה
לִפְנֵי יְהֹוָה וְזָרְקוּ בְּנֵי אַהֲרֹן
הַכֹּהֲנִים אֶת־דָּמוֹ עַל־הַמִּזְבֵּחַ
סָבִיב׃

עלו לבעלים לשם חובה (ibid. 2a); only in the case of פסח or חטאת is the קרבן itself פסול (ibid.). In the case of the other four intentions the law is different: even if one expressed a contradictory intention, the offering is valid from every standpoint (תוספות, ad loc.).

Characteristic of the whole conception of the offerings is that it is not what is in the mind of the one bringing the offering (the בעלים), but what is in the mind of the one performing the *avodah*, that affects the validity of the offering: אין המחשבה הולכת אלא אחר העובד (*Zevachim* 46b). The significance of this halachah is as follows. The procedures of an offering do not express the subjective thoughts found in the mind of the one seeking God's closeness; rather, they embody the objective ideas that emerge from the Sanctuary of the Torah. Through these ideas are to be found the way to God and closeness to Him. One who brings an offering must embrace these ideas; by handing over the offering to the Sanctuary, he expresses his willingness to do so. The *Kohanim* are not primarily שלוחי דידן but, rather, שלוחי דרחמנא: they perform the procedures of the offering as agents of the Sanctuary (see *Nedarim* 35b; *Yoma* 19a–b; תוספות, ad loc., ד"ה מי איכא מידי).

10–13 We pointed out above (v. 3) that offerings brought from צאן represent the human personality from the standpoint of its lot, which is in the hands of God; for a man is like a member of God's flock. Offerings brought from בקר, on the other hand, represent the personality from the standpoint of its tasks; for man was created to work in God's "fields." These two kinds of offerings, then, are connected to the two aspects

12 *He shall cut it up into its parts, with its head and its loose fat, and the priest shall arrange them for the [logs of] wood that are upon the fire that is upon the altar.*	יב וְנִתַּח אֹתוֹ לִנְתָחָיו וְאֶת־רֹאשׁוֹ וְאֶת־פִּדְרוֹ וְעָרַךְ הַכֹּהֵן אֹתָם עַל־הָעֵצִים אֲשֶׁר עַל־הָאֵשׁ אֲשֶׁר עַל־הַמִּזְבֵּחַ׃
13 *And he shall wash the intestines and the feet in water, and the priest shall bring all of it near and turn it into smoke upon the altar; it is an ascent offering, an offering made by fire as an expression of compliance, to* God.	יג וְהַקֶּרֶב וְהַכְּרָעַיִם יִרְחַץ בַּמָּיִם וְהִקְרִיב הַכֹּהֵן אֶת־הַכֹּל וְהִקְטִיר הַמִּזְבֵּחָה עֹלָה הוּא אִשֵּׁה רֵיחַ נִיחֹחַ לַיהוָה׃ פ שני

which, together, comprise the whole of human life. Hence, it is easily understood why עולת בקר and עולת צאן, which share exactly the same *halachos*, are nevertheless treated by Scripture in two separate sections. (These two sections do supplement each other, however; the link between them is emphasized by the conjunctive ו at the opening of the צאן section: וי״ו מוסיף על ענין ראשון וילמד עליון מתחתון [*Zevachim* 48a] — the ו indicates that the laws stated in one section apply to the other as well.) The single task of continual ascent is illuminated here from two standpoints: (1) one's duty (בקר) and (2) the dependence of one's fate in life upon God (צאן). Hence, the law of עולה is taught in two separate sections, and some of its *halachos* (e.g., שחיטה בצפון and פסול חולה זקן ומזוהם) appear only in the second פרשה — as a supplement to the first. If we bear in mind the different inner meaning of these two פרשיות, perhaps we shall also understand the other differences that exist between them — both in content and language.

מן הצאן, מן הכשבים, מן העזים. The selection of animals fit for an offering was limited in verse 2; here, it is limited still further (*Bechoros* 41a) by the repeated partitive term מן, which excludes חולה זקן ומזוהם, the old and infirm (see משנה למלך הל׳ איסורי מזבח, 2:6), the sick and the foul-smelling. רובע ונרבע מוקצה נעבד ונוגח all represent sins; hence, they are excluded in the section of עולת בקר, which teaches of the aspiration to ascend from the standpoint of duties of action. זקן חולה ומזוהם, on the other hand, represent unfortunate strokes of fate; hence, they are excluded in the section of עולת צאן, which teaches of the aspiration to ascend from the standpoint of our fate, which is in the hands of God. From this exclusion we learn: It is not the suffering that one must bear in life that should move him to seek God; rather, it is precisely one who is in possession of his powers, without limitation or hindrance, who should seek God's closeness through continual ascent in the fulfillment of his duty. Not only in old age, illness, and loneliness, but in the freshness of youth, in glowing health, and from the midst of a rich social life are we to seek the path of God and aspire to moral perfection; we are to proceed on this path as a זכר תמים, with virile vigor and with the whole of ourselves.

סמיכה is mentioned in the section on עולת בקר and is not repeated in that of עולת צאן. Why is it not repeated? One who brings an עולת בקר is already cognizant of his duty from the standpoint of בקר. Nevertheless, he needs to be reminded, by the act of סמיכה, that as one of the representatives of the nation he must attest to the binding force of the Torah's commandments vis-à-vis himself (see Commentary to v. 4). Certainly, then, there is need for such a reminder in the case of עולת צאן. One who brings an עולת צאן recognizes only his dependence upon God, and from this standpoint there must be awakened within him the consciousness of his duty. *It goes without saying* that he must be reminded of his duties by the מצוה of סמיכה.

ושחט וגו׳ צפנה. צפון, on the other hand, is mentioned only in the section on עולת צאן, (as it says in our verse ושחט וגו׳ צפנה). The meaning of שחיטה וקבלה בצפון is this: One must surrender the selfish existence of the material and the senses (represented by צפון, the north side where the שולחן stood), in order to bring them into the Divine domain; only thus does one fulfill the first prerequisite for ascending toward God.

Now, one who brings an עולת צאן already recognizes that his whole material-sensory existence is dependent upon God's providence. Yet precisely he must remember that a mere feeling of dependence is not enough, as such a feeling is meaningless if it leads merely to hope — and not to obedience. It does not suffice to feed at God's table and receive from Him the riches of life; rather, one must acquire property and regard it as sacred unto God, to be used for carrying out God's Will by dint of the material and the senses.

It is now clear why סמיכה is mentioned in the section on עולת בקר, whereas צפון appears in that of עולת צאן: סמיכה and בקר both pertain to the realm of action, whereas צפון and צאן relate to the realm of fate.

ונתח אתו לנתחיו. Above (v. 6), it says ונתח אותה לנתחיה. Above, the object is עולה; hence, the object pronoun is feminine. Here, the object is קרבן or צאן; hence, the object pronoun is masculine. What, you may ask, is the significance of stressing עולה as the object in the section on עולת בקר but not in the section on עולת צאן? Above, the עולה-concept of consecrating one's actions is already manifest in the animal to be offered — namely, בקר; hence, the עולה-concept is predominant in the verse. צאן, on the other hand, represents man shepherded by God. Hence, the עולה-concept becomes manifest in the animal only after it is given over to the altar. When it is being cut into its parts, it is still perceived as an animal of pasture, as an animal of an offering in general; it is not yet perceived in the verse as an עולה. Moreover, one who brings a בן בקר, which is a work-animal, already regards himself as "masculine." The offering serves to remind him of his "feminine" dependence, of the need for devotion to the Will of God in his actions. By contrast, one who brings צאן — an animal of pasture — is already conscious of his dependence on God. The offering awakens within him a consciousness of his "masculine" strength, so that he serve God through his deeds.

וערך וגו'. We have already stated above that it is difficult to say with certainty what constitutes עריכת הנתחים על העצים, as the washing of the intestines and lower legs is mentioned only after the עריכה (see above, v. 8). In this פרשה the difficulty is even greater. For it says in verse 13: והקריב הכהן את הכל, which refers to none other than הולכת אברים לכבש (*Yoma* 27a); hence, the עריכה of verse 12 could not even be referring to this הולכה.

Perhaps וערך וגו' refers just to the ordering of the parts of the offering, i.e., their division into groups that bear symbolic meaning. (In our article on the שמונה עשרה prayer (*Collected Writings*, vol. III) we explained the meaning of these groups, showing the parallelism that exists between them and this prayer.) על העצים, then, would mean "*for* the wood," i.e., for the sake of finally delivering the parts onto the wood, and these words hint at the principle by which they are to be ordered: They are to be arranged in accordance with the idea of their being offered on the fire perpetuated in the name of the nation (עצים). Thus, the two aspects of the ordering are: (1) the pairing of the parts, with the constituent parts of the pair interrelated in meaning: the head and the leg, the two forelegs, and so on; (2) the order in which they are conveyed to the altar.

As stated, והקריב הכהן את הכל refers to none other than הולכת איברים לכבש. We explained in our article on the שמונה עשרה as follows. The parts are to be placed on the ramp before being delivered to the altar fire; this way, the mind has pause to recall that the abilities embodied by these parts were given to man by God, and that we are merely giving back to Him what we have received from Him. Thus, we understand why this procedure (הולכת איברים לכבש) is emphasized especially in פרשת עולת צאן (the act of הקרבה is not stated explicitly in the section on עולת בקר), as the idea of God's providential care for us is central to this פרשה.

עלה הוא. In *Toras Kohanim* (ad loc.) it says: עולה, אע״פ שלא הפשיט אע״פ שלא נתח, יכול אע״פ שלא נשחט בצפון ת״ל הוא, מה ראית וכו׳ מפני מה אני מכשיר בהפשט וניתוח שהן לאחר הרציה ופוסל בצפון שהוא לפני הרציה. The offering is valid as an עולה even if it was not skinned and not cut up into parts. However, שחיטה בצפון is required, as indicated by the word הוא. Procedures that come after the זריקה are not required for the offering to be valid, whereas procedures that precede the זריקה are required. This, in turn, calls for interpreting the next words of the verse, אשה ריח ניחח לה׳, as follows. These words do not define עולה, but draw an inference from it. Do not read "It is an עולה *because* it is offered up onto the altar fire" but rather "It is an עולה and *therefore* is to be offered up onto the altar fire." The offering takes on the character of עולה before it is turned into smoke upon the altar — and even without this. The character of עולה is determined by זריקה, which is the הרציה referred to by *Toras Kohanim.* All rites following זריקה are merely למצוה and not לעכב. As mentioned above, at the time of זריקה the possibility of הקטרה must be there. Subsequent to the זריקה, however, even if the איברים and אימורים are lost or disqualified so that no הקטרה at all can be performed, the offering remains valid. This is further confirmation of our view that the concept of עולה is not dependent on the burning upon the altar but on the aspiration of ascending to the heights of the altar, which is expressed through זריקה. (וצ״ע בת״כ על פסוק עולה הוא גבי עולת העוף ועי׳ שם בק״א למטה.)

14 *And if his offering to* God *is an ascent offering of birds, then he shall bring near his offering from the turtledoves or from the young doves.*

15 *And the priest shall bring it near to the altar, nip off its head and turn it into smoke upon the altar, whereas its blood shall have been pressed out on the wall of the altar.*

יד וְאִם מִן־הָעוֹף עֹלָה קָרְבָּנוֹ לַיהוָה וְהִקְרִיב מִן־הַתֹּרִים אוֹ מִן־בְּנֵי הַיּוֹנָה אֶת־קָרְבָּנוֹ׃

טו וְהִקְרִיבוֹ הַכֹּהֵן אֶל־הַמִּזְבֵּחַ וּמָלַק אֶת־רֹאשׁוֹ וְהִקְטִיר הַמִּזְבֵּחָה וְנִמְצָה דָמוֹ עַל קִיר הַמִּזְבֵּחַ׃

14 **ואם מן העוף עלה קרבנו**. All of chapter 1 deals with קרבן נדבה. Now, a נדבה of birds is always an עולה, as עוף are never offered as a שלמים; hence, it does not say here — as it says in verse 10 — ואם מן העוף קרבנו לעולה, but rather ואם מן העוף עולה קרבנו, meaning: קרבנו מן העוף can be only an עולה. "If he wishes to bring this offering מן העוף, in which case it is none other than an עולה, then this is its prescribed procedure …"

מן העוף. מן, here too, sets a restriction, but less restricting than in the case of עולת בהמה. The Gemara says: תמות וזכרות בבהמה ואין תמות וזכרות בעופות, יכול יבשה גפה נקטעה רגלה נחטטה עינה ת״ל מן העוף ולא כל העוף (*Kiddushin* 24b). Thus, only the מום of מחוסר אבר constitutes a disqualification in קרבן העוף.

קרבנו וגו׳ והקריב. Scripture uses the singular here, whereas in the case of קרבן בהמה (v. 2) it uses the plural: תקריבו את קרבנכם. This teaches us that קרבן העוף is brought only by the individual, representing a private personality; a קרבן ציבור cannot consist of birds (*Temurah* 14a; *Toras Kohanim* to our verse).

מן התרים או מן בני היונה. תורים are fit to be offered only when they have reached maturity, and יונים only when they are young; that is why it never says בני תור and never יונים. The age of the birds can be determined by the color of the wings. In the transitional stage, known as תחילת הציהוב, both תורים and יונים are unfit (*Chullin* 22a). Only תורים and בני יונה may be used for bird-offerings (*Toras Kohanim*).

15 **והקריבו**: even one single bird may be offered (*Zevachim* 65a).

והקריבו הכהן וגו׳ ומלק. In the case of קרבן בהמה, the שחיטה may be

16 *He shall remove its crop with its feathers and throw it beside the altar, eastward, to the place of the ashes.*

טז וְהֵסִיר אֶת־מֻרְאָתוֹ בְּנֹצָתָהּ וְהִשְׁלִיךְ אֹתָהּ אֵצֶל הַמִּזְבֵּחַ קֵדְמָה אֶל־מְקוֹם הַדָּשֶׁן׃

performed by a non-*Kohen*. In the case of קרבן עוף, all of the *avodos* must be performed by a כהן — even the מליקה, which corresponds to the שחיטה. The מליקה must be performed בעצמו של כהן (ibid.) — with his fingernail, not with a knife.

והקריבו הכהן אל המזבח ומלק וגו׳ והקטיר. Bringing the bird to the altar precedes מליקה, with no הקרבה interposing between מליקה and הקטרה; hence, מה הקטרה בראש המזבח אף מליקה בראש המזבח (ibid.). מליקה, and מיצוי הדם which follows, are to be performed at the top of the altar, למעלה מחוט הסיקרא בקרן דרומית־מזרחית.

ומלק והקטיר: the מליקה prepares the way for, and makes possible, the הקטרה. Just as at the time of the הקטרה, the head and the body have been separated (as is evident from verses 15 and 17), so have they been separated since the time of the מליקה: in the מליקה of עולת העוף the כהן cuts through both of the סימנים with his fingernail and separates the head from the body. This contrasts with the מליקה of חטאת העוף, of which Scripture says: ולא יבדיל (below, 5:8). מליקה — as opposed to שחיטה — is to be performed ממול ערפו (from the back of the neck below the nape), as specified by Scripture (ibid.) in its discussion of חטאת העוף (*Zevachim* 64b).

ונמצה דמו: דם כולו, the blood of the whole bird — of the head as well as of the body; but only the latter is מעכב (ibid. 66a). This pressing out of the blood על קיר המזבח is stated by Scripture in the passive (ונמצה — not וימצה), perhaps in order to include על קיר המזבח even the blood that flows out, of its own accord, during מליקה; the Gemara (ibid. 64b) gives a similar explanation for the term ימצה at חטאת העוף (below, 5:9).

16 We learn in the Mishnah (*Zevachim* 64b): והסיר את המוראה ואת הנוצה ואת בני המעיים היוצאים עמם. According to the רמב״ן in his commentary to the תורה, this Mishnah is in accordance with אבא יוסי בן חנן, who holds: נוטלה ונוטל קורקבנה עמה (ibid. 65a). The רמב״ן therefore believes that מוראה refers

17 *He shall tear it apart by its wings, but without dividing it completely in half, and the priest shall turn it into smoke upon the altar, on the wood that is on the fire; it is an ascent offering, an offering made by fire as an expression of compliance, to* God.

יז וְשִׁסַּע אֹתוֹ בִכְנָפָיו לֹא יַבְדִּיל
וְהִקְטִיר אֹתוֹ הַכֹּהֵן הַמִּזְבֵּחָה עַל־
הָעֵצִים אֲשֶׁר עַל־הָאֵשׁ עֹלָה הוּא
אִשֵּׁה רֵיחַ נִיחֹחַ לַיהוָה׃ ס

not only to the crop but also to the esophagus and stomach (קורקבן). If we add to these the בני המעיים mentioned in the Mishnah, what we have is the entire digestive apparatus.

According to the רמב״ן, מוראה derives from ראי, excrement. But to us it seems peculiar that the entire nutritive and digestive apparatus should derive its name from that which is discarded as waste, unfit for nourishment. Moreover, no ראי whatsoever is found in the זפק, the crop. It seems more likely that מוראה (like טומאה from טמא) derives from the root מרא; thus מריא, a fattened animal, and the Rabbinic term המראה (*Shabbos* 155b), the fattening of an animal.

The relation of מרה (to oppose) to מרא (to fatten) is not clear. As a mere suggestion we would say: perhaps the word מרא derives from the fact that it is the exact opposite of דם. מרא is food not yet digested, which the body has accepted only mechanically; דם, on the other hand, has been fully assimilated.

והשליך. According to תוספות (*Yoma* 59b, ד״ה והרי [end]), this השלכה is not an actual עבודה and does not require בגדי כהונה.

17 **ושסע** — like ושסעת שסע (below, 11:3), כְּשַׁסַּע הַגְּדִי (*Shoftim* 14:6) — means to split, to tear into two parts. It is related to שסה, as in הוּא יִשְׁסֶה אוֹצַר (*Hoshe'a* 13:15), to spoil. ושסע אותו בכנפיו — he shall tear it apart by its wings.

לא יבדיל. ואם הבדיל כשר (*Zevachim* 64b). *Toras Kohanim* explains: הרצייה (acceptance of the offering) is dependent upon מיצוי הדם, which is parallel to זריקה in עולת בהמה and which is what determines the character of the offering. Thus, a הבדלה that is performed after מיצוי הדם cannot invalidate. The same is true of other illegal procedures: כל ששינה בה מאחר שמיצה את דמה כשרה (ibid.).

When we reflect upon the *halachos* of עולת עוף we find that they differ from those of עולת בהמה — in the great majority of cases they are even diametrically opposed to them — and they are even at odds with the *halachos* of all other offerings. There is no requirement of תמות or זכרות in bird offerings. A bird may be offered as a קרבן עולה or חטאת but not שלמים; a קרבן ציבור may not be brought from birds. סמיכה is not performed. Instead of שחיטה there is מליקה, and מליקה is the very opposite of שחיטה: כל הפסול בשחיטה כשר במליקה (see *Chullin* 19b). מליקת עוף takes the place of שחיטת בהמה, yet מליקה must be performed by a כהן whereas שחיטה כשרה בזר. שחיטת עולת בהמה is בצפון and על ירך המזבח, whereas מליקת עולת עוף is בדרום and בראש המזבח. Instead of זריקה there is מיצוי הדם; instead of ניתוח into natural parts there is שיסוע, a tearing apart. The stomach and intestines of an עולת בהמה are sent up in smoke like the other איברים, whereas the corresponding parts of an עולת עוף are removed and thrown away.

Another distinctive feature of קרבן עוף — a feature that is most striking — is that precisely in the עבודת הדם, which is the essential *avodah* of the offering, the *halachos* of עולה and חטאת are reversed. דם עולת בהמה is בזריקה and למטה מחוט הסיקרא, while דם חטאת בהמה is בנתינה and למעלה על הקרנות. The reverse is true in the case of עוף: דם עולה is למעלה and במיצוי, corresponding to the נתינה of חטאת בהמה, while דם חטאת is למטה and בהזיה, corresponding to the זריקה of עולת בהמה.

All these *halachos* of עולת עוף cannot be attributed to the concept of עולה itself, as this concept is present also in עולת בקר וצאן. Rather, the reason for these *halachos* should be sought in the meaning of עוף as an offering. עולת בקר represents the עולה from the standpoint of בקר — i.e., from the standpoint of a life of work in the service of God. עולת צאן represents the עולה from the standpoint of צאן — i.e., from the standpoint of one's fate in life being in the hands of God. Similarly, עולת עוף represents the עולה from the standpoint of עוף; only from this standpoint will we understand its distinctiveness.

In תנ"ך a bird is often used as a metaphor for a person who is defenseless, who flees before his pursuer; a person whose life is in peril, who is in dire straits. כַּצִּפּוֹר לָנוּד, כְּצִפּוֹר נוֹדֶדֶת מִן־קִנָּהּ, כְּעוֹף־נוֹדֵד (*Mishlei* 26:2, 27:8; *Yeshayahu* 16:2) paint a picture of flight and wandering; צוֹד צָדוּנִי כַּצִּפּוֹר, כַּצִּפֳּרִים הָאֲחֻזוֹת בַּפָּח, כְּצִפּוֹר מִיַּד יָקוּשׁ (*Eichah* 3:53; *Koheles* 9:12; *Mishlei*

6:5) portray life under constant threat or in the thick of trouble. כָּל־בַּעַל כָּנָף, for every winged creature the net is spread out to trap them for their blood, to take their very lives (cf. *Mishlei* 1:17–18). The unfortunate person is כְּצִפּוֹר בּוֹדֵד עַל־גָּג, like a bird alone upon a roof (*Tehillim* 102:8). The dove in particular moans of suffering; thus, אֶהְגֶּה כַּיּוֹנָה (*Yeshayahu* 38:14; see also *Yirmeyahu* 48:28, *Nachum* 2:8, *Yeshayahu* 59:11).

Hence, it would appear that a bird offering, too, represents a state of suffering, or a forlorn individual who is in a state of suffering. Proof of this is in the fact that in קרבן עולה ויורד birds constitute the offering of the poor, and that otherwise we find an obligation to offer birds only in cases of bodily suffering or illness: זב וזבה ויולדת. This would also explain why birds are not used for שלמים, as שלמים represent a state of undisturbed happiness, the exact opposite of what a bird offering represents. Birds are also unfit for a קרבן ציבור, since the national community — especially the nation as represented by the Jewish Sanctuary of the Torah — knows no death or poverty; as our Sages put it: אין ציבור מת ואין ציבור עני (*Temurah* 15b; see also *Yerushalmi*, *Gittin* 3:7). Even in גלות the nation remains alive despite the absence of a מקדש.

In keeping with the theme of suffering which characterizes it, a bird offering requires neither זכרות nor תמות. Nor is סמיכה applicable, as it is observed only at those offerings that are related to the consecration of actions; it is not observed at בכור מעשר ופסח, and is certainly not observed at those offerings that represent man in a condition of weakness and suffering.

It would appear, then, that we may also explain in this way the procedures of עולת עוף; these, too, reflect the character of an offering of one who suffers. We suggest that עולת העוף represents the עולה from the standpoint of one for whom God has ordained a fate of suffering. This parallels what we have discovered about the other עולות: עולת בקר reflects the עולה from the standpoint of one who has dedicated to God his life's work; עולת צאן reflects the עולה from the standpoint of one who has been shepherded by God in his lot in life.

All the offering-procedures of עולת עוף exemplify violently performed actions — מליקה, מיצוי, הסרת מוראה, שיסוע — when compared with the corresponding procedures of עולת בהמה: שחיטה, זריקה, רחיצת קרבים, ניתוח. שחיטה is not intended for killing and destruction but for elevating the animal into the sphere of human-Jewish destiny. The use of the word שחיטה in the sense of killing is secondary. (The meaning of שחט is none other than שחד in an intensified sense, as one who gives שוחד "obtains others for his own use." For this reason great importance is attributed to the personality of the שוחט, and שחיטת נכרי נבילה [*Chullin* 13a].) שחיטה, accordingly, is done by skilled, humane means. מליקה, on the other hand, is performed בציפורן מצד העורף; it is an act that bears the stamp not of skilled, humane treatment but of violent raw destruction, and its analogy can be found only in עריפת פטר חמור and עריפת עגלה.

A similar contrast exists between pressing out the blood on the wall of the altar, on the one hand, and קבלת הדם וזריקתו, on the other; between removing and casting away the crop, on the one hand, and washing and burning the intestines, on the other; between tearing apart the bird by its wings, on the one hand, and cutting the animal into its natural parts, on the other.

These procedures that are performed at עולת עוף are intimately connected with the metaphorical meaning of birds, which reflects a life of suffering and defenselessness.

This initial analysis already explains to us why מליקה, unlike שחיטה, requires a כהן. שחיטה represents a moral action on the part of the בעלים; they themselves must repair their own hearts before they may enter the sphere of the Sanctuary. מליקה, on the other hand — like מיצוי and the other procedures which follow — is representative of the ideal embodied by the Sanctuary; hence, it is performed only by a כהן, a servant of the Sanctuary, and, like הקטרה, at the top of the altar, בראש המזבח.

In light of the preceding discussion let us try to conceptualize the offering-procedures of עולת עוף. It is the one who "suffers" who brings an עולת עוף; it is he who, by this offering, seeks to draw near to God through ascent and advancement; as a "turtledove" or "dove" he surrenders himself to the כהן. The embodiment of his personality is not brought to the north side, which represents the mid-night side of material existence; rather, the servant of the Sanctuary brings it to the south side, which symbolizes the light of the spirit, and from there he takes it up to the very height of the altar. Through מליקה בראש המזבח he teaches us that if it is ordained for a person to endure suffering and violence, this, too, is one of the tasks imposed upon him by the heights of the altar. And this is the moral duty demanded of a person in the midst of his suffering: He must cling with all his strength to the heights of Torah ideals; he must cleave to them even to the point of מיצוי הנפש, the loss of all lifeblood (מיצוי בקיר המזבח העליונה דרומית). Every drop of blood lost in such suffering contributes to the eminence of Jewish destiny. Even if one is stripped of all external protection, denied any possibility of restoring one's soul (הסרת המוראה עם נוצתה); even if one's body is violently torn asunder and left without blood or sustenance (שיסוע בכנפיו), nonetheless, by his very suffering he sustains the holy no less than one who serves God by his deeds. Both aspects — joyful action as well as devoted suffering — play a role in life as lived on Jewish heights. Even the head emptied of its blood, even the body torn asunder, bereft of blood and nourishment, can contribute to the perpetuation of God's fire upon earth (והקטיר אתו הכהן המזבחה על העצים אשר על האש); they, too, can become אשה ריח ניחח לה׳ on earth, which yearns to rise toward God. Truly, יָקָר בְּעֵינֵי ה׳ הַמָּוְתָה לַחֲסִידָיו (*Tehillim* 116:15) — such death, such martyrdom, from those who offer themselves up to Him in love, is precious in God's sight.

Now we can understand why the *halachos* of עולה and חטאת are reversed in קרבן עוף:

As stated above, the location of עבודות הדם in קרבן עוף and קרבן בהמה are reversed: דם עולת בהמה is למטה מחוט הסיקרא, whereas דם עולת עוף is למעלה, on the upper half of the altar; on the other hand, דם חטאת בהמה is למעלה על הקרנות, whereas דם חטאת עוף is למטה, on the lower half of the altar.

Just as the locations of the *avodos* are reversed, so are the *avodos* themselves, i.e., the manner of application. The עבודות הדם of קרבן בהמה suit the character of the offering: the עולה atones for a lack of progress; the חטאת for a lack of steadfastness. Hence, דם עולת בהמה is בזריקה, indicative of the energetic spurring of one's personality toward moral perfection; דם חטאת בהמה is בנתינה, indicative of cleaving to heights already attained. All this is reversed at קרבן עוף. דם עולת עוף is במיצוי — a firm pressing against the wall of the altar — which is nothing but a magnified נתינה, akin to that of חטאת בהמה; it denotes unwavering steadfastness. דם חטאת עוף is בהזיה, which is nothing but a diminished זריקה; it denotes movement toward a goal.

When we grasp the meaning of the עולה and חטאת of the "sufferer," the inversion of all these *halachos* no longer puzzles us. From the standpoint of ordinary life — which is represented by בקר and צאן — עולה is a response to neglect, and חטאת to recklessness in one's active life; עולה, therefore, represents dynamic upward movement, whereas חטאת denotes static repose, a clinging to heights already attained. From the standpoint

2 1 *A person who would bring near an homage offering to God — his offering shall be of fine wheat flour; he shall pour oil upon it and place frankincense upon it.*

ב א וְנֶפֶשׁ כִּֽי־תַקְרִ֞יב קָרְבַּ֤ן מִנְחָה֙ לַֽיהוָ֔ה סֹ֖לֶת יִהְיֶ֣ה קָרְבָּנ֑וֹ וְיָצַ֤ק עָלֶ֙יהָ֙ שֶׁ֔מֶן וְנָתַ֥ן עָלֶ֖יהָ לְבֹנָֽה׃

of a life of suffering, represented by תור ובן יונה, it is just the opposite: The positive task represented by the עולה is none other than steadfastness. The energy that in ordinary life comes to expression in action, in performing one's duty, should, in a condition of suffering, be directed inward, expressing itself in adherence to spiritual heights — despite all the suffering. עולת עוף is a response to a lack of steadfastness; hence, it represents remaining steadily on the heights. On the other hand, the sin of the sufferer is despair. Without hope, he gives up on his future; he rules out the belief in any possibility of ascending. And so he remains passive, ceasing all moral activity. חטאת העוף is directed against such an attitude; hence, it represents dynamic upward movement.

It is unclear what meaningful difference exists between תור and יונה. In *Yirmeyahu* (8:7) the תור is counted among migratory birds; perhaps, then, the name תור derives from the root תור (seek), as the bird seeks out for itself a favorable climate. In any case, תור would appear to be a bird that lives a free life and does not become domesticated like the יונה. It is therefore possible that the תור is to birds what the עז is to the family of צאן. Perhaps related to this is the halachah that תורים are fit as an offering only when mature, and יונים only when young. The significance of the יונה may be inferred from its name, deriving from the root ינה, which denotes weakness and suffering.

CHAPTER 2

1 **ונפש כי תקריב קרבן מנחה לה'**. The term מנחה appears also in contexts other than that of the offerings. In the overwhelming majority of these cases, its meaning is a gift by which the giver recognizes the receiver as the master of his fate, expresses his dependence on the receiver, and submits and subjects himself to the receiver's authority. We are therefore justified in saying that this is also the meaning of the מנחה offering, and

this will enable us to understand the meaning of the various procedures prescribed for the מנחה.

As we have noted in our Commentary to *Bereshis* (4:3–6), it is difficult to say with certainty what comprises the root of the word מנחה. If מנחה derives from the root נחה, its meaning is this: the gift giver acknowledges that the receiver leads him (מנחהו) on his way. However, the common plural form מנחות points to the root מנח, following the pattern of שפחות, שמלות. Accordingly, מנח would be the opposite of מנע (to withhold), in the same way that צלח and נוח are the opposites of צלע and נוע. Thus, the root מנח may be applied to one who withholds nothing from another, having given him the right to all he owns, placed all things at his feet. "Homage" captures the meaning of this root. The מקריב המנחה expresses through his gift that the possessions represented by it are really the property of the "Receiver"; from His hand were they extended to him, and by His Will do they remain with him on loan; with these possessions he submits to the Receiver and is ready to do His Will.

The above enables us to understand the unique wording that opens the chapter on the מנחה offering: ונפש כי תקריב וגו'. In the preceding offerings — עולות בהמה ועוף — the דם, the נפש itself, is given up to the altar as a means of drawing near to God. The נפש itself is the קרבן; the נפש itself is given up to the altar-heights representing our mission. In the מנחה, however, the נפש is not the קרבן but the מקריב; it brings not itself, but its possessions, before the altar of God: ונפש כי תקריב קרבן מנחה לה' — "A soul that would express its desire for God's closeness by bringing an homage-gift ..."

Five kinds of *menachos* are mentioned in this section: מנחת סולת, two kinds of מאפה תנור (namely, חלות and רקיקין), מחבת, and מרחשת. These five *menachos* are made of flour, oil, and frankincense. It is already apparent in the first verse that the essential part of the *minchah* is the flour; the oil and frankincense are merely supplements. It is to the flour, then, that we should turn for the fundamental idea of the *minchah*; the oil and frankincense will merely modify this idea.

There is no need to prove what is well known: flour is the symbol of sustenance; it represents all the material goods upon which human life depends. Thus, the meaning of flour offered at a *minchah* as a sign of homage is this: The condition for our very existence is in the hands of the One to Whom the *minchah* is offered.

If oil is added to the flour, the result is that שמנה חלקו (*Bereshis* 49:20) or, as more generally stated, שָׁמֵן חֶלְקוֹ (*Chavakkuk* 1:16) — "richness" and "oil bread" are added to plain sustenance.

לבונה is one of the ingredients of the קטורת and has a pleasing fragrance. It contributes to the above the further element of "satisfaction," which is not an automatic result of sustenance and richness but a separate blessing in its own right; for one can enjoy the richest foods and yet remain dissatisfied. As the text goes on to state (v. 2), the לבונה is an independent part of the offering — in addition to the flour mixed with oil.

Now, the expression ונפש כי תקריב restricts מנחת נדבה to the lone individual, as it says in *Menachos* (104b): הכל באין בשותפות לא סילק הכתוב אלא מנחה שנאמר נפש. Every other offering, even a single dove, may be brought jointly by two or more; the lone exception is *minchah*, as it says: נפש (a single soul).

The animal-offerings symbolize the human being who has a task to fulfill; the offering represents the נפש together with the body. But this task is something that is common to all, with each person complementing the achievements of his fellow: כל ישראל ערבִים זה בזה (*Shavu'os* 39a). The whole nation should be moved by one spirit, form one body, one soul. Understandably, then, an unlimited number of people may find joint expression in a single offering.

מנחה, however, does not symbolize man, but the means of his existence, prosperity, and satisfaction. For God provides each individual with the necessary conditions of his existence; in this respect, each person stands individually before God. It is the principle of השגחה פרטית which one discovers in this section. אין שנים מתנדבים עשרון אחד (*Menachos* 104b) — because each person gets his own special "עשרון" from God. This idea is reflected in the halachah that applies to all *menachos*: one must meet the *minchah*'s prescribed minimum measure; if one is short of an עשרון by even the slightest amount, the *minchah* is invalid (ibid. 27a).

Now, an עשרון is עשירית האיפה. The *minchah*, then, is like manna, which was collected עומר לגולגולת (*Shemos* 16:16), and the Torah states that "the עמר is עשרית האיפה" (ibid. 16:36). The מן, too, revealed God's providence relating to each individual soul. It would not even be farfetched to say that the name מנחה is merely an extension of מן, as the root of מן is מנה, which is closely related to מנח. מנחה would then mean: the portion allotted by God to man. By offering flour as a מנחה one would be expressing the idea that, even today, the bread that sustains us is none other than "manna"!

As stated above, the word נפש excludes a *minchah* brought jointly by two or more people. It also excludes ציבור from מנחות נדבה, of which this section speaks (*Toras Kohanim*, here). The ציבור brings only מנחת חובה (עומר, שתי הלחם, לחם הפנים) and מנחת נסכים.

There is great significance to the halachah that the ציבור is excluded from מנחות נדבה. For other nations, material independence and material prosperity constitute the main objective — almost the sole objective — of their national unity. Yet, for the Jewish nation, precisely this objective is of secondary import. To be sure, God watches over the national welfare, just as He watches over the welfare of each individual. This aspect of our relationship to God finds constant expression in the שולחן and לחם הפנים, and yearly expression in the עומר and שתי הלחם. It is also a part of מנחת נסכים (see *Bemidbar* 15). When the מרגלים returned from their exploration of the Land, they were found out to be of little faith; they did not believe it was possible to conquer the land that God had promised Israel. Thus, the elite of the people denied the power of God, on Whom the material welfare of the nation was solely dependent. Immediately following this, Israel was given the mitzvah of מנחת נסכים; henceforth, no עולה or זבח was to be brought without an accompanying מנחה and נסכים. This was to teach us that not only our personalities and destinies belong to God, but our material welfare, too, depends solely on Him. It was to ensure that we not assume the misguided mentality of one who says to God: "You are my Master, but טוֹבָתִי בַּל־עָלֶיךָ, my welfare here on earth does not reach up to You" (*Tehillim* 16:2). For this reason we were obligated to bring מנחת נסכים with every עולה, including עולת ציבור (cf. Commentary to *Bemidbar* 15:16).

But that is the full extent of the ציבור's connection to מנחה. Only as חובה, where God has imposed it as a duty, is the nation to remember before Him its material prosperity. But as נדבה the nation is to bring only עולות and to appear before God remembering only the sanctification of deeds. To the עולות the nation is to add מנחת נסכים, so as to give expression also to its material welfare — but only as a secondary consideration and as conditioned by the עולה. But a מנחת נדבה, in and of itself, is not to be brought by the nation. A similar concept is taught by the text of קריאת שמע. In the ואהבת section, which is directed at the individual, it says ובכל מאדך; but in the והיה אם שמע section, which is

2 *And he shall bring it to the sons of Aharon, the priests, one of whom shall take out his handful of its flour and of its oil, along with all its incense; and the priest shall turn its remembrance portion into smoke upon the altar, as an offering made by fire, an expression of compliance, to* God.

ב וְהֵבִיאָהּ אֶל־בְּנֵי אַהֲרֹן הַכֹּהֲנִים
וְקָמַץ מִשָּׁם מְלֹא קֻמְצוֹ מִסָּלְתָּהּ
וּמִשַּׁמְנָהּ עַל כָּל־לְבֹנָתָהּ וְהִקְטִיר
הַכֹּהֵן אֶת־אַזְכָּרָתָהּ הַמִּזְבֵּחָה
אִשֵּׁה רֵיחַ נִיחֹחַ לַיהוָה׃

directed at the nation, it does not say ובכל מאודכם — because the nation of Israel, as such, has neither national might nor national possessions.

It says here כי תקריב קרבן מנחה — and not just כי תקריב מנחה. The Gemara (*Zevachim* 91b) derives from this that a complete קרבן מנחה consists of all three, קמח שמן ולבונה; but שמן alone, or לבונה alone, may also be offered as a *minchah* (see *Toras Kohanim* to our verse).

סלת — see Commentary to *Bereshis* 18:6.

ויצק עליה שמן ונתן עליה לבנה. Scripture repeats the word עליה, which is descriptive of place, in order to distinguish between the place of the oil and the place of the frankincense. The oil is poured on top of all of the flour, whereas the frankincense is concentrated in one place. The repetition of the word עליה thus serves to limit the place of the frankincense, in accordance with the rule: אין ריבוי אחר ריבוי אלא למעט (*Toras Kohanim*).

2 **והביאה אל בני אהרן הכהנים**. יציקה and בלילה are valid even if performed by a non-*Kohen*; מצות כהונה is only מקמיצה ואילך (*Menachos* 18b).

וקמץ. The root קמץ, aside from being employed in connection with קמיצת מנחות, is employed only in *Bereshis* (41:47): ותעש הארץ וגו׳ לקמצים. קמץ is related to גמץ, the root of גומץ (a pit), as in חֹפֵר גּוּמָּץ (*Koheles* 10:8). It is also related to כמס and כמז, which denote the hiding, burying, or enclosure of an object.

The halachah defines the procedure of קמיצה as follows. The כהן sinks his hand into the dough and lifts out as much — and only exactly as much — as can be enclosed in the hollow space formed by closing the three middle fingers onto the palm: חופה ג׳ אצבעותיו עד שמגיע על פס ידו וקומץ (*Menachos* 11a). Thus, we see that קמיצה entails both כמיסה and the creation of a גומץ; for the קומץ is כמוס, enclosed in the palm, and when it is removed from the dough, a גומץ, a hollow space, is formed in its place.

The meaning of קמץ is therefore: to remove something and hold on to it, removing only as much as one is able to hold. But one who wishes to hold something will use — in a natural way — only the three middle fingers; for the little finger does not reach the palm unless by conscious effort. Hence, the measure of a קומץ is defined as the amount which is gripped in the hand by the closing of the three middle fingers.

We should further note: The כהן sinks his entire hand into the dough; then, he rubs away with his thumb and little finger any dough that protrudes beyond the קומץ. In this way he arrives at the exact measure of מלא קמצו — no more and no less. קמיצה — together with מליקה and חפינה — is one of the most difficult procedures to be performed at offerings, אחת מעבודות קשות שבמקדש (ibid.; but see רמב״ם הל׳ מעשה הקרבנות, 13:13, and כסף משנה, ad loc.).

The finger next to the little finger derives its name, קמיצה, from קמיצת מנחות. The little finger itself derives its name, זרת ("span"), from the measure by the same name, as this measure is equivalent to the distance between the little finger and the thumb. The middle finger is called אמה, for the אמה (cubit) is measured from its tip. The index finger is called אצבע; the אצבע הכהן mentioned in connection with the offering procedures refers to this finger. The thumb, which in Scripture is called בוהן, in *Mishnaic* Hebrew is called גודל (*Menachos* 11a).

וקמץ משם, from there, i.e., ממקום שרגלי הזר עומדות — from the place where the non-*Kohen* who brings the *minchah* may stand (ibid. 8b); קמיצה may be performed on any side of the Temple court. קמיצה corresponds to שחיטה, and מנחה — like עולה — is קודש קדשים; nevertheless, קמיצה need not be performed on the north side. An *animal* offering symbolizes *all* aspects of the human personality; hence, when we wish to emphasize in it the material aspect, the animal must be placed in the north, the side of the "Table of our material life." By contrast, the *minchah* offering's whole essence symbolizes just this one aspect; hence, it needs no special emphasis through צפון. We also see from this Gemara that קמיצה does not require דרום־מערב, the southwest corner of the altar. Only הגשה, which is performed between הבאה and קמיצה, requires דרום־מערב (see Commentary to v. 8). Scripture here skips over the intermediate procedure of הגשה, which is set down only in verse 8 vis-à-vis all *menachos*, because קמיצה is the first indispensable *avodah* in the *minchah* offering. קמיצה is directly linked here with הבאה by the omission of הגשה, as if to say: the object of הבאה is קמיצה.

מסלתה ומשמנה — of *its* flour and *its* oil, i.e., the קמיצה should be taken from the prescribed measure of flour and oil; for מיעוטו מעכב את רובו, if even the slightest amount is missing from the prescribed measure of the מנחה, the whole thing is invalid (ibid. 27a). The Gemara states further that a מנחה חסרה is comparable to a בהמה בעלת מום: החסרון כבעל מום דמי (ibid. 9b).

The basic measure for all *menachos* is one עשרון of flour and one לוג of oil. One may bring several עשרונים as מנחת נדבה, with the number of לוגין of oil matching the number of עשרונים (ibid. 88a). But the basic measure remains always one עשרון, and all *menachos* would be measured in a one-עשרון measure. We have already explained above (v. 1) the significance of this measure: it corresponds to the עומר לגולגולת of the manna, and this would explain the strictness with which one must meet the prescribed minimum (one עשרון). What relation exists between this measure and the לוג measure set for oil, we do not know. Perhaps a לוג is simply the proportion of oil to flour that is needed for a perfect mixing, in which case the basic measure of לוג hinges on the basic measure of עשרון.

We learn further from the juxtaposition of the words מסלתה ומשמנה that the קומץ is to be taken ממקום שנתרבה שמנה, from a place where the flour is saturated with the oil (*Sotah* 14b). The קומץ will thus contain מסלתה ומשמנה, and both ingredients will be equally represented in it.

על כל לבנתה — even if a *minchah* consists of sixty עשרונים (the maximum which may be brought in one vessel), only one קומץ לבנה is used for the whole (*Toras Kohanim*).

The procedure for bringing a *minchah* is described in *Sotah* (14b) as follows: סדר מנחות כיצד, אדם מביא מנחה מתוך ביתו בקלתות של כסף ושל זהב ונותנה לתוך כלי שרת לקדשה בכלי שרת ונותן עליה שמנה ולבונתה ומוליכה אצל כהן וכהן מוליכה אצל מזבח ומגישה בקרן דרומית מערבית כנגד חודה של קרן ודיו ומסלק

את הלבונה לצד אחד וקומץ ממקום שנתרבה שמנה ונותנו לתוך כלי שרת לקדשו בכלי שרת ומלקט את לבונתה ונותנה על גביו ומעלהו בכלי שרת להקטירו ומולחו ונותנו על גבי האישים.

From this we learn that between קמיצה and הקטרה would intervene קידוש הקומץ — i.e., נתינת הקומץ לתוך כלי שרת לקדשו — whereby the קומץ was sanctified separately, even though, as a part of the whole *minchah*, it had already been sanctified.

We have already explained, in our Commentary to *Shemos* (29:37; 30:29), the nature of קדושה בכלי שרת: An object that is placed in a כלי שרת belongs to the Sanctuary; and it is invested with קדושת הגוף, which cannot be released through פדיון. Before there is קדושת הגוף, the verbal consecration and the conveyance to the Temple court invest the *minchah*'s contents with קדושת דמים; and if these contents are rendered ritually impure and hence unfit for a *minchah*, their sanctity can be released through פדיון, so that they reassume their ordinary character. But once they are placed in a כלי שרת, they are invested with קדושת הגוף, which cannot be released through פדיון. Among the manifestations of such קדושה is that the object becomes פסול בטבול יום ובלינה (see Commentary below, 22:7; 6:2).

Now, the whole *minchah* had already become קודש in a כלי שרת before the קמיצה; yet the קומץ is then placed in another כלי שרת, to be especially sanctified after the קמיצה. One finds the same phenomenon in the case of an animal offering: The animal had already become קודש, as of the שחיטה, by contact with a knife of the Sanctuary; yet the blood is then especially received (קבלה) in a כלי שרת, to be sanctified for the sake of the זריקה. So, too, with a *minchah*: the קומץ is especially received (נתינה) in a כלי שרת, to be sanctified for the sake of הקטרה, which corresponds to זריקה (*Sotah* 14b; רש״י, ad loc.).

The Gemara (*Menachos* 7a–b) states further: מקדשין מנחה בכלי שעל גבי קרקע; קומצין מכלי שעל גבי קרקע; ואין מקדשין קומץ בכלי שעל גבי קרקע – דילפינן מדם. That is, קידוש מנחה, the sanctification of the whole *minchah*, could be performed in a vessel standing on the floor of the Sanctuary, and so could the קמיצה be taken from such a vessel; but for קידוש הקומץ the כהן had to take a sacred vessel in his hand and receive in it the קומץ for the הקטרה, in the same way that the כהן, in the case of קבלת הדם בכלי שרת, had to receive the blood for the זריקה.

Thus, we find in the *minchah* offering four עבודות that parallel the four עבודות הדם: שחיטה = קמיצה, קבלה = קידוש קומץ, הולכה = הולכה, זריקה = הקטרה.

על כל לבנתה. The כהן adds the whole of the frankincense to the קומץ in the כלי שרת.

והקטיר הכהן את אזכרתה. אזכרתה נזכרים בה נזכרים בקומצה נזכרים בלבונתה (*Toras Kohanim*, our verse). If Scripture had said והקטיר אותם הכהן אזכרה, the concept of אזכרה would have related only to *the parts given over to the fire* and would have expressed the purpose of their being offered: as אזכרה, or for the sake of אזכרה. Scripture, however, refers here to these parts as אזכרתה, the אזכרה *of the minchah*; through them the entire *minchah* is invested with the concept of אזכרה. Through the offering of the קומץ and the לבונה, the שיריים, too — i.e., the נותרת מן המנחה of the next verse — are remembered before God. This is the meaning of the above citation from *Toras Kohanim*: נזכרים בה — the one bringing the offering is to be remembered before God through the entire *minchah*; and this זכירה is to be implemented by means of the קומץ and the לבונה (see קרבן אהרן, ad loc.).

We have here an indication of the intimate relation of the קומץ and לבונה to the שיריים; for הקטרת הקומץ והלבונה is indispensable, and in no respect corresponds to הקטרת אימורים. הקטרת אימורים is an *avodah* of secondary importance: although the בשר הקרבן should not be eaten before הקטרת אימורים, nevertheless, if it becomes impossible to offer up the אימורים — e.g., if נטמאו האימורים — the בשר is מותר באכילה. For it is not the אימורים but the דם which is the מתיר; the מתנות הדם (such as זריקה and the like) constitute the crucial part of the offering.

הקטרת קומץ ולבונה, on the other hand, is an *avodah* of primary importance. It is the מתיר for the שיריים; it is indispensable, like זריקה; and it is the crucial part of the *minchah* (see תוספות, *Zevachim* 43a, ד״ה והלבונה).

Thus, the relation of הקטרת קומץ ולבונה to the שיריים is like that of the דם to the בשר (see above, Commentary to 1:9) — only that here the connection is even more intimate. For זריקת דם may be performed as long as there remains at least a כזית בשר or a כזית חלב to be rendered fit — by the זריקה — for the מזבח or for human consumption. But this is not the case with מנחה; for if even the slightest amount of the שיריים is found to be missing before the הקטרה (שיריים שחסרו בין קמיצה להקטרה), the שיריים are פסולים (only that according to רבי יוחנן the קומץ is nevertheless offered up, whereas according to ריש לקיש there is to be no הקטרת קומץ at all [*Menachos* 9a–b]).

3 *The remainder of the homage offering shall be for Aharon and his sons, a holy of holies from the fire offerings to God.*	ג וְהַנּוֹתֶ֙רֶת֙ מִן־הַמִּנְחָ֔ה לְאַהֲרֹ֖ן וּלְבָנָ֑יו קֹ֥דֶשׁ קָֽדָשִׁ֖ים מֵאִשֵּׁ֥י יְהֹוָֽה׃ ס

As we have said, the crucial part of the *minchah* (הקטרה) is the act that engenders אזכרה. It follows, then, that the concept of אזכרה complements the concept of *minchah*, and that the two concepts, together, form the meaning of the *minchah* offering. The purpose of the act that engenders אזכרה is clear: to elevate the *minchah* 'לזכרון לפני ה, that God may remember the special relationships represented by the *minchah* and let them be the object of His special care and attention. Compare: ונזכרתם לפני ה׳ אלהיכם (*Bemidbar* 10:9). Thus, the *minchah* is not only an expression of allegiance but is at the same time a prayer: that God, in Whose hands rest our daily bread, our prosperity, our satisfaction with life, may remember and bless those things on which all our external happiness depends. In fact, this is the very essence of our allegiance: that we look only to God for our prosperity. Truly, the concept of זכירה conveys the essence of the *minchah*; for this reason one finds that the verb זכר expresses both the intention of the one bringing the *minchah* as well as God's responsiveness to his plea: מַזְכִּיר לְבֹנָה (*Yeshayahu* 66:3); יִזְכֹּר כָּל־מִנְחֹתֶךָ (*Tehillim* 20:4).

3 **והנותרת מן המנחה**. קרב הקומץ שיריה נאכלין (*Sotah* 14b; 15a). The eating of the *minchah* is contingent upon the offering up of the קומץ, which is the מתיר of the שיריים.

מן המנחה. As we noted in verse 2, only if the *minchah* was still there in its entirety at the time of the הקטרה may the שיריים be eaten.

We have already explained, in our Commentary to *Shemos* (29:33), the significance of the *Kohanim*'s eating of the offering. This eating is one of the *avodos* embodying the concept of an offering, as it says: הכהנים אוכלים ובעלים מתכפרין (*Pesachim* 59b). אכילת כהנים is the culmination of שחיטה זריקה והקטרה. The purpose of all three is not the negation of life, but its positive upbuilding. כהנים משולחן גבוה קא זכו (*Menachos* 6a) — as it says at the end of our verse: 'מאשי ה; אכילת כהנים is a continuation of אכילת מזבח. For this is the way to sustain the holy on earth: It is one's duty to use all his powers and all his possessions for the advancement of his life's aspirations, a life sanctified by the rule of the Torah. The *Kohanim*, clothed in holy garments, exemplify this. אכילת כהנים shows man the way to God's closeness, which can be attained only by leading a full life and yet living it with priestlike sanctity.

An offering's positive purpose is all the more striking in the case of *minchah*. For this קרבן relates to those aspects of life about which heathen thought is grossly mistaken; aspects which, in the heathen view, must be negated in order to attain God's closeness. In a *minchah*, not man's personality but his material goods are brought near to God. (According to the heathen conception of God, however, God is resentful of man's happiness; only grudgingly will he grant mortals an abundance of food, prosperity, and joy in life. He is envious of man's happy, refined enjoyment of life, and is gratified only by man's self-limiting sacrifice.) For this reason the requirements of a *minchah* (the "possessions-offering") go beyond those of an animal offering. The remainder of the *minchah* must still be complete at the time of הקטרה במזבח, and a מנחה חסרה is like a זבח בעל מום (ibid. 9b). Only one קומץ — no less but also *no more* (it should not be מבורץ) — is to be given over to the altar fire (ibid. 11a). This constitutes not destruction but אזכרה, the symbolic expression of the *minchah*'s message: partake of life and rejoice in it, but in priestlike sanctity — and rest assured of God's full blessing!

לאהרן ולבניו. We have mentioned several times the relation between the כהן גדול and the other *Kohanim*. The כהן גדול is the nation's representative in the Service of the Sanctuary; the כהנים הדיוטות are merely his assistants. Accordingly, in relation to the other *Kohanim* he is in a class by himself. Therefore, when it says here לאהרן ולבניו it is as though it says מחצה לאהרן ומחצה לבניו, and hence the halachah: כהן גדול מקריב חלק בראש ונוטל חלק בראש (*Yoma* 14a). However, with respect to קדשי גבול, such as תרומה and the like, the status of the כהן גדול is like that of the other *Kohanim* (רמב״ם הל׳ כלי המקדש, 5:12; משנה למלך, ad loc.).

קדשי קדשים. See Commentary to *Shemos* 29:37.

מאשי ה׳. אכילת כהנים is the realization of the idea of אכילת מזבח (see above).

4 *And if you would bring near an homage offering that is baked in the oven, then let it be fine wheat flour mixed with oil in the form of matzah loaves or of thin matzah wafers brushed with oil.*

ד וְכִ֥י תַקְרִ֛ב קׇרְבַּ֥ן מִנְחָ֖ה מַאֲפֵ֣ה
תַנּ֑וּר סֹ֣לֶת חַלּ֤וֹת מַצֹּת֙ בְּלוּלֹ֣ת
בַּשֶּׁ֔מֶן וּרְקִיקֵ֥י מַצּ֖וֹת מְשֻׁחִ֥ים
בַּשָּֽׁמֶן׃ ס

5 *And if your offering is an homage offering baked on a pan, then let it be fine wheat flour mixed with oil, matzah.*

ה וְאִם־מִנְחָ֥ה עַל־הַֽמַּחֲבַ֖ת קׇרְבָּנֶ֑ךָ
סֹ֛לֶת בְּלוּלָ֥ה בַשֶּׁ֖מֶן מַצָּ֥ה תִהְיֶֽה׃

6 *Break it up into pieces and pour oil upon it; it is an homage offering.*

ו פָּת֤וֹת אֹתָהּ֙ פִּתִּ֔ים וְיָצַקְתָּ֥ עָלֶ֖יהָ
שָׁ֑מֶן מִנְחָ֖ה הִֽוא׃ ס שלישי

7 *And if your offering is an homage offering prepared in a deep pot, let it be prepared from fine wheat flour in oil.*

ז וְאִם־מִנְחַ֥ת מַרְחֶ֖שֶׁת קׇרְבָּנֶ֑ךָ
סֹ֖לֶת בַּשֶּׁ֥מֶן תֵּעָשֶֽׂה׃

4–7 Characteristic of מנחת סולת, described in verses 1–3, is that the flour and the oil — the materials of sustenance and prosperity — are offered just as they are; they are subjected to no other preparation beside בלילה. The ensuing verses treat four kinds of מנחות that are prepared through cooking: two kinds of מאפה תנור, baked in the oven — namely, חלות and רקיקין; מנחה על מחבת, baked on a flat pan; and מנחת מרחשת, which is soft-doughed, and prepared in a deep pot.

The etymology of the word חלות is obscure, and it is also a word that is difficult to translate. Whereas cake is baked from special dough and is intended more to appeal to taste than to satisfy hunger, חלה, on the other hand, refers to ordinary bread-dough (*Bemidbar* 15:20); it also alternates with the term ככר (*Shemos* 29:2, 23), which denotes shape or weight. Apparently, חלה refers to any part of a dough that is formed into a separate loaf. Here, חלות is contrasted with רקיקין, as a חלה is thicker than a רקיק, which is a thin, wafer-like bread.

Three different expressions are employed for the application of oil to מנחות. In verses 1 and 6 it says יציקה — ויצק(ת) עליה שמן; in verses 4 and 5 it says בלילה — בלולת (בלולה) בשמן; in verse 7 it says סלת בשמן, i.e., first oil in a vessel, and then flour onto the oil — מתן שמן בכלי. (This is the order in which they appear in Scripture — which is apparently the model for their order in the Mishnah in *Menachos* 74b — though in the preparation of a *minchah* the order of the three applications is reversed; see רש״י [ibid.].)

These expressions refer to three separate applications of oil, which are practiced at all *menachos* except מאפה תנור. First, one puts oil in a vessel (מתן שמן בכלי); then one adds the flour; then more of the oil is poured over the flour and mixed with it (בלילה); and when the *minchah*, in a כלי שרת, is ready for קמיצה, one pours over it the remainder of the לוג of oil (יציקה). Thus, in a מנחת סולת the יציקה follows בלילה and נתינה בכלי שרת (whether בלילה itself also requires a כלי שרת is a question that has not been decided; see משנה למלך הל׳ מעשה הקרבנות, 13:5), whereas in a מנחת מחבת or מרחשת the יציקה follows the פתיתה. In מאפה תנור there is no יציקה, and according to the רמב״ם there is no מתן שמן בכלי either; that is to say, in חלות מאפה תנור there is only בלילה. In the case of רקיקין there is no oil at all in the dough but only משיחה after they are baked (משנה למלך, ibid., elaborates). According to the Mishnah in *Menachos*, this משיחה is executed in the form of the Greek letter X, והשאר נאכל לכהנים, "and the remaining oil is consumed by the *Kohanim*." (For more on this משיחה see Commentary to *Shemos* 29:7. According to a different opinion [*Menachos* 75a], מושחן וחוזר ומושחן עד שיכלה כל שמן שבלוג, "one anoints [the רקיקין] repeatedly until the entire לוג of oil is used up." The רמב״ם accepts this view as the הלכה, despite the general rule that the הלכה follows the anonymous opinion in the Mishnah; see כסף משנה ולחם משנה הל׳ מעשה הקרבנות, 13:9.)

According to what is stated in *Menachos* (63a), a מחבת is flat with a low rim (the רמב״ם avers that it has no rim at all), whereas a מרחשת is deep with a high rim (according to ר׳ יוסי הגלילי it also has a cover). This would explain the wording of the verse (below, 7:9): וכל נעשה במרחשת ועל מחבת — "... *in* a מרחשת and *on* a מחבת." In any event, in the case of מנחה על מחבת the oil evaporates; hence, its dough is hard, whereas that which is cooked in a מרחשת is rich in oil and soft. It is called מרחשת because מעשיה רוחשין (*Menachos* 5:8). רָחַשׁ (*Tehillim* 45:2) signifies an inner stirring (cf. Commentary to *Bereshis* 1:1; in Aramaic, רחש is the word for שרץ and, likewise, signifies movement).

As we have stated, one who brings a מנחה commits himself to God with respect to his sustenance, prosperity, and satisfaction. A מנחה, then, relates to happiness in life. In this light we can understand the differences between the various kinds of מנחות. מנחת סולת represents the general, basic elements of happiness. The other מנחות represent varying degrees of the realization of this happiness, for the manifestations of happiness in life are many and multifarious. But the basic conditions of this happiness remain always the same. Furthermore, only the external manifestations are diverse and multifarious, in quantity as well as quality; but the מלא כף נחת, the basic "handful of satisfaction," is the same in all of them — just as the one קומץ לבונה (handful of frankincense) is the same in all מנחות.

Let us now compare the מנחות prepared in a תנור, on a מחבת, or in a מרחשת. It would seem that their relation to one another is like that of bread, cake, and a cooked dish. מאפה תנור is the bread; it represents ordinary food and the goods of everyday life. מחבת is the cake; it represents extraordinary pleasure — a special and exceptional state of happiness. מרחשת is a cooked dish that is savored in a moment; it represents a temporary, passing moment of joy. From all three together we learn a profound truth: Not only everyday needs but also luxuries and each passing moment of joy — all these are given us by God's special providence; for all of these we commit ourselves to God and offer praises before Him.

As stated above, the preparation of מנחת סולת מחבת ומרחשת begins with מתן שמן בכלי and ends with יציקה; that is, at the beginning flour is added to oil (סלת בשמן), and at the end oil is poured over it (עליה שמן). These מנחות, then — with the oil before and after the flour — highlight the aspects of affluence and prosperity; sustenance is merely an important part of prosperity and is even indicative of affluence: בלולת בשמן.

In מאפה תנור, which represents the needs of daily life, there is no יציקה and, apparently, no מתן שמן בכלי either (see above); there is only בלילה — and even here only with the חלות. With the רקיקין, however, none of the מתנות השמן observed at the other מנחות are applicable; רקיקין are only daubed over externally with oil after they are baked (משיחה לאחר אפיה). This מנחה, then, highlights the aspect of sustenance; the sign of prosperity is merely an added ingredient. In this last regard, חלות differ from רקיקין. In the case of חלות בלולות בשמן, the bread contains elements of, and is indicative of, prosperity. In the case of רקיקין, the bread itself is free of such a sign, as it is just ordinary matzah; prosperity finds expression

ח וְהֵבֵאתָ אֶת־הַמִּנְחָה אֲשֶׁר יֵעָשֶׂה מֵאֵלֶּה לַיהוָה וְהִקְרִיבָהּ אֶל־הַכֹּהֵן וְהִגִּישָׁהּ אֶל־הַמִּזְבֵּחַ׃

ט וְהֵרִים הַכֹּהֵן מִן־הַמִּנְחָה אֶת־אַזְכָּרָתָהּ וְהִקְטִיר הַמִּזְבֵּחָה אִשֵּׁה רֵיחַ נִיחֹחַ לַיהוָה׃

י וְהַנּוֹתֶרֶת מִן־הַמִּנְחָה לְאַהֲרֹן וּלְבָנָיו קֹדֶשׁ קָדָשִׁים מֵאִשֵּׁי יְהוָה׃

8 *You shall bring to* God *the homage offering that is prepared from these [ingredients]; one brings it near to the priest, who [in turn] shall bring it near to the altar.*

9 *The priest shall lift out its remembrance portion from the homage offering and turn it into smoke upon the altar as an offering made by fire, as an expression of compliance, to* God.

10 *The remainder of the homage offering shall be for Aharon and his sons, a holy of holies from the fire offerings unto* God.

in the oil, but the bread itself shows only an external trace of it. The amount of oil and flour is the same for both of these מנחות; but in the case of חלות all of the oil is mixed with the flour, whereas in the case of רקיקין the remaining oil is consumed by the *Kohanim* (according to the halachah taught in the Mishnah משחה כמין כי וכו׳). The חלות and רקיקין of מנחת מאפה תנור, then, represent contentment and moderation in partaking of one's food, as their richness is diverted for other purposes.

8–10 **והבאת וגו׳ והקריבה וגו׳ והגישה וגו׳ והרים וגו׳**. Here, the הגשה is mentioned, the intermediate procedure between הבאה and קמיצה, to which we referred in verse 2.

This is the order of things: The one bringing the *minchah* hands it over in a כלי שרת to the כהן. Before taking the קמיצה, the כהן brings the *minchah*, in a כלי שרת, right up to the southwest corner of the altar; this הגשה is described below (6:7–8) as follows: הקרב אתה בני אהרן לפני ה׳ אל פני המזבח והרים וגו׳. Thus, the whole *minchah* is to be brought near to the altar before the קמיצה. The place where it is to be brought near is לפני ה׳, i.e., on the west side, and אל פני המזבח, i.e., the south; the combination of these two is at the southwest corner, בקרן דרומית מערבית (*Menachos* 19b).

This הגשה is performed at all *menachos* that are brought independently (הבאות בגלל עצמן) and that are either entirely offered, or of which a קומץ is offered, upon the altar (שיש מהן לאישים). Accordingly, it is not performed at מנחת נסכים, which is not brought independently but accompanies a קרבן, nor is it performed at שתי הלחם or לחם הפנים, of which no part is offered upon the altar (ibid. 60a–b).

הגשה is not indispensable to the validity of the offering; nevertheless, it may be performed only by a כהן. It must, then, be of import to the concept of a *minchah*.

In *Melachim* (I, 5:1) it says: וּשְׁלֹמֹה הָיָה מוֹשֵׁל בְּכָל־הַמַּמְלָכוֹת וגו׳ מַגִּשִׁים מִנְחָה וְעֹבְדִים אֶת־שְׁלֹמֹה וגו׳. Thus, הגשה is the act through which a gift becomes an act of homage; the מגיש המנחה lays the offering at the feet of the one for whom it is intended, placing it at his disposal.

This is apparently the significance of the הגשה in קרבן מנחה as well. The *minchah* represents the resources of our material life; but before the כהן lifts out the קומץ and לבונה from the *minchah*, he first places it in God's dominion, at the location representing the spirit that derives from the Torah (the southwest). In this way he symbolically acknowledges that from the hand of God alone have we received the material resources of our lives — sustenance and prosperity, and the satisfaction to be gained from both. We must therefore subordinate all these resources to the spirit illuminated in His Torah. הגשה gives expression to the fundamental idea upon which all the ensuing procedures are based; for in this spirit are קמיצה, נתינה בכלי, הקטרה and אכילת כהנים subsequently to be carried out:

Through קמיצה and נתינה בכלי the Sanctuary symbolically reaches into our material resources and receives them, to be used for its purposes. Through הקטרת הקומץ וכל הלבונה we consecrate a portion of our worldly goods and all the joy of our lives, in order to sustain the holy on earth. We thereby indicate our resolve to give over to God's fire also the resources related to our physical existence and comforts; to merge the joy we take in life with the joy God takes in us; to allow joy in our hearts only if it is consistent with God's joy in us; or better, that God's joy in us be our sole source of joy. אכילת כהנים teaches us that the surrender of our material resources to God in no way entails the renunciation of worldly goods and pleasures, but demands only that they be enjoyed in priestlike sanctity, within the framework and in the spirit of the Torah. It teaches us that such enjoyment, too, is a mitzvah, a way of serving God.

Now, the significance of the הגשה, which precedes all of the above, is this: It teaches that this consecration of our lives to the performance of God's Will is not something above and beyond the call of duty; rather, it is an obligation we owe to God with every fiber of our being. What we consecrate to God at קמיצה and הקטרה we have already acknowledged, at הגשה, as having been received — or as that which will be received — from His hand. Our greatest act of self-dedication to God is nothing more than the fulfillment of our most elementary duty toward Him. As it says: מִמְּךָ הַכֹּל וּמִיָּדְךָ נָתַנּוּ לָךְ, "All is from You, and from Your hand have we given to You" (*Divrei Ha-Yamim* I, 29:14). In this context we can also understand why הגשה is performed only at those *menachos* of which a part is offered upon the altar.

We further note that while in all the previous and subsequent laws the text uses the impersonal third person to refer to the one bringing the offering, here in the case of the *minchah* offering (vv. 6–8, and perhaps already in v. 5) it changes to the second person. The reason for this may be as follows. In the case of all the other offerings it is the person himself (דם = נפש) who seeks to draw closer to God through the קרבן. At the time of the offering, though, he is still far away from God; that is why he is referred to in impersonal terms. In the case of *minchah*, however, the person himself has already drawn closer to God, and he seeks now to bring near to God also the material aspects of his physical life. He stands before God and places before Him the material things of his life. Hence, the more intimate second person is most fitting for him.

The transition in verse 8 from second to third person — **והבאת** ... **והקריבה** — can be explained by the intervening word **יעשה**. Its subject cannot be the preceding **מנחה**, which is feminine; rather, the subject of **יעשה** must be the impersonal "one" ("the *minchah* that one makes from these ..."). The impersonal subject then continues with **והקריבה**, in the third person. We learn from the word **יעשה** the following: **מצות כהונה** is from **הגשה** onward, but the preceding act need not necessarily be performed by the **בעלים** themselves, but can be carried out by anyone on their behalf.

את אזכרתה, i.e., קומץ and לבונה. The קמיצה, the הקטרה, and the **אכילת כהנים** are repeated here to connect them with the הגשה.

11 *Any homage offering that you bring near to* God *must not be prepared leavened, for no leaven or fruit honey may be offered up in smoke as a fire offering to* God.

יא כָּל־הַמִּנְחָה אֲשֶׁר תַּקְרִיבוּ לַיהוָה
לֹא תֵעָשֶׂה חָמֵץ כִּי כָל־שְׂאֹר
וְכָל־דְּבַשׁ לֹא־תַקְטִירוּ מִמֶּנּוּ
אִשֶּׁה לַיהוָה׃

12 *You shall bring these near to* God *as an offering of first fruits, but they must not come upon the altar as an expression of compliance.*

יב קָרְבַּן רֵאשִׁית תַּקְרִיבוּ אֹתָם
לַיהוָה וְאֶל־הַמִּזְבֵּחַ לֹא־יַעֲלוּ
לְרֵיחַ נִיחֹחַ׃

11–12 It has already been said above (vv. 4–5) that מנחת תנור ומנחת מחבת must be matzah. Here, Scripture says of all *menachos* that no part of them may be allowed to leaven. This prohibition is later repeated vis-à-vis baking: לא תאפה חמץ (below, 6:10). Applicable here is the hermeneutic rule דבר שהיה בכלל ויצא מן הכלל ללמד, לא ללמד על עצמו יצא, אלא ללמד על הכלל כולו יצא ("Where something is included in a general statement and is then made the subject of a specific statement, what is specifically stated is not limited to itself alone, but, rather, applies to the whole general statement"). From this we learn that the prohibition of חמץ applies to each one of the procedures in the preparation of a *minchah*, so that one is חייב על לישתה ועל עריכתה ועל אפייתה (*Menachos* 55a). Furthermore, the prohibition stated below (6:10) refers first and foremost to the שיריים — the portion of the *Kohanim*. For Scripture says prior to the prohibition, והנותרת ממנה יאכלו אהרן ובניו, and following the prohibition, חלקם נתתי אתה מאשי; thus, the subject of לא תאפה חמץ is הנותרת. We see, then, that the prohibition applies not only to the portion given over to the altar, but also to the שיריים, the portion of the *Kohanim* (*Menachos* 55a). Watching the *menachos* lest they become *chametz* demands extraordinary vigilance, to be expected only of זריזין (those who are ardent in fulfilling their duty) and במקום זריזין (in the Sanctuary), as "all the *menachos* are kneaded with lukewarm water," כל המנחות נילושות בפושרין (ibid.).

כי כל שאר וגו׳. The prohibition of הקטרת חמץ is the reason for the prohibition of preparing a leavened *minchah*. From the word כל we learn that such הקטרה is prohibited בכל שהוא, in any quantity. From the expression כי כל we learn that there is a special stringency in the prohibition of הקטרת חמץ, as it is the reason for the prohibition of preparing a leavened *minchah*; thus, from here we learn that even תערובת חמץ, any admixture with חמץ, is forbidden to be offered up in smoke (ibid. 58a).

וכל דבש. No דבש may be offered up in smoke, just as שאור may not be so offered. From the contrast, קרבן ראשית וגו׳ (v. 12), it would appear that the term דבש includes only what is fit for ביכורים — and not bee honey. Now, ordinarily the term דבש has a limited, specialized meaning: דבש תמרים (date-honey); but here the term refers to all fruit of trees, as רש״י puts it: כל מתיקת פרי, "all fruit nectar" (for proof from the Gemara see משנה למלך הל׳ איסורי מזבח, 5:1). Apparently this is also the meaning of the term in the expression זבת חלב ודבש, the set designation for the Land of Israel. Here, too, דבש refers to all fruit nectar.

שאור and דבש are אסורים למזבח only if brought as an offering, but it is permissible to use them as fuel in addition to the altar wood, as it is said: לריח ניחוח אי אתה מעלה, אבל אתה מעלה לשם עצים (*Zevachim* 76b). דבש is אסור only for הקטרה, but שיריים mixed with דבש may be eaten; thus, the איסור שאור includes more than the איסור דבש.

קרבן ראשית refers to the שתי הלחם and ביכורים. שתי הלחם are brought on שבועות from the new wheat, and only after they are offered in the מקדש is it permissible to offer a מנחה from new grain; hence, שתי הלחם are called מנחה חדשה and בכורים (below, 23:16–17). (Similarly, only after the עומר is offered is it permissible, outside the מקדש, to partake of new grain.) שתי הלחם are חמץ, as it says: חמץ תאפינה (ibid. 23:17). ביכורים (*Devarim* 26:1ff) are brought from שבח ארץ ישראל, the seven species for which Eretz Yisrael is praised (ibid. 8:8), namely חטה, שעורה, גפן, תאנה, רמון, זית שמן ודבש. They include, then, דבש תמרים and fruit of trees, which are called here דבש and are forbidden to be offered on the altar. קרבן ראשית denotes both שתי הלחם and ביכורים. Our verse states that although שאור and דבש are brought to the altar as קרבן ראשית, nevertheless they may not be given over to the altar fire לריח ניחח. Indeed, שתי הלחם and ביכורים are only "waved" (תנופה) on the east side of the עזרה and then given to the *Kohanim* (*Menachos* 61a).

Let us now try to understand the inner connection between שאור and דבש; for they have been linked here in the prohibition of הקטרה and in the very concept of קרבן ראשית.

The Halachah joins to the above a third — and apparently quite unrelated — law. Like שאור and דבש, this third element, too, is included in the prohibition לא תקטירו ממנו אשה לה׳. In *Menachos* (57b) it says: תנו רבנן, מניין למעלה מבשר חטאת ומבשר אשם ומבשר קדשי הקדשים ומקדשים קלים וממותר העומר וממותר שתי הלחם ומלחם הפנים ומשירי מנחות שהוא בלא תעשה, ת״ל כי כל שאור וכל דבש לא תקטירו ממנו אשה לה׳, כל שהוא ממנו לאישים הרי הוא בבל תקטירו. That is, just as הקטרת שאור ודבש is forbidden, so is the הקטרה of all those portions of offerings from which or for which an offering has been burned upon the altar, rendering them permissible to eat. This prohibition applies to בשר חטאת ואשם וכו׳, since the אימורים have been offered from them; and it applies to שיירי המנחות, since the קומץ has been offered from them. It also applies to שתי הלחם, since חלבי כבשי עצרת have been offered for them; and it applies to לחם הפנים, since בזיכי לבונה have been offered for them.

The Halachah (ibid. 58a) extends the concept of כל שממנו לאישים even further: its application is not limited to those portions of offerings from which an offering has been burned upon the altar; rather, it applies to everything that is called a קרבן, to anything from which some kind of offering has been made, rendering it permissible to eat. Hence, it applies even to בשר חטאת העוף — of which only the blood reached the altar. It applies even to מותר לוג שמן של מצורע, because once some of the oil is sprinkled toward the Holy of Holies and some of it is put on the body of the מצורע (below, 14:15ff), the remainder is given to the *Kohanim* (*Zevachim* 91a; 44a). The common concept in all the above is שיריים. Hence, the prohibition referred to in the statement כל שממנו לאישים הרי הוא בבל תקטירו means this: Anything subsumed under the term שיריים is forbidden to be offered on the altar, just as שאור and דבש are forbidden.

We have here, then, three איסורי מזבח — שאור, דבש and שיריים — sharing some deep inner connection. Let us try to understand the ideas expressed through these *halachos*.

שאור. The significance of חמץ and מצה is historical, as we have already explained in our Commentary to *Shemos* (12:8). מצה symbolizes the lack of political independence, a condition in which our time is not in our own hands, our powers are not at our own disposal. It is a sign of עבדות. By contrast, שאור and חמץ symbolize independence and sovereignty.

Israel's original bread was מצה. Had Israel been left to their own devices, they would still be eating the "bread of servitude." Each year when we celebrate the festival commemorating our deliverance from Egypt, מצה displaces שאור and חמץ from our homes, reminding us anew that not by our own hands did we obtain freedom and independence, but by God's grace, which is perpetual. This same idea must be remembered always when we stand in the Sanctuary, opposite the altar of His Torah. The bread we offer there as a sign of our homage must always be matzah. For only when we exchanged עבדות פרעה for עבדות ה׳ did we merit to receive from God the bread of freedom. The matzah that we hold in our hands is the basis of our whole relationship with God.

Freedom from all other עבדות is the consequence of עבודת ה׳; political independence among the nations is the promised reward for complete subordination to the dictates of His Will. This comes to expression on שבועות, the festival that commemorates the giving of the Torah; for this day is also יום הביכורים, when we acknowledge before God: כי באתי אל הארץ (*Devarim* 26:3). It is then that Israel appears before God with שתי לחם חמץ, the bread of freedom and independence, thereby acknowledging that it enjoys freedom and independence only in return for accepting the yoke of Torah and *mitzvos*. But this is done only once a year. Only on the day that commemorates the giving of the Torah does Israel bring before God the bread of its political independence — a fruit, as it were, ripened on the tree of life; a consequence of Israel's observance of the Torah. ואל המזבח לא יעלו לריח ניחח: this bread, however, may not be brought up to the altar as אשה, to fuel the fire of God; it is not to be the expression of compliance with the Will of God. For what is offered on the altar as אשה ריח ניחוח לה׳ is that which was ours heretofore, which we are now giving up in order to do God's Will. But political independence — embodied by שאור — was not ours, not even a trace of it, by our own power; we obtained it solely by virtue of our complete devotion to Torah. We attained it by means of אשה ריח ניחוח לה׳ — but it cannot itself be offered up to God as אשה ריח ניחוח, for it was never ours without that very closeness to God.

In this way we can also understand the prohibition of offering דבש upon the altar fire. The value of possessing land is represented well by דבש, or מתיקת פרי. For fruits of trees are expressly prepared by nature for man's immediate enjoyment; hence, they are most suited to symbolize possession of land. But possession of its land, like freedom and independence, is not an asset that Israel owes to its own power and prowess. Rather, only by observing God's commandments did Israel gain and retain its land. That is why the festival of the Giving of the Torah marks the beginning of the season at which Israel brings up to the Sanctuary the first fruits of the soil — primarily the first fruits of the trees — and places them before the altar with the declaration to the כהן: הגדתי היום לה׳ אלהיך כי באתי אל הארץ אשר נשבע ה׳ לאבותינו לתת לנו (ibid.). Yet again: ואל המזבח לא יעלו לריח ניחח. For the Land we possess is not something that is inherently our own, which we then part with for the sake of observing the Torah; rather, we possess the Land only by virtue of our observance of the Torah.

To summarize, שאור and דבש, symbolizing independence and possession of the Land, are found in the Sanctuary only as that which is contingent, and not as that which is prerequisite. For this reason they appear in the Sanctuary only as שיריים: the right to partake of them is contingent upon הקטרה — or some other act of relinquishment — which serves as their מתיר, as that which renders them permissible. The idea can be formulated this way: שאור and דבש are the שיריים of the תורה, and the תורה is their מתיר. הקטרת שאור ודבש would divest them of their שיריים character and elevate them to the level of מתירים. Therefore, כל שאר וכל דבש לא תקטירו ממנו אשה לה׳!

The איסור הקטרת שאור ודבש thus becomes part of a more comprehensive halachah. For the prohibition לא תקטירו ממנו אשה לה׳ also includes the הקטרה of those portions of offerings that are permitted as שיריים after the הקרבה of their מתיר: כל שממנו לאישים הרי הוא בבל תקטירו.

We have already mentioned several times the significance of אכילת שיריים where כהנים אוכלים ובעלים מתכפרין. We shall see that שיריים that may be eaten by the בעלים (e.g., בשר שלמים) are no less significant. In all these cases אכילת שיריים is the final flower and result of אכילת מזבח. But the fundamental condition of this idea is the following: Only after the מתיר has been offered is it permitted to partake of the שיריים, and only if something can be defined as שיריים does it become permissible and even obligatory to partake of it. הקטרת שיריים would violate this principle and express the very opposite notion, as it would divest the שיריים of their שיריים character, converting that which needs to be rendered permissible into a מתיר, as though the שיריים had always been at our disposal, ready and available for our enjoyment. The same notion would be expressed by הקטרת שאור ודבש vis-à-vis the things symbolized by שאור and דבש.

The איסור שאור encompasses more than the איסור דבש, as alluded to by the construction of the sentence כל המנחה וגו׳ לא תעשה חמץ כי כל שאור

13 *And any homage offering that you bring near you shall season with salt, and do not allow salt, the covenant of your God, to be lacking from your homage offering; with anything that you offer, you shall offer salt.*

יג וְכָל־קָרְבַּ֣ן מִנְחָתְךָ֮ בַּמֶּ֣לַח תִּמְלָח֒
וְלֹ֣א תַשְׁבִּ֗ית מֶ֚לַח בְּרִ֣ית אֱלֹהֶ֔יךָ
מֵעַ֖ל מִנְחָתֶ֑ךָ עַ֥ל כָּל־קָרְבָּנְךָ֖
תַּקְרִ֥יב מֶֽלַח׃ ס

וכל דבש לא תקטירו וגו׳. (This has already been pointed out by ר׳ נפתלי הרץ וויזל נ״ע in his *Commentary.*) דבש is אסור only בהקטרה, but it is permissible to mix שיריים with דבש and eat them. שאור, on the other hand, as an expression of sovereignty, is entirely antithetical to the homage concept of the *minchah*; hence, שאור is strictly forbidden at every stage in the preparation of a *minchah.* (As for the חלת לחם חמץ of the תודה, see Commentary below, 7:13.)

13 **וכל קרבן מנחתך** means the parts of the מנחה that are given over to the fire, namely קומץ and לבונה. **במלח תמלח** — one should salt them on all sides, as one salts meat to be cooked in a pot (*Menachos* 21a). **ולא תשבית וגו׳** adds a negative precept to the positive one. **על כל קרבנך תקריב מלח** — this extends the law to every offering similar to the קומץ. Anything given over to the fire as an offering is subject to a positive precept of salting and, according to the רמב״ם, to a negative one as well (הל׳ איסורי מזבח, 5:11–12). This excludes דם and יין נסכים, as neither of these are given over to the fire. עצים, too, are excluded, as they feed the fire but are not offered up to it as an offering. Whether קטורת is excluded, since it is not offered on the מזבח החיצון, is a matter of controversy (see *Menachos* 20a–21a; כסף משנה ולחם משנה הל׳ איסורי מזבח, 5:11).

The salt used for offerings — like the עצים — is taken משל ציבור, from the communal supply, even for a private offering. This is due to the ברית-character of the salt (*Menachos* 21b): Just as the לחם הפנים is called ברית and is taken מאת בני ישראל (below, 24:8), so the salt, too, is called ברית — מלח ברית אלקיך — and is even used as an expression for ברית: ברית מלח עולם (*Bemidbar* 18:19).

There can be no doubt as to the general meaning of salt at offerings. Scripture spells it out: מלח ברית אלקיך. And from the accent under the word מלח it is clear that ברית is not genitive, but is in apposition with מלח; not "salt of the covenant," but "salt, the covenant of your God."

Salt is an essential seasoner of foods: הֲיֵאָכֵל תָּפֵל מִבְּלִי־מֶלַח (*Iyov* 6:6). But beside this concrete function, salt has another quality, both tangible and symbolic. It inhibits all plant growth. A field that is sown with salt will yield no vegetation (see *Shoftim* 9:45). An unfruitful land is called מְלֵחָה (*Tehillim* 107:34, et al.). Add to this salt's preservative power, which prevents decay, and remember that decay is the result of the beginning of a new structure. We come to the conclusion that salt represents immutability. For salt forms a protective seal over an object, shielding it from outside influences that would change it. From this standpoint, salt is a perfect symbol for the concept of ברית. For as we have shown in our Commentary to *Bereshis* (6:18), that which is promised in a ברית is isolated and set apart and is not subject to outside influences. A ברית remains in all circumstances and is kept under all conditions and, in the case of a ברית מלח, is unalterable. Something that is concluded in a ברית מלח will not only abide forever, but will also never be subject to change; it is absolute — both in its durability and in its essence. Salt, then, is a sign of the covenant; and if taken from the communal supply, it symbolizes the covenant that is placed in the charge of the community. For the nation as a whole is responsible for the covenant's durability and immutability. Its meaning and authority are not subject to the opinion of the individual; rather, the entire nation is its guardian and guarantor.

Now, this ברית symbolized by מלח at offerings is called ברית אלקיך; hence, it must refer to that which lies in the ארון — which, accordingly, is called ארון ברית ה׳. Salt, then, is the symbol of the Torah, which exists forever and without change. The mitzvah of salting and its meaning are therefore this: One must salt the offering on all sides with the salt of the Torah, with salt received from the nation; that is, the offering must be permeated throughout with the spirit of the eternal Torah, which is guarded and kept, unchanged, by the nation. Only through the Torah can something of our property (קומץ ולבונה) sustain the fire of godliness on earth. Only through the Torah can our aims (אימורים) and endeavors (איברים) lead to the dwelling of God's Presence in this world. The mitzvah of salting does not apply to the דם, to the נפש; for the נפש in itself is unchangeable. Rather, the mitzvah applies to סולת, שמן, לבונה, אימורים, איברים — these must bear the stamp of salt, which symbolizes the eternal, immutable Torah. The external conditions for acquiring wealth do change with the time and the place; the ways of securing a living and attaining prosperity and material happiness do change; accordingly, our aims and endeavors also change. Hence, it is easy to form the mistaken impression that our obligations and our task in life also are constantly changing. The changes of the times affect in particular the material values represented by the *minchah*: material subsistence, prosperity, and happiness. In regard to these, then, one is particularly liable to form such an impression. That is why the Torah says: "If you wish to draw closer to God and to show homage to Him with your material possessions, take salt — representing immutability — from the communal supply and salt your homage offering. In particular, do not omit salt — symbol of God's eternal, immutable covenant — from your homage offering. Moreover, with *every* offering through which you seek God's closeness you are to offer salt — symbol of the immutable covenant."

In light of the above we understand why the mitzvah of salting is first stated vis-à-vis מנחה and only afterward extended to every offering similar to it. The רמב״ם even rules that salt is מעכב only in the case of מנחה, whereas at other offerings salting is a מצוה but is not מעכב. This ruling, however, is not easily reconciled with the Gemara in *Menachos*. כסף משנה explains that the reason for the רמב״ם's ruling is that the term ברית is stated only in reference to מנחה. But this explanation is insufficient; for, according to the רמב״ם, the לא תעשה of לא תשבית מלח ברית אלקיך וגו׳ applies to all offerings. וצ״ע.

We noted above that קטורת is perhaps excluded from the precept of salting, which may be limited to those offerings that are given over to the fire of the מזבח החיצון. This would fit in well with our conception of the קטורת and the מזבח הפנימי. The מזבח החיצון shows us the path leading up to the heights of the Jewish ideal. On that path there is need for a special warning (מלח) as to the everlastingness and immutability of the Torah. But the קטורת represents this ideal itself; it is the embodiment of pure ריח ניחוח. It is offered on the מזבח הזהב, which faces the ארון הברית. Through this מזבח the שולחן and מנורה are united, effecting the realization of the Torah which rests in the ארון. Here there is no need for a special warning concerning the everlastingness and immutability of the Torah; the very essence of the idea of the קטורת presupposes this principle.

14 *If you bring near to* God *an homage offering of first fruits, it shall be brought as soon as it ripens on the stalk; roasted in fire, the kernels freshly ground out of full ears; thus shall you bring near the homage offering of your first fruits.*

יד וְאִם־תַּקְרִ֛יב מִנְחַ֥ת בִּכּוּרִ֖ים לַֽיהוָ֑ה אָבִ֞יב קָל֣וּי בָּאֵ֗שׁ גֶּ֚רֶשׂ כַּרְמֶ֔ל תַּקְרִ֕יב אֵ֖ת מִנְחַ֥ת בִּכּוּרֶֽיךָ׃

14 **מנחת ביכורים** is the מנחת העומר, which is called ראשית קצירכם (below, 23:10). It is offered of the first ripe barley, as evidenced by the term אביב, which denotes the ripening of the barley stalk (*Shemos* 9:31). Furthermore, it must be that the עומר was offered of barley, not of wheat; for the שתי הלחם brought on שבועות from wheat are called ביכורים — and "should you say that the עומר was offered of wheat, then the שתי הלחם would not be ביכורים!" (*Menachos* 68b).

קלוי באש. The barley that was cut for the עומר was not left to dry in the field, but was brought while still fresh on the stalks into the עזרה, where it was beaten out of the ears by reeds and stems of plants, then roasted over a fire in a perforated pipe. Finally, it was spread out in the עזרה and the wind would blow on it (ibid. 66a).

גרש is phonetically related to גרז, גרס — which denote separation via cutting or breaking. One might have understood גרש as גריס, barley groats; and one might have concluded from the expression מגרשה ומשמנה (v. 16) that מנחת העומר is offered in the form of גריסים. But this is not the case. Rather, just as מנחת סולת is offered of wheat flour, so with מנחת העומר: one mixes barley flour with oil, until it forms a dough. And גרש is none other than grain hulled in a ריחיים של גרוסות (*Menachos* 66a). As with the wheat grain, the barley grain is then sifted through several sieves (מנחת העומר is sifted through thirteen sieves, שתי הלחם through twelve, and לחם הפנים eleven) to clear it of all husks, bran, and inferior flour dust (קמח), until only the innermost kernel remains, just as the סולת remains of the wheat. When this kernel is ground, it yields the purest and highest grade of flour (see Commentary, *Bereshis* 18:6). Thus,

15 *You shall put oil upon it and place frankincense upon it; it is an homage offering.*

טו וְנָתַתָּ עָלֶיהָ שֶׁמֶן וְשַׂמְתָּ עָלֶיהָ
לְבֹנָה מִנְחָה הִוא׃

16 *The priest shall offer up in smoke the remembrance portion from the meal made of its kernel, and its oil, along with all its frankincense, as a fire offering, to* God.

טז וְהִקְטִיר הַכֹּהֵן אֶת־אַזְכָּרָתָהּ
מִגִּרְשָׂהּ וּמִשַּׁמְנָהּ עַל כָּל־לְבֹנָתָהּ
אִשֶּׁה לַיהוָה׃ פ רביעי

"גרש and סולת are equivalent terms, only that גרש is applied to מנחת העומר and סולת to the other *menachos*" (*Menachos* 27a, רש״י ד״ה גרש). גרש, then, is not barley groats but, rather, the innermost kernel of the barley, which has been hulled in a ריחיים של גרוסות and sifted in sieves, and which now comprises the finest barley flour.

כרמל. The meaning of this word is known to us only from *Menachos* 84a. According to what is stated there, it denotes a certain stage in the ripening of grain. At this stage, the grains are still soft and easily plucked out of the ears. In *Menachos* 66b the word is interpreted to mean רך ומל — i.e., soft and easy to be shelled — and a support is cited from what is stated in connection with Elisha: לֶחֶם בִּכּוּרִים עֶשְׂרִים־לֶחֶם שְׂעֹרִים וְכַרְמֶל (*Melachim* II 4:42). According to תנא דבי ר׳ ישמעאל (*Menachos* 66b), כרמל means כר מלא, i.e., the full ripening of the grain, when the grains have reached full growth. Apart from the mountain by this name, כרמל always signifies flourishing green meadows — as opposed to forest and desert. Following the analogy of ברזל from the root ברז, גבעל from the root גבע, ערפל from the root ערף, קרסל from the root קרס (קֹרֵס נְבוֹ — *Yeshayahu* 46:1), כרמל may derive from the root כרם. It would then refer to a flourishing region rising in terraces like a vineyard or olive plantation (כרם is close to גרם, a step or degree). But what connection exists between this and a certain stage in the ripening of grain has yet to be clarified. Perhaps כרמל denotes the terrace-like formation of the ears, in which the grains are arranged level upon level.

15 **מנחה הוא**. The עומר is a *minchah* in every respect, as opposed to שתי הלחם which, although they are also called *minchah*, have neither oil nor

3 1 *And if a meal of peace is his offering — if he brings it near from the cattle, whether male or female, he shall bring it whole before* God.

ג א וְאִם־זֶ֥בַח שְׁלָמִ֖ים קׇרְבָּנ֑וֹ אִ֤ם מִן־הַבָּקָר֙ ה֣וּא מַקְרִ֔יב אִם־זָכָר֙ אִם־נְקֵבָ֔ה תָּמִ֥ים יַקְרִיבֶ֖נּוּ לִפְנֵ֥י יְהֹוָֽה׃

frankincense and of which no part is given over to the altar fire — ואל המזבח לא יעלו לריח ניחח (v. 12). For the meaning of these two *menachos* of the first fruits, and for the relationship between them, see our Commentary below, 23:10ff; 23:16ff.

מנחת העומר appears here among the מנחות נדבה and is introduced by the conditional ואם (v. 14) — even though it is a מנחת חובה. According to ר׳ יהודה (*Toras Kohanim*, ad loc.), this alludes to the reality that עתידה מנחת ביכורים לפסק ולחזור, with the loss of the Land there will be a temporary interruption in the offering of מנחת העומר. ר׳ שמעון (ibid.) gives a different explanation: אם אתם מביאים אותה לרצון, מעלה אני עליכם כאלו נדבה הבאתם אותה; ואם אין אתם מביאים אותה לרצון, מעלה אני עליכם כאלו לא הבאתם אותה אלא לצורך עצמכם. That is to say, one should bring an obligatory offering in the same spirit in which one brings a free-will offering (נדבה); and if this spirit is lacking, the offering is regarded as having been brought for ulterior motives — e.g., (in the case of מנחת העומר) in order to render the new produce permissible. See קרבן אהרן.

CHAPTER 3

1 **ואם זבח שלמים**. Outside the context of the offerings, the main meaning of זבח is "meal," generally a meal eaten in company. (זבח seems to be phonetically related to שבע, satiation.) In the context of the offerings, זבח appears mostly juxtaposed to שלמים. This juxtaposition explains the meaning of זבח when used by itself: it generally refers to offerings that are eaten outside the Sanctuary court by those who bring these offerings. זבח, then, is the very opposite of עולה, which is offered in its entirety upon the altar; hence, the common combinations עולה או זבח, עולותיכם וזבחיכם, and the like.

The term זביחה is also used to mean: שחיטה according to law, for the purpose of eating, as in וזבחת מבקרך וגו׳ כאשר צויתך (*Devarim* 12:21). Now, below Scripture says: הזרק את דם השלמים (7:14); המקריב את דם השלמים (7:33). In these verses, the term שלמים is mentioned without the addition of the term זבח, while here it says זבח שלמים. From this we learn in *Zevachim* (4a) that there exists a close connection between the idea of שלמים and the act of זביחה: the זובח is required to bear in mind the שלמים-character of the offering when he performs the זביחה; that is to say, בעינן זביחה לשמה. Similarly, we learn from the above mentioned verses (הזרק וגו׳; המקריב וגו׳) that הקרבה — which includes קבלה and הולכה — and זריקה must also be performed לשמה. The requirement of לשמה applies both to שינוי קודש (e.g., שלמים לשם עולה) as well as to שינוי בעלים (e.g., שלמי ראובן לשם שמעון). And from the summarizing verse זאת התורה לעלה למנחה ולחטאת ולאשם ולמלואים ולזבח השלמים (below, 7:37) we learn that these *halachos* apply to all the offerings. Nevertheless, with the exception of חטאת and פסח, the requirement of לשמה is not indispensable to the כשרות of the offering; as the Mishnah states (*Zevachim* 2a): כל הזבחים שנזבחו שלא לשמן כשרים אלא שלא עלו לבעלים לשם חובה חוץ מן הפסח והחטאת. (Cf. Commentary above, 1:9.)

שלמים. שלם implies a state of completeness, of perfection; as in אבן שלמה (*Devarim* 25:15), et al. This is also the meaning of שלם when used with reference to a human being: it denotes a state in which a person feels there is nothing lacking in any respect; he feels that he is not missing anything, as in ויבא יעקב שלם (*Bereshis* 33:18; see Commentary, ad loc.). שלם, then, is a relative concept; primarily, it describes an object in relation to its parts, and a person in relation to the circumstances and surroundings in which he lives. But on certain rare occasions the term is used to describe not the state of the person, but the state of his affairs and surroundings: they are in harmony with him, since he is in harmony with them. Thus האנשים האלה שלמים הם אתנו (*Bereshis* 34:21) — i.e., the relationship of these people toward us is such that they will not cause us to suffer any loss.

In a state of שלום, one thing does not fulfill itself at the expense of another; rather, things complement each other. We have already shown (*Collected Writings*, vol. VIII, p. 54), based on the phonetic relation of שלם and צלם, that true שלום consists not merely of mutual noninterference, but of an inner, harmonious accord; not of superficial coexistence, but of profound, mutual receptiveness.

שלמים are offerings that derive from a feeling of שלמות. While קרבן עולה symbolizes seeking God's closeness on account of the need to sanctify one's deeds, and קרבן מנחה symbolizes seeking God's closeness by imposing His Will on the means of one's subsistence and happiness, קרבן שלמים symbolizes seeking God's closeness on account of a sense of contentment, a feeling that one lacks nothing, that only God's closeness is missing — and one now seeks this closeness through one's offering. שלמים epitomize the Jewish philosophy of life. Not grief but joy is to form the bridge to God; the highest form of serving God is to enjoy life in the light of His Presence. To seek God, without seeking any particular favors from Him, not even to give thanks to Him for some extraordinary good fortune — that is the idea of a קרבן שלמים.

קרבן שלמים is a distinctively Jewish offering (cf. Commentary, *Bereshis* 46:1). According to one opinion in *Zevachim* 116a, Noachides (בני נח) offered עולות but not שלמים. This is derived from the verse: עוּרִי צָפוֹן וּבוֹאִי תֵימָן (*Shir Ha-Shirim* 4:16). עורי צפון is addressed to Noachides: תתנער ותבוא אומה שמעשיה בצפון is addressed to Israel: ובואי תימן .אומה שמעשיה בצפון ובדרום. That is to say, Noachides sought God in the dark, midnightly side of life (עולה בצפון); the uniqueness of Judaism is that it seeks God in the bright rays of light of midday (no specific side of the Sanctuary courtyard was singled out for שלמים). This opinion accords, apparently, with the law, accepted as the halachah, that שלמי נכרים עולות — i.e., a non-Jew brings in the Sanctuary only עולות; even if he brought an offering as a שלמים, we assume that what he had in mind was an עולה (*Menachos* 73b).

As we have said, a שלמים is an offering that derives from a person's feeling that he lacks nothing in his life. This would explain the halachah that אונן אינו משלח קרבנותיו, one is not permitted to send his offerings to the Sanctuary on the day that he has lost a close relative (husband or wife, father or mother, son or daughter, brother or sister), when he is an אונן, in a state of deep mourning. This halachah is stated with regard to שלמים: שלמים – כשהוא שלם מביא ואינו מביא כשהוא אונן, but it applies to the other offerings as well. It applies even to the קרבן פסח if the one offering it is an אונן at חצות, for it is at this time that the obligation to offer the פסח takes effect (*Zevachim* 99b–100a). The sense of שלום from which the שלמים derives and which it is intended to express must not be lacking at the other offerings: שלמים קרבנו – כל קרבנות שהוא מביא כשהוא שלם הוא מביא ואינו מביא כשהוא אונן (ibid.). One may not enter the Sanctuary gate while one's heart is torn with grief; only one who is at peace and reconciled with his lot can find the way to God's nearness.

Other religions view it as the highest fulfillment of their mission if they can help their adherents overcome grief and sorrow, if they can offer them comfort in their troubles. But in Judaism sorrow must be overcome *before* one enters the Sanctuary; this is, in fact, prerequisite if one is to benefit from its power. For the purpose of the Sanctuary is not to offer us comfort in sorrow but to give us the strength and determination to serve God with joy. Joy pervades the Sanctuary, and man can draw from it courage and good cheer. For God's Sanctuary is the Sanctuary of His Torah. (See Commentary below, 10:19.)

אם מן הבקר וגו׳. See Commentary above, 1:3. One who feels שלם may bring an offering of בקר or of צאן. If he grasps that his mission in life is to labor in God's service, he should bring an offering of בקר. If he wishes to express that his fate is in God's hand, he should bring an offering of צאן. In the latter case, he must choose between the different types of צאן. If he wishes to express only his complete devotion to the Shepherd of his life, he should bring a כבש, and if he also harbors strong resolve to resist any temptation that might lure him away from God's guidance, he should bring an עז. His offering may be either זכר or נקבה, depending on whether he sees his position in life as one of independence or dependence. For a person can feel שלם even if he is in a dependent position. Indeed, the Torah recognizes the position of an עבד who would not want to exchange his condition of servitude for one of freedom and independence! כי טוב לו עמך (*Devarim* 15:16). But in all cases his offering must be תמים: as a "whole" person, with his entire being, must he try to draw near to God, Who guides his actions and shapes his destiny.

Scripture stipulates here **הוא מקריב**. *Toras Kohanim* infers from the word הוא a halachah of great significance: הוא – היחיד מביא שלמים נדבה ואין הצבור מביא שלמים נדבה; i.e., the nation as such, collectively, cannot offer שלמי נדבה. In fact, there are no שלמי ציבור at all except for the שני כבשי עצרת, which are offered on שבועות together with the שתי הלחם. And even in the case of the שני כבשי עצרת, the nation is not represented as one unit (כבש אחד), but as a plurality of individuals (שני כבשים). Even with this modification, the כבשי עצרת differ from שלמים. They are similar in character to the עולה and to the חטאת, as they too are קדשי קדשים. They

2 *He shall lean his hand upon the head of his offering, and he shall slaughter it at the entrance to the Tent of Appointed Meeting, and Aharon's sons, the priests, shall dash the blood against the altar, all around.*	ב וְסָמַךְ יָדוֹ עַל־רֹאשׁ קָרְבָּנוֹ וּשְׁחָטוֹ פֶּתַח אֹהֶל מוֹעֵד וְזָרְקוּ בְּנֵי אַהֲרֹן הַכֹּהֲנִים אֶת־הַדָּם עַל־הַמִּזְבֵּחַ סָבִיב׃

are mentioned together with the חטאת of שבועות (below, 23:19). And they represent communal שלמות as a goal to be longed for, to which one must still aspire; they do not represent this שלמות as something that has already been attained (as in the case of שלמים, where joy is expressed for that which has been attained). After all, they are חובה and קדשי קדשים and שחיטתן בצפון (see *Zevachim* 55a); they represent the Torah's goal, which is yet a vision for the future: !אפס כי לא יהיה בך אביון (*Devarim* 15:4; see Commentary below, 23:19).

The feeling of שלמות that is the basis for שלמים is strictly an actual feeling that can only be experienced by the individual. True, two or more individuals can together bring one שלמים, for it is possible that their partnership and association are the very basis of their שלמות. Indeed, association with other people is essential for a person's happiness; a decent human being will not feel שלם when he is in complete isolation. But the Torah does not subscribe to the fiction of national happiness without the happiness of individuals. A nation as an abstract entity can have no שלמות if its masses of people are suffering and in despair. The שלום of the Jewish nation consists of the שלום of its people. A שלמים offering brought by the nation as an abstract entity has no place on God's altar.

2 **וסמך ידו** (see Commentary above, 1:4). The demands of the Jewish mission are expressed in the offering procedures that follow the סמיכה. Before these procedures, the סומך reminds himself of his standing, as a Man of Israel, vis-à-vis these demands that are addressed to him. This is the meaning of סמיכה in all the offerings; but סמיכה is especially significant in the case of שלמים. Everyone is obligated to stand up for God and to act for the sake of His Torah, but a special obligation is incumbent

upon one who by God's grace has attained שלמות. He for whom God has done everything has to do everything for God. The message of סמיכה, for one who seeks God out of a feeling of שלמות, is this: In your happiness, exemplify God's Word as a Man of Israel.

ושחטו — see Commentary above, 1:5.

פתח אהל מועד. In the case of עולה, שחיטה is to be performed על ירך המזבח צפונה (above, 1:11), and the same applies to all the other קדשי קדשים. They are all offered out of the awareness of moral imperfection. The main cause of all such imperfection is the ascendence of the material, sensual side of our nature. Hence, the first step toward atonement is שחיטה, the renouncement of all selfish, uncontrolled living. The site of שחיטה is בצפון, which is the side of the "Table," representing the material life of the senses.

שלמים, however, do not stem from such an awareness. Rather, a person who has attained wholeness, whose inner perfection has not been marred, seeks God's Presence. In his happiness he appears לפני ה׳, and by entering the Sanctuary he can then attain yet a higher level of happiness. He too, he above all, must dismiss from his heart all selfish feeling and cease living for himself alone (שחיטה). His whole being must rise to a new life sanctified in the setting of the Sanctuary (קבלת דמו בכלי שרת). But שחיטה and קבלה are valid only if performed פתח אהל מועד, before the opened gate of the Tent in which we meet with God. The concept of פתח אהל מועד is extended by what is stated below (vv. 8 and 13), ושחט אתו לפני אהל מועד, to include the entire עזרה. Thus, שחיטת שלמים may be performed בכל מקום בעזרה (*Zevachim* 55a); it is valid even at the צדדים to the north and to the south which are not directly opposite the היכל (ibid. 55b), and according to the רמב״ם it is valid even if performed אחורי ההיכל, behind the היכל (הל׳ מעשה הקרבנות, 5:4). For the entire עזרה is regarded as an "antechamber" before the Sanctuary and is called לפני אהל מועד. Only the צדי צדדים, the לשכות (halls) at the sides of the עזרה, partitioned off for special purposes, are excluded. The words פתח אהל מועד in our verse add only the condition that נפתחו דלתות ההיכל, the doors of the Sanctuary have been opened: שלמים ששחטן קודם שיפתחו דלתות ההיכל פסולין (*Zevachim* 55b). This condition, which is stated in reference to שלמים, is then applied to all the קרבנות (תוספות, *Yoma* 29a). We noted this previously in our Commentary to *Shemos* (27:8).

ג וְהִקְרִיב֙ מִזֶּ֣בַח הַשְּׁלָמִ֔ים אִשֶּׁ֖ה לַֽיהוָ֑ה אֶת־הַחֵ֙לֶב֙ הַֽמְכַסֶּ֣ה אֶת־הַקֶּ֔רֶב וְאֵת֙ כָּל־הַחֵ֔לֶב אֲשֶׁ֖ר עַל־הַקֶּֽרֶב׃	3 *And he shall bring near from the meal of peace a fire offering to* God; *the fat that covers the intestines and all the fat that is attached to the intestines.*

וזרקו וגו׳ סביב (see Commentary above, 1:5). The שלם, the one who feels he has attained שלמות, learns that it is easier to be שלם בגופו ובממונו than to be שלם בתורתו. The service vessel in which the blood was received is brought to the south side of the altar, the side of the מנורה, where one's very being is infused with the spirit of the Torah and illumined by its shining radiance. The procedure observed with דם עולה is now observed with דם שלמים. The כהן turns to his right and circles the altar from the south to the east. In the east, one learns the nature of his own happiness: he is to regard himself as a member of the nation that was charged to live for the sake of the Torah. With the dashing of the blood against the northeast corner one is assigned his first active task: to utilize his material wealth in the context of his belonging to *klal Yisrael.* The כהן continues to circle the altar. From the north, which is the side of the Table, he proceeds to the west, which is the side of the Torah. This way, the one who has attained wholeness and happiness learns that all the power in his possession, all that has been set before him on the table of his life, is to be dedicated to the fulfillment of the Torah, which rests beneath the wings of the cherubim. And with the dashing of the blood against the southwest corner he is assigned a second task: to enlighten his spirit with the light that radiates from the Torah. Finally, there is **שפיכת שיריים ליסוד בדרום** just as at קרבן עולה, and he perceives that the root of his whole being is in the spirit, which is awakened and vitalized by the Torah.

3–5 חֵלֶב (see Commentary to *Bereshis* 4:4) is set aside by the body of the animal so as to sustain itself in a time of deprivation. חָלָב is set aside for a similar purpose — in order sustain the species. חֵלֶב is not identical with שומן; for the latter is integrated with the flesh, whereas the former is set apart unto itself and covered with a thin membrane, which is easily peeled off: תותב קרום ונקלף (*Chullin* 49b).

4 *Also the two kidneys and the fat that rests upon them, which is along the flanks; also the diaphragm upon the liver; he must remove it together with the kidneys.*

ד וְאֵת֙ שְׁתֵּ֣י הַכְּלָיֹ֔ת וְאֶת־הַחֵ֙לֶב֙
אֲשֶׁ֣ר עֲלֵהֶ֔ן אֲשֶׁ֖ר עַל־הַכְּסָלִ֑ים
וְאֶת־הַיֹּתֶ֙רֶת֙ עַל־הַכָּבֵ֔ד עַל־
הַכְּלָי֖וֹת יְסִירֶֽנָּה׃

5 *And sons of Aharon shall turn it into smoke on the altar, upon the ascent offering that is upon the [logs of] wood that are upon the fire; [it is] an offering made by fire as an expression of compliance, to* God.

ה וְהִקְטִ֨ירוּ אֹת֤וֹ בְנֵֽי־אַהֲרֹן֙
הַמִּזְבֵּ֔חָה עַל־הָ֣עֹלָ֔ה אֲשֶׁ֖ר עַל־
הָעֵצִ֣ים אֲשֶׁ֣ר עַל־הָאֵ֑שׁ אִשֵּׁ֛ה
רֵ֥יחַ נִיחֹ֖חַ לַֽיהוָֽה׃ פ

The חלבים mentioned here are (a) החלב המכסה את הקרב, the layer of fat that, like a cloth, is spread over the intestines in the whole abdominal cavity; (b) כל החלב אשר על הקרב, which includes the fat on the בית הכוסות המסס וקיבה and also the fat שעל גבי דקין; and (c) חלב שעל הכליות, the fat over the kidneys, and חלב אשר על הכסלים.

According to רש״י (ibid. 93a), כסלים are apparently distinct from מתניים (loins). For מתניים start directly below the false ribs, whereas כסלים are closer to the hips. The muscle layer of the כסלים is separated from and situated under the loin muscles; sometimes it is covered by the loin muscles: תרבי דתותי מתני (ibid.). Moreover, the תרבא דקליבוסתא, mentioned by the Gemara (ibid.) as belonging to the חלב שעל הכסלים, is situated, according to רש״י, close to the hips; this is also the opinion of the רמב״ם (הל׳ מאכלות אסורות, 7:6), who renders it חלב שבעיקרי הירכים.

According to R. Menachem Asaria (שו״ת, 113), however, מתניים are the צדדי השדרה למטה מהצלעות, and כסלים are the בשר החופים על המתניים. In that case, there is apparently no distinction between כסלים and the loin muscles, וצ״ע.

In any case, it would appear from the wording of verse 4 that the חלב שעל הכליות is connected with the חלב שעל הכסלים, as it does not say ואשר על הכסלים, but אשר על הכסלים.

יותרת is the חצר הכבד (*Targum Onkelos* to our verse; cf. Mishnah, *Yoma* 83a), the diaphragm, which is spread between the respiratory organs and the digestive organs. It directly separates the lungs from the liver, lines the whole chest cavity, and primarily facilitates respiratory movement. Its back surface, which faces the liver, is also important for the process of digestion.

ואת היתרת על הכבד על הכליות יסירנה. It says below (9:10): ואת היתרת מן הכבד, from which we may infer that the liver itself was not offered, and yet in our verse it says על הכבד. *Toras Kohanim* interprets our verse as follows: שיטול מן הכבד על היותרת, i.e., a part of the liver is taken together with the whole diaphragm; יסירנה clearly refers to the יותרת (see קרבן אהרן, ad loc.). The meaning of על הכליות יסירנה remains unclear.

These parts of the קרבן שלמים (as well as those of the חטאת and אשם) that are to be burned upon the altar are called אימורים, as opposed to the parts of the עולה (the whole of which is offered upon the altar), which are called איברים. The derivation of the word אימורים is obscure (see משנה למלך הל׳ מעשה הקרבנות, 1:18).

והקטירו אתו (v. 5), והקטירו (v. 11), והקטירם (v. 16) — the changes in the object pronoun are expounded in *Toras Kohanim*: והקטירו אותו – כשר ולא הפסול; והקטירו – שלא יערב חלבים בחלבים; והקטירם – כולם כאחת. Thus, אימורים may not be offered up unless all the procedures prior to הקטרה have been carried out properly; the אימורים of each offering must be offered up independently, i.e., apart from those of other offerings; and all the אימורים of the same offering are to be offered up together, unlike איברי העולה which are offered up in groups. We infer, then, that all the אימורים together convey one idea.

These are the parts of the קרבן שלמים that are offered upon the altar after זריקת הדם: the כליות, the חלב, the יותרת, and a part of the כבד. Together they form one idea. They all belong to the vegetative system of the organs of digestion and reproduction. Only the diaphragm, which forms the boundary between the lower vegetative and upper animal systems, can also play a role in the animal system. But from the words על הכבד על הכליות it would appear that, in the offerings, the significance of the diaphragm is primarily in respect to the vegetative system.

חלב is the final product of the digestive activity; it consists of surplus nourishing fluids that have not been converted into blood. It provides protection for the digestive organs and also serves as a reserve for a time of deprivation: it is the richness held in store for the animal's use in a time of need. Hence, we also find חלב used as a metaphor for the richest, the choice, and the best — as in חלב יצהר, חלב תירוש (*Bemidbar* 18:12); חֵלֶב חִטִּים (*Tehillim* 147:14); חלב הארץ (*Bereshis* 45:18).

כליות. The importance of the kidneys to the animal organism, besides their role in the production of urine, is unknown. In תנ״ך one finds the combination כליות ולב — e.g., בֹּחֵן לִבּוֹת וּכְלָיוֹת (*Tehillim* 7:10); בֹּחֵן כְּלָיוֹת וָלֵב (*Yirmeyahu* 11:20); צָרְפָה כִלְיוֹתַי וְלִבִּי (*Tehillim* 26:2). Apparently, then, the role of the כליות in the realm of vegetative stimuli and impulses corresponds to the role of the לב in the realm of higher feelings and aspirations. The root of כליות, viz., כלה, which denotes longing and strong desire, also attests to this. The כליות, then, represent the source of sensory desire.

יותרת, the diaphragm, as already mentioned, is the main factor in respiratory movement. Expanding the chest cavity for inhalation and contracting it for exhalation are executed mainly by the muscles of the diaphragm. Here (in v. 4), the diaphragm is mentioned in connection with the kidneys and liver; our verse thus alludes to the vital function of the diaphragm in the service of the vegetative impulses. For, according to our Sages, כבד כועס, the liver is the source of the quality of anger (*Berachos* 61b). Now, one who is angry reacts against something that is loathsome to him. Thus, the כבד is the opposite of the כליות: The כליות represent strong desire for that which is appealing, whereas the כבד represents fierce rejection of that which is loathsome. The combination of both comprises the essence of all of life's physical activity, which is essentially the assimilation of that which is suitable and the rejection of that which is incompatible. היתרת על הכבד על הכליות, then, means: the breath of life in the service of the vegetative impulses of the senses, the ultimate goal of which is represented by חלב.

He whose קרבן is a זבח שלמים seeks God's closeness at the feast of his happiness; he wishes to enjoy his good fortune in the Presence of God. First he learns, through שחיטה and זריקה, the fundamental condition for achieving this aim: He must transform his entire personality and cease living for himself alone. He must commit and devote himself totally to God and to the sacred national mission of fulfilling and understanding the Torah. Then, through הקטרת אימורים he is shown the outcome of his commitment and devotion: On such a level even the

חלב and the כליות and the כבד and the יותרת על הכבד על הכליות — i.e., even the aims and aspirations of the senses — can be freed from subjection to the body; they, too, can be elevated and sanctified to sustain the holy on earth. Only then can the joy of the שלם lead him into God's Presence. Only if החלב המכסה את הקרב ואת כל החלב אשר על הקרב ושתי הכליות והחלב אשר עליהן אשר על הכסלים והיותרת על הכבד על הכליות, all these, become אשה ריח ניחח לה׳ can a זבח שלמים be a קרבן לה׳!

Before הקטרת האימורים, the procedure of תנופה is performed with them. The חזה ושוק are placed upon the אימורים, and they are waved before God (see below, 7:30, et seq.). The חזה ושוק become the property of the כהנים after הקטרת האימורים. The rest of the meat is eaten by the בעלים, who may invite any other Jew to partake. שלמים are eaten outside the עזרה (but see משנה למלך הל׳ שחיטה פ״ב ה״ג בסוף דבריו), in the close vicinity of the Sanctuary: in the wilderness — only within מחנה ישראל; in Shilo — only within the area from which Shilo could be seen; and in Yerushalayim — only within the walls of the city (see *Zevachim* 112b). They may be eaten only within the prescribed time limit of שני ימים ולילה אחד.

והקטירו אתו וגו׳ על העלה וגו׳. It says below (6:5): וערך עליה העלה והקטיר עליה חלבי השלמים, and of the מוספים it says: מלבד עלת הבקר אשר לעלת התמיד תעשו את אלה (*Bemidbar* 28:23). From these two verses we learn (*Pesachim* 58a; *Zevachim* 89a) that all other offerings are to be brought after the תמיד של שחר, the morning daily offering, which is העולה ("*the* עולה"), the עולה *par excellence*: עליה השלם כל הקרבנות. The nation's daily ascent offering, brought morning and evening with the swelling and ebbing rays of daylight, represents the steady breathing of Jewish national devotion. All the other offerings are brought between these two; they are all merely consequences of the nation's perpetual fundamental offering.

Here, too, and for the first time, it says: והקטירו אותו וגו׳ על העלה וגו׳. According to רש״י, this verse, too, expresses only the same negative halachah — the שלמים should not be brought until after "*the* עולה" (עולת התמיד). However, as ר׳ נפתלי הרץ וויזל נ״ע has already noted in his *Commentary*, if this were all that our verse intends, the Talmud (ibid.) would have learned the halachah of עליה השלם כל הקרבנות from our verse.

Therefore, it seems to us that this verse contains a positive statement characterizing the זבח שלמים, the "meal of peace" offering: It, too, finds its place upon, and belongs to, the national עולה — in spite of the apparent intrinsic contrast that exists between them. Like all the other

ו וְאִם־מִן־הַצֹּאן קָרְבָּנוֹ לְזֶבַח שְׁלָמִים לַיהוָה זָכָר אוֹ נְקֵבָה תָּמִים יַקְרִיבֶנּוּ׃	6 *If his meal-of-peace offering to* God *is from the flock, he shall bring it near, male or female, whole.*

offerings it, too, is bounded by תמידים. The תמיד is a national offering and is burned in its entirety upon the altar. The שלמים, on the other hand, as mentioned earlier, is an offering brought by the individual, and only its אימורים are offered upon the altar, as the main part is returned to the בעלים and eaten by them. Nevertheless, the אימורים of the individual's "meal of peace" are joined to the community's ascent offering; they are offered upon it as are all the other offerings. We have here an expression of a great truth: The national devotion to the Torah is realized through the pure joy of families and individuals; and the idea expressed in הקטרת הכליות והחלב — that when an individual sanctifies his sensual drives, the Divine Presence may be found even in his personal happiness — is one of the major consequences of the collective national devotion.

The allusions in this verse may be interpreted as follows: בני אהרן are the *national* servants of the Sanctuary of the Torah. העלה is the קרבן התמיד and expresses the whole *nation's* devotion to God. Even the wood that is used to sustain the altar fire is taken from the communal supply. Yet the אשה (v. 3) that is offered here (v. 5) is taken from the שלמים of the *individual*. אותו — it, too, shall be offered by בני אהרן המזבחה על העלה אשר על העצים אשר על האש; like the עולה, it, too, becomes אשה ריח ניחח לה׳.

6 See Commentary to verse 1, where we explained that קרבן שלמים is a distinctively Jewish offering. This is evident in the קרבן פסח, the offering by which Israel was constituted by God into His nation, by which Israel entered into a national covenant with God, and which is offered each year on the day that the nation was founded. Fundamentally, the קרבן פסח is a form of זבח שלמים. Hence, מותר הפסח — an animal that was consecrated for use as a קרבן פסח, was lost at the time of the offering, and later found — is קרב שלמים, brought as a שלמים. Now, in our verse there would seem to be a superfluous statement; for it says below אם כשב (v. 7), ואם עז (v. 12), and there would seem to be no need for the introductory ואם מן הצאן קרבנו. Rather, Scripture teaches us through this

7 *If it is a sheep that he brings near as his offering, then he [himself] must bring it near before* God.

ז אִם־כֶּ֥שֶׂב הֽוּא־מַקְרִ֖יב אֶת־קָרְבָּנ֑וֹ וְהִקְרִ֥יב אֹת֖וֹ לִפְנֵ֥י יְהוָֽה׃

8 *And he shall lean his hand upon the head of the offering, and he shall slaughter it in front of the Tent of Appointed Meeting, and sons of Aharon shall dash its blood against the altar, all around.*

ח וְסָמַ֤ךְ אֶת־יָדוֹ֙ עַל־רֹ֣אשׁ קָרְבָּנ֔וֹ וְשָׁחַ֣ט אֹת֔וֹ לִפְנֵ֖י אֹ֣הֶל מוֹעֵ֑ד וְ֠זָֽרְקוּ בְּנֵ֨י אַהֲרֹ֧ן אֶת־דָּמ֛וֹ עַל־הַמִּזְבֵּ֖חַ סָבִֽיב׃

statement that even an offering not consecrated for use as שלמים, but whose origin is in קרבן פסח, e.g., מותר פסח, is treated with all the laws of שלמים — e.g., סמיכה ונסכים ותנופת חזה ושוק — laws that apply exclusively to שלמים and not to פסח (*Menachos* 83b).

8 See Commentary to verse 2. **ושחט אתו** — so, too, above (v. 2) it says ושחטו and below (v. 13) ושחט אתו. We have here a repeated emphasizing of the object, the offering that is slaughtered in the עזרה. Elsewhere (see Commentary to *Devarim* 12:21) we learn the prohibition שלא ישחט חולין בעזרה (*Kiddushin* 57b). שלמים — which are the offerings closest to the level of חולין and, like חולין, are eaten outside the עזרה — are slaughtered inside the עזרה; but a חולין animal may not be slaughtered in the עזרה. The repeated emphasis in the verses of our chapter extends this prohibition to include animals that are unfit to be used for offerings, such as בעלי מומין וחיה ועופות (ibid.). Moreover, not only שחיטת חולין בעזרה but even the bringing of חולין objects of any kind into the עזרה is forbidden. (According to the רשב״א it is forbidden to bring in a חולין object only if there exists, of this type of object, one that is fit for an offering — e.g., bread, fruit, and the like; see משנה למלך הל׳ שחיטה, 2:3.) Only symbolic acts and symbolic objects are to appear in the Sanctuary. If one brings into the Sanctuary an ordinary, profane object — or, especially, if he performs there in a mundane way an act whose counterpart, when performed there, is laden with the symbolism of the Sanctuary — he debases, even desecrates, the place and the act. Hence, חולין שנשחטו בעזרה are אסורין בהנאה. שחיטת חולין בעזרה deprives שחיטת קדשים of its symbolic meaning.

ט וְהִקְרִיב מִזֶּבַח הַשְּׁלָמִים אִשֶּׁה
לַיהוָה חֶלְבּוֹ הָאַלְיָה תְמִימָה
לְעֻמַּת הֶעָצֶה יְסִירֶנָּה וְאֶת־הַחֵלֶב
הַמְכַסֶּה אֶת־הַקֶּרֶב וְאֵת כָּל־
הַחֵלֶב אֲשֶׁר עַל־הַקֶּרֶב׃

9 *He shall then bring, of the meal of peace, as a fire offering before* God, *its fat: he shall remove the entire tailpiece up to the backbone, and the fat that covers the intestines and all the fat that is attached to the intestines.*

9–10 **חלבו**. It is difficult to understand the meaning of this word here. According to רבי עקיבא (*Toras Kohanim* to our verse) it refers to a specific piece of fat near the אליה: חלב שבין הפקוקלות. However, this is also how רבי עקיבא interprets חלב שעל הכסלים of verse 4 — and yet, in verse 10, חלב שעל הכסלים is mentioned in addition to חלבו of verse 9. According to ר׳בי יהודה (ibid.) the word חלבו lends the status of חלב to the אליה of מוקדשין; hence, האוכל אליה של מוקדשין violates the אכילת חלב prohibitions in addition to the לאו דזרות — even though אליה של חולין is permitted to be eaten and is not included among the forbidden חלבים (below, 7:23, et seq.). We have structured the translation of our verse in a similar sense — והקריב מזבח השלמים אשה לה׳ [את] חלבו: האליה תמימה וגו׳ ואת החלב וגו׳ ואת כל החלב וגו׳ ואת שתי הכליות וגו׳. Thus, the parts listed here constitute the "חלב" that is to be offered up in the case of a כבש. Scripture introduces this list of parts with "חלבו," a general term; for the idea of חלב is broadened here by the inclusion of האליה, which is counted among the אימורים only in the case of כבש. This explanation of the verse, however, does not necessarily lead to the opinion of רבי יהודה that האוכל אליה מן המוקדשים חייב משום חלב. For the word חלב, in a broader sense, includes all of the אימורים — as in והקטיר עליה חלבי השלמים (below, 6:5) — and yet כליות יותרת וכבד are not called חלב in the limited sense of איסור חלב (see רמב״ם הל׳ מאכלות אסורות, 7:5).

האליה occurs only in this connection, and it is only by tradition that we know that it refers to the tail. **העצה** is the backbone close to the kidneys, as the Gemara says: מקום שהכליות יועצות (*Chullin* 11a). **עצה**, then, might derive from the root עוץ (עֻצוּ עֵצָה — *Yeshayahu* 8:10), with a ה appended, as in צֹנֶה וַאֲלָפִים (cf. *Tehillim* 8:8, צנה derived from צאן). Offering the אליה among the אימורים is the distinguishing feature of קרבן

10 *Also the two kidneys and the fat that rests upon them, which is along the flanks; also the diaphragm upon the liver; he must remove it together with the kidneys.*

י וְאֵת֙ שְׁתֵּ֣י הַכְּלָיֹ֔ת וְאֶת־הַחֵ֨לֶב֙
אֲשֶׁ֣ר עֲלֵהֶ֔ן אֲשֶׁ֖ר עַל־הַכְּסָלִ֑ים
וְאֶת־הַיֹּתֶ֨רֶת֙ עַל־הַכָּבֵ֔ד עַל־
הַכְּלָיֹ֖ת יְסִירֶֽנָּה׃

11 *And the priest shall turn it into smoke upon the altar, an offering that is made to God by being delivered into the fire.*

יא וְהִקְטִיר֥וֹ הַכֹּהֵ֖ן הַמִּזְבֵּ֑חָה לֶ֥חֶם
אִשֶּׁ֖ה לַֽיהוָֽה׃ פ

הכבש. Apparently, this extension of the idea of חלב — with the אימורי הכבש — is connected with the very meaning of the כבש as the expression of our trust in God, Who shepherds and upholds us in our life and lot. It is also possible that the חלב of the קרב, the חלב on the כליות, the חלב on the כסלים, as well as the חלב of the אליה do not merely represent the idea of חלב in general, but, rather, particularize this idea through the parts on which these חלבים are found. For example: חלב הכליות is the חלב of the lower urges; חלב הקרב is the חלב of nourishment. Unfortunately, we do not know the physiological function of the כסלים and אליה and, hence, cannot explore this theory further with regard to these parts.

11 **לחם אשה לה׳**. Similarly, in the section on שלמי עז Scripture says: לחם אשה לריח ניחח (v. 16), while in the section on שלמי בקר it says: אשה ריח ניחח לה׳ (v. 5). The expression common to all three verses is אשה. From this common term, *Toras Kohanim* (on our verse) derives that the varying expressions לחם, ריח ניחח, לה׳ apply to all three kinds of שלמים. In other words, these verses are complementary. The complete sentence in each case would then be: לחם אשה (ל)ריח ניחוח לה׳.

First, let us examine what the concept of לחם adds to the concept of אשה. If it were possible to interpret אשה to mean "fire," or, particularly, the "fire that is kept burning on the altar," then לחם אשה would be the "fuel of the fire" — that which is given over to the fire in order to keep this fire alive. God's Torah is the אש דת; its perpetuation is dependent on our committing to it the חלב and the כליות — all our aims and aspirations. However, an analysis of all the places in which the word אשה is mentioned leaves no room for doubt: אשה does not mean "fire" but "that which is given over to the fire"; it means the same as לחם אש. It remains for us to explain what is meant by the combination לחם אשה. It must be that לחם and אשה are two aspects of the offering, which differ in nuance. Conclusive proofs by which to support this approach are found in chapter 21. These terms, לחם and אשה, occur there repeatedly and in various contexts. First, the כהן is prohibited from defiling himself by טומאת מת even outside the Sanctuary, and the prohibitions of קרחה, פאת זקן and שריטה are especially emphasized in his regard (vv. 1–5). The reason given for these prohibitions (v. 6) is this: קדשים יהיו לאלקיהם ולא יחללו שם אלקיהם כי את אשה ה׳ לחם אלקיהם הם מקריבים והיו קדש. Second, the nation is commanded to keep the כהן holy in two aspects: They should not allow him to violate the special marriage prohibitions, which sanctify him even in his private life outside the Sanctuary (v. 7). On the other hand, they must honor him as someone holy (v. 8). This commandment is stated as follows: וקדשתו כי את לחם אלקיך הוא מקריב וגו׳. Finally, the prohibition excluding a כהן בעל מום from serving at the altar (vv. 17 and 21) reads: איש וגו׳ אשר יהיה בו מום לא יקרב להקריב לחם אלקיו. כל איש וגו׳ לא יגש להקריב את אשי ה׳ מום בו את לחם אלקיו לא יגש להקריב. Clearly, אשה and לחם here represent two different aspects of the offering. לחם is not linked with אשה; rather, both words are related directly to God — it consistently says אשי ה׳ and לחם אלקיך or לחם אלקיו. And the concept of לחם is an important part of the reason for the sanctity of the כהן and for treating him as holy (below, 21:8, 17).

Giving the offering over to the altar fire produces a double effect: (1) the effect of the fire on the parts given over to it and (2) the effect of the parts on the fire. The symbolic meaning of these two effects is this: (1) The fire of the Torah penetrates and rules man's entire being; it penetrates and rules all the aspects represented by the parts of the offering. At the same time, (2) the fire is kept alive — a place is made for God to dwell on earth. The first is embodied by אשה, the second by לחם.

אש and אשה apparently derive from two different roots. אש derives from the root אשש, which is closely related to עשש, to consume (thus, עש, the moth); it is the consuming fire, which is sustained by the fuel that is fed it. אשה, on the other hand, derives from the root אשה, which is closely related to עשה; it is the material that is fashioned by the fire.

Thus, אש is sustained by the material, which is the לחם, whereas אשה is the material that is fashioned by the fire.

לחם related directly to God — as in לחם אלקיו, לחם אלקיך, and also לחמי לחם (*Bemidbar* 28:2) — is, as it were, the table that you set in My honor to please Me; it is that which you prepare for Me on earth when I "come to you," so as to "dwell among you." אשי ה׳, on the other hand, is that which is given over to the fire of the Torah in accordance with God's Will in order to be purified, fashioned, and brought to life. The objective in both cases is the same. What is destined to be לחם אלקיך must become אשי ה׳, and what becomes אשי ה׳ thereby becomes לחם אלקיך. When the fire of the Torah rules over the material, the material becomes a bearer of godliness on earth; God's Presence comes to rest upon the work of our hands only if the fire of the Torah rules them. Similarly, we find written about the wings of the cherubim: והיו הכרבים פרשי כנפים למעלה סככים בכנפיהם על הכפרת (*Shemos* 25:20) — i.e., they become bearers of the Divine Presence from above (פרשי כנפים למעלה) *by* shielding the Torah below (סככים בכנפיהם על הכפרת). (See Commentary to *Shemos* 25:17–20.)

If this approach is not mistaken, then we understand well what we have already noted above (from chapter 21). There are *mitzvos* whose whole intention is to bring about an ideal harmony between (a) the life of the כהן outside the Sanctuary, including his personal appearance, and (b) his function in the Service of the Sanctuary. And precisely in connection with these *mitzvos* is this function called הקרבת לחם אלקיהם, הקרבת לחם אלקיך. This indicates to us the following: The כהן's service in the Sanctuary shows symbolically how the whole of our lives and our deeds are to be לחם אלקינו, worthy of leading to God's Presence abiding among us, as it says: ושכנתי בתוכם. Hence, there must not be a contradiction between the life of the כהן outside the Sanctuary and the concept of his service inside the Sanctuary. Otherwise, his real life makes a sham of the ideal expressed in the Sanctuary through his symbolic actions: קדשים יהיו לאלקיהם ולא יחללו שם אלקיהם כי את אשי ה׳ לחם אלקיהם הם מקריבים והיו קדש. That is to say, outside the Sanctuary, as well, they are to be holy unto God, in Whose Name they call inside the Sanctuary. They should not desecrate, outside, the Name of God which they teach inside. For in the Sanctuary they bring near unto God earthly matter, and master it with the fire of the Torah so that it be worthy of God's Presence. Therefore, they themselves must become a "sanctuary" — even when they are outside the Sanctuary (see Commentary to chapter 21).

12 *And if his offering is a goat, he shall bring it near before* God.

יב וְאִם־עֵז קׇרְבָּנוֹ וְהִקְרִיבוֹ לִפְנֵי
יְהֹוָה׃

13 *And he shall lean his hand upon its head, and he shall slaughter it in front of the Tent of Appointed Meeting, and sons of Aharon shall dash its blood against the altar, all around.*

יג וְסָמַךְ אֶת־יָדוֹ עַל־רֹאשׁוֹ וְשָׁחַט
אֹתוֹ לִפְנֵי אֹהֶל מוֹעֵד וְזָרְקוּ בְּנֵי
אַהֲרֹן אֶת־דָּמוֹ עַל־הַמִּזְבֵּחַ
סָבִיב׃

14 *He shall then bring near his offering from it as a fire-offering to* God: *the fat that covers the intestines and all the fat that is attached to the intestines.*

יד וְהִקְרִיב מִמֶּנּוּ קׇרְבָּנוֹ אִשֶּׁה לַיהֹוָה
אֶת־הַחֵלֶב הַמְכַסֶּה אֶת־הַקֶּרֶב
וְאֵת כׇּל־הַחֵלֶב אֲשֶׁר עַל־הַקֶּרֶב׃

We know from chapter 21 that this concept of לחם applies to all the offerings that are offered upon the altar; nevertheless, in our chapter, לחם is mentioned only in connection with שלמים. This can be explained by what has been stated above. The procedures of the שלמים offering include partaking of it at home. This transforms the family table into an altar, the home into a sanctuary, and elevates those who partake to the level of כהנים and כהנות. Thus, the very offering procedures of שלמים represent God's Presence in all the joy of our life on earth. And the essential prerequisite to this end is the ideal symbolized by לחם; for God's Presence will not grace our lives on earth unless our aims and endeavors are worthy of that Presence.

A fitting German translation of לחם would be *Opfer* (offering) in its original, literal sense, denoting the offering of a gift or, more precisely, a gift that has been offered; that is to say, a gift given in accordance with the will of the receiver. לחם אשה, then, means a gift that is offered by being delivered into the fire. (See Commentary above, 1:2.)

12–15 **שלמי עז** differ from שלמי כבש only in respect to the offering of the אליה, as the אליה is offered in the case of כבש but not in the case of עז. Scripture therefore repeats here, in the case of עז, all the offering procedures

15 *Also the two kidneys and the fat that rests upon them, which is along the flanks; also the diaphragm upon the liver; he must remove it together with the kidneys.*

טו וְאֶת֙ שְׁתֵּ֣י הַכְּלָיֹ֔ת וְאֶת־הַחֵ֨לֶב֙
אֲשֶׁ֣ר עֲלֵהֶ֔ן אֲשֶׁ֖ר עַל־הַכְּסָלִ֑ים
וְאֶת־הַיֹּתֶ֨רֶת֙ עַל־הַכָּבֵ֔ד עַל־
הַכְּלָיֹ֖ת יְסִירֶֽנָּה׃

16 *The priest shall turn them into smoke upon the altar as an offering made by fire, as an expression of compliance; all the fat belongs to God.*

טז וְהִקְטִירָ֥ם הַכֹּהֵ֖ן הַמִּזְבֵּ֑חָה לֶ֤חֶם
אִשֶּׁה֙ לְרֵ֣יחַ נִיחֹ֔חַ כָּל־חֵ֖לֶב
לַיהֹוָֽה׃

17 *It shall be an everlasting statute for your descendants in all your dwelling places: You shall not eat any fat, nor any blood.*

יז חֻקַּ֤ת עוֹלָם֙ לְדֹרֹ֣תֵיכֶ֔ם בְּכֹ֖ל
מוֹשְׁבֹתֵיכֶ֑ם כָּל־חֵ֥לֶב וְכָל־דָּ֖ם
לֹ֥א תֹאכֵֽלוּ׃ פ חמישי

mentioned above in the case of כבש — to teach us that only this difference exists between them (*Toras Kohanim*).

16 **כל חלב לה'** — all that is offered as "חלב" belongs to God; that is to say, anything counted among the אימורים (see Commentary to v. 9) is holy unto God, and any other use of it would come under the category of מעילה (see Commentary below, 5:14, et seq.).

This law is stated especially here, in the case of שלמים, for the following reason. As קדשים קלים they are ממון בעלים, the property of the ones who bring the offering; they are ultimately eaten by the בעלים, and even בחייהם, while the animals are alive, no מעילה applies to them. However, once זריקת דם takes place, the אימורים — here called חלב — belong to God; that is to say, they are holy unto God and included in the category of קדשי ה' (below, 5:15); their profane use constitutes מעילה (*Chullin* 117a).

17 **חקת עולם וגו'**. The details of the law concerning חלב are explained below (7:23, et seq.). Here, the intention is only to juxtapose the איסור חלב ודם to what is stated in the previous verse, כל חלב לה'. Scripture thus alludes

to the fact that there is a connection between the prohibition of eating these materials and the precept of offering them on the altar (see below). In addition, *Toras Kohanim* interprets our verse as follows: חקת עולם – לבית עולמים; לדרתיכם – שינהג הדבר לדורות; בכל מושבותיכם – בארץ ובחוצה לארץ. Even though the use of these materials in offerings is limited in time and place, the prohibition of eating חלב ודם remains in force לדרתיכם בכל מושבותיכם — both בפני הבית and שלא בפני הבית (i.e., regardless of whether the Sanctuary is in existence or not), both בארץ and בחוצה לארץ; it applies after the destruction of the Sanctuary and also outside of the Holy Land — even though the Service of the Sanctuary is forbidden there (*Kiddushin* 37b; וצ״ע בכריתות ד ע״ב). According to this interpretation of *Toras Kohanim*, the words חקת עולם are the continuation of the final words of the preceding verse, כל חלב לה׳; that is to say, the mitzvah of offering all חלב to God is not limited to the משכן, but is, rather, a חקת עולם — it applies also to the בית עולמים, i.e., the בית המקדש, which is the site of the *avodah* לעולם, for all time. To this halachah is linked the second halachah of the verse: לדרתיכם בכל מושבותיכם כל חלב וכל דם לא תאכלו.

The connection between these two *halachos* is as follows. Just as the בית המקדש is called בית עולמים, so, too, the laws concerning the offerings and the mitzvah of offering them have been given to us as a חקת עולם; hence, all the laws deriving from these *halachos* also apply for all time. Although we have been exiled from our Land and our Sanctuary has been violated, all this is only temporary. Only temporarily are we prevented from fulfilling these *halachos*; the conditions necessary for their fulfillment are temporarily lacking. But this does not mean that these *halachos* and their ramifications have been abrogated. Just as the mitzvah כבד את אביך is not abrogated for one whose father is temporarily absent; just as the mitzvah ולמדתם אותם את בניכם is not abrogated for one who does not yet have children of his own — so it is with הלכות מקדש וקדשיו: they are in effect and incumbent upon us even today. This is evidenced by the laws of חלב ודם, which apply לדרתיכם בכל מושבותיכם. By refraining from eating blood and חלב we attest to the eternal validity of the laws of the offerings, affirm confidence in the ultimate restoration of the *avodah* in the Sanctuary, and lodge the most effective protest against any attempt to justify efforts at so-called reform by the pretense that the laws of the offerings are obsolete and were abrogated long ago.

4 1 God *spoke to Moshe, saying:*	ד א וַיְדַבֵּר יְהֹוָה אֶל־מֹשֶׁה לֵּאמֹר:
2 *Speak to the Children of Israel,*	ב דַּבֵּר אֶל־בְּנֵי יִשְׂרָאֵל לֵאמֹר נֶפֶשׁ

The connection between the prohibition of eating חלב and the laws of the offerings is especially apparent in that this prohibition applies only to animals fit to be used as offerings (cf. below, 7:25); it applies only to שור כבש ועז, and not to חיה ועוף.

The prohibition of eating blood is different. Although this prohibition, like that of חלב, is linked here with the bringing of the offerings, it entails more than what may be deduced from this context. For, as opposed to the חלב prohibition, it is not limited to animals fit for use as offerings, but is applicable also to חיה ועוף, to all warm-blooded animals. There must, then, be another reason for the prohibition of eating blood, a reason unconnected with the laws of the offerings. (See Commentary below, 17:10–12. Cf. Commentary below, 7:26–27; to *Bereshis* 9:4–5; and to *Devarim* 12:23.)

The idea expressed here by the linking of the prohibition of חלב and דם with the precept of offering them is as follows. Blood and חלב-fat are the two poles of the animal organism: The very essence of the animal is concentrated in the blood — כי הדם הוא הנפש (*Devarim* 12:23); חלב-fat is the final product of the organic life of the animal — the animal produces it for its own needs. (חֵלֶב is blood converted for selfish purposes, while חָלָב is blood converted for purposes of kindness. Both are forms of the root חלף.) Symbolically, in an animal offering, animal blood can represent the essence of a human being, and animal חלב can represent human aims. But, actually, the essence of an animal can never become the essence of a human being, and animal aims are not to become human aims. Precisely because חלב and דם, in offerings, symbolically represent aspects of man, they must never actually be assimilated by man, lest we entertain the notion that human nature can be identified with animal nature.

CHAPTER 4

2 **נפש כי תחטא וגו׳ ועשה וגו׳.** נפש, the soul, is the very essence of the human personality. It manifests itself through man's mind and will. The body, with its organs and powers, is entrusted to its rule and

saying: If a person inadvertently transgresses some of all the things that God has commanded that they shall not be done, and he commits any one of them.	כִּֽי־תֶחֱטָ֤א בִשְׁגָגָה֙ מִכֹּל֙ מִצְוֺ֣ת יְהוָ֔ה אֲשֶׁ֖ר לֹ֣א תֵעָשֶׂ֑ינָה וְעָשָׂ֕ה מֵאַחַ֖ת מֵהֵֽנָּה׃

guidance. The duty of the נפש is to exercise its rule and extend guidance only in accordance with God's Will. To do so, it, too, must subject itself to the "fire" of the Torah, in order to be ruled by its light. If the body is subservient to the soul, and the soul is subservient to God, then all of man's activities, spiritual and physical, are conducted in the service of God. Man's will, ruling his body, carries out God's Will in complete moral freedom. But if the נפש withdraws (תחטא) from the light of Torah fire (this is the literal meaning of חטא, as we argued — based on the phonetic relation of חטא to חתה — in our Commentary to *Bereshis* 39:9), there is danger that the body's organs and powers, which should be activated only within the limits hallowed by God's Will, will act contrary to His Will. This, then, is the meaning of קרבן חטאת: A soul, having strayed from the rule of God's Will, now seeks to regain God's closeness on which the purity of its active life depends. קרבן חטאת is the expression of this quest. Through this seeking after God's closeness (=קרבן), the soul atones for having drawn away from the אש דת (=חטאת).

However, one brings an offering for his sin only if the act is begun and completed in inadvertence, בשגגה (see *Shabbos* 102a). בשגגה means not only *on account of* inadvertence, but *in the midst of* inadvertence — i.e., תחילתו וסופו שגגה (ibid.). But if either at the beginning or at the end of the act there is awareness of its forbidden nature (זדון), one is exempt from a חטאת, even if this awareness comes when it is no longer possible to prevent the act from being completed, e.g., הזורק אבן לרשות הרבים בשבת ונזכר לאחר שיצתה מידו (ibid.); and certainly one is exempt where תחילתו וסופו זדון, the entire act is carried out with this awareness. In these latter cases *the sin is beyond the sphere in which an offering can atone.*

We have already noted (Commentary to *Bereshis* 8:1) the difference between שגג and שגה. The שוגג is one who errs through carelessness.

It was his obligation to make sure that his actions be in accordance with the law, but he did not relate to this obligation with all due seriousness. At the time of his שגגה he was not חָרֵד עַל דְּבַר ה׳ (see *Yeshayahu* 66:2). Lack of concern for the fitness of one's deeds is the sin at the root of every שגגה; it is the פשע found in every חטא, as it says: ומפשעיהם לכל חטאתם (below, 16:16).

There is a שוגג who errs in regard to the halachah — e.g., he is unaware that חלב is אסור, or that one who eats חלב is liable to כרת; viz., שגג בלאו או שגג בכרת (see *Shabbos* 69a). And there is a שוגג who is well-versed in the halachah but the nature of the object escapes him — e.g., he is aware of the איסור חלב and of its severity, but he thinks that he is eating שומן (permitted fat).

Some Sages hold that one is liable to a חטאת only if he knew the halachah and subsequently forgot it (הכיר ולבסוף שכח). Others hold that even one who had grown up among non-Jews (תינוק שנשבה בין הנכרים) is liable. In such a case, one sinned because he never had knowledge of Judaism; even he, when he becomes aware of his obligation as a Jew, must bring a חטאת for his שגגה (ibid. 68b). This latter opinion is accepted by the רמב״ם as the halachah (הל׳ שגגות, 2:6).

Even a שוגג בלא מתכוון is liable to a חטאת. In such a case one is called a מתעסק: not only is he unaware of transgressing, but he performs the act without any intention of doing so — e.g., he had חלב in his mouth וקסבר רוק הוא ובלעו (*Shabbos* 73a). He, too, is a שוגג who brings a חטאת for his שגגה. The Gemara says: מתעסק בחלבים ובעריות חייב שכן נהנה, for he nonetheless has committed the transgression. The law is different only with regard to שבת, as מלאכת מחשבת אסרה תורה, only a מלאכה entailing the fulfillment of one's intent constitutes חילול שבת. Hence, המתעסק בשבת is פטור מחטאת — e.g., if one intended to lift, or even to cut, something detached from the ground, and he cut something attached to the ground. His act — חתיכת המחובר — entails no fulfillment of any intent, as he had no intention whatsoever to perform this act (*Kerisos* 19b).

מכל מצות ה׳ אשר לא תעשינה. It is difficult to interpret the phrase אשר לא תעשינה as an expression for negative commandments. From the grammatical construction it appears as though מצות were the subject of אשר לא תעשינה, in which case the phrase would mean "commandments that are not to be fulfilled"! We therefore must conclude that

אשר refers not to מצות, but to the objects of the מצות, "God's commands with regard to the things that are not to be done."

It is also difficult to explain the construction of the sentence נפש כי תחטא וגו׳ מכל מצות ה׳ וגו׳. The verb חטא is usually not followed by the sin, in the accusative. Nor can the מ in מכל be taken to indicate a distancing of self from the *mitzvos*, as there is no analogous construction in connection with the verb חטא. We therefore have no alternative but to conclude that מצות ה׳ is actually the object of the verb חטא, and that the מ of מכל is a partitive term, meaning *some of* all the *mitzvos* (the use of מ in this sense is quite common in the sections dealing with the offerings). This is also what the Halachah teaches: not every offense that is committed inadvertently makes one liable to a חטאת; rather, the obligation to bring a חטאת is limited to the inadvertent violation of a לא תעשה שיש בו מעשה שחייבין על זדונו כרת, a negative precept entailing an action that when done willfully carries the penalty of כרת. Thus are excluded all negative precepts for whose willful violation one would not be liable to כרת — even if one would be liable to the death penalty, e.g., מכה אב ואם and גונב נפש מישראל. פסח and מילה are also excluded — even though they carry with them the penalty of כרת — since they are positive, not negative, precepts. Finally, even מגדף, blasphemy, is excluded — even though it is a negative precept for which one is liable to כרת — since it entails no action but only speech (ibid. 2a). All this is derived from the case of עבודה זרה, which is the archetype for this halachah; for עבודה זרה is the only sin whose שגגה is mentioned explicitly in the Torah as making one liable to a חטאת (*Bemidbar* 15:22, et seq.; see Commentary, ad loc.). The Torah uses the phrase תורה אחת (ibid. 15:29): תורה אחת יהיה לכם לעשה בשגגה; והנפש אשר תעשה ביד רמה וגו׳ ונכרתה הנפש וגו׳. Thus, הוקשה כל התורה כולה לעבודה זרה (*Kerisos* 3a) vis-à-vis the obligation to bring a חטאת in the case of שוגג.

The limitation of the חטאת obligation to cases of לא תעשה שיש בו כרת may be explained by the natural weakness of man. For there is not a righteous man on earth who does only good and does not sin. No man can be expected never to err unintentionally; on the contrary, of man it is said: שְׁגִיאוֹת מִי־יָבִין (*Tehillim* 19:13). Hence, his שגגה requires no special atonement — unless he is careless with or indifferent toward a mitzvah punishable by כרת; for in such a case, the severity of כרת should keep him from even an inadvertent violation.

There is, however, another explanation. The limitation of the חטאת

obligation to שגגה in a לא תעשה שזדונו כרת highlights before us this group of *mitzvos* in particular and demands of us to relate to them with special concentration and seriousness. Elsewhere (see Commentary below, 20:9), we shall prove that חיובי כרת are essentially sins of a specifically Jewish character — and this applies even to sins punishable by both כרת and מיתת בית דין, as the כרת derives from their uniquely Jewish aspect. Consider, for example, מילה, פסח, חלב, דם, נדה. Consider also all איסורי עריות that are only בכרת; in keeping with our assumption, בני נח are not included in these prohibitions, as it says: כל ערוה שבית דין של ישראל ממיתין עליה בן נח מוזהר עליה אין בית דין של ישראל ממיתין עליה אין בן נח מוזהר עליה (*Sanhedrin* 57b. According to רמב"ם הל' מלכים, 9:5, אחותו מן האם is the only exception, but see כסף משנה, ad loc.).

Now, we do not have permission to know or conjecture anything about the penalty of כרת, which is in the hands of God alone. Nevertheless, it would appear that הכרת מעמיה should be understood according to its plain sense: the uprooting of the נפש from the future of its people — in this world and the next. One who commits an offense punishable by כרת is not worthy of being rooted in the soil of his people's future. The penalty of כרת, then, is profoundly related to the specific nature of Judaism (cf. Commentary above, 1:5 [end]). This accords with what is stated in *Toras Kohanim* to our verse: While the word נפש includes everyone who has entered the covenant of Israel, including גרים and עבדים, the term בני ישראל excludes non-Jews. Although the עולות of non-Jews are offered on the altar, they may not bring a חטאת. Thus, we can allude to a possible connection between the very concept of חטא and the penalty of כרת: According to our understanding, one who inadvertently sins allows himself to be disconnected from the enlightening and life-giving fire of the Torah; the חטאת brings his נפש back to this fire. One who willfully sins disconnects himself from this Divine fire; and the penalty of כרת uproots the נפש entirely from the source of light and life.

ועשה מאחת מהנה. ועשה מאחת can mean only that he performed part of some forbidden act. For example, in the case of prohibited work on Shabbos, once one has performed a complete part of some prohibited work — e.g., written שם from שמעון, דן from דניאל, נח from נחור, or woven two threads of a garment — he is liable to a חטאת (*Shabbos* 103a–b).

3 *If the anointed priest sins,* ג אִם הַכֹּהֵן הַמָּשִׁיחַ יֶחֱטָא לְאַשְׁמַת

Just as the מ of מאחת indicates part of a whole, so does the מ of מהנה; only that in the latter case the part indicated is a part in the logical sense, something derived from a primary concept, a part of a collective idea — e.g., pruning (זומר), which is a derivative (תולדה) of planting (נוטע); for pruning furthers the growth of trees and thus derives from the collective idea (אב) of planting. Hence the interpretation: הנה אבות מהנה תולדות (ibid. 103b, 70a–b).

At the same time, the combination מאחת מהנה draws attention to the matter of determining the number of errors committed. This can be אחת מהנה or מאחת הנה. There is the case of one who performs a number of forbidden acts all of which derive from one error (אחת מהנה) — e.g., he forgets that today is Shabbos and performs a number of מלאכות of various אבות (see Commentary to *Shemos* 35:1): שגגת שבת וזדון מלאכות. In such a case all the מלאכות that are performed derive from one error, and he is liable to only one חטאת. And then there is the case of one who knows that today is Shabbos and yet performs a number of אבות מלאכות because he forgets that they are forbidden on Shabbos. In this case the violation of the prohibition of working on Shabbos derives from a number of errors — זדון שבת ושגגת מלאכות (מאחת הנה) — and one is liable to a number of חטאות according to the number of errors made (*Shabbos* 103b, 70a–b).

The חיוב חטאת is not dependent on the number of acts but on the number of errors. One who performs prohibited work on יום הכיפורים that falls out on שבת is liable to two חטאות; yet one who forgets the prohibition against eating חלב and eats חלב several times — without awareness of his sin between violations (בהעלם אחד) — is liable to only one חטאת. According to one opinion of the Sages תמחויין וגופין מוחלקין: if one error is repeated with separate objects, the number of חטאות is determined by the number of objects (*Kerisos* 11b; 15b). This opinion is not accepted by the רמב"ם as the halachah (הל' שגגות, 6:1).

3 **הכהן המשיח** refers only to one who was anointed with שמן המשחה for the sake of serving in the Sanctuary. That is to say, it refers neither to

bringing guilt to the people, he shall bring near for the sin he has committed a young bull, whole, to God *as an offering for the sin.*	הָעָם וְהִקְרִ֗יב עַ֣ל חַטָּאתוֹ֙ אֲשֶׁ֣ר חָטָ֔א פַּ֧ר בֶּן־בָּקָ֛ר תָּמִ֥ים לַיהֹוָ֖ה לְחַטָּֽאת׃

a מרובה בבגדים — like the כהנים גדולים in the days of the Second Temple (who, in the absence of שמן המשחה, were inducted into office by investiture with the eight priestly garments), nor to a משוח מלחמה, who is anointed for the sole purpose of exhorting the people before battle (*Devarim* 20:2ff.; *Horayos* 11b–12a). הכהן המשיח, then, refers to the most complete and highest priestly representative of the nation. This does not, however, exclude משוח שעבר — one who was anointed only so as to substitute for the temporarily disqualified כהן גדול, and who ceases to serve in his stead when the first one is ready to resume his duties; or one who ceases to serve as the כהן גדול on account of advanced age or a מום (*Horayos*, ibid., and 9b. The question of the לחם משנה הל׳ שגגות, 15:7, is resolved by what is stated in *Horayos* 9b).

לאשמת העם. אשמה leads to שממה, desolation, and the אָשֵׁם bears within himself the seed of his desolation. We have explained this matter previously, in our Commentary to *Bereshis* (42:21–22), based on the etymology of the word אשם. What is stated here is that the inadvertence of the כהן המשיח leads to אשמת העם, or is itself considered as אשמת העם. This can be understood if we remember that the כהן גדול represents the nation in its ideal realization (see Commentary to *Shemos* 28); hence, חטאת הכהן המשיח needs atonement as אשמת העם, as a sin that imperils the future of the nation.

Truly, the כהן המשיח is the symbolic embodiment of the national idea. This becomes evident when we compare the first section of this chapter (vv. 3–12) with the second section (vv. 13–21). The offerings and offering procedures in these two sections are identical. Both offerings are פרים. Both are חטאות פנימיות, as their blood is not placed on the קרנות מזבח החיצון but is taken into the היכל. There, two procedures are performed with the blood: הזיה על הפרוכת and מתנות על קרנות מזבח הקטורת. Both offerings are פרים הנשרפים: except for the אימורים, which are offered up on the altar, they are burned in their entirety outside the שלוש מחנות. They both differ in their laws from the חטאות החיצוניות, which are treated in the succeeding sections (vv. 22–26 and 27–35); there is nothing in common between חטאות פנימיות and חטאות חיצוניות except for שחיטה, שפיכת שיריים ליסוד, and הקטרת אימורים.

The "personality" to be atoned for in the second section is the national community in its concrete reality. The two elements that constitute this community — viz., (a) עיני הקהל, the spiritual leadership, i.e., the סנהדרין and בית דין הגדול; and (b) the קהל whose actions are guided by this leadership, i.e., the whole nation — were the cause of sin. There is no obligation to bring this חטאת unless בית דין הגדול inadvertently errs in a ruling (שגגו בהוראה) regarding a דבר שחייבין על זדונו כרת, and the people actually sin as a result of this ruling. These two elements — the national spiritual leadership and the national conduct — are embodied by the בית דין הגדול and by the ציבור, and they are symbolically united in the כהן גדול, who is the representative of the whole nation.

Now, the כהן המשיח, too, is liable to this חטאת if he inadvertently errs in a ruling for himself in a matter for which one is חייב כרת and then acts in accordance with that decision (הורה לעצמו שוגג ועשה שוגג בדבר שחייבין על זדונו כרת); for the ruling of the כהן משיח for himself is like the ruling of the בית דין for the community (שהוראת כהן משיח לעצמו כהוראת בית דין לצבור) (*Horayos* 6b). This parallel is expressed by what is stated in our verse: לאשמת העם (ibid.). The Gemara (ibid. 7a–b) says further that הוראת כהן משיח לעצמו makes him liable to a חטאת only if he is a מופלא — i.e., only if he is versed in the Halachah and qualified and authorized to rule for himself. But if he is not a מופלא, then הוראה דידיה ולא כלום היא, his ruling has no legal force whatsoever; it is nothing but meaningless pretension, and his sin falls into the category of an ordinary שגגה, which, in the case of the כהן גדול, has no atonement through an offering. The same is true of the חטאת of the קהל: the ruling of a בית דין that is not מופלא is meaningless — הוראה דלהון ולא כלום. If a community sins on the basis of an erroneous decision issued by a בית דין that is not מופלא, then the sin committed is an ordinary שגגה, which is not atoned for by means of a פר העלם דבר של ציבור (the name for the פר החטאת discussed in the second section); rather, each individual atones for his sin by bringing a חטאת יחיד. For it is not office and honor but knowledge of the Torah which grants authority in Israel.

והקריב על חטאתו אשר חטא. Whereas the words לאשמת העם liken the חטאת of the כהן המשיח to that of the קהל, the words על חטאתו אשר חטא differentiate between them; as it says in *Horayos* (7a): לאשמת העם הרי הוא משיח כצבור, מה צבור אינו מביא אלא על העלם דבר עם שגגת מעשה, אף משיח אינו מביא אלא על העלם דבר עם שגגת מעשה. אימא מה ציבור הורה ועשו אחריו בהוראתו חייבין, אף משיח כשהורה ועשו אחריו בהוראתו יהא חייב, ת״ל והקריב על חטאתו אשר חטא, על מה שחטא הוא מביא, ואין מביא על מה שחטאו אחרים. This halachah distinguishes between the standing of the כהן גדול and that of בית דין הגדול. Neither the כהן nor even the כהן גדול is granted any authority by virtue of his priestly office. It is not the task of the כהן גדול to interpret the Torah. His word as a כהן does not have binding authority לאסור ולהתיר. Only in the Sanctuary does he symbolically represent the unity of בית דין and ציבור, the ideal of the nation guided by the spirit of the Torah. But his הוראה is authoritative only for himself; in the Sanctuary הוראת כהן משיח לעצמו כהוראת בית דין לצבור — and he atones for it with the same חטאת. But in everyday life, in the midst of his people, the position of the כהן גדול in relation to the Torah is no different from that of the lowliest hewer of wood. The only difference is that an ordinary שגגת מעשה of a כהן גדול is not atoned for by means of an offering.

The foregoing does away with all the mindless talk about a Jewish hierarchy — as though the Jewish priesthood were the source of all hierarchical pretentiousness. This false claim, which has passed from mouth to mouth, is utterly discredited by Jewish law and by the facts of Jewish history. Throughout all the thousands of years of Jewish history the influence of priestly authority in the shaping of the community was not pronounced. The overwhelming majority of men who had impact on the life of the Jewish nation as its leaders and teachers were not כהנים; and those among them who were כהנים exerted influence not by virtue of their priestly position but on account of their personal qualities — which would have opened the nation's hearts to them even had they not been descendants of Aharon.

Now, it does say in *Devarim* (17:9) of one who turns to the highest legal authority: ובאת אל הכהנים הלוים ואל השופט וגו׳. However, this is explained by *Sifre* (ad loc.) in a manner consistent with the basic halachah that is written here: If there are *Kohanim* and *Levi'im* who are qualified to serve on the Sanhedrin, it is a mitzvah to have them among its members; but their presence is not indispensable to the authority of the Sanhedrin, and certainly the Sanhedrin need not be composed entirely of כהנים: מצות בית

דין שיהיו בו כהנים ולוים . . . אעפ״י שאין בו כהנים ולוים כשר We learn further (*Sanhedrin* 52b), from the juxtaposition of השופט with הכהנים in the above-quoted verse, that בית דין הגדול does not have its full powers unless the *avodah* of the כהנים is in place in the Sanctuary. The Gemara also states that the authority of the סנהדרין הגדולה is dependent upon the site of the Sanctuary: מלמד שהמקום גורם (ibid. 14b). For, in Judaism, justice is not a political-national expediency; rather, its source is in the same Will of God Who commanded that an altar be built for His Torah, and Who commanded that the fulfillment of His Will be represented symbolically in His Sanctuary by the offerings given to the fire of His Torah. What the כהן teaches in the Sanctuary through symbols is implemented by the Sanhedrin in actual life. Both functions are forms of עבודת ה׳.

True, the Torah expects the כהנים and the entire tribe of Levi to know that "God is their inheritance" (cf. *Devarim* 10:9). Since the Service of the Sanctuary is entrusted to them, and since they have no inheritance in the Land, they are to become men imbued with the knowledge and spirit of the Torah — so that those who "place incense for Your perception and whole offerings upon Your altar" (ישימו קטורה באפך וכליל על מזבחך) will also "teach Your laws to Ya'akov and Your Teaching to Yisrael" (יורו משפטיך ליעקב ותורתך לישראל) (*Devarim* 33:10). As Malachi, last of the prophets, exhorted the corrupt כהנים of his day: שִׂפְתֵי כֹהֵן יִשְׁמְרוּ־דַעַת וְתוֹרָה יְבַקְשׁוּ מִפִּיהוּ (*Malachi* 2:7). But the function of the כהן is to teach, to exhort, to reprove, to turn the hearts of the people back to God and to make peace between one person and another: תּוֹרַת אֱמֶת הָיְתָה בְּפִיהוּ וְעַוְלָה לֹא־נִמְצָא בִשְׂפָתָיו בְּשָׁלוֹם וּבְמִישׁוֹר הָלַךְ אִתִּי וְרַבִּים הֵשִׁיב מֵעָוֺן (ibid. 2:6). It is not the function of the כהן, however, to wield the authority of the Law. The Sages, based on the above verse, expressed this distinction as follows: משה היה אומר יקוב הדין את ההר אבל אהרן אוהב שלום ורודף שלום ומשים שלום בין אדם לחברו, "The principle of Moshe is: 'The law must cut through the mountain,' but that of Aharon is: 'To love peace, pursue peace, and bring peace between one person and another'" (*Sanhedrin* 6b). The Sages said further, based on the verse מֶלֶךְ בְּמִשְׁפָּט יַעֲמִיד אָרֶץ וְאִישׁ תְּרוּמוֹת יֶהֶרְסֶנָּה (*Mishlei* 29:4): The כהן is an איש תרומות, he is dependent upon others, and such dependency disqualifies him from serving in the office of judge (see *Kesubos* 105b). At any rate, nowhere do we find even the slightest hint of such an idea that the כהן גדול was a prototype for the authority of a "pope." The Urim and Tummim made known God's Word in the case of certain national ventures, but they were consulted only in regard to the success or failure of these ventures and not on questions of law (see *Eruvin* 45a, רש״י ד״ה הרי שמואל ובית דינו קיים).

Let us bear in mind that the פר כהן המשיח is brought only for the כהן's own sin (על חטאתו אשר חטא) due to an error on his part in interpreting the law, unlike the פר העלם דבר של ציבור which is brought for הוראה לאחרים ושגגת אחרים. The task of the כהן גדול, then, is this: His *life* should serve as an *example* of proper understanding and proper observance of the Torah. That which בית דין הגדול is to *teach* the nation to fulfill, the כהן גדול is to *exemplify* in his life. It is fitting that he be מופלא בהוראה; but his primary task is to be a model for his people and to actualize, in his life, his knowledge of Torah. For this reason the כהן גדול must be a "complete" person: as a husband and father he must lead the full life of a man and citizen in the midst of his people. The כהן גדול is not permitted to remain unmarried (see *Yoma* 13a).

פר בן בקר. His offering is to be a פר, a working animal. For he brings his offering not as a private individual but as one appointed to work in the field of God. He must appreciate his transgression in terms of his position as כהן המשיח and undertake to be true to this calling in the future. Symbolically, he draws near to the entrance of God's Sanctuary as a "פר," for it is his task to work in God's service. By leading a life consistent with his service in the Sanctuary, he is to open the hearts of his people and enlighten their eyes with Torah and is to draw near to God as a "פר בן בקר."

According to *Toras Kohanim* on our verse, פר denotes a mature animal, and בן בקר a young animal. The combination פר בן בקר, then, denotes a "young mature bull" — i.e., a bull in the first year of its maturity, namely, a בן שלש, an animal in its third year of life, having completed two full years but not yet three (see also *Rosh Hashanah* 10a).

Even as the nation must remain always a "yearling" (בן שנה) and sustain its youthfulness before God, even as there is nothing of which the Torah is more wary than ונושנתם בארץ (*Devarim* 4:25), that the community's relationship with God might grow old and stale (on the contrary, our mission in life should renew in our hearts, each day, fresh vigor and enthusiasm), so must the leaders of the people, despite ripe maturity, remain ever "young." They must constantly reexperience the greatness of their calling and never grow "old" in their position, too settled. For precisely such settling into old routine is the cause of the

ד וְהֵבִ֣יא אֶת־הַפָּ֗ר אֶל־פֶּ֛תַח אֹ֥הֶל
מוֹעֵ֖ד לִפְנֵ֣י יְהֹוָ֑ה וְסָמַ֤ךְ אֶת־יָדוֹ֙
עַל־רֹ֣אשׁ הַפָּ֔ר וְשָׁחַ֥ט אֶת־הַפָּ֖ר
לִפְנֵ֥י יְהֹוָֽה׃

4 *He shall bring the bull to the entrance of the Tent of Appointed Meeting before* God, *lean his hand upon the head of the bull and slaughter the bull before* God.

ה וְלָקַ֛ח הַכֹּהֵ֥ן הַמָּשִׁ֖יחַ מִדַּ֣ם הַפָּ֑ר
וְהֵבִ֥יא אֹת֖וֹ אֶל־אֹ֥הֶל מוֹעֵֽד׃

5 *The anointed priest shall then take some of the bull's blood and bring it into the Tent of Appointed Meeting.*

---

errors for which atonement is here sought. Long years of studying the Torah and practicing it can turn it into a mere routine, and the monotony of routine easily leads to arrogance. One no longer weighs each step in his life; one ceases to refresh and renew his learning, which would provide the right standard to gauge his conduct. The כהן המשיח who errs in ruling for himself (טעה בהוראה לעצמו) and as a result errs in practice (שגג במעשה) must present himself before God as a פר בן בקר, and undertake to avoid the arrogance of growing old and stale in the study and practice of the Torah.

4 **ושחט את הפר לפני ה׳** — in the north (בצפון), as it says above (1:11) regarding קרבן עולה: ושחט אתו וגו׳ צפנה לפני ה׳, and as it says below (4:29) in the case of חטאת יחיד: ושחט את החטאת במקום העלה. This law is extended to include every חטאת: זה בנה אב לכל חטאות שיהו טעונות צפון (*Zevachim* 48b; see *Toras Kohanim* and קרבן אהרן to our verse). Not only purely practical errors but even practical errors that are a result of errors in theory derive from an intensification of the material-sensual side of our nature. Hence, even in the case of פר כהן המשיח the very first prerequisite is שחיטה וקבלה בצפון (see Commentary above, 1:11).

5 **ולקח הכהן המשיח**. In the following verses (6 and 7) it says merely הכהן. *Toras Kohanim* derives from this that although it is a מצוה for the כהן המשיח himself to perform the offering procedures of his חטאת, nevertheless, if another כהן performed them, they are valid.

ולקח מדם הפר: מדם הנפש ולא מדם העור ולא מדם התמצית (*Zevachim* 25a). That is to say, only דם הפר, the blood in which the individuality of the פר, its נפש, is concentrated; the blood with which the נפש departs, דם שהנפש יוצאת בו (see קרבן אהרן, to our verse) — only this blood is valid for use in the blood *avodah*. This is the blood that spurts out in a stream (מקלח); but not דם העור — or as it is called in *Toras Kohanim*, דם הבשר — the blood that exudes from the skin and flesh of the neck *before* the windpipe and esophagus are cut; and not דם התמצית, which trickles out (שותת) *after* the דם הקילוח, the stream (*Kerisos* 22a).

(וצ״ע דמשמע שם דאיכא נמי דם התמצית קודם דם הקילוח ואם כן כיון שהשוחט צריך שיתן וורדין לתוך הכלי אי אפשר שלא יהא בו מדם התמצית הראשון, וצ״ל או דלא ממעט אלא דם התמצית האחרון או דלא ממעט אלא כשיש דם התמצית לבד אבל עם דם הנפש לא פסל ואפשר דלא קאמר אלא דלא צריך לקבל גם דם העור ודם התמצית ולא דצריך לכוון שלא לקבלן וצ״ע עיין זבחים עט: דאם לא רבה דם התמצית על דם הנפש לא פסל ופליגי אי שכיח לרבות דם התמצית ע״ש.)

A further comment on מדם הפר: The מ in this case is not a partitive term; it does not serve to indicate that only part of the blood (מקצת הדם) need be received in the כלי שרת. For even after the הזיות ומתנות, Scripture still speaks of כל דם הפר (v. 7). Moreover, the halachah states: השוחט צריך שיקבל את כל דמו של פר (*Zevachim* 25a). Rather, the מ is locative; it serves to indicate that the דם הפר must pass directly מהפר, from the animal, into the כלי שרת, as though instead of מדם הפר it were written דם מהפר. Hence, נשפך הדם על הרצפה ואספו פסול, if the blood spilled to the ground and he gathered it up, it is פסול (ibid.). This hermeneutic rule, which renders מדם הפר as though it were written דם מהפר, is called גורעין ומוסיפין ודורשים (ibid.) — i.e., we subtract the letter מ from the word מדם and add it to the word הפר and then expound it as though it were written so. It would seem, however, that this rule was cited only for didactic clarity. For in reality the construction מדם הפר expresses the full depth of the nature of קבלת הדם: The blood received in a כלי שרת has moved out of the category of דם הפר and directly into the category of דם הקדש. Through שחיטה it ceases being דם הפר, and through קבלה it becomes דם הקדש. Just as until now it belonged to the פר, now it belongs to קודש. Henceforth it will serve the purposes of קודש, as hitherto it served the needs of the פר. This removes from שחיטה any suggestion of killing and destruction; the whole purpose of שחיטה is to afford entry to a higher existence, to a life that is governed and "received" by קודש. Until now the פר was the vessel containing the blood; henceforth, קודש becomes for the blood its living organism, which gives

6 *The priest shall dip his finger into this blood and sprinkle some of this blood seven times before God toward the dividing curtain of the Sanctuary.*

ו וְטָבַ֧ל הַכֹּהֵ֛ן אֶת־אֶצְבָּע֖וֹ בַּדָּ֑ם
וְהִזָּ֨ה מִן־הַדָּ֜ם שֶׁ֤בַע פְּעָמִים֙ לִפְנֵ֣י
יְהוָ֔ה אֶת־פְּנֵ֖י פָּרֹ֥כֶת הַקֹּֽדֶשׁ׃

7 *Then the priest shall put some of the blood upon the horns of the spice incense altar before God, which is in the Tent of Appointed Meeting; but he shall pour all the [remaining] blood of the bull onto the base of the ascent offering altar, which is next to the entrance to the Tent of Appointed Meeting.*

ז וְנָתַן֩ הַכֹּהֵ֨ן מִן־הַדָּ֜ם עַל־קַ֠רְנוֹת
מִזְבַּ֨ח קְטֹ֤רֶת הַסַּמִּים֙ לִפְנֵ֣י יְהוָ֔ה
אֲשֶׁ֖ר בְּאֹ֣הֶל מוֹעֵ֑ד וְאֵ֣ת ׀ כָּל־דַּ֣ם
הַפָּ֗ר יִשְׁפֹּךְ֙ אֶל־יְסוֹד֙ מִזְבַּ֣ח
הָעֹלָ֔ה אֲשֶׁר־פֶּ֖תַח אֹ֥הֶל מוֹעֵֽד׃

it its direction and aim (cf. first explanation of the רשב״ם, *Bava Basra* 111b, ד״ה אלא אמר רבא וד״ה לשארו).

והביא אתו. See below.

6–7 **וטבל**. Only once in תנ״ך (*Melachim* II, 5:14) is this verb used in the sense of its common Rabbinic usage, bathing (טבילה). In all other instances, bathing is termed רחיצה, and the meaning of טבל is to dip an object into liquid in order that some of the liquid adhere to it. So ויטבלו את הכתנת בדם (*Bereshis* 37:31); וְטָבַלְתְּ פִּתֵּךְ בַּחֹמֶץ (*Ruth* 2:14). Moreover, below it is written: וטבל וגו׳ מן הדם (v. 17), and there the meaning of טבל is plainly to wet by dipping. Thus, we see the relationship between טבל and טפל, which means to join one thing to another so that they are loosely linked. So, too, the meaning of תפל is not far from this; cf. טוח תָפֵל, which appears repeatedly in *Yechezkel* 13. The term וַיִּטְבֹּל used in the account of Na'aman (*Melachim* II, 5:14) may also be explained in this light. Grudgingly and indignantly, Na'aman carried out the רחיצה prescribed to him by the prophet. In an incomplete performance, he went in and out of the water seven times (cf. ibid. 5:10, 13). The same applies to the term נִטְבְּלוּ in *Yehoshua* (3:15): the feet of the כהנים hardly got wet. Our translation of וטבל is therefore not "to immerse" but "to dip," which includes the notion of becoming moistened and colored by liquid.

וטבל והזה: על כל הזיה טבילה (*Toras Kohanim*) — the dipping must be repeated before each הזיה.

אצבעו: המיומנת שבימין (ibid.) — the strongest and most dexterous finger, or the first one to the right, on the right hand, i.e., the index finger of the right hand (קרבן אהרן).

והזה. נזה is an intransitive verb, meaning "to spray," always in the sense of "spraying upon." Small particles of some substance move toward an object and are sprayed upon it. Thus, נזה is related to נשה ["to lend"]. The נושה gives voluntarily (ש) something of his own to another, but without it ceasing to belong to him. הזה is a transitive verb, meaning "to sprinkle." הזיה, then, is a lesser form of זריקה.

וטבל וגו' בדם והזה מן הדם: וטבל – ולא מספיג; בדם – שיהא בדם שיעור טבילה מעיקרו; מן הדם – מן הדם שבענין (*Menachos* 7b). The כהן must wet his finger in the blood by dipping (טבילה), not by collecting blood from the sides of the vessel. At the first dipping, the whole prescribed quantity of blood must be already in the vessel (this quantity must be received all at once from the animal into the vessel — see משנה למלך הל' מעשה הקרבנות, 5:9). Finally, each הזיה must be performed with blood taken afresh from the vessel (דם שבענין means that which was mentioned in verse 5) and not with the blood remaining on the finger from the previous sprinkling (see *Menachos* 7b); i.e., על כל הזיה טבילה as stated above.

את פני פרכת הקדש — toward the place where the פרוכת isolates and shields the קדש, i.e., the ארון: מלמד שהוא מכוון כנגד [בין] הבדים (*Toras Kohanim*) — he sprinkles the blood toward the space between the two staves of the ארון. He has only to sprinkle the blood toward the פרוכת; there is no need for the blood to touch the פרוכת: כשהוא מזה לא היו נוגעין בפרוכת ואם נגעו נגעו (*Yoma* 57a).

ונתן הכהן מן הדם: מן הדם שבענין (*Toras Kohanim*) — i.e., for the מתנות on the קרנות מזבח הזהב as well he must dip afresh before each מתנה.

מזבח קטרת הסמים. The altar must first have been used at least once for offering up the daily קטורת — that is, all the incense indispensable to the validity of the קטורת offering (*Zevachim* 40b).

(*Yoma* 58b) מזבח לפני ה׳ ואין כהן לפני ה׳, הא כיצד עומד חוץ למזבח ומזה :**לפני ה׳** — i.e., even when executing the הזיות toward the פרוכת (v. 6), the כהן would be standing before the מזבח הקטורת, with the altar between him and the פרוכת. On יום הכיפורים, however, he would perform the הזיות toward the פרוכת when standing between the altar and the פרוכת, with the altar behind him. Hence, in describing עבודת יוה״כ Scripture says that when he had finished the הזיות toward the פרוכת then ויצא אל המזבח in order to perform the מתנות on the horns of the altar (below, 16:18).

אשר באהל מועד. The מתנות on the horns of the altar must be carried out in respect to its whole standing in the היכל — i.e., to all four of its horns (*Zevachim* 40a).

The עבודות הדם prescribed here differ from those of all the other offerings — not only in respect to their place of procedure but also in the actual עבודות themselves. They differ in respect to their place of procedure, for they are performed in the היכל, in the אוהל מועד, and for this reason these offerings are called חטאות פנימיות — as opposed to the other חטאות, which are performed only in the עזרה on the מזבח החיצון. But, more essentially, they differ in respect to the עבודות themselves. In all the other חטאות there is only נתינה: מתנות על קרנות המזבח; in the חטאות פנימיות there is both הזיה and נתינה. We pointed out above that הזיה is akin to a diminished זריקה.

צ״ע לרמב״ם מתנות דם על קרנות מזבח הקטרת היו ג״כ בהזיה – עי׳ הל׳ מעשה הקרבנות פ״ה הי״ב והל׳ יוה״כ פ״ג ה״ה. ולא ידעתי מקור לדבר זה, הלא הכתוב מחלק בפירוש וקרא לנתינות על בין הבדים ועל הפרוכת ועל טהרו של מזבח הזהב הזיה ולמתנה על קרנות מזבח הזהב קרא נתינה וצלע״ג. מרש״י יומא נח: נראה לענ״ד בבירור שס״ל ג״כ שמתנות על הקרן היו בנתינה ולא בהזיה ע״ש. וצ״ע במשנה פ׳ איזהו מקומן איתא ודמן טעון הזיה על בין הבדים ועל הפרכת ועל מזבח הזהב זה משמע לכאורה כרמב״ם ונראה שאין ראיה משם דהא לא באה המשנה רק להורות מקום השחיטה והמתנות לא איכות המתנות למחלקותם וכן המשנה ג׳ לא מחלקת בין מתנות חטאת שהם בנתינה באצבע ובין מתנות עולה שהם בהזיה בכלי וע״ש.

In הזיה, as in זריקה, the blood is set in motion in a certain direction, as opposed to נתינה באצבע, which signifies cleaving to a certain high point. We have already explained above (1:5, 17) that נתינה is the characteristic *avodah* of the חטאת, which atones for active deviation (sins of commission). נתינה reminds the sinner that he must cleave to the heights of moral duty. זריקה, on the other hand, is the characteristic *avodah* of the עולה, which atones for neglect of duty (sins of omission). זריקה challenges the sinner to take dynamic action and advance toward the prescribed goal. In the case of פר כהן המשיח — as well as in the case of פר העלם דבר של ציבור — both הזיה and נתינה are prescribed. It must be, then, that the sin for which these offerings atone consists of both of these elements (omission and commission): הזיה must atone for neglect of duty, and נתינה must atone for active transgression. And in fact, it is so. In both cases — פר כהן המשיח and פר העלם דבר של ציבור — the שגגה to be atoned for consists of two elements: שגגת הוראה (העלם דבר) and שגגת מעשה. שגגת הוראה, which is the error of faulty theory, is a sin of omission, a lack of devotion in the study of the Torah. שגגת מעשה, on the other hand — like the שגגה of every other חטאת — is a sin of commission, of actual transgression. שגגת הוראה is atoned for by הזיה את פני פרכת הקדש, whereas שגגת מעשה is atoned for by נתינת הדם על קרנות המזבח.

שבע פעמים הזיה את פני פרכת הקדש — and according to the halachah this הזיה was כנגד בין הבדים. The פרוכת, the cherubim-curtain, is positioned between the קודש הקדשים and the קודש — i.e., between the דביר, the place of the Word, and the היכל, the place of the Power and the Faculty (see *Shemos* 26:33). The function of the פרוכת is to separate and to shield. It *separates* and distinguishes between God's Torah, on the one hand, and the Table and the Menorah of national prosperity and spiritual development, on the other; for God's protection is extended to the Torah absolutely, whereas to the Table and the Menorah it is granted only conditionally. And the פרוכת *shields* the Torah itself from material and spiritual errors. Both functions — to separate and to shield — are subsumed in the concept of שמירה. Like the cherubim "east of the Garden of Eden," so do God's cherubim stand guard at the gates of the Torah לשמר את דרך עץ החיים (*Bereshis* 3:24; see Commentary, ad loc.).

The כהן המשיח (and similarly the בית דין הגדול in the case of פר העלם דבר) stands לפני ה׳ as a "פר" and sprinkles of "his" blood seven times את פני פרכת הקדש, toward the פרכת הקדש. He learns from this experience that it is his duty to become a "פר," a "worker in the service of Divine sowing." שמירת התורה is his foremost duty. Therefore, he must unceasingly direct toward this שמירת התורה the noblest powers of his נפש; he must do so "seven times" — i.e., to the utmost perfection — until he perceives the light of Divine truth, even while pursuing earthly endeavor. But the שמירת התורה that is incumbent upon man is realized primarily through לימוד התורה, through "learning." Indeed, we find that wherever

שמירה precedes עשייה — as in ושמרתם ועשיתם (see Commentary, below, 22:31; 26:3; *Devarim* 4:6) — שמירה is understood to mean תלמוד.

The כהן המשיח, because of insufficient knowledge of the law, erred in a ruling for himself (הורה לעצמו שוגג). As a result, he inadvertently violated (עשה שוגג) a prohibition of such importance that its willful violation carries with it the penalty of כרת. By sprinkling דם הפר toward the פרכת הקדש, he learns the following: בדי הארון, the staves of the ארון, stretching out toward the nation as a whole, expect him to be the leading bearer. He is bidden to study the Torah day and night — for only study leads to practice: שבע הזיות את פני הפרוכת כנגד הבדים. He should endeavor always to understand the true meaning of the Torah, even though only the very few achieve this goal to perfection. He should sprinkle the blood כנגד הפרוכת, not על הפרוכת — yet ואם נגעו נגעו. He has fulfilled his duty if he has done his utmost.

Yet even he has not fulfilled his duty unless he has met three requirements, upon which the attainment of the goal — true understanding of Torah — depends:

(a) וטבל ולא המספיג: The energy he devotes to Torah study should be drawn from the wellspring of his soul. It should not be energy that has already been depleted by use for some other purpose and is no longer of any value.

(b) על כל הזיה טבילה: Not only the first step, but each subsequent stride forward — even the final step toward the goal — must be taken with equally fresh force.

(c) ויהא בדם שיעור טבילה מעיקרו: A spiritual venture can reach its goal only by *gradual* progress — and this applies even to the gifted individual *brimming* with spiritual resources. Even if the whole quantity of blood is there at the beginning, nevertheless, the הזיה has to be performed in seven הזיות. Recognizing the truth is such a lofty goal that even the מופלא, the fully qualified — of whom Scripture here speaks — cannot attain it in a flash. He, too, must always go back and reexamine the first premises of his thought. Perhaps it was precisely as a מופלא that he erred — because he ascribed to himself הפלאה.

And further: עומד חוץ למזבח ומזה. At these הזיות — which symbolize energy devoted to Torah study — the מזבח should not be behind him but in front of him. For the מזבח represents practical fulfillment. Indeed, the purpose of Torah study is not theoretical knowledge alone. Rather, our goal must be the מעשה, the practical fulfillment; we should learn in order to observe and to do — to fulfill our mission in the realm of action. The מזבח קטרת הסמים לפני ה׳ stands in front of the כהן המשיח. The כהן must aspire to fulfill the Jewish mission לריח ניחוח לה׳. When he devotes his energy to the study of Torah, he should be ever mindful of this mission. Over the מזבח הקטורת must he sprinkle the הזיות את פני פרכת הקדש. And so it is said in regard to all of us: תלמוד גדול שהתלמוד מביא לידי מעשה (*Kiddushin* 40b); and it is written: שֵׂכֶל טוֹב לְכָל־עֹשֵׂיהֶם (*Tehillim* 111:10) — true understanding is granted only to those whose whole object is correct conduct.

But the error was not only theoretical in nature, a שגגת הוראה; rather, it led to a שגגת מעשה. Therefore, the finger of the Sanctuary directs the כהן המשיח to the "heights" of the incense altar. As we explained in *Shemos* (chap. 30), the incense altar represents the Jewish ideal in its purest fulfillment. For it symbolizes the Torah permeating the Table and Menorah — לריח ניחוח לה׳; it symbolizes the spirit of the Torah permeating the material and spiritual life of the individual and the community. Now, the imperfection of reality tends to obscure the purity of this ideal. Therefore, at least once a year, on יום הכיפורים, the nation must be reminded of the ideal in all its grandeur (*Shemos* 30:10). But there is nothing that mars the purity of this ideal more than the sin that is mentioned here: The כהן המשיח, who is also מופלא בתורה, errs in a ruling regarding an איסור כרת and as a result errs in his practice. There is nothing that mars it more than the sin mentioned in the next section: בית דין הגדול, which is entrusted with the authority to interpret the Torah, errs in a ruling regarding an איסור כרת and as a result causes the nation to sin. In both of these cases a serious offense is given legal sanction by the spiritual leaders of the nation! That is why the finger of the Sanctuary points to *all* the heights of this ideal (the horns on all four sides of the altar). *Together* they represent the highest goal: giving satisfaction, on earth, to God. We can realize this goal through all the blessings — spiritual and material — that we receive by virtue of the Torah and for the sake of the Torah. Only with the realization of this goal does the אהל become an אהל מועד. The כהן המשיח and the בית דין הגדול, who "serve God" as a "פר," should be ever mindful of this ideal. With complete and ever-fresh devotion they should learn God's Will from the Torah (הזיות כנגד פרכת הקדש, as mentioned above). The כהן המשיח should not cause himself to sin, and בית דין הגדול should not lead the nation to sin; they should not bring down the ideal from its lofty heights. Rather, they should uphold it in all its eminence, in every direction, by coming to know the true meaning of the Torah: ונתן הכהן מן הדם על קרנות מזבח קטרת הסמים לפני ה׳ אשר באהל מועד!

But first, the מזבח לפני ה׳ must be dedicated as מזבח קטרת הסמים. It must first be used at least once for offering up קטרת הסמים, to be invested with its meaning as מזבח קטרת; only then is it permissible to put the blood on its horns. For מתנות הדם are not the main purpose of this altar. The נפש — which, through שחיטה, nullified its egocentric being and took the first step toward closeness to God — finds on the מזבח החיצון the way to the highest ideal. The מזבח הפנימי, on the other hand, represents this ideal in its full realization, and that is what is expressed by קטרת הסמים. Here, in our verse, the נפש of the כהן המשיח is warned never again to obscure, through careless error, the purity of this ideal; that is the meaning of putting blood upon the horns of this altar. Hence, this altar must first be invested with its ideal meaning as מזבח קטרת הסמים, and only afterward is it permissible to put upon its horns the דם פר כהן המשיח.

ואת כל דם הפר ישפך אל יסוד מזבח העלה אשר פתח אהל מועד. The הזיות ומתנות הפנימיות are intended only to remind the כהן המשיח of the ideal spiritual and practical heights. As a spiritual leader of the nation he should be ever mindful of these heights, so that he not come to err — in a ruling or in practice. But his position in everyday life resembles that of the rest of his people. He, too, is in the Sanctuary courtyard — not in the אהל מועד but at the פתח אהל מועד — where the מזבח העולה merely shows the way that leads up to the heights of Torah fulfillment. כל דם הפר, too, is to be poured אל יסוד מזבח העלה. By completing the הזיות ומתנות הפנימיות, he merely ensures for himself his place in the national community of all נפשות בית ישראל. They constitute the base on which Jewish life is built, a life that ascends and draws closer to God, and it was from this base that he was in danger of being "uprooted" on account of his error (see Commentary above, 1:5). The only difference between the שפיכת שיריים of חטאות פנימיות and that of חטאות חיצוניות is this: The שיירי הדם of חטאות פנימיות are poured onto the יסוד מערבי, the western base, which is closest to the היכל; as it says in our verse: אשר פתח אהל מועד (*Zevachim* 51a). The שיירי הדם of חטאות חיצוניות, however, are poured onto the יסוד דרומי (see below, v. 25).

8 *He shall lift out from it all the fat of the bull, the offering that clears of sin: the fat that covers the intestines and all the fat that is attached to the intestines.*

ח וְאֶת־כָּל־חֵלֶב פַּר הַחַטָּאת יָרִים
מִמֶּנּוּ אֶת־הַחֵלֶב הַמְכַסֶּה עַל־
הַקֶּרֶב וְאֵת כָּל־הַחֵלֶב אֲשֶׁר עַל־
הַקֶּרֶב׃

9 *Also the two kidneys and the fat that rests upon them, which is along the flanks; also the diaphragm upon the liver; he must remove it together with the kidneys.*

ט וְאֵת שְׁתֵּי הַכְּלָיֹת וְאֶת־הַחֵלֶב
אֲשֶׁר עֲלֵיהֶן אֲשֶׁר עַל־הַכְּסָלִים
וְאֶת־הַיֹּתֶרֶת עַל־הַכָּבֵד עַל־
הַכְּלָיוֹת יְסִירֶנָּה׃

10 *Just as it was lifted off the bull of the meal of peace; and the priest shall turn them into smoke upon the altar of ascent offering.*

י כַּאֲשֶׁר יוּרַם מִשּׁוֹר זֶבַח הַשְּׁלָמִים
וְהִקְטִירָם הַכֹּהֵן עַל מִזְבַּח הָעֹלָה׃

11 *But the skin of the bull, and all its*

יא וְאֶת־עוֹר הַפָּר וְאֶת־כָּל־בְּשָׂרוֹ

8–10 ואת כל חלב פר החטאת וגו׳. With the conclusion of the עבודות הדם (vv. 5–7), the כפרה is completed; the נפש of the one seeking atonement is reestablished on the basis of Judaism in the Sanctuary. Then, through הקטרת אימורים, the נפש learns the consequence of this reinstatement: Henceforth, even חלב and כליות and יותרת הכבד — i.e., even material aims and aspirations — can be raised out of the realm of abject bodily desire; even they can, and should, fuel the fire of the Torah. Past error will not stand in the way of a pure and joyous future. Rather, אימורי חטאת, like אימורי שלמים, are to be surrendered joyfully and happily to the power of God's guidance (cf. Commentary above, 3:3–5). We have explained previously, based on the phonetic relation of חטא to חתה, that subjecting the חלב and כליות to the ruling power of God's fire is the essence of rectification of חטא, which disturbs one's relationship to God's Torah (see Commentary to *Bereshis* 39:9).

11–12 ואת עור הפר וגו׳. One would expect that, as a further consequence of this reinstatement, the flesh of the bull would now be given to the כהנים

עַל־רֹאשׁ֖וֹ וְעַל־כְּרָעָ֑יו וְקִרְבּ֖וֹ
וּפִרְשֽׁוֹ׃

flesh, along with its head and its feet, along with its intestines and its dung.

יב וְהוֹצִ֣יא אֶת־כָּל־הַ֠פָּר אֶל־מִח֨וּץ
לַֽמַּחֲנֶ֜ה אֶל־מָק֤וֹם טָהוֹר֙ אֶל־
שֶׁ֣פֶךְ הַדֶּ֔שֶׁן וְשָׂרַ֥ף אֹת֛וֹ עַל־
עֵצִ֖ים בָּאֵ֑שׁ עַל־שֶׁ֥פֶךְ הַדֶּ֖שֶׁן
יִשָּׂרֵֽף׃ פ

12 *He shall take [this], the whole bull, out to a pure place outside the camp, where the ashes are poured out, and burn it on [logs of] wood with fire; where the ashes are poured out shall it be burned.*

to eat in a holy place — as we find in the case of all the other חטאות (below, 6:19). In such cases, this eating of the flesh teaches us the following. First, the דם and the אימורים — i.e., the spiritual nature and the inner desires — find their place before God. They have but one aim: to sustain the holy on earth. Then, the whole human being is to be hallowed with priestlike sanctity. All of his personal desires are to be impressed with the seal of priestlike sanctity. All of his actions are to be holy, and in all of them he should seek to ascend toward God. All this is represented by the כהן, clothed in the priestly garments, in the Sanctuary courtyard.

חטאות הפנימיות, however, differ. Their blood applications do not remind the נפש of the ascent to the ideal, for this ascent is represented by the Sanctuary courtyard. Rather, they remind the נפש of the ideal that has already been realized, which is represented by the Sanctuary. Now, there is not a כהן in the world who is worthy of even symbolically representing, through his eating, such a level of perfection; certainly not after the leaders of the nation have sinned, as חטאות הפנימיות are brought solely in order to atone for the error of the כהן המשיח or בית דין הגדול. Therefore, while the flesh of חטאות חיצוניות is eaten by the כהנים, that of חטאות פנימיות is taken out of the camp, חוץ לשלש מחנות (*Toras Kohanim*); there, outside the national area around the Sanctuary, it is burned in a ritually pure place.

ואת עור הפר ואת כל בשרו וגו׳. After the אימורים have been removed, the whole animal — without being flayed or cut into parts — is taken out, חוץ לשלש מחנות (see *Zevachim* 105b). The עזרה is one מחנה: מחנה שכינה; the הר הבית is the second מחנה: מחנה לויה; the whole city up to the walls is the third מחנה: מחנה ישראל. That is to say, the פר is taken outside of Yerushalayim אל שפך הדשן, to the בית הדשן, the place where the ashes of the altar are poured out (below, 6:4); and it is necessary that ashes from the altar already be there — שיהא לשם דשן (*Yoma* 68b). The place must be טהור; ואם טמא יטהרנו (*Toras Kohanim*). Before the פר is burned it should be sectioned into its parts, in the same way that the עולה is sectioned. This is alluded to by the words על ראשו ועל כרעיו וגו׳. Nevertheless, the animal is not flayed (*Yoma* 68a).

Scripture says further **על עצים באש** — and not על העצים אשר על האש as in the case of עולה (above 1:8). The inference is that it is not necessary to use עצים כשרים למערכה, wood that was selected for use on the altar fire; rather, any wood is suitable for this burning, even straw — אפילו בקש אפילו בתבן. Burning by means other than fire is excluded — e.g., בסיד רותח (quicklime) or בגיפסיס רותח (other chemical means) — but burning by fire is valid in any form (*Pesachim* 75a; *Toras Kohanim*; קרבן אהרן, our verse).

It is expounded further: ושרף אותו - כשר ולא הפסול. Only if the פר is כשר is it burned בבית הדשן outside of Yerushalayim; if it becomes פסול it is burned within the confines of the Sanctuary, like the other פסולי המוקדשין. Hence the halachah: פרים הנשרפים ושעירים הנשרפים בזמן שהן נשרפין כמצותן נשרפין בבית הדשן ומטמאין בגדים; ואם אינן נשרפין כמצותן נשרפין בבית הבירה ואינן מטמאין בגדים. In the latter case (אינן נשרפין כמצותן), the halachah is as follows: If the פסול occurred before the זריקה (or, according to לוי, before the יציאה), they are burned in the עזרה, like other פסולי קדשי קדשים ואימורי קדשים קלים. If the פסול occurred after the זריקה (or, according to לוי, after the יציאה), they are burned בהר הבית (*Zevachim* 104a–b).

A further halachah that is applicable here is spelled out below (16:27–28) in the case of פר ושעיר של יום הכיפורים. (These קרבנות — like the פר כהן המשיח and the פר העלם דבר של צבור — are חטאות פנימיות. They, too, are burned — except for their אימורים — outside the שלש מחנות.) Scripture says there: והשרף אתם יכבס בגדיו ורחץ את בשרו במים וגו׳. In other words, all those who engage in bringing out and burning the פרים הנשרפים ושעירים הנשרפים (the שעירים are the שעיר של יום הכיפורים and the שעירי עבודה זרה — see *Bemidbar* 15:22, et seq.) become טמא לטמא בגדים וכלים במגע; i.e., their טומאה is conveyed also to the clothes and כלים that they touch while engaged with the פרים ושעירים הנשרפין. This טומאה, then, is similar to טומאת משא נבילה. They become טמא as soon as they exit the first מחנה, viz., the עזרה. This טומאה, too, applies only to פרים ושעירים הנשרפין כמצותן. פסולים are not מטמא.

All these laws are connected with the reason for burning the חטאות פנימיות. They clarify the reason behind the mitzvah and at the same time serve as an antidote against mistaken notions that might come to mind. Let us now elaborate.

One would expect that חטאות פנימיות, like חטאות חיצוניות, would be given to the כהנים and that אכילת כהנים — which symbolizes אכילת הבעלים — would complete אכילת המזבח. Yet there is no man worthy of representing — even if only symbolically — the lofty ideal of חטאות פנימיות, and certainly not after the spiritual leaders of the nation have sinned. For it is the imperfection of these leaders — as opposed to the perfection of the Torah ideal — which has made them liable to this חטאת. The same applies to פר ושעיר של יום הכיפורים, as we shall later make clear. There is no one in the whole national area around the Sanctuary — neither in מחנה שכינה, in מחנה לויה, nor in מחנה ישראל — who is on a level commensurate with this high ideal. The removal and burning of these offerings חוץ לשלש מחנות reflects the inadequacy of the entire national community. In the actual life of the nation, no one is found to be worthy of eating this offering; no personality is found to be on a level commensurate with the high ideal represented by these חטאות.

Now it is clear why these halachos apply only when נשרפין כמצותן. Should פרים ושעירים הנשרפין become פסול — e.g., on account of טומאה — they would be unfit to be eaten even if there *were* to be a כהן worthy of eating them. (The Gemara's question לינה מהו שתועיל בפרים הנשרפין [*Zevachim* 104b] is left unresolved, despite the fact that in such a case פרים הנשרפין would be unfit to be eaten even if there *were* to be a כהן worthy of eating them. The assumption that לינה פוסלת would strengthen our view considerably.) Thus, in the case of נשרפין שלא כמצותן the whole reason for burning חטאות פנימיות is obscured and neutralized; hence, their שריפה is like that of all other פסולי המוקדשין.

הנשרפין כמצותן בבית הדשן are to be taken out אל שפך הדשן and burned על שפך הדשן, where ashes that can be burned no further by the altar fire are deposited. These offerings (חטאות פנימיות), also, are regarded as "דשן" — but for an entirely different reason: they have no אוכלים. They are sectioned, just as the עולה is sectioned; thus, even while they are burned, their character as an offering is maintained, and man's imperfection is pronounced, as it were, upon each of the parts: Man must come to know his inadequacy in the tasks represented by the various parts. However, the sectioning is to be done without flaying the body and without cleansing the קרב וכרעיים, and even the laws regarding the עצים — which apply to the עולה — are inapplicable here, lest one think that this is an ideal burning in accordance with the ideal purpose of the offering. On the contrary, these are parts of an offering that are burned because there are no אוכלים.

Finally, we come to the halachah: פרים הנשרפין ושעירים הנשרפים בזמן שהן נשרפין כמצותן ... מטמאין בגדים (*Zevachim* 104a); or, as רבי puts it in *Toras Kohanim* (אחרי מות, 16:28): כל שדמו נכנס לפנים השורפו מטמא בגדים. As we shall explain later in great detail (פרשת הטומאה in שמיני), טומאה is an expression of the lack of moral freedom, and the laws of טומאה are intended to refute the notion that we lack such freedom; for these laws apply wherever external circumstances are liable to give rise to such a notion.

For example, let us say that one comes into contact with a human corpse, or with the carcass of one of the mammals, which physically resemble man. That corpse or that carcass exposes man — or that which physically resembles man — as having succumbed, powerless, to the external, compelling forces of nature. This leads to the thought that man *generally* has no freedom. The condition of death carries over, as it were, into the realm of life, and man is perceived as a mere puppet in the hands of the physical forces that rule him. For is he not lying dead before us, now, in utter helplessness? One gets the impression that life and death, both, are merely different effects of the one force of nature.

Such a notion undermines the foundations of the entire Torah, for it denies man's moral freedom. The laws of טומאה are intended to counter this notion. Toward this end, especially, we have been charged with טבילה במקוה, which separates the spheres of life and death: One must immerse and purify himself of his impurity before re-entering the sphere of the Sanctuary. For the foundation of the Sanctuary is man's moral freedom, which rises above all physical compulsion.

13 *And if the entire council of Israel* יג וְאִם כָּל־עֲדַת יִשְׂרָאֵל יִשְׁגּוּ

But such a notion — that man lacks moral freedom — can easily be fostered by פרים ושעירים הנשרפין כמצותן. For the very basis of the שריפה, the mitzvah to burn them, is that in the whole nation there is not a single person who is on a level commensurate with the perfection of the Torah ideal. The *truth* about man's nature is that godliness prevails over sensuousness only through a struggle — an inevitable step in the attainment of any and all moral freedom (see Commentary, *Bereshis* 2:7,9; 4:7). But, oh, how close to this truth is the *false* notion of man's innate lack of freedom! For so goes the argument, based on the fact that אָדָם אֵין צַדִּיק בָּאָרֶץ אֲשֶׁר יַעֲשֶׂה־טּוֹב וְלֹא יֶחֱטָא (*Koheles* 7:20): Sin is innate in man; by his very nature he is incapable of doing what is good! This is the delusion lurking in שריפת חטאות פנימיות, a delusion that imperils the whole moral mission of the Sanctuary. In response, the Torah has ordained that one may not enter the מחנה שכינה under such a demoralizing influence. Rather, השרף אתם יכבס בגדיו ורחץ את בשרו במים ואחרי כן יבוא אל המחנה (below, 16:28). Only the מתעסקין ביציאתן ובשריפתן are טמאים. The פרים ושעירים הנשרפין themselves, however, are not מטמא; hence, even the place where they are burned must be טהור. Indeed, the ultimate goal of man's whole development is that he is destined to attain a lofty level, higher than the present stage which is characterized by struggle with sensuality. At that time the human ideal will be fully realized: not only will death disappear from the world, בִּלַּע הַמָּוֶת לָנֶצַח (*Yeshayahu* 25:8), but the holiness emanating from God's Sanctuary will penetrate all areas of life. At that time the separation between קודש and חול will fall away, and the מחנה שכינה will extend to every place in which people live. בַּיּוֹם הַהוּא יִהְיֶה עַל־מְצִלּוֹת הַסּוּס קֹדֶשׁ לַה׳ וְהָיָה הַסִּירוֹת בְּבֵית ה׳ כַּמִּזְרָקִים לִפְנֵי הַמִּזְבֵּחַ: וְהָיָה כָּל־סִיר בִּירוּשָׁלַםִ וּבִיהוּדָה קֹדֶשׁ לַה׳ צְבָאוֹת וּבָאוּ כָּל־הַזֹּבְחִים וְלָקְחוּ מֵהֶם וּבִשְּׁלוּ בָהֶם. "On that day קדש לה׳ will shine upon the bells of the horses (as upon the forehead of the כהן גדול), and the pots of the Sanctuary will be like the basins of the altar. All the cooking vessels in Yerushalayim and Yehudah will be so holy unto God that all who come to bring an offering will be able to use them for their offerings" (*Zecharyah* 14:20–21).

13 **כל עדת ישראל**. As a rule, the community of Israel is called עדת בני ישראל — the community that comprises all the children of Israel. In *Shemos*

וְנֶעְלַם דָּבָר מֵעֵינֵי הַקָּהָל וְעָשׂוּ אַחַת מִכָּל־מִצְוֹת יְהוָה אֲשֶׁר לֹא־תֵעָשֶׂינָה וְאָשֵׁמוּ׃

errs, and something is hidden from the community, and they commit one of all the things concerning which God has commanded that they shall not be done, and they have thus incurred guilt.

12, however, at the nation's founding, the community is repeatedly called עדת ישראל — i.e., a multitude united by a common destiny inherent in the name ישראל. On two other occasions, also, the whole nation is called עדת ישראל: (a) When Korach seeks a higher rank for himself, Moshe reminds him of the privilege already granted to the *Levi'im*: they were awarded with a higher station despite the common destiny of the entire people, which should dictate equal rights for all: המעט כי הבדיל אלקי ישראל אתכם מעדת ישראל וגו׳ (*Bemidbar* 16:9). (b) Before the tribes of Reuven and Gad request for themselves special rights, they recognize that the whole nation has equal rights to the conquered territory: הארץ אשר הכה ה׳ לפני עדת ישראל וגו׳ (ibid. 32:4).

Elsewhere in Scripture the whole nation is always referred to as עדת בני ישראל. Here, in our verse, the term עדת ישראל, therefore, refers not to the whole nation but to the "community" that has been charged with the guardianship of Israel's mission, namely, בית דין הגדול, the סנהדרין. In *Bemidbar* (35:24–25), the court that is empowered to try capital cases (i.e., a בית דין of 23 members) is called simply העדה. But the term that is employed in our verse is not עדה but עדת ישראל. From this we learn that our verse speaks of the court of all Israel, namely, the 71-member Sanhedrin. Similarly, *Toras Kohanim* (to our verse) states: יכול בכל העדה הכתוב מדבר ת״ל כאן עדה ולהלן נאמר עדה, מה עדה אמורה להלן בית דין אף כאן בית דין, או מה עדה אמורה להלן בעשרים ושלשה אף כאן בעשרים ושלשה ת״ל עדת ישראל העדה המיוחדת שבישראל; ואיזו זו סנהדרי גדולה היושבת בלשכת הגזית.

From the words כל עדת וגו׳ we learn an additional halachah, which in any case is implied by the very concept עדת ישראל: The full plenum — quantitative as well as qualitative — of בית דין הגדול must commit this error. But if one of the members of the court was legally unfit to judge, or if the מופלא של בית דין was not present (and someone else substituted for him), or if one of the members had said "איני יודע" or had declared the others to be in error, then it is not the type of error that is atoned for as an "error of the Sanhedrin" (ibid.; *Horayos* 4b). The case of "איני יודע" is not cited in *Horayos* (ibid.). אך האי דקאמר איני יודע כמאן דליתיה דמי ולא היה צריך להזכירו במתניתין, עי׳ סנהדרין יז. ורמב״ם הל׳ סנהדרין פ״ח ה״ב כ״מ שם. והגאון באר שבע ס״ל דלא איתותב ר׳ יונתן אלא בהא דקאמר מאה שישבו להורות אבל ע״א שהוא מנין המיוחד לסנהדרין גדולה בעינן לכ״ע שיהו כולם בהוראה, שאף המיעוט שידעו שטעו הסכימו לפחות בהרכנת ראש בהוראה, ולא כדמשמע מכל הפוסקים דסגי שישתקו ע״ש בפירושו להוריות ג: וד: במתניתין הורו ב״ד וידע אחד מהן שטעו ע״ש מילתא בטוב טעם ודעת ע״ש.

ישגו ונעלם וגו׳. We have already remarked on the difference between שגג and שגה (Commentary to *Bereshis* 8:1). שגה denotes an error of faulty theory. The mind is caught up with some idea and thus is distracted from all other matters. Hence, the stronger form, שגע — a wrong idea, fixed in the mind. This error of faulty theory is explained further by the words ונעלם דבר מעיני הקהל וגו׳. The בית דין הגדול functions as עיני הקהל, the eyes of the nation. The wisdom of the nation resides with them. They draw knowledge from the Torah, and from this knowledge they draw conclusions as to how the people should act. In the case of our verse, "something" (דבר) escapes the knowledge of the nation's greatest sages. They are caught in a misconception of the law (ישגו) and as a result overlook some aspect of it (ונעלם מהם דבר).

The Gemara in *Horayos* 7b, however, seems to take the word ישגו to imply a שגגת מעשה, an error in practice. But since ישגו undoubtedly refers here to עדת ישראל, the Sanhedrin, and since it is immaterial in this case whether the members of the Sanhedrin commit the מעשה or not, it would appear that the Gemara's intention is this: If Scripture had said just ישגו ועשו, we would have concluded that it was referring to an error in practice committed by the Sanhedrin. Scripture, however, says ישגו ונעלם; from this we infer that there was a שגגת הוראה on the part of the Sanhedrin, a העלם דבר, which led to a שגגת מעשה on the part of the קהל (see below).

The nature of this שגגת הוראה is explained more fully in *Horayos* 3b–4a: הורו בית דין לעקור את כל הגוף, אמרו אין נדה בתורה אין שבת בתורה אין עבודה זרה בתורה, הרי אלו פטורין; הורו לבטל מקצת ולקיים מקצת הרי אלו חייבין. If their error negates the entire "body" of a law and would nullify that whole law, then the atonement described here does not apply. It applies only if their error pertains to a part of a law — e.g., if they said that carrying out מרשות לרשות is forbidden on Shabbos, but throwing מרשות לרשות is permitted. For Scripture says ונעלם דבר ולא שתתעלם מצוה כולה (ibid.). The Gemara adds: אין בית דין חייבין עד שיורו בדבר שאין הצדוקין מודין בו (ibid.). An erroneous ruling of the Sanhedrin must be atoned for as prescribed here only if it pertains to something that the Sadducees would not acknowledge. But something that the Sadducees would acknowledge — since it is explicitly stated in the Torah — זיל קרי בי רב הוא, every schoolchild should know it, and every Jewish child would know it; it is not a matter for the הוראה of the Sanhedrin.

ונעלם דבר מעיני הקהל ועשו וגו׳. The erroneous ruling of the בית דין הגדול need only be atoned for if such a ruling results in an error in practice on the part of the קהל: מעשה תלוי בקהל והוראה תלויה בבית דין (ibid. 3a). It makes no difference whether the members of the בית דין themselves act in accordance with their הוראה or not. But the בית דין is held responsible for the sin of the community only if בית דין issues its ruling in order that it be put into practice: It is not enough that they say מותרים אתם; rather, they must say מותרים אתם לעשות (ibid. 2a). If they did not say this; or if someone knew that בית דין had erred (ידע שטעו) but nevertheless acted in accordance with its erroneous ruling, because he thought that מצוה לשמוע דברי חכמים, or because he generally was מבעט בהוראה and would defy the authority of בית דין (ibid. 2b; רש״י, ad loc.) — in all these cases the individual who sinned is held responsible and not the בית דין.

According to ר׳ שמעון בן אלעזר (ibid. 3a; 5a), קהל means the majority of the nation — either the majority of the Jews in the Land of Israel, even if this consists of a minority of the tribes, or the majority of the tribes, even if this consists of a minority of the Jews in the Land of Israel. His opinion is accepted by the רמב״ם as the halachah (הל׳ שגגות, 12:1).

ואשמו: the nation's sin, caused by the error of the nation's sages, places guilt upon the whole nation. This חטאת הקהל, like all other חטאות, is brought only על דבר שחייבין על זדונו כרת.

14 *And the sin that they have committed has become known, then the community shall bring near a young bull as an offering for the sin, and they shall bring it before the Tent of Appointed Meeting.*

יד וְנֽוֹדְעָה֙ הַֽחַטָּ֔את אֲשֶׁ֥ר חָֽטְא֖וּ
עָלֶ֑יהָ וְהִקְרִ֨יבוּ הַקָּהָ֜ל פַּ֤ר בֶּן־
בָּקָר֙ לְחַטָּ֔את וְהֵבִ֣יאוּ אֹת֔וֹ לִפְנֵ֖י
אֹ֥הֶל מוֹעֵֽד׃

15 *The elders of the council shall lean their hands upon the head of the*

טו וְסָמְכ֞וּ זִקְנֵ֧י הָעֵדָ֛ה אֶת־יְדֵיהֶ֖ם

---

14 **והקריבו הקהל פר וגו׳**. According to ר׳ יהודה (*Horayos* 4b), whose view is accepted as the halachah, the national community — not the בית דין הגדול — is to bring the offering that atones for the error of בית דין. The nation acts here as a unified, organic whole. The בית דין הגדול is the rational soul of the national body (עיני הקהל). Hence, the nation provides the פר for the use of the בית דין and exhorts itself — and the בית דין — to serve God as a "פר."

Significantly, the nation appears here as one unit of twelve tribes: The nation brings not one פר but twelve פרים (ibid.). We have already pointed out on several occasions that Israel, in realizing its ideal national life, is not considered merely one unit but a קהל עמים, a קהל גוים (see Commentary, *Bereshis* 28:3, 35:11–12, 48:3–6). The same is true here, in the case of atoning for the sin caused by the error of the nation's greatest sages. Each tribe — even the minority which did not sin — provides one פר for the use of בית דין הגדול. Efrayim and Menashe are considered one tribe — viz., שבט יוסף — as they are in Ya'akov's blessing and on the אפוד and חושן of the כהן גדול (*Horayos* 6b). Each tribe, in accordance with its own unique mission, calls upon the בית דין הגדול to fulfill itself as a פר. The funds for these פרים are not taken from the תרומת הלשכה, as in the case of the other קרבנות ציבור, but are collected from every individual (ibid. 3b). In this way the error of בית דין הגדול is brought to the awareness of each individual in Israel.

15 **זקני העדה**. The סמיכה is not performed by all the members of the Sanhedrin. Rather, three (according to ר׳ יהודה, five; see לחם משנה הל׳ מעשה

עַל־רֹאשׁ הַפָּר לִפְנֵי יְהֹוָה וְשָׁחַט אֶת־הַפָּר לִפְנֵי יְהֹוָה׃

bull before God, *and the bull shall be slaughtered before* God.

טז וְהֵבִיא הַכֹּהֵן הַמָּשִׁיחַ מִדַּם הַפָּר אֶל־אֹהֶל מוֹעֵד׃

16 *The anointed priest shall bring some of the blood of the bull into the Tent of Appointed Meeting.*

יז וְטָבַל הַכֹּהֵן אֶצְבָּעוֹ מִן־הַדָּם וְהִזָּה שֶׁבַע פְּעָמִים לִפְנֵי יְהֹוָה אֵת פְּנֵי הַפָּרֹכֶת׃

17 *And the priest shall dip his finger in some of the blood and sprinkle [it] seven times before* God *toward the dividing curtain.*

יח וּמִן־הַדָּם יִתֵּן | עַל־קַרְנֹת הַמִּזְבֵּחַ אֲשֶׁר לִפְנֵי יְהֹוָה אֲשֶׁר בְּאֹהֶל מוֹעֵד וְאֵת כָּל־הַדָּם יִשְׁפֹּךְ אֶל־יְסוֹד מִזְבַּח הָעֹלָה אֲשֶׁר־פֶּתַח אֹהֶל מוֹעֵד׃

18 *He shall put some of the blood upon the horns of the altar which stands before* God, *in the Tent of Appointed Meeting; but he shall pour all the [remaining] blood onto the base of the altar of ascent offering, which is next to the entrance to the Tent of Appointed Meeting.*

הקרבנות, 3:10) of its most prominent members represent the whole בית דין. We noted above (1:4) that the פר העלם דבר של צבור is one of the two exceptions in which סמיכה is observed at a קרבן ציבור. סמיכה is very significant in this offering: סמיכה indicates that the בית דין is the בעלים seeking atonement, even though the funds for the פרים are collected from the tribes, who are party to the sin. Still, the סמיכה is performed by representatives of the בית דין and not by all seventy-one of its members (whereas in other קרבנות שותפין, all must perform סמיכה), in order to teach us that this is not an offering for seventy-one individuals but an offering of the בית דין as a whole.

16–21 The offering procedures stated here resemble in every respect those of the פר כהן המשיח, and in our discussion of the פר כהן המשיח we explained the relation of these procedures to the פר העלם דבר של צבור. The כהן המשיח

19 *He shall lift out all its fat from it and turn it into smoke upon the altar.*	יט וְאֵת כָּל־חֶלְבּוֹ יָרִים מִמֶּנּוּ וְהִקְטִיר הַמִּזְבֵּחָה׃
20 *And he shall do with this bull as he did with the bull of the offering that clears of sin, exactly so shall he do with it. The priest will effect atonement for them, and they will be forgiven.*	כ וְעָשָׂה לַפָּר כַּאֲשֶׁר עָשָׂה לְפַר הַחַטָּאת כֵּן יַעֲשֶׂה־לּוֹ וְכִפֶּר עֲלֵהֶם הַכֹּהֵן וְנִסְלַח לָהֶם׃
21 *One shall take out the bull [to a place] outside the camp and burn it, even as one burned the first bull; it is an offering that clears the community of sin.*	כא וְהוֹצִיא אֶת־הַפָּר אֶל־מִחוּץ לַמַּחֲנֶה וְשָׂרַף אֹתוֹ כַּאֲשֶׁר שָׂרַף אֵת הַפָּר הָרִאשׁוֹן חַטַּאת הַקָּהָל הוּא׃ פ

and the בית דין הגדול are the foremost spiritual leaders of the nation. The כהן המשיח is the symbolic embodiment of the national ideal. He must be a model for his people — in knowledge of the Torah and observance of the *mitzvos*. The members of בית דין הגדול are the nation's greatest sages, who are entrusted with teaching Torah to Israel. What the כהן המשיח was told regarding his own life, the בית דין הגדול should be told regarding the life of the nation: They should be ever mindful of the ideal of the Torah, which rests beneath the wings of the cherubim. They should be ever mindful of guarding the Torah (פרוכת); of life's ideal material and spiritual perfection (מזבח הזהב); and of the moral endeavor to ascend to this ideal (מזבח העולה). And akin to what was said in the case of פר כהן המשיח is said also in the case of פר העלם דבר: There exists no one who is on a level commensurate with the national ideal represented by this offering, no one who is worthy of the symbolic act of eating this offering. פר העלם דבר, like פר כהן המשיח, is one of the פרים הנשרפין חוץ לשלש מחנות. The reason for and purpose of this שריפה are stressed by the concluding words חטאת הקהל הוא: בנין אב לכל חטאות הקהל שישרפו (*Toras Kohanim*). That is to say, all חטאות פנימיות (including שעירי עבודה זרה — *Bemidbar* 15:24) call to mind the imperfection of the na-

22 *But if a prince commits a sin and inadvertently does one of the things concerning which* God, *his* God, *has commanded that they shall not be done, then he has incurred guilt.*

כב אֲשֶׁר נָשִׂיא יֶחֱטָא וְעָשָׂה אַחַת מִכָּל־מִצְוֺת יְהוָה אֱלֹהָיו אֲשֶׁר לֹא־תֵעָשֶׂינָה בִּשְׁגָגָה וְאָשֵׁם׃

tional reality as opposed to the national ideal. Therefore, they are to be burned outside the national area around the Sanctuary.

What remains to be explained is the fact that "קרנת" is written חסר in verse 18; for in the other חטאות פנימיות, "קרנות" is written מלא. We have remarked on this previously in our Commentary to *Bereshis* 1:14. On the כתיב חסר of "קרנת" in חטאות חיצוניות (below, vv. 25, 30, and 34) see also חידושי הר"ן to *Sanhedrin* 4a.

22 The two preceding offerings, פר כהן המשיח and פר העלם דבר של ציבור, are brought to atone for the sin of the community; the חטא כהן המשיח is also לאשמת העם (v. 3). Both cases are marked not only by errors in practice, but also by acts committed as the result of erroneous rulings by the highest authorities confirmed as experts in the law: כהן משיח מופלא and בית דין הגדול.

Two other cases now follow: חטאת נשיא and חטאת יחיד. In both cases there is שגגת מעשה, error in practice, without שגגת הוראה. Both are brought to atone for the sin of the individual. And in contrast to the preceding offerings, which are חטאות פנימיות, these are categorized as חטאות חיצוניות.

The נשיא of whom Scripture here speaks is the one "who has no one above him but God," שאין על גביו אלא ה׳ אלקיו. That is to say, he is not the prince of a tribe, but the ruler who stands at the head of the entire nation, namely, the king. Our Sages (*Horayos* 11a–b) derive this from the seemingly superfluous wording in the expression מצות ה׳ אלקיו, which is the same expression applied to the king in *Devarim* 17:19: למען ילמד ליראה את ה׳ אלקיו. Even when the nation was divided, both the King of Yehudah and the King of Yisrael were considered נשיאים vis-à-vis this mitzvah (*Horayos* 11b).

The expression ה׳ אלקיו links God's Name to a particular individual, thus indicating a special relationship that exists between God and that individual — in that he is His messenger, does His bidding, or calls out with His Name. We find this expression applied to the כהן גדול (below,

23 *Or if his sin which he has* כג אוֹ־הוֹדַע אֵלָיו חַטָּאתוֹ אֲשֶׁר

21:12), to כהנים in general (ibid. 21:17 and 22; *Devarim* 18:7), to the king (ibid. 17:19; *Shemuel* I, 30:6; *Melachim* I, 5:17; et al.), and to the prophet (ibid. II, 5:11, et al.). Here, too, in our verse, this expression identifies the נשיא as one who does God's bidding and who is a special officer in His service. It points to the king, who is at the head of the nation, holds all its powers, and — with none above him but Hashem his God — directs his people in the way of God's service: שום תשים עליך מלך–שתהא אימתו עליך (*Sanhedrin* 20b; see Commentary to *Devarim* 17:14). We find in other places as well that the king is called נשיא: *Melachim* I, 11:34; *Yechezkel* 34:24, 37:25, and chapters 45 and 46.

From the order of the פרשיות החטאות one learns about the role of the king: he is first in the fulfillment of the Torah. Just as the כהן המשיח is first in knowledge of the Law, so the first one to obey the Law is to be the king. However, since his חטאת is not connected with a שגגת הוראה, it follows that his position as king does not grant him authority to interpret the Torah. When he wishes to know what is permissible according to the Law, then, like any other יחיד, he must turn to the בית דין. He is the first יחיד among all the יחידים. Of the כהן המשיח's sin and of the community's sin caused by בית דין הגדול, Scripture says: לאשמת העם (v. 3), ואשמו (v. 13), and חטאת הקהל (v. 21); but of the king's sin Scripture says: אשר נשיא יחטא וגו׳ ואשם. For the king's sin jeopardizes only his own future. No matter how high he has been raised above the nation by virtue of the powers invested in him, he must stand alone before God to answer for his sins, just as the humblest citizen. Thus ר׳ יוחנן בן זכאי's comment on the words אשר נשיא יחטא: אשרי הדור שהנשיא שלו מביא קרבן על שגגתו. אם נשיא שלו מביא קרבן, צריך אתה לומר מהו הדיוט; ואם על שגגתו מביא קרבן, צריך אתה לומר מהו זדונו. "Fortunate the generation whose ruler seeks atonement by making an offering for the wrong he has committed in error! How must the conscience of the ordinary citizen be stirred by the conscientious conduct of the king; and if he is so deeply affected by a transgression he has committed in error, how much more deeply will he be affected if he has been guilty of an intentional sin!" (*Horayos* 10b).

23 **או הודע אליו וגו׳**. או is in contrast with ואשם of the preceding verse. Read the two verses together as follows: "... he remains guilty without

committed was made known to him, he shall bring as his offering a whole, male goat.	חָטָ֖א בָּ֑הּ וְהֵבִ֤יא אֶת־קָרְבָּנוֹ֙ שְׂעִ֥יר עִזִּ֖ים זָכָ֥ר תָּמִֽים׃

atonement; or, if he becomes aware of his sin, he can atone for it by bringing a חטאת." הודע אליו — the sin comes or is brought to his knowledge, or at least he does not disclaim the sin when others testify that he has committed it. But if even two witnesses testify that he had eaten חלב, and he denies it and asserts לא אכלתי, he is not חייב קרבן. Witnesses cannot obligate a person to bring a חטאת; for a מזיד has no atonement through an offering, and only in one's own heart is it known whether he acted inadvertently or deliberately. Two can testify אכלת חלב, but they cannot claim חייב אתה קרבן. Hence, he is believed even when he contradicts two witnesses, so long as the issue is strictly the obligation to bring an offering: מה אם ירצה לומר מזיד הייתי (*Kerisos* 11b; *Yevamos* 87b).

The Torah equates here the law of the king with that of the הדיוט (below, v. 28) and stipulates that in neither case do witnesses have the power to make one liable to an offering. This corroborates the principle, known to us from another source as well, that the king — like any other citizen — is subject to the judicial authority of the court: דנין אותו ומעידין אותו. Even though the Mishnah in *Sanhedrin* (18a) states: המלך לא דן ולא דנין אותו לא מעיד ולא מעידין אותו, "The king may neither judge nor be judged; he may neither testify nor be testified against," the Gemara (ibid. 19a) explains: לא שנו אלא מלכי ישראל אבל מלכי בית דוד דן ודנין אותן, דכתיב בית דוד כה אמר ה׳ דינו לבקר משפט (ירמיהו כא:יב), ואי לא דיינינן ליה, אינהו היכי דייני, והכתיב התקוששו וקושו ואמר ריש לקיש קשט עצמך ואחר כך קשט אחרים. The king's exclusion from judgment and testimony — both as giver and as object — is but a late decree, due to the defiant attitude of King Yannai, and is not in accordance with Torah law. Indeed, the prophet (ibid.) exhorts the House of David to judge the people justly — and yet one who is not subject to the authority of the court is not entitled to judge others! It must be, then, that — according to Torah law — the king may both judge and be judged (see לחם משנה הל׳ מלכים, 3:7).

אשר חטא בה. It is not sufficient that he knows in general that he has committed a sin for whose willful violation one is liable to כרת. Rather, he must know the specific sin אשר חטא בה. It is not sufficient that he knows that he has eaten חלב or נותר — e.g., היו חלב ונותר לפניו ואכל אחד מהן ואינו יודע איזה מהן אכל; rather, he must know that he has eaten חלב, or he must know that he has eaten נותר (*Kerisos* 19a). Shortly it will be made clear, in our discussion of verse 24, how greatly the Torah limits the right to bring a חטאת. This requirement — that one must recognize the specific sin — relates to that discussion and confirms that a חטאת יחיד is brought not on account of sinfulness in general but on account of a certain definite act; it is brought to inspire conscientiousness in certain definite actions.

והביא את קרבנו שעיר עזים זכר תמים. He should seek God's closeness by presenting himself in the Sanctuary as a שעיר עזים זכר תמים. We have seen above (1:10–13) that צאן — as opposed to בקר — represent the human personality not according to its works but according to the lot assigned to it and the guidance provided it by the "Shepherd of Israel." Among the types of צאן, the עז represents stubborn resistance to strangers and compliant obedience to its owner. The stubborn resistance to strangers is utmost in the male of the species, the שעיר. For the חטאת נשיא, a male animal is required not merely למצוה but לעיכוב, as derived from the seemingly superfluous word זכר (see קרבן אהרן on *Toras Kohanim* to our verse).

The קרבן נשיא consists of a שעיר, whereas the קרבן of the כהן המשיח and of the בית דין הגדול consists of a פר. Accordingly, the king's task and attendant duty to be careful in his conduct derive not from his high office (see Commentary to v. 3, end) but from the national role assigned to him by God. He has been raised to the very height of power in order to be a "שעיר," to defend and stand on guard, to protect the nation and God's Word which is in its midst. Indeed, the king's function in foreign affairs is not to conquer and enlarge the nation's territory; ירושה and ישיבה precede the appointment of a king (see *Devarim* 17:14). The national power concentrated in his hands in foreign affairs is meant to be used solely for defense, for standing guard at the borders. He is to be a "שעיר." In internal affairs, as well, the first and foremost function of the king is to be a "שעיר." His duty is to represent God's Word — which forms the sum of the national mission — and to defend it, by the power of his position, against any infringement or perversion within the nation. The national power in his hands should function like a

24 *And he shall lean his hand upon the head of the he-goat and slaughter it at the place where the ascent offering is slaughtered, before* God; *it is an offering that clears one of sin.*	כד וְסָמַ֤ךְ יָדוֹ֙ עַל־רֹ֣אשׁ הַשָּׂעִ֔יר וְשָׁחַ֣ט אֹת֔וֹ בִּמְק֛וֹם אֲשֶׁר־יִשְׁחַ֥ט אֶת־הָעֹלָ֖ה לִפְנֵ֣י יְהוָ֑ה חַטָּ֖את הֽוּא׃

"שעיר," to stand up to any attack on God's Word within the nation. In this way, too, רש״י (*Sanhedrin* 20b, ד״ה עמי הארץ קלקלו) understands the word "לשפטינו" (*Shemuel* I, 8:5) as a just demand (כהוגן שאלו) on the part of the זקנים שבדור; they requested a king לשופטם ולרדות הסרבנים שבהם. But he who would represent God's Word and protect it from others must first protect it from himself. He must beware of moral carelessness — which is the literal meaning of שגגה — so that he not fall from the קרנות מזבח העולה, the moral heights which are the goal of all ascent and advancement (cf. our Commentary on *Tehillim* 58 and 72).

שעיר עזים. *Toras Kohanim* to verse 28 teaches us that all שעירי חטאות — including that of the נשיא — must be בני שנה. The king, too, must never grow "old" in his position of power. He must sustain fresh enthusiasm for his task. We shall see there, however, that this halachah is not derived from the expression שעיר עזים but from other verses. Accordingly, there is no difference in age between an animal that is referred to as שעיר and one that is called שעיר עזים (the משנה למלך in הל׳ מעשה הקרבנות, 1:14 remains in doubt on this question).

24 **ושחט אתו**. From the limiting word אותו and from the similar ושחט אתה (v. 33) *Toras Kohanim* derives the halachah (which is also cited in *Temurah* 15a and 21b) that only *this* animal — once it is set aside by the חוטא to be offered as atonement for his חטא — is fit for an offering; but ולד חטאת, a kid or lamb born from a female חטאת (the חטאת יחיד is a female goat or a female sheep), or תמורת חטאת, the animal exchanged for a חטאת, or חטאת שמתו בעליה, a חטאת whose owner has died, or חטאת שכפרו בעליה, a חטאת that was lost and whose owner then gained atonement through another animal — all these are unfit for any offering, even indirectly (i.e., they are not ירעה עד שיסתאב וימכר ויפלו דמיו לנדבה),

and are left to die (מתות). In the Mishnah in *Temurah* (15a) and in *Toras Kohanim* (to our verse) yet a fifth category is named: שעברה שנתה; thus the generally used expression חמש חטאות מתות. The Gemara (*Temurah* 22a) explains, however, that this last category, too, is a חטאת אבודה and that the Mishnah there (ibid. 21b) should be understood as referring to אבודה שעברה שנתה and אבודה שנמצאת בעלת מום. According to רש״י on the Mishnah (ibid.), these last two form one special category, distinct from חטאת שכפרו בעליה באחרת, and constitute the fifth category of the חטאות המתות, as they must be left to die even if found קודם שכפרו בעלים באחרת. According to תוספות (ibid.), however, they are identical with חטאת שכפרו בעליה, and it becomes difficult to find the fifth category of חטאות המתות.

The halachah of חטאות מתות is unique to חטאת. All the other offerings — עולה, שלמים, תודה — transmit their own character to animals that derive from them by birth or exchange, ולדותיהן ותמורותיהן כיוצא בהן, and these animals are offered up as עולה, שלמים, or תודה in exactly the same way as the animals from which they derive (ibid. 17b and 18b). So, too, עולה ושלמים שמתו בעליהם must be offered by the heirs (*Zevachim* 5a; *Menachos* 4b). Even for אשם, which resembles חטאת in respect to that which precipitates it, we find in parallel cases (e.g., תמורת אשם, אשם שמתו בעליו) that although the animal itself is unfit for an offering, it does — at least indirectly — become an offering. It is left to graze until it develops a מום and is then sold, and the proceeds go to the Sanctuary fund (שופרות), from which עולות נדבת צבור are then bought: כל שבחטאת מתה באשם ירעה עד שיסתאב וימכר ויפלו דמיו לנדבה (*Temurah* 20b). The difference between חטאת and אשם is even more pronounced according to רבינו תם (*Zevachim* 5b, תוס׳ ד״ה הגה״ה; *Menachos* 4b, תוס׳ ד״ה אשם). In his opinion the whole principle of רעייה is only a תקנת חכמים, whereas מדאורייתא an אשם שכפרו בעליה וכו׳ may itself be offered as עולת נדבה של ציבור (קיץ המזבח), and the halachah originally was worded: כל שבחטאת מתה באשם קרב עולה.

The halachah of חטאות המתות is apparently connected with another halachah which is also characteristic of חטאת and which is derived (*Zevachim* 7b–8a) from the phrases ושחט אתה לחטאת and ולקח הכהן מדם החטאת (below, vv. 33–34): A חטאת whose עבודות הדם — the שחיטה, the קבלה, the הולכה, the זריקה — were performed שלא לשמה is פסולה, whether it be a חטאת ראובן שנזבחה לשם עולה (a שינוי קודש), or חטאת חלב שנזבחה לשם חטאת דם שמעון (a שינוי בעלים), or perhaps even a חטאת חלב שנזבחה לשם חטאת דם (*Zevachim* 7a; 9b; see כסף משנה הל׳ פסולי המוקדשים, 15:6). In the case of all other offerings, however, a קרבן that is brought שלא לשמה is כשר, but the one who brought it has not fulfilled his obligation and must bring another offering: כל הזבחים שנזבחו שלא לשמן כשרים אלא שלא עלו לבעלים לשם חובה (*Zevachim* 2a). In this respect only פסח is similar to חטאת, as פסח, too, is פסול שלא לשמו (תוספות, ad loc.). אשם — in this respect as well — resembles not חטאת but עולה and the other קרבנות (*Zevachim* 2a).

All of these *halachos* may be explained by the unique characteristic that, in our opinion, marks the very essence of the חטאת. The חטאת is the lone offering that may only be brought as an obligation arising from a specific cause. (In the case of חטאות המוספים, the cause lies in the special significance of the particular day.) It may only be brought as an obligation, as a חובה, and never as a נדבה. (See also v. 23, אשר חטא בה.) All the other offerings — עולה, שלמים, תודה, מנחה — may also be brought as free-will offerings without any compelling cause. Even אשם — in the case of אשם תלוי — is offered on account of only a doubtful cause. Moreover, according to the view of ר׳ אליעזר — which is taught in the Mishnah in *Chullin* (41b) and is accepted as halachah by טור אורח חיים 1 and יורה דעה 5 (but not by the רמב״ם in הל׳ מעשה הקרבנות, 14:8 and הל׳ שחיטה, 2:18) — מתנדב אדם אשם תלוי בכל יום. אשם, then, is also a דבר שנידר ונידב, an offering that can be brought as a vow offering or a free-will offering.

It would thus seem logical that since חטאת cannot be offered as a נדבה, it therefore cannot suffer the intermediate status in which an offering is כשר but is not עולה לחובה. Indeed, it would appear that this intermediate status is assigned to חטאת in only one case — חטאת ששחטה לשם חולין (*Zevachim* 46b), and the explanation for this must be sought. True, the רמב״ם is of the opinion that this status was assigned to חטאת in two additional cases: שחטה לשם אחד שהוא מחויב עולה and שחטה לשם מת (הל׳ פסולי המוקדשים, 15:8–9). In both of these cases, however, the Gemara (*Zevachim* 7a; 9b) simply says כשרה, and it is difficult to maintain — considering the whole course of the discussion there — that what the Gemara means to say is כשר ואינו מרצה. For the Gemara (ibid. 5a) explicitly asks, regarding this intermediate status that applies to other קרבנות: אם אין מרצין למה באין, and the Gemara answers — based on the verse מוצא שפתיך וגו׳ (*Devarim* 23:24) — that an offering that does not count לחובה is considered a נדבה; and we do, in fact, find in the case of עולות לאחר מיתה that they are כשרין ואין מרצין. Yet neither of these two points applies to חטאת: It cannot be brought בנדבה, and it cannot be offered לאחר מיתת בעליה. This has already been pointed out by the commentary צאן קדשים (*Zevachim* 5a).

It would also appear that the חמש חטאות המתות are intimately connected with this basic characteristic of the חטאת. They, too, may be accounted for by the fact that a חטאת is brought only as a result of a specific cause. The common denominator of the five חטאות המתות is that they all bear the character of a חטאת but are not connected to a specific cause. Therefore, they — and even the proceeds from their sale — are unfit to be used for an offering. ולד החטאת and תמורת החטאת received their חטאת-character by birth or exchange, but they never corresponded to a sin requiring atonement. In the cases of חטאת שמתו בעליה and שכיפרו בעליה באחרת, the sin has already vanished with the death of the one seeking atonement or with his attainment of atonement through another animal. They are all חטאות that do not correspond to a sin.

This fundamental characteristic of the חטאת precludes a חטאת from being offered even indirectly upon the altar, so long as the חטאת-character of the animal is intact and only external factors have severed its connection to the cause of its being brought. In the parallel cases in all other offerings, the animal is left to graze until it develops a מום and is then sold, and the proceeds are used for purchasing עולות נדבת צבור (קיץ המזבח). The same applies to a חטאת that lost its חטאת-character because of a מום, or to a חטאת that never definitely received the character of a חטאת — e.g., where (for security's sake) one had set aside two animals for his one חטאת, lest one of the two be lost or become unfit (מותרות חטאת). But a complete and fit חטאת that lacks the connection to its cause is left to die, and it is unfit for the altar even by way of metamorphosis into an עולה, even if it was אבודה and a פסול מום was added to it (see תוספות, *Temurah* 21b, ד״ה ולד).

There is yet another aspect from which to consider this distinction between קרבן חטאת and all other קרבנות. All the other offerings are easily transformed into עולות, as they resemble the עולה in the עבודות הדם that are essential to the atonement: they are all בזריקה למטה. חטאת is the exception, as it alone is בנתינה למעלה.

Now, if we consider that any offering — other than a חטאת that is undiminished in its character — can be transformed into an עולה, and that the עולה, more than any other offering, is liable to be brought as a נדבה (as only the עולה can be offered also as נדבת ציבור), we come to the conclusion that עולה is the basic, regular form of all the offerings, and that חטאת, by contrast, is the exception. יחיד and ציבור can bring עולות whenever they wish. Any offering that is unfit to be offered can be transformed and converted into an עולה. The altar, too, is generally called מזבח העולה; and the daily offering, the תמיד, is an עולה. The idea embodied by the עולה, then, can and must, with each and every breath, fill the consciousness of Jews — as individuals and as a community. This idea is the expression of the spirit that is the purest, most natural consequence of our relationship with God, and upon this spirit rests the full realization of that relationship. The idea embodied by the חטאת, however, should inform our consciousness in exceptional cases only; it is justified only under special circumstances.

Let us remember, as we noted above (1:3), that עולה מכפרת על מצות עשה ועל הרהורי הלב; that עולה embodies the positive ascent toward greater moral perfection and the positive infusion of good and pure thoughts into the mind — by which alone one is saved from useless and evil thoughts, as the mind never rests. This reflects the basic premise of our relationship with God, the premise that governs our moral life from the first to the final breath, namely, continuous ascent — in thought and deed — toward the ideal of moral and spiritual perfection. Awareness of our inadequacy in light of the never attained ideal, recognition of the need for and possibility of continual ascent, and the zest for unceasing ascent — the qualities embodied by the "ascent offering" — can, should, and must remain with us always. In the moral-spiritual realm, ascent means — life!

The חטאת, on the other hand, stems from an awareness of descent, and it emphasizes — as an antidote to descent — the duty of steadfastness, of remaining steadily up on moral heights. If this duty, embodied by נתינה על קרנות המזבח as the future mission of the morally fallen, if this standing firm — which is requisite in the life of the Jewish soul — is not connected with a sin that has been committed, then it spells nothing but death to all moral life. For if ascent in the moral realm means life, then standing still in this realm means death. Connection with a specific sin or a specific fall lends a different connotation to the כהן's pointing to the horns of the altar, a connotation of heights that are relative to a fall, which has been revealed by sin. Without this connection, though, the horns of the altar represent the absolute height of the moral ideal, and to identify with them would be to say: "The ideal of remaining steadily up on the heights has been attained!" But even the slightest hint of such a thought — that the moral ideal has already been attained to perfection — would be the demise of all moral perfection.

We understand, then, why עולה, and not חטאת, embodies the underlying idea of the offerings; why the תמיד is an עולה and not a חטאת; why, in all the other offerings, the עבודות הדם that are essential to atonement resemble those of עולה and not חטאת — so that all the other offerings are, as it were, modified עולות, inasmuch as אכילת הכהנים והבעלים completes אכילת המזבח, and כהנים משולחן גבוה קזכו. We understand, finally, why all the other offerings can be transformed and converted into עולות; why only עולה may be offered, without any conditions, as נדבה — בין ביחיד ובין בציבור. Not by a permanent חטאת-consciousness of sin and guilt, not by a permanent state of penitent contrition, will the heart be moved to yearn for God, or the spirit be uplifted with inspiration to serve God and work for the rectification of His world. עולה, עולה, עולה — up! upward! aloft! Up to the light of God's closeness, and higher, for ever and ever! That is the call that comes continually from God's Sanctuary to the sons and daughters of Israel, a call that awakens and revives and dispels depression and death. This call of the living God of the Jewish Sanctuary is the loudest, most forceful protest against all the heathen theories of mortification and against the doctrine of the self-deprecation of unrectifiable sinfulness, which the blasphemers impute to the Sanctuary of offerings of the eternally living God.

It is not for naught that whenever Scripture mentions the הקטרת אימורים of the חטאת, it emphasizes the resemblance to the זבח השלמים. (We already noted this above, on vv. 8–10; see also below, vv. 26, 31, and 35.) The basis of חטאת is but a temporary state — a passing illness. Once the עבודות הדם have been performed, the חלב וכליות are ריח ניחוח לה׳.

Now we understand why the Torah keeps away from the altar any חטאת — and precludes it from being offered even indirectly, via grazing and redemptive sale — if that חטאת has no relation to the precipitating cause, or if this cause no longer exists. To offer such a חטאת would mean one of two things: either it would represent the condition of חטא, sinfulness, as the normal condition of the human being, or it would express the very opposite extreme, that man is sinless. Such spiritual arrogance, no less than the idea of unrectifiable sinfulness, means the demise of all moral perfection. Both lead to moral death. The one — because one believes there is no *need* for ascent; the other — because one believes there is no *possibility* of ascent. ולד חטאת, תמורת חטאת, חטאת שמתו בעליה, ושכיפרו בעליה באחרת — in short, any חטאת that does not correspond to a sin is not fit to be offered on the altar of the God of Israel and is left to die.

What remains to be explained is the halachah that the law of the

25 *The priest shall take, with his finger, some of the blood of the offering that clears of sin and put it upon the horns of the altar of ascent offering; he shall then pour [the remainder of] its blood onto the base of the altar of ascent offering.*

כה וְלָקַח הַכֹּהֵן מִדַּם הַחַטָּאת בְּאֶצְבָּעוֹ וְנָתַן עַל־קַרְנֹת מִזְבַּח הָעֹלָה וְאֶת־דָּמוֹ יִשְׁפֹּךְ אֶל־יְסוֹד מִזְבַּח הָעֹלָה:

ולד חטאת ותמורת חטאת ושמתו בעליה. חטאות מתות does not apply to חטאות ציבור in any case do not apply בציבור: for חטאת ציבור is never a נקבה, תמורה is not effective for a ציבור, and אין ציבור מתים — "a community never dies" (*Temurah* 16a). However, חטאת שכיפרו בעליה באחרת — e.g., פר ושעיר של יום הכיפורים שאבדו והפרישו אחרים תחתיהן — is not left to die but is itself offered as an עולה for קיץ המזבח, according to Torah law; רעייה was introduced as a Rabbinic measure, גזירה לאחר כפרה אטו לפני כפרה (ibid. 15a, et seq.; *Shevuos* 12a). Perhaps it may be said that an erroneous conception of man's relation to his task — as reflected by a חטאת without חטא — is suggested only by the חטאת of the individual and not by that of the ציבור. The two extremes, spiritual arrogance and resigned sinfulness, are found primarily in the individual. The community, however, includes a spectrum of diverse individuals, and corresponding to every חטאת ציבור there is always a sin requiring atonement. There cannot be a חטאת ציבור that has no sin whatsoever corresponding to it; hence, it is fit at least as an עולה and is not left to die.

במקום אשר ישחט את העלה — i.e., בצפון; see Commentary above, 1:5 and 1:11.

חטאת הוא: חטאת – שיהיו כל מעשיו לשם חטאת; הוא – פרט לשחטו שלא לשמו (*Toras Kohanim*). The Halachah here elaborates the principle that we mentioned previously — namely, חטאת שנזבחה שלא לשמה פסולה.

25 **ולקח הכהן מדם החטאת וגו'**. Only part of the blood of the חטאת is applied to the קרנות — as opposed to the blood of the עולה, which is thrown entirely. This fits in with what has been stated above: The חטאת instructs

man to maintain his level — but this level is only a partial and relative one. To hold one's position, to *remain* on a moral level already attained — this, too, is one of man's tasks, but its importance is of a merely negative character. This task is just a natural outgrowth of the moral energy of man, whose whole being is oriented toward positive progress and whose whole aim is advancement and ascent. But all progress becomes illusory if it is not accompanied by an appreciation of the level attained; all progress is illusory if a level once attained is then lost out of carelessness. The חטאת itself rests on the basis of the עולה. Hence: ולקח הכהן מדם החטאת באצבעו ונתן על קרנת מזבח העולה ואת דמו ישפך אל יסוד מזבח העולה.

Earlier (1:5), we explained the meaning of זריקת הדם of the עולה, and in that connection we also explained the blood applications of the חטאת and שפיכת השיריים. Here, we shall note only the following: עולה relates to the four sides of the altar, but encompasses them in two dashings — שתים שהן ארבע. The מתנות of the חטאת, however, are performed on each of the four corners individually: ארבע מתנות על ארבע קרנות (*Zevachim* 52b). One who has erred בשגגה, through carelessness, should focus his attention on the four aspects which together fashion Jewish life. The כהן's finger points out to him each one of these aspects: the spirit of the Torah permeating the life of the people of the Torah (southeast); the material and sensory powers developed by the nation of the Torah (northeast); the Torah that will be realized through these powers (northwest); and the spirit that will be enlightened by the Torah (southwest). Each one of these is a moral height, which must be appreciated seriously if one is to avoid failure.

If our approach to the meaning of the four sides of the altar is correct, they would appear to be identical with the four fundamentals of the פרשיות התפילין, which are the fundamentals of Jewish thought and practice. In תפילין של יד they are included jointly; in תפילין של ראש they are placed separately on one base. קדש = the people of the Torah (east); והיה כי יביאך = material prosperity (north); שמע = the Torah (west); והיה אם שמוע = study of Torah, תלמוד תורה (south). After ascending the ramp at the south, the כהן would turn right and circle the altar; thus, the order of the sides of the altar is east, north, west, south. This corresponds precisely with the accepted order in תפילין של רש״י.

The שתי מתנות of the עולה and the ארבע מתנות of the חטאת are only למצוה, as the כפרה is effected with one מתנה: כל הניתנין על מזבח החיצון שנתן במתנה אחת כיפר (ibid. 36b; see above, Commentary to vv. 17–21).

כו וְאֶת־כָּל־חֶלְבּוֹ יַקְטִיר הַמִּזְבֵּחָה
כְּחֵלֶב זֶבַח הַשְּׁלָמִים וְכִפֶּר עָלָיו
הַכֹּהֵן מֵחַטָּאתוֹ וְנִסְלַח לוֹ׃ פ ששי

26 *He shall turn all its fat into smoke upon the altar, as with the fat of the meal-of-peace offering; the priest will effect atonement for him for his sin, and he will be forgiven.*

כז וְאִם־נֶפֶשׁ אַחַת תֶּחֱטָא בִשְׁגָגָה
מֵעַם הָאָרֶץ בַּעֲשֹׂתָהּ אַחַת
מִמִּצְוֺת יְהוָה אֲשֶׁר לֹא־תֵעָשֶׂינָה
וְאָשֵׁם׃

27 *And if any person from among the people of the land inadvertently sins by doing one of the things concerning which God commanded that they shall not be done, he has incurred guilt.*

כח אוֹ הוֹדַע אֵלָיו חַטָּאתוֹ אֲשֶׁר
חָטָא וְהֵבִיא קָרְבָּנוֹ שְׂעִירַת עִזִּים
תְּמִימָה נְקֵבָה עַל־חַטָּאתוֹ אֲשֶׁר
חָטָא׃

28 *Or if his sin which he has committed was made known to him, then he shall bring as his offering a whole, female goat, for the sin which he has committed.*

26 **ואת כל חלבו וגו'**. See above, Commentary to verses 8–10.

וכפר עליו הכהן וגו'. The כהן will protect him from his sin (see Commentary, *Bereshis* 6:14), ונסלח לו, and he will be forgiven. That is to say, if not for the מתנות על קרנות המזבח, which remind him of his duty to adhere to the heights of the Torah, one sin would lead to another, and his carelessness would steadily increase; repentance would suffice only after cathartic suffering. These developments are avoided, once the כהן effects atonement for him. His past will not imperil his future, and so he is forgiven. סלח is closely related to שלח and צלח: there will be no obstacle on his life's path.

27–35 These verses deal with the חטאת יחיד of any individual in Israel, **נפש אחת וגו' מעם הארץ**. This חטאת of the individual resembles in *every respect* the חטאת of the נשיא. For in regard to the responsibility of observing the *mitzvos*, the king and the commoner are on equal footing before God.

29 *He shall lean his hand upon the head of the offering that clears of sin, and he shall slaughter the offering that clears of sin at the place of the ascent offering.*

כט וְסָמַךְ אֶת־יָדוֹ עַל רֹאשׁ הַחַטָּאת וְשָׁחַט אֶת־הַחַטָּאת בִּמְקוֹם הָעֹלָה׃

30 *The priest shall take, with his finger, some of its blood and place it upon the corners of the altar of ascent offering, and he shall then pour all [the remainder of] its blood onto the base of the altar.*

ל וְלָקַח הַכֹּהֵן מִדָּמָהּ בְּאֶצְבָּעוֹ וְנָתַן עַל־קַרְנֹת מִזְבַּח הָעֹלָה וְאֶת־כָּל־דָּמָהּ יִשְׁפֹּךְ אֶל־יְסוֹד הַמִּזְבֵּחַ׃

31 *He shall remove all its fat, even as the fat was removed from the meal-of-peace offering, and the priest shall turn it into smoke upon the altar as an expression of compliance, to* God; *the priest will effect atonement for him, and he will be forgiven.*

לא וְאֶת־כָּל־חֶלְבָּהּ יָסִיר כַּאֲשֶׁר הוּסַר חֵלֶב מֵעַל זֶבַח הַשְּׁלָמִים וְהִקְטִיר הַכֹּהֵן הַמִּזְבֵּחָה לְרֵיחַ נִיחֹחַ לַיהוָה וְכִפֶּר עָלָיו הַכֹּהֵן וְנִסְלַח לוֹ׃ פ

32 *If he brings a sheep as his offering for an offering that clears of sin, then he shall bring it female and whole.*

לב וְאִם־כֶּבֶשׂ יָבִיא קָרְבָּנוֹ לְחַטָּאת נְקֵבָה תְמִימָה יְבִיאֶנָּה׃

33 *He shall lean his hand upon the head of the offering that clears of sin, and one slaughters it (the female sheep) as an offering that clears of sin, at the place where the ascent offering is slaughtered.*

לג וְסָמַךְ אֶת־יָדוֹ עַל רֹאשׁ הַחַטָּאת וְשָׁחַט אֹתָהּ לְחַטָּאת בִּמְקוֹם אֲשֶׁר יִשְׁחַט אֶת־הָעֹלָה׃

The only difference between the two **חטאות** is in the type of animal representing the personality of the offerer. The king draws near to God as a "**שעיר**," which reflects the nature of his national role (see Commen-

לד וְלָקַח הַכֹּהֵן מִדַּם הַחַטָּאת
בְּאֶצְבָּעוֹ וְנָתַן עַל־קַרְנֹת מִזְבַּח
הָעֹלָה וְאֶת־כָּל־דָּמָהּ יִשְׁפֹּךְ אֶל־
יְסוֹד הַמִּזְבֵּחַ׃

34 *The priest shall take, with his finger, some of the blood of the offering that clears of sin, and he shall put it upon the horns of the altar of ascent offering; he shall then pour all [the remainder of] its blood onto the base of the altar.*

לה וְאֶת־כָּל־חֶלְבָּהּ יָסִיר כַּאֲשֶׁר
יוּסַר חֵלֶב־הַכֶּשֶׂב מִזֶּבַח
הַשְּׁלָמִים וְהִקְטִיר הַכֹּהֵן אֹתָם
הַמִּזְבֵּחָה עַל אִשֵּׁי יְהוָה וְכִפֶּר
עָלָיו הַכֹּהֵן עַל־חַטָּאתוֹ אֲשֶׁר־
חָטָא וְנִסְלַח לוֹ׃ פ

35 *He shall remove all its fat, even as the fat of the sheep of the meal-of-peace offering is to be removed, and the priest shall turn them into smoke on the altar, on the fire offerings to* God; *the priest will effect atonement for him for his sin, and he will be forgiven.*

tary to v. 23). The personality of the commoner, however, is represented by a שעירה or כבשה, a female goat or a female sheep, as he chooses. The femininity of the animal represents his subordinate social standing — as opposed to the standing of the נשיא, which is represented as masculine. Yet the commoner is allowed to choose between a שעירה and a כבשה. If he wishes to express his independence among his people, he brings a שעירה; and if he regards himself as merely one of the flock, as one who requires God's guidance, he brings a כבשה.

In any case, the three פרשיות of the חטאת יחיד teach us this: Differences in social standing do not affect a person's moral dignity and do not influence the attainment or preservation of God's closeness. The שעיר of the king, the שעירה of the leading citizen, and the כבשה of the lowliest commoner all must submit, in שחיטה, to the sharp knife of moral dictates. The king and commoner alike must be representatives of the Torah and must sanction its authority vis-à-vis themselves (סמיכה). The דם השעיר of the king, the דם השעירה of the prominent citizen, and the דם הכבשה of the common person receive the same direction via the finger of the כהן — to adhere to the heights of the Torah. Blood of all of them is poured onto the יסוד דרומי. There, they find the foundation of the building that is life, a building to be raised in the spirit of the Torah. After the "atonement of the personality," the חלב וכליות of all of them are offered up on the altar fire: All their aims and aspirations bring satisfaction to God; through their being and desire, they do God's Will on earth. The פרשה of the חטאת כבשה concludes with the words על אשי ה׳ (v. 35): The desires and aspirations of the lowliest commoner are joined on the altar to אשי ה׳; if the moral level of his desires and aspirations is maintained, they are equal in value to all the other deeds performed for God's sake.

From the wording of verse 27 we learn several *halachos* which complete the law of the חטאת. With repeated emphasis, Scripture stresses the *individual* who sins: נפש, אחת, בעשתה. From this we learn (*Shabbos* 93b, et seq.) that one is not liable to a חטאת unless he performs by himself a forbidden act. For example, מלאכת הוצאה on Shabbos consists of two basic factors: עקירה, removing an object from one רשות, and הנחה, setting it down in another רשות. Now, if one person performs the עקירה and another the הנחה — זה עוקר וזה מניח — neither of them is liable to a חטאת. Similarly, if two people together perform a מלאכה, and each one of them is capable of performing it by himself (זה יכול וזה יכול) — e.g., they together hold a pen and write with it — they are exempt. But if two together perform a מלאכה, and each one is not capable of performing it by himself (זה אינו יכול וזה אינו יכול) — e.g., they carry out a heavy beam into רשות הרבים — they are both liable to a חטאת. Where one of them is capable of performing the מלאכה by himself and the other is not (זה יכול זה אינו יכול), the one who is capable is liable to a חטאת, but the one who is not capable is regarded as one who renders unnecessary assistance, which is legally insignificant (מסייע אין בו ממש). This principle — מסייע אין בו ממש (ibid. 93b) — applies to other *halachos* as well, but it requires more precise definition (see ט״ז on או״ח 328, 1; יו״ד 198, 21, with נקודות הכסף, ad loc.).

Furthermore, the word מכם (above, 1:2) excludes a מומר (a Jew who has estranged himself from the Torah) from bringing an עולה; here, Scripture repeats this halachah in the case of חטאת: מעם הארץ – פרט למומר (*Chullin* 5b). Even a חטאת, which is an obligatory offering (קרבן חובה), may not be offered by a מומר — whether a מומר with respect to the whole Torah or just with respect to the particular sin he committed. One who seeks atonement must be one who would be שב מידיעתו or — as *Toras Kohanim* puts it — יושב לו מידיעתה; that is to say, had he known

5 1 *And if a person sins and hears a* ה א וְנֶפֶשׁ כִּי־תֶחֱטָא וְשָׁמְעָה קוֹל

that the act was forbidden, he would have refrained from doing it. For it is not sufficient that he did it בשגגה; rather, it is necessary that he did it *because of* שגגה. The Halachah distinguishes between different types of מומרים: מומר לכל התורה כולה (which includes מומר לעבודה זרה and מומר לחלל שבתות בפרהסיא); מומר לאותו דבר; מומר לדבר אחד; and further: מומר לתיאבון, מומר להכעיס, and the middle case of מומר שלא לתיאבון ושלא להכעיס. A מומר להכעיס לדבר אחד, one who, on principle, holds in contempt even one of the laws of the Torah, is treated as one who estranged himself from the whole Torah (*Chullin* 5b; יו״ד 2, 4–7). Permission to bring an offering depends on what the character of the offerer was like when he committed the sin. If at that time he was a מומר לכל התורה or a מומר לאותו דבר, he is not allowed to bring a חטאת, even if afterwards he was חוזר בתשובה. For although he sinned בשגגה, he did not sin because of שגגה (see *Chullin* 5b, תוספות ד״ה אינו שב; משנה למלך הל׳ שגגות, 3:7). It goes without saying that he may not be a מומר at the time of the offering, and that he must have remorse especially for the sin that he committed and undertake never to repeat it. This, of course, is already included in the general principle of זֶבַח רְשָׁעִים תּוֹעֵבָה (*Mishlei* 21:27). Here, in our verse, we learn a new halachah: permission to bring an offering depends also on what the character of the offerer was like at the time of sin. If, at that time, he was a מומר with respect to the whole Torah, or a מומר with respect to that sin, he is not allowed to bring a חטאת (*Chullin* 5b).

ואת כל חלבה יסיר וגו׳. So it says in verses 31 and 35. In the case of פר כהן המשיח (v. 8) and פר העלם דבר (v. 19), Scripture uses the term ירים. The reason for this may be as follows: In the case of the פרים הנשרפים, only the חלבים reach their true destination — as they attain אכילת מזבח, like חלבי השלמים. The rest of the offering, however, is נשרף מחוץ למחנה. הרמת החלבים, the lifting out of the חלבים, is the antithesis of that שריפה: they are preserved for their true destination.

CHAPTER 5

1 The חטאות discussed in the previous chapter are brought to atone for sins whose willful violation (מזיד) carries with it the penalty of כרת. The rule is this: כל שחייבין על זדונו כרת חייבין על שגגתו חטאת. Each one of these חטאות is

demand of an oath, and he is a witness — having seen or known [something] — so that, if he does not testify, he will bear his iniquity.	אָלָה וְהוּא עֵד אוֹ רָאָה אוֹ יָדָע אִם־לוֹא יַגִּיד וְנָשָׂא עֲוֹנוֹ׃

a חטאת קבועה, a "fixed" חטאת, and is not linked to the financial capability of the one obligated to bring the חטאת. One who cannot afford to bring a שעירה or a כבשה should fulfill his obligation when he does have the means.

This chapter (vv. 1–13) discusses three offenses, two of which are not punishable by כרת. He who violates one of these offenses is liable to a קרבן עולה ויורד, an offering that "rises and falls" — i.e., one that varies according to the means of the person obligated to bring the offering. The three offenses — which form a special category of liability to an offering — are as follows: (a) שבועת העדות, also called שמיעת קול (v. 1); (b) טומאת מקדש וקדשיו (vv. 2 and 3); (c) שבועת ביטוי, also called ביטוי שפתים (v. 4). In all three cases one brings, if one is affluent (בעשירות), a שעירה או כבשה לחטאת; if one is poor (בדלות), שתי תורים או בני יונה אחד לחטאת ואחד לעולה; if one is very poor (בדלי דלות), עשירית איפה סולת למנחת חטאת (*Kerisos* 10b). שבועת העדות is unique among the three in that מביא על הזדון כשגגה (ibid. 9a), one brings an offering even if he committed the offense as a complete מזיד, whereas other חטאות are brought only for שגגה.

First, let us examine the wording of Scripture and acquaint ourselves with the basic *halachos*; then, we shall attempt to understand the reasons underlying these *halachos*.

ושמעה קול אלה. If Scripture had said ושמעה אלה, the meaning would have been that one merely hears an oath. ושמעה קול אלה, however, means that one hears a demand of an oath; satisfying such a demand would be worded ושמעה לקול אלה. The construction שמע קול meaning "hearing a demand or request" is quite common — e.g., וישמע ה׳ את קול דבריכם (*Devarim* 1:34); שמע ה׳ קול יהודה (ibid. 33:7); שָׁמַע ה׳ קוֹל בִּכְיִי (*Tehillim* 6:9). The words קול אלה denote that the oath is directed at the hearer and includes a demand. (For more on אלה in the sense of oath, see Commentary to *Bereshis* 21:23; see also Commentary to *Shemos* 20:7).

והוא עד. עד derives from the root עוד. Its basic meaning is to be lasting. Thus, we get עוד, which is indicative of continuity of time or action;

עוֹדֵד, to encourage someone so that he be able to endure; הָעִיד, to give permanence to something passing. This is the function of an עֵד. An עד observes a fleeting event, capturing it in his mind; in his consciousness the event lives on. Even after it has expired from an external standpoint, he can reproduce the event in words via הגדה and present it before his listeners (מעיד), and in this way give it prolonged life (עוד).

או ראה או ידע is a parenthetical statement, which serves to explain how a person becomes a witness. He may have seen the act with his own eyes (ראה) — e.g., he saw that Reuven gave money to Shimon, but he did not know whether it was given as a loan, as payment, or as a deposit. This is ראיה without ידיעה. Such testimony can be meaningful if, for instance, Shimon denies altogether that he had received any money from Reuven. Alternatively, the witness may have heard with his own ears an admission from Shimon that he owed Reuven a sum of money. Thus, he knows that a legal claim existed, but he did not see the act that caused this claim. This is ידיעה without ראיה. The Gemara (*Shevuos* 33b and 34a) proves from here that the halachah of שבועת העדות applies only to monetary cases (דיני ממונות). For capital cases (דיני נפשות) are not decided based on circumstantial evidence, which is the very essence of ידיעה בלא ראיה; and ראיה without ידיעה does not suffice either in such cases, as the witnesses in capital cases must testify also about the circumstances that render the act punishable.

אם לוא יגיד ונשא עונו is not a consequence of ושמעה קול אלה, as though withholding testimony were a sin only if preceded by *adjurement*, i.e., by a demand *in the form of an oath*. Rather, אם לוא יגיד ונשא עונו is a further explanation of והוא עד: he knows of evidence which, were he to withhold it, would amount to his bearing sin. From this we learn that even without שמיעת קול אלה, i.e., even if they were not *adjured* to do so, witnesses are obligated to testify (although the liability for a קרבן עולה ויורד applies only in the case of שמיעת קול; see below).

Our verse speaks only of a case where there are two witnesses (*Bava Kamma* 56a, רש״י ד״ה אם לא יגיד, כל מקום שנאמר עד הרי כאן שני עדים וכו׳). However, even if there is only one witness, who can merely obligate the defendant to take an oath, of him our Sages say (ibid. 55b): היודע עדות לחברו ואינו מעיד לו פטור מדיני אדם וחייב בדיני שמים, he who knows of evidence but withholds it and does not testify is exempt from the judgments of human courts, but is subject to the judgments of Heaven (see תוספות,

ibid. 56a, ד״ה פשיטא). They say further (*Pesachim* 113b): שלשה הקב״ה שונאן המדבר אחד בפה ואחד בלב והיודע עדות בחבירו ואינו מעיד לו והרואה דבר ערוה בחברו ומעיד בו יחידי, There are three whom God hates: he who says one thing with his mouth but another in his heart; he who knows of evidence that he could give but withholds it; and he who, as a single witness, offers testimony in a criminal case in which such testimony is of no use whatsoever and constitutes הוצאת שם רע, slander.

We learn further from אם לוא יגיד ונשא עונו that בראויין להגדה הכתוב מדבר, "Scripture speaks of witnesses who are fit to testify." But if they know of evidence עד מפי עד — i.e., their evidence is based not on their own observation but on what they have heard from others — or if one of them is a קרוב או פסול, a relative or otherwise ineligible, they are exempt (*Shevuos* 35a).

We also learn from here that withholding testimony is a sin only where the testimony could be of use, and only where the witnesses cannot retract their claim that אין אנו יודעים לך עדות. For only in such a case can it be said that אם לא הגידו then נשאו עוונם. Thus, witnesses bear sin for denying they know evidence only if they deny this in the court, for it is there that כיון שהגיד שוב אינו חוזר ומגיד (תוספות, *Bava Kamma* 56a, ד״ה פשיטא, and also שו״ת הראש, 59:1). According to ר״ן (פרק שבועת העדות, 14b) and בית יוסף (טור חושן משפט 29), witnesses who say אין אנו יודעין are allowed to backtrack (חזרה) and say יודעין אנו; it is only in our case, after a preceding שבועה, that חזרה is ineffective (see כסף משנה to הל׳ עדות, 3:5).

The case under discussion here involves more than the general obligation of giving evidence; for the demand that the witnesses testify is stated here in the form of an oath: משביע אני עליכם אם לא תבואו ותעידוני וכו׳ (*Shevuos* 33a). They need not reply אמן to the oath; rather, once they are adjured — even out of court — to give evidence (מושבע מפי אחרים) and then in court declare that they have no evidence to give (אין אנו יודעין לך עדות), they violate שבועת העדות, the oath of testimony. (According to the רמב״ם, however, they are liable without replying אמן only if adjured in court, but if adjured out of court they must reply אמן [הל׳ שבועות, 9:1; see כסף משנה and לחם משנה, ad loc.].) If the witnesses are liable in the case of מושבע מפי אחרים, then certainly they are liable if they are called upon to give evidence and they themselves take an oath that they have no evidence to give (שבועה שאין אנו יודעין לך עדות); or if they are adjured משביע אני עליכם and they reply אמן, in which case it is as though they themselves take an oath, as כל העונה אמן אחר שבועה כמוציא שבועה בפיו דמי (*Shevuos* 29b).

ב אוֹ נֶפֶשׁ אֲשֶׁר תִּגַּע בְּכָל־דָּבָר
טָמֵא אוֹ בְנִבְלַת חַיָּה טְמֵאָה אוֹ
בְּנִבְלַת בְּהֵמָה טְמֵאָה אוֹ בְּנִבְלַת
שֶׁרֶץ טָמֵא וְנֶעְלַם מִמֶּנּוּ וְהוּא
טָמֵא וְאָשֵׁם׃

2 *Or if a person touches some impure object, be it the carcass of an impure animal, or the carcass of impure livestock, or the carcass of an impure creeping thing, and it escapes his awareness, but he is impure and [therefore] guilty.*

The witnesses are not liable to an offering unless they are adjured by the one who stands to gain from the testimony. This is alluded to by the מלא spelling of לוא in the phrase אם לוא יגיד; it is as though Scripture had said אם לו לא יגיד (ibid. 35a). Another halachah in שבועת העדות — and, similarly, in שבועת הפקדון (vv. 21 and 22) as well — is that the witnesses are liable to an offering only if they directly caused the claimant a monetary loss, i.e., only if their testimony would have obligated his opponent to pay (*Shevuos* 34a). Hence, as mentioned previously, a single witness who refrains from testifying is not liable to an offering — even though his testimony would have obligated the defendant to take a judiciary oath and perhaps, as a consequence, would have caused the defendant to admit liability. Nevertheless, this witness is not liable to an offering, as his refraining from testifying causes the claimant a monetary loss only indirectly. The following general rule applies here: דבר הגורם לממון לאו כממון דמי. Had the witness testified, the claimant would have had a right to obligate the defendant to take a judiciary oath. The claimant is deprived of this right by the refraining witness. But the loss of this right is not considered a monetary loss (ibid. 32a).

Another halachah applicable to שבועת העדות is that the testimony must pertain to things that are subject to judiciary oaths; this excludes עבדים שטרות וקרקעות. Hence, משביע עדי קרקע פטור (ibid. 37b; see Commentary to *Shemos* 22:8).

2 **בנבלת חיה טמאה וגו׳**. The modifier טמאה, attached here to חיה and בהמה, does not limit the discussion to those animals that may not be eaten (see below, 11:4–8); for, in the continuation of the verse, שרץ טמא is mentioned also, and yet *all* שרצים are forbidden as food. Rather, the

טומאה mentioned here denotes the ability to convey ritual impurity by contact (טומאת מגע). Accordingly, the phrase בנבלת שרץ טמא refers only to the שמונה שרצים listed below (11:29–30) — החלד והעכבר, etc. But then there should be no need to attach the modifier טמאה to נבלת חיה ובהמה, as the נבלה of *every* חיה and בהמה conveys impurity by contact. Moreover, the very mention of בהמה טמאה is superfluous, as it is included in חיה (בהמה בכלל חיה). In *Shevuos* 7a, the superfluous words בהמה טמאה are employed in a גזירה שוה with what is stated below (7:21): ונפש כי תגע בבהמה טמאה וגו׳ ואכל מבשר זבח השלמים. They teach us that the טומאה mentioned here has impinged upon מקדש וקדשיו: After becoming ritually impure, one entered the Sanctuary or ate of its holy things (excluding קדשי גבול such as תרומה). (See also *Chullin* 70b–71a, according to רבנן דרבי יוסי הגלילי, and רש״י there.)

ונעלם ממנו. In *Shevuos* (14b) we learn that one becomes liable to a חטאת on account of טומאה only if he had awareness in the beginning (ידיעה בתחילה) — i.e., he knew that he had become טמא and that this place was the Sanctuary or this food was קדשים — but when he entered the מקדש or ate the קדשים he had lost awareness of his state of טומאה or of the קדושה of the place or object (העלם בינתים — ibid. 4a). This type of שגגה — which the Gemara (ibid. 14b) terms ידיעות קמייתא דליתנהו בכל התורה כולה — differs from the שגגות that make one liable to a חטאת קבועה (chapter 4). Take, for example, חטאת חלב: it is sufficient that he have ידיעה בסוף and become aware of the facts only after he has sinned. Even if he never knew, before he sinned, that this was a piece of חלב, he is liable to a חטאת. The same is true of all other שגגות. However, liability to a קרבן עולה ויורד because of טומאת מקדש וקדשיו is contingent upon prior ידיעה. This is derived (*Shevuos* 5a) from the expression ונעלם מכלל: שידע. At the same time, the assumption is that every Jew already knows the *law* of מגע נבלה from what he learned in school (ידיעת בית רבו — ibid.); vis-à-vis *halachic* knowledge, the requirement of ידיעה בתחילה is considered already fulfilled — so that even if he had forgotten the halachah before he became טמא, he is still liable to an offering. (Parenthetically, it is clear from here that women, too, in their youth, were taught these *halachos*. For the laws of this offering apply equally to men and women, and yet when the Gemara [ibid.] asks מי איכא דלית ליה ידיעת בית רבו, "Is there anyone who has not been taught Torah in his youth?" it answers only with the rare case of תינוק שנשבה לבין הנכרים, a child who

3 *Or if he touches the impurity of a human being, whatever state of impurity it be by which he becomes impure, and it escapes his awareness, but he becomes aware and incurs guilt.*	ג אוֹ כִּי יִגַּע בְּטֻמְאַת אָדָם לְכֹל טֻמְאָתוֹ אֲשֶׁר יִטְמָא בָּהּ וְנֶעְלַם מִמֶּנּוּ וְהוּא יָדַע וְאָשֵׁם׃

was taken captive and brought up among gentiles and so has grown up knowing nothing of Judaism.) According to תוספות, every Jew in possession of this ידיעת בית רבו is regarded as having met the condition of ידיעה בתחילה — even if he had not been aware of the fact that he came into contact with something טמא. But this opinion seems difficult. For according to this opinion the fundamental difference between this case of שגגה (קרבן עולה ויורד בטומאת מקדש וקדשיו) and all other שגגות is blurred, as ידיעת בית רבו is present also in the case of שגגת חלב. The only difference between them is in the exceptional case of תינוק שנשבה, and even this difference disappears according to the view that a תינוק שנשבה is considered אנוס (*Shabbos* 68b). We therefore interpreted above in accordance with the opinion of רש״י. (See *Shevuos* 5a, 14b with תוספות ד״ה או דלמא, and 19b; cf. תוספות יום טוב to *Shevuos* 2:1 and לחם משנה to הל׳ שגגות, 11:1.)

והוא טמא ואשם. His טומאה brought him to guilt, as he entered the מקדש or ate קדשים while he was in a state of ritual impurity. Both of these acts are punishable by כרת.

3 **בטמאת אדם**: טומאה caused by a human corpse — either by the מת itself or by a טמא מת, a person who touched a corpse. A טמא מת, too, is an אב הטומאה; hence, the מת itself is called אבי אבות הטומאה.

לכל טמאתו: טומאות caused by certain states of living human beings — e.g., זבים וזבות נדות ויולדות (*Toras Kohanim*).

בה: לרבות נבלת עוף טהור. This carcass does not convey טומאה by contact but, rather, בבית הבליעה, by being swallowed (ibid.; *Shevuos* 7b). Later (chapter 11) we will note that the טומאה of מאכלות אסורות is generally referred to by the expression טמא ב-, whereas טומאת מגע is referred to by

ד אוֹ נֶפֶשׁ כִּי תִשָּׁבַע לְבַטֵּא בִשְׂפָתַיִם לְהָרַע ׀ אוֹ לְהֵיטִיב לְכֹל אֲשֶׁר יְבַטֵּא הָאָדָם בִּשְׁבֻעָה וְנֶעְלַם מִמֶּנּוּ וְהוּא־יָדַע וְאָשֵׁם לְאַחַת מֵאֵלֶּה׃

4 *Or if a person swears, uttering [it] with his lips, to deny or to grant something, with regard to anything that a man may utter in an oath, and it escapes his awareness, and then he becomes aware of it, and he incurs guilt regarding one of these.*

the expression טמא ל-. Similarly, here, טומאה that is precipitated only by אכילה is referred to by the words יטמא בה.

אדם וכלים become טמא only through an אב הטומאה. The additional phrase אשר יטמא בה thus defines the level of טומאה discussed in verses 2 and 3: One came into contact with the kind of טומאה by which he can be rendered ritually impure, אשר יטמא בה — i.e., he touched an אב הטומאה and so became טמא. Then he forgot about his טומאה, or forgot about the sanctity of the place or object, and entered the מקדש or ate קדשים. These cases are called in the Mishnah (*Shevuos* 2a and 14a) ידיעות הטומאה שתים שהן ארבע. They are called ידיעות because ידיעה בתחילה is their distinguishing feature. Scripture here deals with one ידיעה that results in two cases — ידיעת הטומאה that slipped his mind in regard to מקדש or in regard to קדשים: העלם טומאה וזכור את המקדש או את הקודש. ר׳ ישמעאל, whose view is accepted as the halachah, adds the other two cases, where it is not the טומאה that slipped his mind, but the sanctity of the place or object: העלם מקדש או קודש וזכור את הטומאה (ibid. 14b).

והוא ידע. This is the ידיעה בסוף (ibid. 4b): after the act he becomes aware that he has sinned.

4 **לבטא**. בטא occurs only here and in *Bemidbar* (30:7 and 9) in connection with vows and oaths. In addition, this root occurs in *Mishlei* (12:18): יֵשׁ בּוֹטֶה כְּמַדְקְרוֹת חָרֶב, and in *Tehillim* (106:33): וַיְבַטֵּא בִּשְׂפָתָיו. The utterances referred to in the latter two verses are ones that were better had they not been uttered. Vows, too, are utterances that are generally undesirable. It follows, then, that the utterances referred to in our verse, as well, are in themselves undesirable. This is confirmed by the content of

this halachah: It relates to promissory oaths (שבועות להבא) — which are generally undesirable — and false assertive oaths (שבועות שקר לשעבר).

בטא is related to בדה and to פתה, פתא, פתע, פתח. The common meaning of the four latter roots is to be outwardly unprotected. This meaning is included also in the root בדה: Fabrications (דברים בדויים) are contrary to the external, objective truth, yet the fabricator (בדאי) does not refrain from uttering them. The related root בטח has a similar meaning: One who is trusting (בוטח) feels no need for protection from the outside world; he does not fear something that comes from without. The relation of בטא – בטח can be compared to the relation of שגג – שכך, של – שלו, which we already noted in commenting on *Bereshis* (8:1): Rash, hasty action (שגג, של) is the sign of unworried carelessness (שכך, שלו). This is also the meaning of the relation of בטא – בטח: One who gives utterance to something (מבטא) is not worried about the consequences of his words or about their objective worth.

The ביטוי referred to in our verse is expressed in the form of an oath: כי תשבע לבטא בשפתים. The addition בשפתים teaches us a halachah in regard to promissory oaths (of which the text here primarily speaks): גמר בלבו צריך שיוציא בשפתיו (*Shevuos* 26b), taking an oath in your mind is not binding unless you actually utter it with your lips. The only exceptions to this rule are תרומה and קדשים, of which Scripture says כל נדיב לבו (*Shemos* 35:5) and וְכָל־נְדִיב לֵב עֹלוֹת (*Divrei Ha-Yamim* II, 29:31); see Commentary to *Shemos*, ad loc.

להרע או להיטיב is not to be understood in a halachic sense; for if one takes an oath to commit a transgression, his oath is invalid and is called שבועת שוא (see Commentary to *Shemos* 20:7). An oath relating to something impossible — whether morally or physically — has no validity whatsoever. Rather, להרע או להיטיב is to be understood in a personal sense: to do something positive or negative for a person. The structure of the sentence או נפש כי תשבע לבטא בשפתים להרע או להיטיב לכל אשר יבטא האדם בשבעה is expounded in *Shevuos* (25a, et seq.) according to the hermeneutic rule ריבה ומיעט וריבה. The first part of the sentence — או נפש וגו׳ — in itself, includes any type of oath, assertive or promissory; similarly, the last part — לכל אשר יבטא וגו׳ — is an unlimited amplification. The middle part — להרע או להיטיב — would, by itself, include only promissory oaths entailing something positive or negative. However, since להרע או להיטיב is written between two amplifications, it loses its narrow sense and serves as an example that limits the scope of the amplifications. Thus, the first and last part includes an assertive oath (לשעבר, e.g., לא נתתי and נתתי ,לא אכלתי and אכלתי) and a promissory oath (להבא, e.g., לא אתן and אתן ,לא אוכל and אוכל) — even if it entails nothing positive or negative (אין בה הרעה והטבה — e.g., לא אזרוק צרור לים, אזרוק צרור לים; לא זרקתי, זרקתי). The middle part, להרע או להיטיב, which serves as an example, excludes דבר מצוה, everything that the Torah commands or forbids us to do. And just as it excludes the morally impossible, so it excludes the physically impossible. In short, anything included under שבועת שוא is excluded from שבועת ביטוי.

A שבועת ביטוי, then, relates only to optional acts (רשות), which are left to man's free choice; where one is free to decide to do the act or not to do it. Moreover, a שבועת ביטוי applies only where the oath, whether it were formulated in the positive or in the negative, would remain a שבועת ביטוי (איתיה בהן ולאו). Thus, שבועה שאני יודע לך עדות, for example, is excluded also, for if this oath were formulated in the negative, it would be a שבועת העדות. This is רב's view, which is accepted as the halachah. According to שמואל, however, שבועת ביטוי relates only to those acts that are subject to the free choice of the oath-taker; that is to say, it must be an oath that can be taken whether it were formulated in the past case or in the future case (איתיה בלהבא). Thus, an oath asserting זרק פלוני צרור לים is excluded also, for one could not swear יזרוק פלוני צרור לים. According to שמואל, then, דבר מצוה is excluded even in the case of an assertive oath (לשעבר), since it is excluded in the case of a promissory oath (להבא). For example, שבועה שלא הנחתי תפלין is not a שבועת ביטוי, since if one were to swear לא אניח תפלין it would be a שבועת שוא.

(It appears that these conditions formulated by רב and שמואל — איתיה בלאו והן, איתיה בלהבא — are merely identifying marks of and identical with the concept of רשות. This resolves the question of תוספות [ibid. 26a] ד״ה מיעט.)

לכל אשר יבטא האדם בשבעה ונעלם ממנו is expounded in *Shevuos* (26a) as follows: תנו רבנן, האדם בשבועה פרט לאנוס, ונעלם פרט למזיד, ממנו שנתעלמה ממנו שבועה, יכול שנתעלמה ממנו חפץ תלמוד לומר בשבועה ונעלם, על העלם שבועה הוא חייב ואינו חייב על העלם חפץ. The oath-taker is called here האדם, in order to teach us that he took the oath with full awareness and was worthy of the name אדם. That is to say, one is not liable to an offering on account of a שבועת ביטוי unless he was aware of the prohibition of false oaths;

and in the case of an assertive oath (לשעבר), one is not liable unless he was also aware of the falseness of his words.

Now, where one takes an assertive oath innocently, thinking that he is telling the truth, and afterwards it becomes clear that he had erred, obviously he is free of any sin and is considered אנוס. For one can swear only to *the best of his knowledge.* Even though he was merely in error, he *could* not have sworn to anything else; he was under the *constraint* (אונס) of his error and is absolved of all responsibility.

Even awareness of the prohibition of false oaths is of the essence of this sin. If, at the time of the oath, he had forgotten this prohibition, he is not considered a שוגג who requires atonement but, rather, an אנוס who is totally exempt. This halachah is unique to שגגת שבועה, inadvertent violation of oaths; there is nothing like it in all other שגגות (*Shabbos* 69b; רש״י, ad loc., ד״ה הא מני מונבז). For example, if someone ate חלב, or performed מלאכה on Shabbos, forgetting that these acts are prohibited and punishable by כרת (שגג בלאו וכרת שבהם), he requires atonement; for the forgetting of the prohibition and of the punishment is the שגגה that makes one liable to a חטאת קבועה (above, chapter 4). But if one took a false oath, forgetting that this is prohibited, he is considered אנוס and is not liable to a קרבן.

This halachah, which is unique to the laws of oaths, is connected to the very concept of an oath. For the meaning of השבע is this: The oath-taker accepts upon himself Divine punishment if he has spoken falsely or fails to actualize his words (see Commentary to *Bereshis* 21:23 and *Shemos* 20:7). It follows, then, that the basis of every שבועה is the awareness that one who swears falsely defies God's Will. Without this awareness the act of השבע has not been carried out, and the oath has no meaning.

Nevertheless, Scripture says ונעלם ממנו — which excludes a מזיד (פרט למזיד). Cases of such העלמה can be constructed easily in promissory oaths (שבועת ביטוי להבא): One took the oath with full awareness; he was an אדם בשבועה. *Only afterwards* did he forget the oath, נעלמה ממנו השבועה, and, as a consequence, violate his oath. Again it is characteristic that על העלם שבועה הוא חייב ואינו חייב על העלם חפץ (*Shevuos* 26a). If, for example, one takes an oath not to eat wheat, and then he eats wheat under the impression that it is oats, he is exempt from a קרבן עולה ויורד. In other שגגות, the law of one who errs as to the nature of the object is the same as the law of one who errs in a matter of halachah. One who ate חלב

5 *Then it shall be that if he incurs guilt regarding one of these, he shall admit to himself that regarding which he has sinned.*

ה וְהָיָה כִי־יֶאְשַׁם לְאַחַת מֵאֵלֶּה וְהִתְוַדָּה אֲשֶׁר חָטָא עָלֶיהָ׃

is liable to a חטאת, whether he thought that it is permissible to eat חלב or that he was eating שומן. One is not liable to a קרבן עולה ויורד on account of a שבועת ביטוי, however, unless he was oblivious to the oath itself: נעלמה ממנו שבועה (ibid.).

In assertive oaths (שבועת ביטוי לשעבר) it is more difficult to construct a case of העלמה such that the oath-taker is not a מזיד. For in assertive oaths העלמה can be found only at the time of the oath, when, at the same time, the oath-taker must be האדם בשבועה — he must know the facts as they are and also must be aware of the halachic implication of a false oath. Hence, העלמה is found in assertive oaths only where — at the time of the oath — the oath-taker is aware that swearing falsely is prohibited but is unaware that it makes one liable to an offering: באומר יודע אני ששבועה זו אסורה אבל איני יודע אם חייבין עליה קרבן או לאו (ibid. 26b). In general, the liability to a חטאת on account of שבועת ביטוי is quite exceptional; for, as a rule, חטאת is applicable only at חייבי כריתות. (Our approach here follows that of רש״י. The רמב״ם takes a different approach — but there are several problems with it.)

5 **והתודה**. The mitzvah of וידוי (confession) appears almost always in the reflexive: התודה. Not to another man must the sinner confess his sin; essentially, not even to God, as He knows of the sin and does not need the confession. Rather, *to himself* must the sinner admit that he has sinned. The sinner's admission *to himself* is his first step toward mending his ways. Indeed, one may not bring an offering unless he has resolved to correct his ways. For the decision to repent, to do תשובה, is fundamental to an offering; the offering is merely its outward expression. Without this resolve, the offering is meaningless (see Commentary above, 1:2; 4:3). But one can come to such a decision only if he sees himself without illusions and admits the sin he has committed. So long as he deceives himself and covers up his sin, he will not succeed in purifying his heart.

6 *And he shall bring to* God *as an expression of his guilt, regarding the sin which he committed, a female from the flock, a female sheep or a female goat as an offering that clears of sin, and the priest will effect atonement for him from his sin.*

ו וְהֵבִ֣יא אֶת־אֲשָׁמ֣וֹ לַֽיהוָ֡ה עַ֣ל חַטָּאתוֹ֩ אֲשֶׁ֨ר חָטָ֜א נְקֵבָ֨ה מִן־הַצֹּ֥אן כִּשְׂבָּ֛ה אֽוֹ־שְׂעִירַ֥ת עִזִּ֖ים לְחַטָּ֑את וְכִפֶּ֥ר עָלָ֛יו הַכֹּהֵ֖ן מֵֽחַטָּאתֽוֹ׃

Rather than merely admitting in general terms that he has sinned (התודה אשר חטא), he must admit to the sin אשר חטא עליה, he must specify the matter regarding which he has sinned. Only in this way will repetition of the sin be avoided in the future.

וידוי is practiced at every חטאת אשם ועולה and is uttered at the moment of סמיכה (*Yoma* 36a). This התוודות is far removed from the non-Jewish conception of "confession to a priest"; for the whole essence of התוודות is man's admission *to himself*. He who confesses before others to sins שבין אדם למקום is called insolent, as these sins are between man and God and should be revealed before Him alone. He who truly repents of them will remain ashamed of them in the secrecy of his heart; he will not put them on display (see *Berachos* 34b; *Yoma* 86b).

ידה — the root of התודה — is related to ידע, and it is also the root of יד, hand; thus, יְדוּ (*Yirmeyahu* 50:14), וַיַּדּוּ־אֶבֶן בִּי (*Eichah* 3:53) connote the forceful throwing of an object to another person; וידוי is the bringing out of what was hidden until now in the secrecy of his heart.

6 **והביא את אשמו לה׳ וגו׳ לחטאת**, and similarly in verse 7. The term אשמו here does not refer to the name of the offering; for this offering is not an אשם, but is a חטאת in every respect. It must be, then, that אשמו here refers to the condition of the sinner before he has gained atonement for his sin. This condition is called here אשמו and חטאתו. It is called אשמו, from the standpoint of the external consequences of sin; and it is called חטאתו, from the standpoint of the sinner's inner decline. Why a קרבן חטאת is referred to here by אשמו may be explained as follows:

All three of the sins that make one liable to a קרבן עולה ויורד are close to being זדונות. שמיעת קול (v. 1) and שבועת ביטוי are not שגגות גרידה, for

ז וְאִם־לֹא תַגִּיעַ יָדוֹ דֵּי שֶׂה וְהֵבִיא
אֶת־אֲשָׁמוֹ אֲשֶׁר חָטָא שְׁתֵּי
תֹרִים אוֹ־שְׁנֵי בְנֵי־יוֹנָה לַיהוָה
אֶחָד לְחַטָּאת וְאֶחָד לְעֹלָה׃

7 *And if his means are not sufficient for a sheep, he shall bring as an expression of his sin which he has committed, two turtledoves or two young doves to* God, *one as an offering that clears of sin, and one as an ascent offering.*

ח וְהֵבִיא אֹתָם אֶל־הַכֹּהֵן וְהִקְרִיב
אֶת־אֲשֶׁר לַחַטָּאת רִאשׁוֹנָה
וּמָלַק אֶת־רֹאשׁוֹ מִמּוּל עָרְפּוֹ
וְלֹא יַבְדִּיל׃

8 *He shall bring them to the priest, and the latter shall bring near first the one intended as an offering that clears of sin; he shall nip off its head near its neck without severing it completely.*

the qualification האדם בשבועה applies to both. In the case of טומאת מקדש וקדשיו there is ידיעה בתחילה, and the העלמה of this ידיעה is a more severe sin than an ordinary שגגה (see below, Commentary to v. 13). Moreover, Scripture here enables even the very poor to offer atonement for their sin; it appears, then, that the need for atonement is greater here, from which one may infer the greater severity of these sins. This is expressed by the word אשמו: The sinner should be aware that the sin will have serious consequences for his future. When he brings his offering to God, he should bear in mind אשמו; he should bear in mind that by violating the principles implicit in these *halachos* he is bringing upon himself desolation: "א שם." See Commentary to *Bereshis* 42:21 and also below, 5:15ff. (We should note further in regard to שמיעת קול, שבועת ביטוי, and other violations of oaths that כפרת קרבן and even the punishment of judicial מלקות do not offset what was said at Sinai: כי לא ינקה ה׳ [*Shemos* 20:7]. He who violates an oath במזיד desecrates God's Name [חילל את השם], for which there is no complete atonement except by the punishment meted out by God's justice. See רמב״ם הל׳ שבועות, 12:1; כסף משנה and לחם משנה, ad loc.)

8–9 **והקריב את אשר לחטאת ראשונה**: זה בנה אב לכל חטאות שיהו קודמות לכל עולות הבאות עמהן, "This establishes a general rule that whenever חטאת and עולה are offered together, the חטאת is to be offered first" (*Pesachim* 59a). חטאת,

ט וְהִזָּ֞ה מִדַּ֤ם הַֽחַטָּאת֙ עַל־קִ֣יר
הַמִּזְבֵּ֔חַ וְהַנִּשְׁאָ֣ר בַּדָּ֔ם יִמָּצֵ֖ה אֶל־
יְס֣וֹד הַמִּזְבֵּ֑חַ חַטָּ֖את הֽוּא׃

9 *He shall sprinkle some of the blood of the offering that clears of sin upon the wall of the altar, and what remains of the blood shall be pressed out onto the base of the altar: it is an offering that clears of sin.*

which atones for a negative precept, precedes עולה, which atones for a positive precept; as first one must fulfill סור מרע, and only then is it possible to aspire to עשה טוב.

ומלק את ראשו וגו׳. (See Commentary on עולת העוף, above, 1:15.) How does מליקה at חטאת העוף differ from מליקה at עולת העוף? At עולת העוף one cuts through both of the סימנים — the windpipe and the esophagus — and separates the head from the body, whereas at חטאת העוף one cuts through only one סימן, as it says ולא יבדיל. (According to the רמב״ם [הל׳ מעשה הקרבנות, 6:23 and 7:6] the difference is only in the separation of the head from the body.) Furthermore, at an עולה, מליקה is performed בראש המזבח, and מיצוי הדם, too, is performed למעלה; at a חטאת, מליקה is performed below at the southwest corner — but it is valid in any place, and the essential עבודת הדם is not מיצוי but הזיה, sprinkling (which is a lesser form of זריקה), למטה מחוט הסיקרא. This is alluded to by the wording in verse 9: והנשאר וגו׳ יִמָּצֵה וגו׳ (not יַמְצֶה). The wording indicates that the blood is to reach the יסוד as a natural result of the הזיה. Thus, the הזיה should be performed in such a way that blood of the הזיה will reach the יסוד. One must say, then, that the הזיה should be למטה מן החוט; for if it were performed למעלה מן החוט, the blood would flow down onto the סובב and would not reach the יסוד: קיר שהשירין שלו מתמצין ליסוד (*Zevachim* 64b). Still, מיצוי should be performed after the הזיה, and it is not resolved whether מיצוי is מעכב, like הזיה, or is merely למצוה, like שפיכת שיריים. The latter possibility appears to be the correct one (see ibid. 63a, et seq.). The הזיה of חטאת העוף is to be performed at the southwest corner — בקרן דרומית מערבית; we learn this from the מנחה of דלי דלים (v. 12), which is brought instead of חטאת עוף (ibid. 63b). Only the blood of חטאת העוף reaches the altar; the rest of the bird is eaten by the כהנים, as in the case of בשר חטאת בהמה.

10 *And he shall offer the second as an ascent offering as prescribed; the priest will effect atonement for him for his sin which he has committed, and he will be forgiven.*

י וְאֶת־הַשֵּׁנִי יַעֲשֶׂה עֹלָה כַּמִּשְׁפָּט
וְכִפֶּר עָלָיו הַכֹּהֵן מֵחַטָּאתוֹ
אֲשֶׁר־חָטָא וְנִסְלַח לוֹ: ס שביעי

11 *And if his means are not sufficient for two turtledoves or two young doves, he shall bring — as an expression of coming near to* God *again, which he has squandered by his sin — one tenth of an* efah *of fine flour as an offering that clears of sin; he shall put no oil upon it and place no frankincense upon it, for it is an offering that clears of sin.*

יא וְאִם־לֹא תַשִּׂיג יָדוֹ לִשְׁתֵּי תֹרִים
אוֹ לִשְׁנֵי בְנֵי־יוֹנָה וְהֵבִיא אֶת־
קָרְבָּנוֹ אֲשֶׁר חָטָא עֲשִׂירִת הָאֵפָה
סֹלֶת לְחַטָּאת לֹא־יָשִׂים עָלֶיהָ
שֶׁמֶן וְלֹא־יִתֵּן עָלֶיהָ לְבֹנָה כִּי
חַטָּאת הִוא:

12 *He shall bring it to the priest, and the priest shall take out his*

יב וֶהֱבִיאָהּ אֶל־הַכֹּהֵן וְקָמַץ הַכֹּהֵן ׀

10 **כמשפט**. According to its plain meaning, this refers to the laws spelled out for עולת עוף (above, 1:14, et seq.). But the Sages interpreted: כמשפט חטאת בהמה (*Chullin* 21a), since the עולת עוף and חטאת עוף are brought instead of חטאת בהמה. קרבן אהרן (on *Toras Kohanim* to our verse) reasons that if Scripture were referring to the laws of עולת נדבה, it would have said כמשפטו.

11 **את קרבנו אשר חטא**. Let us compare the following sources: ואת אשר חטא מן הקדש (below, 5:16); חוֹטְאוֹ נַפְשׁוֹ (*Mishlei* 20:2); וְחוֹטֵא נַפְשֶׁךָ (*Chavakkuk* 2:10). In these verses, the object of the verb חטא is not the sin itself but the thing that was made defective by the sin: an object against which one has sinned, which one has violated by his sin. Accordingly, את קרבנו אשר חטא means: the expression of God's closeness, which he has squandered by his sin.

12 **והביאה אל הכהן**. See Commentary above, 2:2. מנחת חוטא, like all other מנחות requiring קמיצה, requires הגשה to the southwest corner prior to the קמיצה (*Menachos* 60a–b).

מִמֶּנָּה מְלוֹא קֻמְצוֹ אֶת־
אַזְכָּרָתָהּ וְהִקְטִיר הַמִּזְבֵּחָה עַל
אִשֵּׁי יְהוָה חַטָּאת הִוא׃
יג וְכִפֶּר עָלָיו הַכֹּהֵן עַל־חַטָּאתוֹ
אֲשֶׁר־חָטָא מֵאַחַת מֵאֵלֶּה וְנִסְלַח
לוֹ וְהָיְתָה לַכֹּהֵן כַּמִּנְחָה׃ ס

handful, its remembrance portion, and turn it into smoke on the altar, on the fire offerings to God; *it is an offering that clears of sin.*

13 *The priest will effect atonement for him for his sin which has committed, and he will be forgiven. And it shall belong to the priest, like the homage offering.*

---

13 **והיתה לכהן כמנחה**. The שיריים are eaten by the כהן, like those of a מנחת נדבה (above, 2:3). If the מנחה is brought by the כהן, he himself can offer it, just as he offers a מנחת נדבה. A מנחת חטאת of a כהן — like his מנחת נדבה — is burned in its entirety (כליל), without קמיצה (*Menachos* 73b; see below, 6:16).

שמיעת קול, טומאת מקדש וקדשיו, and שבועת ביטוי seem to belong to disparate categories of *mitzvos*. Yet the Torah singles them out from all the other *mitzvos* and prescribes for them a separate קרבן. It must be, then, that these three *mitzvos* are intrinsically related and form a special category of halachic concepts.

The common denominator of these three *mitzvos* is that they all relate to ידיעה שבלב, knowledge. The offender in the case of these *mitzvos* denies having certain knowledge or overlooks it. In the case of שמיעת קול he refrains from testifying about something that he knows through ראיה or ידיעה. In the case of טומאת מקדש וקדשיו he has ידיעת טומאה or ידיעת מקדש וקדשיו, and this knowledge then escapes his mind. In שבועת ביטוי לשעבר he tells a lie against the truth that is known to him. The foregoing cases represent one aspect of man's inner self: his knowledge and awareness. שבועת ביטוי להבא adds the other aspect: the exercise of his will (בחירה). We have here, then, the sum of man's inner powers — his knowledge and his will.

The חטאת section (chapter 4, above) opens with שגגת הוראה on the part of the nation's leaders — the כהן המשיח and the בית דין הגדול. The people, however, bring atonement only for actual sins committed. The חטאת section concludes with קרבן עולה ויורד. It takes us into the realm of that awareness which must be the possession of every Man of Israel. This awareness bears the seal of God, and one must guard it from all distortion. According to one view (*Horayos* 8b) — which may not be accepted as halachah (see רמב"ם הל' שגגות, 10:7) — the בית דין, כהן המשיח, and נשיא do not bring a קרבן עולה ויורד. For the values embodied by this offering are the spiritual treasure of the entire people; if the nation's leaders deny these values — even if only inadvertently — they cannot gain atonement through an offering.

Let us consider the spheres with which the sins that make one liable to a קרבן עולה ויורד are concerned. שמיעת קול concerns society — and the underlying principle of society is justice. טומאת מקדש וקדשיו concerns the Sanctuary — and the underlying principle of the Sanctuary is moral freedom. שבועת ביטוי concerns the human spirit — and the underlying principle of the human spirit is truthfulness in thought and will. These three principles are included in the concept of "truth": the truth of justice, the truth of morality, and the truth inherent in the human spirit. The obligation to be faithful to these truths does not derive from considerations of social or personal expediency. Rather, God demands that every נפש in Israel be bound by this charge — in his relationship to society, to the Sanctuary, to himself, and to God. These ידיעות turn the נפש into a Jewish personality, and he who denies them will be held accountable before God.

The offering on account of שמיעת קול confronts the man of Israel with society. It shows him that God is the Guarantor of society and of the *justice* upon which it is founded. For God obligates every individual in society to promote the welfare of all other individuals; a person should seek the welfare of his fellow man and help him by means of his knowledge and word. This is the spiritual bond that holds society together. Now, the importance of man's justice toward his fellow man reaches its zenith in the obligation to give testimony. This obligation was chosen to embody the social bond established by God. One can call upon his fellow man to offer testimony on his behalf in court, and one may do so in the Name of God — even out of court. If the person thus called upon knows of evidence and denies this knowledge in court, then even if he does not swear to this himself and does not answer "amen" to an adjurement, he has committed the sin of a false oath. He has sinned not only against his fellow man, but also against God. For it is God Who represents before him the rights of his fellow man; it is

God Who informs man's awareness of the truth of justice — which is the basis for justice among men. **The truth of *justice* in the consciousness of man derives from God.**

The offering on account of טומאת מקדש וקדשיו confronts man with God's Sanctuary. It shows him the Sanctuary and its holy things, whose basis is *moral freedom*. And it also shows him the טומאה of death, which represents physical servitude. And the offering says to man: The end of all *physical* life is death. But do not, as a consequence of this reality, deny the freedom of your *moral* life. Do not forget the freedom of your moral being, which is close to God and does not submit to the compelling force of death. For God has established for you His Sanctuary and entrusted to you its holy things. They represent God's guarantee to you of the truth of your moral consciousness. They challenge the free, moral aspect of your personality to serve God in freedom, despite your narrow physical surroundings.

Both spheres — the טומאה of physical servitude and the טהרה of moral freedom — are truths. Both were created by the one God, Who created physical nature and moral life. Only if you mingle them will you turn them into falsehood. Physically you are fettered, but morally you are free; as long as you are alive God weds within you these two forces. Your physical faculties, which are bound by the constraints of nature, He has subordinated to your free will, in order that you may serve God in the Sanctuary. Physical truths are valid only for physical existence; but your existence as a human being extends beyond the sphere of the purely physical. For God has ennobled you with the breath of life and endowed you with a share of His freedom, and in the realm of this freedom the physical laws of matter and energy have no validity. The teachings of טהרה are known to you מבית רבך. You know that only a טהור is permitted to enter the מקדש and partake of its קדשים; you learned that a person must choose between טומאה and טהרה; for טומאה blocks the way to the מקדש and bars the eating of its קדשים. Every Jewish child is familiar with this teaching, by which he first came to know that he was born to enter the Sanctuary and enjoy its blessings. This teaching that you learned in your youth — do not dismiss it as a children's fairy tale. Let ידיעת בית רבך accompany you throughout your adult life. Do not deny the truth of the Sanctuary of moral freedom; do not enter the Sanctuary or partake of its holy things while your mind is filled with impure thoughts awakened by contact with death. Sustain the consciousness that leads to distinguishing between קדושה and טומאה. **The truth of *moral freedom* in the consciousness of man derives from God.**

The offering on account of שבועת ביטוי confronts the inner self of the Jew with God. It says to him: Your whole spiritual, inner self, all your thoughts and aspirations, belong to God. Your slightest thoughts, the slightest stirrings of your will, are known to Him. He demands of you truth — in thought and will. He is aware of every thought you have expressed, every resolution you have declared. He does not want you to take lightly a thought or resolution that you have enunciated. Even in דבר הרשות — which is of no importance per se — you are *free* to call upon God as the Guarantor of your word or resolution. And if you *do* call upon Him to act as your Guarantor — even in insignificant matters which do not affect the interests of your fellow — and your word is not true, or you fail to carry out your resolution, heaven and earth will be the bearers of His judgment against you; they will requite you for every falsehood you have uttered, for every oath you have not actualized. **The truth inherent in the *human spirit*, as expressed in the thoughts and aspirations of man, derives from God.**

Justice is the basis of society; *moral freedom* is the basis of the Sanctuary; *truth* is the basis of the human spirit with its capacity for thought and will — all these *bear the seal of God, and He is their champion*: This is the basis of faith upon which Jewish life is founded. If a Jew lacks one of these, אחת מאלה (v. 5), he has been unfaithful to his destiny. If he, rich or poor, violates one of these basic principles — even if he does so out of a certain unawareness (העלם) — the Torah dictates that he recognize that he is אשם לאחת מאלה; he should recognize that by disregarding one of these principles he has reached the brink of "desolation." For everyone in Israel, from the wealthy to the very poor, is responsible for justice in society, for morality within the Sanctuary, and for truth within the human spirit. One is spared from desolation only if והתודה, he admits to himself, אשר חטא עליה: He should remind himself of the sacred, timeless principles that he violated by his actions. He should express, with an offering, his resolve to be mindful of his duty and to be faithful to it. And then, on the heights of the altar in the Sanctuary, he will regain what he has lost of God's closeness.

This offering, when brought by an individual of ordinary means, is a כשבה או שעירה לחטאת (see Commentary, 4:27ff.). A poor person brings a חטאת עוף and an עולת עוף — in place of a חטאת בהמה; and the very poor bring a מנחת חוטא.

In our discussion of עולת עוף נדבה (1:14ff.) we explained the meaning of bird-offerings, the offering procedures of עולת עוף, and the distinctiveness of חטאת עוף. Here, we should consider several other *halachos* unique to the offering procedure of חטאת עוף, and we should also consider why a חטאת עוף and an עולת עוף are brought in place of a חטאת בהמה.

תור and יונה are an offering from the standpoint of one who suffers, who does not sense God's providential care as represented by כבשה and שעירה. Thus, the offering of a poor person is a bird. In this light we explained why, in bird-offerings, the *halachos* of the עבודת הדם are reversed — relative to the corresponding *halachos* in עולת בהמה and חטאת בהמה — such that דם עולת עוף is במיצוי למעלה, while דם חטאת עוף is בהזיה למטה. The reversal of these *halachos* is related to the standpoint of the sufferer, which is represented by the bird-offering. For a person in a state of suffering will sin because of despair, loss of hope, and resultant indifference. הזיה למטה is directed against these characteristics, and suggests a reawakening of the aspiration to ascend to the heights. The sufferer's challenge in the realm of action, however, is to adhere with all his might to moral heights, and this challenge is embodied — in עולת העוף — by מיצוי למעלה. From these considerations we see at once that active sin on the part of a poor and suffering person generally stems from these two factors: He presumes that God has abandoned him and left him to his fate; hence, he, too, abandons himself and no longer has the energy and vigor to adhere to a high moral level. On the other hand, because he despairs of himself he loses all feeling of self-worth; he sinks into indifference and, falling, actively sins; he falls, because he no longer believes in advancing. Or, to employ the terminology of the offering procedures: he falls because he denies the lifestream of his personality (דם נפשו) the aspiration for ascent to the heights (הזיה למטה of חטאת); he therefore fails to adhere to moral heights and, thus, fails to meet his special challenge in the realm of action (מיצוי למעלה of עולה). This explains why a poor person brings both a חטאת עוף and an עולת עוף instead of a חטאת בהמה.

As we have already stated, the offering procedures of עולת העוף convey a profound truth: that intense *suffering*, too — if it does not lead to moral decline — constitutes an act of *avodas Hashem*; it, too, is worthy of ascending the altar לריח ניחוח לה'. Hence, there is מליקה בראש המזבח — a מליקה with complete הבדלה — followed by מיצוי, שיסוע, etc.

חטאת העוף, by contrast, does not champion *suffering*, but, rather, the aspiration to *action* in spite of suffering. Hence, it lacks the violent procedures of the עולה. מליקה is secondary and merely בסימן אחד, as it says: ולא יבדיל (v. 8). There is only הזיה, which is performed at the south-west corner (דרומית מערבית), the place designated for הגשת מנחה, at "the corner of joy before God" — אל פני המזבח and לפני ה׳ — where the spirit emanating from the מנורה-light is illumined by the Torah and turns to its study and fulfillment. This is followed by מצוי שיריים אל יסוד המזבח; for the life-pulse of the poor person who lives for God and His Torah is also joined to the base of our national life. Finally, there is אכילת הבשר לכהנים; for the life of the poor person, too, despite the leanness of its style, can be priest-like. If he lives for God and His Torah, he, too, will be privileged to eat and rejoice before God (see Commentary above, 2:8).

The חטאת הבהמה of the wealthy person, as well as the חטאת העוף and עולת העוף of the poor person, are called אשם. They represent what a person takes upon himself in order to save his future from desolation. Not so the עשירית האיפה of the very poor. For, as we explained in the section on מנחה (above, chapter 2), one who brings a מנחה brings not himself, but his possessions — with which he meets his physical needs — near to God. That is why the מנחה is not called here אשם but קרבנו אשר חטא (v. 11). For it restores to man God's closeness (קרבת ה׳), which man denied — and squandered — with his sin. The poor man, in his poverty, considers himself far removed from God's closeness. Hence, he is likely to think that he is not important in God's sight: it is not *he* who has been obligated to be responsible for justice in society, to uphold the morality of the Sanctuary, or to guard the truth of his spirit. And because he is contemptible in his own sight, he carelessly sins in one of these domains. Once he admits his sin, he should bring עשירית האיפה סולת, which is the manna-measure for the needs of one day. For even a small measure of material goods, even the means of one single day's existence, testify to God's nearness no less than does a profusion of possessions and comforts. For God is near also to the very poor and watches over them with His providence. They, too, are called upon to serve God — in society, in the Sanctuary, and in spiritual life. Even the עשירית האיפה of the poorest person, which has neither oil nor frankincense, is accepted and sanctified in a Service vessel (קידוש בכלי). It, too, is brought near to God by the כהן to the ray of light of His Torah (הגשה

בקרן דרומית מערבית). Thus, the life of even the poorest person is dedicated to the study of Torah and its fulfillment. He opens his store of resources to the claims of the Sanctuary, and the כהן removes a handful (קומץ). When this handful is delivered to the altar, the lot of the poor man, too, is remembered — along with every rich contribution that sustains the holy (אזכרתה - על אשי ה'; cf. Commentary above, 4:27–35). When, in this way, he recognizes his self-worth, the poor man, too, is privileged to rejoice in his portion — in priest-like sanctity (והיתה לכהן כמנחה).

One might have understood simply that the offering of the very poor consists only of סולת — the means of bare existence — without שמן, the symbol of prosperity, and without לבונה, the symbol of satisfaction, as this offering represents God's nearness even under circumstances of the most bare existence. Yet Scripture expressly *forbids* putting oil or frankincense on the סולת: לא ישים עליה שמן ולא יתן עליה לבונה (5:11) — with each of these constituting a separate prohibition: חייב על השמן בפני עצמו וחייב על לבונה בפני עצמה (*Menachos* 59b). Moreover, the reason given for these prohibitions is not that this is an offering of the very poor, but, rather: כי חטאת היא! (similar to מנחת סוטה, *Bemidbar* 5:15).

Apparently, then, the meaning of the prohibition is this: Had the poor man remained free of sin, he would not have felt the lack of the "oil" and of the "frankincense"; for even the poorest person can consider himself rich, and in great poverty can attain happiness. Not poverty but sin precludes oil and frankincense. Where there is sin, even a wealthy man will not attain true wealth and happiness: לא ישים עליה שמן ולא יתן עליה לבנה כי חטאת היא!

This would also explain the following halachah (*Menachos* 59b): נתן משהו שמן על גבי כזית מנחה פסל, נתן כזית לבונה על גבי משהו מנחה פסל. The prohibition of שמן is stated in terms of general שימה (לא ישים עליה שמן); thus, if one puts on the מנחה even the slightest amount of oil, משהו, he violates the prohibition. The prohibition of לבונה, however, is stated in terms of נתינה (ולא יתן), and a נתינה is no less than a כזית. With regard to the prescribed measure of the מנחה itself, the reverse is true. The word עליה suggests a quantity large enough to represent the whole מנחה — i.e., at least a כזית. In the case of לבונה, however, עליה is repeated; thus, the requirement of כזית מנחה that applies in the case of oil does not apply in the case of לבונה, and the word עליה (in the case of לבונה) is to be understood in a general sense — על משהו מנחה (in accordance with the rule: אין ריבוי אחר ריבוי אלא למעט — ibid. 60a).

14 God *spoke to Moshe, saying:* יד וַיְדַבֵּר יְהֹוָה אֶל־מֹשֶׁה לֵּאמֹר׃

15 *If a person commits a breach of trust and thoughtlessly trespasses against any of* God's *holy things,* טו נֶפֶשׁ כִּי־תִמְעֹל מַעַל וְחָטְאָה בִּשְׁגָגָה מִקָּדְשֵׁי יְהֹוָה וְהֵבִיא

The meaning of the two prohibitions is as follows: One should not put even a drop of oil on a piece of *minchah* that is large enough to be nourishing; and one should not put frankincense — in a quantity large enough to be satisfying — on even a grain of *minchah*. And the reason? כי חטאת היא, it is an offering that clears one of sin. This is the idea: It is not poverty that robs the poor of a sense of wealth and of the happiness of satisfaction. Were the poor man to remain free of sin, he would have a sense of wealth with every portion that nourishes him, and every grain would give him happiness and satisfaction. But where there is sin, all the "oil" is removed from the nourishing food and not a grain gives satisfaction.

(According to another tradition cited in *Menachos* [ibid.], whether the prohibition of putting oil on the minchah applies to even a single drop is a question that the Sages raised but did not resolve.)

14 **וידבר**. The preceding verse concludes God's Word (that begins at 4:1) regarding the חטאות. God's Word here (וידבר ה׳) begins a new category of offerings — the אשם. Three אשמות are mentioned here: אשם מעילה, אשם תלוי, and אשם גזילה — and the last is itself introduced by God's Word (below, v. 20). The sins for which these offerings are brought differ one from the other in character, yet the same offering is brought for all three sins. There must be, then, an inner connection between them. We can discern the nature of this connection only after we clarify to ourselves the basic *halachos* of these offerings.

15 **אשם מעילה: נפש כי תמעל וגו׳**. נפש includes everyone of Israel; thus the teaching: נפש – לרבות כהן משיח למעילה (*Toras Kohanim*).

כי תמעל מעל. מעל is related to מעיל, the term for the robe of the כהן גדול. Similarly, בָּגַד, to be faithless, is related to בֶּגֶד, garment. Here we have an excellent example of the harmonious logic on which the roots

אֶת־אֲשָׁמוֹ לַיהוָה אַיִל תָּמִים מִן־הַצֹּאן בְּעֶרְכְּךָ כֶּסֶף־שְׁקָלִים בְּשֶׁקֶל־הַקֹּדֶשׁ לְאָשָׁם׃

he shall bring to God, *as an expression of his guilt, one ram, whole, selected from among the flock, according to your valuation of silver shekels, according to the shekel of the Sanctuary, as a guilt offering.*

of Hebrew words are based. בגד is the garment of a human being; בגידה is a breach of trust in ordinary human affairs. מעיל is the robe worn by the כהן גדול; מעילה is a breach of trust in sacred, priestly matters. It appears, then, that one who is a בוגד behaves as a "garment," and one who is a מועל behaves as a "robe." The garment worn by an individual points to his human character. If someone puts his trust in me as a human being and I betray that trust, then I have shown myself to be merely the "outer garment" of a human being. Outwardly I have the appearance of a human being, but this is merely a mask. Similarly מועל: One would rightfully expect that a priestly spirit would move within me, but I merely wear a priestly mask.

In *Mei'lah* (18a) we learn: אין מעל אלא שינוי, וכן הוא אומר (במדבר ה:יב) איש איש כי תשטה אשתו ומעלה בו מעל, ואומר (דברי־הימים א׳ ה:כה) וימעלו באלקי אבותיהם ויזנו אחרי הבעלים. The term מעילה is used to denote the unfaithfulness of a woman to her husband and the unfaithfulness of Israel to God. Thus, מעילה means שינוי: the מועל *deviates* from the behavior that is rightfully expected of him. Similarly, as regards קדשי ה׳: the מועל treats them improperly, in a way that is contrary to what was called for, considering what they were meant to be.

מקדשי ה׳. These include two types: (a) קדשי מזבח, sacred things for the altar, i.e., things that one has dedicated to be used as offerings, such as animals or מנחות that have קדושת הגוף, that are *themselves* to be used for sacred purposes; (b) קדשי בדק הבית, things that have been dedicated for the upkeep of the Sanctuary. Such articles are not sacred in themselves, but, rather, are sacred only in their *value* to the Sanctuary's purposes; they have only קדושת דמים and are to be sold for the benefit of the Sanctuary treasury.

God's Sanctuary and its holy things are entrusted to the care of the entire nation. It is expected of all of us to treat them in a high-priestly manner, to reserve them exclusively for their destined purpose and not to use them for another purpose. If we betray this trust, we have committed מעילה, for we have not behaved in a priest-like manner.

The comparison of מעילת קדשים with מעילה of עבודה זרה and of סוטה (*Mei'lah* 18a), and the גזירה שוה with תרומה (חטא חטא מתרומה — *Mei'lah* 18b), define the sin of מעילה as (a) שינוי רשות without direct הנאה — e.g., selling the article, lending it, or giving it as a gift, and thus transferring it from the Sanctuary's possession to an ordinary party's possession (similar to the transfer from רשות הקב״ה to רשות עבודה זרה); (b) נהנה ולא פגם, using the article without diminishing its value — e.g., wearing a piece of jewelry belonging to the Sanctuary (similar to סוטה); or (c) נהנה ופגם, using the article and diminishing its value (similar to אכילת תרומה, below, 22:14).

We learn further from the גזירה שוה with תרומה that פגם ולא נהנה — i.e., causing damage to הקדש without deriving any benefit — does not constitute מעילה; for so it is also with תרומה: ואיש כי יאכל קדש פרט למזיק (see *Mei'lah* 19a; תוספות, ad loc.). We noted previously (on *Shemos* 21:35) the halachah that causing damage to הקדש is beyond the jurisdiction of any human court.

The law of נהנה ולא פגם applies to objects whose importance to the Sanctuary is not dependent on their value, so that even if one diminishes them in value they lose nothing vis-à-vis their designated purpose — e.g., an animal to be used as an offering. It also applies to objects that show depreciation in value only after a very long time — e.g., a golden cup or golden jewelry. The law of נהנה ופגם, by contrast, applies to objects the use of which normally entails depreciation. As the Mishnah says (*Me'ilah* 18a): כל דבר שיש בו פגם לא מעל עד שיפגום, ושאין בו פגם כיון שנהנה מעל.

We also learn via גזירה שוה from תרומה that just as תרומה when separated by a שליח is valid, so מעילה when committed by a שליח obligates the משלח (ibid. 18b and 20a). מעילה, then, is one of the few exceptions where יש שליח לדבר עבירה; we explained this halachah previously, in commenting on *Shemos* 21:37. Furthermore, מעילה — like תרומה — applies only to that which is תלוש מן הקרקע. Yet in other respects מעילה exceeds תרומה. For example, the obligation to pay קרן וחומש for תרומה applies only to אכילה, whereas מעילה includes every kind of הנאה.

וחטאה בשגגה. From this we learn that the law of מעילה stated here — קרבן ותשלומי קרן וחומש — applies only to the case of שוגג. In the case of הזיד במעילה the law is לוקה or משלם (see רמב״ם הל׳ מעילה, 1:3).

The limitation of this law of מעילה to the case of שוגג is reflected also in the following halachah: קדשי בדק הבית — which have only קדושת דמים and are not sacred in themselves — lose their קדושה via מעילה and become חולין (according to the רמב״ם this is true only where מעילה was committed via הוצאה מרשות הקדש, but where מעילה was committed by other means — נהנה ופגם, or נהנה alone where פגם is inapplicable — הקדש does not lose its קדושה; see משנה למלך on הל׳ מעילה, 6:4). Items having קדושת הגוף (such as בהמה וכלי שרת) — being sacred in themselves — do not lose their sanctity via מעילה; hence, it is possible to commit מעילה with them again and again. קדשי בדק הבית, however, having only קדושת דמים, are deconsecrated by one act of מעילה and are then considered חולין. Thus the halachah: אין מועל אחר מועל במוקדשין אלא בהמה וכלי שרת בלבד (*Mei'lah* 19b). Now, as we have stated, this law of מעילה applies only in the case of שוגג; thus the halachah is that הקדש בשוגג מתחלל במזיד אין מתחלל (*Kiddushin* 55a). A willful profanation of a sacred object does not rob it of its sanctity; only an inadvertent profane use of an object brings about the loss of its sanctity!

מעילה applies only to קדשי ה׳; hence, הקדש that has not *yet* been consigned exclusively לגבוה, or that has *already* been handed over to be eaten by the כהנים or בעלים, is not subject to מעילה. קדשים קלים are ממון בעלים; hence, they are subject to מעילה only after זריקת הדם, for at that time the אימורים are fit for the מזבח. Furthermore, מעילה in the case of קדשים קלים can be committed only with their אימורים after זריקה, as their בשר is handed over at once to be eaten by the כהנים and בעלים. By contrast, קדשי קדשים are ממון גבוה from the moment they are dedicated as offerings (משהוקדשו); hence, they are subject to מעילה even before זריקה. After זריקה — in the case of חטאת and אשם — מעילה applies only to their אימורים, whereas their בשר is not subject to מעילה, as יש היתר לכהנים, it is permitted to the כהנים immediately after זריקה (*Me'ilah* 7b).

Furthermore, אין לך דבר שנעשית מצותו ומועלין בו, an object whose prescribed procedure has been carried out is not subject to מעילה. The only exceptions are תרומת הדשן, בגדי כהן גדול on יום הכיפורים, and עגלה ערופה (ibid. 11a–b).

Blood that is to be applied to the altar — בהזיה, בנתינה, or בזריקה — is not subject to מעילה, for it is not *property* that has been dedicated,

16 *And he shall make restitution for that which he has trespassed against the holy things, and shall add to it one fifth and give it to the priest; the priest will effect atonement for him with the ram of the guilt offering, and he will be forgiven.*	טז וְאֵת אֲשֶׁר חָטָא מִן־הַקֹּדֶשׁ יְשַׁלֵּם וְאֶת־חֲמִישִׁתוֹ יוֹסֵף עָלָיו וְנָתַן אֹתוֹ לַכֹּהֵן וְהַכֹּהֵן יְכַפֵּר עָלָיו בְּאֵיל הָאָשָׁם וְנִסְלַח לוֹ: פ

rather, it represents the *personality* of the one who dedicates himself. In this respect it is exceptional among all the sacred objects of the Sanctuary (ibid. 11a; *Zevachim* 46a). In *Toras Kohanim* this law is derived from the letter מ in מקדשי ה׳. וכן אימעיט דם מנותר ומטומאה לאוכל בטומאת הגוף (*Zevachim* 45b).

והביא את אשמו לה׳ איל. איל is the male of the sheep, once it has reached the thirty-first day of its second year. During the first thirty days of its second year it is called פלגס and is brought neither as a כבש nor as an איל (*Parah* 1:3).

בערכך. In our opinion the ך in ערכך is the pronominal suffix of the second person: your valuation — i.e., the valuation of the nation; that is to say, the worth of the object according to national valuation. This valuation is performed by the representatives of the nation, the כהנים, for national purposes, as we find here and below, 27:12; or it is a fixed national valuation, as we find several times in chapter 27.

כסף שקלים. The ram for the אשם must be worth at least two שקלים.

לאשם. As will be explained in chapter 7, the אשם resembles the עולה as regards שחיטה and זריקה, and it resembles the חטאת as regards הקטרת אימורים and אכילת בשר לכהנים. The three אשמות discussed here (as well as אשם שפחה חרופה, below, 19:21) differ from עולה and חטאת only in this: these אשמות must consist of an איל valued minimally at two שקלים (both אשם נזיר and אשם מצורע consist of a כבש).

16 **ואת אשר חטא מן הקדש**. תשלומין applies even for פחות משוה פרוטה, whereas אשם and חומש apply only for שוה פרוטה (*Me'ilah* 18a).

17 *And a person who sins and commits one of all these acts concerning which God has commanded that they shall not be done, but he is not certain, yet he has incurred guilt and must bear his iniquity.*

יז וְאִם־נֶ֙פֶשׁ֙ כִּ֣י תֶחֱטָ֔א וְעָֽשְׂתָ֗ה
אַחַת֙ מִכָּל־מִצְוֺ֣ת יְהֹוָ֔ה אֲשֶׁ֖ר לֹ֣א
תֵעָשֶׂ֑ינָה וְלֹֽא־יָדַ֥ע וְאָשֵׁ֖ם וְנָשָׂ֥א
עֲוֺנֽוֹ׃

ואת חמישתו — the fifth that it is presently lacking. We regard the principal as though it were four fifths of the whole sum, and we add the missing fifth: שיהא הוא וחומשו חמשה (*Toras Kohanim*). This חומש is called חומש מלבר. It is not a fifth of the sum as the sum stands now (חומש מלגיו), but the fifth that lies outside it; it is the fifth that is missing, which must be supplied in order to complete the whole. A fifth מלבר is equivalent to a quarter מלגיו.

באיל האשם. The איל and the קרן — but not the חומש — are indispensable to the כפרה (as in *Bemidbar* 5:7–8; see *Bava Kamma* 111a).

Let us now summarize the *halachos* of אשם מעילה: If one forgets about the sanctity of an article (whether it be sacred in itself, or sacred in its value) and as a result removes it from the Sanctuary's possession (by sale, loan, or gift) or benefits from the article בשוה פרוטה with or without reducing its value (depending on the nature of the object), he must bring an offering of a ram worth two shekels as an אשם. He must also pay הקדש the value of this misappropriation and add to it another fifth. (ויש לעיין אי נהנה בשוה פרוטה ופגם במה שנהנה בשוה פרוטה אי משלם ב׳ פרוטות? ונראה דודאי לא משלם ב׳ פרוטות דהא פגם ולא נהנה פטור משום דאיתקיש לתרומה כי יאכל פרט למזיק ואי אפשר לחייבו לשלם מה שפגם, עי׳ מעילה יט.) An object that is sacred only in its value loses its sanctity through inadvertent misuse. Willful misuse does not deprive the object of its sanctity and does not obligate the offender to bring an offering or to pay a חומש; he is only באזהרה (see הל׳ מעילה on משנה למלך, 1:3).

17 Verses 17–19 deal with **אשם תלוי**, the offering that must be brought when a person is in doubt whether he has committed an offense that makes him liable to a חטאת. As long as he is not sure that he has com-

mitted it, he is obligated to bring an אשם, which is called אשם תלוי because of the act that remains "suspended" in doubt. In Scripture this doubt is called ולא ידע, as opposed to הודע אליו (above, 4:28) which makes one liable to a חטאת.

Even though he remains in doubt whether he has sinned, he is אשם and on the verge of "desolation"; the very state of doubt is a sin for which he is responsible. This idea is repeated at the end of the section: אשם הוא אשם אשם לה' (v. 19). Scripture underscores to us with repeated emphasis: the very fact that we are in doubt as to whether we have acted lawfully entails guilt which leads to desolation.

The way in which a case of doubt is presented in *Bemidbar* 5:14 offers an illuminating parallel to our verse. There, the two sides of the ספק (נטמאה או...לא נטמאה?) are expressed via two definite statements (והיא לא נטמאה, והיא נטמאה). Here also, the ספק (עשתה?) is expressed via a definite statement (ועשתה) — but Scripture mentions only this one side (namely, ועשתה; Scripture does not add: או...לא עשתה, but instead adds: ולא ידע). Suffice it to say that the sinner here requires atonement even if he does not know for certain that he has sinned.

In fact, ר' אליעזר is of the opinion — which is not accepted as the halachah — that מתנדב אדם אשם תלוי בכל יום ובכל עת שירצה, "One may bring an אשם תלוי as a free-will offering at any time he pleases" (*Kerisos* 25a), lest he had sinned and the sin remained unknown to him.

According to the accepted halachah, however, one may not bring a חטאת or אשם without an external, compelling cause; thus, these offerings are brought always as a חובה, an obligatory offering (see above, 4:24, Commentary on חמש חטאות המתות). To such an extent does Judaism reject all guilt-consciousness that begets melancholy! Even אשם תלוי may be brought only if preceded by a specific act that creates the doubt and that carries with it an *obligation* to offer an אשם. For example, one eats a piece of fat (in the specific case explained below) and then is in doubt whether it was שומן, which is permitted to be eaten, or חלב, which is forbidden; or one performs מלאכה during בין השמשות — when there is doubt whether it is day or night — and now does not know whether it was then שבת or חול, etc.

Morevoer, in *Kerisos* (17b) it is explained (and this view is accepted as the halachah [רמב"ם הל' שגגות, 8:2]) that חתיכה משתי חתיכות שנינו — e.g., two pieces were before him, one permitted and the other forbidden (איקבע איסורא), and he ate one of them, and then he is in doubt whether

18 *He shall bring one ram, whole, from among the flock, according to your valuation, as a guilt offering, to the priest. The priest will effect atonement for him for his act of negligence which he has committed and concerning which he is still uncertain, and he will be forgiven.*

יח וְהֵבִיא אַיִל תָּמִים מִן־הַצֹּאן
בְּעֶרְכְּךָ לְאָשָׁם אֶל־הַכֹּהֵן וְכִפֶּר
עָלָיו הַכֹּהֵן עַל שִׁגְגָתוֹ אֲשֶׁר־שָׁגָג
וְהוּא לֹא־יָדַע וְנִסְלַח לוֹ:

he ate the one or the other — only in such a case of doubt is one obligated to bring an אשם תלוי. It is not necessary, however, that (as ר׳ זירא explains there) it also be possible to resolve the doubt by examining the remaining piece (אפשר לברר איסורא). Rather, one brings an אשם תלוי even where he had eaten one of the pieces, and a non-Jew had eaten the other piece; for in such a case איקבע איסורא, even though it is not possible לברר איסורא.

In light of the above it appears that the wording of our verse is even more precise. It does not say that he did something and does not know whether it was forbidden. Rather, it says that he did something unlawful and does not know (i.e., does not know whether perhaps it was permitted). That is to say, the איסור lay before him — איקבע איסורא (or as it is often put: איתחזק איסורא) — yet, since היתר was also present, he does not know for certain whether he committed an offense. Hence, in our view, the two words ולא ידע combine to form one idea: a "not-knowing," a "not-knowing-for-certain."

18 **בערכך**. The אשם תלוי — like the אשם מעילה mentioned before it — must be valued minimally at כסף שקלים (*Kerisos* 22b).

וכפר וגו׳ אשר שגג והוא לא ידע וגו׳. The אשם תלוי atones only for uncertainty. If, afterwards, he realizes that he did sin — that he did commit an offense for whose willful violation one is liable to כרת — he must bring a חטאת as prescribed. If he resolves the uncertainty before the offering of the אשם, the אשם is not offered. But if he is still uncertain

19 *It is a guilt offering. He is surely guilty before* God.	יט אָשָׁ֖ם ה֑וּא אָשֹׁ֥ם אָשַׁ֖ם לַיהֹוָֽה׃ פ
20 God *spoke to Moshe, saying:*	כ וַיְדַבֵּ֥ר יְהֹוָ֖ה אֶל־מֹשֶׁ֥ה לֵּאמֹֽר׃
21 *If a person sins and commits a breach of trust against* God *by making a denial to his neighbor with regard to an article that was entrusted to him, or a loan, or an object taken by robbery, or he has withheld something from his neighbor.*	כא נֶ֚פֶשׁ כִּ֣י תֶחֱטָ֔א וּמָעֲלָ֥ה מַ֖עַל בַּיהֹוָ֑ה וְכִחֵ֨שׁ בַּעֲמִית֜וֹ בְּפִקָּד֗וֹן אוֹ־בִתְשׂ֤וּמֶת יָד֙ א֣וֹ בְגָזֵ֔ל א֖וֹ עָשַׁ֥ק אֶת־עֲמִיתֽוֹ׃
22 *Or he has found a lost article and denies it, and has sworn to a lie regarding anything of that which a man may do to sin in this respect.*	כב אֽוֹ־מָצָ֧א אֲבֵדָ֛ה וְכִ֥חֶשׁ בָּ֖הּ וְנִשְׁבַּ֣ע עַל־שָׁ֑קֶר עַל־אַחַ֗ת מִכֹּ֛ל אֲשֶׁר־יַעֲשֶׂ֥ה הָאָדָ֖ם לַחֲטֹ֥א בָהֵֽנָּה׃

at the time of זריקה, the offering is considered already offered בחובה and should be completed as prescribed, even if the uncertainty was resolved after זריקה (ibid. 23b).

21–22 Verses 20–26 deal with **אשם גזילה**, which is brought under the following circumstances: A person denies, under oath, a monetary claim against him and later admits that he swore falsely. In such a case he must return the object; or, if the object can no longer be returned, he must pay its value. If he had denied a debt, he must pay it. He must add an "external" fifth, i.e., a quarter of the principal (see Commentary above, v. 16) and bring an אשם גזילה.

כי תחטא ומעלה מעל בה׳. Any dishonesty in the relations between man and his fellow is considered a breach of trust against God. God is the שלישי שביניהם (*Toras Kohanim*), the unseen third party Who is present wherever one man has business dealings with another — even if no other witnesses are present. For God is the Guarantor of honesty between men. Here in our case, this Guarantor is invoked as a witness when one man makes a false denial to his neighbor. Hence, this is not just בגידה. For the offender here pledges his priestly character, his relationship to God, as surety for his honesty; and when this priestly character is exposed as a hollow mask, this is full-fledged מעילה (see Commentary above, v. 15).

וכחש. כחש is related to כעס. כעס is genuine and justified indignation at behavior that is improper. כחש, on the other hand, is artificial indignation at a justified claim — to which the defendant ascribes impropriety. Accordingly, כחש ב- means "to deny a justified claim," and, generally, "to behave in a manner that is contrary to justified expectations" — as in וּבְשָׂרִי כָּחַשׁ מִשָּׁמֶן (*Tehillim* 109:24); כִּחֵשׁ מַעֲשֵׂה־זַיִת (*Chavakkuk* 3:17). Thus, בְּנֵי־נֵכָר יְכַחֲשׁוּ־לִי (*Tehillim* 18:45) should be rendered: "I claim that they are hostile to me, but they dismiss my claim with mock indignation." In only two instances does כחש appear to denote simply deceit: לְמַעַן כַּחֵשׁ (*Zecharyah* 13:4); כִּחֵשׁ לוֹ (*Melachim* I, 13:18).

בפקדון או בתשומת יד וגו׳. תשומת יד is that which is put in the hand in order to be used — i.e., a loan (הלוואה). Examples are given here from different legal categories. פקדון and תשומת יד came into the possession of the defendant with the knowledge and will of the claimant. גזל came into the possession of the defendant with the knowledge of the claimant but against his will. עושק is a monetary claim on the property of the defendant, where the claimant is definite in his claim — e.g., withheld wages. אבידה found its way by itself into the possession of the defendant, and it is possible that the claimant is not definite in his claim. All these are cited as mere examples and include all claims that, if admitted to, obligate the defendant to a payment — i.e., claims that relate to ממון and not to קנס, inasmuch as מודה בקנס פטור (see Commentary, *Shemos* 22:3). They relate only to objects concerning which judicial oaths are taken — which excludes עבדים שטרות וקרקעות; הקדש is also excluded, as alluded to by the word עמיתו (see Commentary, ibid. 21:35).

The oath mentioned here in our verse is called שבועת הפקדון. It applies in court and out of court, whether the defendant took the oath on his own initiative or in response to the claimant's demand. Moreover, even if the claimant presses his claim by adjuring the defendant, the denial by the defendant is considered a false oath.

כג וְהָיָה כִּי־יֶחֱטָא וְאָשֵׁם וְהֵשִׁיב
אֶת־הַגְּזֵלָה אֲשֶׁר גָּזָל אוֹ אֶת־
הָעֹשֶׁק אֲשֶׁר עָשָׁק אוֹ אֶת־
הַפִּקָּדוֹן אֲשֶׁר הָפְקַד אִתּוֹ אוֹ
אֶת־הָאֲבֵדָה אֲשֶׁר מָצָא׃ מפטיר

23 *Then it shall be, if he has sinned and he recognizes his guilt, that he shall return that which he took by robbery, or that which he withheld, or that which was entrusted to him for safekeeping, or the lost article which he has found.*

The אשם וחומש mentioned here apply in cases of complete מזיד and of partial שוגג, but not in cases of complete שוגג, of שגגה גרידא — i.e., not when the oath-taker is unaware of the falseness of his words or ignorant of the prohibition of false oaths; for the qualification האדם בשבועה applies in this regard as well (see Commentary above, v. 4).

23 **והיה כי יחטא ואשם**. The completion of this law appears in *Bemidbar* 5:5ff. The case discussed there is that of גזל הגר — i.e., where the claimant, who died, was a גר and hence had no heirs. Scripture says there (v. 7): והתודו את חטאתם. From this we learn that a person does not bring the אשם or add the חומש unless he voluntarily admits his guilt. But if witnesses testify against him that he had sworn falsely, he cannot seek atonement through אשם and חומש; rather, he pays only קרן, the capital, and in the case of טוען טענת גנב בפקדון he pays כפל (see Commentary, *Shemos* 22:6–7; *Shevuos* 49a). As regards the sin of swearing falsely, the full weight of the warning לא ינקה ה׳ (*Shemos* 20:7), pronounced at Sinai, applies to him. Accordingly, we have translated ואשם (here, v. 23): "and he recognizes his guilt," and ביום אשמתו (v. 24): "on the day he admits his guilt."

והשיב את הגזלה אשר גזל. If the article is still extant in the same condition and has not been altered, he must return it as it is; if it has undergone a שינוי שאינו חוזר לברייתו, he must pay its monetary equivalent. This law is derived (*Bava Kamma* 67a) from the wording of the verse: והשיב את הגזלה מה ת״ל אשר גזל אם כעין שגזל יחזיר ואם לאו דמים בעלמא בעי שלומי. We learn further from the words אשר גזל that one pays חומש only for his own act of גזילה, but a son does not pay חומש for גזל committed by his father (ibid.).

24 *Or anything else concerning which he has sworn to a lie; he shall pay for it in capital, equivalent to its value, and shall add one fifth to it. He shall give it to the one whose rightful due it is, on the day he admits his guilt.*

כד אוֹ מִכֹּל אֲשֶׁר־יִשָּׁבַע עָלָיו
לַשֶּׁקֶר וְשִׁלַּם אֹתוֹ בְּרֹאשׁוֹ
וַחֲמִשִׁתָיו יֹסֵף עָלָיו לַאֲשֶׁר הוּא
לוֹ יִתְּנֶנּוּ בְּיוֹם אַשְׁמָתוֹ׃

25 *But as for his guilt offering, he shall bring it to* God, *a ram, whole, from among the flock, according to your valuation, as a guilt offering, to the priest.*

כה וְאֶת־אֲשָׁמוֹ יָבִיא לַיהוָה אַיִל
תָּמִים מִן־הַצֹּאן בְּעֶרְכְּךָ לְאָשָׁם
אֶל־הַכֹּהֵן׃

26 *The priest will effect atonement for him before* God, *and he will be forgiven regarding any one of all the things which he has done to incur guilt through them.*

כו וְכִפֶּר עָלָיו הַכֹּהֵן לִפְנֵי יְהוָה
וְנִסְלַח לוֹ עַל־אַחַת מִכֹּל אֲשֶׁר־
יַעֲשֶׂה לְאַשְׁמָה בָהּ׃ פפפ

24 **וחמשתיו** — in the plural; it can happen that he has to pay several fifths. For example, he repeatedly denies, under oath, the same claim (ibid. 65b); or he takes an oath that he no longer owes a fifth that he was previously obligated to pay (ibid. 103a–b).

לאשר הוא לו יתננו: הגוזל את חבירו שוה פרוטה ונשבע לו יוליכנו אחריו למדי, "He who robs his neighbor — even if only to the value of a *perutah* — and swears falsely in this regard must travel even as far as Media in order to restore it to him" (ibid. 103a). He cannot gain atonement through the **אשם** and the **חומש** unless he first sees to it that what he had taken is returned to the rightful owner himself.

25 **בערכך**. The value of this **אשם** — as in the case of the preceding two **אשמות** — must be at least two shekels.

26 **ונסלח לו**. See comments on verse 6.

The chapter opened with **שמיעת קול**, **טומאת מקדש וקדשיו**, and **שבועת**

ביטוי. These were singled out from all the other *mitzvos* and assigned a special offering — קרבן עולה ויורד; thus, they form a special group. Just as the chapter opened with three *mitzvos*, it now closes with three *mitzvos*: מעילה, ספק, and שבועת הפקדון. These, too, were singled out from all the other *mitzvos* and assigned a special offering — קרבן אשם; and just as they find their atonement through the same offering, so must they be related in their inner nature.

The common denominator of these three *mitzvos* is that the offender displays indifference about the legality of his property and actions.

If a person inadvertently commits מעילה — by using a sacred object or by transferring it to another's possession — this shows that he has not distinguished properly between the sacred and the profane in his possession; sacred and profane objects were not separated from one another. Indeed, the duty of guarding the sanctity of sacred objects should have moved him to make an exacting and careful separation.

מעילה is a thoughtless enrichment of oneself at the expense of the Sanctuary. Even if one loans a sacred object or gives it as a gift, he has enriched himself at the Sanctuary's expense; for he has used sacred property as though it were his own.

The ספק, uncertainty, that makes us liable to an אשם תלוי reveals this same attitude of indifference; for we were careless in regard to *mitzvos* that carry with them the severe penalty of כרת — and the carelessness is especially pronounced if it was a case of חתיכה אחת בין שתי חתיכות (איקבע איסורא). The very existence of the uncertainty proves that we lacked a proper measure of conscientiousness, for we failed to separate properly between the permitted and the prohibited so as to keep far from sin. We allowed the forbidden and the permitted to be placed side by side, where they were indistinguishable from each other; we performed מלאכה during בין השמשות, at the border where the forbidden and the permitted meet. This shows that we failed to fashion our lives — in time and space — in such a way that our hands not come to sin. He who falls into the ספק of אשם תלוי unwittingly enriches himself at the cost of religious infraction.

He who violates שבועת הפקדון — and becomes liable to an אשם גזילה — enriches himself at his neighbor's expense and scorns God by his action.

Now it is clear why אשם מעילה and אשם תלוי (vv. 15–19) are grouped together under one advent of God's Word (v. 14), whereas אשם גזילה (vv. 21–26) is introduced by a separate advent of God's Word (v. 20).

For the first two arise from a culpable carelessness in separating between the sacred and the profane, the permitted and the forbidden. The offender who is liable to an אשם גזילה, however, deliberately enriched himself by prohibited means. This concept of enrichment fits in with the halachah, mentioned previously, that one is liable to an אשם גזילה only if he denied under oath a claim relating to ממון; for if he had freely admitted this claim, he would have been obligated to pay. But if he denied under oath a claim relating to קנס, he is not liable to an אשם גזילה; for if he had freely admitted liability to קנס, he would have been absolved from paying. שבועת הפקדון, then, is not simply a false oath; if that were the case, it would be included in שבועת ביטוי. Rather, it is self-enrichment by means of a false oath. Similarly, we have seen that פגם ולא נהנה does not constitute מעילה.

When we compare the offenses that obligate the bringing of an עולה ויורד to the offenses that obligate the bringing of an אשם, we find common ground between the two groups. For the values that are safeguarded there in the sphere of ידיעה (see Commentary on verse 13) are the very same values safeguarded here in the sphere of רשות — i.e., the sphere of man's control or self-interest. The parallel between מעילה בקדשי ה׳ and טומאת מקדש וקדשיו is obvious, as is the parallel between שבועת הפקדון and שמיעת קול; but there is also a basic parallel between the ספק of אשם תלוי and שבועת ביטוי. Let us now elaborate:

The offering on account of טומאת מקדש וקדשיו addresses the Jew's consciousness: Man must guard the principle of the Sanctuary and its holy things, as befitting a truth pronounced by God; let him not distort this truth through false conceptions induced by טומאה. Similarly, אשם מעילה safeguards God's holy things; let them not be thoughtlessly encroached upon in the sphere entrusted to our control.

The offender in שמיעת קול commits his offense for selfish reasons. Through his offering he learns that he must put his consciousness at the service of the rights of his fellow man. Similarly, in שבועת הפקדון the offender learns through his offering that the whole sphere of man's control and self-interest is restricted by the rights of others.

The offering on account of שבועת ביטוי calls for truth in thought and deed — even in דבר הרשות, matters that do not affect anyone's interests. אשם תלוי, too, calls for clarity that leads to distinctions in time and place. This clarity is required throughout the entire range of goods and means that are vital to man's actions.

It may be said, then, that the עולה ויורד group confronts the *personality* with eternal values pronounced by God: justice, moral freedom, and truth. These are the very values safeguarded by the אשם group — in the sphere of man's *control* and *interests.*

The respective offerings, also, are in accordance with this distinction. The חטאת relates to the *personality,* which has sunk in forgetfulness and carelessness. The offering restores the personality to its position on the heights of its moral calling. The אשם, as its name implies, relates to the sphere of man's *control* and *self-interest,* which is *threatened with desolation* on account of his sin. The offering shows man the sole conditions under which he can hope to thrive and flourish in this sphere.

A man seeks to advance in the sphere of his control and interests, but thinks only of his *own* good and is indifferent to the demands of the Sanctuary or the Torah. Consequently, he fails to distinguish properly between sacred and profane, between the prohibited and the permitted. As a result, he enriches himself thoughtlessly at the expense of the Sanctuary; with total indifference he falls into a situation wherein he is likely to violate the Law in the course of serving himself or taking action; or he enriches himself with property that does not belong to him and then rejects the claim for payment by mockingly submitting (through an oath) all his property to Divine punishment.

והיה כי יחטא ואשם. Now he has strayed far from the fire of the Torah, and he finds himself on the verge of desolation. For he appropriated a *perutah* that belonged to the Sanctuary, or he robbed his neighbor of a *perutah* and in doing so scorned God, or he was indifferent toward God's commandments and left his observance of them to chance. Now he knows that such conduct undermines the very existence of all wealth. He must now approach God with an אשם, through which he expresses this awareness and undertakes to live by it.

In this offering he represents himself as an איל. We noted previously (Commentary on *Shemos* 29:1) that the איל, the ram, by virtue of its strength, leads the rest of the flock. It represents the wealthy individual endowed with possessions and power. The connection between these אשמות and the possessions of the offerer is emphasized especially by the halachah of בערכך — these offerings were assigned a minimum value of שתי כסף. Such a halachah was stipulated for no offering other than the אשם.

אשם, like חטאת and עולה, is קודש קדשים, and its שחיטה likewise is בצפון. The offering procedures of the אשם resemble in part those of the עולה and in part those of the חטאת. The עבודות הדם of the אשם resemble those of the עולה — viz., זריקת שתי מתנות שהן ארבע למטה — but הקטרת אימורים ואכילת בשר לכהנים apply, as in the case of חטאת. Although it is brought to atone for violation of negative precepts, the אשם has no מתנות חטאת on the horns of the altar — מתנות which signify adhering to lofty heights; rather, it has the זריקה of עולה, which signifies the aspiration to progress and ascend. For man's task in the realm of material possessions is to make diligent progress; indeed, the Sanctuary's symbol of the material — the שולחן עצי שיטים (see Commentary, *Shemos* 25:23) — signifies steady progress and prosperity. He who errs in the dimension represented by the איל, in aspiring to accumulate wealth and to advance his interests, will find atonement not by remaining static and holding his position, but by making ardent progress — progress marked also by ascent to the heights of his moral mission. Hence, the blood of the איל אשם is dashed (בזריקה) like the blood of the עולה. But precisely for this reason הקטרת אימורים and אכילת בשר לכהנים apply to the אשם, as to the חטאת. For the sinner should take the following to heart: If his material advancement is also a moral ascent to the heights of the altar, then his חלב and כליות — his material aims and aspirations — will become לחם אשה לריח ניחוח לה'; they, too, will be worthy of increasing holiness and pleasing God, on earth. Even his own enjoyment of the fruit of his labors to attain prosperity will be a form of serving God in priestlike sanctity — as reflected by אכילת בשר איל האשם לכהנים.

A person commits מעילה בהקדש; there is doubt whether, in the sphere of his possessions and activities, he has acted lawfully; he even scorns God and retains what does not belong to him. He thereby demonstrates that his material interests are at odds with the ideal possessions of the Sanctuary; with the practical realization of the Torah; with social justice, which was pronounced by God and which derives from the equality between man and his fellow man (עמיתו — see Commentary below, 19:15 and 17). In this way he will not succeed in protecting his material interests. On the contrary, by turning his back on the Torah's requirements, by divorcing material aspirations from moral values, he has brought only "desolation" to his material world. The success of his material aspirations depends on their subordination to moral ideals.

Therefore, he must now approach the Sanctuary as an איל שוה שתי כסף. As an איל שוה שתי כסף he must surrender himself בצפון, the side of the material (שחיטה), to be received into the sphere of the Sanctuary (קבלה). The Sanctuary will direct him to ascend and progress like an איל שוה שתי כסף; his חלב וכליות will be offered upon the altar, and his בשר will be eaten by the כהנים in the Sanctuary. From this he will learn the following: Even an איל שוה שתי כסף, a man of wealth in pursuit of wealth, must stand within the Sanctuary. His material advancement should be strictly a moral ascent to the heights of the altar. His material aims and aspirations should be offered on the altar of doing God's Will. His enjoyment of the fruit of his material labors should itself be a form of serving God in priestlike sanctity. Only then will his material interests be spared from desolation, and God's blessing will rest upon his works.

In the case of אשם מעילה and אשם גזילה, payment of the קרן (full restitution) must precede the offering of the אשם. Another obligation related to כפרה is that one must add a fifth to the קרן and pay this sum to the Sanctuary or to the person who was robbed (in the event of his death one must pay his heirs). Payment of such an additional fifth is found also in the cases of זר שאכל תרומה (below, 22:14) and redemption of מעשר שני or הקדש by the בעלים (below, 27:13, 27, and 31). All of these five cases have this in common: We impinged upon a sacred domain (even the possessions of our neighbor are termed sacred, once we have sworn or been adjured in God's Name). We increased our assets at the expense of הקדש. We repaid the principal. Now, the חומש reminds us that instead of impinging upon הקדש or upon our fellow men, we should have increased their assets and even given them of our own. Redemption of הקדש by the בעלים also resembles such impingement. For he who restores to himself an article that he had consecrated is likely to form the mistaken impression that הקדש, to which he had consecrated the article, is undeserving of the article. When we are allowed to redeem the article and restore it to our possession, we must counter any thought that would undermine the prestige of הקדש; toward this end we add a חומש.

Perhaps we should view the חומש as a double tenth. This may explain the phenomenon of חומש מלבר, which is actually a quarter. The idea that all our possessions are pledged toward the *realization* of the concepts represented by the Sanctuary is generally expressed by our giving up one tenth. The dedication of this tenth signifies that we do not use any "ten" — i.e., any complete sum — without first having *furthered* the aims of the Sanctuary. So it is with מעשר ראשון, מעשר שני, מעשר עני, מעשר בהמה. We do not call nine our own unless, corresponding to them, we have given one to הקדש (cf. Commentary, *Bereshis* 14:20). Here, in our case, one atones for *impinging* on the domain of הקדש; hence, the expression of our *commitment* to הקדש is doubled. We do not call eight our own unless, corresponding to them, we have given two to הקדש — and this amounts to חומש מלבר. The idea expressed here is this: Not only must we refrain from misappropriating property of the Sanctuary or of our neighbors so as to gain at their expense, but on the contrary, even were this sum ours by right, we would not call it our own unless we had first given them something of our own.

Let us now consider two characteristic and interrelated *halachos*: First, inadvertent misappropriation of a sacred object profanes it, whereas willful misappropriation does not, but allows the object to retain its sanctity: הקדש בשוגג מתחלל במזיד אינו מתחלל (see *Kiddushin* 55a). Second, Scripture treats the case of ספק more severely than it does the case of ודאי: אשם תלוי, which is brought to atone for a questionable transgression, is assigned a minimum value of שתי כסף, whereas חטאת, which atones for a definite transgression, is not assigned a value (*Toras Kohanim* on v. 17; *Zevachim* 48a).

The Sanctuary does not fear transgression — it fears indifference! That is the thought expressed by the halachah that הקדש בשוגג מתחלל במזיד אינו מתחלל. For the Sanctuary is exalted far above the designs of transgressors, and they will never be able to detract from its sanctity. Indeed, their very opposition to the Sanctuary testifies to its sanctity. But שגגה that comes as a result of indifference, שגגה that is thoughtless inattentiveness to the sanctity of the Sanctuary and to its rightful claims upon our conduct — these are the things that undermine the sanctity of the Sanctuary. For only the consciousness of those who recognize the Sanctuary will give it mastery and reign in all walks of life.

Similarly, in the observance of the *mitzvos*, the uncertainty that perhaps a transgression was committed is more serious than the certainty of it. How extreme is the indifference of a person who confuses objects, persons, and times — without the slightest consideration of the Halachah's requirements — to the point that a situation can arise that leads to a ספק of אשם תלוי (*Kerisos* 17a–b).

According to the overwhelming majority of our Masters, ספק

6 1 God *spoke to Moshe, saying:* | ו א וַיְדַבֵּר יְהוָה אֶל־מֹשֶׁה לֵּאמֹר׃

מדאורייתא מדאורייתא לחומרא; that is to say, not only a ספק that obligates one to bring an אשם תלוי (e.g., ספק חתיכה משתי חתיכות where איקבע איסורא), but also other ספקות (e.g., חתיכה אחת ספק חלב ספק שומן) are forbidden by Torah law. According to the רמב״ם (see הל׳ טומאת מת, 9:12), however, a ספק that does not obligate one to an אשם תלוי (לא איתחזק איסורא) is not forbidden by Torah law, and we treat it stringently only by Rabbinic law (מדרבנן לחומרא). But according to this opinion, too, the obligation to keep far from any possibility of transgression — i.e., even from a case of doubt — is part of the precept of ובכל אשר אמרתי אליכם תשמרו (*Shemos* 23:13; see Commentary, ad loc.). For the Torah has entrusted to us its precepts and charged us to be conscientious about observing them. The Torah expects us to watch our step and "to place a fence around the Law." Indeed, this is what we learn from the section on אשם תלוי: If we are careless and haphazard about our actions — so that doubt arises whether we have acted lawfully — then we already "bear sin" and threaten the whole sphere of our endeavor with "desolation." From this we infer the duty to be conscientious, to carefully consider all our actions, so that we keep far from transgression and from everything that might lead to it. This duty derives from the gravity of the *mitzvos*, as well as from concern for our own well-being. The duty of conscientiousness is perhaps expressed in the words of Elifaz: וְיָדַעְתָּ כִּי־שָׁלוֹם אָהֳלֶךָ וּפָקַדְתָּ נָוְךָ וְלֹא תֶחֱטָא, "If you wish to know that all is well in your home, then be attentive to your household so that you not come to sin" (*Iyov* 5:24).

צו

CHAPTER 6

1 The preceding *parashah* (chapters 1–5) describes the various kinds of offerings (קרבנות נדבה [free-will offerings], namely עולה, מנחה, and שלמים; and קרבנות חובה [obligatory offerings] that atone for sin, viz., חטאת and אשם) and explains various *halachos* of the offerings. Knowledge of these *halachos* is vital also to the בעלים, who seek to draw closer to God through these offerings.

2 *Command Aharon and his sons as follows: This is the teaching with regard to the ascent offering: It is an ascent offering upon the place where the offerings are burned upon the altar throughout the night until the morning, when the altar fire shall be rekindled upon it.*	ב צַו אֶת־אַהֲרֹן֙ וְאֶת־בָּנָ֣יו לֵאמֹ֔ר זֹ֥את תּוֹרַ֖ת הָעֹלָ֑ה הִ֣וא הָעֹלָ֡ה עַל֩ מוֹקְדָ֨ה עַל־הַמִּזְבֵּ֤חַ כָּל־הַלַּ֙יְלָה֙ עַד־הַבֹּ֔קֶר וְאֵ֥שׁ הַמִּזְבֵּ֖חַ תּ֥וּקַד בּֽוֹ׃ מ"ם זעירא

The *halachos* explained in the next two chapters complement those of the preceding chapters, but concern primarily the כהנים, who are charged with offering the קרבנות. Hence, these *halachos* are addressed especially to אהרן ובניו. Accordingly, the order of the offerings is changed: They are not arranged according to the motive for bringing them — חובה or נדבה — but according to the degree of their sanctity: קדשי קדשים or קדשים קלים. Thus, עולה, מנחה, חטאת, and אשם are treated first, followed by שלמים.

2 **זאת תורת העלה**. This supplement to the laws of the offerings — which is addressed especially to the כהנים — begins with the laws pertaining to the *night*, which is the time when the Sanctuary is entrusted exclusively to the כהנים and closed to the rest of the nation.

The laws of the offerings conclude (below, 7:37–38) with the words **זאת התורה לעלה למנחה וגו׳ אשר צוה ה׳ את משה בהר סיני ביום צותו את בני ישראל להקריב את קרבניהם לה׳ במדבר סיני**. This sentence emphasizes the *place* where Israel offered their first offerings; the Halachah emphasizes also the *time* when Israel received the mitzvah of the offerings. It was **יום צותו** — it was "day" when they received this command. Similarly, we find that the Torah distinguishes between the prophecy of Moshe, who received the Torah, and the prophecy of all the other prophets of Israel: **פה אל פה אדבר בו ומראה ולא בחידת** (*Bemidbar* 12:8). For God did not speak to Moshe through the twilight of a dream; not **בחלום אדבר בו** (ibid. 12:6). Rather, the Word of God that came to Moshe reached the lucid intellect of an aware individual. Moshe, too, relayed God's Word to the clear minds of aware individuals. Similarly — says the Halachah — with a clear mind and with full awareness should a person bring near his offering to God; with clear thought and from free choice should he dedicate himself to fulfilling the Torah. אשר צוה ה׳ את משה בהר סיני ביום צותו – למדנו לכל הקרבנות שאין כשרים אלא ביום (*Toras Kohanim*, below, 7:38; see *Megillah* 20b–21a). All הקרבה — all drawing closer to God through an offering — is fit only by day (see רש״י, *Megillah* loc. cit.).

Night, לילה, is the time when things are "commingled" (see Commentary, *Bereshis* 1:5), when man, too, reverts to the bondage of physical forces. Hence, the night brings heathen man close to his gods; at night he senses their power, as he is held in their sway along with all the other creatures. During the day — יום — however, man walks upright (יום is related to קום — see Commentary ibid.). He becomes aware of *himself*, and he struggles to subdue the world. Hence, to the heathen mind, the day is the time of man's struggle with the gods.

The Jewish perception is the antithesis of the heathen perception. Not in the resignation of night does the Jew sense God's power. Rather, in clarity of thought, in creative action that conquers worlds, in the upright posture of daytime endeavor — precisely in these does he attain closeness to God. The light of his clear intellect, the force of his free will, the creativity of his endeavors — indeed, the whole of his free personality standing tall throughout the day — all these were given to him by the grace of the Creator. For the one God has granted man a share of the infinite outpouring of His Intellect, a share of His holy free Will, a share of His creative Power which dominates the world. Thus God has raised man beyond the bonds of the physical world, set him upright, and made him master of the world — in order that he serve God in it. In the very carrying out of a day's work, a man fulfills the Will of God.

In the heathen perception, the day is a struggle of mortals against the power of the gods. To the Jew, day means serving God, and through his work he brings God satisfaction. Hence, in the Sanctuary אין היום הולך אחר הלילה, rather, הלילה הולך אחר היום; day does not follow night, rather, night follows day. For the night, which symbolizes the stillness of death, cannot drag the day down after it; rather, the day, which symbolizes a life of closeness to God, raises with it the night.

Physical nature is not the intermediary between the Jew and his God. For the man of Israel stands above physical nature; he stands directly before God. It was במדבר, in the wilderness — where a person has nothing and no one but himself — that God drew near to Israel and established with them the covenant of His Torah. It was there, במדבר — where a person has nothing to offer to God except himself, his own personality — that God commanded Israel to make offerings to Him. It is the unfettered personality — the one who subordinates his thought, will, and action, to God — who is bound by the Torah and from whom offerings are expected: זאת התורה לעלה למנחה ולחטאת ולאשם ולמלואים ולזבח השלמים, אשר צוה ה׳ את משה בהר סיני ביום צותו את בני ישראל להקריב את קרבניהם לה׳ במדבר סיני [below, 7:37-38].

"ביום צותו" — "the offering at the time of the command" — this is the abbreviation of the principle that limits all הקרבות of offerings to the daytime. The idea reflected by this principle appears also in other *halachos* of the offerings and is deeply connected with the antithesis of טומאה and מקדש.

An exception to this principle is established here by the words היא העלה על מוקדה על המזבח כל הלילה. Let us elaborate:

סמיכה, שחיטה, תנופה, הגשה, קמיצה, הקטרת קומץ (קמיצה corresponds to שחיטה, זריקה to הקטרת קומץ; see Commentary above, 2:2), מליקה, קבלה, זריקה, and הזיה all are fit only during the day (in several cases this is specially alluded to by Scripture). The common denominator of all these procedures is that they renew the relationship between the offerer — or certain aspects of his personality — and God and His Torah. They all are הקרבות — in the wider sense of this term; hence, they all are fit only during the day.

Our verse, however, says: היא העלה על מוקדה על המזבח כל הלילה. From this we learn that איברים (the parts) of עולה, and חלבים (the kidneys and fat) of חטאת, אשם, and שלמים — all of which are included in the concept of עלה על מוקדה — are burned upon the altar כל הלילה עד הבוקר, all night until daybreak; and that if פקעו, if they slip off the altar fire, they are placed back upon the fire all night. For the כפרה has been completed already by the הקרבות; all that remains is to draw the proper conclusions from these הקרבות. Hence, these procedures (הקטרת חלבים ואיברים and החזרת איברים שפקעו) are fit also at night.

For the night dimension of human life is not distant from God; the dimension of day is not the only dimension related to God. לְךָ יוֹם אַף־לְךָ לָיְלָה (*Tehillim* 74:16) — both day *and night* are His. Just as He forms light, יוֹצֵר אוֹר, so He creates darkness, בּוֹרֵא חֹשֶׁךְ (*Yeshayahu* 45:7).

The Torah rejects only the reverse idea: that the dimension of night alone turns to God, and only in it can one seek God. יום, the time when man rises up, when he creates and acts and thinks and wills with freedom and independence — *that* is the foremost time for serving God. In the dimension of day, one must again seek God; in that dimension — as a first and foremost condition — one must again seek to draw near to God.

But when independent man, who walks upright, *has* found God again; when, through שחיטה קבלה וזריקה ביום, he has already surrendered to the Sanctuary his whole personality and all his might, then the sanctification of the day dimension of his personality includes within God's covenant the night dimension as well — הלילה הולך אחר היום — and the sun never sets for earthly man who remains close to God in the deep of the night. For the נפש has already waged its struggle during the "day" and succeeded in ascending and drawing closer to God. Henceforth, the חלבים ואיברים — the "aims and aspirations" and the "deeds" (see Commentary above, 1:8; 3:9) — will fuel God's fire at night as well, and will bring satisfaction to Him.

The same applies to offerings upon the fire that do not represent the consequence of closeness to God already attained, but, rather, themselves represent drawing close to God — e.g., הקומץ והלבונה והקטורת ומנחת כהנים ומנחת כהן משוח ומנחת נסכים (*Menachos* 26b). All these are things that are to be offered during the day, yet מעלן ומקטירן עם בא השמש ומתעכלין והולכין כל הלילה, they may be offered up and burned just before sunset and gradually be consumed by the fire throughout the night (ibid.). This is alluded to in the general introductory statement: זאת תורת העלה, from which we learn that whatever goes up onto the altar may stay there throughout the night.

Inclusion of the night within the day's sphere of influence is characteristic of all the procedures performed in the Sanctuary. This accounts for the following halachah, which applies to all that is given over to the fire and burned during the night, as a consequence of the preceding day: If it tarries off the altar until the break of a new Sanctuary day, it is disqualified from the altar fire: כל שלן חוץ למזבח פסול בלינה.

Perhaps this is the significance of the small מ in the word מוקדה. This מ reflects the diminutive role of the place, the altar hearth during the night. For the night is dependent on the preceding day; what takes place atop מוקדה merely completes what has already taken place on the base and on the sides.

There is another halachah implicit in the words היא העלה על מוקדה על המזבח כל הלילה — namely, the rule that once an offering has been placed on the altar, it is not to be taken down. The word היא alludes to

3 *The priest shall put on his linen garments and his linen breeches* ג וְלָבַ֨שׁ הַכֹּהֵ֜ן מִדּ֣וֹ בַ֗ד וּמִֽכְנְסֵי־בַד֮

the regular עולה discussed in the preceding chapters; this rule, then, applies to a regular עולה that has been offered as prescribed. The general heading זאת תורת העלה, however, extends the application of this rule to anything that can be included in the concept of עולה. Thus the halachah: המזבח מקדש הראוי לו, i.e., כל הראוי לאישים אם עלה לא ירד. That is to say, anything that was once destined for the altar fire (ראוי לאישים) — even if afterwards it becomes פסול and unfit to be offered — if placed on the altar is not to be taken down. (Only one condition is attached to this halachah: it must be a case of פסולו בקדש; but in cases of פסולים where לא היו פסולן בקדש — e.g., הרובע והנרבע והמוקצה והנעבד, etc. — אין הקודש מקבלן, i.e., אפילו עלו ירדו [*Zevachim* 83a, 84a].) Indeed, the role of the Sanctuary is to sanctify all aspects of human existence; we have already explained this matter in our Commentary to *Shemos* 29:37.

At sunset the *avodah* of the altar was closed, and new offerings were no longer accepted upon it. But the fire kept burning on the altar כל הלילה, throughout the night, to complete the *avodah* of the offerings of the day. These offerings fueled God's fire עד הבקר, until the morning, and then ואש המזבח תוקד בו, the altar fire was to be kindled afresh for the *avodah* of the new day.

Previously, we mentioned the mitzvah of kindling the altar fire and maintaining it, and we explained the detailed *halachos* of this mitzvah and what it signifies (see Commentary above, 1:7). There were three מערכות (fires): (a) The מערכה גדולה — here called מוקדה — was the main fire of the altar. On this fire the offerings were accepted as fuel for the אש דת, "the fire of the Torah," to be ריח ניחוח לה׳. (b) אש המזבח, viz., the מערכה שניה של קטורת, was arranged at the southwest corner. From this fire, glowing coals were taken for the קטורת of the inner altar (see Commentary to v. 6). (c) The מערכה של קיום האש expressed the idea that the altar fire must be kept continually burning and must never be allowed to go out: והאש על המזבח תוקד בו לא תכבה (below, v. 5; see *Yoma* 45a).

3 But before the arranging of the pyre and the kindling of the altar fire, the mitzvah of תרומת הדשן is performed. The purpose of תרומת הדשן is

on his body, and shall take up the ashes into which the fire has consumed the ascent offering upon the altar, and shall lay them down at the side of the altar.	יִלְבַּשׁ עַל־בְּשָׂרוֹ וְהֵרִים אֶת־הַדֶּשֶׁן אֲשֶׁר תֹּאכַל הָאֵשׁ אֶת־הָעֹלָה עַל־הַמִּזְבֵּחַ וְשָׂמוֹ אֵצֶל הַמִּזְבֵּחַ׃

not to prepare the altar for the *avodah* of the day *that is to begin*; that is the role of הוצאת הדשן (v. 4). Rather, תרומת הדשן concludes the *avodah* of the day *that has passed*. תרומת הדשן, in itself, is an *avodah*, and may be performed only by a כהן כשר wearing priestly garments.

Just as Scripture says of the מנחה (v. 8): והרים ממנו בקמצו, so it says here: והרים את הדשן. For the כהן is to lift a whole קומץ out of the ashes of yesterday's offering-fire, ושמו אצל המזבח, and lay it down beside the altar — on the east side, next to the ramp — ושמו בנחת ושמו כולו ושמו שלא יפזר (see *Yoma* 23b–24a; *Tamid* 28b; *Temurah* 34a). Just as the קומץ of the מנחה serves as אזכרה for the entire מנחה, so does the קומץ of תרומת הדשן serve as remembrance of the offerings made yesterday to God and His Torah. The ashes are placed במזרח, the side of the entrance for the people, the side that represents the nation. The ashes remind the nation — at the transition to the *avodah* of the day that is about to begin — that the new day does not bring new tasks. For the task that is incumbent upon us today is the same task that was incumbent upon us yesterday. The most recent Jewish grandchild stands in the place where his first ancestors already stood, and each new day adds its contribution to the fulfillment of the one task assigned to all generations of the House of Israel. Each day receives its mission from the hand of the previous day.

This relation between תרומת הדשן and קומץ המנחה explains the entreaty expressed in *Tehillim* (20:4): יִזְכֹּר כָּל־מִנְחֹתֶךָ וְעוֹלָתְךָ יְדַשְּׁנֶה סֶלָה, "May He accept the אזכרה of all your מנחות and the תרומת הדשן (that is the literal meaning of דשן) of your עולה." That is to say, may the remembrance of all your acts of homage and your ascent toward God remain ever before Him.

Thus, תרומת הדשן forever calls to mind the days gone by that were dedicated to God. This explains the exception of תרומת הדשן from the rule that כל היכא דנעשית מצותו אין בו משום מעילה, an object whose prescribed procedure has been carried out is not subject to מעילה. The דשן — even after it has been taken up and deposited as prescribed — remains קדוש and is subject to מעילה (*Pesachim* 26a; see Commentary above, 5:15, et seq.). For, in a deeper sense, the purpose of lifting out the ashes is not completed by depositing them. They serve to recall the past throughout the future, and this sustains their קדושה forever.

מדו בד. מדו refers to the כתונת, the robe that covers the whole body down to the feet (see *Yoma* 23b). Here, this robe is called מדו — to teach us that it must be כמידתו, "made to measure," neither too short nor too long. Its purpose is to cover the body, not to add external dignity. That is why it may not be too short, but also not too long. A trailing train would give it a different meaning. בד — see Commentary to *Shemos* 28:43.

ילבש על בשרו: שלא יהא דבר חוצץ בינו לבשרו (*Zevachim* 19a). The significance of the priestly garments is not outward, for the eyes of others, but inward, for the consciousness of the כהן himself. When he puts on his robe, he is to wrap himself in the purity of the holy (see Commentary to *Shemos* 28:43). Only מכנסים and כתונת are mentioned here, but all the priestly garments are required, including אבנט and מגבעת (see *Yoma* 23b).

The continuity of verses 2 and 3 proves that הקטרת אברים and תרומת הדשן are valid throughout the night. The new מערכה (v. 5), on the other hand, is arranged only in the morning. Yet the Gemara says that the first half of the night is for הקטרה, and the second half is for הרמה. Thus the triple halachah: (a) איברים שיש בהם ממש, parts that have not been consumed by the fire, that have substance and have fallen out of the fire, must be returned to the fire even after midnight. (b) Parts that have already become charcoal need not be returned even before midnight. (c) שרירין, parts that have been hardened completely by the fire but have not yet become charcoal, חצות עושה בהם עיכול: before midnight they must be returned to the fire, but after midnight we regard them as though their mitzvah had been fulfilled, and they need not be returned to the fire; hence, אין מועלין בהם, in accordance with the law of כל דבר שנעשה מצותו (*Zevachim* 86; *Yoma* 20a).

Usually תרומת הדשן was performed at the time of קריאת הגבר or near to it, whether before or after it (ibid.). The term קריאת הגבר can refer to the call of the rooster, but here it refers to the call of the herald, who cries: עמדו כהנים לעבודתכם ולוים לדוכנכם וישראל למעמדכם (ibid. 20b). On יום הכיפורים the תרומת הדשן was performed from midnight, and on the רגלים

4 *He shall then take off his garments and clothe himself in other garments and take the ashes out of the camp to a pure place.*	ד וּפָשַׁט אֶת־בְּגָדָיו וְלָבַשׁ בְּגָדִים אֲחֵרִים וְהוֹצִיא אֶת־הַדֶּשֶׁן אֶל־מִחוּץ לַמַּחֲנֶה אֶל־מָקוֹם טָהוֹר׃

from the first watch of the night; and before קריאת הגבר on רגלים the עזרה would already be full of Israelites who had come with their offerings (ibid. 20a).

4 **בגדים אחרים**: these, too, are בגדי כהונה, but they are פחותים, inferior to the בגדי הרמה, which themselves could be — perhaps should be — שחקים, older and more worn-out than the priestly garments worn throughout the day (see ibid. 23b; 12b; לחם משנה and משנה למלך on הל' תמידין ומוספין, 2:10).

The הוצאת הדשן prescribed here clears the altar of the remains of the previous day's offerings, thus preparing it for the *avodah* of the new day (the previous day's offering parts that were not consumed by the fire were laid at the side of the מערכה גדולה). Apparently, הוצאת הדשן, too, is an *avodah* (see משנה למלך, ibid.).

תרומת הדשן begins the *avodah* of the new day by recalling the *avodah* of the previous day. הוצאת הדשן, on the other hand, signifies that, at the same time, the Jewish nation must begin its task anew each day. The start of every new day summons us to set out upon our task with full and fresh devotion as though we had never accomplished anything before. The memory of yesterday's accomplishments must not inhibit today's performance. Thoughts of what has already been accomplished are likely to choke off all initiative for new accomplishments. Woe to him who is smug with satisfaction over his past achievements, who does not begin the work of each new day as though it were the very first day of his life's work!

והוציא את הדשן. Every trace of yesterday's devotion must be removed from the altar, so that the new day's *avodah* can begin on an entirely new basis. This explains the halachah that the כהנים must wear humble, worn garb when occupied with yesterday's *avodah* — i.e., when per-

5 *And the altar fire shall be kindled upon it; it must not go out. Early in the morning the priest shall lay upon it [logs of] wood to burn [there]; he shall arrange the ascent offering upon it and shall offer up in smoke upon it the fat parts of the peace offering.*	ה וְהָאֵ֨שׁ עַל־הַמִּזְבֵּ֤חַ תּֽוּקַד־בּוֹ֙ לֹ֣א תִכְבֶּ֔ה וּבִעֵ֨ר עָלֶ֧יהָ הַכֹּהֵ֛ן עֵצִ֖ים בַּבֹּ֣קֶר בַּבֹּ֑קֶר וְעָרַ֤ךְ עָלֶ֙יהָ֙ הָֽעֹלָ֔ה וְהִקְטִ֥יר עָלֶ֖יהָ חֶלְבֵ֥י הַשְּׁלָמִֽים׃

forming הוצאה and apparently also הרמה. We should not pride ourselves in past accomplishments. The past must give way to the new task, to which every new day summons us.

The פוסקים differ as to whether הוצאת הדשן to a place outside the city must be performed every day. Every day the ash was removed from the hearth to the center of the altar and heaped up into an ash pile, called תפוח. From there the ash was taken outside the city (according to one opinion this was done only if the תפוח had grown too large — see משנה למלך ibid., 2:13). At times there were כשלוש מאות כור (2520 cubic feet) of ashes on the תפוח, and on the רגלים they would not clear away the ash because it was considered נוי למזבח (*Tamid* 28b).

According to the רמב״ם (הל׳ תמידין ומוספין, 2:15) the ash removed to a place outside the city has the same law as the ash taken up at תרומת הדשן: it, too, has to be carefully deposited so that it will not scatter, and it is subject to מעילה. (In *Jeschurun*,* vol. 1, p. 549, a report is filed of ash heaps recently discovered outside Yerushalayim. Analysis of the ash has revealed that it is of animal origin. Most probably this is the שפך הדשן mentioned in Scripture. It brings to us — after thousands of years — a remembrance of the offerings of our ancestors!)

אל מחוץ למחנה אל מקום טהור. See Commentary above, 4:11–12.

5 **והאש על המזבח תוקד בו** — see Commentary to verse 2. **ובער עליה הכהן** — see Commentary above, 1:7. **בבקר בבקר** intensifies the concept of morning — i.e., very early in the morning (see *Yoma* 33a).

---

*A monthly journal (1854–1870), edited by Rav Hirsch. (Ed.)

'ויערך עליה העלה וגו. We have already explained above (1:7) the meaning of the fire flaming atop the altar. It motions to us to "fuel the אש דת" — i.e., to carry out the Torah — in all phases of life, as individuals and as a nation. Fulfillment of this duty is represented daily by the עולת התמיד, the obligatory national offering, which was made incumbent upon us from the very beginning (see Commentary to *Shemos* 29:38–39). The bringing of the עולת התמיד was the culmination and objective of the building of the Dwelling Place and the sanctification of the altar and the כהנים. Accordingly, it is with this offering that we are to begin the daily Service of the offerings. The עולת התמיד is העולה ("*the* עולה"), the עולה *par excellence*. Hence, our Sages say (*Pesachim* 58b): מנין שלא יהא דבר קודם לתמיד של שחר תלמוד לומר וערך עליה העולה, מאי תלמודא אמר רבא העולה עולה ראשונה. In our view the עולת התמיד is called ראשונה on account of the verse (in *Shemos*) cited above — as we were commanded in regard to the עולת התמיד before all the offerings. (Perhaps רש״י's comment [ibid.] — which at first glance appears difficult — should also be interpreted in this way.)

Now it does not say והקטיר עליה העולה — as it says immediately afterwards והקטיר עליה חלבי השלמים — but, rather, 'וערך עליה העלה והקטיר וגו. From this we infer that as the מערכה (וערכו עצים על האש — above, 1:7) forms a base for the תמיד, so, too, the תמיד forms a base for all the offerings that follow it. For the pronoun in the phrase והקטיר עליה refers back to the preceding word העלה. Our Sages (*Pesachim* 58b) say as follows: ומנין שאין דבר קרב אחר תמיד של בין הערבים ת״ל והקטיר עליה חלבי השלמים. That is to say, the morning daily offering is arranged on the fire, and all the other offerings — even חלבי השלמים — are burned upon the morning daily offering. Thus, the Service of the offerings of each day concludes with the afternoon daily offering, after which no other offering may be brought: עליה שלמים ולא על חבירתה שלמים; or as רבא expounds, taking the word השלמים in the sense of השלם: עליה השלם כל הקרבנות (ibid.).

The תמיד offering, then, begins and concludes the Service of the altar, and all the other offerings — even שלמים of the individual — fit in between the two תמידים. Thus, the whole Service of the altar may be regarded as one continuous national offering that lasts the whole day. עולת תמיד של ציבור represents unceasing consecration of the nation's actions. It is the element with which everything begins and ends, and upon which all other aspects of national and private life depend. עולת

6 *A fire is to be kept continually burning on the altar, where it must never go out.*	ו אֵ֗שׁ תָּמִ֛יד תּוּקַ֥ד עַל־הַמִּזְבֵּ֖חַ לֹ֥א תִכְבֶּֽה׃ ס

תמיד של ציבור expresses the meaning of every Jewish day: to continuously ascend to the height of the Torah ideal with all the powers and talents inherent in the nation. In this way satisfaction will be brought to God, and God's Presence will dwell on earth. And in the achievement of this goal, every individual Jew's joyful dedication finds its national significance. Consecration of the nation's actions — עולה ראשונה — is the basis and the objective of everything. והקטיר עליה חלבי השלמים: on this עולה, in this consecration, the aims, aspirations, and happiness of each individual are to be spent or invested. The consecration of the nation — i.e., all the individuals who live and strive in its midst — is Israel's task before God. That is what is represented by the morning and afternoon daily offerings, with all the other offerings in between.

There is only one offering that is brought after the afternoon daily offering — namely, the קרבן פסח (see *Pesachim* 59a). With this offering the nation returns each year to the hour of its birth; in awe it awaits the hour of exodus. All its members offer their פסחים as one man and go off to meet the night in which they went forth — and continue to go forth — from death unto life and from bondage unto eternal freedom.

6 **אש תמיד תוקד וגו׳**. In the preceding verses, the preparation of the fire for the Service of the altar has already been completed; also, the instructions regarding the offerings to be brought on it have already been given. The Halachah therefore infers (*Yoma* 45b) that this verse contains more than the requirements of the fire used for the offering altar itself; it teaches us that all fire — even the fire for the incense altar (already alluded to in verse 2) and for the נר תמיד of the מנורה, and even the coals for the קטורת brought in the קודש קדשים on יום הכיפורים — all these have to be taken from the offering altar in the עזרה.

From the accentuation in our verse it appears that לא תכבה is an addition to the word המזבח; accordingly, the verse should be rendered: "A fire is to be kept continually burning on the altar, where it must never go out."

7 *And this is the teaching of the homage offering: Aharon's sons shall bring it near before God at the front of the altar.*	ז וְזֹ֥את תּוֹרַ֖ת הַמִּנְחָ֑ה הַקְרֵ֨ב אֹתָ֤הּ בְּנֵֽי־אַהֲרֹן֙ לִפְנֵ֣י יְהֹוָ֔ה אֶל־פְּנֵ֖י הַמִּזְבֵּֽחַ׃

Thus, there is only one place for the fire of the Torah, and from there one must kindle all other fire in the Sanctuary. That place is the source of the fire of the קטורת-ideal, the source of the light of the מנורה-spirit, and the source of the fire of the highest devotion on יום הכיפורים. In order for the spiritual to permeate life, actions must be consecrated to the Torah. Without אש של עולה על מזבח החיצון there can be no life on the מזבח הזהב, on the מנורה, or בין הבדים in the Sanctuary of the cherubim. Without an offering on the altar of duty there can be no elevation of soul, no illumination of spirit, no soaring to the ideal of the Torah, which rests beneath the wings of the cherubim.

7 **וזאת תורת המנחה**. Of the laws pertaining to the מנחה that are stated here, some are intended to apply generally to a whole category; some are laws repeated here to signal indispensability; and some are supplementary to laws stated previously.

An example of those intended to apply generally is the law that the כהנים partake of שיירי המנחה (v. 9). This law is stated here in regard to all *menachos* that require קמיצה and thus applies even to מנחת חוטא (above, 5:12) — even though this law is not expressly stated there (see *Menachos* 72b).

An example of those repeated here to signal indispensability (שנה הכתוב לעכב) is the law of הקטרת הלבונה, which was already mentioned above (2:2) and is repeated here (v. 8). From this repetition we learn that הקומץ והלבונה מעכבין זה את זה (*Menachos* 27a).

Examples of supplementary laws are קביעת מקום ההגשה, the assignment of the place for the הגשה (v. 7) — **לפני ה׳ אל פני המזבח** — which is missing above (2:8); also, the extension of the prohibition of חמץ to שיירי המנחה as well (vv. 9 and 10), and the assignment of the place for partaking of שיירי המנחה (v. 9), which is not mentioned above (2:3).

We have already explained, in chapter 2, the underlying ideas of all

8 *He shall take out from it his handful of the fine flour of the homage offering and of its oil, along with all the frankincense that is upon the homage offering, and he shall turn its remembrance portion into smoke upon the altar, as an expression of compliance, to* **God.**	ח וְהֵרִ֨ים מִמֶּ֜נּוּ בְּקֻמְצ֗וֹ מִסֹּ֤לֶת הַמִּנְחָה֙ וּמִשַּׁמְנָ֔הּ וְאֵת֙ כָּל־הַלְּבֹנָ֔ה אֲשֶׁ֖ר עַל־הַמִּנְחָ֑ה וְהִקְטִ֣יר הַמִּזְבֵּ֗חַ רֵ֣יחַ נִיחֹ֛חַ אַזְכָּרָתָ֖הּ לַיהוָֽה׃

these *halachos.* Here we will consider only a few details that were not treated there.

הקרב וגו׳ לפני ה׳ אל פני המזבח: this is הגשה בקרן דרומית מערבית, presenting the *minchah* at the southwest corner of the altar. Sustenance and prosperity, and the satisfaction that hinges on them, have been given us by God. We now present them to God and submit them to the spirit of His Torah (see Commentary, chapter 2).

8 **והרים ממנו**: מן המחובר. The whole of the מנחה that is remembered before God by means of the קומץ must be in one vessel; as a result, the קומץ will relate to the whole מנחה. All — not only part — of the material aspects of our lives must be related to God (*Menachos* 24a).

בקמצו: with his hand, not with a vessel that holds the measure of his handful (see ibid. 19b). For the קמיצה represents not only the objective sanctification of material resources but also the very act of sanctification. It is not the prosperity per se, but the man who utilizes it, that gives the *minchah* the character of קדשי קדשים — an offering that consecrates our actions (see Commentary to *Shemos* 29:37). Thus, we derive from בקמצו a second halachah: בקומצו — not מבורץ (=מפורץ); one should not take more than a handful (*Menachos* 11a; see תוספות, ibid. 19b, ד״ה בקומצו). For the focus here is on material goods — in the measure that man uses them.

והרים וגו׳ בקמצו וגו׳ ואת כל הלבנה: מקיש לבונה להרמה (ibid. 106b). Thus we infer: לבונה לא יפחות מקומץ (ibid.), the frankincense is not to be less

ט וְהַנּוֹתֶ֣רֶת מִמֶּ֔נָּה יֹאכְל֖וּ אַהֲרֹ֣ן וּבָנָ֑יו מַצּ֤וֹת תֵּֽאָכֵל֙ בְּמָק֣וֹם קָדֹ֔שׁ בַּחֲצַ֥ר אֹֽהֶל־מוֹעֵ֖ד יֹאכְלֽוּהָ׃

9 *Whatever is left of it, Aharon and his sons shall eat; it shall be eaten as* matzos *in a holy place, in the forecourt of the Tent of Appointed Meeting shall they eat it.*

י לֹ֤א תֵֽאָפֶה֙ חָמֵ֔ץ חֶלְקָ֛ם נָתַ֥תִּי אֹתָ֖הּ מֵֽאִשָּׁ֑י קֹ֤דֶשׁ קָֽדָשִׁים֙ הִ֔וא כַּֽחַטָּ֖את וְכָאָשָֽׁם׃

10 *It must not be baked leavened; I have given it as their portion from the fire offerings made to Me; it is a holy of holies, like the offering that clears of sin, and like the guilt offering.*

יא כָּל־זָכָ֞ר בִּבְנֵ֤י אַהֲרֹן֙ יֹֽאכְלֶ֔נָּה חָק־עוֹלָם֙ לְדֹרֹ֣תֵיכֶ֔ם מֵֽאִשֵּׁ֖י יְהוָ֑ה כֹּ֛ל אֲשֶׁר־יִגַּ֥ע בָּהֶ֖ם יִקְדָּֽשׁ׃ פ שני

11 *Every male among the sons of Aharon may eat it; it is an everlasting due for your descendants from the fire offerings to* God; *everything that touches them shall become holy.*

in quantity than the קומץ. We will draw satisfaction from sustenance and prosperity only if we devote them to God; and the measure of the satisfaction will correspond to the measure of the devotion.

9–11 אכילת שיירי מנחה is a מצוה, as is the eating of all offering parts handed over to the כהנים. It is also a symbolic act, and it is the conclusion of the offering procedures and their culmination. It shows the nature of the closeness to God that a person attains via the preceding offering procedures: Even personal enjoyment can become a way of serving God in priestlike sanctity and does not distance a person from the sphere of the Sanctuary.

שיירי מנחות — as well as בשר קדשי קדשים — are to be eaten only by זכרי כהונה in the עזרה. The profusion of place descriptions — במקום קדש בחצר אהל מועד — extends the site of the eating: התורה ריבתה חצירות הרבה אצל אכילה אחת (*Zevachim* 56a). We learn from here that the concept of עזרה vis-à-vis אכילת קדשים includes also the לשכות הבנויות בחול ופתוחות לקודש

— chambers, at the sides of the Sanctuary, that are built on non-sacred ground and open into sacred ground. For this is the message of אכילת כהנים: Even one who stands on non-sacred ground is obliged to remain close to the Sanctuary; the Sanctuary should never leave his sight.

לא תאפה חמץ חלקם וגו׳ — see Commentary above, 2:11–12. אתה refers back to the subject of לא תאפה חמץ. We see, then, that the prohibition of allowing *menachos* to become חמץ applies not only to the *minchah* before קמיצה והקטרה but also to שיירי המנחה, which are handed over to the כהן: אפילו חלקם לא תאפה חמץ (*Menachos* 55a).

We have already explained above (2:11–12) that חמץ, which is the bread of independence, represents the antithesis of dependence on God, which is the idea embodied by the מנחה. This accounts for the חמץ prohibition that applies to the מנחה generally. But it is necessary to mention this prohibition specifically with respect to שיירי מנחה, as these are not offered on the altar, rather, their מתיר is offered in their stead (see our comments, ibid., vis-à-vis כל שממנו לאשים). The reason for the prohibition in the case of שיירי מנחה is alluded to by the juxtaposition of לא תאפה חמץ and חלקם נתתי אתה מאשי: אכילת כהנים is but a symbolic continuation of אכילת מזבח. At the same time, the כהנים are supported through this gift, which they receive משולחן גבוה. Thus, they — more than the rest of the nation — are dependent on the Sanctuary for their very existence; they must remember always that their existence depends on God's Sanctuary.

קדש קדשים הוא כחטאת וכאשם. מנחה, too — like חטאת and אשם — serves to consecrate our actions. And שיירי מנחה, too — like בשר חטאת ואשם — may be eaten only by זכרי כהונה, in places invested with the sanctity of the עזרה.

כל אשר יגע בהם יקדש. בהם, in the plural, can refer only to מאשי ה׳ of the same verse or to קדשים of the previous verse. Indeed, this halachah is not limited to מנחה, but applies universally to all קדשים. The universality of application is derived (*Zevachim* 97b) from the general concluding statement: זאת התורה לעלה למנחה וגו׳ ולזבח השלמים (below, 7:37).

The halachah stated here is this: Any foodstuff that comes into contact with one of the קדשים and, as a result, absorbs some קודש substance is treated in the same manner as the קודש it absorbed. For example, if half a זית of חולין absorbs half a זית of קודש, the whole is treated as a כזית

קודש. Hence, if a זר eats it, he is חייב; or if the קודש was פסול — e.g., נותר — then anyone who eats it is חייב. This is the principle that היתר מצטרף לאיסור — which applies only to קדשים.

This halachah is repeated below in regard to חטאת (v. 20) — כל אשר יגע בבשרה יקדש — and is spelled out, on the basis of that verse, by a ברייתא in *Zevachim* (97a–b) and *Pesachim* (45a): ת״ר כל אשר יגע יכול אפילו שלא בלע ת״ל בבשרה עד שיבלע בבשרה ... יקדש להיות כמוה הא כיצד אם פסולה היא תפסל ואם כשרה היא תאכל כחמור שבה. The word בשרה in the text refers to בשר החטאת; and the case, then, is that of something of the היתר penetrating into the איסור as a result of contact between them. But as regards the principle that היתר מצטרף לאיסור, there is no difference between היתר שנבלע באיסור and איסור שנבלע בהיתר.

This halachah (אוכל שבלע מחומר הקודש), however, requires further investigation, for יגע ב- is taken to mean penetration — not external contact without any transfer. Now, it is difficult to maintain that the expression יגע בבשרה alludes to penetration; for נגע ב- in parallel passages — כל הנגע במזבח יקדש (*Shemos* 29:37), כל הנגע בהם יקדש (ibid. 30:29) — entails similar consequences and yet denotes mere external contact. Moreover, external contact is the meaning of נגע ב- in all of Scripture.

It appears, therefore, that this halachah is known to us *by way of tradition*, and the ברייתא's inference — בבשרה עד שיבלע בבשרה — attaches the halachah to the Scriptural text merely as a mnemonic device.

Nonetheless, there would appear to be agreement between the meaning of נגע ב- in the parallel passages we have cited and the meaning of this expression, as taught by tradition, in our verse. For the halachah stated in the parallel passages is that contact (נגיעה) with the מזבח or with a כלי שרת imparts קדושה to the touching article. But this contact is not merely external contact; rather, the following condition is attached to it: Only ראשו של מזבח, the top of the altar (whose purpose is to receive consecrated things), or the כבש, the ramp leading up to it (איברי העולה are placed on the ramp before they are burned atop the altar) impart קדושה by contact. Similarly, only תוכן, the inside of the כלי שרת (which receives things that are to be sanctified), imparts קדושה by contact. Moreover, not every object becomes sanctified by contact, but only that which is fit for the particular site: on the מזבח, only הראוי לאישים; in כלי הלח, only לח; in מידות היבש, only יבש (see *Zevachim* 83a; 88a). Thus, we see that there exists a close, mutual relationship between the two objects in contact — a conceptual penetration, as it were. And as conceptual

12 God *spoke to Moshe, saying:*	יב וַיְדַבֵּר יְהוָה אֶל־מֹשֶׁה לֵּאמֹר׃
13 *This is the offering of Aharon and his sons which they shall bring near to* God, *each one on the day he is initiated into office: one tenth of an* efah *of fine flour as a perpetual homage offering, half of it in the morning and half of it in the evening.*	יג זֶה קָרְבַּן אַהֲרֹן וּבָנָיו אֲשֶׁר־יַקְרִיבוּ לַיהוָה בְּיוֹם הִמָּשַׁח אֹתוֹ עֲשִׂירִת הָאֵפָה סֹלֶת מִנְחָה תָּמִיד מַחֲצִיתָהּ בַּבֹּקֶר וּמַחֲצִיתָהּ בָּעָרֶב׃

penetration functions there (in the parallel passages), so material penetration functions here (in our verse).

As we commented on *Shemos* 29:37, the conveying of קדושה is of the essence of קודש הקדשים and is its driving force. Here, however, actual penetration operates in all קדשים — including קדשים קלים.

13 The offerings described in this and the following verses are (a) חביתי כהן גדול — a מנחה that the כהן גדול brings each day in the morning and in the afternoon; and (b) מנחת חינוך לכהן הדיוט — a מנחה that every כהן brings on the day he is initiated into the priestly service. This is how these offerings are interpreted by the Halachah, and only this interpretation can resolve the difficulties that arise in these verses.

The difficulties are as follows: In this verse, the offering is called קרבן אהרן ובניו. Now, the expression אהרן ובניו always denotes the כהן גדול and the other כהנים who serve together with him — i.e., Aharon and his attendant sons. It never denotes Aharon and his successors in the office of כהן גדול; indeed, these are mentioned separately in verse 15. Yet from verse 15 it appears that this offering is brought only by הכהן המשיח — viz., the כהן גדול. Moreover, from the expression ביום המשח אתו it would appear that this offering is brought only on the day of initiation into the priestly service; and yet right afterwards it is called מנחה תמיד — a מנחה that is offered daily, similar to עלה תמיד (*Bemidbar* 28:3).

The Halachah says as follows: This offering is to be brought each day by the כהן גדול. The other כהנים, however, bring it only once — on the day of their initiation into the priestly service; and only after this initiation

14 *It shall be prepared on a pan in oil; you shall bring it boiled to* יד עַל־מַחֲבַת בַּשֶּׁמֶן תֵּעָשֶׂה

are they permitted to bring any other offering. We, therefore, think that the word אשר (v. 13) refers not to קרבן but to אהרן ובניו, whereas עשירית האפה is the object of יקריבו. This offering, which is brought every day as a מנחה תמיד by the כהן גדול (v. 15), is the same offering brought by אהרן ובניו on the day of their initiation into the priestly service. Accordingly, on the day the כהן גדול assumes the office of כהונה גדולה he must bring this offering twice; and if he has not yet officiated at an offering as an ordinary כהן, he must bring this offering three times (*Menachos* 78a): אחת לחינוכו לעבודת כהן הדיוט ואחת לחינוכו לעבודת כהן גדול ואחת לחביתין (רש"י כת"י, שם).

מנחה תמיד. With this expression Scripture equates this offering with the קרבן תמיד, which is brought each day by the nation. Both must be brought even on Shabbos (דוחים את השבת). Both must be brought, even if it is not possible to bring them in ritual purity (דוחים טומאת מת). (On the suspension of טומאה see Commentary to *Bemidbar* 9:10; see *Menachos* 50b.)

מחציתה בבקר ומחציתה בערב. This applies only to the חביתין brought by the כהן גדול as a מנחה תמיד. The *minchah* of initiation (מנחת חינוך), however, is offered שלימה, all at once.

עשירת האפה וגו׳. חביתי כהן גדול always have to be brought as one half of a whole (מחצה משלם). Therefore, he does not bring one twentieth of an *efah* in the morning and offer it, and one twentieth in the afternoon and offer it; rather, he brings a whole tenth of an *efah* and divides it and offers half in the morning and half in the afternoon (מביא עשרון שלם וחוצהו ומקריב מחצה בבקר ומחצה בין הערבים). Hence, if a כהן גדול offers his חביתין in the morning and dies, and his successor takes office the same day, the latter must bring a whole tenth and offer of it only half (ibid.).

14 **על מחבת בשמן וגו׳**. The מנחה is to be prepared in three ways:

(a) It is to be fried על מחבת בשמן, in oil in a pan (טיגון). Since על מחבת by itself already denotes frying in oil (above, 2:5), the addition of

softness, baked variously after the manner of the homage offering that is to be broken into pieces shall you bring it near, as an expression of compliance, to God.	מֻרְבֶּ֖כֶת תְּבִיאֶ֑נָּה תֻּפִינֵי֙ מִנְחַ֣ת פִּתִּ֔ים תַּקְרִ֥יב רֵֽיחַ־נִיחֹ֖חַ לַֽיהוָֽה׃

the word בשמן signifies an extra amount of oil. How much oil? Three לוגין, similar to the amount in the מנחת נסכים of the תמיד, which is triple the quantity in an ordinary מנחת נדבה.

(b) Before the טיגון, one fulfills the requirement of מרבכת by scalding the *minchah* (חליטה) thoroughly in boiling water — שנעשית ברותחין כל צרכה (*Toras Kohanim* to our verse).

The root רבך is related, apparently, to רבק, fatten; thus, עֶגְלֵי מַרְבֵּק (*Yirmeyahu* 46:21). The Rabbinic term רפק means to loosen and to soften (thus, perhaps: מִתְרַפֶּקֶת עַל־דּוֹדָהּ [*Shir Ha-Shirim* 8:5] — the heart melts from great longing; מסס, too, is used in this sense). Accordingly, רבך refers to the softening of the dough, which causes it to swell. מרבכת, then, is similar to מרחשת of מנחת נדבה (above, 2:7), only that מרחשת is prepared in oil.

(c) A further requirement is תופיני, a word that derives from the root אפה with a ת prefixed to it. It means baked in an oven (see *Menachos* 50b).

Thus, חביתי כהן גדול resemble the חלת לחם שמן of the מילואים (*Shemos* 29:2 and 23; see Commentary ad loc.), which is also prepared in these three ways: חליטה, טיגון, and אפייה. Of these, חליטה is performed first. This is indicated, apparently, by the expression מרבכת תביאנה: at the beginning of its הבאה it should be מרבכת, and only then should one meet the requirements of עשייה and אפייה. In *Menachos* (50b) there is a dispute whether טיגון precedes אפייה, or vice versa.

תפיני מנחת פתים. These words present many difficulties (see מזרחי and קרבן אהרן on our verse; לחם משנה and משנה למלך to הל׳ מעשה הקרבנות, 13:4). We learn in *Menachos* (75b) that חביתי כהן גדול — like all other מנחות כהנים — are not broken into pieces at all. פתות אתה פתים, "Break it up into pieces" (above, 2:6), applies only to *menachos* that require קמיצה — *menachos* of which only a קומץ is offered up on the altar. Thus, the Mishnah states: מנחת ישראל כופל אחד לשנים ושנים לארבעה ומבדיל, ordinary *menachos* were folded over twice and then broken, so that each cake or

15 *The priest who will be anointed from among his sons in his place shall do it. It shall be given as an everlasting tribute to* God *to go up entirely in smoke.*

טו וְהַכֹּהֵן הַמָּשִׁיחַ תַּחְתָּיו מִבָּנָיו יַעֲשֶׂה אֹתָהּ חָק־עוֹלָם לַיהוָה כָּלִיל תָּקְטָר׃

loaf is broken up into four pieces. By contrast, מנחת כהנים כופל אחד לשנים ושנים לארבעה ואינו מבדיל, the *minchah* of כהנים was folded over twice but was *not* broken through. Moreover, מנחת כהן משיח לא היה מקפלה, the *minchah* of the כהן גדול was not folded over — i.e., as the ברייתא interprets: "it was not folded into four but it was folded into two" (*Menachos* 75b). In any case, מנחת כהן was not broken into pieces — and yet in our verse it is called מנחת פתים!

We therefore venture to say that מנחת פתים is a general term for all מנחות that are broken into pieces — i.e., for all מנחות ישראל that require קמיצה, of which only a קומץ is offered up on the altar, and which are broken up for this purpose (to allow for קמיצה). מנחת פתים, then, is a general term for the three מנחות נדבה described above (2:4–7): מאפה תנור, מחבת, and מרחשת. תופיני is a plural noun in the construct state and denotes: "the ways of baking." תפיני מנחת פתים, then, means "the ways in which the broken *menachos* are baked" — i.e., the ways in which מנחת מאפה תנור מחבת ומרחשת are prepared. The three ways of preparation are united in חביתי כהן גדול: they are baked in an oven, like מאפה תנור; they are fried in a pan, like מנחה על מחבת; and they are made from soft dough, like מנחת מרחשת. Thus, all the kinds of *menachos* are combined in חביתי כהן גדול. The חביתי כהן גדול themselves are not מנחת פתים, but they are prepared in the way that one prepares the *menachos* that are so termed. The one מנחת כהן גדול combines all of מנחות ישראל.

Verses 13 and 15 are in the third person. They relate to the כהן, to whom these *mitzvos* apply. Verse 14, however — which describes the preparation of the מנחה — is in the second person. This verse, then, addresses Moshe or the nation as a whole: תקריב ,תביאנה. We will come back to treat this point in our discussion of the meaning of this offering.

15–16 **המשיח תחתיו מבניו**. The office of כהונה גדולה is bequeathed from father to son — provided that the son is qualified to succeed his father (ממלא

16 *Every homage offering of a priest, then, must be offered up in its entirety; it must not be eaten.*

טז וְכָל־מִנְחַ֥ת כֹּהֵ֛ן כָּלִ֥יל תִּהְיֶ֖ה לֹ֥א תֵאָכֵֽל׃ פ

מקום אביו), in his character and spiritual abilities. Even so, the son does not assume office automatically. Rather, first the representatives of the nation clarify whether he is suitable for the position; then, he is inducted into office by anointment. In the absence of שמן המשחה, he is inducted by investment with the garments of the כהן גדול: ריבוי בגדים (see Commentary to *Shemos* 29:30).

חק עולם: The term חוק is not strictly synonymous with "law"; rather, it also denotes an obligation that one party has toward another — as in *Bereshis* 47:22 (see Commentary, ad loc.); below, 10:13–14; *Mishlei* 30:8. In our view, this is how the term should be understood here, too. שיירי מנחות ישראל — as well as the other מתנות כהונה — are handed over to the sons of Aharon as חק. In מנחת כהן המשיח they return again to God in an expression of homage.

לחם הפנים is also called חק עולם (below, 24:9). From this we learn (*Menachos* 76a), via גזירה שוה, that חביתי כהן גדול — like לחם הפנים — are brought as twelve loaves, representing the placing of the national welfare before the Presence of God. The number twelve attached to the חביתין gives them a national meaning, similar to that of the לחם הפנים.

כליל תקטר: in its entirety — i.e., unbroken and without קמיצה.

In the case of מנחת חינוך the whole עשרון is offered at once, whereas in the case of חביתין half is offered in the morning and half in the afternoon. As regards other laws — the amount of oil, חליטה, טיגון, and אפייה — it is not clear whether מנחת חינוך resembles חביתין. According to *Toras Kohanim*, their laws are not the same: מנחת חינוך consists only of one עשרון סולת and one לוג of oil. However, from *Menachos* 78a it appears that the preparation of מנחת חינוך resembles the preparation of חביתין. There are other approaches in רש"י, ad loc. (see רמב"ם הל' מעשה הקרבנות, 13:4; הל' כלי המקדש, 5:17, and משנה למלך, ad loc.). In the case of חביתין as well as מנחת חינוך a קומץ לבונה is added, as in the case of every מנחת יחיד (see *Menachos* 59a). The law of the לבונה is like the law of the עשרון:

half a קומץ is offered in the morning and half a קומץ in the afternoon (ibid. 52a).

We have already seen in פרשת מילואים (*Shemos* 29) that Aharon and his sons were initiated into the כהונה through the offering of a פר and two אילים. The פר represented the task assigned to them, whereas the אילים represented the honor that was granted them. There were two aspects to this honor: They were granted influence over the people; this was represented by איל העולה. And they were granted material benefits; these were represented by איל המילואים (which was an offering of the שלמים variety). Together with איל המילואים they also brought a סל מצות; these מצות represented the means of material existence which were promised to the כהנים. Among the three kinds of מנחות of לחם המילואים, the לחם שמן resembled חביתי כהן גדול.

Thus, לחם שמן — one of the offerings that constituted the consecration of the priestly tribe — was singled out from among the other קרבנות המילואים, and was ordained as a mitzvah for all time: Every כהן, upon entering the priestly service, must — through this offering — refer back to the original act of the מילואים; he must, as it were, experience it anew. (We are assuming that מנחת חינוך is prepared in the same way as חביתין. This assumption is contrary to *Toras Kohanim*'s formulation, which, however, is not cited as halachah by the רמב״ם.) Moreover, the כהן גדול is to continue each day the original act of the מילואים — through one of its essential features, as follows.

It is characteristic that precisely the material benefits connected with כהונה are represented by this offering. Before entering the priestly service, the כהן is to symbolically offer up these benefits on the altar fire לריח ניחוח לה׳. And the כהן גדול, as the representative of the כהנים, is to do so each day for all time. What is more, according to one version in *Toras Kohanim*, if a כהן performs *avodah* before he has brought a מנחת חינוך, his *avodah* is פסולה! (see רמב״ם הל׳ כלי המקדש, 5:16; משנה למלך, ad loc.). In this way the כהן will recognize and take to heart that he should not perform the duties of his office for the sake of its attendant benefits; rather, he may partake of these benefits as unavoidable prerequisites for his physical existence — but he must devote them entirely to the Divine purposes of his office. The כהן's service is his inheritance and the whole basis of his existence. Nevertheless, he should not devote his service to his existence; rather, he should devote his existence to his service. וכל מנחת כהן כליל תהיה לא תאכל!

Indeed, every man of Israel must devote all his resources to God. He must place before God all of his material assets and allow the Sanctuary to take out its "handful," in accordance with God's command, to sustain the holy on earth. It is this devotion of his possessions to the Sanctuary that makes a man a Jewish man. For he places his physical existence, too, in God's care, and he takes no joy in life if through this life he has not brought God satisfaction.

In the case of the כהן, however, not only part, but the *whole* of his existence, including *all* the material aspects of his life and welfare, must be spent serving God. His life — even outside the Sanctuary — must be a model for the whole people. This is corroborated by the special *mitzvos* addressed to כהנים (below, chapter 21). His mission is to "prepare" (כונן) a place for God's Presence to dwell among us, as his very name (כהן) implies (see Commentary, *Bereshis* 14:17–18). Hence, there must be nothing about him that is unworthy of the כהונה and its sanctity. When he brings to the Sanctuary his own *minchah* — representing his own sustenance, prosperity, and satisfaction — not just a portion of it, for remembrance, is to be brought to the altar, but, rather, all of it is to be consumed in the flame of godliness.

The obligatory *minchah* that the כהן גדול brings each day is the richest of all the *menachos* (ג' לוגין שמן), and it comprises a combination of all the kinds of *menachos*. It represents, then, man's portion in whatever measure Providence has allotted to him: basic needs (מאפה תנור), luxuries (מחבת), and moments of joy (מרחשת=מרבכת; see Commentary above, 2:4–7). This is not because the כהן גדול considers himself, as an individual, to be in a state of great wealth, but because he represents the nation and gives it symbolic expression.

The meaning of the חביתין is like the meaning of לחם הפנים, only that לחם הפנים relates to the national community in its concrete reality [i.e., as a nation of individuals], whereas the חביתין relate to the national idea, the nation viewed as one unit. This idea is represented by the כהן גדול. That is why both לחם הפנים and the חביתין consist of twelve חלות, but with this difference: לחם הפנים, which relates to the national community as individuals, is baked in pairs, whereas the חביתין, which relates to the nation as one unit, are apparently baked אחת אחת (see רמב"ם הל' מעשה הקרבנות, 13:3; משנה למלך, ad loc.).

From this national perspective we can also explain what we pointed out above: the mitzvah of preparing the מנחה is addressed to Moshe or to the nation — and not to the כהנים: תביאנה, תקריב (v. 14). For it is the nation that encourages the כהן גדול to bring his חביתין so richly prepared. This duty is incumbent upon the nation in actual life as well: גדלהו משל אחיו (see Commentary below, 21:10–12) — the nation must see to it that the כהן גדול appear in a manner befitting the dignity of his people even in his external life. The pages of Jewish history teach us that the source of every moral decline is in the corruption of the upper classes of society. The standing of the כהן and particularly of the כהן גדול — who must be married and have a "home" — proves that they are to exert a moral, ennobling influence through their exemplary home life, and for this reason are to live in the midst of national society. Thus we may gather that the Torah's intention is this: The כהן גדול must be allowed to lead a wealthy life. This will enable him to join the more affluent circles of society — in his home life, in the education of his children, and in the whole course of his civil life. As a result, his influence at the hub of the moral life of the nation will be pronounced. To carry out this intention of the Torah is the כהן גדול's duty; his מנחת חביתין reminds him of it each morning and afternoon.

We have explained previously, in our Commentary to *Shemos* 29:38–39, that the *tamid* offering represents the unity that prevails in the world and in man's relationships. Now, the basic phenomena of physical existence — e.g., the contrast between day and night — appear to be antithetical to this unity. The *tamid* offering, therefore, represents the unity of God's governance of the world — in the very midst of the phenomena that appear antithetical to this unity. At the waxing rays of morning and at the waning rays of evening, man — embodied as a sheep in the flock of the one Shepherd — remains one and the same, as do the symbols of his sustenance, prosperity, and happiness (see ibid. 29:38–41).

This message of unity is even more imperative here, where there is special need to show the unity of the physical relationships in the world and in life. For this is the very essence of מנחת חביתין: it represents these physical relationships by means of an independent *minchah* that is offered each day. Hence, the morning and afternoon *minchah* constitutes a unified whole. It must be brought complete and undivided (שלמה), all together one עשרון; thus, each one of the two *menachos* — of the morning and of the afternoon — forms only half of one whole. For this reason, even where a כהן גדול offers the morning *minchah* and then

17 God *spoke to Moshe, saying:*

יז וַיְדַבֵּ֥ר יְהֹוָ֖ה אֶל־מֹשֶׁ֥ה לֵּאמֹֽר׃

18 *Speak to Aharon and to his sons, saying: This is the teaching of the offering that clears of sin. At the place where the ascent offering is slaughtered shall the offering that clears of sin also be slaughtered before* God; *it is a holy of holies.*

יח דַּבֵּ֤ר אֶֽל־אַהֲרֹן֙ וְאֶל־בָּנָ֣יו לֵאמֹ֔ר
זֹ֥את תּוֹרַ֖ת הַֽחַטָּ֑את בִּמְק֡וֹם אֲשֶׁ֣ר
תִּשָּׁחֵ֣ט הָעֹלָ֠ה תִּשָּׁחֵ֨ט הַֽחַטָּ֜את
לִפְנֵ֣י יְהֹוָ֔ה קֹ֥דֶשׁ קָֽדָשִׁ֖ים הִֽוא׃

dies, and his successor brings the afternoon *minchah*, the latter must consecrate a whole עשרון in order to bring half of it for the afternoon *minchah* (see *Menachos* 50b).

We have clarified the national meaning of חביתי כהן גדול. This may explain why the times of morning and evening are called עֲלוֹת הַמִּנְחָה (*Melachim* I, 18:36; ibid. II, 3:20), and it may also explain the recurring expression מנחת הערב. These expressions refer, apparently, to מנחת החביתין, as מנחת הנסכים of the *tamid* offering is secondary to, and merely an accompaniment to, the עולה. (See, however, our Commentary to *Tehillim* 141:2.)

18 **זאת תורת החטאת**. These words extend the mitzvah of washing out חטאת blood that has splashed onto a garment (v. 20) — the only mitzvah in verses 18–22 that relates exclusively to חטאת — to all חטאות בהמה, whether פנימיות or חיצוניות. Only חטאת העוף is excluded, as this section deals only with חטאות הנשחטות (see *Zevachim* 92a).

במקום אשר תשחט וגו׳. שחיטת חטאת — like שחיטת עולה — is performed בצפון, on the north side. Earlier (see Commentary above, 1:10–13), we attempted to explain the significance of שחיטה וקבלה בצפון in the case of עולה as follows: The surrender of selfish existence and the transition to Sanctuary existence are aims that relate primarily to the material and sensual side of life. This, then, is the meaning of the analogy Scripture draws between חטאת and עולה: The עולה is occasioned by the failure to actualize moral aims. The חטאת is occasioned by the lack of adherence to moral values. And the source of the problem in both instances is the

19 *The priest whose function it is to offer it as an offering that clears of sin shall eat it; in a holy place shall it be eaten, in the forecourt of the Tent of Appointed Meeting.*	יט הַכֹּהֵן הַמְחַטֵּא אֹתָהּ יֹאכְלֶנָּה בְּמָקוֹם קָדֹשׁ תֵּאָכֵל בַּחֲצַר אֹהֶל מוֹעֵד׃

heightened influence of the material and of the senses. Only self-sacrifice in the material and sensual side of life leads to adherence to moral values, as it also leads to ascent and advancement. קדש קדשים הוא: the basis of the חטאת — like that of the עולה — is the consecration of actions, and what underlies this consecration is the sanctification of the material and the sensual.

19 **הכהן המחטא אתה וגו׳**. One cannot say that the issue here is *permission* to partake of the חטאת — as though only the כהן who performs the offering procedure may partake of the בשר. For immediately afterwards (v. 22) this permission is granted to all male כהנים; and even בעלי מומים are permitted to partake (below, 21:22), although they are unfit to perform the offering procedures.

Rather, Scripture speaks here of the *legal right* to share in the בשר חטאת. Of this right, it says in *Devarim* (18:8): חלק כחלק יאכלו לבד ממכריו על האבות — i.e., all כהנים have equal rights, except in that which will be ceded to the family groups. Let us explain:

Originally, all the כהנים had equal rights in the Sanctuary, but with the growth of the priestly population there arose a need for mutual renunciation. From that time onward only certain family groups had the right, at a given time, to perform the *avodah* and partake of the offering. This was the procedure: From the time of Moshe to that of David, the כהנים were divided into eight משמרות. Shemuel and David then divided them into twenty-four משמרות. These משמרות took weekly turns serving in the Sanctuary. Each משמר was divided into בתי אב, family groups, and each day a different בית אב would perform the *avodah* (see *Ta'anis* 27a; רמב״ם הל׳ כלי המקדש, 4:1). Only during the רגלים, when all of Israel assembled in the Sanctuary, were the קרבנות ציבור treated according to the original rule: חלק כחלק יאכלו (*Sukkah* 56a).

Thus, הכהן המחטא of our verse refers to a כהן of the משמר that is

20 *Anything that touches its flesh shall become holy, and if any of its blood splashes on a garment, you shall wash that on which it is splashed, in a holy place.*	כ כֹּל אֲשֶׁר־יִגַּע בִּבְשָׂרָהּ יִקְדָּשׁ וַאֲשֶׁר יִזֶּה מִדָּמָהּ עַל־הַבֶּגֶד אֲשֶׁר יִזֶּה עָלֶיהָ תְּכַבֵּס בְּמָקוֹם קָדֹשׁ׃

serving during the current week, or, more precisely, to a כהן of the בית אב that is serving today (see רמב״ם הל׳ מעשה הקרבנות, 10:14–15; לחם משנה, ad loc.), whose responsibility it is to perform the *avodah*. All members of the משמר have a share in the offering, but there is one condition: they must be ראויים לחיטוי ולאכילה at the time the offering is made, i.e., provided that they are not טמאים or אוננים and hence unfit to serve or to partake. Thus, an אונן and a טבול יום, although permitted to partake of the offering after nightfall, are not entitled to a share; for when the offering was made they were not fit to serve and to partake. As for a בעל מום, see our Commentary to verse 22, and see *Zevachim* 99a.

במקום קדש תאכל וגו׳. See our Commentary to verses 9–11.

Scripture here equates אכילת חטאת with עבודת חטאת. The right to partake depends on the eligibility to perform *avodah* and partake of the offering at the time of offering (a כהן גדול אונן is excluded from the חלוקה, even though he is permitted to perform the *avodah* as an אונן; for while he is an אונן he is forbidden to partake of the offering). This equation clearly demonstrates the great importance of אכילת כהנים — that it is in itself an עבודה. Taken together, verses 18 and 19 teach us the following: The basis of the חטאת — like that of the עולה — is the renunciation of uncontrolled sensuality. In the case of חטאת, however, the objective of the offering procedures is not abstention from sensuality, but, rather, the sanctification of its pleasures in priestlike sanctity.

20 **כל אשר יגע בבשרה יקדש**: see our Commentary to verses 9–11.

ואשר יזה וגו׳: יזה is the קל of נזה. נזה is an intransitive verb, whereas הזה is a transitive verb; see Commentary above, 4:6–7. Scripture states here that חטאת blood that has splashed onto a garment must be washed out, in the עזרה. This halachah applies only to דם חטאת בהמה and not to other דם קדשים or to דם חטאת עוף. It applies only to דם חטאת כשר שנתקבל בכלי כלי וראוי למתנות הדם — blood, of a חטאת כשרה, that has been received in a כלי שרת for the מתנות הדם: הזיה, נתינה, זריקה; blood before קבלה or after מתנה does not require washing. Furthermore, only an object that is ראוי לקבל טומאה (potentially susceptible to טומאה) and ראוי לכיבוס (washable) requires washing. The entire garment need not be washed, but only the blood spot. (First, the spot is washed in water; then, מעבירים עליו שבעה סממנים, seven substances are applied to it: רוק תפל, מי רגלים, נתר, בורית, אשלג, קמוניא, אהל. No blood can withstand this process; hence, this process is also employed to determine whether a stain is a bloodstain. See *Niddah* 61b; *Zevachim* 92a, 93a–b, 95a–b. A כלי that is not ראוי לכיבוס requires גרידה [scraping]; see ibid. 94a.)

Let us now ask: What is the underlying idea of all these *halachos*? It must hinge on the nature of the חטאת. More precisely, it must hinge on that quality that is represented by מתנות הדם of חטאת בהמה.

The answer to our question, then, is as follows: The fact that blood that was destined for מתנה falls instead upon a כלי הראוי לקבל טומאה (even a vessel that is potentially but not yet actually susceptible to טומאה — e.g., if מחשבה was lacking; see ibid. 94a) is entirely antithetical to that quality of חטאת represented by מתנות הדם. Hence, the antithetical idea must be negated by כיבוס; and this כיבוס is a positive Sanctuary procedure, which must be performed within the precincts of the Sanctuary — במקום קדוש.

Now, if we are not mistaken in our approach, דם חטאת בהמה המקובל בכלי שרת differs from both דם חטאת העוף and דם of other קדשים. The blood of all the other offerings is ניתן למטה. It symbolizes, then, the נפש that is still on a low level and that still needs to undertake uplifting action. On such a level the נפש is still reaching to attain its goal, and no concrete human reality — represented by any plain garment or vessel — is considered antithetical to this level. The very opposite is the case. דם המקובל במזרק shows symbolically that every mundane aspect of human life can be brought near and elevated to the heights of holiness. Hence, in the case of the other offerings, דם שניתז על הבגד does not constitute a violation of the idea embodied in the blood.

In the case of דם חטאת בהמה, however, which is ניתן למעלה על קרנות המזבח, things are different. Particularly in the case of דם הפנימיות, which is ניתן על קרנות מזבח הזהב, and — on a higher level — in the case of דם

הזייה על הפרוכת כנגד בין הבדים, things are different. These דמים represent moral perfection, which one must guard more than anything else. דם הפנימיות symbolizes a moral level that is forever held aloft as a shining example, but which no human being can actually attain. This, then, is the meaning of דם חטאת בהמה שניתז על הבגד after having been readied for מתנה or הזיה: Instead of reaching קרנות המזבח, the blood reaches a garment or a vessel. Thus, a discrepancy is created between the level of the garment or vessel and the lofty level represented by the blood. The result is the debasement of this lofty moral level, and only כיבוס במקום קדוש can restore the idea embodied in the blood to its pristine state.

This theory would seem to be disproved by the halachah that even דם שניתז על בגדי כהן גדול — e.g., the מעיל — requires כיבוס; for the מעיל itself symbolizes an ideal level of moral perfection. But this objection may disappear when we consider that בגדי כהונה ניתנו ליהנות בהם and that it is permissible to wear them שלא בשעת עבודה (*Yoma* 68b); thus, they are not to be entirely separated from the actual personality of the כהן. (וצ״ע מאבנט לסברת הרמב״ם שאסר שלא בשעת עבודה עי׳ הל׳ כלאים פ״י הל״ב וע״ש בראב״ד ובכסף משנה. The אבנט [the priestly sash], however, does not represent perfection already attained but, rather, the ideal, for whose full realization one must strive. The level of the אבנט, then, is like that of the עולה, and — from the perspective of חטאת — constitutes a disturbing contrast. See Commentary, *Shemos* 28:43.)

We mentioned above the halachah that דם requires כיבוס only before זריקה, נתינה, or הזיה — but not after the completion of the עבודה. This halachah is apparently related to the rule that אין לך דבר שנעשה מצותו ומועלין בו (see Commentary above, verse 3). קדושה resides in an object only for as long as the object is a means to a מצוה that is to be performed; but once the mitzvah has been completed, the object loses its sanctity. Thus, Judaism opposes the superstitions of heathen mysticism, which ascribes magical powers to sanctified objects. Sanctified objects are a means in the service of an idea — and this idea alone is holy. Only so long as they serve as a means of expressing this idea do they partake of its holiness. The sanctity conveyed to them is not tangible and does not attach to them forever. Nevertheless, one should not go to the other extreme: In treating a sacred or mitzvah object, one should do nothing that appears to be demeaning to the idea it served. Hence we learn that תשמישי מצוה אינן נזרקין and תשמישי קדושה נגנזין (*Megillah* 26b; see רמ״א on או״ח 21:1).

21 *And an earthenware vessel in which it was cooked must be broken, but if it was cooked in a copper vessel, it shall be purged and rinsed in water.*	כא וּכְלִי־חֶרֶשׂ אֲשֶׁר תְּבֻשַּׁל־בּוֹ יִשָּׁבֵר וְאִם־בִּכְלִי נְחֹשֶׁת בֻּשָּׁלָה וּמֹרַק וְשֻׁטַּף בַּמָּיִם׃

As we have stated, only a כלי הראוי לקבל טומאה requires כיבוס. Only a כלי הראוי לקבל טומאה bears the stamp of man and relates to the human dimension. Such a כלי, by its very purpose, represents an aspect that is antithetical to the idea embodied in דם חטאת. (See Commentary below, 11:32 and the summary of that chapter.)

21 **וכלי חרש אשר תבשל בו**. According to *Zevachim* 95b, this should be understood as though it had said: "And an earthenware vessel that absorbs of the חטאת by way of cooking"; for the same law applies even if עירה לתוכו רותח, one poured boiling broth into the vessel. This is connected to the question of whether, even in other עירוי ,איסורין (pouring hot liquid onto something) is considered akin to "cooking" — i.e., whether it has the status of a כלי ראשון or a כלי שני (see תוספות, there, and ש״ך to יו״ד 105:2).

ישבר. That which is absorbed into an earthenware vessel cannot be removed by הגעלה (purging), as התורה העידה על כלי חרס שאינו יוצא מידי דופיו לעולם (*Pesachim* 30b).

ומרק ושטף. מרק is related to מרג. A מורג is a tool that frees grain of its husk. מרק means "to free a material of foreign elements which it has absorbed" — cf. Commentary to *Shemos* 21:25. Thus, מרק can mean "to polish": נְחֹשֶׁת מָרוּק (*Divrei Ha-Yamim* II, 4:16), and — in connection with smoothing skin treatment: וּבְתַמְרוּקֵי הַנָּשִׁים (*Esther* 2:12). Thus, also, מָרָק (*Shoftim* 6:19) — the liquid mixed with the gravy of cooked meat. In our verse מריקה means purging in boiling water (הגעלה), whereas שטיפה (ושטף) means rinsing in cold water (see *Zevachim* 97a). The requirement for שטיפה after מריקה is prescribed for all קדשי מזבח, but not for תרומה (ibid. 96b). מריקה ושטיפה as well as שבירת כלי חרס must be performed במקום קדוש — in the עזרה (ibid. 93b).

22 *Every male among the priests shall eat it; it is a holy of holies.*

כב כָּל־זָכָר בַּכֹּהֲנִים יֹאכַל אֹתָהּ קֹדֶשׁ קָדָשִׁים הִוא׃

The הגעלה prescribed for קדשים differs from the הגעלה prescribed for other איסורים (*Bemidbar* 31:23). In the case of other איסורים, no שטיפה is necessary after הגעלה. Furthermore, מריקת קדשים is valid only when performed with water, whereas הגעלה — at least in the case of תרומה — is valid even when performed with other liquids. Furthermore, as regards קדשים we learn that בישל במקצת הכלי טעון מריקה ושטיפה כל הכלי (*Zevachim* 96b; see תוספות, there). The halachah in cases of איסור והיתר depends on whether שאר איסורים are to be treated like תרומה or like קדשים (see בית יוסף on טור או״ח 452).

When we search for the reason behind the mitzvah of מריקה ושטיפה in קדשים, we encounter serious obstacles. For the reason behind a mitzvah derives from its laws, yet in the case of this mitzvah there remain unresolved questions about some of its basic laws. Take, for example, the question of whether מריקה ושטיפה should be performed immediately or only after the absorption has become נותר (see *Zevachim* 97a; תוספות, ad loc., ד״ה ממתין; רמב״ם הל׳ מעשה הקרבנות, 8:14, and לחם משנה, ad loc.); and especially the question of whether מריקה ושטיפה are required even in the case of תלאו באויר התנור (where there is only בישול, without בילוע). וצ״ע.

22 **כל זכר בכהנים** — see Commentary to verse 19. Here, too, יאכל אתה refers to the right to participate in the חלוקה. Permission to eat the offering will later (21:22) be granted to all of the כהנים — including בעלי מום. Here, an exception is made in the case of בעל מום: even though he is not ראוי לחיטוי, nevertheless, he is entitled to participate in the חלוקה (*Zevachim* 102a); see Commentary below, 21:17ff.

The juxtaposition of this verse to the preceding verse teaches us that מריקה ושטיפה applies only to קדשים כשרים, which are fit to be eaten (see *Zevachim* 96b, רש״י ד״ה מריקה ושטיפה אינה בפנימיות). The מיעוט אחר מיעוט (אתה and קדש קדשים הוא) — which is always taken as a limitation of the limitation and hence an extension — serves to include all קדשים, with the exception of תרומה alone (*Zevachim* 96b; תוספות, ad loc., ד״ה חומר).

The halachah that only זכרי כהונה are allowed to partake applies to all קדשי קדשים — including שלמי ציבור (see *Zevachim* 55a).

כג וְכָל־חַטָּאת אֲשֶׁר יוּבָא מִדָּמָהּ אֶל־אֹהֶל מוֹעֵד לְכַפֵּר בַּקֹּדֶשׁ לֹא תֵאָכֵל בָּאֵשׁ תִּשָּׂרֵף׃ פ

23 ***Every offering that clears of sin, from which any of the blood is brought into the Tent of Appointed Meeting to effect atonement in the Sanctuary, must not be eaten; it must be burned in fire.***

23 Scripture already stated above (4:12 and 21) that the flesh of **חטאות פנימיות** — unlike the flesh of other **חטאות** — is not to be eaten but burned. The halachah stated here, however, relates to all the **חטאות** — including the **חיצוניות**, whose blood is destined for the **מזבח העולה**: If blood of these **חטאות** is brought **במזיד** into the **היכל** and placed upon the **פרוכת** or the **מזבח הזהב**, then the flesh of these offerings is not to be eaten but burned. Moreover, in the case of **חטאות חיצוניות**, if the blood destined for the **מזבח החיצון** is brought into the **היכל** to effect atonement, the entire offering becomes **פסול**; and even if some of the blood is not brought into the **היכל** but is left in the **עזרה** — e.g., **שקבל דמה בשני כוסות** — one may not continue with the offering procedures of this **חטאת** (*Zevachim* 82a). The same is true of those **חטאות פנימיות** — e.g., **פר העלם דבר** (above, 4:16) — whose blood is destined for the **היכל**: if any of their blood is brought into the **קודש הקדשים**, the offering becomes **פסול** (see *Zevachim* 82b).

It is difficult to say, though, that our verse (which seems to refer to a **קרבן** that normally would be eaten) speaks only of this **פסול** of the **חטאות חיצוניות**. For this **פסול** precludes the whole continuation of the offering procedure — **נתינת דם על הקרנות** and **הקטרת אימורים** — and not only **אכילת הבשר**; why, then, does the verse mention only an **איסור אכילה**?

ר׳ יוסי הגלילי (ibid. 82a) offers a different interpretation of our verse: **כל הענין כולו אינו מדבר אלא בפרים הנשרפים ושעירים הנשרפים לשרוף פסוליהן אבית הבירה ולעמוד בלא תעשה על אכילתן**. According to **ר׳ יוסי הגלילי**, our verse is speaking only of **חטאות פנימיות** that became unfit; the **פסול** of the **חטאות חיצוניות** of which blood has been brought into the **היכל** is derived from 10:18, below. According to those who dispute him, the **פסול** of **חטאות חיצוניות** is derived from our verse. It appears, however, that they, too, agree with the essence of his interpretation, only that in their view both *halachos* are included in our verse — both חטאת פנימית, whose blood is brought lawfully into the היכל, and חטאת חיצונית, whose blood is brought in unlawfully: וכל חטאת אשר יובא מדמה אל אהל מועד לכפר בקדש לא תאכל. In these cases, instead of אכילה בקודש (v. 19) there is to be שריפה בקודש. See *Pesachim* 82b: בקדש באש תשרף and רש״י there ד״ה פסולי שאר קדשים (cf. לחם משנה to הל׳ מעשה הקרבנות, 11:3). In their view, then, we have here two *halachos*: (a) כל חטאת — whether פנימית or חיצונית — from which any blood is brought into the היכל to effect atonement may not be eaten, לא תאכל; and the implication is that such a חטאת חיצונית is פסולה. This accounts also for what is stated below (10:18): הן לא הובא וגו׳. (b) Every חטאת פסולה — including חטאות פנימיות that have become פסול (חטאות which in the case of נעשו כמצותן would have been burned outside the שלוש מחנות; see Commentary above, 4:11–12) — as well as all קדשי קדשים שנפסלו (see *Pesachim* 82b) are to be burned בקדש, i.e., in the עזרה.

For a discussion of שריפת חטאות פנימיות שנעשו כמצותן, see Commentary above, 4:11–12. Here, Scripture adds only a prohibition against אכילתן, partaking of them; and the meaning of this prohibition is self-evident in light of the explanation we have offered there.

שריפת קדשי קדשים שנפסלו — like אכילתם בכשרותם — must be performed in the עזרה. It follows, then, that this שריפה is a positive offering procedure. For the idea represented by the פסול contradicts the idea of קודש, and the purpose of the שריפה is to refute and negate this anti-קודש idea. Hence, the שריפה of the major פסולים — viz., נותר ופיגול — must be performed during the day, as befits an offering procedure (see *Zevachim* 56b).

As we have stated, חטאות שנכנס מדמן לפנים and even פנימיות שנכנס מדמן לקדשי קדשים are פסולות. In the case of other קרבנות, however, the law is different: נתן את הניתנין בחוץ בפנים, if blood that was intended to be applied outside was applied inside, נתכפרו הבעלים — and only the בשר is פסול (see ibid. 26b). It appears that the reason behind this halachah of חטאת is the same as the reason behind כיבוס דם חטאת (v. 20). Let us elaborate:

The דם of all other קרבנות represents the נפש that still needs to advance. Hence, the idea represented by this דם is neither debased nor desecrated by הזייה על הכלי; for every aspect of human life is summoned to ascend in the realm of the Sanctuary. Similarly, in all other קרבנות the symbolic demonstration of a higher, even the highest purpose (נתן את הניתנין בחוץ בפנים) entails no arrogance on the part of any נפש; nor does it constitute a debasement of the idea of that purpose. For this דם

7 1 *And this is the teaching with regard to the guilt offering: it is a holy of holies.*

ז א וְזֹאת תּוֹרַת הָאָשָׁם קֹדֶשׁ קָדָשִׁים
הוּא׃

2 *In the place where they slaughter the ascent offering they shall also slaughter the guilt offering, and he shall dash its blood against the altar, all around.*

ב בִּמְקוֹם אֲשֶׁר יִשְׁחֲטוּ אֶת־הָעֹלָה
יִשְׁחֲטוּ אֶת־הָאָשָׁם וְאֶת־דָּמוֹ
יִזְרֹק עַל־הַמִּזְבֵּחַ סָבִיב׃

3 *He shall bring near all of its fat, the tailpiece and the fat that covers the intestines.*

ג וְאֵת כָּל־חֶלְבּוֹ יַקְרִיב מִמֶּנּוּ אֵת
הָאַלְיָה וְאֶת־הַחֵלֶב הַמְכַסֶּה אֶת־
הַקֶּרֶב׃

---

represents the נפש still in need of advancement, and every man is summoned to attain the highest moral purpose.

חטאת, however, is different. Its blood represents the נפש that has already attained a high moral level, and the challenge for the נפש is to adhere to this level and maintain its eminence. Now, if דם חטאת reaches a level that is higher than the level befitting it, this entails arrogance on the part of that נפש and also constitutes a debasement of the idea of that lofty level. The עזרה is to the היכל, and the היכל is to the קודש הקדשים, as the lower levels are to the level of highest perfection.

The only thing that argues against this conception is the law of חטאת העוף. For if this conception is not mistaken, then we would expect that a חטאת העוף שנכנס מדמה לפנים would not be פסולה, just as דם חטאת העוף is not טעון כיבוס. But this is an issue that is not resolved (see *Zevachim* 92b).

CHAPTER 7

1–7 These verses complete the *halachos* of the אשם. They describe the אשם's offering procedures that were not detailed above (5:14–26).

As regards שחיטה and זריקה, the laws of the אשם parallel those of the עולה; as regards הקטרת אימורים and אכילת בשר לכהנים, its laws parallel those of the חטאת. And since an אשם is brought only from צאן, its הקטרה (vv. 3 and 4) resembles that of חטאת כבש (4:35). For our analysis of these *halachos*, see above (5:26).

4 *The two kidneys and the fat that rests upon them, which is along the flanks; also the diaphragm upon the liver; he must remove it together with the kidneys.*

ד וְאֵת שְׁתֵּי הַכְּלָיֹת וְאֶת־הַחֵלֶב אֲשֶׁר עֲלֵיהֶן אֲשֶׁר עַל־הַכְּסָלִים וְאֶת־הַיֹּתֶרֶת עַל־הַכָּבֵד עַל־הַכְּלָיֹת יְסִירֶנָּה׃

5 *The priest shall turn them into smoke upon the altar, a fire offering to* God: *It is a guilt offering.*

ה וְהִקְטִיר אֹתָם הַכֹּהֵן הַמִּזְבֵּחָה אִשֶּׁה לַיהוָה אָשָׁם הוּא׃

6 *Every male among the priests shall eat of it. In a holy place shall it be eaten: it is a holy of holies.*

ו כָּל־זָכָר בַּכֹּהֲנִים יֹאכְלֶנּוּ בְּמָקוֹם קָדוֹשׁ יֵאָכֵל קֹדֶשׁ קָדָשִׁים הוּא׃

7 *As is the offering that clears of sin, so is the guilt offering; one law applies for them: the priest who is to effect atonement with it, it shall be his.*

ז כַּחַטָּאת כָּאָשָׁם תּוֹרָה אַחַת לָהֶם הַכֹּהֵן אֲשֶׁר יְכַפֶּר־בּוֹ לוֹ יִהְיֶה׃

We also mentioned above (4:24) — in explaining the halachah of כל שבחטאת מתה באשם ירעה — that אשם mediates between חטאת and the other offerings. For an אשם that does not relate to a specific offense (e.g., שנתכפרו באחר or שמתו בעליו or תמורת אשם) is not itself offered (as כיפרו באחר or שמתו בעליו or תמורת עולה is offered); rather, it is offered only indirectly — and only after it has been transformed into an עולה: It must be put out to pasture (ניתק לרעייה) until it develops a מום and is then sold, and the proceeds are used to purchase an עולה. The Gemara in *Zevachim* (5b) says further that if one slaughters it after it is put out to pasture but before it develops a מום (שחטו סתם), it is כשר and is offered as an עולה, as this was its ultimate destination. Before it is put out to pasture, however, it is still called an אשם; and — since it does not relate to a specific sin — if one slaughters it, it is פסול. This is derived from verse 5: אשם הוא – בהווייתו יהא. That is to say, as long as it is not ניתק לרעייה it is considered an אשם.

ח וְהַכֹּהֵן הַמַּקְרִיב אֶת־עֹלַת אִישׁ עוֹר הָעֹלָה אֲשֶׁר הִקְרִיב לַכֹּהֵן לוֹ יִהְיֶה׃

8 *And [as for] the priest who brings any man's ascent offering, the skin of the ascent offering that he has brought near shall belong to the priest; it shall be his.*

ט וְכָל־מִנְחָה אֲשֶׁר תֵּאָפֶה בַּתַּנּוּר

9 *Also every homage offering that is baked in the oven, and every one*

All of the offerings — except חטאת — are capable of metamorphosing into עולות. Earlier (4:24), we attempted to explain this phenomenon. We also mentioned there the view of רבינו תם. In his opinion the whole procedure of רעייה prescribed for אשם is only דרבנן, whereas according to the original halachah, אשם שמתו בעליו וכו׳ is itself offered as an עולה. According to this view, בהווייתו יהא means as follows: Since it is destined to become an עולה, let it have this status even now; there is no need for ניתוק לרעייה in order to transform it into an עולה. (See also לחם משנה to הל׳ פסולי המוקדשין, 4:15.)

8 עלת איש. This expression — instead of the usual term עולה — excludes two things: פרט לעולה שלא עלתה לאיש and פרט לעולת הקדש (see *Zevachim* 103a–b). That is to say, the כהנים do not acquire the right to the hide of the עולה — or to the hides of the other קדשי קדשים — unless the בעלים fulfill their obligation, i.e., unless no פסול befalls the offering until after זריקה. Similarly, the כהנים do not acquire the right to the hide in cases where the proceeds from its sale go to בדק הבית — e.g., התפיס עולה לבדק הבית.

The term המקריב — like the term המחטא above (6:19) — includes every כהן who is ראוי להקרבה. It is necessary to expressly repeat this halachah in connection with עור העולה. For in other offerings, the ones who acquire the right to the meat are also the ones who acquire the right to the hide: in קדשי קדשים the כהנים acquire it, and in קדשים קלים the בעלים acquire it. In the case of עולה, however, the כהנים do not acquire the right to the meat.

9–10 A similar halachah is stated in verse 9 as regards מנחות: They are to be divided among all who are ראויים להקרבה. This excludes אונן and טבול יום,

that is prepared in a deep pot and on a pan, shall belong to the priest who brings it near; it shall be his.	וְכָל־נַעֲשָׂה בַמַּרְחֶשֶׁת וְעַל־מַחֲבַת לַכֹּהֵן הַמַּקְרִיב אֹתָהּ לוֹ תִהְיֶה׃

even though they are permitted to partake of the מנחה after nightfall. Verse 10 adds the halachah that כל מנחה, every single מנחה, is to be divided among all who have rights to it, איש כאחיו: All the כהנים of the בית אב of that day receive a portion of each one of the מנחות. It is forbidden to apportion מנחה against מנחה, even where the מנחות are alike — e.g., מנחת מרחשת כנגד מנחת מרחשת. If it were permitted to do so, one כהן would take this whole מנחה, and another כהן would take that whole מנחה. But such a division is forbidden; rather, each מנחה is to be apportioned among all the members of the בית אב, even if this means that each share will amount to very little. This halachah applies to all מנחות and all offerings, but it is mentioned in Scripture in connection with מנחה בלולה וחרבה to stress its application even in extreme cases; for in the cases of מנחה בלולה וחרבה it can often happen that each כהן's portion will amount to merely a little bit of unbaked dough or a pinch of flour (see *Menachos* 73a; רמב״ם הל׳ מעשה הקרבנות, 10:15–16).

This halachah clearly demonstrates the symbolic nature of the כהנים's partaking of the offerings. Indeed, we have already seen several times that אכילת כהנים is itself an integral part of the ritual of the offerings. Were this אכילה intended to be merely a payment for service, the halachah would be just the opposite: The כהנים would be permitted — even obligated — to see to it that each portion be worthy in itself and not lose all its value as a result of the division. It would certainly be permitted to apportion *minchah* against *minchah*, offering against offering. But אכילת כהנים is more than just a payment for service: it is a מצוה and an עבודה, which repeats itself in each offering. Hence, each one of those called upon to serve must take part in the fulfillment of the mitzvah. Only the apportionment of עורות קדשים is unconnected with the symbolism of the עבודה. It appears to be strictly a payment for service rendered. Hence, it is permissible to apportion the עורות קדשים according to the preferences of those entitled to a share (*Pesachim* 57a; *Bava Kamma* 110a).

10 *And, likewise, every homage offering, be it mixed with oil or dry, it shall belong to all sons of Aharon, one as well as another.*

י וְכָל־מִנְחָה בְלוּלָה־בַשֶּׁמֶן וַחֲרֵבָה
לְכָל־בְּנֵי אַהֲרֹן תִּהְיֶה אִישׁ
כְּאָחִיו׃ פ שלישי

11 *And this is the teaching of the meal-of-peace offering which he brings near to* God.

יא וְזֹאת תּוֹרַת זֶבַח הַשְּׁלָמִים אֲשֶׁר
יַקְרִיב לַיהוָה׃

12 *If he offers it by reason of thanksgiving, he shall bring near — with the thanksgiving offering — matzah loaves mixed with oil and thin matzah wafers brushed with oil, and loaves of bread made from fine flour boiled to softness, mixed with oil.*

יב אִם עַל־תּוֹדָה יַקְרִיבֶנּוּ וְהִקְרִיב ׀
עַל־זֶבַח הַתּוֹדָה חַלּוֹת מַצּוֹת
בְּלוּלֹת בַּשֶּׁמֶן וּרְקִיקֵי מַצּוֹת
מְשֻׁחִים בַּשָּׁמֶן וְסֹלֶת מֻרְבֶּכֶת
חַלֹּת בְּלוּלֹת בַּשָּׁמֶן׃

---

11 **וזאת תורת זבח השלמים וגו׳**. From here we learn (*Zevachim* 120b) that, in the *halachos* of פיגול and נותר elaborated in the following verses, one law applies for all שלמים. These *halachos* apply to every שלמים and תודה — even when offered on a במה at the time of היתר הבמות. (See also Commentary to *Devarim* 12:5ff and *Shemos* 27:8.)

12–14 **אם על תודה יקריבנו**. We have already learned in chapter 3 about the שלמים offering. This offering is the expression of a person who, in a state of שלמות, seeks God's closeness. Here, Scripture introduces the קרבן תודה, the thanksgiving offering, which is a special type of שלמים. One who brings a תודה has attained a state of שלמות, after having been in danger and then delivered from it — e.g., those who survive the wilderness, are freed from prison, recover from illness, or survive the perils of the sea. These four are duty bound to give thanks (ארבעה צריכין להודות — see רש״י here), and of them Scripture says (*Tehillim* 107:21–22): יוֹדוּ לַה׳ חַסְדּוֹ וְנִפְלְאוֹתָיו לִבְנֵי אָדָם, וְיִזְבְּחוּ זִבְחֵי תוֹדָה וִיסַפְּרוּ מַעֲשָׂיו בְּרִנָּה. "Let them thank God for the lovingkindness He shows and the wonders He performs

13 *He shall bring his offering together with loaves of leavened bread, together with his meal-of-peace offering of thanksgiving.*

יג עַל־חַלֹּת לֶחֶם חָמֵץ יַקְרִיב
קָרְבָּנוֹ עַל־זֶבַח תּוֹדַת שְׁלָמָיו׃

14 *He shall bring from it one out of each offering, as an uplifted gift to* God; *it shall belong to the priest who dashes the blood of the peace offering [against the altar].*

יד וְהִקְרִיב מִמֶּנּוּ אֶחָד מִכָּל־קָרְבָּן
תְּרוּמָה לַיהוָה לַכֹּהֵן הַזֹּרֵק אֶת־
דַּם הַשְּׁלָמִים לוֹ יִהְיֶה׃

for human beings. Let them offer thanksgiving offerings and recount with great joy what God has done for them."

The conditional clause אם על תודה יקריבנו refers back to תורת זבח השלמים; from this we learn that the תודה is a type of שלמים. Thus, Scripture here elaborates only the *halachos* unique to תודה, but the *halachos* prescribed for all שלמים apply also to תודה — e.g., סמיכה ונסכים ותנופת חזה ושוק (*Toras Kohanim*).

והקריב על זבח התודה חלות וגו׳. The animal of the שלמים (זבח התודה) forms the center, to which the bread prescribed here is added. This bread is what gives the שלמים its character as a תודה.

First, three kinds of מצה are mentioned here (v. 12). Two of these, חלות and רקיקים, were mentioned above in the case of מנחה מאפה תנור (2:4), while the third — מרבכת — is known to us from חביתי כהן גדול (6:14). The three are identical to the three kinds of matzah mentioned at the מילואים (*Shemos* 29:2; see *Menachos* 78b).

Together with the *matzos*, one must also bring leavened bread, *chametz*. Scripture states (v. 13): על חלת לחם חמץ יקריב קרבנו; from this we learn that the three kinds of matzah form one קרבן group (קרבנו), and that together with and parallel to them one must bring *chametz* loaves, which form a second group. And all four kinds of bread accompany the animal of זבח תודת שלמיו. According to the Mishnah in *Menachos* (76b), the quantity of flour used for the three kinds of matzah is the same quantity used for the one kind of *chametz*: על חלות לחם חמץ – כנגד חמץ הבא מצה (ibid. 78a).

We find only one other offering that contains לחם חמץ — namely, שתי הלחם of Shevuos. It, too, is connected with קרבן שלמים, as it is brought with the שני כבשי עצרת. It appears that שלמי ציבור with לחם חמץ resemble שלמי תודה with לחם חמץ — only that the meaning of שלמי ציבור is for the nation, whereas the meaning of שלמי תודה is for the individual. Once a year, on the *Atzeres* of the festival of מתן תורה, the nation brings (תביאו — below, 23:17) its לחם חמץ before God, as the individual does on the other days of the year, when he comes to express תודה. Each one of the שתי הלחם is prepared from one עשרון, as Scripture says: שתים שני עשרונים (ibid.). Similarly, according to *Menachos* 77b, each one of the *chametz* loaves of the תודה is prepared from one עשרון.

Verse 14 states that one חלה from each of the four kinds of bread of the תודה — including the *chametz* loaves — is to be given, as תרומה לה׳, to the כהן. The Gemara in *Menachos* (ibid.) draws an equation between this תרומה and תרומת מעשר — where Scripture employs similar language: והרמתם ממנו תרומת ה׳ (*Bemidbar* 18:26) — and infers that תרומת תודה, also, is one out of ten. That is to say, each of the four kinds of bread consists of ten loaves, and one of each kind is taken as תרומה. We are speaking here, then, of forty loaves: ten of *chametz* and thirty of matzah. As stated above, each *chametz* loaf is prepared from one עשרון, and the quantity of flour used for all the matzah loaves is the same quantity used for the *chametz* loaves. Thus, the forty תודה loaves are made from twenty עשרונים: ten עשרונים for the ten *chametz* loaves, and ten עשרונים for the thirty matzah loaves (see *Menachos* 77a–b).

A relatively small amount of oil was used for the ten עשרונים of the תודה *matzos*. In other *menachos*, each עשרון receives one לוג. Here, the ten עשרונים together receive only half a לוג: half of this amount goes to the חלות and רקיקין (each receives an eighth of a לוג), and the other half to the רביכין (ibid. 89a).

The four kinds of bread of the תודה form one complete concept, and each one of them is indispensable for the validity of the whole, מעכבין זה את זה (ibid. 27a). Scripture, too, refers to them as one unit: והקריב ממנו (v. 14), from which we learn (ibid. 77b) that all the loaves must be together when the תרומה is lifted out: והקריב ממנו מן המחובר.

The bread is merely an accessory to the זבח. Hence, the bread becomes קדוש only with שחיטת הזבח — providing that the bread has formed a crust (קרמו פניה) by this time (see ibid. 78b).

Previously, in the chapter on מילואים (*Shemos* 29), we analyzed the *matzos* of the תודה, which are identical to לחם המילואים. We found that they represent sustenance and prosperity in various degrees — from the simple רקיק, which is just painted over externally with the oil of prosperity, to the oil-rich רביך, which is skillfully prepared. Sustenance and prosperity are the two elements that, more than anything else, reflect the condition of well-being. The *matzos* of the תודה signify that each and every degree of external well-being bears the meaning of matzah: its source and purpose is the service of God.

But the meaning of the תודה is not expressed by matzah alone; rather, it is expressed by two groups of bread: by *chametz* and by matzah. Both groups are made out of the same amount of flour, and the two together form the תודה unit. A life saved from danger by God's grace is embodied in the תודה by both *chametz* and matzah.

From the standpoint of man's position in the world, a life saved from danger is embodied by *chametz.* But this same position is itself embodied by matzah, when a person stands before God; and only as "matzah" does he take a share, large or small, in true prosperity. For *chametz* — as opposed to matzah — denotes a condition of independence. It represents man in control of all that is his, with nothing to impede him. He was delivered from some צרה that had inhibited his step. He emerged from dire straits and attained broad independence. This full independence that one enjoys in a condition of external well-being has no means of expression more fitting than ten *chametz* loaves. "Ten" is a round, closed number. In essence it is the quantitative expression of qualitative שלמות — immaculate and impeccable perfection. The ten *chametz* loaves represent the state of well-being of the person delivered from צרה; this state of well-being is what occasioned his bringing of a תודה. But he would not have offered a תודה, had he not conceived of this well-being as follows: What appears to be as *chametz* from the standpoint of his position in the world appears to him as "matzah" when he stands before God. For he knows that only by God's grace does he regain *chametz* — independence. Thus, as he regains worldly independence, his sense of dependence on God is renewed, and he commits himself anew to dedicate his whole life and all his independent powers to the service of God. He brings matzah in the same measure in which he brings *chametz*; and only this halachah of מצה נגד חמץ makes his offering a תודה. By bringing the same measure of matzah and *chametz,* he avoids all pride of independence, in respect to the condition of שלמות he has recovered. He feels that his regained independence only magnifies his obligation to serve God.

15 *And the flesh of his meal-of-peace offering of thanksgiving shall be eaten on the day it is offered; he must not leave any of it until the morning.*	טו וּבְשַׂ֗ר זֶ֚בַח תּוֹדַ֣ת שְׁלָמָ֔יו בְּי֥וֹם קָרְבָּנ֖וֹ יֵאָכֵ֑ל לֹֽא־יַנִּ֥יחַ מִמֶּ֖נּוּ עַד־בֹּֽקֶר׃

Now, this awareness of our dependence on God does not diminish our happiness or the richness of our lives. On the contrary, it is precisely this that lends value to our position in the world. The very fact that only by God's grace did we survive and reclaim our happiness, and that we will dedicate our lives to His service — this is what lends value to our happiness and enriches our lives. Indeed, only through "matzah" will our daily bread receive the "oil."

The forty loaves represent our external well-being, and one out of each ten must be separated as תרומה לה' and given to the כהן — i.e., to the בית אב serving on the day of the offering. תרומת לחמי תודה is similar in meaning to ביכורים, תרומה, and חלה, but with this difference: Those three relate to the blessings of the field, the threshing floor, and the home. תרומת לחמי תודה, however, relates to deliverance and all that this entails. It signifies that the deliverance and the resulting awareness of indebtedness — the whole relation of our lives to God as expressed by the חמץ and מצה of the תודה — come to us only by merit of the Torah, whose laws the כהן teaches. That is to say, our past is rooted only in the Torah, and our future is committed solely to its fulfillment. Only by performing the *mitzvos* of the Torah do we pay our debt of gratitude to God.

In *Menachos* 77b it is not resolved whether תרומת לחמי תודה is like תרומה in every respect — even as regards the penalty of מיתה and חומש.

15 Verses 15–18 elaborate upon the *halachos* concerning the time when the flesh of the offerings should be eaten: Scripture distinguishes between נאכלין ליום אחד and נאכלין לשני ימים ולילה אחד. In addition, other, related *halachos* are elaborated: נותר, פיגול (חוץ לזמנו), and פסול (חוץ למקומו). Scripture records these *halachos* in the section on תודה and שלמים because the eating of the meat is especially characteristic of these offerings, which is why they are called זבח (a meal, an offering that includes a meal).

טז וְאִם־נֶ֣דֶר ׀ א֣וֹ נְדָבָ֗ה זֶ֚בַח קָרְבָּנ֔וֹ
בְּי֛וֹם הַקְרִיב֥וֹ אֶת־זִבְח֖וֹ יֵאָכֵ֑ל
וּמִֽמָּחֳרָ֔ת וְהַנּוֹתָ֥ר מִמֶּ֖נּוּ יֵאָכֵֽל׃

16 *But if his meal offering is a vow or a free-will offering, it shall be eaten on the day it is brought near as an offering, and on the following day whatever is left of it may be eaten also.*

ביום קרבנו יאכל. These words serve to create a close relationship between the **אכילה** of the offering and its קריבה לה׳. This relationship is expressed in action: the **אכילה** and the קריבה must be performed on the same day. On the same day that the offering is "brought near to God," its flesh must be eaten by man. Yet Scripture does not employ a verb, such as **ביום הקריבו** of verse 16. Rather, the "bringing near to God" is expressed through a noun that serves as the general term for every offering: ביום קרבנו — "on the day that it becomes a קרבן." From this we learn that the relationship between **אכילה** and קריבה applies to everything that is termed קרבן and that involves human consumption. In all such cases, the time of eating is limited to יום קרבנו. Thus, this rule applies not only to תודה but also to לחמי תודה, on the one hand, and to חטאת, אשם, and מנחה, on the other. שלמים, too, would be included in this concept, but Scripture excluded them and extended the time frame in which they are to be eaten (v. 16).

The קריבה of animal קרבנות is accomplished through זריקה and the עבודות הדם that lead up to it (שחיטה, קבלה, הולכה, and זריקה), whereas the קריבה of מנחות is accomplished through the parallel קמיצה procedures — from קמיצה to הקטרת הקומץ, which corresponds to זריקת הדם. The day of the offering is defined as that day and the night that follows, up to the next morning. This is evident from what our verse states: לא יניח ממנו עד בקר. For in the Sanctuary the day is reckoned from morning unto morning, הלילה הולך אחר היום, in contrast to the ordinary day which is reckoned from night unto night, היום הולך אחר הלילה (see Commentary to *Shemos* 12:1–2; above, 6:2).

16 **ואם נדר או נדבה**. נדר — see Commentary to *Bereshis* 28:20–21; נדבה — see Commentary to *Shemos* 25:2, 35:5. Both offerings are completely voluntary, brought without any compelling cause. The נודר accepts upon himself an obligation using the verbal formula הרי עלי, "I take upon

myself to bring an offering"; the נודב dedicates an object via the formula הרי זו, "This is to be an offering."

נדר, then, is a personal obligation. Responsibility (אחריות) for the נדר rests upon the נודר until he fulfills the obligation he has undertaken. Accordingly, if one undertakes to bring an offering — e.g., he says הרי עלי שלמים — and the animal that he dedicates dies or becomes פסול, he is obligated to bring another animal.

נדבה, by contrast, is an obligation strictly in regard to an object. Accordingly, if one dedicates an animal — e.g., he says הרי זו שלמים — and then it dies or becomes פסול, he is free of responsibility, as his obligation related strictly to *this* animal.

Both — נדר and נדבה — are placed here in contrast to תודה. תודה is a שלמים that is brought because of an external factor. A person's deliverance from danger obligates him to express his gratitude by means of an offering. שלמים of נדר or נדבה, however, are not brought because of an external factor; they are not brought as an expression of gratitude for deliverance from danger. Rather, they represent a state of harmony that is maintained continually, without interruption.

ביום הקריבו את זבחו יאכל. שחיטה gives an offering the character of a זבח, as שחיטה is identical to זביחה, which primarily means "killing for the purpose of human consumption." Furthermore, as we have stated, the special import of הקרבה is זריקה, as זריקה shows the נפש the way to קרבת אלקים. Now, Scripture does not say here ביום הקריבו יאכל זבחו but, rather, ביום הקריבו את זבחו יאכל. From this manner of combining all three elements (שחיטה, זריקה, אכילה) the Gemara (*Zevachim* 56a–b) derives that the אכילה is connected not only with the זריקה, but also with the שחיטה; thus, זריקה, too, is permitted only on the day of the זביחה: ,ביום שאתה זובח אתה מקריבו ביום שאי אתה זובח אי אתה מקריבו. It follows, then, that דם נפסל בשקיעת החמה; and if, by the time of sunset, blood has not yet been offered, it may not be offered on the next day either. (שחיטה and זריקה, in any case, are not to be performed at night; see Commentary above, 6:2. See תוספות, *Zevachim* 56a, ד״ה מנין לדם שנפסל בשקיעת החמה. רבינו תם differentiates between the expressions שקיעת החמה and משתשקע החמה: שקיעה denotes the beginning of sunset; משתשקע denotes the end of sunset, which marks the beginning of night. Between the two שקיעות there is time to walk four מילין = 4 times 18 minutes, or one tenth the relative length of the day.)

17 *But whatever is left of the flesh of the meal offering shall be burned in fire on the third day.*	יז וְהַנּוֹתָ֖ר מִבְּשַׂ֣ר הַזָּ֑בַח בַּיּוֹם֙ הַשְּׁלִישִׁ֔י בָּאֵ֖שׁ יִשָּׂרֵֽף׃
18 *And if any of the flesh of his meal-of-peace offering should be eaten*	יח וְאִ֣ם הֵאָכֹ֣ל יֵ֠אָכֵל מִבְּשַׂר־זֶ֨בַח

What is stated here, then, is that זריקה and אכילה should be carried out on the day of the שחיטה, only that in the case of שלמי נדר ונדבה the אכילה is permitted also on the following day (וממחרת). This license, however, is stated in Scripture in דיעבד terms: Only that which is נותר ממנו, left over and not eaten on the first day, may still be eaten on the following day; but — even in the case of שלמים — it is a מצוה to eat the meat on the day of the זביחה (see *Toras Kohanim* here).

Even so, the וי״ו החיבור in והנותר remains difficult. Perhaps it can be said that יאכל in verses 15 and 16 refers not to the *actual* eating but to the *intention* of eating (מחשבת אכילה) — i.e., to the intention (in regard to eating) that a person has at the time of הקרבה. (This, in any case, is the explanation of יאכל in verse 18.) In this light, the וי״ו החיבור in והנותר becomes perfectly clear, and the explanation of verses 15 and 16 runs as follows: "The meat of his thanksgiving שלמים should be intended to be eaten on the day of the offering ... But if it is a נדר or a נדבה, then the intention must be to eat it on the day of the offering and also on the following day; and what *actually is* left over (on the following day) is permitted to be eaten."

17 **ביום השלישי באש ישרף**. One may not eat the meat of שלמים on the night following the second day. It may be eaten שני ימים ולילה אחד, two days and the intervening night. Nevertheless, it is to be burned only after daybreak of the third day, as פיגול and נותר (and — according to *Toras Kohanim* here — all other פסולים, too) are burned only by day (see *Shemos* 12:10). According to the Mishnah in *Zevachim* (56b) בכור and מעשר, too, are eaten for two days and a night — the same as שלמים.

18 **ואם האכל יאכל**. In *Zevachim* 28–29 the tradition is recorded that our verse speaks not of actual eating but of the intention to eat: If, at the

on the third day, it will not be accepted for him who offers it as being in accordance with the Divine Will. It will not be credited to him. It shall be a rejected thing. The person who eats of it will bear his iniquity.	**שְׁלָמָיו בַּיּוֹם הַשְּׁלִישִׁי לֹא יֵרָצֶה הַמַּקְרִיב אֹתוֹ לֹא יֵחָשֵׁב לוֹ פִּגּוּל יִהְיֶה וְהַנֶּפֶשׁ הָאֹכֶלֶת מִמֶּנּוּ עֲוֺנָהּ תִּשָּׂא׃**

time of the הקרבה, one intended to eat the meat beyond the prescribed time limit, this very intention (מחשבת חוץ לזמנו) renders the offering פסול. Even if, subsequently, this intention is not carried out, and all the other offering procedures are performed properly, the קרבן is פסול, and one who eats of it — even within the prescribed time limit — incurs the penalty of כרת (which is called here נשיאת עון, as it says: עונה תשא).

This interpretation of our verse is in accordance with the principle — which applies to all offerings — that once זריקה is performed, the בעלים gain atonement, and the offering is essentially valid; and no act performed afterwards, including partaking of the offering after the prescribed time limit, can retroactively nullify this validity. Moreover, from the text of Scripture it is evident that האכל יאכל ביום השלישי and the resulting פסול relate to the time of the הקרבה rather than the time of אכילה. For our verse states: המקריב אתו לא יחשב לו; from this we learn that בשעת הקרבה הוא נפסל ואינו נפסל בשלישי.

Furthermore, from the amplification האכל יאכל we learn that the אכילה referred to here should be taken in the wider sense, to include both consumption by man and consumption by the altar: אחד אכילת אדם ואחד אכילת מזבח. אכילת מזבח includes any procedure that entails giving to the altar; thus, it includes זריקה שפיכת שיריים והקטר חלבים. From the expression האכל יאכל we learn further (in *Zevachim* 13a) that this פסול מחשבה applies at all procedures that bring about the אכילה (מביאין לידי אכילה); that is to say, it applies not only during זריקה, but also during שחיטה קבלה והולכה, as all of these are indispensable to אכילת הקרבן. זריקה is cited here (המקריב אתו) merely as an example (יצתה להקיש אליה), to teach us that מחשבה פוסלת only at those עבודות that — like זריקה — are indispensable to the כפרה; this excludes שפיכת שיריים, which is only למצוה but not לעכב (see Commentary above, 1:5). The פסול caused by מחשבת

חוץ לזמנו is expressed here in three ways — פגול יהיה, לא יחשב לו, לא ירצה — which we will now consider:

לא ירצה. זריקה, when performed as prescribed, represents the person who is in accord with God's Will and who is ready to do His Will. But if — during זריקה or during one of the עבודות prior to זריקה — there occurs a מחשבת חוץ לזמנו, this relation between the person and רצון ה׳ is voided, and the purpose of the זריקה is defeated. The implication is that the פסול פיגול applies only if the הרצאה (i.e., the זריקה) is completed in all other respects. לא ירצה: the הרצאה is blocked solely by מחשבת הזמן; only in such a case does מחשבת הזמן lead to פיגול: ומה פסול הרצאת כן כשר כהרצאת הרצאת כשר עד שיקריבו כל מתיריו אף הרצאת פסול עד שיקריבו כל מתיריו (*Zevachim* 28b). (The מתיר is that *avodah* upon which אכילת מזבח and אכילת אדם depend — viz., זריקת הדם in קרבנות בהמה, and הקטרת הקומץ in מנחות.) For example: if there is מחשבת פיגול during שחיטה, קבלה, or הולכה, but then the זריקה is not performed, the offering is not rendered פיגול.

לא יחשב לו. זריקה, when performed as prescribed, connects the קרבן with the one who brings it; for the דם represents the נפש of the one bringing the offering. But if there is a מחשבת זמן during one of the עבודות הדם, this connection is voided. לא יחשב לו: a conceptual relationship is not established between the offering and the offerer. The implication is that, apart from this מחשבת פיגול, there must be no other cause that severs this connection: לא יערב בו מחשבות אחרות. For example: if, during the עבודות הדם, one had in mind some other thought capable of invalidating the offering — e.g., מחשבת חוץ למקומו (for more on this concept, see below), or שלא לשמה in the case of a פסח or חטאת — the offering is not rendered פיגול. These are two conditions upon which the law of פיגול depends: עד שיקריבו כל מתיריו and שלא יערב בו מחשבות אחרות. Both conditions can be formulated in one sentence: ובלבד שיקריב המתיר כמצותו (see Mishnah, *Zevachim* 29b).

פגול יהיה. The primary meaning of the root פגל is not clear. (The word appears only here and in a similar halachic context below [19:7]. In addition, we find: וּמְרַק פִּגֻּלִים [*Yeshayahu* 65:4]; וְלֹא־בָא בְּפִי בְּשַׂר פִּגּוּל [*Yechezkel* 4:14]. Clearly, both of these verses, too, allude to what is prohibited here in the Torah.) Nor does phonetic affinity yield an analogy. Perhaps פגל is identical with פלג, in which case פגול means division, separation, and extreme alienation. This we venture to suggest only as a possibility. Light support can be adduced from the Rabbinic term פקל; for it, too, signifies division and detachment via peeling: הבצלים משיפקל (*Maaseros* 1:6).

עונה תשא. Similarly, in the section on נותר, which is related to the section on פיגול, Scripture says: ואכליו עונו ישא — and then explains: ונכרתה הנפש ההוא מעמיה (below, 19:8). From this we learn that אכילת פיגול ונותר is punishable by כרת (see *Zevachim* 28b).

In *Zevachim* (ibid.) the further tradition is recorded that not only מחשבת חוץ לזמנו but also מחשבת חוץ למקומו (e.g., חישב לזרוק דמו או להקטיר חוץ לעזרה, or חישב לאכול בשר קדשי קדשים חוץ לעזרה או לאכול בשר קדשים קלים חוץ לירושלים) renders the offering פסול — with this difference: מחשבת חוץ למקומו invalidates the offering, but one who eats of it is not liable to כרת, whereas מחשבת חוץ לזמנו makes one who eats of it liable to כרת. In the Talmud, חוץ לזמנו is always referred to as פיגול, whereas חוץ למקומו is referred to simply as פסול.

The halachah of חוץ למקומו per se is accepted unanimously. Opinions differ only on the question of where פסול חוץ למקומו appears in Scripture. For, both the verse here, which is called קרא אריכא, and the shorter verse in פרשת קדושים (19:7) — according to their plain meaning — deal only with פסול חוץ לזמנו. The opinion finally accepted is that of רבא (*Zevachim* ibid.), who explains the view of his teacher רבה (ibid. 28a). According to this view, both פסולים are indicated in the קרא אריכא (our verse): שלישי - זה חוץ לזמנו; פיגול – זה חוץ למקומו. The term שלישי repeated in פרשת קדושים teaches that מחשבת חוץ למקומו invalidates the offering only if the intention concerns a place that is משולש בדם בבשר ובאימורין (ibid. 29a; see below).

This view raises many difficulties. For, according to this view, the term פיגול in Scripture refers to חוץ למקומו. Yet the context of our verse seems to indicate that פיגול relates only to חוץ לזמנו. Moreover, the term פיגול in the Talmud refers exclusively to חוץ לזמנו.

We have suggested, however, that the basic meaning of פיגול is separation. Indeed, both חוץ לזמנו and חוץ למקומו can be construed as a "separation" of אכילת אדם or אכילת מזבח from the שחיטה. The primary meaning of פיגול, then, could be *spatial* separation. (He who consumes the offering חוץ למקומו separates the זביחה in the עזרה from אכילת אדם or אכילת מזבח, which takes place in an unlawful place. This separation is concrete and apparent to the eye. It is different in the case of one who consumes the offering חוץ לזמנו. He, too, separates אכילה from זביחה. But this separation is not readily apparent and is known only to one who knows the day of the זביחה.) And the explanation of our verse, according to רבא, could be as follows: If one intends during the הקרבה to separate the time of the אכילה from the time of the שחיטה, then פיגול יהיה — it is as though he separates them spatially. That is to say, even though he plans to consume the offering within the Sanctuary, and he intends merely to postpone the time of the אכילה, the separation in time counts as a separation in place. Moreover, the punishment in this case is more severe: one who eats of the offering is liable to כרת. And from this we deduce that if one intends to consume the offering חוץ למקומו — to separate the place of the אכילה from the place of the שחיטה — the offering is פסול, but one who eats of it is not liable to כרת.

Various approaches are taken in רש״י and תוספות to explain the condition מקום שיהא משולש וכו׳ (ibid.), which relates to מחשבת חוץ למקומו. The chief difficulty is this: יום השלישי undoubtedly refers to חוץ לזמנו, yet רבא (ibid.) relates it to חוץ למקומו. If, however, our interpretation of רבא is correct, then both of these פסולים are included in the verse, and חוץ לזמנו is but an intensified aspect of חוץ למקומו. In this light we can understand the יש מפרשים cited and rejected by תוספות (ibid. ד״ה למקום שיהא משולש בדם ובבשר ואימורים); we can interpret and clarify their words as follows: יום השלישי means יום המשולש. That is to say, only a time that is forbidden for all three of the offering's אכילה-components – דם בשר ואימורים – is called חוץ לזמנו. But יום השלישי is repeated in פרשת קדושים. From this repetition we learn that a similar halachah applies also to חוץ למקומו. That is to say, only a מקום משולש, a place where all three אכילה-components are forbidden, is called חוץ למקומו. In a word: מחשבת חוץ לזמנו as well as מחשבת חוץ למקומו relate to a time or place that is מופגל — i.e., מופלג, beyond the bounds of the offering — where דם and בשר and אימורים are all forbidden. For the halachic ramifications of this conception, see תוספות (ibid.).

The whole preceding discussion is summarized in two sentences of the Mishnah (*Zevachim* 27b; 29b): השוחט את הזבח לזרוק דמו בחוץ או מקצת דמו בחוץ, להקטיר אימוריו בחוץ או מקצת אימוריו בחוץ, לאכול בשרו בחוץ או כזית מבשרו בחוץ ... פסול ואין בו כרת; לזרוק דמו למחר, מקצת דמו למחר, להקטיר אימוריו למחר או מקצת אימוריו למחר, לאכול בשרו למחר או כזית מבשרו למחר ... פיגול וחייבין עליו כרת. זה הכלל: כל השוחט והמקבל והמהלך והזורק לאכול דבר שדרכו לאכול, ולהקטיר דבר שדרכו להקטיר, כזית חוץ למקומו פסול ואין בו כרת, חוץ לזמנו פגול וחייבין עליו כרת, ובלבד שיקריב המתיר כמצותו.

We have already mentioned that the four עבודות הקומץ of the מנחה offering (קמיצה, נתינה בכלי, הולכה, and הקטרת הקומץ) correspond to the four עבודות הדם of קרבן בהמה; hence, the law of מחשבת חוץ לזמנו ומקומו applies also to these four עבודות הקומץ — e.g., הקומץ ... לאכול שיריה בחוץ (see *Menachos* 11b, et seq.).

The פוסקים differ as to whether מחשבה alone — without verbal expression — suffices to invalidate the קרבן. See משנה למלך to הל׳ פסולי המוקדשין, 13:1.

Let us now attempt to find the idea that is expressed in the *halachos* of verses 15–18. Their common subject is the relationship between שחיטת הקרבן and the offering procedures included in the concept of אכילה (or the relationship between קמיצת המנחה and its אכילה).

First we are told that תודה — and all other offerings except בכור מעשר ושלמים — may be eaten only on the day of the שחיטה and on the night that follows (יום ולילה). Similarly, מנחה may be eaten only on the day of the קמיצה and the night that follows. שלמים — and also בכור ומעשר — may be eaten one day longer (שני ימים ולילה אחד). That which is not consumed within these times must be burned by day.

Relatedly, זריקה, too, must be performed on the day of the שחיטה, before sunset — as זריקה, too, is included in the concept of אכילת מזבח. As for the second act of אכילת מזבח — viz., הקטר חלבים ואיברים — we learned previously (in chapter 6) that it is permitted also throughout the night that follows, as the night, too, is included in the day of the offering.

To summarize: אכילת אדם and אכילת מזבח are valid only on the offering-day of the שחיטה. Only in the case of שלמים is אכילת אדם permitted also on the following day. From this we learn of the close connection between אכילת אדם ומזבח and שחיטה. And great importance is attached to this connection. We see its importance from the fact that if, during any of the עבודות הדם, one intends to perform, or says that he will perform, an action that would disrupt this connection, he thereby invalidates the entire offering; and the intention to consume the offering beyond the prescribed time limit makes the one who eats of it liable to כרת.

שחיטה, זביחה, represents the renouncement of selfish, uncontrolled living. It is the negative side of the offering procedures; it is the negation of a former mode of being. זריקה, הקטרה, and אכילת בשר — in short: אכילת מזבח ואדם — are the positive side. They provide שחיטה with its positive purpose. For the purpose of renouncing the life led formerly is to lead a more noble life presently, for the sake of the holy. Moreover, through אכילת אדם man regains what he had relinquished, and the very life that he had offered up to God is uplifted and sanctified.

These two sides — the positive and the negative — are interconnected and interdependent. The Torah asks of man that he cease living a purely physical life, only in order that he rise to a more exalted life, lived for God and the fulfillment of His Will. At the same time, one cannot sanctify his earthly existence unless he ceases living a purely physical life ruled by physical drives. The sole purpose of זביחה is אכילה, and there can be no אכילה without זביחה. If the connection between these two elements is severed, then זביחה without אכילה represents self-destruction without any moral purpose; and אכילה without זביחה represents deification of the flesh, with the uncontrolled emancipation of the senses becoming an ideal, becoming the mission of the person seeking God's closeness. If this is how a person brings his קרבן, if this is how he seeks to draw near to God, then זביחה without אכילה represents the metaphysical lie of heathenism, which claims that willful self-destruction appeases the anger and jealousy of the gods; and אכילה without זביחה represents the ethical lie of heathenism, which deifies sensual drives and exalts the unbridled yielding to them as a sacred ritual. זביחה without אכילה lowers the conception of God to a blood-thirsty deity; אכילה without זביחה desecrates the Sanctuary and consecrates within it orgies of unbridled license.

We understand the requirement that ביום הקריבו את קרבנו יאכל, זבחו יאכל. For the close connection between זריקה-אכילה and זביחה safeguards the purity of the moral idea of both. This halachah — which upholds the truth and morality of the whole idea of the offerings — is written in the section on תודה and שלמים. This, too, we now understand. For what moves us to bring these offerings is the sense that our fate depends on God; and their central theme is consecration of the joy we take in our lot. Precisely this awareness and this aspiration are fertile soil for those heathen lies that distort the truth and destroy morality. Accordingly, it is in the very idea of these offerings that the perniciousness of those fallacious notions shows itself; and this law of אכילה and זביחה serves to counteract such notions.

We also understand the halachah that נותר ביום באש ישרף and אכליו עונו ישא כי את קדש ה׳ חלל ונכרתה הנפש ההוא מעמיה (below, 19:8). נותר — viz., בשר קודש separated from the זביחה — represents אכילה that does not stem from זביחה; that is to say, it represents uncontrolled satisfaction of the senses, not subjected to Divine disciplines. He who eats נותר as בשר קודש violates the holiness of the Sanctuary, which is none other than the Sanctuary of the Torah. Even the very existence of נותר threatens the holiness of the Sanctuary, and the destruction of נותר by fire restores its sanctity. Therefore, this burning must be done by day — like all other holy rituals in the Sanctuary.

We still must consider why a time extension is granted for אכילת אדם in the case of שלמים. The extension is not for a whole extra day, as שלמים are not eaten for שני ימים ושני לילות but only שני ימים ולילה אחד, two days and the intervening night. At nightfall of the second day שלמים become נותר, but they are not burned until the next day, as שריפת קדשים is performed by day. Thus, only the day following the first night is added to the time that is fit for eating שלמים.

We know that in the Sanctuary the night belongs to the preceding day, while outside the Sanctuary the day belongs to the preceding night. Now, the fundamental character of שלמים consists in the fact that their בשר may be eaten also outside the Sanctuary, נאכלין בכל העיר; for they signify God's closeness in ordinary, family life, and they transform the home into a sanctuary of God. Hence, just as the Sanctuary is extended spatially, and the site of family life is sanctified with the holiness of the Sanctuary, so is there an extension in terms of time; and the time extension granted for אכילת שלמים represents the sanctification of ordinary, family life and its integration into the holiness of the Sanctuary. Through שני ימים ולילה אחד the civil day is added to the Sanctuary day, and we have a complete day according to two ways of reckoning the day. It begins in the morning, like the beginning of the Sanctuary day, and ends in the evening, like the end of the civil day. It consists of a day, from morning until morning, as observed in the Sanctuary, and to this is added the following day until sunset; for, outside the Sanctuary, this day, too, belongs to the preceding night.

It is different in the case of תודה. For one who brings a תודה was saved by God's grace; the delivering hand of God manifested itself in his life. Hence, the need is felt in this case to join the אכילה to the זביחה. He should enjoy his regained happiness only on the basis of surrendering and committing himself totally to God; for he undertakes to devote himself to God with all his strength — after all that has happened to him. Scripture therefore limits the time for אכילת תודה and equates it with אכילת קדשי קדשים — in respect to the intimate connection between אכילה and זביחה.

Now, if — during one of the עבודות הדם, which represent the new relation of the נפש to God — one intends to separate זביחה from אכילה, and אכילה from זביחה, and even if one intends this only in regard to the smallest portion worth mentioning (כזית הראוי לאכילה או להקטרה), such an intention is the antithesis of the idea of the offering and contradicts its whole truth and moral purity. לא ירצה ולא יחשב לו: such זביחה and such אכילת מזבח ואדם are incapable of representing the fulfillment of God's Will or the realization of man's destiny. Self-destruction, on the one hand, and lack of restraint, on the other, are the very opposite of the Will of God and the destiny of man.

פיגול יהיה: Although the separation is only in intention, only in time, and all is to be kept within the bounds of the Sanctuary, nevertheless the offering is considered "torn asunder" in its essential elements — as though it had been subjected to actual, spatial separation. Moreover, the offerer introduces into the Sanctuary itself the antithesis of the idea of the offering; he seeks sanction for this antithetical idea within the bounds of the Sanctuary. Thus, the separation of the offering's elements in time (מחשבת חוץ לזמנו) is worse than the separation in place (חוץ למקומו); the former — more so than the latter — undermines the conceptual foundation of the Sanctuary. He who has in mind a מחשבת חוץ למקומו intends to perform זריקה, הקטרה, or אכילת בשר קודש outside of the Sanctuary. Thus, he turns his back on God's Sanctuary — but he does not think that separation of these elements is possible in the setting of God's Sanctuary. He who has in mind a מחשבת חוץ לזמנו, however, intends to tear asunder the basic elements of the Sanctuary *within* the bounds of the Sanctuary. The Sanctuary itself is asked to sanction the undermining of its moral foundation. חוץ למקומו only invalidates the offering; one does not become liable to כרת on its account. חוץ לזמנו is פיגול and makes one liable to כרת. Similarly, he who leaves Judaism and turns his back on the Sanctuary does not bring ruin upon the holy things of Israel. But the Sanctuary *is* threatened when apostasy is introduced into its midst; when arbitrariness is sanctioned within the Sanctuary itself. People stand within the Sanctuary, as it were — even though they have already turned it into the very opposite; and the Sanctuary itself is asked to sanction the undermining of its moral foundations. Such is פיגול. That is why it is פיגול only if קרב המתיר כמצותו: only if everything else

19 *And the flesh that touches any impure thing shall not be eaten; it shall be burned in fire. As for the flesh, anyone who is pure may partake of it.*

יט וְהַבָּשָׂר אֲשֶׁר־יִגַּע בְּכָל־טָמֵא לֹא יֵאָכֵל בָּאֵשׁ יִשָּׂרֵף וְהַבָּשָׂר כָּל־טָהוֹר יֹאכַל בָּשָׂר׃

20 *But the person who eats of the flesh of the meal-of-peace offering that is* God's, *while his impurity is still upon him, that person will be uprooted from his people.*

כ וְהַנֶּפֶשׁ אֲשֶׁר־תֹּאכַל בָּשָׂר מִזֶּבַח הַשְּׁלָמִים אֲשֶׁר לַיהוָה וְטֻמְאָתוֹ עָלָיו וְנִכְרְתָה הַנֶּפֶשׁ הַהִוא מֵעַמֶּיהָ׃

21 *A person who touches anything impure — whether the impurity of a human being, an impure animal, or any impure creeping thing — and then eats of the flesh of the meal-of-peace offering that is* God's, *that person shall be uprooted from his people.*

כא וְנֶפֶשׁ כִּי־תִגַּע בְּכָל־טָמֵא בְּטֻמְאַת אָדָם אוֹ | בִּבְהֵמָה טְמֵאָה אוֹ בְּכָל־שֶׁקֶץ טָמֵא וְאָכַל מִבְּשַׂר־זֶבַח הַשְּׁלָמִים אֲשֶׁר לַיהוָה וְנִכְרְתָה הַנֶּפֶשׁ הַהִוא מֵעַמֶּיהָ׃

has been done as prescribed and the offering has not been invalidated for other reasons. Only then does it appear as though the separation of the basic elements of the offering has been sanctioned as a perfectly normal proceeding.

19–21 These verses add two more instances in which it is forbidden to partake of the meat of the offering. Verse 19 deals with the case of בשר קדשים שנטמא, whereas verses 20–21 deal with the case of בשר קדשים טהור בטומאת הגוף. The former, טומאת עצמו, is בלאו; the latter, בטומאת הגוף, is בכרת.

והבשר — and similarly בשר in the latter part of the verse — refers to בשר קדשים, which was mentioned in the preceding verses. This is evident also in verse 20. Thus, in the laws of טומאה and טהרה — which relate to אכילת בשר קדשים — the meat of offerings is called simply בשר. From this we learn something about the concepts of טומאה and טהרה. These concepts are rooted in the depth of human existence, in its very nature and purpose. The Halachah gives symbolic expression to this — in קדשים alone; but what is taught in קדשים as a symbol must be actualized in the life of man. Indeed there were men in Israel who, seeking to attain moral purity, applied the symbolic laws of טהרה — which the Torah prescribes only for קדשים — to everyday life: היו אוכלין גם את חוליהן בטהרה. As early as the time of Sha'ul and David, we find this code of conduct observed in all its glory (see *Shemuel* I, 21:6).

On various occasions we have defined the concepts signified by טומאה and טהרה. Clearly, טומאה signifies a lack of freedom. For man is destined to live in moral freedom; but whenever a living organism succumbs to compelling physical forces, this is liable to give rise to the notion that man lacks freedom. And there is nothing that fosters this notion more than a dead body.

Etymologically it appears that טמא can be explained based on its relation to טמע, דמע, and טמה (cf. the Rabbinic idiom יורד לטמיון), all of which denote an object's loss of independence, its sinking and assimilation into something else. This concept is related also to the meaning of דמה — particularly the passive נדמה: to be the same, to be silenced. טמא, then, in the concrete sense, denotes that which has lost the freedom of its vital, independent existence (in Aramaic, טמיא actually means the bone of a dead body). In the symbolic sense, the טמא signifies loss of moral freedom for him who comes in contact with it; the טמא drags him down, too, into the abyss of a lack of freedom.

טהור, by contrast, appears to be an extension of טור, a row (cf. the relation between בהן and בון; כהן and כון; קהל and קול; רהב and רוב; and the like). It denotes a state in which the connection between constituent parts is fixed according to their own qualities. The parts are joined together, according to this connection, without external constraint, and the principle that governs the whole is also the sole governing principle of the parts (cf. תור and תואר). טהור, then, in the concrete sense, denotes that which is free of external constraint and can develop in freedom under its own governing principle. In the symbolic sense, the טהור represents a state of moral freedom unfettered by any external constraint. (Previously we interpreted that טמא is related to טמם, and טהור to צהר [see Commentary, *Bereshis* 7:2]; but now the etymology expounded here appears to us to be the correct one.)

Yevamos 74b cites תלתא קראי, three verses, that describe the purification of a ritually impure person. It appears from these verses that a person is rendered ritually pure in three stages: (a) ולא יאכל מן הקדשים כי אם רחץ בשרו במים (below, 22:6), where אכילת קדשים depends on טבילה alone; (b) ובא השמש וטהר ואחר יאכל מן הקדשים (below, 22:7), where the setting of the sun is required before אכילת קדשים; and (c) וכפר עליה הכהן וטהרה (below, 12:8), where טהרה depends on the bringing of an offering. The significance of these three successive stages is explained there as follows: After טבילה, but before הערב שמש, one may eat מעשר שני but not yet תרומה or קדשים. With הערב שמש one may eat תרומה; but if his טומאה makes him liable to a קרבן (as in the case of זב וזבה יולדת ומצורע) he may eat קדשים only after he has brought the קרבן. Thus, a מחוסר כפרה may eat תרומה but not קדשים. These are three stages in which a person is purified of his טומאה.

Parallel to these three stages, there are also three degrees of טומאה conveyed from one object to another. These degrees derive their names from the number of objects through which the טומאה has been conveyed, and the magnitude of the degree decreases in direct proportion to the number of objects conveying the טומאה. The source of the טומאה — e.g., a נבילה — is called אב הטומאה. What touches it is called ראשון. What touches the ראשון is called שני, and so on, שלישי and רביעי. And an object's susceptibility to טומאה escalates with its degree of sanctity: חולין contract טומאה solely from a ראשון, and אין שני עושה שלישי בחולין. תרומה contracts טומאה from a שני as well, whereas קדשים contract טומאה even from a שלישי. It follows, then, that a טבול יום (a ritually impure person who has immersed, but must wait until nightfall to regain ritual purity in order to eat תרומה) has the degree of a שני, and a מחוסר כפרה (who cannot eat קדשים) has the degree of a שלישי. An object that becomes טמא but cannot convey טומאה is called פסול rather than טמא, and here all depends on the object's degree of sanctity: שני is פסול in חולין, שלישי is פסול in תרומה, רביעי is פסול in קדשים (see *Pesachim* 18b; *Chagigah* 24a; according to רש״י [ibid., ד״ה אינו דין] מחוסר כפרה and שלישי are merely מעלות דרבנן in קודש, but תוספות [ibid., ד״ה מנין] disagree, and so does the רמב״ם [הל׳ אבות הטומאות, 11:4]).

Here, Scripture says: והבשר אשר יגע בכל טמא וגו׳. Below (11:33), Scripture says: כל אשר בתוכו יטמא — i.e., the contents of a כלי חרס that has been rendered טמא by a שרץ are pronounced "טמא." Now, the שרץ is an אב, the כלי חרס is ראשון, and its contents are שני. From this we derive that בכל טמא of our verse includes at least שני, and that שני עושה שלישי בקודש. And we derive further, by קל וחומר from מחוסר כיפורים, that טמא of our verse includes also שלישי, and that שלישי עושה רביעי בקודש (*Pesachim* 18b–19a; *Chagigah* 24a).

According to *Sotah* 29a, our verse distinguishes between טומאת בשר and טומאת הגוף. The Gemara says as follows: והבשר אשר יגע בכל טמא לא יאכל, ודאי טמא הוא דלא יאכל הא ספק טמא וספק טהור יאכל, אימא סיפא והבשר כל טהור יאכל בשר, ודאי טהור הוא דיאכל בשר הא ספק טמא וספק טהור לא יאכל. From this, רב גידל — on רב's authority — derives a major principle in הלכות טומאה: דבר שיש בו דעת לישאל ספקו טמא; דבר שאין בו דעת לישאל ספקו טהור. ר' יוחנן completes this הלכה in *Pesachim* 19b–20a: ספק טומאה הבאה בידי אדם נשאלין עליה, אפילו בכלי המונח על גבי קרקע כדבר שיש בו דעת לישאל. In sum: A case of doubtful טומאה concerning an object devoid of reason — e.g., a piece of meat lies near a שרץ טמא, and there is doubt whether they came in contact — is ruled טהור. By contrast, a case of doubtful טומאה concerning the state or actions of a person endowed with reason — e.g., there is doubt whether an adult came in contact with טומאה; or there is doubt whether, as a result of his actions, something טמא touched something טהור — is ruled טמא.

The Gemara in *Sotah* also discusses ספק טומאה — in the corresponding case of סוטה — that is not symbolic טומאה but actual, moral טומאה. This ספק, too, is treated as אסור, and Scripture says of it ונסתרה והיא נטמאה (*Bemidbar* 5:13). From here we learn that a doubt in regard to a דבר שיש בו דעת לישאל is treated as טמא, only if it arises במקום סתירה, i.e., ברשות היחיד. But if doubt over a person's state or actions arises ברשות הרבים, or ברשות היחיד when there are at least two other persons (according to the רשב״א, in his commentary to *Niddah* 5b: two other men) present beside himself (in which case they count as רבים), the doubt is not treated as טמא. This is the rule: – דבר שיש בו דעת לישאל ברשות היחיד ספיקו טמא, ברשות הרבים ספיקו טהור; ושאין בו דעת לישאל – בין ברשות היחיד בין ברשות הרבים ספיקו טהור (*Sotah* 28b).

According to תוספות (*Niddah* 2a, ד״ה מעת לעת) and the רמב״ם (הל' אבות הטומאות, 16:3 et seq.) it appears that a case of doubtful טומאה concerning an object devoid of reason is ruled טהור, even in an instance of a ספק השקול, whereas a case of doubtful טומאה concerning a person endowed with reason is ruled טמא, even if there was a חזקת טהרה, presumption of טהרה.

Thus, a case of doubtful טומאה concerning an object devoid of reason is ruled more leniently than a case of doubt in all other איסורים. For the rule in all other איסורים is ספק דאורייתא לחומרא; and according to the overwhelming majority of authorities, this very rule applies מדאורייתא (see Commentary above, end of chap. 5). The Torah here (as in other laws of טומאה, which we will discuss below, 11:29 et seq.) is apparently signaling to us, to keep us from mistaken notions: We should not think that when טומאה touches an object, it exerts upon that object an actual, magic and invisible influence. For were טומאה to exert a harmful, actual and magic influence, doubtful טומאה would not be treated more leniently than all other ספקות. On the contrary, טומאה would lead to סכנה, and the Gemara says: חמירא סכנתא מאיסורא (*Chullin* 10a). This is one of the proofs that הלכות טומאה belong to the category of symbolic laws; i.e., they call to mind and make us conscious of the most important truths. As further proof we cite the fact that the Torah does not forbid a ישראל to become טמא, and even a כהן is forbidden only in regard to טומאת מת. Otherwise, כהנים and ישראלים are prohibited in regard to טומאה only when they are about to come in contact with מקדשיו וקדשיו.

On the other hand, a case of doubtful טומאה concerning the state or actions of a person endowed with reason (דבר שיש בו דעת לישאל) is ruled more strictly. This is an idea with which we are familiar; for ידיעת הטומאה — along with שמיעת קול and שבועת ביטוי — was singled out from all the other *mitzvos* and assigned a קרבן עולה ויורד. הלכות טומאה are intended to heighten our consciousness of personal, autonomous God and of personal, autonomous man. This consciousness is the basis for all of Jewish belief, and the purpose of מקדש וקדשיו is to lead us to this belief. Hence, forgetfulness of these *halachos* obligates one to seek atonement through a special offering. Here, too, a Jew endowed with intelligence is not allowed to partake of קדשים unless it is clear to him — beyond the shadow of a doubt — that he is free of all טומאה. Similarly, any object which comes in contact with a person endowed with intelligence, or any object for which such a person causes contact, cannot be called טהור unless its טהרה is absolutely clear to him.

As we have stated, the חומרא of דבר שיש בו דעת לישאל applies only in רשות היחיד, whereas ספק טומאה ברשות הרבים is טהור. The ירושלמי (see תוספות, *Sotah* 28b) and also the רמב״ם (הל׳ אבות הטומאות, 16:1) connect this halachah (ספק טומאה ברשות הרבים) with the law that טומאה דחויה בציבור, טומאה retreats before the public, and ציבור עושין פסח בטומאה בזמן שרובו של טומאה

ציבור טמאין, the nation — when the majority is טמא — brings the Pesach offering בטומאה (see Commentary, *Bemidbar* 9:2).

This law (טומאה דחויה בציבור) graphically demonstrates the spiritual and moral stature of the human community. אין ציבור מת, a community does not die; the nation knows no death. Even the individual, by devoting his actions to the welfare of the community, redeems the spiritual fruit of his earthly labors and saves it from the clutches of death. He, too — while yet in this world — partakes of immortality. Such a view obviously does not conceive of the community as a union of individuals cooperating in order to achieve material power. If that were so, the nation, too, would be in the power of death; the nation and its aspirations would be transitory — no less than the individual and his desires. Rather, the nation is the eternal bearer of the abiding values of mankind; the community represents the everlastingness of man with all of his spiritual and moral values. These values comprise the essence of what unites the individuals and transforms them into a people. The very idea of the community, then, represents the moral freedom of man. Hence, טומאה דחויה בציבור. For the idea of the community allays the threat to moral freedom-consciousness; one need not fear that the physical subjection of טומאה will carry over into the moral realm. The טהרה represented by the idea of the community exerts a positive influence. Hence, if a case of doubtful טומאה arises under the aegis of the community — ברשות הרבים, בפני שלשה — the idea of the community tips the scale in favor of טהרה. That is why, as the ירושלמי puts it, ספק טומאה דחויה בציבור — i.e., ספק טומאה ברשות הרבים טהור.

As we have stated, אכילת בשר בטומאת הגוף, when the *person* is טמא, is punishable by כרת, whereas אכילת בשר שנטמא, when the *meat* is טמא, is only בלאו. The reason for this seems to be as follows: In the case of טומאת בשר, the קודש idea has already been tarnished by טומאה. In the case of טומאת הגוף, however, the person deliberately contradicts the קודש idea. Moreover, he does so at the very time, and through the very act by which, he is supposed to absorb this idea by means of אכילת קדשים. Once a person has become טמא, he is forbidden to enter the Sanctuary and to eat קדשים; and if he violates this prohibition, even if only in error, he must seek atonement by means of a קרבן עולה ויורד. And since אכילת בשר בטומאת הגוף is an איסור כולל (see Commentary below, v. 24), this איסור extends even to קודש that has already become

טמא; hence הטמא שאכל בין קדש טמא בין קדש טהור חייב (*Zevachim* 106a; 108a).

בשר שנטמא, and also נותר (v. 17), must be burned; and by way of tradition we know that this applies to all פסולי הקודש, both קדשים קלים and קדשי קדשים. They, too, require שריפה in order to restore the קודש idea, which has been impinged upon by the פסול (see *Pesachim* 82b). If the פסול hinges on the בשר itself — as in לן (נותר), יוצא, טמא, and also פיגול — then it is burned immediately: כל שפסולו בגופו ישרף מיד. But if the source of the פסול is external to the בשר — e.g., if all the blood has been spilled, and זריקה cannot be performed; or if בשר הפסח, which may be eaten only למנויו, has no אוכלים, as all the בעלים have become טמא — then the בשר is held over until the next day; as a result, the בשר becomes נותר as well, and the פסול hinges on the בשר itself. This holding over of the בשר overnight is called עיבור צורה: the בשר is to lose its freshness, so that the פסול is recognizable in the בשר itself. Thus כל שפסולו בגופו ישרף מיד, בדם ובבעלים תעובר צורתן ויוצאין לבית השריפה (ibid. 34b). The same applies to בשר that is פסול because of doubt: through עיבור צורה it becomes definitely פסול (ibid. 34a).

From the sentence כל טהור יאכל בשר (v. 19) *Toras Kohanim* learns further that anyone who is טהור may partake of the family meal of שלמים, which need not be restricted — like the similar פסח — to a closed company, decided upon beforehand.

As we have stated, verse 20 speaks of טומאת הגוף and not of טומאת בשר. In *Zevachim* (43b) this is proven also from the expression וטמאתו עליו ("while his טומאה is still upon him"), which depicts טומאה as a temporary state: מי שטומאה פורחת ממנו. From this we infer that the verse speaks only of טומאת הגוף, which has an antidote — namely, טהרה במקוה, unlike בשר שנטמא, which has no טהרה במקוה.

21 The expression וטמאתו עליו in verse 20 relates primarily to טומאה שיצאה עליו מגופו — e.g., מצורע, זב, etc. Verse 21 adds טומאה that is conveyed via נגיעה. The latter verse mentions טומאות קלות as well as חמורות: קלות, such as טומאת שרץ; חמורות, such as טומאת אדם (מצורע, זב, מת, etc.); and between the two of them it mentions טומאת נבילה (בהמה טמאה). From this we learn that, in the case of טומאת הגוף, one is liable to כרת even on account of קלות; and that in the case of טומאת בשר one violates only a לאו and is not liable to כרת even on account of חמורות (*Toras Kohanim*; see *Zevachim* 43b).

22 God *spoke to Moshe, saying:*

23 *Speak to the Children of Israel, saying: You shall not eat any fat of oxen, sheep, or goats.*

כב וַיְדַבֵּר יְהֹוָה אֶל־מֹשֶׁה לֵּאמֹר׃

כג דַּבֵּר אֶל־בְּנֵי יִשְׂרָאֵל לֵאמֹר כָּל־חֵלֶב שׁוֹר וְכֶשֶׂב וָעֵז לֹא תֹאכֵלוּ׃

22 The *halachos* mentioned until now in chapters 6 and 7 complete the laws of the offerings; hence, they are addressed to the כהנים (cf. 6:2, 18), who are charged with fulfilling them. The next two sections (vv. 22–27; 28–36), however, are addressed directly to the people. The second section (vv. 28–36) supplements the laws of the שלמים offering and deals mainly with responsibilities of the people. This section, then, is closely connected with the שלמים laws of verses 11–21. Similarly, the first section (vv. 22–27), which intervenes between the two שלמים sections, supplements the laws of חלב and דם (prohibited above, 3:17) and is closely connected with the laws of the offerings. Its whole purpose is to draw conclusions from these offering laws, vis-à-vis the people.

Similarly, we find that כל חלב וכל דם לא תאכלו (3:17) is the concluding sentence of the laws of שלמים. This sentence is essentially a consequence of the preceding כל חלב לה׳ (3:16). From this perspective we explained (above, 3:17) the reason for the prohibition of חלב and דם: This prohibition is a consequence, unlimited by time or place — חקת עולם לדרתיכם בכל מושבותיכם — of the offering laws, which apply for all time.

23 Here, first of all, the prohibition of חלב is restricted. It applies only to an animal of a kind that is fit for an offering: שור וכשב ועז. In other words: in the case of עוף and חיה, חלב is not forbidden; and in the case of כוי, which is a cross between a חיה and a בהמה, חלב is אסור out of doubt. Furthermore, only חלב that is offered from all three kinds of animals is forbidden; this excludes אליה, as only אלית הכבש is counted (above, 3:9) among the חלבים offered on the altar (see *Chullin* 117a).

On the other hand, the prohibition is extended by the words כל חלב. For the עונש, the punishment (v. 25), is worded כי כל אכל חלב and not כי כל אכל כל חלב; thus (as we know from tradition), one does not become liable to כרת unless he eats at least a כזית, and this is also the law in other אכילה prohibitions. Yet the אזהרה, the prohibition, is worded כל חלב

24 *And the fat of an animal that has died of itself and the fat of that which was seized to be devoured may be used for any other purpose, but for [both] these reasons you must not eat it.*

כד וְחֵלֶב נְבֵלָה וְחֵלֶב טְרֵפָה יֵעָשֶׂה לְכָל־מְלָאכָה וְאָכֹל לֹא תֹאכְלֻהוּ׃

לא תאכלו; thus, in the case of חלב and also other אכילה prohibitions חצי שיעור אסור מן התורה, even the smallest quantity is forbidden by Torah law, despite the fact that punishment is incurred only if one eats a כזית (*Yoma* 74a).

24 **וחלב נבלה וחלב טרפה יעשה לכל מלאכה וגו׳**. The combined case of חלב נבלה וגו׳ teaches several things. Here we see that חלב as well as נבילה and טרפה are forbidden only to be eaten, but may be used for any other purpose (מותרים בהנאה). For according to ר׳ אבהו (*Pesachim* 21b), whose view is accepted as halachah, wherever אכילה is forbidden הנאה also is forbidden, unless the Torah expressly permits it as in the case of נבילה (see *Devarim* 14:21).

However, the permissibility of הנאה in the case of the three איסורים mentioned in our verse is known to us from other sources. In the case of נבילה, express permission is granted in *Devarim* (ibid.); and according to ר׳ עקיבא (*Pesachim* 23b) this implies a היתר הנאה for חלב as well, since כשהותרה נבילה חלבה וגידה נמי הותרו — i.e., the היתר הנאה in the case of נבילה applies to all parts of the animal, including its חלב. The היתר הנאה in the case of טריפה, too, is stated elsewhere: לכלב תשלכון אתו (*Shemos* 22:30); from this we learn that one may feed טריפה to animals.

Hence, according to ר׳ עקיבא, our verse here teaches only that חלב נבילה is not subject to טומאת נבילה and can be used לכל מלאכה, even for מלאכת הקדש: איסור והיתר לא צריך קרא וכי איצטריך קרא לטומאה ולטהרה.

The exemption of חלב from טומאת נבילה, however, is mentioned here in connection with חלב טריפה and with the prohibition of eating either of them: ואכל לא תאכלהו. From this we learn that our verse speaks only of חלב of a בהמה טהורה — an animal of the kind for which the condition of טריפה is halachically meaningful, and whose חלב is forbidden to be eaten. This excludes a בהמה טמאה, whose condition as טריפה is halachically meaningless; and this also excludes a חיה, whose חלב is permitted to be eaten. Thus, חלב בהמה טמאה וחלב חיה are not exempt from טומאת נבילה, and only חלב בהמה טהורה is טהור מטומאת נבילה (see *Zevachim* 70a and b).

ואכל לא תאכלהו. Although טומאת נבילה does not extend to the חלב, the איסור אכילת נבילה does extend to it; and one who eats חלב נבילה violates both an איסור נבילה and an איסור חלב. The same applies to חלב טריפה: אמרה התורה יבא איסור נבלה ויחול על איסור חלב, יבא איסור טרפה ויחול על איסור חלב (*Chullin* 37a). This is a major principle in all Torah איסורים: איסור חל על איסור — both in respect to the איסור itself and in respect to its punishment. This principle applies, however, only in the case of an איסור מוסיף, an איסור כולל, or an איסור בבת אחת.

What is an איסור כולל and what is an איסור מוסיף? If the second איסור includes (כולל) an object that was not included in the first איסור, the second איסור is an איסור כולל. In such a case, the second איסור takes effect even on those objects already included in the first איסור. In our verse, the איסור of נבילה and of טריפה is an איסור כולל vis-à-vis the איסור חלב. For the איסור חלב applies to only a specific part of the animal; and if the animal then dies or suffers a terminal ailment or injury, the איסור נבילה or the איסור טריפה will apply also to the other parts of the animal. And since it applies to these, it applies also to that part that was already forbidden as חלב.

By contrast, if the second איסור applies only to the same object that was already forbidden, but renders it forbidden in other respects as well — this is an איסור מוסיף. For example, an איסור קדשים is an איסור מוסיף vis-à-vis an איסור חלב. For חלב is only אסור באכילה; but once an animal is consecrated as שלמים and its חלב becomes fit for the altar, the חלב becomes אסור בהנאה as well. Now, since the איסור קדשים takes effect upon the חלב in respect to prohibiting it בהנאה, it takes effect upon it also to the whole extent of the איסור — and prohibits it באכילה as well: איסור קדשים חל על איסור חלב, and חלב של קדשים is אסור באכילה on both accounts.

Hence, the Mishnah in *Kerisos* (13b) says: יש אוכל אכילה אחת וחייבין עליה ארבעה חטאות ואשם אחד: טמא שאכל חלב והיה נותר מן המוקדשין ביום הכפורים. The איסור קדשים renders the חלב forbidden בהנאה also. The איסור נותר renders the חלב forbidden לגבוה (i.e., למזבח) also. These איסורים, then, are איסורים מוסיפים. On the other hand, טומאת הגוף prohibits the eating of all קודש, and יום הכיפורים prohibits also the eating of חולין. These, then, are איסורים כוללים (see רש״י [ibid.]; *Shevuos* 24b; *Yevamos* 32b, 33a).

25 *For whoever eats the fat of an animal of which a fire offering can be brought near to God, that person who eats it will be uprooted from his people.*

כה כִּי כָּל־אֹכֵל חֵלֶב מִן־הַבְּהֵמָה אֲשֶׁר יַקְרִיב מִמֶּנָּה אִשֶּׁה לַיהוָה וְנִכְרְתָה הַנֶּפֶשׁ הָאֹכֶלֶת מֵעַמֶּיהָ׃

It is different, however, if the second איסור is no more comprehensive than the first — neither in respect to the objects included in it nor in respect to the actions prohibited by it. Take, for example, אבר מן החי and טריפה, both of which are אסורים באכילה and apply to the entire animal. These איסורים can take effect on one object, only if they arise simultaneously, בבת אחת — e.g., a part is severed from a living animal, and this severance makes the animal טריפה. The assumption in this example is that the איסור of אבר מן החי takes effect only with the severance of the part and is not considered to be existing always with every living animal (בהמה בחייה לאו לאברים עומדת). According to the dissenting opinion, however — which holds that the איסור of אבר מן החי takes effect from the moment of birth — the two איסורים do not arise simultaneously unless the part is severed at the moment of birth (see *Chullin* 103a).

25 **כי כל אכל חלב וגו׳**. It is impossible to interpret that the words אשר יקריב וגו׳ restrict the prohibition of חלב to animals actually brought as offerings. For Scripture has already stated (above, 3:17) that this prohibition is חקת עולם לדרתיכם בכל מושבותיכם; it applies, then, even in times and in places where the bringing of offerings is forbidden. Furthermore, the previous verse (v. 24) prohibits the חלב of נבילה and טריפה, even though these are unfit to be brought as offerings. And, finally, the wording of our verse itself precludes such an interpretation. For the חלב of an animal actually brought as an offering is itself אשה לה׳; hence, if Scripture had intended to prohibit only the חלב of offerings, it would have been sufficient to say simply: כי כל אוכל חלב אשר יקריב לה׳.

Clearly, then, the words חלב מן הבהמה אשר יקריב ממנה אשה לה׳ denote merely the kind of animal whose חלב is prohibited; and they denote also the kind of חלבים that are prohibited by the law of חלב. Only the fat of animals *of a kind* that is fit for an offering, and only those fats that are fit to be אשה לה׳, are forbidden by the law of חלב; only the eating

26 *And you shall eat no kind of blood in all your dwelling places, whether it be of bird or beast.*

כו וְכָל־דָּם֙ לֹ֣א תֹאכְל֔וּ בְּכֹ֖ל מֽוֹשְׁבֹתֵיכֶ֑ם לָע֖וֹף וְלַבְּהֵמָֽה׃

27 *Any person who eats any kind of blood, that person will be uprooted from his people.*

כז כָּל־נֶ֖פֶשׁ אֲשֶׁר־תֹּאכַ֣ל כָּל־דָּ֑ם וְנִכְרְתָ֛ה הַנֶּ֥פֶשׁ הַהִ֖וא מֵעַמֶּֽיהָ׃ פ

of such חלב is punishable by כרת. Moreover, the words כי כל אכל וגו׳ provide the reason for the preceding וחלב נבלה וחלב טרפה וגו׳. It follows, then, that the חלב prohibition applies to animals of a kind that is fit for an offering, even if they themselves were rendered unfit by some external cause — e.g., בעלי מומין, which in this respect resemble נבילה וטריפה (see *Pesachim* 43b; רמב״ן here). At the same time, the חלב prohibition applies only to fats that are fit for the altar. These fats are listed above 3:3–4 (see Commentary there). Their distinguishing feature is that they form a separate layer and are covered with a thin membrane, which is easily peeled off: תותב קרום ונקלף. Certain membranes and threads (קרומין וחוטין) that are attached to the חלב are likewise אסורים באכילה, but not under the penalty of כרת.

It is characteristic that, whereas the blood of a fetus is אסור from the earliest stage of embryonic formation, the חלב of a fetus is considered חלב only when its development is completed (חדשים גרמי — *Chullin* 75a); and according to תוספות (ibid., ד״ה לדברי; ibid. 103a, ד״ה דאיסור) only at its complete maturity and birth.

26–27 Although the prohibition of blood — like that of חלב — is connected (above, 3:17) with the laws of the offerings, nevertheless the prohibition of דם exceeds that of חלב, in respect to the range of animals subject to the איסור. The expression בכל מושבתיכם makes it clear that the prohibition of blood — like that of חלב — is not limited exclusively to קדשים. Moreover, the words לעוף ולבהמה extend the prohibition of blood to include all higher mammals (בהמה וחיה) and all birds. Blood of the lower creatures, however, is regarded as their flesh. Hence, it is permissible to eat the blood of kosher fish and locusts. But he who eats such blood when it is collected (e.g., in a vessel) must — due to מראית עין — indicate its source; e.g., he must leave fish scales beside the fish blood. The prohibition of blood is mentioned again, in full detail, below (17:10, et seq.) and in *Devarim* (12:23, et seq.).

A חיוב כרת applies only in the case of דם הנפש — i.e., דם שהנשמה יוצאת בה (*Kerisos* 20b; see תוספות there ד"ה דם הקזה, and לחם משנה to הל' מאכלות אסורות, 6:3). The other blood of the animal is prohibited בלאו.

As regards טומאת נבילה, the law of דם is the same as the law of חלב — i.e., דם נבילה is not טמא (see *Eduyos* 8:1). כן הוא לרמב"ם וראב"ד ויש שיטה אחרת עי' תוספות יום טוב שם.

Earlier (3:17), we attempted to explain the reason for the prohibition of eating חלב and דם. It seemed to us that דם and חלב embody the essence and aim of animal life. One can say as follows: In animal life, the blood is the נפש; and the נפש rules all the other organs and materials, for the sake of producing חלב. Now, all the other organs and materials of the animal can be assimilated by man; in the human body, the נפש האדם dominates them and harnesses them for Divine purposes. As for דם הבהמה, it can be used in an animal offering to represent symbolically נפש האדם; and חלב הבהמה, which is אשה לה', can symbolize the surrender of all attainments to the אש דת. But, actually, נפש הבהמה represented by דם must never become נפש האדם; and animal aims — represented by חלב הבהמה — must never actually be assimilated by man. Rather, כל חלב לה' (above, 3:16). All the aims of man are holy unto God; man must devote himself exclusively to serving God, without any selfish motives.

It appears that the reason for the prohibition of eating חלב and דם is also the reason for their exemption from טומאת נבילה. Let us explain:

Clearly, the prototype of all טומאה is the human corpse, which represents man's submission to the compelling physical forces of nature. An animal carcass, by contrast, is טמאה only if it resembles a human corpse. Hence, טומאת נבילה applies only to the higher mammals, whose bodies resemble the human body. Of the lower mammals, only eight, שמנה שרצים — mice, weasels, etc. (below, 11:29–30) — are טמאים. But טומאה does not apply to all the other kinds of creatures — e.g., fish, amphibians, insects, and worms; nor does טומאה apply to birds, except for נבלת עוף טהור בבית הבליעה.

As regards the organs and materials of the higher mammals, the Torah recognizes their analogy to those of the human body and hence assigns to them טומאה similar to that which was assigned to the human corpse. But as regards animal blood, the Torah rejects any such analogy.

28 God *spoke to Moshe, saying:* כח וַיְדַבֵּר יְהֹוָה אֶל־מֹשֶׁה לֵּאמֹר׃

Human blood cannot be represented by animal blood, which is on a lower level than human blood. Indeed, had טומאה been assigned to דם נבילה, this would have lent support for that mistaken notion which all the laws of טומאה and טהרה are intended to refute. As for חלב, it is a layer of fat stored in the body for use in a time of need; it represents the aims of animal life. As such, the prohibition of חלב is mentioned only in the case of שור כבש ועז, which can be brought as קרבנות. Now, what is true of any analogy between animal and human דם is true also of חלב: Do not think for a moment that there exists an analogy between this חלב and the nature of man. Hence, the Torah tells us to treat חלב and דם as materials that are totally inconsonant with man. The foregoing clarifies for us verse 25, which provides the reason for what is stated in verse 24. The words כי כל אכל חלב provide the reason for the preceding two *halachos*: יעשה לכל מלאכה and ואכל לא תאכלהו; for the reason behind the prohibition of eating חלב is also the reason for its exemption from טומאה.

The prohibition of eating חלב hinges solely on the symbolic meaning of חלב in offerings. The prohibition of eating דם, however, is different. It does not derive solely from the relation of דם to the offerings, but hinges also on the actual physical quality of דם. For this reason it applies to all the higher species of animals, even to those that are not fit to be used as offerings. Later (below, 17:10; *Devarim* 12:23), our task will be to explore this aspect of the blood prohibition.

Since the prohibition of eating חלב is purely symbolic, the prohibition therefore takes effect only upon the completion of the animal's independent formation; for only then have all its materials and organs attained their unique organic significance. Hence, חלב שליל מותר, the חלב of a fetus may be eaten. The physical aspect of the prohibition of eating דם, however, makes this איסור operative even in the very earliest stages of the animal's formation.

28 The prohibition of חלב is introduced above (3:17) only as the consequence of the preceding כל חלב לה׳ (3:16). Thus, the negative command of חלב signals to all future generations that a Jew must remember the

29 *Speak to the Children of Israel, saying: He who brings a meal-of-peace offering near to* God *shall bring to* God *his offering from his meal-of-peace offering.*	כט דַּבֵּ֛ר אֶל־בְּנֵ֥י יִשְׂרָאֵ֖ל לֵאמֹ֑ר הַמַּקְרִ֞יב אֶת־זֶ֤בַח שְׁלָמָיו֙ לַיהוָ֔ה יָבִ֧יא אֶת־קָרְבָּנ֛וֹ לַיהוָ֖ה מִזֶּ֥בַח שְׁלָמָֽיו׃

sanctity of the offerings even during his every-day, ordinary meals. Similarly here, after mentioning the negative command of חלב, Scripture adds positive laws that apply to חלבי הקרבנות, and thus brings to a close all the laws of the offerings. For Scripture completes here the offering laws of אשי ה׳, the אימורים. We have already stated above (4:8–10; 4:27–35) that אימורי הקרבנות are included in the general concept of חלב. This is indicated by what is said here (v. 30ff.) that חלבי השלמים require "waving" (תנופה) before their הקרבה, and the חלב should be waved together with the חזה ושוק.

Previously (Commentary to *Shemos* 29:26, et seq.), we explained the meaning of the gift of the חזה ושוק and the meaning of the תנופה that is performed with them. Here, we shall comment only on the close connection between these *mitzvos* and the prohibition of חלב. While the prohibition of חלב teaches that self-centeredness must be barred from the ultimate aims of our life's work, תנופת חזה ושוק ואימורים teaches us to devote to God and to our fellow men all the drives and aims of our senses (אימורים), all the thoughts and desires that these stimulate (חזה), and all our efforts and accomplishments (שוק). It teaches us to direct them to mankind all around us (תנופה, horizontally) and to God above us (תרומה, vertically). But these procedures that are performed with the offering, and these gifts that are given to the כהן, are mentioned only at קרבן שלמים. We have here, then, an important allusion: A person is not entitled to rejoice in his happiness before God unless he has fulfilled with it תנופה and תרומה — i.e., devoted it to the service of God and to the communal aims determined by Him. The very juxtaposition of the two sections — the mitzvah of תנופה and the prohibition of חלב — can explain why תנופה is assigned solely to the שלמים offering.

29 **המקריב וגו׳**. The laws of תנופת חזה ושוק in these verses stress the significance of זבח as a "meal." The thought conveyed here is this: He who

30 *His [own] hands shall bring the fire offerings to* God; *the fat upon the breast, he [himself] shall bring it, [and] the breast, in order to perform with it a waving before* **God.**	ל יָדָיו תְּבִיאֶינָה אֵת אִשֵּׁי יְהֹוָה אֶת־הַחֵלֶב עַל־הֶחָזֶה יְבִיאֶנּוּ אֵת הֶחָזֶה לְהָנִיף אֹתוֹ תְּנוּפָה לִפְנֵי יְהֹוָה׃

would bring near to God the meal that symbolizes the peace he enjoys must bring his offering from that meal — i.e., he must make God a partner, as it were, to his meal. His enjoyment of the peace that has been given him must not only be free of selfishness (in the negative) but must also further God's purposes (in the positive).

30 **ידיו תביאינה**. The law of תנופה is like the law of סמיכה, in that the בעלים themselves must fulfill the mitzvah of תנופה in the עזרה. סמיכה differs from תנופה, however, in the case of a woman's שלמים and in the case of a joint offering (בחוברין); for the כהן performs the waving instead of the woman, and — in a joint offering — one of the members performs the waving instead of all the members (see *Menachos* 61b; 93b).

The תנופה procedure is performed jointly with the כהן: הא כיצד כהן מניח ידו תחת ידי הבעלים ומניף. כיצד עושה מניח אימורין על פיסת היד וחזה ושוק עליהן (*Menachos* 61b–62a). The כהן places his hands under the hands of the בעלים and performs the תנופה. The אימורין are placed on the hands of the בעלים with the חזה ושוק placed on the אימורין. The תנופה procedure consists of two motions — one horizontal and the other vertical: מוליך ומביא מעלה ומוריד (ibid. 61a). It is the כהן who guides the בעלים in performing the תנופה motions.

לפני ה׳: במזרח (ibid.), on the side of the life of the people facing God. At the הגשה of מנחות (above, 6:7), however, לפני ה׳ denotes מערב. The reason is that הגשת מנחות is in closer relationship to the altar and must be performed both לפני ה׳ (in the east) and אל פני המזבח, (in the south). It would have been logical, then, for הגשה to be performed at the south-east corner. But at this corner there was no יסוד (see Commentary above, 1:5), and the מנחה — like the חטאת — requires the יסוד (*Menachos* 61a). Hence, we say that לפני ה׳ there (in the case of מנחה) is the side closest

31 *The priest shall turn the fat into smoke upon the altar, and the breast shall then belong to Aharon and his sons.*	לא וְהִקְטִיר הַכֹּהֵן אֶת־הַחֵלֶב הַמִּזְבֵּחָה וְהָיָה הֶחָזֶה לְאַהֲרֹן וּלְבָנָיו׃
32 *And the right thigh you shall give as an uplifted gift to the priest, from your meal-of-peace offerings.*	לב וְאֵת שׁוֹק הַיָּמִין תִּתְּנוּ תְרוּמָה לַכֹּהֵן מִזִּבְחֵי שַׁלְמֵיכֶם׃

to the היכל, whereas לפני ה׳ here is the east, the side of the life of the people facing God.

31 **והקטיר וגו׳**. First comes הקטרת האימורים (provided they have not been lost or rendered impure); only then are the כהנים entitled to the חזה ושוק (see *Pesachim* 59b).

32 **ואת שוק הימין וגו׳**. The תנופה procedure is performed with the חזה and the שוק simultaneously. תנופה and הרמה are performed with both; as it says in פרשת מילואים, in which חזה ושוק first appear: אשר הונף ואשר הורם (*Shemos* 29:27; see Commentary, ad loc.). Also in verse 34 they are mentioned together in complete equality. Here (vv. 30–31 and 32–33), however, they are mentioned separately, one after the other. Clearly, the concept of giving the breast to the כהן is not identical to the concept of giving the thigh. For the כהן is given the חזה as the final consequence of הקטרת אימורים: והקטיר וגו׳ והיה וגו׳ (v. 31), whereas the gift of the שוק is called תרומה מזבחי שלמים — similar to the תרומה from grain.

In verse 35 we will see that the כהן's right to the חזה ושוק is not the same as his right to the meat of חטאת and אשם. For, as regards חטאת and אשם, אכילת כהנים itself is one of the symbolic acts of the offering; it is a kind of continuation and culmination of אכילת מזבח: כהנים אוכלים ובעלים מתכפרים (*Pesachim* 59b). By contrast, חזה ושוק are given to the כהן as an expression of appreciation for the task to which he was chosen. They are משחת אהרן ומשחת בניו (v. 35): As it were, through חזה ושוק the initiation of the כהן into his כהונה is constantly renewed. חזה ושוק, then, must be intimately related to the meaning of his office. For this reason they are mentioned as early as ימי המילואים, when the כהנים were first inducted into office; as early as then, the gift of חזה ושוק was instituted for all time.

Of the איל המילואים, the שוק was offered on the altar, whereas the חזה was given to Moshe, who officiated בכהונה. In the case of all subsequent שלמים, however, both the חזה and the שוק were given to the כהן (see *Shemos* 29:27–28).

חזה, the breast, symbolizes all of man's thoughts and aspirations. It represents, then, on the one hand, the moral and spiritual source of all human accomplishment achieved in moral freedom; and, on the other hand, it represents that human sphere to which the whole function of the כהן is addressed. For all our thoughts and aspirations must be enlightened by the light of the Torah taught by the כהן. Now, all of our life's aims — and all the impulses channelled toward the attainment of these aims — must become לחם אשה לה׳; through them we must bring satisfaction to God and sustain the holy on earth. Indeed, this is the whole essence of הקטרת אימורים. But the fulfillment of this duty is itself the fruit — of thought and will — that ripened in the light of the Torah taught by the כהן. Hence, when we offer up the אימורים of the שלמים offerings that reflect our personal happiness, it is only natural that we present the חזה to the כהן; and we should express our appreciation before him as follows: The world view represented by הקטרת אימורים is the foundation of our personal happiness. But we have attained this view thanks only to the Torah, which is entrusted to the כהן.

By contrast, שוק, the thigh, symbolizes power and progress; we have mentioned previously the parallel between שוקי האיש and גבורת הסוס (see Commentary, *Shemos* 29:22–25). שוק, then, represents man's strength (גבורת האיש) and his external position of power. This is a sphere that seems far removed from the כהן's influence — just as the riches of the produce of the field seem far removed from such influence.

Actually, though, the analogy to the field proves just the opposite. For at each stage in which one enjoys the produce of his field, he gives the כהן a gift: ביכורים, תרומה, חלה. The gift is merely symbolic, for even a single kernel is sufficient: חטה אחת פוטרת את הכרי (*Chullin* 137b). This gift is of dual significance: (a) It symbolizes the recognition that even material prosperity is gained thanks only to the Torah — which is entrusted to the כהן. (b) It reminds the giver that material blessings, too, should be devoted to promoting knowledge of Torah — which is taught

33 *One among the sons of Aharon who brings near the blood of the peace offering and the fat, he shall have the right thigh as a portion.*

לג הַמַּקְרִ֞יב אֶת־דַּ֧ם הַשְּׁלָמִ֛ים וְאֶת־הַחֵ֖לֶב מִבְּנֵ֣י אַהֲרֹ֑ן ל֥וֹ תִהְיֶ֛ה שׁ֥וֹק הַיָּמִ֖ין לְמָנָֽה׃

by the כהן. This symbol — of recognition and reminder — is called, for the most part, תרומה. For תרומה "uplifts" (מרימה) material things and subordinates them to godly, moral and spiritual purposes.

Now, this is also the significance of שוק הימין, which is תרומה לכהן מזבחי שלמיכם (v. 32). When the individual who feels happy and content (בעל השלמים) gives this תרומה to the כהן, he should give it with this same dual intent: (a) as an expression of his recognition that he has gained happiness thanks only to the Torah, which is entrusted to the כהן; and (b) as an expression of his commitment to devote "the strength of his thigh" (גבורת השוק) — the power afforded him by his secure position — to the support of the Torah, taught by the כהן.

Thus, the חזה and the שוק are given to the כהן out of divergent conceptions: It is only natural that he should receive the חזה, but he receives the שוק only as תרומה. We now also understand the consistent terminology חזה התנופה and שוק התרומה, although the two motions — תנופה and תרומה — are performed with both the חזה and the שוק (as noted previously in our Commentary to *Shemos* 35:22.)

33 Here, too, המקריב means הראוי להקרבה (see above, 6:19; 7:8,9; Commentary, ad loc.). In אבא שאול's view, which is accepted by the רמב״ם as halachah (הל׳ מעשה הקרבנות, 10:21), Scripture adds here that the כהן — to have the right to participate in the division of בשר — must be ראוי not only at the time of זריקה but also בשעת הקטרה (see *Zevachim* 102b).

מבני אהרן — but not all בני אהרן. To be entitled to a share of קדשים, it is not enough to be born a כהן. For the law is that כל כהן שאינו מודה בעבודה אין לו חלק בכהונה (*Menachos* 18b). A כהן must be wholehearted toward the Sanctuary service, to which he was born. He must believe that God has commanded us to offer to Him offerings, and that the Sanctuary service fulfills a Divine purpose (see רש״י, *Chullin* 132b, ד״ה שאינו מודה בעבודה).

לד כִּ֩י אֶת־חֲזֵ֨ה הַתְּנוּפָ֜ה וְאֵ֣ת ׀ שׁ֣וֹק
הַתְּרוּמָ֗ה לָקַ֙חְתִּי֙ מֵאֵ֣ת בְּנֵֽי־
יִשְׂרָאֵ֔ל מִזִּבְחֵ֖י שַׁלְמֵיהֶ֑ם וָאֶתֵּ֣ן
אֹ֠תָם לְאַהֲרֹ֨ן הַכֹּהֵ֤ן וּלְבָנָיו֙ לְחָק־
עוֹלָ֔ם מֵאֵ֖ת בְּנֵ֥י יִשְׂרָאֵֽל׃

34 *For I have taken the breast of the wave [offering] and the thigh of the uplifted gift from the Children of Israel from their meal-of-peace offerings, and I have given them to Aharon the priest and to his sons as an everlasting due from the Children of Israel.*

לה זֹ֣את מִשְׁחַ֤ת אַהֲרֹן֙ וּמִשְׁחַ֣ת בָּנָ֔יו
מֵאִשֵּׁ֖י יְהֹוָ֑ה בְּיוֹם֙ הִקְרִ֣יב אֹתָ֔ם
לְכַהֵ֖ן לַיהֹוָֽה׃

35 *This is the consecration of Aharon and the consecration of his sons from the fire offerings to* God, *on the day on which He drew them near, to serve* God *as priests.*

34 **ואתן אתם וגו׳ מאת בני ישראל**: מאת בני ישראל – מרצון כל ישראל (*Toras Kohanim*). Although מתנות כהונה are given to the כהנים by God, they should not demand them as a right to be forcibly taken as their due; rather, they are as gifts from the people to the כהן: אין הכהנים רשאין ליטול אותם בזרוע אלא כמו מתנה הם משלמי ישראל שהם נותנין מתנה לכהן (פי׳ ראב״ד שם).

35 **זאת משחת אהרן וגו׳**. This gift of the חזה ושוק from the שלמים offering represents a constant renewal of the consecration of the כהונה.

The gift signals to the כהן that the nation's "breast" — i.e., the nation's thoughts and aspirations — should be the field of his labors; the nation's strength, as symbolized by the thigh, will support and implement his teachings; and the climate in which the seeds of the teachings of His Sanctuary will thrive is not one of contrition and gloom but one of good cheer, of vibrant joy in the awareness of a life lived in the presence of God.

At the same time, the gift to the כהן signals to the nation that, although the כהן makes no direct, tangible contribution to the nation's prosperity, nevertheless, the prosperity of every individual in the nation finds its basis and purpose in the Torah, which is entrusted to the כהן. For a man's happiness and prosperity have a firm foundation only if his "breast" belongs to the Torah; and they have meaning and value

לו אֲשֶׁר צִוָּה יְהוָה לָתֵת לָהֶם בְּיוֹם מָשְׁחוֹ אֹתָם מֵאֵת בְּנֵי יִשְׂרָאֵל חֻקַּת עוֹלָם לְדֹרֹתָם׃

36 *It is this that* God *commanded on the day He consecrated them, that it shall be given them by the Children of Israel: an everlasting statute for their descendants.*

לז זֹאת הַתּוֹרָה לָעֹלָה לַמִּנְחָה וְלַחַטָּאת וְלָאָשָׁם וְלַמִּלּוּאִים וּלְזֶבַח הַשְּׁלָמִים׃

37 *This is the teaching for the ascent offering, for the homage offering, for the offering that clears of sin, and for the guilt offering; and for the offering of investiture, and for the meal-of-peace offering.*

---

only if he uses his "thigh" — the power of his position — to support the Torah, whose Sanctuary is served by the כהן.

ביום הקריב אתם וגו׳. The gift of חזה ושוק was instituted immediately on the day of the מילואים, so that through this gift the consecration of the כהנים would be constantly renewed. For the procedure observed with the איל המילואים was that the כהנים dedicated the חזה and the שוק to God — and gave to Moshe the symbol of their appreciation and commitment (see Commentary, *Shemos* 29:26). Henceforth, every שלמים offering sanctifies the family circle, transforming the home into a sanctuary and the family members into כהנים. And the family members give the חזה and the שוק of their offering to the כהנים — just as the כהנים, at their consecration, gave them to the altar (שוק) and to Moshe (חזה).

37–38 **זאת התורה וגו׳**. These verses conclude the second major group of laws given at Sinai — the laws of the offerings. Before them came the משפטים, the laws regulating the life of the individual and of society. The משפטים are the ultimate purpose of the laws of the offerings, and the key to understanding them (cf. Commentary to *Shemos* 21:1).

The retrospective summary (v. 37) mentions all the types of offerings that have been elucidated:

Mentioned first are עולה and מנחה, חטאת and אשם: offerings that (a) consecrate actions (עולה) or (b) acknowledge provision of a liveli-

38 *Which God had already commanded to Moshe on Mount Sinai, on the day He commanded the Children of Israel to bring near their offerings to* God, *in the wilderness of Sinai.*

לח אֲשֶׁר צִוָּה יְהֹוָה אֶת־מֹשֶׁה בְּהַר סִינָי בְּיוֹם צַוֹּתוֹ אֶת־בְּנֵי יִשְׂרָאֵל לְהַקְרִיב אֶת־קָרְבְּנֵיהֶם לַיהֹוָה בְּמִדְבַּר סִינָי: פ רביעי

hood (מנחה); offerings that (a) atone for errors of action (חטאת), or (b) atone for offenses related to the means of a livelihood (אשם). The division into these two kinds corresponds to the relation between חזה and שוק: עולה and חטאת = חזה; מנחה and אשם = שוק.

Mentioned last are מילואים and שלמים, which combine both of the above two elements: they (a) consecrate actions (b) out of a feeling of exaltation over the livelihood provided by God.

It is significant that the concluding chapter (chap. 7) takes שלמים (presented in chap. 3) out of the order of all the offerings that have been elucidated, for the purpose of concluding the laws of the offerings with שלמים. The retrospective summary (v. 37), too, mentions שלמים last, in order to join them to the very first offering, קרבן המילואים. Thus, the root and the flower are joined together — the first of all the offerings together with their culmination. And, indeed, these two offerings are related in their meaning (see Commentary to v. 35). Moreover, the very mention of the מילואים constitutes an introduction to the next chapter, which returns to the dedication of the Dwelling Place and the consecration of the כהנים, and resumes the account that was interrupted with the end of the book of *Shemos* (see Commentary, *Shemos* 40:18–38).

This grouping together of all the classes of offerings teaches us halachah as well. For there are laws that are specified at only certain offerings — e.g., שינוי בעלים ושינוי קודש, the laws of בלוע in קדשים, פיגול, and many others. But since in this verse הוקשו כל הקרבנות זה לזה, as a result these laws apply to them all (see *Zevachim* 4b, 7b, 8a, 97b, 98a; *Menachos* 83a).

אשר צוה ה׳ את משה וגו׳. The offering laws that were proclaimed here מאהל מועד (above, 1:1) had already been given to Moshe at Sinai along with all the other *mitzvos*, of which these form an integral part. They

8 1 God *spoke to Moshe, saying:*

ח א וַיְדַבֵּר יְהוָה אֶל־מֹשֶׁה לֵּאמֹר׃

2 *Take Aharon and his sons with him, and the garments and the anointing oil; the bull of the offering that clears of sin and the two rams and the basket of* matzos.

ב קַח אֶת־אַהֲרֹן וְאֶת־בָּנָיו אִתּוֹ
וְאֵת הַבְּגָדִים וְאֵת שֶׁמֶן הַמִּשְׁחָה
וְאֵת ׀ פַּר הַחַטָּאת וְאֵת שְׁנֵי
הָאֵילִים וְאֵת סַל הַמַּצּוֹת׃

3 *And gather the entire community together at the entrance of the Tent of Appointed Meeting.*

ג וְאֵת כָּל־הָעֵדָה הַקְהֵל אֶל־פֶּתַח
אֹהֶל מוֹעֵד׃

are neither a temporary concession to a generation still under the influence of paganism, nor do they constitute a separate chapter that is all magic and mystery. Rather, they are *mitzvos* like all the other *mitzvos*. Their purpose is to educate the nation to observe and keep the *mitzvos*. Accordingly, they, too, had already been given at Sinai like all the other *mitzvos*. But since the offering laws are integral to the *halachos* of the Dwelling Place, they were reiterated מאהל מועד after its erection (according to ר׳ ישמעאל, that is where the details of these laws were first given): ר׳ ישמעאל אומר כללות נאמרו בסיני ופרטות באהל מועד, ר׳ עקיבא אומר כללות ופרטות נאמרו בסיני ונשנו באהל מועד (זבחים קטו:). In this regard as well, all the categories of offerings and the laws concerning them are placed together with the מילואים — whose laws had already been stated at Sinai (*Shemos* 29): מה מלואים נאמרו כללותיהם ודקדוקיהם מסיני אף כולן נאמרו כללותיהם ודקדוקיהם מסיני (*Toras Kohanim*).

ביום צותו וגו׳ במדבר סיני — see Commentary above, 6:2.

CHAPTER 8

1 As we noted at the end of *Shemos* (40:18–38), Scripture there concludes the description of the erection of the Dwelling Place, and in the process skips over the dedication of ימי המילואים. Then, at the beginning of *Vayikra* (chap. 1–7), Scripture teaches the *halachos* of the offerings, these being the main purpose of the Dwelling Place. Only after completing these *halachos* does Scripture return to the beginning of the account of

4 *Moshe did as* God *had commanded him, and the community gathered at the entrance of the Tent of Appointed Meeting.*

ד וַיַּעַשׂ מֹשֶׁה כַּאֲשֶׁר צִוָּה יְהֹוָה אֹתוֹ וַתִּקָּהֵל הָעֵדָה אֶל־פֶּתַח אֹהֶל מוֹעֵד׃

5 *And Moshe said to the community: This is what* God *has commanded to be carried out.*

ה וַיֹּאמֶר מֹשֶׁה אֶל־הָעֵדָה זֶה הַדָּבָר אֲשֶׁר־צִוָּה יְהֹוָה לַעֲשׂוֹת׃

6 *Thereupon, Moshe made Aharon and his sons come nearer, bathed them in water.*

ו וַיַּקְרֵב מֹשֶׁה אֶת־אַהֲרֹן וְאֶת־בָּנָיו וַיִּרְחַץ אֹתָם בַּמָּיִם׃

7 *Put upon him the tunic, girded him with the sash, clothed him with the robe, put upon him the* efod, *girded him with the band of the* efod *and encircled him with it.*

ז וַיִּתֵּן עָלָיו אֶת־הַכֻּתֹּנֶת וַיַּחְגֹּר אֹתוֹ בָּאַבְנֵט וַיַּלְבֵּשׁ אֹתוֹ אֶת־הַמְּעִיל וַיִּתֵּן עָלָיו אֶת־הָאֵפֹד וַיַּחְגֹּר אֹתוֹ בְּחֵשֶׁב הָאֵפֹד וַיֶּאְפֹּד לוֹ בּוֹ׃

8 *He placed the breastplate upon him, and put the Urim and the Tummim into the breastplate.*

ח וַיָּשֶׂם עָלָיו אֶת־הַחֹשֶׁן וַיִּתֵּן אֶל־הַחֹשֶׁן אֶת־הָאוּרִים וְאֶת־הַתֻּמִּים׃

---

the dedication. For a general account of the dedication was given previously at the end of *Shemos*: ויעש משה ככל אשר צוה ה׳ אתו כן עשה (*Shemos* 40:16), and now Scripture returns to describe it in detail.

According to the רמב״ן, Scripture returns to this account at the beginning of *Vayikra*; for the term אהל מועד mentioned there (1:1) refers not to the Dwelling Place that was finally erected and consecrated, but to the Dwelling Place on the first of the seven days of investiture. Just as the consecration of the כהנים (*Shemos* 29:30 and 35; below, 8:33) and of the altar (*Shemos* 29:37) was repeated daily for seven days, and only on the eighth day were they consecrated for all time, so have we learned

9 *He placed the turban upon his head, and upon the turban, in front, he placed the golden showplate, the diadem of the Sanctuary, as God had commanded Moshe.*

ט וַיָּ֥שֶׂם אֶת־הַמִּצְנֶ֖פֶת עַל־רֹאשׁ֑וֹ
וַיָּ֨שֶׂם עַל־הַמִּצְנֶ֜פֶת אֶל־מ֣וּל פָּנָ֗יו
אֵ֚ת צִ֣יץ הַזָּהָב֙ נֵ֣זֶר הַקֹּ֔דֶשׁ כַּאֲשֶׁ֛ר
צִוָּ֥ה יְהוָ֖ה אֶת־מֹשֶֽׁה׃

10 *Then Moshe took the anointing oil and anointed the Dwelling Place and all that was within it, and sanctified them.*

י וַיִּקַּ֤ח מֹשֶׁה֙ אֶת־שֶׁ֣מֶן הַמִּשְׁחָ֔ה
וַיִּמְשַׁ֥ח אֶת־הַמִּשְׁכָּ֖ן וְאֶת־כָּל־
אֲשֶׁר־בּ֑וֹ וַיְקַדֵּ֖שׁ אֹתָֽם׃

11 *He sprinkled [some] of it upon the altar seven times and anointed the altar and all its vessels, and the basin and its base, to sanctify them.*

יא וַיַּ֥ז מִמֶּ֛נּוּ עַל־הַמִּזְבֵּ֖חַ שֶׁ֣בַע
פְּעָמִ֑ים וַיִּמְשַׁ֨ח אֶת־הַמִּזְבֵּ֜חַ
וְאֶת־כָּל־כֵּלָ֗יו וְאֶת־הַכִּיֹּ֛ר וְאֶת־
כַּנּ֖וֹ לְקַדְּשָֽׁם׃

12 *He poured [some] of the anointing oil upon Aharon's head and anointed him, to sanctify him.*

יב וַיִּצֹק֙ מִשֶּׁ֣מֶן הַמִּשְׁחָ֔ה עַ֖ל רֹ֣אשׁ
אַהֲרֹ֑ן וַיִּמְשַׁ֥ח אֹת֖וֹ לְקַדְּשֽׁוֹ׃

13 *And Moshe made Aharon's sons draw nearer, clothed them with the tunics, girded them with a sash and bound tall turbans upon them, as God had commanded Moshe.*

יג וַיַּקְרֵ֨ב מֹשֶׁ֜ה אֶת־בְּנֵ֣י אַהֲרֹ֗ן
וַיַּלְבִּשֵׁ֤ם כֻּתֳּנֹת֙ וַיַּחְגֹּ֤ר אֹתָם֙ אַבְנֵ֔ט
וַיַּחֲבֹ֥שׁ לָהֶ֖ם מִגְבָּע֑וֹת כַּאֲשֶׁ֛ר צִוָּ֥ה
יְהוָ֖ה אֶת־מֹשֶֽׁה׃ חמישי

---

by way of tradition in regard to the אוהל מועד: It was erected anew on each of the seven days of investiture, and only on the eighth day was it erected and consecrated for all time.

Thus, according to the רמב״ן, the offering laws were given on the first of the seven days of the מילואים, immediately after the Dwelling Place was first erected. Indeed, it is only logical that the teaching of the offering laws should precede the offering up of the מילואים offerings; for

14 *He then brought closer the bull of the offering that clears of sin; Aharon and his sons leaned their hands upon the head of the bull of the offering that clears of sin.*

יד וַיַּגֵּ֕שׁ אֵ֖ת פַּ֣ר הַֽחַטָּ֑את וַיִּסְמֹ֨ךְ
אַהֲרֹ֤ן וּבָנָיו֙ אֶת־יְדֵיהֶ֔ם עַל־רֹ֖אשׁ
פַּ֥ר הַֽחַטָּֽאת׃

15 *He slaughtered [it] and Moshe took, with his finger, the blood and put [some] of it upon the horns of the altar, all around, and purged the altar of sin; and he poured the [rest of the] blood onto the base of the altar and sanctified the altar, so that atonement could be effected upon it.*

טו וַיִּשְׁחָ֗ט וַיִּקַּ֨ח מֹשֶׁ֥ה אֶת־הַדָּ֛ם
וַ֠יִּתֵּן עַל־קַ֨רְנ֤וֹת הַמִּזְבֵּ֙חַ֙ סָבִ֙יב֙
בְּאֶצְבָּע֔וֹ וַיְחַטֵּ֖א אֶת־הַמִּזְבֵּ֑חַ
וְאֶת־הַדָּ֗ם יָצַק֙ אֶל־יְס֣וֹד הַמִּזְבֵּ֔חַ
וַֽיְקַדְּשֵׁ֖הוּ לְכַפֵּ֥ר עָלָֽיו׃

16 *He took all the fat that is attached to the intestines, the diaphragm of the liver and the two kidneys along with their fat, and Moshe turned them into smoke upon the altar.*

טז וַיִּקַּ֗ח אֶֽת־כָּל־הַחֵ֘לֶב֮ אֲשֶׁ֣ר עַל־
הַקֶּ֒רֶב֒ וְאֵ֨ת יֹתֶ֣רֶת הַכָּבֵ֔ד וְאֶת־
שְׁתֵּ֥י הַכְּלָיֹ֖ת וְאֶת־חֶלְבְּהֶ֑ן וַיַּקְטֵ֥ר
מֹשֶׁ֖ה הַמִּזְבֵּֽחָה׃

17 *But the bull, along with its skin, its flesh and its dung, he burned in fire outside the camp, as* God *had commanded Moshe.*

יז וְאֶת־הַפָּ֤ר וְאֶת־עֹרוֹ֙ וְאֶת־בְּשָׂר֣וֹ
וְאֶת־פִּרְשׁ֔וֹ שָׂרַ֣ף בָּאֵ֔שׁ מִח֖וּץ
לַֽמַּחֲנֶ֑ה כַּאֲשֶׁ֛ר צִוָּ֥ה יְהֹוָ֖ה אֶת־
מֹשֶֽׁה׃

---

the מילואים offerings included most of the classes of offerings: חטאת, עולה, מנחה, שלמים.

וידבר וגו' קח וגו'. We noted previously, in our Commentary to *Shemos* 40:17, that the Dwelling Place was erected finally on the first of Nissan, after the seven days of investiture. Thus, the beginning of the dedication of which Scripture here speaks was on the twenty-third of Adar.

18 *He thereupon brought near the ram of the ascent offering, and Aharon and his sons leaned their hands upon the head of the ram.*

יח וַיַּקְרֵ֕ב אֵ֖ת אֵ֣יל הָעֹלָ֑ה וַֽיִּסְמְכ֞וּ
אַהֲרֹ֧ן וּבָנָ֛יו אֶת־יְדֵיהֶ֖ם עַל־רֹ֥אשׁ
הָאָֽיִל׃

19 *He slaughtered [it] and Moshe dashed the blood against the altar, all around.*

יט וַיִּשְׁחָ֑ט וַיִּזְרֹ֨ק מֹשֶׁ֧ה אֶת־הַדָּ֛ם
עַל־הַמִּזְבֵּ֖חַ סָבִֽיב׃

20 *And he cut up the ram into its parts, and Moshe offered up in smoke the head, the parts and the fat.*

כ וְאֶת־הָאַ֕יִל נִתַּ֖ח לִנְתָחָ֑יו וַיַּקְטֵ֤ר
מֹשֶׁה֙ אֶת־הָרֹ֔אשׁ וְאֶת־הַנְּתָחִ֖ים
וְאֶת־הַפָּֽדֶר׃

21 *He washed the intestines and the feet in water, and Moshe turned the entire ram into smoke upon the altar. It is an ascent offering to express compliance; it is a fire offering to* God, *as* God *had commanded Moshe.*

כא וְאֶת־הַקֶּ֥רֶב וְאֶת־הַכְּרָעַ֖יִם רָחַ֣ץ
בַּמָּ֑יִם וַיַּקְטֵ֨ר מֹשֶׁ֜ה אֶת־כָּל־
הָאַ֣יִל הַמִּזְבֵּ֗חָה עֹלָ֨ה ה֤וּא לְרֵֽיחַ־
נִיחֹ֙חַ֙ אִשֶּׁ֥ה הוּא֙ לַֽיהוָ֔ה כַּאֲשֶׁ֛ר
צִוָּ֥ה יְהוָ֖ה אֶת־מֹשֶֽׁה׃ ששי

22 *He then brought near the second ram, the ram of investiture, and Aharon and his sons leaned their hands upon the head of the ram.*

כב וַיַּקְרֵב֙ אֶת־הָאַ֣יִל הַשֵּׁנִ֔י אֵ֖יל
הַמִּלֻּאִ֑ים וַֽיִּסְמְכ֞וּ אַהֲרֹ֧ן וּבָנָ֛יו
אֶת־יְדֵיהֶ֖ם עַל־רֹ֥אשׁ הָאָֽיִל׃

23 *He slaughtered [it], and Moshe took [some] of its blood and placed it upon the right ear cartilage of Aharon, upon the thumb of his right hand and upon the big toe of his right foot.*

כג וַיִּשְׁחָ֓ט ׀ וַיִּקַּ֤ח מֹשֶׁה֙ מִדָּמ֔וֹ וַיִּתֵּ֛ן
עַל־תְּנ֥וּךְ אֹֽזֶן־אַהֲרֹ֖ן הַיְמָנִ֑ית
וְעַל־בֹּ֤הֶן יָדוֹ֙ הַיְמָנִ֔ית וְעַל־בֹּ֖הֶן
רַגְל֥וֹ הַיְמָנִֽית׃

The command as to the consecration of the כהנים and as to the מילואים offerings is mentioned in *Shemos* 29. See our Commentary there, where we tried to understand what these signify.

24 *He then made the sons of Aharon draw closer, and Moshe placed [some] of the blood upon the cartilage of their right ears, upon the thumbs of their right hands and upon the big toes of their right feet, and Moshe dashed the blood against the altar, all around.*

כד וַיַּקְרֵב אֶת־בְּנֵי אַהֲרֹן וַיִּתֵּן מֹשֶׁה
מִן־הַדָּם עַל־תְּנוּךְ אָזְנָם הַיְמָנִית
וְעַל־בֹּהֶן יָדָם הַיְמָנִית וְעַל־בֹּהֶן
רַגְלָם הַיְמָנִית וַיִּזְרֹק מֹשֶׁה אֶת־
הַדָּם עַל־הַמִּזְבֵּחַ סָבִיב׃

25 *He took the fat, the tailpiece and all the fat that is attached to the intestines, the diaphragm of the liver, and the two kidneys along with their fat, and the right thigh.*

כה וַיִּקַּח אֶת־הַחֵלֶב וְאֶת־הָאַלְיָה
וְאֶת־כָּל־הַחֵלֶב אֲשֶׁר עַל־הַקֶּרֶב
וְאֵת יֹתֶרֶת הַכָּבֵד וְאֶת־שְׁתֵּי
הַכְּלָיֹת וְאֶת־חֶלְבְּהֶן וְאֵת שׁוֹק
הַיָּמִין׃

26 *From the basket of* matzos *that stood before* God *he took one matzah loaf, one loaf of oil bread, and one thin wafer and placed it upon the fat parts and upon the right thigh.*

כו וּמִסַּל הַמַּצּוֹת אֲשֶׁר ׀ לִפְנֵי יְהוָה
לָקַח חַלַּת מַצָּה אַחַת וְחַלַּת לֶחֶם
שֶׁמֶן אַחַת וְרָקִיק אֶחָד וַיָּשֶׂם
עַל־הַחֲלָבִים וְעַל שׁוֹק הַיָּמִין׃

27 *And put it all upon the hands of Aharon and upon the hands of his sons, and he waved them as a wave [offering] before* God.

כז וַיִּתֵּן אֶת־הַכֹּל עַל כַּפֵּי אַהֲרֹן וְעַל
כַּפֵּי בָנָיו וַיָּנֶף אֹתָם תְּנוּפָה לִפְנֵי
יְהוָה׃

28 *Moshe then took them from their hands and turned them into smoke upon the altar, upon the ascent offering; they are offerings of investiture, to express compliance; it is a fire offering to* God.

כח וַיִּקַּח מֹשֶׁה אֹתָם מֵעַל כַּפֵּיהֶם
וַיַּקְטֵר הַמִּזְבֵּחָה עַל־הָעֹלָה
מִלֻּאִים הֵם לְרֵיחַ נִיחֹחַ אִשֶּׁה הוּא
לַיהוָה׃

29 *Moshe then took the breast, and waved it as a wave [offering] before* God. *This was Moshe's portion of the ram of investiture, as* God *had commanded Moshe.*

כט וַיִּקַּח מֹשֶׁה אֶת־הֶחָזֶה וַיְנִיפֵהוּ
תְנוּפָה לִפְנֵי יְהוָה מֵאֵיל הַמִּלֻּאִים
לְמֹשֶׁה הָיָה לְמָנָה כַּאֲשֶׁר צִוָּה
יְהוָה אֶת־מֹשֶׁה׃ שביעי

30 *Last of all, Moshe took [some] of the anointing oil and of the blood that was upon the altar and sprinkled it upon Aharon, upon his garments, upon his sons and upon the garments of his sons, and he sanctified Aharon, his garments, his sons and the garments of his sons with him.*

ל וַיִּקַּח מֹשֶׁה מִשֶּׁמֶן הַמִּשְׁחָה וּמִן־
הַדָּם אֲשֶׁר עַל־הַמִּזְבֵּחַ וַיַּז עַל־
אַהֲרֹן עַל־בְּגָדָיו וְעַל־בָּנָיו וְעַל־
בִּגְדֵי בָנָיו אִתּוֹ וַיְקַדֵּשׁ אֶת־אַהֲרֹן
אֶת־בְּגָדָיו וְאֶת־בָּנָיו וְאֶת־בִּגְדֵי
בָנָיו אִתּוֹ׃

31 *Then Moshe said to Aharon and to his sons: Cook the flesh at the entrance of the Tent of Appointed Meeting and there you shall eat it and the bread that is in the basket of the investiture offerings, as I transmitted the command: Aharon and his sons shall eat it.*

לא וַיֹּאמֶר מֹשֶׁה אֶל־אַהֲרֹן וְאֶל־בָּנָיו
בַּשְּׁלוּ אֶת־הַבָּשָׂר פֶּתַח אֹהֶל
מוֹעֵד וְשָׁם תֹּאכְלוּ אֹתוֹ וְאֶת־
הַלֶּחֶם אֲשֶׁר בְּסַל הַמִּלֻּאִים
כַּאֲשֶׁר צִוֵּיתִי לֵאמֹר אַהֲרֹן וּבָנָיו
יֹאכְלֻהוּ׃

---

31 **כאשר צויתי וגו'**. The substance of the command is expressed in the third person: אהרן ובניו יאכלהו. Since the beginning of the verse states that Moshe is speaking to אהרן ובניו, it appears that צויתי should be understood as "I transmitted the command." Scripture employs this wording for the following reason:

During the seven days of the מילואים, Moshe did not serve in the capacity of transmitter of the Torah; rather, he himself was involved in fulfilling the mitzvah, as he was the officiating כהן. The כהנים, who ate the בשר איל מלואים and the לחם out of the סל המלואים, were being prepared for the כהונה and were partaking of their כהונה offering (see Commentary

32 *Whatever is left of the flesh and the bread you shall burn in fire.*

לב וְהַנּוֹתָ֥ר בַּבָּשָׂ֖ר וּבַלָּ֑חֶם בָּאֵ֖שׁ
תִּשְׂרֹֽפוּ׃ מפטיר

33 *And you shall not go out from the entrance of the Tent of Appointed Meeting for seven days, until the day on which the days of your investiture are completed; for He shall perform your investiture for seven days.*

לג וּמִפֶּ֨תַח אֹ֜הֶל מוֹעֵ֗ד לֹ֤א תֵֽצְאוּ֙
שִׁבְעַ֣ת יָמִ֔ים עַ֚ד י֣וֹם מְלֹ֔את יְמֵ֖י
מִלֻּאֵיכֶ֑ם כִּ֚י שִׁבְעַ֣ת יָמִ֔ים יְמַלֵּ֖א
אֶת־יֶדְכֶֽם׃

---

to *Shemos* 29:31–33). It was just at this time that they were told that it is Moshe who is the transmitter of the Torah; and thereafter, as well, the כהן was subject to the authority of the Torah and its teachers. The כהן's essential mission is in implementing the Torah, rather than in teaching it. For, the teaching of Torah is not dependent on lineage; as the Mishnah says: ממזר תלמיד חכם קודם לכהן גדול עם הארץ, "A learned bastard takes precedence over an unlearned High Priest" (*Horayos* 13a). This saying clearly defines the position of the כהן vis-à-vis the teaching of Torah. Anyone who speaks of a priestly hierarchy in Israel — like that which exists in other circles — is drawing this strictly from his own imagination (see Commentary above, 4:3).

33 ומפתח וגו׳. According to the רמב״ן, leaving the Dwelling Place is prohibited here by Scripture only **בשעת עבודה**; for that is how *Toras Kohanim* interprets a similar verse later on (10:7). But one must wonder at his comment. For Scripture states here explicitly: **ופתח אהל מועד תשבו יומם ולילה שבעת ימים** (v. 35), which implies that the **כהנים** had to abide in the Sanctuary at all times. Moreover, during those seven days Aharon and his sons were assigned no **עבודה** whatsoever; it was assigned entirely to Moshe. Only on the eighth day did they assume their priestly duties. Hence, only the command relating to that day (below, 10:7) can prohibit leaving **בשעת עבודה**. Indeed, the command to abide in the Dwelling Place at all times was never stated in regard to the eighth day.

לד כַּאֲשֶׁר עָשָׂה בַּיּוֹם הַזֶּה צִוָּה יְהוָה לַעֲשֹׂת לְכַפֵּר עֲלֵיכֶם׃

34 *As He has done this day, so has* God *commanded to do repeatedly, in order to effect atonement for you.*

לה וּפֶתַח אֹהֶל מוֹעֵד תֵּשְׁבוּ יוֹמָם וָלַיְלָה שִׁבְעַת יָמִים וּשְׁמַרְתֶּם אֶת־מִשְׁמֶרֶת יְהוָה וְלֹא תָמוּתוּ כִּי־כֵן צֻוֵּיתִי׃

35 *You shall abide in the entrance of the Tent of Appointed Meeting day and night, and you shall keep God's charge, so that you will not die, for so it was commanded to me.*

34 **כאשר עשה וגו׳**. Since Moshe is the speaker here, the subject of עשה is none other than God; and from this we infer that all that was done here at God's command and in His Name is as though it were done by God Himself. Similarly, we find: כל אשר עשים שם הוא היה עשה (*Bereshis* 39:22) — all was done at Yosef's command. Why does Scripture emphasize here that God is the Doer? Because what is being discussed here is the consecration of the כהנים to their כהונה, and this consecration has no meaning unless it is God Who has wrought it. In the preceding verse, as well, it is God Who is the subject of ימלא את ידכם.

צוה ה׳ לעשת וגו׳ — henceforth as well, throughout all of the seven days mentioned in the preceding verse.

According to the Gemara (*Yoma* 2a, 3b), לעשות alludes to פרישת כהן for מעשה פרה, while לכפר alludes to פרישת כהן גדול for מעשה יום הכיפורים. From the end of the Gemara's discussion (*Yoma* 4a, 8a), however, it appears that this is only an אסמכתא, and those פרישות are merely מעלה בעלמא — i.e., פרישה לטהרה and פרישה לקדושה, instituted on the model of פרישת המילואים (see *Yoma* 8b).

35 **ופתח אהל מועד תשבו וגו׳**. Let us compare our verse to what is written elsewhere: אַשְׁרֵי יוֹשְׁבֵי בֵיתֶךָ וגו׳ בָּחַרְתִּי הִסְתּוֹפֵף בְּבֵית אֱלֹקַי (*Tehillim* 84:5,11); שִׁבְתִּי בְּבֵית־ה׳ כָּל־יְמֵי חַיַּי לַחֲזוֹת וגו׳ (ibid. 27:4; see our Commentary there). From these verses it appears that he who "abides in God's House" gives himself up entirely to the idea embodied by the Sanctuary and saturates

36 *Aharon and his sons carried out all the things that God had commanded through Moshe.*	לו וַיַּעַשׂ אַהֲרֹן וּבָנָיו אֵת כָּל־הַדְּבָרִים אֲשֶׁר־צִוָּה יְהוָה בְּיַד־מֹשֶׁה: ססס
9 1 *And it came to pass on the eighth day that Moshe called Aharon and his sons and the elders of Israel.*	**ט** א וַיְהִי בַּיּוֹם הַשְּׁמִינִי קָרָא מֹשֶׁה לְאַהֲרֹן וּלְבָנָיו וּלְזִקְנֵי יִשְׂרָאֵל:

his mind with thoughts and resolutions learned in God's House. For only thus can abiding in God's House be an object of great longing. Hence, in our view, this abiding at the entrance of the אהל מועד for seven days included this task also: The כהנים absorbed a host of holy ideas that impact upon the consciousness and will, ideas that are embodied by the אהל מועד-Sanctuary. Safeguarding these ideas is the essence of the service of the כהונה, for which the abiding at the entrance of the Tent was preparation.

ושמרתם את משמרת ה׳. We find a similar expression used in connection with the nation's obedience to God — when to camp and when to journey forth — during the long wandering in the wilderness (*Bemidbar* 9:23). The expression is applied particularly to the camping — in regard to the patient waiting for the signal to break camp: ובהאריך הענן וגו׳ ושמרו בני ישראל את משמרת ה׳ ולא יסעו (ibid. 9:19).

שמיני

CHAPTER 9

1 **ויהי ביום השמיני**. In our essay on מילה (*Collected Writings*, vol. III) we explained the symbolic significance of the eighth day, which is preceded by seven consecutive days. We argued that the completion of a count of seven days symbolizes the conclusion and completion of the condition that has prevailed until now; the eighth day marks a new beginning on a higher level — the beginning of a higher "octave," as it were.

2 *And he said to Aharon: Take for yourself a calf born of cattle as an offering that clears of sin and a ram as an ascent offering, [both] whole, and bring them near before* **God.**

ב וַיֹּאמֶר אֶל־אַהֲרֹן קַח־לְךָ עֵגֶל
בֶּן־בָּקָר לְחַטָּאת וְאַיִל לְעֹלָה
תְּמִימִם וְהַקְרֵב לִפְנֵי יְהוָה׃

The same is true here. Seven days the כהנים abided at the entrance of the Tent of Meeting. This brought to a close the condition in which the כהנים lived only the personal lives of individuals. On the eighth day they entered a new, loftier phase of life, consecrated to God and to His people.

2 **עגל בן בקר** — according to Rosh Hashanah 10a — is a two-year old calf, i.e., in its second year. It is more developed than an עגל סתם (that which is denoted by the simple term עגל), which is only in its first year; but it has not yet reached the maturity of a פר בן בקר, which begins only in the third year. According to *Bechoros* 19b, cattle mature for breeding only in their third year. Accordingly, the term בן בקר — as a designation of age — may denote those years in which an animal is still regarded as בן ובת and not yet as אב ואם. Perhaps, then, the terms פר and פרה derive from the root פרה, to be fruitful. פר בן בקר, then, would denote the age at which an animal is characterized by both aspects: when it is in the process of making the transition from בן to פר; and, in light of the above, that would be the third year. (According to the רמב״ם in הל׳ מעשה הקרבנות, 1:14, an animal is termed a פר in its second year; see כסף משנה there, and משנה למלך הל׳ פרה אדומה, 1:1, end.)

This is the only offering where the obligation is to bring an עגל; and, as we have stated, it must be an עגל that is nearly a פר. It is fitting that the כהן who is *about* to serve in the Sanctuary should represent himself with such an offering. Later, however, when he has already assumed the office of כהן המשיח, he represents himself as a פר (above, 4:3). So, too, during the days of the מילואים, when he contemplated the "field" of his future labors, he saw himself as a פר at work (see Commentary to *Shemos* 29:1).

Thus did Aharon draw near to God — with an עגל לחטאת and with an איל לעולה. He pledged that, in the responsibilities of his office, he would always adhere to the lofty heights of his calling (חטאת); and, in the dignity of his office, he would always be a model for the community, striding before them and guiding them to the heights of Jewish perfection (עולה).

According to our Sages in *Toras Kohanim*, this offering was brought to atone also for חטא העגל, even though atonement had already been effected for this sin. Let us explain:

Previously, in our Commentary to *Shemos* 8:22, we stressed the sharp contrast between Judaism and all ancient and modern heathenism. The essence of this contrast is this: That which the heathen idolizes, and to which he offers himself and all that he owns, the Jew masters and offers to the one and only God.

The same applies here. Aharon had made the עגל as a symbol of one of the powers subservient to the one, sole God. But heathen belief, which idolizes the forces of nature, turned the עגל into a divine power, ruling coordinately with God. In our verse, Aharon offers to God an עגל representing *himself*. Through שחיטה he masters this, *his* עגל. Through זריקה he devotes it to the one God, so as to serve before Him in freedom. He thus expresses the following: This same physical force to which the heathen world bends the knee, rules also within man. But the man who is close to God rules over it with his moral freedom; and once nature is mastered by man's free will, it, too, is sanctified and joined to God's service. When man grasps this truth, he atones for the sin of idolizing nature. For the false god of nature is then subordinated not only to God but also to the man whose moral freedom has brought him close to God.

There is a deep connection between חטא העגל and the erecting of the Dwelling Place. This sin occurred between the issuing of the command to erect the Dwelling Place and the implementation of this command. It constitutes historical proof, for all time, of the very need for the atonement of the nation and the כהנים; and lo, this is the whole purpose of the Sanctuary: to serve as a place of כפרה for Israel. We noted this previously in our Commentary on חטא העגל.

Bearing in mind this sin of Aharon, we can explain his offerings here — the עגל לחטאת and the איל לעולה — as follows: In a moment of weakness he fell, and did not adhere to the lofty heights of his calling.

3 *And to the Children of Israel you shall speak, saying: Take a he-goat for an offering that clears of sin, and a calf and a sheep in their first year, [both of them] whole, for an ascent offering.*

ג וְאֶל־בְּנֵי יִשְׂרָאֵל תְּדַבֵּר לֵאמֹר
קְחוּ שְׂעִיר־עִזִּים לְחַטָּאת וְעֵגֶל
וָכֶבֶשׂ בְּנֵי־שָׁנָה תְּמִימִם לְעֹלָה׃

4 *And an ox and a ram for a peace offering, to perform a meal offering before* God, *an homage offering mixed with oil, for today* God *will appear to you.*

ד וְשׁוֹר וָאַיִל לִשְׁלָמִים לִזְבֹּחַ לִפְנֵי
יְהוָה וּמִנְחָה בְּלוּלָה בַשָּׁמֶן כִּי
הַיּוֹם יְהוָה נִרְאָה אֲלֵיכֶם׃

Instead of leading the people, he yielded to them and submitted to their will. Henceforth, he vows to adhere always to the lofty altar-heights of his calling (חטאת); to always walk before them, to show them the way that leads to God (עולה).

3–4 **ואל בני ישראל תדבר וגו׳**. First, the כהן brings his offering (v. 2). For upon assuming his new office, he must recognize the new responsibility thrust upon him by his exalted position — vis-à-vis God and the nation. Then, the nation, too, must bring its offering to God. It, too, must recognize its responsibility to God, and its standing as a nation amidst the nations. For it is not to the כהן that God's Presence will appear here; rather, God will appear to the nation, which is assuming an historical task among the nations. God allows His Presence to dwell where His Torah finds a Sanctuary and a people.

The nation's offering consists of two groups: (a) שעיר לחטאת ועגל וכבש לעולה and (b) שור ואיל לשלמים ומנחה בלולה בשמן. The first group reflects the nation's posture toward God, while the second group reflects the nation's position as a nation amidst the other nations.

Standing before God, the nation undertakes as follows:

Through the שעיר עזים לחטאת the nation signifies that it will stubbornly resist all temptations of strangers. Obediently and faithfully it will hold fast to its position, to which the one Shepherd has assigned it.

Through the עגל וכבש בני שנה לעולה the nation signifies that with freshness of youth and with manly strength it will follow God's lead, ever upwards. In its actions and in its lot it will commit itself to God, Who guides its actions and supports it in its lot, in order that it reach the goal that God has set for it in His Torah.

Through the שור ואיל לשלמים לזבח לפני ה׳ the nation joyfully gives expression to the special position it has attained among the nations, thanks to its unwavering steadfastness and faithful devotion. The young עגל that stands before God, becomes a virile שור when confronting the nations — by virtue of its energetic endeavors. And the כבש that follows its one and only Shepherd, becomes the איל that leads the flock of nations. Israel will recognize with joy this aspect of its task among the nations; this is expressed through the national זבח השלמים, "meal of peace before God" offering.

מנחה בלולה בשמן, "flour soaked in oil," symbolizes the means that afford the nation a prosperous existence. They, too, must be presented to the altar as a sign of homage.

Although מנחה here is joined with שלמים, in verse 17 it is connected to עולה and cited between עולה and שלמים. Thus, the מנחה complements the עולה and at the same time is the basis of the שלמים. For the total commitment of the personality, as expressed in the עולה, is complemented by the recognition that all the possessions that afford one a prosperous existence belong to God and are in His hands (this is also expressed by מנחת נסכים); and a person's joy in life before God — as expressed in שלמים — is rooted in the very recognition that all sustenance and prosperity are a gift from God (see Commentary below, v. 17).

It is significant that the only communal offering that represents the joy of action before God is designated here as שור — a general term — and not פר (there are no other שלמי ציבור except for כבשי עצרת, which, as כבשים, represent not the idea of service but our lot which is supported by God). The general term שור signifies that the duty of serving God applies to all ages. For the community includes every individual, at every age and at every level of strength.

If this communal offering, too, is related to חטא העגל, then its meaning is as follows: The nation undertakes, through the offering of שעיר עזים לחטאת, never again to be induced by an ערב רב to turn away from God and His Torah. Through the עגל of the עולה and through the שור of the שלמים, the nation atones directly for the חטא העגל (see Commentary

5 *They took that which Moshe had commanded to the Tent of Appointed Meeting; the entire community drew near, and they stood before* God.

ה וַיִּקְחוּ אֵת אֲשֶׁר צִוָּה מֹשֶׁה אֶל־פְּנֵי אֹהֶל מוֹעֵד וַיִּקְרְבוּ כָּל־הָעֵדָה וַיַּעַמְדוּ לִפְנֵי יְהֹוָה׃

6 *And Moshe said: Do this thing that* God *has commanded, and* God's *glory will reveal itself to you.*

ו וַיֹּאמֶר מֹשֶׁה זֶה הַדָּבָר אֲשֶׁר־צִוָּה יְהֹוָה תַּעֲשׂוּ וְיֵרָא אֲלֵיכֶם כְּבוֹד יְהֹוָה׃

on Aharon's offering, above, v. 2), as *Toras Kohanim* here says: Aharon had intended to make it an עגל, but the people elevated it to the level of an independent שור. Through the כבש of the עולה and through the איל of the שלמים, the nation places its destiny in the hands of God, the one and only Shepherd. Thus, with selfless devotion the nation will lead the flock of mankind to God — with manly strength and joyful courage. For the "flour and oil" of its existence and prosperity, the nation thanks God alone, the one and only God, and to Him alone will it render homage and praise.

6 **זה הדבר אשר צוה ה׳ תעשו וגו׳**. As קרבן אהרן on *Toras Kohanim* (to our verse) has pointed out, these words — which are addressed to the nation — cannot refer to the physical performance of the offering. For the nation has already performed all that was required of it in regard to this offering. Therefore, *Toras Kohanim* says as follows: ויאמר משה זה הדבר אשר צוה ה׳ תעשו. אמר להם משה לישראל אותו יצר הרע העבירו מלבכם ותהיו כולכם ביראה אחת ובעצה אחת לשרת לפני המקום, כשם שהוא יחידי בעולם כך תהא עבודתכם מיוחדת לפניו שנאמר ומלתם את ערלת לבבכם. מפני מה כי ה׳ האלקים הוא אלקי האלקים ואדוני האדונים, עשיתם כן וירא אליכם כבוד ה׳.

Apparently, this explanation of *Toras Kohanim* conceives of all the offering procedures prescribed here as one single act. They all are included in זה הדבר. They all express one דבר, one Word of God, whose actualization is our responsibility. The principle that emerges from all the *mitzvos* prescribed to us in the rites of the offerings is this: להעביר מלבנו, we must remove from our hearts, אותו יצר הרע, that uncontrolled animal sensuality, which is symbolized by the animal we present as an offering. We must not leave room for it in our hearts. Rather, we must subordinate our sensuous impulses to the power of our moral will, as symbolized by שחיטה, נתינה or זריקה, and הקטרה. Thus, fear of God, יראה, will deliver us from all sin (חטאת), and our hearts will be of one resolve, בעצה אחת, to fulfill our duties to God (עולה).

And just as, here, one offering represents the community before the one, sole God, so are we to attain inner and outer harmony through our very attachment to God. Every individual with all his facets, and the community with all its members, are in connection with the one, sole God. It is through this very connection that each individual is to attain an inner harmony, reconciling the dichotomous nature of his being, and the whole community is to attain unity and equality. As it says of the unity in the life of the individual: ומלתם את ערלת לבבכם וערפכם לא תקשו עוד, כי ה׳ אלקיכם הוא אלקי האלקים ואדני האדנים וגו׳ (*Devarim* 10:16–17).

Circumcise the ערלה of your heart (with all your might, resist sensuality: תהיו כולכם ביראה אחת – חטאת) and no longer be stiff-necked (do good willingly and joyfully: בעצה אחת לשרת לפני המקום – עולה). For your God is God of gods (your lives are entrusted to Him alone) and Master of masters (consciously or unconsciously, willingly or by force).

Clearly, the idea expressed in these verses is that the unity of one's life's work is a direct result of God's unity; and one does not attain unity in his life's work unless he does God's Will through commission and omission. As *Toras Kohanim* concludes: עשיתם כן, if you devote yourselves, one and all, to God, translating into reality the ideal symbolized by the offerings, then וירא אליכם כבוד ה׳: the united community, devoting itself to God, will be privileged to behold the Divine Presence. And when God will dwell in your midst before your very eyes, the purpose of erecting the Dwelling Place will have been achieved: ועשו לי מקדש ושכנתי בתוכם (*Shemos* 25:8).

In our opinion, this passage from *Toras Kohanim* expresses the basic idea of all the offerings and the symbolic significance of the offering procedures.

From our verse, *Yoma* 5b derives that מקרא פרשה מעכב: they would read aloud פרשת המילואים (*Shemos* 29) during the procedure of the offerings, and this reading was an indispensable part of the ritual. For the reading of this פרשה lent to the performance of these procedures the aura of קיום מצוה: None of them were fabricated by man, according

7 *And Moshe said to Aharon: Draw near to the altar and perform your offering that clears of sin, and your ascent offering, and effect atonement for yourself and for the people, and then perform the offering of the people and effect atonement for them, as* God *has commanded.*

ז וַיֹּאמֶר מֹשֶׁה אֶל־אַהֲרֹן קְרַב אֶל־
הַמִּזְבֵּחַ וַעֲשֵׂה אֶת־חַטָּאתְךָ
וְאֶת־עֹלָתֶךָ וְכַפֵּר בַּעַדְךָ וּבְעַד
הָעָם וַעֲשֵׂה אֶת־קָרְבַּן הָעָם
וְכַפֵּר בַּעֲדָם כַּאֲשֶׁר צִוָּה יְהוָה׃

8 *And Aharon drew near to the altar and slaughtered the calf of the offering that clears of sin that was his.*

ח וַיִּקְרַב אַהֲרֹן אֶל־הַמִּזְבֵּחַ וַיִּשְׁחַט
אֶת־עֵגֶל הַחַטָּאת אֲשֶׁר־לוֹ׃

9 *The sons of Aharon brought the blood close to him, he dipped his finger into the blood and put it*

ט וַיַּקְרִבוּ בְּנֵי אַהֲרֹן אֶת־הַדָּם אֵלָיו
וַיִּטְבֹּל אֶצְבָּעוֹ בַּדָּם וַיִּתֵּן עַל־

---

to his subjective feelings; they served solely to fulfill God's command. Similarly, the כהן הגדול on יום הכיפורים — between the עבודת היום and the עבודות חוץ — would read aloud פרשת אחרי מות. In doing so, he signified that the procedures he had performed were strictly the realization of God's command (*Yoma* 68b, רש״י).

7 **וכפר בעדך ובעד העם**. Aharon's offerings atoned also for the people. This constitutes proof of the special connection between these offerings and חטא העגל. For the people were partners to Aharon's sin, as they forced their will upon him: עשו את העגל אשר עשה אהרן (*Shemos* 32:35; see Commentary there, 32:1). Thus, the sin of the people themselves was atoned for by the offering of the people, while their share in Aharon's sin was atoned for by Aharon's offering.

9 In verse 12, speaking of the עולה, it says: וימצאו — they presented the blood to him; for he had to take the vessel containing the blood in order to dash the blood against the sides of the altar. Here, of the חטאת,

קַרְנ֣וֹת הַמִּזְבֵּ֔חַ וְאֶת־הַדָּ֣ם יָצַ֔ק אֶל־יְס֖וֹד הַמִּזְבֵּֽחַ׃

upon the horns of the altar, and he poured the [remainder of the] blood toward the base of the altar.

י וְאֶת־הַחֵ֨לֶב וְאֶת־הַכְּלָיֹ֜ת וְאֶת־הַיֹּתֶ֤רֶת מִן־הַכָּבֵד֙ מִן־הַ֣חַטָּ֔את הִקְטִ֖יר הַמִּזְבֵּ֑חָה כַּאֲשֶׁ֛ר צִוָּ֥ה יְהוָ֖ה אֶת־מֹשֶֽׁה׃

10 *The fat and the kidneys along with the diaphragm of the liver of the offering that clears of sin he offered up in smoke upon the altar, as* God *had commanded Moshe.*

יא וְאֶת־הַבָּשָׂ֖ר וְאֶת־הָע֑וֹר שָׂרַ֣ף בָּאֵ֔שׁ מִח֖וּץ לַֽמַּחֲנֶֽה׃

11 *But the flesh and the skin he burned in fire outside the camp.*

יב וַיִּשְׁחַ֖ט אֶת־הָעֹלָ֑ה וַ֠יַּמְצִאוּ בְּנֵ֨י אַהֲרֹ֤ן אֵלָיו֙ אֶת־הַדָּ֔ם וַיִּזְרְקֵ֥הוּ עַל־הַמִּזְבֵּ֖חַ סָבִֽיב׃

12 *He then slaughtered the ascent offering; the sons of Aharon presented the blood to him and he dashed it against the altar, all around.*

יג וְאֶת־הָעֹלָ֗ה הִמְצִ֧יאוּ אֵלָ֛יו לִנְתָחֶ֖יהָ וְאֶת־הָרֹ֑אשׁ וַיַּקְטֵ֖ר עַל־הַמִּזְבֵּֽחַ׃

13 *They had presented to him the ascent offering in its parts, and the head, and he turned them into smoke upon the altar.*

יד וַיִּרְחַ֥ץ אֶת־הַקֶּ֖רֶב וְאֶת־הַכְּרָעָ֑יִם וַיַּקְטֵ֥ר עַל־הָעֹלָ֖ה הַמִּזְבֵּֽחָה׃

14 *He then washed the intestines and the feet, and turned them into smoke upon the ascent offering on the altar.*

---

it says merely ויקרבו: they brought the blood close to Aharon, so that he could dip his finger into it.

11 **ואת הבשר ואת העור וגו׳**. Although it was a חטאת חיצונית, it was treated like the פר כהן המשיח: its meat was not eaten, but burned מחוץ למחנה. For there did not yet exist a כהן fit to eat the חטאת; only as a result of this חטאת would a כהן arise who would be fit for this. The חטאת of ימי המילואים,

15 *Thereupon he brought near the offering of the people, took the he-goat of the offering that clears of sin that was the people's, slaughtered it and offered it as an offering that clears of sin, like the first one.*

טו וַיַּקְרֵב אֵת קָרְבַּן הָעָם וַיִּקַּח אֶת־
שְׂעִיר הַחַטָּאת אֲשֶׁר לָעָם
וַיִּשְׁחָטֵהוּ וַיְחַטְּאֵהוּ כָּרִאשׁוֹן׃

16 *He brought near the ascent offering, and offered it as prescribed.*

טז וַיַּקְרֵב אֶת־הָעֹלָה וַיַּעֲשֶׂהָ
כַּמִּשְׁפָּט׃ שני

17 *He brought near the homage offering, filled his hand from it, and turned it into smoke upon the altar, in addition to the morning's ascent offering.*

יז וַיַּקְרֵב אֶת־הַמִּנְחָה וַיְמַלֵּא כַפּוֹ
מִמֶּנָּה וַיַּקְטֵר עַל־הַמִּזְבֵּחַ מִלְּבַד
עֹלַת הַבֹּקֶר׃

also, was treated in this manner — for the very same reason (see Commentary above, 4:11–12 and *Shemos* 29:14).

16 כמשפט: as prescribed above (chap.1) for עולת נדבה.

17 וימלא כפו ממנה. From *Menachos* 9b and 19b it is evident that this means קמיצה. We noted previously (vv. 3–4) that the idea of the מנחה generally complements the idea of the עולה and the שלמים, through מנחת נסכים. Here, however, this idea is expressed through an independent מנחה. Hence, while מנחת נסכים is burned in its entirety upon the altar, the מנחה mentioned here requires קמיצה — as in the case of מנחת נדבה — and its שיריים are eaten. This מנחה and מנחת העומר, which is similar in meaning, are the only מנחות ציבור of which only a קומץ is offered on the altar. So, too, the שלמי ציבור mentioned here have no parallel except for כבשי עצרת. According to *Toras Kohanim* here, all the עולות (according to the ראב״ד ad loc., the שלמים too) were accompanied by מנחות נסכים appropriate to them, and this is indicated (as regards עולות) by the word כמשפט (v. 16).

יח וַיִּשְׁחַט אֶת־הַשּׁוֹר וְאֶת־הָאַיִל
זֶבַח הַשְּׁלָמִים אֲשֶׁר לָעָם וַיַּמְצִאוּ
בְּנֵי אַהֲרֹן אֶת־הַדָּם אֵלָיו
וַיִּזְרְקֵהוּ עַל־הַמִּזְבֵּחַ סָבִיב׃

18 *He then slaughtered the ox and the ram, the meal-of-peace offering that was the people's; the sons of Aharon presented the blood to him, and he dashed it against the altar, all around.*

יט וְאֶת־הַחֲלָבִים מִן־הַשּׁוֹר וּמִן־
הָאַיִל הָאַלְיָה וְהַמְכַסֶּה וְהַכְּלָיֹת
וְיֹתֶרֶת הַכָּבֵד׃

19 *Also the fat parts of the ox, and the tailpiece of the ram, the membrane and kidneys and diaphragm of the liver.*

כ וַיָּשִׂימוּ אֶת־הַחֲלָבִים עַל־הֶחָזוֹת
וַיַּקְטֵר הַחֲלָבִים הַמִּזְבֵּחָה׃

20 *They placed the fat parts upon the breast pieces; he turned the fat parts into smoke upon the altar.*

כא וְאֵת הֶחָזוֹת וְאֵת שׁוֹק הַיָּמִין הֵנִיף

21 *But Aharon had [already] waved the breast pieces and the right*

מלבד עלת הבקר. The עולות ונסכים and the independent מנחה were brought in addition to the morning תמיד offering and its attendant נסכים (see *Toras Kohanim*). On Shabbos and the festivals, the מוספים express the special thoughts of devotion inspired by the sanctity of the day. But these do not exclude the thoughts of devotion awakened in us every morning by the simple gift of a new day, as expressed by the תמיד. The מוספים merely supplement the daily expression of devotion attached to the daily morning offering: מלבד עלת הבקר אשר לעלת התמיד (*Bemidbar* 28:23). Similarly here, the offerings prescribed for the eighth day of the מילואים were like the מוספים for that day; they were brought מלבד עלת הבקר.

19 **והמכסה**. According to the רמב״ן, this is not short for חלב המכסה את הקרב, but a name for all the חלב that is offered on the altar. For the distinguishing characteristic of חלב is that it is not integrated with the flesh, but lies upon the organs and covers them. See Commentary above, 3:3–5.

21–22 תנופת חזה ושוק of the שלמים was performed together with תנופת האימורים — before their הקטרה. Here, however (in vv. 20–21), Scripture ends with

thigh in a wave [offering] before God, *as Moshe had commanded.*	אַהֲרֹ֛ן תְּנוּפָ֖ה לִפְנֵ֣י יְהוָ֑ה כַּאֲשֶׁ֖ר צִוָּ֥ה מֹשֶֽׁה׃

the תנופה, and places the הקטרה before it. (The sense of verse 21, then, is as follows: Aharon had already waved the חזה and the שוק — before the הקטרה mentioned in verse 20.) There can be only one reason for this order: to connect this ritual (תנופת חזה ושוק) with the immediately following ברכה. According to *Toras Kohanim* here, this ברכה was none other than the ברכת כהנים prescribed for all time (*Bemidbar* 6:22ff.). Clearly, then, there is a connection between the חזה ושוק and this ברכה. What is this connection?

Previously (7:30ff.), we explained the significance of the gift of חזה ושוק of שלמים to the כהנים, and the significance of תנופת חזה ושוק: The individual who rejoices in his happiness before God devotes to Him all of his thoughts and aspirations (חזה), all of his material power and prominence (שוק). All these he devotes to God and to the communal aims determined by Him (תרומה ותנופה). And when he gives the חזה ושוק to the כהן, he recognizes and acknowledges that all his material and spiritual assets — which are the source of his שלמות and of the joy of his שלמים — have come to him thanks only to God's Torah, which proceeds from the mouth of the כהן. He thereby devotes everything to this Torah.

To this is now joined ברכת כהנים, to teach us the following: It is only thanks to this recognition that he will continue to be blessed with material security (יברכך וישמרך), with spiritual gifts (יאר ויחנך), and with the שלמות that flows from the combination of the two (ישא וישם לך שלום). Hence, the Gemara (*Sotah* 38b) regards ברכת כהנים as the conclusion of the עבודה, as it says: וישא אהרן וגו׳ וירד מעשות וגו׳; see רש״י there (unlike *Toras Kohanim* here, which explains this verse as a מקרא מסורס). From this we learn the halachah that כל כהן שאינו עולה בעבודה שוב אינו עולה (*Sotah* 38b). If a כהן does not move toward the דוכן by רצה, he may not participate in ברכת כהנים. ברכת כהנים is not an independent act which stands on its own. For the blessings pronounced in it can be attained only as a result of the עבודה that preceded it, and only in close association with the עבודה may ברכת כהנים be recited.

22 *And Aharon lifted up his hands toward the people and blessed them, and then he came down from performing the offering that clears of sin, the ascent offering and the peace offering.*

כב וַיִּשָּׂא אַהֲרֹן אֶת־יָדָו אֶל־הָעָם
וַיְבָרְכֵם וַיֵּרֶד מֵעֲשֹׂת הַחַטָּאת
וְהָעֹלָה וְהַשְּׁלָמִים׃

23 *Thereupon, Moshe and Aharon went into the Tent of Appointed Meeting; they came out again, blessed the people — and God's glory revealed itself to all the people.*

כג וַיָּבֹא מֹשֶׁה וְאַהֲרֹן אֶל־אֹהֶל
מוֹעֵד וַיֵּצְאוּ וַיְבָרְכוּ אֶת־הָעָם
וַיֵּרָא כְבוֹד־יְהוָה אֶל־כָּל־הָעָם׃
שלישי

וישא אהרן את ידו: בנשיאות כפים, "With hands raised" (ibid. 38a). The כהן's hands do not possess any inherent power to bestow blessings. Perhaps this is why ידו is spelled חסר. The hand of the כהן merely points to God, Who has promised the blessing. For more on ברכת כהנים see Commentary to *Bemidbar* 6:22ff.

23 **ויבא משה וגו'**. The purpose of their entry into the אהל מועד is not explained in Scripture. When we consider only what is explicitly mentioned in the text, it appears that the ביאה and the יציאה were preparatory to ויברכו; and the ברכה, in turn, was preparatory to 'וירא כבוד ה. Perhaps there is truth, then, in the following interpretation:

The Dwelling Place was consecrated, and the כהנים and the people brought their offerings. The people were promised that, as a result, God's Presence would appear to them, sealing the covenant whereby the Divine Presence would dwell in their midst, on account of the place prepared for the Torah.

God's Presence, however, did not appear immediately upon the completion of the offerings. If that had happened, it might have lent credence to the pagan superstition that in the offering procedures there is a mysterious quality that has a magical effect upon God and produces an appearance of God to man, in a kind of physical cause-and-effect. But this is not the case. For the one, personal, and autonomous God willfully promised to appear to the people; and He made this promise not on account of the offering, but on account of the commitment expressed in the offering.

So it was that the offerings had been brought and Aharon had blessed the people that their material and spiritual resources would blossom, and that peace would be granted them by God through His blessing and protection, grace and providential care — all this as a result of the promised ושכנתי בתוכם. But the Divine Presence had not yet appeared. Rather, first Moshe and Aharon entered the place that had just been completed as an אהל מועד, where God — as He promised — would meet with His people. This promise was symbolized, as God ordained, by the ארון, שולחן, מנורה, and the מזבח הקטורת in the משכן הכרובים. These signify the following: Wherever the Torah finds a home, in steadfastness and in life full of vitality; wherever the people's prosperity and spirit are devoted to the Torah, so that all of life ascends בריח ניחוח לה׳ — there the כרובים descend from God, and God's Presence becomes manifest in the form of blessing and protection. Imbued with the idea of the אהל מועד, Moshe and Aharon went out to the people and, in this spirit, blessed them. That is to say, they expressed the wish to the people that the אהל מועד idea be realized in them and by them. And, indeed, it was realized: וירא כבוד ה׳ אל כל העם וגו׳!

Just as the ברכה pronounced by Aharon is identified as ברכת כהנים by the preceding חזה ושוק, so was the ברכה pronounced by Moshe and Aharon rendered a ברכת אהל מועד by the preceding ביאה אל אהל מועד. This ברכה was then realized by the appearance of כבוד ה׳, and thus the Dwelling Place was completed and became, literally, an אהל מועד.

In *Toras Kohanim* we find the following: ויבא משה ואהרן אל אהל מועד, למה נכנס משה ואהרן ביחד ללמדו על מעשה הקטורת, או לא נכנס אלא לדבר אחר הריני דן ירידה טעונה ברכה וביאה טעונה ברכה מה ירידה מעין עבודה אף ביאה מעין עבודה וכו׳ הא למה נכנס משה עם אהרן ללמדו על מעשה הקטורת. According to *Toras Kohanim*, ברכת משה ואהרן (v. 23) is connected with the ביאה אל אהל מועד, just as ברכת אהרן (v. 22) is connected with the ירידה מעשות החטאת וגו׳. Hence, just as this ירידה (which — according to *Toras Kohanim* — preceded the ברכה, as we mentioned earlier) is connected with the עבודה, so this ביאה — from which flowed the ברכה of Moshe and Aharon — is connected with the עבודה; and, according to *Toras Kohanim*, this connection is reflected in the teaching of מעשה הקטורת.

Now, if we bear in mind that the whole idea of the היכל reaches its

24 *Fire went forth from before* God *and consumed the ascent offering and the fat parts upon the altar; the people saw [it] and shouted for joy, and they fell upon their faces.*

10 1 *And Aharon's sons, Nadav and Avihu, each took his pan, put fire into them and placed incense upon it, and they brought near before* God *strange fire which He had not commanded them.*

כד וַתֵּצֵא אֵשׁ מִלִּפְנֵי יְהֹוָה וַתֹּאכַל
עַל־הַמִּזְבֵּחַ אֶת־הָעֹלָה וְאֶת־
הַחֲלָבִים וַיַּרְא כָּל־הָעָם וַיָּרֹנּוּ
וַיִּפְּלוּ עַל־פְּנֵיהֶם׃

י א וַיִּקְחוּ בְנֵי־אַהֲרֹן נָדָב וַאֲבִיהוּא
אִישׁ מַחְתָּתוֹ וַיִּתְּנוּ בָהֵן אֵשׁ
וַיָּשִׂימוּ עָלֶיהָ קְטֹרֶת וַיַּקְרִיבוּ
לִפְנֵי יְהֹוָה אֵשׁ זָרָה אֲשֶׁר לֹא צִוָּה
אֹתָם׃

loftiest conception in the מעשה הקטורת upon the מזבח הזהב, and further, that ללמדו על מעשה הקטורת relates apparently to the conceptual meaning of the ritual and not to its actual performance, as this was not the proper time for offering קטורת, we conclude that this passage in *Toras Kohanim* is not far from our own interpretation of the purpose of Moshe and Aharon's entry into the אהל מועד.

CHAPTER 10

1 We have already noted elsewhere (*Bereshis* 4:3–6) that in the account of the very first offering, and again at every renewal of the offerings, Scripture distinguishes, by deed or word, between an offering that was rejected and an offering that was accepted. This renders groundless that blasphemous notion in which our present-day reformers wish to pride themselves. The understanding that the offerings have only relative worth, they claim, did not come until the time of the prophets, who had advanced beyond the "primitive" conception of the Pentateuch. But consider the fact that Kayin's offering was rejected while that of Hevel was accepted. Consider the warnings addressed to Shlomo during the construction and following the completion of the Sanctuary (*Melachim* I, 6:12–13; 9:3–9). These cases declare unequivocally that the value of the Sanctuary and its offerings depends on how dutiful we are

to God. Consider, further, Aharon's sons who died because of the sin of their offering: God's fire consumed them, at the same time that this very fire accepted the offering of the people, thereby expressing God's approval and demonstrating God's presence in the midst of the people. This refutes such a mistaken conception of the value of the offerings. The death of Aharon's sons is also a clear protest against all subjective arbitrariness in the sphere of our ritual worship of God.

ויקחו בני אהרן וגו׳: בני אהרן – שלא חלקו כבוד לאהרן, נדב ואביהוא – לא נטלו עצה ממשה, איש מחתתו – איש מעצמו יצאו ולא נטלו עצה זה מזה (*Toras Kohanim*). From the very wording of Scripture we learn that Aharon's sons behaved arrogantly. For the text does not read: ויקחו נדב ואביהוא מחתות ויתנו בהן אש וגו׳. Rather, it first stresses their filial relationship to Aharon: בני אהרן. The phrase איש מחתתו, also, is indicative of arrogance; thus, the words נדב ואביהוא have a similar connotation. Let us explain:

They were בני אהרן — yet they did not consult with their father before acting. Or, precisely because they were sons of Aharon they felt they were under no obligation to seek advice from anyone else. Actually, they were נדב ואביהוא — merely individual members of the nation, and yet they did not seek advice from the nation's leaders. Perhaps they had an exaggerated sense of self-worth, and so relied exclusively on their own reasoning. Moreover, איש מחתתו, each of them acted solely on his own initiative. They did not consult even with one another!

To be sure, their intention was praiseworthy, for even after their sin they are called קרובי (v. 3). Their praiseworthy intention is expressed in *Toras Kohanim* as follows: אף הם בשמחתם כיון שראו אש חדשה עמדו להוסיף אהבה על אהבה. The fact is, however, that when the entire *nation* was privileged to witness a revelation of God's closeness, Nadav and Avihu felt the need to make a *separate* offering of their own. This shows that they were not moved by the true spirit of priesthood. For in Judaism the priests are completely identified with the nation. They have no standing in their own right. The whole essence of the כהנים is that they stand in the midst of the people, and this accounts for their standing before God.

Thus, in their very "drawing near," Nadav and Avihu were at fault. Moreover, their offering per se was illegal in every respect. These two aspects of their sin are inferred by *Toras Kohanim* (to 16:1) from the differing Scriptural expressions used to describe their act: בקרבתם לפני ה׳

וימתו (ibid.) and וימת נדב ואביהוא וגו׳ בהקרבם אש זרה וגו׳ (*Bemidbar* 3:4). Both the subjective קריבה, the "drawing near," and the objective הקרבה, the offering per se, entailed sin.

Indeed, the הקרבה was illegal with respect to the מחתות, the אש, the קטורת — all were against the Halachah. All כלי שרת must be של ציבור and לשם קודש (see רמב״ם הל׳ כלי המקדש, 8:7; הל׳ בית הבחירה, 1:20). Upon surrendering his offering to a sacred vessel of the nation, the offerer stands on the sacred ground of the nation and of its Torah, and surrenders himself to the demands of the Sanctuary by renouncing all personal caprice. The מחתה of Nadav and of Avihu, however, was מחתתו; each used his own fire pan. They did not bring their offering in vessels of the Sanctuary, but in their own vessels — without self-renunciation.

ויתנו בהן אש — more precisely: אש זרה; as ר׳ עקיבא explains in *Toras Kohanim*: מן הכיריים. They did not take fire from the altar, as was prescribed for the daily קטורת and for the קטורת of יום הכיפורים. That is to say, they did not take "fire of the Torah," which demands the devotion of the entire community, great and small. Rather, it was fire from their own hearths.

Finally, to the קטורת itself. קטורת is the only offering that is never brought as נדבה, neither by the community nor by individuals. It is offered only as the community's obligatory offering each day, and as the כהן גדול's obligatory offering on יום הכיפורים (*Menachos* 50a–b). For the קטורת symbolizes the person who is *completely* absorbed in bringing God satisfaction, who ascends *entirely*, לריח ניחוח לה׳ (see Commentary to *Shemos* 30:1ff; 30:34ff.). So long as this idea is a goal set by God, it represents the ideal of His requirements. But if it is given expression by one's own choice, as a נדבה, this idea entails great arrogance. Now, as regards this disastrous offering of Nadav and Avihu, the Torah stresses, above all else, that it was one which God had not commanded them to make: אשר לא צוה אתם. Even if the details of the offering had not been forbidden (as we have seen they indeed were), the mere fact that this offering had not been commanded by God would have been sufficient to make it forbidden.

In the service of the offerings, there is no place for subjective arbitrariness. Even the קרבנות נדבה, the free-will offerings, must comply with prescribed forms. One who brings an offering seeks קרבת אלקים, closeness to God, but this can be attained only through obedience to God and

2 *Then fire went forth from before* God *and consumed them, and they died before* God.

ב וַתֵּצֵא אֵשׁ מִלִּפְנֵי יְהֹוָה וַתֹּאכַל אוֹתָם וַיָּמֻתוּ לִפְנֵי יְהֹוָה׃

3 *And Moshe said to Aharon: This is what* God *spoke, saying: I will be sanctified through those near to Me, and thus I will be honored by all the people. And Aharon was silent.*

ג וַיֹּאמֶר מֹשֶׁה אֶל־אַהֲרֹן הוּא אֲשֶׁר־דִּבֶּר יְהֹוָה ׀ לֵאמֹר בִּקְרֹבַי אֶקָּדֵשׁ וְעַל־פְּנֵי כָל־הָעָם אֶכָּבֵד וַיִּדֹּם אַהֲרֹן׃

acceptance of the yoke of His commandments. This is precisely the point that separates Judaism from paganism. The pagan, through his offering, seeks to make his deity subservient to his will, while the Jew, through his offering, places himself in the service of God and accepts upon himself the yoke of His commandments. Hence, all offerings in Judaism are formulas of Divine imperatives; and the offerer, through his offering, undertakes to adopt the Divine imperative as his guiding light. Offerings of one's own devising would be a subversion of that very truth which the offering is intended to represent. Such offerings would glorify personal caprice instead of obedience to God and acceptance of the yoke of His commandments.

Now we understand the death of Aharon's sons. Their death at the time of the first dedication of the Sanctuary is a warning to all future כהנים. It bars all arbitrariness, all personal caprice, from the precincts of the Sanctuary, whose whole purpose is to be a Sanctuary for the Torah! In Judaism the priest's function is not to introduce innovations in the Service, but to carry out God's command.

3 **בקרבי אקדש**. From *Yechezkel* 20:41, 28:22 and 25, 36:23, 38:16, 39:27 and also *Bemidbar* 20:13 it appears that the expression הִקָּדֵשׁ ב־, used in reference to God, means as follows: His קדושה becomes known through His strong actions against or on behalf of someone. Through His strong actions it becomes manifest that He is קדוש and absolute, and that whatever He wills He does. For the great among the nations do His bidding, and world powers cannot stand up to Him. The mitzvah ונקדשתי בתוך

בני ישראל (below, 22:32) also is to be understood in this way: A person must be willing to sacrifice everything in order to do God's Will.

Now, we might have interpreted בקרבי אקדש וגו׳ along the lines of the verse just cited (viz., *Vayikra* 22:32): My קדושה becomes known through those who are near to Me. Through them and through their actions it becomes manifest that a person must overcome all obstacles and must be willing to sacrifice all that is dear to him, in order to do God's Will. This duty of קידוש ה׳ is incumbent upon קרובי, for they are appointed to be the teachers of the people in their relationship with God. Had Nadav and Avihu fulfilled this duty, God would have appeared בכבודו — in the full "weight" of His majesty and commands.

But this interpretation is difficult. It is difficult to maintain that, by merely refraining from bringing their offering, Nadav and Avihu would have effected such a קידוש השם. For such refraining would not seem to require extraordinary self-control. And even if we grant that a great spirit moved within them and a surge of inspiration took hold of them, nevertheless, had they restrained themselves, this would have been strictly an inner process, and God alone would have been witness to it. The nation, however, would not have known a thing about it. Thus, it would not have effected כבוד ה׳ על פני כל העם.

We could posit, though, that בקרבי אקדש is a euphemistic, positive expression — instead of the negative בקרובי לא יחולל שמי. Indeed, the less their refraining from bringing their offering would have been a קידוש השם the more their offering was in fact a חילול השם, especially since it was performed by קרובי ה׳, whose task it was to teach the people obedience to God.

What appears more likely, however, is that our verse should be interpreted in the sense of the verses cited above from *Yechezkel*: אקדש, through My strong actions against My close ones, My sanctity becomes known. For by not overlooking the sins of My close ones — and even decreeing upon them death — it becomes manifest that My Will is absolute. For even the greatest persons, those close to Me — and precisely they — are not allowed the slightest deviation from My Will. ועל פני כל העם אכבד: as a result, the people will recognize the true weightiness of the obedience they owe Me.

Seen in this light, these words of God contain consolation for Aharon; hence, our verse continues: וידם אהרן. The consolation is this: Had his sons not been קרובי ה׳, perhaps their sin would have been forgiven, and the Divine decree that was dealt them would not have been a warning of such solemn import to the people. These words of God are antithetical to the modern point of view that grants immunity to great men of intellect in the matter of their moral lapses. According to this view, men of intellect are entitled to be treated with great leniency if they should violate God's moral law. According to Judaism, the greater the person, the greater his moral responsibilities. As the Gemara (*Yevamos* 121b) expounds on the verse in *Tehillim* (50:3): וּסְבִיבָיו נִשְׂעֲרָה מְאֹד – מלמד שהקב״ה מדקדק עם סביביו כחוט השערה. "'And round about Him it is exceedingly stormy.' This teaches us that God is exacting — even to a hairbreadth — with those who are around Him." Similarly, it is written (ibid. 89:8): אֵל נַעֲרָץ בְּסוֹד־קְדֹשִׁים רַבָּה וְנוֹרָא עַל־כָּל־סְבִיבָיו. "God, Whose majesty is felt even in the council of the holy ones, Who stands in awesome grandeur above all that are round about Him." Psalm 99, too, deals with God's holiness, which excludes from His Presence all that is profane. For holiness is the foremost duty of anyone who attains closeness to God. In verses 6–8 of this Psalm it says: "Moshe and Aharon were outstanding among His priests, and Shemuel among those who proclaim His Name." They were close to God; hence, "they called upon God and He answered them. He spoke to them from a pillar of cloud" and appointed them "keepers of His testimonies," transmitters of His statutes. In their pleas for others, He listened to them and was a forgiving God; but for their own misdeeds, He exacted justice: ונקם על עלילותם!

הוא אשר דבר ה׳. It is difficult to explain this phrase, for the Torah has not mentioned, up till now, that God had spoken such words. Hence, the רמב״ן holds that this sentence serves to explain the death of Aharon's sons, and he interprets the sentence as follows: "This is what God has expressed through this event." However, we find similar expressions elsewhere in Scripture — הוא הדבר אשר דברתי (*Bereshis* 41:28), הוא הדבר אשר לא דברו ה׳ (*Devarim* 18:22); and from these examples we infer that here, also, Scripture refers to words spoken previously. If Scripture's meaning had been in line with the רמב״ן, it should have said: זה אשר וגו׳. It appears, then, that from here we have again evidence that not all of God's Words to Moshe are recorded in the Written Law. Rather, Moshe here repeats these words because of the event that occurred; and as a result of the account of this event, they are also mentioned in the Torah.

4 *And Moshe called Mishael and Eltzafan, sons of Aharon's uncle, Uzziel, and said to them: Draw near and carry your brethren from before the Sanctuary, out of the camp.*

ד וַיִּקְרָא מֹשֶׁה אֶל־מִישָׁאֵל וְאֶל
אֶלְצָפָן בְּנֵי עֻזִּיאֵל דֹּד אַהֲרֹן
וַיֹּאמֶר אֲלֵהֶם קִרְבוּ שְׂאוּ אֶת־
אֲחֵיכֶם מֵאֵת פְּנֵי־הַקֹּדֶשׁ אֶל־
מִחוּץ לַמַּחֲנֶה׃

5 *They drew near and carried them out in their tunics, out of the camp, as Moshe had spoken.*

ה וַיִּקְרְבוּ וַיִּשָּׂאֻם בְּכֻתֳּנֹתָם אֶל־
מִחוּץ לַמַּחֲנֶה כַּאֲשֶׁר דִּבֶּר מֹשֶׁה׃

Otherwise, however, these — like many other Words of God — would have remained in the תורה שבעל פה.

4 **מאת פני הקדש**. In Scripture it is not clear where Aharon's sons offered incense. We know of only two places for such offerings: on the מזבח הזהב in the היכל, on which the daily קטורת was offered, and in the קודש הקדשים, in which the כהן גדול offered incense on יום הכיפורים. Since this latter offering had not yet been prescribed, it seems probable that Nadav and Avihu offered the incense on the מזבח הזהב in the היכל. Nevertheless, in *Toras Kohanim* it says: נטלו אש זרה ונכנסו לבית קדשי הקדשים. Nothing can be concluded from the juxtaposition of verses 1 and 2 in chapter 16, as there Scripture actually forbids כניסה להיכל שלא בשעת עבודה (see Commentary there). In any case, it is clear that they entered at least the היכל.

Here, however, the place where the bodies lay is identified as פני הקדש; and since the קודש is the היכל, and פני הקדש is east of the היכל (see *Menachos* 27b), it follows that they died in the חצר in front of the אהל מועד. This supports the view of ר׳ אליעזר in *Toras Kohanim* that נגפן מלאך ודחפן לחוץ והוציאם. Accordingly, וימתו לפני ה׳ (v. 2) means that the decree struck them inside the היכל, and they were forced outside, where they died in the עזרה.

בכתנתם. Their clothes were untouched by the fire. According to one opinion in *Toras Kohanim*, their bodies, too, were untouched; the fire struck them as lightning strikes: שריפת נשמה וגוף קיים.

6 *Moshe said to Aharon and to his sons, Elazar and Isamar: Do not let your heads remain unshorn and do not make a rent in your garments, lest you die and lest He be angry with the entire community; but your brethren, the entire House of Israel, shall bewail the burning that* God *has kindled.*

ו וַיֹּאמֶר מֹשֶׁה אֶל־אַהֲרֹן וּלְאֶלְעָזָר
וּלְאִיתָמָר ׀ בָּנָיו רָאשֵׁיכֶם אַל־
תִּפְרָעוּ ׀ וּבִגְדֵיכֶם לֹא־תִפְרֹמוּ
וְלֹא תָמֻתוּ וְעַל כָּל־הָעֵדָה יִקְצֹף
וַאֲחֵיכֶם כָּל־בֵּית יִשְׂרָאֵל יִבְכּוּ
אֶת־הַשְּׂרֵפָה אֲשֶׁר שָׂרַף יְהוָה׃

6 **ראשיכם אל תפרעו**. The כהן גדול, in every generation, is commanded — even at the death of his closest relatives — as follows: את ראשו לא יפרע ובגדיו לא יפרם (below, 21:10). Here, פריעה and פרימה are forbidden both to Aharon and to his sons. For on this יום השמיני the sons — otherwise regarded as כהנים הדיוטות — are also included in the level of כהן גדול.

פריעת ראש means גדל פרע שער ראשו (*Bemidbar* 6:5), "allowing the hair of one's head to grow wild" — i.e., refraining from cutting one's hair.

פרם in Scripture occurs only here, in connection with אבל, and later on (13:45), in connection with מצורע. The Mishnah in *Sotah* (7a) says: אם נקרעו נקרעו ואם נפרמו נפרמו. Clearly, then, פרימה is not the same as קריעה. According to רש״י there, פרימה is more extensive than קריעה: it is a tearing into many pieces. According to the ערוך, however, פרימה is merely a tear in the seam. From the prescribed method of קריעה for an אבל it appears that פרם does not mean to tear into pieces, but, rather, to tear without severing.

פרם may be related to the Aramaic ברם. ברם is a word that signals objection, spoken by one who argues and takes issue with his fellow. In Rabbinic usage it may also mean "in truth." All these meanings are related — according to the conception of the Hebrew language — in the sense of separating, making a cut, cutting into pieces.

In the case of a מצורע, פריעה represents the devaluation of his individual personality, whereas פרימה represents his social devaluation. This is also the meaning of these acts when they are performed upon the death of relatives: They express the sense of loss that death brings to the relative of the deceased. For the deceased had been this person's

שאר, a "complement" to him personally and socially. He, the surviving relative, has suffered a personal and social loss; he has been devalued, as it were. And he must demonstrate — in his external appearance — this sense of loss by refraining from cutting the hair of his head (including the beard) and by rending his garment. This שאר feeling is not only justified, but is a duty according to Jewish law. Although מן התורה the laws of mourning apply only on the first day — apparently only if מיתה וקבורה הם ביום אחד — whereas שבעה and שלושים apply only מדרבנן, nevertheless, like all מצוות דרבנן they have been accepted by the nation as a sacred, binding duty. They demonstrate, for Jewish family life, what *should* be the relationship between husband and wife, between parent and child, between brothers and sisters.

But the כהן גדול is different; and on this first day of their completed consecration, Aharon's sons, too, were כהנים גדולים. The כהן גדול's task is to represent before God the ideal of an eternal nation. It is therefore his duty to suspend his personal feelings on account of the concept of God and the idea of the nation. For he who is close to God will not meet with death, and his passing away is merely a change in the place of his existence. The nation, too, knows no death: אין ציבור מת (see *Temurah* 15b). In the nation's heart live all the generations that have passed, and from its midst will spring all the generations that are to come. In it, past and future are ever present. The source of this immortality — in this world and the next — is in God's Sanctuary; and the כהן גדול, whose forehead bears the proclamation קדש לה׳, is to teach this lesson by refraining from פריעה and פרימה. For this reason he was told for all times — and on יום השמיני his sons, too, were told: ראשיכם אל תפרעו ובגדיכם לא תפרמו!

ועל כל העדה יקצף. Compare: אם הכהן המשיח יחטא לאשמת העם (above, 4:3). If the spiritual elite of the nation sin, it is the sin of the entire nation; and if they are found to be deserving of death, and are torn away by their death from their national work, their death is a calamity for the entire nation. This applies especially when they are called upon to represent the entire nation in its ideal unity before God. Hence, it says here that their death would be a קצף על כל העדה. In this reference to their national importance before God lies also the reason for prohibiting their פריעה ופרימה, as we have tried to indicate.

ז וּמִפֶּתַח אֹהֶל מוֹעֵד לֹא תֵצְאוּ פֶּן־
תָּמֻתוּ כִּי־שֶׁמֶן מִשְׁחַת יְהֹוָה
עֲלֵיכֶם וַיַּעֲשׂוּ כִּדְבַר מֹשֶׁה: פ

7 *And do not move away from the entrance of the Tent of Appointed Meeting, lest you die, for the oil of* God's *consecration is upon you. They did according to Moshe's word.*

ח וַיְדַבֵּר יְהֹוָה אֶל־אַהֲרֹן לֵאמֹר:

8 God *spoke to Aharon, saying:*

ט יַיִן וְשֵׁכָר אַל־תֵּשְׁתְּ | אַתָּה | וּבָנֶיךָ
אִתָּךְ בְּבֹאֲכֶם אֶל־אֹהֶל מוֹעֵד
וְלֹא תָמֻתוּ חֻקַּת עוֹלָם
לְדֹרֹתֵיכֶם:

9 *Drink no wine or strong drink, you and your sons who stand by you, when you go into the Tent of Appointed Meeting, so that you will not die; [this is] an everlasting statute for your descendants.*

י וּלְהַבְדִּיל בֵּין הַקֹּדֶשׁ וּבֵין הַחֹל
וּבֵין הַטָּמֵא וּבֵין הַטָּהוֹר:

10 *And this is also in order to differentiate between the sanctified and the unsanctified, and between impure and pure.*

יא וּלְהוֹרֹת אֶת־בְּנֵי יִשְׂרָאֵל אֵת
כָּל־הַחֻקִּים אֲשֶׁר דִּבֶּר יְהֹוָה
אֲלֵיהֶם בְּיַד־מֹשֶׁה: פ רביעי

11 *And to teach the Children of Israel all the laws that* God *has uttered for them through Moshe.*

---

7 See Commentary above, 8:33.

9–11 **יין ושכר**. In *Kerisos* (13b) we find various opinions as to the objects and the extent of this prohibition. According to the halachah as stated by the רמב״ם (הל׳ ביאת מקדש, 1:1–2), **שכר** includes not only wine but any intoxicating drink. There is no **חיוב מיתה** or **חילול עבודה**, however, unless one drinks wine in an intoxicating quantity — which is defined as a **רביעית** of unmixed (i.e., undiluted) wine, or more than a **רביעית** of diluted wine.

יב וַיְדַבֵּ֨ר מֹשֶׁ֜ה אֶֽל־אַהֲרֹ֗ן וְאֶ֣ל
אֶלְעָזָ֣ר וְאֶל־אִיתָמָ֣ר ׀ בָּנָיו֮
הַנּֽוֹתָרִים֒ קְח֣וּ אֶת־הַמִּנְחָ֗ה
הַנּוֹתֶ֙רֶת֙ מֵאִשֵּׁ֣י יְהוָ֔ה וְאִכְל֥וּהָ
מַצּ֖וֹת אֵ֣צֶל הַמִּזְבֵּ֑חַ כִּ֛י קֹ֥דֶשׁ
קָֽדָשִׁ֖ים הִֽוא׃

12 *Moshe spoke to Aharon and to his surviving sons Elazar and Isamar, saying: Take the homage offering that is left over from the fire offerings of God and eat it as* matzos *beside the altar, for it is a holy of holies.*

The discussion here, then, is not of full-fledged drunkenness, but of reasonable grounds for suspecting the clouding of mental clarity. Hence, he who drinks יין ושכר is forbidden to serve in the מקדש (v. 9), to make legal decisions regarding the מקדש (v. 10), or to decide any practical halachic question (v. 11). For what is required for the practice of God's commandments is not hazy and excited emotion and imagination, but a clear mind and a sharp and sober intellect. The symbols of the Sanctuary speak not to the imagination, but to the clear and lucid mind. For only the mind — which comprehends clearly, reaches accurate conclusions, and places every detail in its proper category — is capable of guiding us to carry out God's commandments.

Aharon's sons died because they were captivated by the exhilaration of their own hearts. This is a lesson for all future כהנים and teachers of the Law: See yourselves only as servants of the Sanctuary and as teachers and realizers of Torah. Do not teach what your own heart tells you; rather, teach God's laws and His Torah. Be agents for and guides to the fulfillment of *mitzvos*; do not follow the dictates of misguided and misleading imagination. כִּי־שִׂפְתֵי כֹהֵן יִשְׁמְרוּ־דַעַת וְתוֹרָה יְבַקְשׁוּ מִפִּיהוּ כִּי מַלְאַךְ ה׳־צְבָאוֹת הוּא (*Malachi* 2:7). The Jewish *teacher* of the Law must remain a *student* of the Torah all his life.

12 **הנותרים**. Elsewhere (Commentary to *Shemos* 16:19), we analyzed the difference between נותר and נשאר. In our view, that which is נותר was likewise destined for destruction. Consider, for example, what our verse says next: המנחה הנותרת מאשי ה׳; the מנחה is characterized as being נותר from the מזבח, as we indeed find, כהנים משולחן גבוה קא זכו (*Bava Kamma*

13 *Eat it in a holy place, for this is your [due] and your sons' due from the fire offerings of* God, *for so I was commanded.*

יג וַאֲכַלְתֶּם אֹתָהּ בְּמָקוֹם קָדוֹשׁ כִּי
חָקְךָ וְחָק־בָּנֶיךָ הִוא מֵאִשֵּׁי יְהוָה
כִּי־כֵן צֻוֵּיתִי׃

14 *And you shall eat the breast of the wave [offering] and the thigh of the uplifted gift in a pure place, you and your sons and your daughters with you; for they have been given as your due and your sons' due from the meal-of-peace offerings of the Children of Israel.*

יד וְאֵת חֲזֵה הַתְּנוּפָה וְאֵת | שׁוֹק
הַתְּרוּמָה תֹּאכְלוּ בְּמָקוֹם טָהוֹר
אַתָּה וּבָנֶיךָ וּבְנֹתֶיךָ אִתָּךְ כִּי־
חָקְךָ וְחָק־בָּנֶיךָ נִתְּנוּ מִזִּבְחֵי
שַׁלְמֵי בְּנֵי יִשְׂרָאֵל׃

13a). Hence *Toras Kohanim* (here) learns from the expression בניו הנותרים that Elazar and Isamar, too, were on the verge of falling for this sin, but they recovered and were saved.

את המנחה: This is the מנחת ציבור mentioned above (9:4). (As we have stated [Commentary to 9:17], there is no other מנחת ציבור הנקמצת except for מנחת העומר.) In addition, מנחת נחשון (see *Bemidbar* 7:13) was also offered on this day.

13–14 כי כן צויתי: באנינות יאכלוה (*Zevachim* 101a). Special commands to eat שיירי המנחה (v. 13) and to eat the חזה ושוק (vv. 14–15) are necessary here for two reasons:

First, as we noted previously (9:3–4), מנחת ציבור and שלמי ציבור are quite unique among the offerings. Hence, it is impossible to apply to them the laws of מנחת יחיד and שלמי יחיד (above, 6:7ff., and 7:28ff.), except by explicit command.

Second, the כהנים were אוננים at this time. Even the כהן גדול, who is allowed to perform עבודה as an אונן, is not allowed to eat קדשים when he is in a state of אנינות: כהן גדול מקריב אונן ולא אוכל (see *Horayos* 12b). Only during עבודה is he required to transcend personal feelings of grief, for the sake of national God-consciousness; indeed, this is the whole meaning of the עבודה. Not so during the אכילה. For the purpose of the

15 *Let them bring the thigh of the uplifted gift and the breast of the wave [offering] upon the fire offerings of the fat parts, in order to make a wave [offering] before* God, *and it shall be an eternal due for you and for your sons who stand by you, as* God *has commanded.*

טו שׁ֣וֹק הַתְּרוּמָ֞ה וַחֲזֵ֣ה הַתְּנוּפָ֗ה עַ֣ל
אִשֵּׁ֤י הַחֲלָבִים֙ יָבִ֔יאוּ לְהָנִ֥יף
תְּנוּפָ֖ה לִפְנֵ֣י יְהוָ֑ה וְהָיָ֨ה לְךָ֜
וּלְבָנֶ֤יךָ אִתְּךָ֙ לְחָק־עוֹלָ֔ם כַּאֲשֶׁ֖ר
צִוָּ֥ה יְהוָֽה׃ חמישי

אכילה is to elevate subjective enjoyment to the level of symbolic עבודה. The אונן, however, unavoidably feels grief; from a subjective point of view, his heart is broken. It is impossible for him to attain that joy to which אכילת קדשים is intended to give expression. (For the meaning of these אכילות, see Commentary above, 6:7ff; 7:28ff.)

כי חקך וחק בניך הוא מאשי ה׳ (v. 13); similarly, **כי חקך וחק בניך נתנו מזבחי שלמי בני ישראל** (v. 14). Through these אכילות, the כהנים attained their special status vis-à-vis אשי ה׳ and זבחי שלמי ישראל. These were the first שיריים and the first חזה ושוק that the כהנים acquired of the offerings. Partaking of them was one of the characteristic procedures essential to the יום השמיני. חזה ושוק in particular are repeatedly emphasized here. For whenever they are given and received, they lead to an ever-recurring awareness of and admonition about the task of the כהונה and its significance in the nation. These two אכילות were essential to the meaning of this day; hence, the אנינות prohibition was nullified in their case.

Regarding שיירי מנחה Scripture says במקום קדוש, while regarding חזה ושוק it says במקום טהור. For שיירי מנחה may not be eaten outside the עזרה — here the חצר — which encompasses the site of the altar. חזה ושוק, however, may not be eaten outside ירושלים — here the מחנה ישראל — whose טהרה is shown by the expulsion of מצורעים (*Bemidbar* 5:1–4).

שיירי מנחה, being קדשי קדשים, may be eaten only by זכרי כהונה. חזה ושוק, being קדשים קלים, may be eaten also by בנותיך, but the right to participate in the distribution is restricted to the males: חק לבנים ואין חק לבנות (*Toras Kohanim*).

טז וְאֵת ׀ שְׂעִיר הַחַטָּאת דָּרֹשׁ דָּרַשׁ
מֹשֶׁה וְהִנֵּה שֹׂרָף וַיִּקְצֹף עַל־
אֶלְעָזָר וְעַל־אִיתָמָר בְּנֵי אַהֲרֹן
הַנּוֹתָרִם לֵאמֹר:
יז מַדּוּעַ לֹא־אֲכַלְתֶּם אֶת־הַחַטָּאת
בִּמְקוֹם הַקֹּדֶשׁ כִּי קֹדֶשׁ קָדָשִׁים
הִוא וְאֹתָהּ ׀ נָתַן לָכֶם לָשֵׂאת
אֶת־עֲוֺן הָעֵדָה לְכַפֵּר עֲלֵיהֶם

16 *Moshe inquired [in detail] about the he-goat of the offering that clears of sin, and lo! it had [already] been burned. And he was angry with Elazar and Isamar, the surviving sons of Aharon, and he said:*

17 *Why did you not eat the offering that clears of sin in the place of the Sanctuary, seeing that it is a holy of holies, and that He gave it to you precisely in order to lift away the sin of the community, to*

---

16 **ואת שעיר החטאת וגו׳ והנה שרף**. According to *Zevachim* 101a–b, on that day there were three שעירי חטאת whose meat would normally have been given to the כהנים to eat: (a) the שעיר חטאת of the nation (9:3); (b) the שעיר of נחשון, prince of Yehudah, who brought his offering on the first day of חנוכת המזבח, which was יום השמיני of the מילואים. It was a שעיר עזים לחטאת (see *Bemidbar* 7:16), and was offered after קרבנות המילואים. And since it was then also ראש חדש ניסן, they offered also (c) the שעיר חטאת של ראש חדש. The first two שעירים were קדשי שעה, as they were occasioned by the unique importance of that day — the חנוכה. The last שעיר, however, was of קדשי דורות, as it is one of the regular obligations of ראש חדש, which apply for all time. The Gemara (*Zevachim* 101b) derives from the verse ואתה נתן לכם לשאת את עון העדה לכפר עליהם לפני ה׳ (v. 17) that only the שעיר של ראש חדש was burned. For only this שעיר served to atone for actual עון העדה. The others, שעירי קדשי שעה, more than serving to atone for the past, expressed commitment for the future.

17 **במקום הקדש**. Had it been taken outside the sacred area, outside the חצר (the עזרה), it would have become פסול on account of יוצא, in accordance with the law of קדשי קדשים, and would rightly have been burned.

effect atonement for them before **God?**	לִפְנֵ֥י יְהוָֽה׃

לשאת את עון העדה. The כהן's eating of the בשר חטאת represents the final consequence of offering the חלב and the דם — namely, that *every phase* of human life is to be hallowed with priestlike sanctity (cf. Commentary above, 4:11–12). Thus, this eating is one of the acts that effect atonement for past sins.

Here, however, in the case of שעיר של ראש חדש, there is a unique, additional element, which is rooted in the very essence of this חטאת. For this offering is a שעיר לחטאת לה׳ (see *Bemidbar* 28:15); it atones for sins against the Sanctuary that are known only to God, חטא שאין מכיר בו אלא ה׳ (*Shevuos* 9a) — i.e., שאין בו ידיעה לא בתחילה ולא בסוף, a sin that one committed unwittingly and about which one never became aware.

Accordingly, ואתה נתן לכם לשאת את עון העדה — which is said of no other offering — can be interpreted in two ways:

(a) It can be interpreted in the sense of תשאו את עון המקדש וגו׳ תשאו את עון כהנתכם (*Bemidbar* 18:1): You *bear the responsibility* for this sin. Similarly here, this eating was given to you in order to bear the responsibility for the sin of the community. This eating is to warn you to see to it that the people do not inadvertently grow more and more distant and estranged from the Sanctuary.

(b) It can be interpreted in the sense of ונשא אהרן את עון הקדשים (*Shemos* 28:38). The positive statement קדש לה׳, which is engraved on the ציץ that is upon Aharon's forehead, contradicts the erroneous beliefs that stem from עון הקדשים. Hence, the ציץ atones (הציץ מרצה) for this sin — namely, the sin of טומאת הקדשים (see Commentary to *Shemos* 28:38). Similarly here, the eating of the שעיר של ראש חדש was given to you in order to atone for the sin of the community. The כהן's eating of the meat of the חטאת in the עזרה represents the hallowing of physical life; hence, it atones for the thoughtlessness that leads to the estrangement of life from the Sanctuary.

Later, we will show that Aharon's reply (v. 19) supports the second interpretation. In any case, it is clear that Moshe stresses here the special purpose of the שעיר של ראש חדש. For its importance magnifies the grievance against Aharon and his sons for their failure to partake of its meat.

18 *See, its blood was not brought into the interior of the Sanctuary; you should have eaten it in a holy place, as I had commanded.*

19 *And Aharon said to Moshe: See, today they brought near their offering that cleared of sin, and their ascent offering, to* God, *and then such befell me. If I had eaten today offerings that clear of sin, would that have been what is right in the eyes of* God?

יח הֵן לֹא־הוּבָא אֶת־דָּמָהּ אֶל־
הַקֹּדֶשׁ פְּנִימָה אָכוֹל תֹּאכְלוּ
אֹתָהּ בַּקֹּדֶשׁ כַּאֲשֶׁר צִוֵּיתִי׃
יט וַיְדַבֵּר אַהֲרֹן אֶל־מֹשֶׁה הֵן הַיּוֹם
הִקְרִיבוּ אֶת־חַטָּאתָם וְאֶת־
עֹלָתָם לִפְנֵי יְהוָה וַתִּקְרֶאנָה אֹתִי
כָּאֵלֶּה וְאָכַלְתִּי חַטָּאת הַיּוֹם
הַיִּיטַב בְּעֵינֵי יְהוָה׃

18 **הן לא הובא וגו'**. Had any of its blood been brought into the interior of the Sanctuary, the offering would have become פסול, in accordance with the law explained above (6:23; see Commentary there), and would have rightly been burned.

כאשר צויתי. I commanded to do so specifically in regard to שיירי המנחה (vv. 12–13), that they be eaten despite the אנינות; and בשעת מעשה, immediately after the tragedy, I commanded to do so generally (see *Zevachim* 101a): ומפתח אהל מועד לא תצאו (v. 7) — your אנינות is not to cause a break in your relation to the Sanctuary.

19 **הן היום הקריבו את חטאתם ואת עלתם** — the חטאת and עולה of Aharon, who had earlier (9:2) been commanded to bring them. From here we learn that the כהונה of the sons was included in the כהונה of their father.

In our view, Aharon's reply should be understood as follows: Precisely in the special purpose of the שעיר של ראש חדש — which Moshe had stressed to strengthen his reproach — Aharon sees justification for his actions. Let us elaborate:

He and his sons had this very day entered the priesthood by offering חטאת and עולה. Through these offerings they had undertaken to adhere always to the lofty heights of their calling and to go before the people as examples and models. Then, suddenly — ותקראנה אתי כאלה, something happened which exposed the disparity between the actual moral state of the כהנים, on the one hand, and what they had undertaken through their offerings, on the other. For the כהנים committed a capital offense, and were cut down during the first moments of their consecration. ואכלתי חטאת היום? Can we now — in the face of our own failure — consider ourselves worthy of eating חטאת to atone for thoughtless errors of the people?

To be sure, all the offerings that they offered for the sake of consecrating the Dwelling Place and the כהנים — and this includes the שיירי מנחה, the חזה ושוק, as well as the שעיר חטאת העם and the שעיר נחשון — all these were קדשי שעה, which were prescribed for the special occasion of the day, and which were to be eaten even in a state of אנינות. The grief of אנינות must be set aside for the sake of the mitzvah of אכילת חטאות קדשי שעה. Nevertheless, one cannot infer from these offerings the law of the שעיר של ראש חדש, which is one of the קדשי דורות. The reason why one cannot infer this is as follows:

קדשי שעה do not serve to atone for an actual offense of the past or present. Rather, their whole purpose is to relate to the yet unformed future, which is to receive a pure foundation through resolutions undertaken on the occasion of the offering. Hence, Aharon and his sons were commanded to partake of these קדשי שעה. Not by virtue of their present level were they to partake of these offerings; rather, by virtue of partaking they were to attain a higher level. The eating itself was to exhort them to their calling. Hence, even though they were beset by feelings of unworthiness, which were intensified by the אנינות, this did not prohibit them from eating; for the whole purpose of the eating was to exhort them as to what was expected of them in the future.

חטאת של ראש חודש, however — being one of the קדשי דורות — is different. The eating of its meat in the Sanctuary completes the atonement for actual offenses committed. Hence, the כהן who partakes must be a model of perfection. Yet the כהנים had just committed a capital offense, which exposed the disparity between their actual state and the moral ideal represented by their offering. Thus, Aharon was right in asking: Is this the proper time for the eating of the חטאת? This question seemed to him even more justified since even his own חטאת — which was of קדשי שעה — was not eaten but was burned outside the camp, as in the case of פר כהן המשיח (above, 9:11).

Aharon's reply is explained similarly in *Zevachim* (101a): שמא לא שמעת אלא בקדשי שעה דאי בקדשי דורות ק״ו ממעשר הקל, ומה מעשר הקל אמרה תורה

לא אכלתי באוני ממנו, בקדשי דורות לא כל שכן? And the Gemara there states a general rule, that קדשי דורות are not to be eaten in a state of אנינות. In our view, this prohibition is strengthened even more by the special character of the death described here.

That the כהן who partakes of the meat of the offering must appear as a model to the offerer is expressed in the words of Hoshea (4:8–9): חַטַּאת עַמִּי יֹאכֵלוּ וְאֶל־עֲוֹנָם יִשְׂאוּ נַפְשׁוֹ: וְהָיָה כָעָם כַּכֹּהֵן וגו׳. "The sin-offering of My people they eat; thereby, unto their sins they lift their souls. And the people become like the priest..."

We should also mention two opinions cited in the Gemara (*Zevachim* 101a):

One opinion is that מפני אנינות נשרפה, the חטאת של ראש חדש was burned because of אנינות. According to this opinion, אנינות לילה is דאורייתא, the condition of אנינות lasts through the night מן התורה; and since a חטאת may be eaten only יום ולילה, this חטאת was not fit to be eaten at all and therefore was burned. According to this opinion the Gemara states further that the word היום in the phrase ואכלתי חטאת היום cannot refer to the incident that occurred (since the חטאת could not be eaten even at night) but defines the חטאת as one of קדשי דורות: it is חטאת היום, an offering of the day, one of the מוספי ראש חדש.

According to the other opinion, אנינות לילה is only דרבנן. Thus, they were prohibited from eating only during the day, but not at night, and ואכלתי חטאת היום can then be taken to refer to the incident that occurred. Rather, מפני טומאה נשרפה, this חטאת was burned only because of טומאה. On account of אנינות they had to wait until night to eat it, and in the meantime it became טמא through no fault of theirs — טומאה באונס באתה — and therefore was burned.

הייטב בעיני ה׳. The first י has a *dagesh*. Hence, the הַ is not interrogative but a ה״א הידיעה. And since it is used here in conjunction with a verb, it has the meaning of אשר, as in הבאה מצרימה (*Bereshis* 46:27), הַנִּמְצְאוּ־פֹה (*Divrei Ha-Yamim* I, 29:17), and elsewhere. Aharon, then, is asking: [Is this] that which would be pleasing in God's eyes? We have here an allusion to the law to which Aharon — according to the Gemara in *Zevachim* — refers. The meaning of his words is: Granted, the eating of קדשי שעה is pleasing in God's sight; but this offering is of קדשי דורות, and is not included in the mitzvah of באנינות יאכלוה.

20 *When Moshe heard this, it was right in his eyes.*

כ וַיִּשְׁמַע מֹשֶׁה וַיִּיטַב בְּעֵינָיו: פ

ששי

11 1 God *spoke to Moshe and to Aharon, in order to say to them:*

יא א וַיְדַבֵּר יְהֹוָה אֶל־מֹשֶׁה וְאֶל־אַהֲרֹן לֵאמֹר אֲלֵהֶם:

20 **וייטב בעיניו**: לא בוש משה לומר לא שמעתי אלא שמעתי ושכחתי (*Zevachim* 101b). Moshe admitted that Aharon was right. He, too, had been told of the abrogation of the אנינות prohibition only in regard to קדשי שעה. He had been told, but had forgotten.

CHAPTER 11

1 The whole preceding chapter is closely connected with the dietary laws, which are discussed in this chapter. There (10:1–2) we learned that even individuals who are worthy of the priesthood are liable to err and incur the penalty of death, if they become captivated by their own sentiments. Related to this is the halachah that כהנים and teachers of the Law — whenever they are called upon to serve in the Sanctuary or to render a halachic decision — must sanctify themselves by exercising self-restraint even in matters that are permitted; they must refrain from wine and strong drink, which muddle the mind and agitate the emotions (10:9–11). Finally, the preceeding chapter teaches that the sanctification of life achieved by the Sanctuary culminates in the sanctification of physical pleasure, and that the meal eaten by the כהנים in the sacred area completes the atonement effected by the offerings. All of this has prepared us to understand that the fulfillment of our spiritual and moral mission — to be a ממלכת כהנים וגוי קדוש — depends, in no small measure, also on the food that we eat.

The opening verse of this new chapter accords with this idea. It expresses the great significance the Torah attaches to the dietary laws. The very fact that these laws are given both to Moshe and to Aharon testifies to their importance: וידבר ה׳ אל משה ואל אהרן.

We find similar formulations — in sections reporting transmittal of *mitzvos* — only in the case of the first, fundamental laws of the New Moon and of the Pesach offering (*Shemos* 12:1 and 43), and also in the

2 *Speak to the Children of Israel, saying: This, if it has vitality, is what you may eat of all the animals that live on land:*	ב דַּבְּרוּ אֶל־בְּנֵי יִשְׂרָאֵל לֵאמֹר זֹאת הַחַיָּה אֲשֶׁר תֹּאכְלוּ מִכָּל־הַבְּהֵמָה אֲשֶׁר עַל־הָאָרֶץ:

case of the laws of טומאת נגעים זיבה ונדה (below, 13:1; 14:33; 15:1), which are closely related to the dietary laws. But the formulation that we find here in the opening verse of our chapter — וידבר ה׳ אל משה ואל אהרן לאמר אלהם — we find nowhere else.

This formulation indicates that these laws were given first to Moshe and to Aharon. They must pay special attention to these laws, in accordance with their respective positions in the nation as regards the Torah. Moshe is the transmitter and teacher of Torah, whereas Aharon is the educator for fulfillment of the *mitzvos*; and the success of their work with the nation depends especially on these laws. Moshe's mission addresses the nation's intellect and knowledge; Aharon's mission addresses the nation's spirit and will. Both missions depend on the nation's observance of these laws. Through them, the nation's foundation is laid for a second time — on a higher level. חודש and פסח created the body of the nation. פרשת משפטים arranged its social life. From פרשת תרומה until chapter 11 in פרשת שמיני, the Dwelling Place was established, which raised the Torah ideal as the highest aim in the nation. The whole essence of this aim is that the entire people — with all its individual members — become "a kingdom of priests and a holy nation." This ideal must not be merely the symbol of the Sanctuary, but must become a reality in every phase of life of every individual son and daughter of the nation. The community encamped around the Sanctuary must be worthy of the call addressed (below, 19:2) to all its sons and daughters: קדשים תהיו כי קדוש אני ה׳ אלקיכם! But this requires people conceived, born, and nourished especially for this purpose. A special regimen must be followed to produce people born and nourished for the sacred ideal of the Torah. This regimen is laid down by God in פרשיות שמיני תזריע מצורע ואחרי מות, the chapters leading up to קדשים תהיו.

2 **זאת החיה אשר תאכלו מכל הבהמה וגו׳**. We noted previously (*Bereshis* 1:24–25) that בהמה and חיה are two different classes of mammals. The

בהמה submits to the service of man; it serves as a "במה" to man's ascendance. The other mammals are included in חיה. They possess "independent life" and are not subject to man's control. Thus, we find: וכל החיה למינה וכל הבהמה למינה (ibid. 7:14); ואת כל החיה ואת כל הבהמה (ibid. 8:1).

The term חיה, however, is used also as a general term for all living creatures, as in: כל החיה אשר אתך וגו׳ כל החיה כל הרמש וגו׳ (ibid. 8:17 and 19). Similarly, we find, at the end of our chapter, that the term חיה is used to include all the animals mentioned in the chapter: להבדיל וגו׳ ובין החיה הנאכלת ובין החיה אשר לא תאכל (below, 11:47).

The term בהמה, as well, is used in a wider sense to include the whole animal world that is on a lower level than man. So we find in *Bereshis* 6:7 — מאדם עד בהמה — and also in *Bereshis* 7:23, in *Shemos* 9:25, and elsewhere.

In our verse, however, these two terms appear one after the other: זאת החיה וגו׳ מכל הבהמה וגו׳. This formulation was undoubtedly chosen with special intent. Our Sages (*Chullin* 70b–71a) comment on our verse, and on the parallel verse in *Devarim* (14:4–5), as follows: Here, Scripture opens with חיה and concludes with בהמה — to teach us that בהמה בכלל חיה. There, Scripture opens with בהמה and concludes with חיה (זאת הבהמה אשר תאכלו שור וגו׳ איל וצבי וגו׳) — to teach us that חיה בכלל בהמה. In other words, these two verses complement each other. From both together we learn that the terms חיה and בהמה are at times to be understood in a wider sense; and that a בהמה may be regarded as a חיה, and a חיה as a בהמה . Scripture teaches this to us precisely in the section on the dietary laws, in order to indicate something about these laws. The terms חיה and בהמה, in their wider sense, characterize the mammals that are permitted as food. These mammals are included under חיה in respect to their bodies, and under בהמה in respect to their natures. For a בהמה may not be eaten unless it is also a חיה; and a חיה may not be eaten if it does not also possess the character of a בהמה, in the wider sense of this term. Thus, a טריפה may not be eaten, as it cannot live (טריפה אינה חיה); as the Gemara (*Chullin* 42a) says: חיה אכול שאינה חיה לא תיכול. So, too, a חיה may be eaten only if it possesses the character of a בהמה — i.e., there is no antagonism between it and man, but it tends to submit to his authority.

מכל הבהמה אשר על הארץ — animals that live on land, as opposed to creatures that live in water (v. 9).

3 *Whatever forms a hoof and cleaves it completely into two hoofs and at the same time chews the cud among the animals, this you may eat.*	ג כֹּ֣ל | מַפְרֶ֣סֶת פַּרְסָ֗ה וְשֹׁסַ֤עַת שֶׁ֨סַע֙ פְּרָסֹ֔ת מַעֲלַ֥ת גֵּרָ֖ה בַּבְּהֵמָ֑ה אֹתָ֖הּ תֹּאכֵֽלוּ׃

3 **כל מפרסת פרסה וגו׳**. We noted previously, in our Commentary to *Shemos* 10:26, that since the hoof of the horse, too, is called פרסה, this term applies to any hoof, even if it is not cleft. The term derives from the root פרס = פרש, cover over; for the hoof is like a covering of horn that is spread over the toes. This is also the meaning of the verbs הפריס, מפריס; as it says: מַקְרִן מַפְרִיס (*Tehillim* 69:32). Just as מקרין means "horned," מפריס means "hoofed." Wessely, too, in his *Commentary* on this verse, interprets it in this way.

This interpretation — that מפרסת פרסה means "has hoofs" and not "has cleft hoofs" — seems to be contradicted, however, by the following verses: ופרסה לא הִפְרִיסָה, ופרסה לא יפריס, ופרסה איננו מפריס; for it seems that Scripture refers to cases where the *cleft* hoof is not present. Actually, though, the animals we assume to be the שפן and the ארנבת have no hoofs at all, and in the camel, too, the hoof formation is by no means complete. Moreover, our verse goes on to explain that the hoof to which it refers is fully cleft, as it says: כל מפרסת פרסה ושסעת שסע פרסת. Hence, the expression מפריס פרסה that appears in the succeeding verses relies on this explanation and refers only to the fully cleft hoof mentioned here. Similarly, והוא גרה לא יגר (v. 7) is to be interpreted in this way. For Scripture there leaves out the key word מעלה. In *Devarim* (14:8), too, Scripture — in reference to the חזיר — employs abbreviated wording: כי מפריס פרסה הוא ולא גרה.

ושסעת שסע. Similarly, Scripture says: ושסע אתו בכנפיו (above, 1:17). ושסעת שסע פרסת means: the one hoof is split into two hoofs. As it says in *Devarim* (14:6): ושסעת שסע שתי פרסות.

מעלת גרה. גרה derives from גרר — as גזה, זמה, derive from גזז, זמם. גרר is the root of מְגֵרָה, the saw; גרר, then, means "to saw." Accordingly, the word גרה in and of itself contains the characteristic feature of a בהמה טהורה. All true ruminants also have fully cleft hoofs and so are permitted to be eaten. They all lack incisors in the upper jaw. Instead, they have

4 *But this you may not eat from among those that chew the cud and that are thus hoofed: The camel, because it chews the cud but does not form the proper hoof; it is impure to you.*

ד אַךְ אֶת־זֶה לֹא תֹאכְלוּ מִמַּעֲלֵי הַגֵּרָה וּמִמַּפְרִסֵי הַפַּרְסָה אֶת־הַגָּמָל כִּי־מַעֲלֵה גֵרָה הוּא וּפַרְסָה אֵינֶנּוּ מַפְרִיס טָמֵא הוּא לָכֶם׃

a hard rough plate in the upper jaw, on which by grinding circular movements the incisors of the lower jaw cut up their food. In our opinion, food that is chewed up in this fashion is called גרה. This term, then, is indicative of the lack of incisors in the upper jaw, and this lack is a sufficient distinguishing feature of a בהמה טהורה. As it says in *Chullin* (59a): כל בהמה שאין לה שינים למעלה בידוע שהיא מעלת גרה ומפרסת פרסה וטהורה.

The שפן and ארנבת, mentioned in the succeeding verses, are not true ruminants, as they possess a complete set of upper incisors; and the camel, too, lacks only the centrals and laterals but has the canines, called ניבי (*Chullin* 59a). Only in young camels, in the first dentition or milk teeth, are all incisors missing. Hence, one can determine that an animal is kosher based on the feature of the teeth, if he knows that it is not a young camel: ובלבד שיכיר בן גמל (ibid.).

In this light, the Scriptural formulations cited above — והוא גרה לא יגר (v. 7) and the even more abbreviated ולא גרה (*Devarim* 14:8) — are self-explanatory. Since the pig has complete upper incisors, it does not chew the cud.

Animals that chew the cud have four stomachs. The food is masticated by mere "sawing" and reaches the paunch (כרס), where it is softened. Then it is passed into the second stomach (בית הכוסות), formed into balls, and brought up into the mouth again. Only at this point is it chewed properly. It then descends into the tripe stomach (המסס) and finally reaches the rennet bag (קיבה), where it is digested by the stomach juices. This bringing up again — from the second stomach to the mouth — of food that was merely "sawed" is called העלאת גרה.

4 **ופרסה איננו מפריס**. The camel does not have complete hoofs. They cover the toes on top but do not surround them like a shoe. Also, the toes

are divided only above, and are joined together again below on the soles.

טמא הוא לכם. Since this verse is introduced with אך את זה לא תאכלו, the concluding phrase טמא הוא לכם must contain the reason for the prohibition. That reason is expressed here by the term טמא. The prohibition, then, does not hinge on nutritional considerations; rather, one should search for its reason in that sphere in which the concept of טומאה is meaningful. This is none other than the sphere of קדושה, moral holiness.

As we have seen (Commentary above, 5:13 and 7:19–21), this קדושה is symbolized by מקדש וקדשיו, the Sanctuary and its holy things; and symbolical טומאה, which is expressed by טומאת מגע, must be kept away from them. If food is prohibited on account of it being טמא, then this prohibition hinges on our mission to become holy; the forbidden food is antithetical to the קדושה for which we are duty bound to strive. טומאת מאכלות is the actual antithesis of our actual moral holiness, just as טומאת מגע is the symbolic antithesis of the holiness symbolized by the Sanctuary.

These two types of טומאה are evident in *Toras Kohanim*'s introduction to the section dealing with the שמונה שרצים (v. 29): אלה הטמאים לכם בכל השרץ (יא:לא) מה ת״ל? לפי שנאמר לא תטמאו בהם ונטמתם בם (יא:מג) שומע אני טומאת הגויות וטומאת הקדושות ת״ל החולד והעכבר והצב למינהו. In our view, the expression טומאת הגויות וטומאת הקדושות refers to these two types of טומאה: (a) טומאת מאכלות, which brings to the body actual טומאה, and (b) טומאת מגע, which is antithetical to the מקדש from a symbolic standpoint. And since the term טמא can be applied to both types, one might have erred in understanding the language of Scripture. One might have thought that the sentence that concludes the שרץ prohibition — ולא תטמאו בהם (v. 43) — refers to both types of טומאה, and that all שרצים convey not only טומאת הגוויות but also טומאת הקדושות. Scripture therefore states: אלה הטמאים וגו׳ (v. 31) — to teach us that only the eight שרצים listed there (in vv. 29–30) convey טומאת הקדושות.

This connection — between the dietary laws and moral holiness — is underscored in the very first of Israel's dietary laws, namely in *Shemos* 22:30. That is why this law is placed among the משפטים, which lay the foundations of Israel's society. Scripture there says: ואנשי קדש תהיון לי ובשר בשדה טרפה לא תאכלו לכלב תשלכון אתו. This verse from *Shemos* implies the following: We must not share our table with the elemental and animal world. Our eating should not be a merely physical process, but a moral act. Not merely physical considerations but moral considerations, considerations of our calling to become אנשי קדש, are to determine our choice of food. This is the principle whose foundations are laid down there (in *Shemos*) and whose detailed *halachos* are spelled out here. There, a positive criterion is given for the choice of our food: ואנשי קדש תהיון לי. According to this criterion Scripture here determines — in the negative — what is טמא and unfit for our food.

Scripture does not, however, say here טמא הוא, absolutely, but טמא הוא לכם. Unlike the prohibition of אבר מן החי, which, as one of the ז׳ מצוות בני נח, hinges on the general task of mankind (see our Commentary, *Bereshis* 9:4), the prohibition of forbidden food applies only to the people of the Torah. This food is declared טמא only for אנשי קודש, to whom the Torah was given; for this food is incompatible with the קדושה to which they aspire.

Compare the letter ן in the words תהיון, תשליכון (*Shemos* 22:30), and see our Commentary there.

We learn something further from the expression טמא הוא לכם: The nature and character of the animal are the causes of it being forbidden to eat. The chewing of the cud and the cleft hoof are mere symptoms; in and of themselves, they do not cause permissibility, and their absence does not cause prohibition. They merely indicate the presence of that character upon which the permission to eat depends. Therefore, if the character of the animal is established by any other proof, there is no need to examine the animal further for its סימני טהרה.

In our view, this conception underlies the teaching in *Bechoros* (6b): טמא הוא – הוא טמא ואין טמא הנולד מן הטהור טמא. From this דרשה we learn a general principle: היוצא מן הטמא טמא והיוצא מן הטהור טהור, "That which issues from the impure is impure, and that which issues from the pure is pure" (ibid. 5b). Thus, בהמה טהורה שילדה כמין בהמה טמאה מותר באכילה וטמאה שילדה כמין בהמה טהורה אסור באכילה (ibid.), if a kosher animal gives birth to young that lacks the signs of kosher animals, it is permitted to be eaten; and if an unkosher animal gives birth to young that has all the signs of a kosher animal, it is forbidden to be eaten. In both cases the character of the young is established by the character of the mother, and the presence or absence of the signs of טהרה is of no consequence.

The principle that כל היוצא מן הטמא טמא is derived also from other verses. It applies not only to the animal itself but to any substance that

5 *And the rabbit, because it chews the cud but does not form a hoof; it is impure to you.*

ה וְאֶת־הַשָּׁפָן כִּֽי־מַעֲלֵה גֵרָה הוּא
וּפַרְסָה לֹא יַפְרִיס טָמֵא הוּא
לָכֶם׃

6 *And the hare, because it chews the cud but does not form a hoof; it is impure to you.*

ו וְאֶת־הָאַרְנֶבֶת כִּֽי־מַעֲלַת גֵּרָה
הִוא וּפַרְסָה לֹא הִפְרִיסָה טְמֵאָה
הִוא לָכֶם׃

7 *And the pig, because it forms a hoof and cleaves the hoof completely but does not chew the cud; it is impure to you.*

ז וְאֶת־הַחֲזִיר כִּֽי־מַפְרִיס פַּרְסָה
הוּא וְשֹׁסַע שֶׁסַע פַּרְסָה וְהוּא גֵּרָה
לֹא־יִגָּר טָמֵא הוּא לָכֶם׃

8 *You shall not eat of their flesh and not touch their carcasses; they are impure to you.*

ח מִבְּשָׂרָם לֹא תֹאכֵלוּ וּבְנִבְלָתָם
לֹא תִגָּעוּ טְמֵאִים הֵם לָכֶם׃

issues organically from an unkosher animal — e.g., milk and eggs. Bee's honey, however, is permitted to be eaten, because it is not produced organically in the body of the bee, but is collected from outside sources: מפני שמכניסות אותו לגופן ואין ממצות אותו מגופן (ibid. 7b).

5–6 Of the camel Scripture says: ופרסה איננו מפריס; it has the beginning of a hoof, but not a complete hoof. Of the שפן, however, Scripture says: ופרסה לא יפריס, and of the ארנבת: ופרסה לא הפריסה. Neither of these are hoofed at all. There is surely a connection between this change of expression in Scripture and the toe formation in these animals.

Scripture also says of both that they are מעלי גרה. Now, שפן is commonly translated "rabbit," and ארנבת "hare." But these translations are impossible unless both these animals chew the cud, which is difficult to claim.

8 **ובנבלתם לא תגעו**. Even מגע טומאת מת, a most severe kind of טומאה, is forbidden only to the כהנים (below, chap. 21, et seq.). Can it be, then, that here the less severe מגע נבילה is forbidden to the entire nation? It must be

9 *This you may eat of all that lives in the water: whatever has fins*

ט אֶת־זֶה תֹּאכְלוּ מִכֹּל אֲשֶׁר בַּמָּיִם כֹּל אֲשֶׁר־לוֹ סְנַפִּיר וְקַשְׂקֶשֶׂת

that this prohibition applies only at times when a person is about to approach מקדש וקדשיו — e.g., ברגל. Thus the halachah: חייב אדם לטהר את עצמו ברגל (*Rosh Hashanah* 16b). Nevertheless, see below, at the end of the chapter, about אכילת חולין בטהרה: Although the *halachos* of טומאה and טהרה apply by law only in the sphere of the Sanctuary, people who lived on a high spiritual level applied these *halachos* to their everyday lives as well.

מבשרם לא תאכלו ובנבלתם לא תגעו. From here we learn that the בשר, the meat, of an impure animal is always נבילה, as שחיטה does not deliver it from נבילה. A בהמה טהורה, however, is נבילה only if it dies without proper שחיטה.

מבשרם וגו׳. The prohibition applies only to the edible parts of the animal, but not to the עצמות גידין וטלפים, the bones, sinews and claws (*Toras Kohanim*).

טמאים הם לכם. All of the בהמות טמאות — already identified individually as טמאות — are here subsumed under the common term טמאים. From this we learn that מצטרפים זה עם זה, the flesh of different animals (including all their edible material) can be combined to form the minimum forbidden measure, כזית. And since Scripture repeats here that these materials convey טומאה, without hinging this on the special character of camel flesh, rabbit flesh, etc., we learn that they are prohibited in any form: לאסור צירן ורוטבן וקיפה שלהם — juices, gravy, and sediment that are mixed with them all come under this prohibition. This does not apply, however, if the taste of the forbidden material is no longer present: הם פרט לשאין בהם בנותן טעם. As a rule we assume that in a mixture of one in sixty the taste disappears, and the material may be regarded as nonexistent, בטל בששים. Finally, from the word לכם we learn that although these animals are forbidden to be eaten, nevertheless מותרים הם בהנאה — they may be used for any other purpose (*Toras Kohanim*).

9 The root of סנפיר, fin, is obscure. If we assume that the letter ר was added to the root — as, perhaps, also in the case of טפסר and עכבר —

and scales in the water, in seas and in rivers, these you may eat.	בַּמַּיִם בַּיַּמִּים וּבַנְּחָלִים אֹתָם תֹּאכֵלוּ׃

then the root of the word is סנף. סנף, related to זנב, gives us the Rabbinic term סניף, which means: an appendage which is subordinate to another thing. This meaning suits the external form of fins.

קשקשת, scales, as in וְשִׁרְיוֹן קַשְׂקַשִּׂים (*Shemuel* I, 17:5); the Gemara (*Chullin* 66b), too, explains the word by means of this verse.

The root קשש is related to גזז. It is indicative of something that can be removed by mechanical means. This supports the view of the רמב״ן on our verse that the קשקשת is not fixed to the skin of the fish, but can be removed easily by hand or knife. This view is adopted by all the ראשונים and also in יורה דעה (83:1); נודע ביהודה (מהדורה תניינא י״ד סי׳ כח), however, raises an objection.

It appears that support for the רמב״ן's position can be adduced also from the Halachah itself. For the rule cited in *Chullin* (66b) is: כל שיש לו קשקשת יש לו סנפיר. Yet *Toras Kohanim* states that our verse includes also amphibians, הגדלים בים והגדלים ביבשה. Now, if the term קשקשת were to include fixed, unremovable scales, the rule כל שיש לו קשקשת יש לו סנפיר would be disproved by the many species of amphibians that have such scales but do not have fins.

את זה וגו׳ במים, כל וגו׳ במים בימים ובנחלים וגו׳. The verse begins with מים and ends with ימים ונחלים. We seem to have here, then, a case of כלל ופרט, and the rule is that אין בכלל אלא מה שבפרט. When a general term is followed by enumeration of particulars, the scope of the general term is limited to the things specified. Accordingly, the prohibition in our verse would apply only to those creatures found in ימים ונחלים, seas and rivers.

However, the general term מים is stated here twice, before the specification, and the rule is that כל מקום שאתה מוצא שני כללים סמוכין זה לזה הטל פרט ביניהם ודונם בכלל ופרט וכלל. Thus, the specification serves merely to illustrate the general term; for in כלל ופרט וכלל, the general statement applies to all things similar to the specification (כעין הפרט). Accordingly, the prohibition includes anything that has the characteristics of ימים ונחלים.

Opinions differ as to the scope of the concept illustrated by the פרט

in a כלל ופרט וכלל. Everything depends on whether כללא קמא דוקא or כללא בתרא דוקא (see *Eruvin* 28a). If כללא קמא דוקא, then a כלל ופרט וכלל consists of a כלל ופרט sentence that is extended by the second כלל. If כללא בתרא דוקא, then a כלל ופרט וכלל consists of a פרט וכלל sentence that is restricted by the first כלל.

Now, if a כלל ופרט וכלל includes a כלל ופרט, the rule is that אין בכלל אלא מה שבפרט, only that this פרט is then extended by the second כלל and becomes an exemplification of the כלל. Accordingly, the halachah applies to anything resembling the פרט in all its essential features. In our verse, the essential features of the פרט (ימים ונחלים) are as follows: מים נובעים and גדלין על גבי קרקע, they spring from a natural source and form on the earth's surface. This would include חריצין ונעיצין, artificially dug canals and lakes into which natural water is diverted or collected; for they possess both of these essential features. And this would exclude בורות שיחין ומערות; for although their waters are גדלים על גבי קרקע, they are not נובעים. Certainly, then, כלים are excluded; that is to say, creatures bred in water that is contained in vessels are not prohibited.

If, on the other hand, a כלל ופרט וכלל includes a פרט וכלל, the rule is that נעשה הכלל מוסיף על הפרט: the כלל is given its widest application, and is then restricted by the first כלל. This would exclude anything that does not resemble the פרט in any essential feature, and would include anything that resembles the פרט in at least one of its essential features. In our verse, even בורות שיחין ומערות would be included; for although their waters are not נובעים, they are גדלים על גבי קרקע. Only כלים would be excluded. However, even according to this opinion, the words את זה תאכלו at the beginning of the verse limit the scope of the prohibition. As a result, this opinion reaches the same conclusion: The requirement of fins and scales applies only to creatures produced in waters springing from a natural source — i.e., in ימים ונחלים and in חריצין ונעיצין that are fed by natural wells or springs.

תנא דבי ר׳ ישמעאל has a different approach. In his view, when שני כללים are סמוכין זה לזה — as in the case of במים במים here — the operating principle is not כלל ופרט but ריבוי ומיעוט, and we have an amplification that is restricted only slightly. According to this approach, the halachah applies to all flowing waters, even those not coming from springs. That is to say, the law applies also to חריצין ונעיצין שאינם נובעים. Only כלים and בורות שיחין ומערות שהן צעורין ככלים are excluded (*Chullin* 67a and תוספות, ad loc.; יורה דעה 84:2). On the difference between the two opinions —

י וְכֹל אֲשֶׁר אֵין־לוֹ סְנַפִּיר וְקַשְׂקֶשֶׂת בַּיַּמִּים וּבַנְּחָלִים מִכֹּל שֶׁרֶץ הַמַּיִם וּמִכֹּל נֶפֶשׁ הַחַיָּה אֲשֶׁר בַּמָּיִם שֶׁקֶץ הֵם לָכֶם׃

10 *But whatever does not have fins and scales in seas and in rivers, of all small creatures of the water and of all animal life that lives in the water, they shall be an abomination to you.*

יא וְשֶׁקֶץ יִהְיוּ לָכֶם מִבְּשָׂרָם לֹא תֹאכֵלוּ וְאֶת־נִבְלָתָם תְּשַׁקֵּצוּ׃

11 *And they shall be an abomination to you, you shall not eat of their flesh, and their bodies removed from their element you shall hold in abomination.*

כללא בתרא דוקא or כללא קמא דוקא — and on the relation of the latter opinion to ריבוי מיעוט וריבוי, see תוספות, in *Chullin* 65b, ד״ה וכי תימא.

10–11 **שקץ הם לכם**. Cf. Commentary above, verse 8: טמאים הם לכם. The ציר of דגים טמאים, however, is אסור only מדרבנן: שאני ציר דזיעה בעלמא הוא (ibid. 99b and תוספות, ad loc.).

In *Devarim* 14:10 the forbidden water creatures, too, are classed under the general term טמא. Here, however, a more specific term is attached to them: שקץ. שקץ is not the same as קוץ. The term קוץ is applied also to something that is physically loathsome, as in the verse: ונפשנו קצה בלחם הקלקל (*Bemidbar* 21:5). שקץ, by contrast — in all places in Scripture — refers only to that which is morally loathsome.

Just as it says here ואת נבלתם תשקצו, so it says in *Devarim* (7:26) in regard to idolatry שקץ תשקצנו. The words שקץ תשקצנו express the extreme contrast between our sanctity and the טומאה of idolatry. Hence, in the books of the prophets שקוץ and שקוצים are code words for idols and idolatry. Indeed, it can be said that שקץ refers exclusively to forbidden creatures and to idolatry. Only once do we find כִּי לֹא־בָזָה וְלֹא שִׁקַּץ עֱנוּת עָנִי (*Tehillim* 22:25), and there too it apparently means: He answers the call of the poor, and — contrary to the claim of their enemies — does not regard this as something shameful or antithetical to His righteousness and holiness.

It follows, then, that if food — in the context of the prohibition against eating it — is termed שקץ, such eating is antithetical to that morality which must be the basis of our existence. Whereas טומאה only impedes קדושה, שקץ leads to its very opposite. שקץ, then, is synonymous with "abomination," and we have translated it accordingly.

שקץ הם לכם ושקץ יהיו לכם. By their nature they are שקץ, and therefore you are to treat them as שקץ. The prohibition against eating such creatures rests on the actual contrast between their nature and your nature.

From the words ושקץ יהיו לכם the Gemara (*Pesachim* 23a) derives further that one must treat such creatures as שקץ even in regard to possessing and acquiring them. They — as well as anything forbidden to be eaten מדאורייתא — are forbidden to be purchased for the sake of trade. Only if they come into our possession by chance, במזדמן, are we then permitted to sell them. This prohibition, however, applies only to things that are used primarily as food, but not to animals such as horses and donkeys and the like, which are used primarily for work. Among all the things that are forbidden to be eaten מדאורייתא, only חלב is permitted for סחורה (see Commentary above, 7:24).

מבשרם לא תאכלו. Here, too, the prohibition applies only to the edible parts, but not to the bones and the like (see *Toras Kohanim*).

ואת נבלתם תשקצו. Since שחיטה is inapplicable to water creatures, and their dead bodies do not convey טומאה by contact, the meaning of the word נבילה here is not the same as in the section on בהמה טמאה (v. 8). Rather, *Toras Kohanim* expounds as follows: ואת נבלתם תשקצו – להביא את היבחושין שסיננן. That is, from ואת נבלתם תשקצו we learn that aquatic creatures lacking scales are forbidden to be eaten, once they are removed from their element. For verses 9 and 10 deal only with scale-less creatures living in natural or standing waters, but gnat-like creatures (יבחושין) which breed in standing waters collected in closed containers are not included in the prohibition stated there. From our verse we now learn that they, too, are permitted only while they are still in their element. But once they leave the element in which they were produced and lived — e.g., one passes the fluid through a strainer (סינן) — then תשקצו, they must be treated as שקץ; henceforth, according to *Chullin* 67a, they are included in the category of כל השרץ השרץ על הארץ (v. 41).

In accordance with this conception of נבלתם, the Gemara (*Shabbos* 107b) says that one who takes a fish out of water is considered to have

12 *Whatever does not have fins and scales in the water shall be an abomination to you.*

יב כֹּל אֲשֶׁר אֵין־לוֹ סְנַפִּיר
וְקַשְׂקֶשֶׂת בַּמָּיִם שֶׁקֶץ הוּא לָכֶם׃

13 *And these you shall hold in abomination from among the fowl; they shall not be eaten; they are an abomination: the* nesher, *the* peres, *and the* azniyah.

יג וְאֶת־אֵלֶּה תְּשַׁקְּצוּ מִן־הָעוֹף לֹא
יֵאָכְלוּ שֶׁקֶץ הֵם אֶת־הַנֶּשֶׁר
וְאֶת־הַפֶּרֶס וְאֵת הָעָזְנִיָּה׃

14 *The* da'ah *and the* ayah *according to its species.*

יד וְאֶת־הַדָּאָה וְאֶת־הָאַיָּה לְמִינָהּ׃

15 *Any* orev *according to its species.*

טו אֵת כָּל־עֹרֵב לְמִינוֹ׃

16 *The* bas ha-ya'anah, *the* tachmas *the* shachaf, *and the* netz *according to its species.*

טז וְאֵת בַּת הַיַּעֲנָה וְאֶת־הַתַּחְמָס
וְאֶת־הַשָּׁחַף וְאֶת־הַנֵּץ לְמִינֵהוּ׃

17 *The* kos, *the* shalach *and the* yanshuf.

יז וְאֶת־הַכּוֹס וְאֶת־הַשָּׁלָךְ וְאֶת־
הַיַּנְשׁוּף׃

18 *The* tinshemes, *the* ka'as *and the* racham.

יח וְאֶת־הַתִּנְשֶׁמֶת וְאֶת־הַקָּאָת
וְאֶת־הָרָחָם׃

19 *The* chasidah, *the* anafah *according to its species, the* duchifas *and the* atalef.

יט וְאֵת הַחֲסִידָה הָאֲנָפָה לְמִינָהּ
וְאֶת־הַדּוּכִיפַת וְאֶת־הָעֲטַלֵּף׃

---

killed it; and, according to **בית שמאי** (*Chullin* 75a), a fish taken out of water is considered dead.

12 **במים**. It is sufficient that it has scales while in the water, even if it sheds them upon leaving the water (see *Toras Kohanim*).

13–19 We left the names of the birds listed here untranslated. For all the other kinds of birds, which are not listed here, are permitted to be eaten (see

20 *Any winged creeping thing that goes upon four legs is an abomination to you.*

כ כֹּל שֶׁרֶץ הָעוֹף הַהֹלֵךְ עַל־אַרְבַּע שֶׁקֶץ הוּא לָכֶם׃

21 *Only this may you eat of all the winged creeping things that go upon four legs; those that have jointed legs above their feet, to hop with them upon the earth.*

כא אַךְ אֶת־זֶה תֹּאכְלוּ מִכֹּל שֶׁרֶץ הָעוֹף הַהֹלֵךְ עַל־אַרְבַּע אֲשֶׁר־לֹא כְרָעַיִם מִמַּעַל לְרַגְלָיו לְנַתֵּר בָּהֵן עַל־הָאָרֶץ׃

לוֹ קרי

Chullin 61a, et seq.); hence, any mistake in the translation of one of these names could lead to transgression.

The common translation of most of these names is based solely on conjecture. תוספות (ibid. 63a, ד״ה נץ; 62b, ד״ה מאי ספיקייהו) even doubt whether the common translation of נשר as eagle and עורב as raven is correct.

From an anatomical and physiological comparison of the permitted יונה and the forbidden נשר, three positive signs and one negative sign of a kosher bird are transmitted to us in *Chullin* (61a): אצבע יתרה, זפק, קורקבנו נקלף, אינו דורס. A bird that has all these signs — and in certain cases even if it has only some of them — is assuredly kosher. However, we are well versed in only two of these signs: זפק (the presence of a crop) and קורקבנו נקלף (the inner skin of the stomach is easily peeled off); the commentators differ on the meaning of the other two signs, אצבע יתרה and אינו דורס. Since the time of the *Amora'im* the rule has been: עוף טהור נאכל במסורת (ibid. 63b), birds may be eaten only on the basis of a reliable tradition that they are kosher.

20 **כל שרץ העוף ההלך על ארבע**. Winged insects have at least six feet. We therefore presume that the number four mentioned here serves only to teach us that they have more than two feet; for this multiplicity of feet is what distinguishes שרץ העוף from עוף. It appears that this is also the רמב״ן's understanding here. Nevertheless, see Commentary below, verse 23.

21–22 Verse 21 cites only "jointed legs" as the characteristic sign of permitted שרץ העוף. Yet, verse 22 names particular species, and to each one adds

כב אֶת־אֵלֶּה מֵהֶם֙ תֹּאכֵ֔לוּ אֶת־
הָאַרְבֶּ֣ה לְמִינ֔וֹ וְאֶת־הַסָּלְעָ֖ם
לְמִינֵ֑הוּ וְאֶת־הַחַרְגֹּ֣ל לְמִינֵ֔הוּ
וְאֶת־הֶחָגָ֖ב לְמִינֵֽהוּ׃
כג וְכֹל֙ שֶׁ֣רֶץ הָע֔וֹף אֲשֶׁר־ל֖וֹ אַרְבַּ֣ע
רַגְלָ֑יִם שֶׁ֥קֶץ ה֖וּא לָכֶֽם׃
כד וּלְאֵ֖לֶּה תִּטַּמָּ֑אוּ כָּל־הַנֹּגֵ֥עַ

22 *These of them you may eat: the* arbeh *according to its species; the* sal'am *according to its species; the* chargol *according to its species and the* chagav *according to its species.*

23 *Every winged creeping thing that has four legs is an abomination to you.*

24 *And with regard to these you shall consider yourselves impure; whoever touches their carcass*

למינהו ,למינו. Thus, verse 22 limits the generalization stated in verse 21, and then generalizes beyond this limitation by adding the words למינו and למינהו. Hence, according to *Chullin* 65ff., the structure here is that of כלל ופרט וכלל, and the species named in verse 22 illustrate the כלל. From these species we learn characteristic signs of permitted שרץ העוף — in addition to the כרעים (called קרצולין in the Mishnah) mentioned in verse 21. These signs are common to all the species mentioned. These, then, are the signs of permitted שרץ העוף: ארבע רגלים, ארבע כנפים, קרצולים, וכנפין חופין את רובו. To these, a fifth condition is added: ושמו חגב. For the other signs are already derived from the preceding species (ארבה, סלעם, חרגל); why, then, does the Torah add ואת החגב? To teach us that it must be known by the name חגב (see Mishnah, *Chullin* 59a; ibid. 66b).

לו in verse 21 is written לא, to teach us that locusts are permitted even at the stage when the jointed legs are not yet developed, אין לו עכשיו ועתיד לגדל לאחר זמן (ibid. 65a).

23 **וכל שרץ העוף וגו׳**. On verse 20 we raised the following difficulty: As far as we know, all winged insects have at least six feet. This difficulty is compounded by the words of רבי in *Toras Kohanim* here: אם יש לו חמש הרי זה טהור. An explanation in accordance with the actual facts is much to be desired.

בְּנִבְלָתָ֑ם יִטְמָ֖א עַד־הָעָֽרֶב׃

shall remain impure until evening.

כה וְכָל־הַנֹּשֵׂ֖א מִנִּבְלָתָ֑ם יְכַבֵּ֥ס בְּגָדָ֖יו וְטָמֵ֥א עַד־הָעָֽרֶב׃

25 *And whoever carries [part] of their carcass shall wash his garments and remain impure until evening.*

24–25 **ולאלה תטמאו**. Until now the discussion has been of טומאת הגוויות — i.e., forbidden foods that transmit to the body actual טומאה. In this connection Scripture cites mammals, fish, and birds, and to the latter appends winged insects. To these should be added wingless creeping things, whose laws are set forth only later (vv. 41–42). Verse 41 (וכל השרץ השרץ על הארץ), then, is the direct continuation of verses 20–23 (כל שרץ העוף וגו׳), only that the Torah interrupts here (v. 24ff.) with a different subject, which is related to the previous subject: The Torah elaborates upon the relation of the creatures mentioned until now to טומאת הקדושות.

טומאת הקדושות is strictly symbolical טומאה that is antithetical to the קדושה of מקדש וקדשיו. In this regard Scripture now says (v. 24): All those mentioned until now *bring actual* טומאה via אכילה, but only לאלה תטמאו — only one who has come into relation with those that will now be mentioned must *consider himself* טמא and conduct himself as a טמא. Details of this halachah now follow: כל הנגע בנבלתם יטמא עד הערב — i.e., one must observe the טומאה laws until the end of the day. These laws will be enlarged upon later, in chapter 22: the טמא must keep away from all קדשים.

As the הרכסים לבקעה correctly points out, symbolical טומאה is generally referred to in Scripture by the expression טמא ל-. Thus, it says here: ולאלה תטמאו. Further examples are לה יטמא (below, 21:3); לאביו ולאמו לא יטמא (below, 21:11); וכל טמא לנפש *(Bemidbar* 5:2). By contrast, actual טומאה of מאכלות אסורות and עריות is always referred to by the expression טמא ב-. For example: ולא תטמאו בהם (below, v. 43); ולא תטמאו את נפשתיכם בכל השרץ (below, v. 44); לטמאה בה (below, 18:20); אל תטמאו בכל אלה (below, 18:24).

In טומאת הגוויות, the object beginning with the letter ב is the concrete cause of the טומאה, and the טומאה is its concrete effect: a person is rendered טמא *by* the object. In טומאת הקדושות, it is different. Here, the letter ל of the object expresses the cause of the טומאה. The relation between the person and the object — *that* is what produces the טומאה. The very fact that the person becomes לו, related to the object, and appears to pertain to it — *that* is what causes טומאה. Thus, the cause of the טומאה is a concept, a relation — a conceptual relation engendered by an external action. Hence, the effect, too, is in the conceptual realm, and can be removed as soon as the said relation is negated by certain procedures — i.e., as soon as the connection between the person and the object is severed in time and place. The procedures that remove this connection — in time and place — are טבילה and הערב שמש (see below).

The meaning of ולאלה תטמאו, then, is this: When you have come into relation with these, consider yourselves טמאים.

כל הנגע בנבלתם וגו׳ וכל הנשא מנבלתם וגו׳. Scripture distinguishes here between מגע (contact) and משא (carrying). מגע is *direct* contact, but contact only. The body of a living human being approaches the dead body of one of these creatures and touches it without moving it. The contact is with the outer parts of one's body. Contact with the inner parts or folds of the body — מגע בית הסתרים — is not called מגע in this regard (see *Niddah* 42b–43a and תוספות, there, ד״ה למימרא).

משא, according to רש״י (*Chullin* 20b, ד״ה מלק; see ר״ש on *Zavim* 5:3 and *Kelim* 1:2), is not a mere passive bearing of an object; that is, it is not sufficient that the object rests on the person. Rather, he must carry it actively and move it from place to place, which also includes היסט, moving an object without carrying it. (According to the רמב״ם in his commentary to *Kelim* 1:2, משא also includes the mere passive bearing of the object, without moving it. In הל׳ טומאת מת, 1:6, his opinion on this issue is not clear.) According to the ר״ש, the mere passive bearing of an object is included in the concept of אבן מסמא, which will be discussed in the context of טומאת זב (below, 15:4).

Neither משא nor היסט require direct contact. Rather, a person becomes טמא by merely causing the movement of a נבילה.

כלים and אוכלים are also rendered טמא by contact (מגע); the טומאה of משא and היסט, however, apply only if a person moved the נבילה.

We learn further from these two verses that טומאת משא is more severe than טומאת מגע. Of מגע it says: כל הנגע בנבלתם יטמא, only those that touch the נבילה directly — whether they are אדם, כלים, or אוכלים — become טמא. In the case of טומאת משא, however, the טומאה extends to all כלים or אוכלים that are in contact with the person at the time of the משא, and they are treated as though they themselves were in contact with the נבילה; hence, they too, like the person, become ראשונים לטומאה. This transference of the טומאה is called טומאה בחיבורין: the טומאה is transferred directly to all objects that are in contact with the person during the moving of the נבילה. This law is expressed in Scripture by the words יכבס בגדיו. בגד, here, is taken in the widest sense of the term. It includes all the objects that comprise the image of man during his creative activity (and during the activities from which he derives benefit? [see below]); man, as it were, is enclothed by them. These are the כלים (and אוכלים?) which complement the בגד in its narrow sense. Only אדם and כלי חרס are excluded.

צ״ע אי הנושא נבלה מטמא אוכלין בחיבורין להיות תחלה מדאורייתא, דהא אפילו כלי חרס ממעט ליה בת״כ מפני שאינו דומה לבגד שיש לו טהרה במקוה אע״פ שהוא דומה לו בהיותו כלי כ״ש אוכלין ומשקין שאינו דומה לבגד כלל והא דקאמר פ״ה דזבים מ״א כל המטמא בגדים בשעת מגעו מטמא אוכלין ומשקין להיות תחלה אפשר דרק מדרבנן קאמר תדע דהא מיירי שם ג״כ מידים שהוא ודאי רק דרבנן וצ״ע דממפרשי המשנה והברייתא בת״כ פרשת זבים משמע דס״ל שהוא דאורייתא.

What a person touches after he is no longer in contact with the נבילה becomes a שני לטומאה. This applies only to אוכלים, as אדם וכלים can be rendered טמא only by an אב הטומאה (see *Toras Kohanim* here).

יכבס בגדיו. טהרה is restored to the בגד via טבילה — i.e., by immersing it completely in a מעיין or in מי מקוה (see Commentary to vv. 32 and 36). This טבילה is called here כביסה, a term that is frequently employed elsewhere, as well, in connection with טהרת כלים — even though the primary meaning of this term is none other than the ordinary washing of כלים. We presume that this term is used here to keep us from the error of thinking that טבילה is effective also for טהרת אוכלין. This erroneous assumption might have come to mind here since, as we have stated, both כלים and אוכלים are נטמאים בחיבורין and are included in the term בגדיו. טבילה, however, restores the טהרה of כלים but not of אוכלים. Hence, it is called here כביסה, a term that normally applies only to כלים.

וטמא עד הערב. The טבילה of all טמאים (except נדה ויולדת — see *Pesachim* 90b) must take place during the day. He who is טמא for only one day may immerse immediately; he who is טמא for seven days may immerse on the seventh day; and one may not immerse until after sunrise (see *Megillah* 20a).

After טבילה the restoration of טהרה begins, but the טהרה is not complete until nightfall of the new day. Until then the טמא is called טבול יום,

26 *As regards any animal that has hoofs but does not cleave them*	כו לְכָל־הַבְּהֵמָה אֲשֶׁר הִוא מַפְרֶסֶת פַּרְסָה וְשֶׁסַע ׀ אֵינֶנָּה שֹׁסַעַת וְגֵרָה

and his status is like that of a שני לטומאה: he may eat מעשר שני, but not תרומה or קדשים. When night begins — at הערב שמש — these, too, are permitted to him.

A different law applies to four טמאים — namely, זב וזבה מצורע ויולדת: The completion of their טהרה depends on the bringing of certain offerings. Accordingly, they are called מחוסרי כפרה. They, too, may eat תרומה at הערב שמש, but they are forbidden to eat קדשים until they have brought their offerings. These *halachos* are stated in *Yevamos* 74b: טבל ועלה אוכל במעשר, העריב שמשו אוכל בתרומה, הביא כפרה אוכל בקדשים.

The restoration of טהרה in stages is derived (ibid.) from three verses: (a) ולא יאכל מן הקדשים כי אם רחץ בשרו במים (below, 22:6) — the eating of קדשים is dependent on טבילה; (b) ובא השמש וטהר ואחר יאכל מן הקדשים (below, 22:7) — eating is permitted only at הערב שמש; (c) וכפר עליה הכהן וטהרה (below, 12:8) — the טהרה is contingent on the bringing of offerings. The first verse relates to מעשר, the second to תרומה, and the third to קדשים.

A יולדת (of whom the third verse speaks), from the time of her טבילה until she has brought her offerings, is called טבולת יום ארוך.

Toras Kohanim (here) states that the טומאת נבילה referred to here is טומאת אבר מן החי. Indeed, these two טומאות are similar. The only difference between them is this: אבר מן החי conveys טומאה only in its complete state as an אבר, but בשר הפורש מן אבר מן החי (flesh that separates from that אבר) does not convey טומאה. בשר הפורש מן הנבילה, however, does convey טומאה. Accordingly, the נבילה referred to here is not an animal that died, but a part that was severed from the animal and thus "died."

The Gemara (*Chullin* 128b), however, does not derive טומאת אבר מן החי from our verse, but from what is stated later: וכי ימות מן הבהמה (v. 39); for that expression denotes an animal part that has died. Accordingly, our verse deals with טומאת נבילה; and even though this law was already mentioned above (v. 8) in general terms, Scripture here explains it in greater detail.

26 **לכל בהמה**. This verse refers back to verse 24; and the meaning of the ל in לכל, here, is the same as in ולאלה תטמאו, there.

אֵינֶ֫נָּה מַעֲלָ֔ה טְמֵאִ֥ים הֵ֖ם לָכֶ֑ם כָּל־הַנֹּגֵ֥עַ בָּהֶ֖ם יִטְמָֽא׃

and does not chew the cud, they are impure to you; whatever touches them shall be impure.

כז וְכֹ֣ל ׀ הוֹלֵ֣ךְ עַל־כַּפָּ֗יו בְּכָל־הַֽחַיָּה֙ הַהֹלֶ֣כֶת עַל־אַרְבַּ֔ע טְמֵאִ֥ים הֵ֖ם לָכֶ֑ם כָּל־הַנֹּגֵ֥עַ בְּנִבְלָתָ֖ם יִטְמָ֥א עַד־הָעָֽרֶב׃

27 *And whatever goes upon its paws among all animals that go upon four legs, they are impure to you; whoever touches their carcass shall remain impure until evening.*

כח וְהַנֹּשֵׂא֙ אֶת־נִבְלָתָ֔ם יְכַבֵּ֥ס בְּגָדָ֖יו וְטָמֵ֣א עַד־הָעָ֑רֶב טְמֵאִ֥ים הֵ֖מָּה לָכֶֽם׃ ס

28 *And whoever carries their carcass shall wash his garments and remain impure until evening; they are impure to you.*

טומאת נבילה is presented in four groups in verses 26–40. First mentioned are the animals that are forbidden to be eaten. They are arranged in three groups according to their descending degree of closeness to man. Verse 26 mentions hoofed animals whose hoofs are not cleft and who are not ruminants. Being hoofed they stand closest to man among the impure animals. Next mentioned, in verse 27, are the unhoofed quadrupeds, and finally in verses 29–30 the eight lower creeping things, which are the furthest from man. Verse 39 adds the fourth group, נבלת בהמה טהורה.

טמאים הם לכם. A comparison with verse 31 (אלה הטמאים לכם וגו׳) proves that both this verse and the similar verses 27–28 deal only with **טומאת מגע** and not with **איסור אכילה**. The reason for these repetitions still needs to be understood.

28 All **נבלות בהמה טמאה** are **מטמא במגע ובמשא**. We should point out further that all animals are **מטמא** only after their death; they neither convey nor contract **טומאה** while they are still alive. Only man conveys and contracts **טומאה** even while he is still alive.

29 *And this is what is impure to you among the creeping things that creep upon the earth: the weasel, the mouse and the toad according to its species.*	כט וְזֶה לָכֶם הַטָּמֵא בַּשֶּׁרֶץ הַשֹּׁרֵץ עַל־הָאָרֶץ הַחֹלֶד וְהָעַכְבָּר וְהַצָּב לְמִינֵהוּ׃
30 *The hedgehog, the* ko'ach, *the lizard, the* chomet *and the mole.*	ל וְהָאֲנָקָה וְהַכֹּחַ וְהַלְּטָאָה וְהַחֹמֶט וְהַתִּנְשָׁמֶת׃
31 *These are those that are impure to you among all creeping things; whoever touches them when they are dead shall be impure until evening.*	לא אֵלֶּה הַטְּמֵאִים לָכֶם בְּכָל־הַשָּׁרֶץ כָּל־הַנֹּגֵעַ בָּהֶם בְּמֹתָם יִטְמָא עַד־הָעָרֶב׃

29–31 **בשרץ השרץ על הארץ** — the lower creeping things. Although all of them are אסורים באכילה, only the eight kinds named here are מטמאים במגע. The correct translation of their names is not certain. חלד, weasel, and עכבר, mouse, are known. צב, according to רש״י (*Kesubos* 15a) and ר״ש (*Tohoros* 5:1), resembles a frog. אנקה, according to רש״י (here), is a hedgehog. כח is unknown. הלטאה, according to רש״י (here), is a lizard. חמט, according to רש״י (*Chagigah* 11a), is a snail. From *Chullin* 128b, however, it appears that all the שרצים mentioned here are vertebrated animals, for their characteristic feature is that they possess בשר גידים ועצמות, "flesh, tendons, and bones." Yet snails are definitely invertebrates; hence, it is difficult to say that a חמט is a snail. תנשמת is mentioned also among the birds (above, v. 18). According to רש״י (there), the one counted among the birds is a bat, and the one counted among the שרצים is a mole. Both of these, according to Oken (the zoologist), belong to the same order, which may be the explanation of the common name.

The שמונה שרצים are מטמאים only במגע but not במשא, and, like all other animals, only במותם, but not while alive. אבר מן החי is מטמא also in the case of שרץ, as it suffers partial מיתה (see *Chullin* 128b). The blood of שרצים, like the flesh, is טמא — אין דמם חלוק מבשרם (see *Kerisos* 4b), whereas דם נבילה is not טמא. The special law of טומאת דם that is applicable to שרצים is derived (in *Me'ilah* 17a) from the words וזה לכם הטמא; for from here we learn that the שרץ — with all its components — is called טמא (see Commentary below, v. 46).

כל הנגע בהם וגו׳ יטמא. The word בהם in this verse implies that, to become טמא, one must come into contact with a complete dead שרץ, while the word מהם in the next verse — וכל אשר יפל עליו מהם וגו׳ (v. 32) — implies that even part of a שרץ conveys טומאה by contact. This contradiction is resolved in *Chagigah* (11a) as follows: A part of a שרץ is טמא if the part is large enough to represent the whole, מקצתו שהוא ככולו. The Sages estimated this to be the size of a lentil, כעדשה; for the חומט at first is the size of a lentil. By contrast, in the case of נבלת בהמה the minimum size is כזית. Furthermore, מקצתו של שרץ is מטמא only if it is still fresh, לח; but when a שרץ is יבש (dry) or שרוף, only כולו — the complete שרץ — is מטמא, provided that שלדו קיים, its form remains intact (*Niddah* 56a).

From the repeated mention in Scripture of שרץ that creeps על הארץ we learn (*Chullin* 126b, et seq.) that the eight שרצים named here live on land — which excludes עכבר ים and the like. From the combination of words בשרץ השרץ על הארץ (compare v. 43 which, discussing איסור אכילה, states generally בכל השרץ השרץ) we learn (ibid. and *Nazir* 64a) that טומאת מגע depends on two factors: השורץ and על הארץ. The Gemara (ibid.) says: כתיב בכל השרץ השרץ (v. 43; similar wording appears in v. 29 in connection with טומאת מגע: בשרץ השרץ), which implies כל מקום שהוא שורץ — i.e., שרץ is מטמא anywhere. וכתיב על הארץ (v. 29), which implies that שרץ is מטמא only while on the ground. The Gemara resolves the contradiction as follows: הא כיצד? ודאי מגעו טמא, ספק מגעו טהור. One who definitely touched a source of טומאה is טמא no matter where this source was located. But if there is doubt whether contact was made, the person is טהור if the source was floating in water. And even though the rule is that ספק טומאה ברשות היחיד שיש בו דעת לישאל טמא (see Commentary to *Bemidbar* 5:14), this applies only if the טומאה-conveying object rests on the ground (על הארץ) but not if it is floating in water (צפה) or is thrown in the air (נזרק). Thus the *halachos*: כל הניטלין והנגררין ספיקן טמא מפני שהן כמונחין, והנזרקין ספיקן טהור; ספק טומאה צפה בין בכלים בין בקרקע טהורה(*Nazir* 63b, 64a). Similarly, it says in *Tohoros* (4:3): השרץ בפי החולדה והנבלה בפי הכלב ועברו בין הטהורין או שעברו טהורין ביניהן – ספקן טהור מפני שאין לטומאה מקום. (See ר״ש, there and Mishnah 7.)

This halachah applies to all טומאת מגע, including טומאת מת, but not

32 *And everything upon which any part of them falls when they are dead — of any wooden vessel, or a garment, or articles of leather, or a sack, any utensil with which work is done — shall be put into water, remain impure until evening and then be pure.*

לב וְכֹל אֲשֶׁר־יִפֹּל עָלָיו מֵהֶם ׀ בְּמֹתָם
יִטְמָא מִכָּל־כְּלִי־עֵץ אוֹ בֶגֶד אוֹ־
עוֹר אוֹ שָׂק כָּל־כְּלִי אֲשֶׁר־יֵעָשֶׂה
מְלָאכָה בָּהֶם בַּמַּיִם יוּבָא וְטָמֵא
עַד־הָעֶרֶב וְטָהֵר׃ שביעי

to מאהיל על המת or to עליונו ותחתונו של זב. (See ר״ש, *Tohoros* 4:3. From רמב״ם הל׳ אבות הטומאות, 15:7, it appears that the law of ספק צפה applies only in the case of שרץ. וצ״ע.)

32 **וכל אשר יפל עליו מהם במתם**. This verse elucidates the detailed *halachos* of טומאת נבלת שרץ, and the case discussed teaches us also about טומאת אבר מן החי, which resembles טומאת נבילה.

Scripture does not say וכל אשר יגע בו במתם, but, rather, וכל אשר יפל עליו מהם במתם — i.e., a part of the שרץ falls off of it. This is אבר מן החי. This "falling off" is equated here with מיתה: like מיתה, its effect must be irreparable — כעין מיתה שאין לה חליפין (*Toras Kohanim*). From this we learn that טומאת אבר מן החי applies only in the case of a whole limb (אבר), but not in the case of flesh that separates from a living animal (בשר הפורש מן החי), which the body can replace. Moreover, according to ר׳ עקיבא and רבי, the definition of אבר is even more limited: it must be an epitome of the whole body — i.e., it must contain the components of the whole body. According to ר׳ עקיבא it must contain at least sinews and bones; according to רבי — flesh, sinews, and bones: מה שרץ גידים ועצמות וגו׳, or מה שרץ בשר גידים ועצמות וגו׳ (*Chullin* 128b).

Furthermore, Scripture implies that the limb separated upon the death (אשר יפול כו׳ במתם) of the שרץ. This is none other than אבר מדולדל, a limb that was broken while the שרץ was still alive, but that remained loosely attached to the living body. Upon the death of the שרץ, the law is that מיתה עושה ניפול — we regard the limb as though it had been severed while the שרץ was still alive; the death of the שרץ first affects the limbs dangling from it, and they are regarded as though they had "died" (fallen off) prior to the death of the שרץ. [טומאת אבר מן החי requires an אבר שלם while טומאת אבר מן המת requires merely a כזית.]

In the case of בהמה טהורה, however, the effect of the שחיטה extends also to the אבר המדולדל: שחיטה spares the dangling limb from טומאת אבר מן החי, just as it spares the entire animal. מן התורה it spares the limb from איסור אבר מן החי as well: אין שחיטה עושה ניפול (ibid. 74a).

(It appears that שחיטה is like מיתה in that both affect also the אבר המדולדל, only that in the case of מיתה the אבר "dies," whereas in the case of שחיטה the אבר is "slaughtered" in a שחיטה כשרה. According to the opinion that שחיטה עושה ניפול, however, the אבר in the case of שחיטה, too, is accorded the status of אבר מן החי; for the שחיטה affected the אבר before affecting the animal as a whole.)

מכל כלי עץ או בגד או עור או שק כל כלי וגו׳. כלי עץ — any vessel made of wood. בגד — any woven material whose threads are of plant or animal origin, כל טווי ואריג. Linen or woolen material is considered a בגד if it is at least שלש על שלש (אצבעות), three fingerbreadths square. Other material is considered a בגד if it is at least שלשה על שלשה (טפחים), three handbreadths square. This applies to pieces of cloth; but as regards a complete garment, its size is immaterial (*Shabbos* 26b–27a; 64a). כלי עור — an article made of skin or leather. שק — an article made of woven goats' hair; in *Bemidbar* 31:20 it is called מעשה עזים. Not only goats' hair, but any material of animal origin — e.g., hair, bones, horns, claws, and the like — is included in this category, provided that it comes from land animals such as עזים. Articles made of the bones or the feathers of birds, or made of fish, are not מקבל טומאה (*Chullin* 25b; *Kelim* 17:13).

Among the four categories mentioned here — כלי עץ, בגד, עור, שק — only שק denotes both a material and a form; and from שק we infer to the other categories that their form must resemble its form. A sack has two characteristic features: יש לו בית קיבול and מיטלטל מלא וריקן, its structure is that of a receptacle, and it can be moved whether empty or full. Hence, articles — made of the materials stated here — that lack even one of these two characteristics are not מקבלים טומאה. Examples of such articles are (a) פשוטי כלי עץ, כלי עצם, and כלי עור, which are flat and do not have a receptacle (in the case of עור, only if it is so rigid that one cannot wrap anything in it; see תוספות, *Shabbos* 63b, ד״ה מניין לאריג); (b) כלי עץ העשוי לנחת, which holds ארבעים סאה בלח (it is also called כלי הבא

במידה) and when filled is so heavy that it cannot be moved (see *Chullin* 25a; *Shabbos* 83b; *Chagigah* 26b; *Kelim* 15:1).

A special law is stated in regard to articles that are ראויים ומיוחדים למדרס (i.e., fit and designated for one to lie, sit, ride, or stand on), which are subject to טומאת משכב ומושב ומרכב of a זב וזבה נדה ויולדת (see chap. 15). Such articles are also susceptible to טומאת מגע even when they are פשוטים, without a בית קיבול, and — according to תוספות in *Menachos* 31a, ד"ה שידה — even if they are extremely large and are not מיטלטלין מלא וריקן. This law is derived by קל וחומר from פכים קטנים (*Shabbos* 84b; see *Bechoros* 38a).

(According to תוספות in *Menachos* 31a, an article is called מיוחד למדרס only if it serves the body when it is at rest; this excludes stilts or ladders and the like, which serve the body when it is in motion.)

As regards פשוטי כלי עץ, there is a distinction between those that are strictly משמשי אדם, used exclusively for man (e.g., a ladder) and those that are משמשים גם את האדם וגם את משמשי האדם, used for both man and his appurtenances (e.g., a table): the latter are מקבלים טומאה. According to תוספות (*Eruvin* 31a, ד"ה בפשוטי), however, this טומאה is only מדרבנן, and so it seems also from the רמב"ם (הל' כלים, 4:1).

ר' יוסי states a further rule in regard to משמשי משמשיו של אדם — e.g., utensil covers: If they remain on the utensil בשעת מלאכה ושלא בשעת מלאכה, both when the utensil is in use and when it is not in use, they are considered to be the same as the utensil, and they, too, are מקבלים טומאה (see *Kelim* 16:7). This rule, too, relates to פשוטי כלי עץ — e.g., a flat cover to a vessel, or a flat plate underneath it. It appears that this טומאה, also, is מדרבנן.

כל כלי אשר יעשה מלאכה בהם: it must be an independent כלי; חפויי כלים, coverings which serve merely to protect vessels, are excluded (*Toras Kohanim* here).

Our verse speaks primarily of moveable vessels that have a receptacle; hence, it appears that the מלאכה referred to here is the transportation of objects by means of these vessels. Indeed, this is called מלאכה in the case of שבת as well.

Among the materials from which vessels are made, metals (מתכות) are omitted here; but they are mentioned in *Bemidbar* 31:22: אך את הזהב ואת הכסף את הנחשת וגו' (see *Shabbos* 16b).

(According to the Gemara in *Avodah Zarah* 75b, the words וטהר and

במי נדה יתחטא in *Bemidbar* 31:23 refer to טבילת כלי מדין. This immersion applies to כלי סעודה של מתכות that pass from non-Jewish to Jewish possession, and has nothing to do with טומאה. The Gemara in *Shabbos* 16b seems to support the view that טבילת כלי מדין is מדרבנן; accordingly, the Scriptural sources cited in *Avodah Zarah* are merely אסמכתא. See כסף משנה to הל׳ מאכלות אסורות, 17:5. However, it appears that the word אך [*Bemidbar* 31:22] which opens that section connects it with the preceding section as follows: וכל בגד וכל כלי עור וגו׳ תתחטאו [ibid. 31:20] — everything that is not כלי סעודה של מתכות — requires only purification from טומאה; but כלי סעודה של מתכות require both הגעלה and טבילת כלי מדין [ibid. 31:22–23]. This connection between the two sections is made even more obvious by the omission of the term כלי in the second section: one can discern that the second section is discussing כלים, only through its connection with the preceding section.)

כלי מתכות, then, are not included in the analogy to שק; hence, neither the feature of בית קיבול nor that of טלטול מלא וריקן applies to them. Therefore, even פשוטיהן and vessels that are עשויין לנחת are טמאין (see *Chullin* 25a; *Chagigah* 26b).

There is another difference between כלי מתכות and כלי עץ. All כלים are מקבלי טומאה only when נגמרה מלאכתן, when they have the status of a כלי — i.e., when their manufacture is completed. But the necessary degree of completion (for קבלת טומאה) differs for כלי עץ and כלי מתכות. כלי עץ are מקבלי טומאה as soon as they are fit for their intended use, even if they are not yet painted or polished and are in a raw, unfinished state (גולמי כלי עץ). By contrast, כלי מתכות are מקבלי טומאה only when they are completely finished and do not require polishing. Hence the statement: גולמי כלי עץ טמאין, פשוטיהן טהורין; גולמי כלי מתכות טהורין, פשוטיהן טמאין; נמצא טהור בכלי עץ טמא בכלי מתכות, טהור בכלי מתכות טמא בכלי עץ (*Chulin* 25a). Two explanations are offered for the greater degree of finish required for כלי מתכות: (a) because לכבוד עשויין; apart from their utility, the idea of beauty, ornamentation, is predominant in their manufacture; or (b) because דמיהן יקרים; they are a more expensive, better class of vessel than common wooden ones (ibid. 25b).

במים יובא וטמא עד הערב וטהר. In *Toras Kohanim* we find: – במים יובא כולו כאחת, יכול מקצתו ת״ל ובא השמש וטהר (ויקרא כב:ז), מה טהרה האמורה למטן ביאת שמש כולו כאחת, אף כאן ביאת כלי כולו כאחת. Thus, a parallel is drawn between the sinking of the sun and the sinking of the כלי (in water), both of

33 *And any earthenware vessel into whose cavity any part of them falls, whatever is within its cavity becomes impure, and you shall break it.*	לג וְכָל־כְּלִי־חֶרֶשׂ אֲשֶׁר־יִפֹּל מֵהֶם אֶל־תּוֹכוֹ כֹּל אֲשֶׁר בְּתוֹכוֹ יִטְמָא וְאֹתוֹ תִשְׁבֹּרוּ׃

which are necessary for טהרה: in both cases, the sinking must be complete. This parallel explains the significance of the two elements upon which טהרה depends: טבילה and הערב שמש (see below).

One should also note that our verse does not say ובא השמש וטהר (as in 22:7) or וטהר בערב (as in *Bemidbar* 19:19), but וטמא עד הערב וטהר. The word וטהר, then, can also relate back to the preceding phrase עד הערב. From this we learn that, after טבילה until הערב שמש, a mixed state of טומאה and טהרה prevails: the כלי is טהור למעשר and טמא לתרומה — as we saw earlier (Commentary to v. 25) in the case of a person, a טבול יום (see *Yevamos* 75a).

33 **וכל כלי חרש** — vessels made of baked clay; vessels made of unbaked clay are classified as כלי אדמה, which — like כלי אבנים — are not susceptible to טומאה.

אשר יפל מהם אל תוכו: a כלי חרס becomes טמא only through its inner space (אוירו), but not through its outer surface (גביו). A שרץ renders an earthenware vessel טמא as soon as it enters the inner space of the vessel — even if it is not touching the vessel. For this is also how טומאה is conveyed by the vessel: כל אשר בתוכו יטמא, everything inside it becomes טמא. For example, if the vessel is filled with mustard seeds, even the top and middle seeds — which do not touch the surface of the vessel — become טמא, since they, too, are within its interior space: התורה העידה על כלי חרס ואפילו מלא חרדל. The manner in which the vessel receives טומאה is derived from the manner in which it imparts טומאה: ילפינן תוכו לִיטַמֵא מתוכו לְטַמֵא (*Chullin* 24b).

Thus an earthenware vessel that is closed with a tightly fitting lid, אשר צמיד פתיל עליו (see *Bemidbar* 19:15), is protected from the טומאה contracted in אהל המת, and protects its contents from this טומאה (מציל באהל המת).

34 *Of any food that is eaten, on which water comes, becomes impure when this happens, and so, too, any beverage that is drunk, in any vessel, becomes impure.*

לד מִכָּל־הָאֹכֶל אֲשֶׁר יֵאָכֵל אֲשֶׁר יָבוֹא עָלָיו מַיִם יִטְמָא וְכָל־מַשְׁקֶה אֲשֶׁר יִשָּׁתֶה בְּכָל־כְּלִי יִטְמָא:

The law of כלי חרס, then, differs from the law of all other כלים: טהור בכלי חרש טמא בכל הכלים, טהור בכל הכלים טמא בכלי חרש; אויר כלי חרש טמא וגבו טהור, אויר כל הכלים טהור וגבן טמא (*Chullin* 24b). The foregoing applies only to susceptibility to טומאה. Once a כלי חרס becomes טמא via תוכו, however, גבו also becomes טמא: כלי חרס שנטמא תוכו נטמא גבו (*Bechoros* 38a). Henceforth, even what touches the outer surface of the vessel becomes טמא: מרובה מדת לְטַמֵּא ממדת לִיטַּמֵּא שהוא מטמא את אחרִים מאחוריו ואינו מיטמא מאחוריו (תורת כהנים כאן; ועי׳ משנה למלך הל׳ כלים א:יג). Accordingly, פשוטי כלי חרס — which have no תוך — are not susceptible to טומאה; and since אין מדרס לכלי חרס, they have no טומאה at all (see *Bechoros* 38a).

A כלי חרס can never become an אב הטומאה. Other כלים can become אב הטומאה either by becoming משכב ומושב של זב or by touching a corpse. Neither means are available, however, to a כלי חרס. A כלי חרס is not ראוי למדרס; and only those כלים that have טהרה במקוה become אב הטומאה by contact with a מת, but a כלי חרס that becomes טמא can never regain טהרה, as it says here: ואתו תשברו (see *Eruvin* 104b).

These characteristics account for the halachah, unique to כלי חרס, that המכניס כלי חרס טמא למקדש פטור — he is פטור from the prohibition of bringing כלים טמאים into the מקדש. Two reasons are given for this halachah: (a) because לית ליה טהרה במקוה, or (b) because אינו נעשה אב הטומאה. According to תוספות in *Niddah* (28b, ד״ה פרט), the conclusion of the סוגיא in *Eruvin* is in accordance with the first reason; consequently, even המכניס שרץ למקדש is פטור. It appears, however, that this is only according to the version of רבינו חננאל, which is cited by תוספות in *Eruvin* (104b, ד״ה לא דכ״ע חייב). תוספות themselves, however, prefer the version of רש״י. According to this version, the conclusion of the סוגיא is in accordance with the second reason, and המכניס שרץ חייב. This is also the view of the רמב״ם (הל׳ ביאת מקדש, 3:16).

כל אשר בתוכו יטמא. The vessel itself is ראשון לטומאה and renders its contents שני לטומאה. That is why the contents are described, in the next verse, only as אוכלין and משקין, for only these become טמא through a ולד הטומאה (e.g., the כלי חרס here); כלים, however — like אדם — become טמא only through an אב הטומאה (*Pesachim* 20a–b; *Shabbos* 138b).

34 **מכל האכל אשר יאכל**. The words אשר יאכל are interpreted in *Yoma* (80a) as a statement about quantity. They indicate a quantity that represents one אכילה, namely, a volume equal to that of a hen's egg, כביצה — although as regards איסור the minimum measure of אכילה is an olive's worth: כל השיעורין כולן בכזית חוץ מטומאת אוכלין ששינה הכתוב במשמען ושינו חכמים בשיעורן.

According to רבינו תם (תוספות ישנים, ibid. and תוספות, *Pesachim* 33b, ד״ה לאימת), שיעור כביצה applies both לקבל טומאה (the law discussed in our verse) and לטמא אחרים. רש״י, however, mentions another opinion, which holds that this minimum measure is prescribed only for conveying טומאה. Thus, אוכלין, to receive טומאה, may be in any volume, כל שהוא, but to convey טומאה their volume must be at least כביצה. This view is also adopted by the רמב״ם in הל׳ טומאת אוכלין, 4:1. But it is difficult to explain our verse in accordance with this view. For from our verse we derive that the שיעור in טומאת אוכלין is כביצה, and yet our verse discusses אוכלין *receiving* טומאה. According to ה״ר יוסף (תוספות, *Pesachim* 33b), however, even this view grants that the minimum measure for הכשר טומאה (see below) is כביצה. This resolves the difficulty of interpreting our verse, as the words אשר יבוא עליו מים teach us the law of הכשר לקבל טומאה.

From the wording of our verse *Toras Kohanim* derives laws relating to quality: האוכל — i.e., אוכל המיוחד, namely human food (מאכל אדם); animal fodder (מאכל בהמה), however, is not מקבל טומאה. אשר יאכל, it must be edible — פרט לאוכל סרוח; if the food is rotten, it is not מקבל טומאה. Moreover, even if the food becomes טמא before it rots, it loses its טומאה when decay sets in. This applies even to טומאת נבילה: דלכי מסרחה פרחה טומאתה. One must distinguish, however, between various degrees of decay: between that which is not ראוי לגר and that which is not even ראוי לכלב; also between הסריחה מעיקרא, where the decay set in before the טומאה, and הסריחה לאחר מכן, where the decay set in after the טומאה (*Menachos* 23a; *Bechoros* 23b — see רש״י ד״ה הסריחה מעיקרא). מאכלות אסורות, too, are מקבלות טומאת אוכלין, even though they are not fit to be eaten by Jews. Even איסורי הנאה — which are not אוכל שאתה יכול להאכילו לאחרים, i.e., which one may not feed to others — are מקבלים טומאת אוכלין (see *Menachos* 101b).

אשר יבוא עליו מים. אוכלים are מקבלים טומאה only if they have once come into contact with liquid — intentionally or at least with agreement. This contact with liquid is called הכשר. (For the details of this law, see Commentary below, v. 38.)

וכל משקה אשר ישתה וגו'. In *Pesachim* 16a, et seq., three opinions are stated in regard to the טומאה of liquids: (a) מדאורייתא they are both מקבלים טומאה and מטמאים אחרים; (b) מדאורייתא they are מקבלים טומאה, but they cannot convey it to other things, they are not מטמאים אחרים; (c) מדאורייתא they have no טומאה at all, אין טומאה למשקין כל עיקר. According to the last opinion, the words וכל משקה וגו' do not deal with טומאת משקין, but with הכשר קבלת טומאה, and they serve to extend and limit the concept of מים mentioned earlier in the verse: Just as מים renders אוכלין susceptible to טומאה, so does כל משקה אשר ישתה render them susceptible; and just as כל משקה is בכל כלי (i.e., תלוש מן הקרקע, detached from the ground), the same applies to מים. Thus, water does not render אוכלין susceptible to טומאה unless it is תלוש, and not מחובר לקרקע; and certain other liquids — besides water — are מכשירים לטומאה. Altogether there are seven such liquids: dew, water, wine, oil, blood, milk, and bee's honey (*Machshirin* 6:4; as for blood, remember that — as stated above — even מאכלות אסורות are susceptible to טומאת אוכלין). The blood listed here is strictly דם חולין, not דם קדשים; and only דם שהנפש יוצאה בו, not דם התמצית (*Pesachim* 16a–b; see Commentary above, 7:26).

The רמב"ם (הל' אבות הטומאות, 7:1) rules that משקין מקבלין טומאה ואינן מטמאין אחרים מדאורייתא. Accordingly, our verse deals with טומאת משקין, and from here we learn that not only אוכל but also כל משקה אשר ישתה is susceptible to טומאה, if the משקה is בכל כלי — i.e., תלוש מן הקרקע. Here, too, only the seven liquids mentioned above are included in the category of משקה אשר ישתה: שבעה משקין טמאים ושאר כל המשקין טהורין (*Terumos* 11:2). Thus, the law of משקה אשר ישתה is stated here in regard to טומאת משקין, but not in regard to הכשר. Nevertheless, *Toras Kohanim* (to v. 38) states that the term מים in the passage on הכשר זרעים includes the ז' משקין — and them alone. The result is that both הכשר and טומאה apply only to these seven liquids (see the רמב"ם's commentary to *Terumos* 11:2).

As we have said, not every drinkable liquid is considered משקה vis-à-vis טומאה. The same is true of the term אוכל: it, too, does not include all foods. Materials that serve only to flavor the food — מילי דעביד לטעמא — are not מטמא טומאת אוכלין (*Niddah* 51b).

35 *And anything upon which part of the carcass falls shall be impure, even an oven and a hearth must be demolished; they are impure and only as impure may they serve you.*

לה וְכֹל אֲשֶׁר־יִפֹּל מִנִּבְלָתָם ׀ עָלָיו
יִטְמָא תַּנּוּר וְכִירַיִם יֻתָּץ טְמֵאִים
הֵם וּטְמֵאִים יִהְיוּ לָכֶם׃

Furthermore, just as משקין do not — מן התורה — convey טומאה, so אוכלין convey טומאה only in a limited way. For this is the rule: אין אוכל טמא עושה כיוצא בו, it does not convey טומאה to objects in its own category. Hence, אין אוכל מטמא אוכל; only משקין can become טמא by contact with אוכל טמא (*Pesachim* 14a; 18a–b). And according to the opinion that מדאורייתא there is no טומאת משקין at all, אוכלים — מן התורה — only receive but do not convey טומאה.

35 **תנור וכירים**. The ovens referred to here were movable earthenware vessels, like large pots without bottoms. They would attach them to the ground with clay and cover the walls with a coat of clay, which was called טפילה. The attachment of these ovens to the ground was only temporary, however. Hence, Scripture mentions them especially, to teach us that their temporary attachment to the ground does not cancel their status as movable vessels; rather, they are considered כלי חרס and as such are מקבלים טומאה: דסלקא דעתך אמינא כיון דחבריה בארעא כגופא דארעא דמי קמ״ל (*Shabbos* 125a; see רש״י, there, ד״ה נתנו על פי הבור and ד״ה ההוא לאידך גיסא.)

יתץ. נתץ always denotes the demolition of immovable objects, as in: ונתץ את הבית (below, 14:45). Scripture employs this term — instead of שבירה, the term employed (v. 33) in reference to כלים — to teach us that the oven and range are מחוסרי נתיצה, i.e., מחוברין (*Shabbos* 125a).

יתץ and similarly ואתו תשברו (v. 33) are not absolute commands, as though every earthenware כלי and תנור that becomes טמא must be demolished. Rather, Scripture immediately adds וטמאים יהיו לכם: as טמאים they may be used for חולין purposes — i.e., where there is no contact with מקדש וקדשיו. Only restoration of טהרה hinges on שבירת הכלי, or on נתיצת התנור.

כלי חרס have no טהרה במקוה as do all the other vessels, which accordingly are called כלי שטף. (This term derives from the language of Scripture below [15:12]: וכל כלי עץ ישטף במים, in contrast with וכלי חרס וגו׳ ישבר.) The foregoing is according to רש״י, *Chullin* 25a. According to רש״י, *Bechoros* 38a, however, only כלי עץ are termed כלי שטף (see תוספות, there).

Note further that all vessels — and not only כלי חרס — regain their טהרה via שבירה; and all vessels, while they are שבורים, cannot become טמאים. It is not necessary for the vessel to be completely broken; rather, it is sufficient that the vessel loses the form that makes it fit for its intended use, and so ceases to be a כלי. In this respect, all depends on the intended use of the כלי. If a כלי חרס was intended to contain solid food, a hole כמוציא זית — large enough for an olive to fall through — suffices. If the כלי was intended to contain liquids, a hole ככונס משקה or כמוציא משקה — large enough for liquid to enter or exit — suffices (כמוציא משקה is smaller than ככונס משקה). And if the כלי was intended to contain larger fruit, it loses its טומאה only on account of a hole כמוציא רימון, large enough for a pomegranate to fall through (*Shabbos* 95b).

Susceptibility to טומאה, and also continuation of the state of טומאה, are dependent, then, on the intended use of the vessel. The same applies to גמר מלאכה (the required degree of the vessel's completion, mentioned in the Commentary to v. 32), upon which susceptibility to טומאה depends: it, too, depends on the intended use of the vessel. For example, a hide that is to be used as a carpet is considered finished as soon as it is fit for this purpose, and thereupon becomes fit to receive טומאה. But if the hide is to be cut up for straps or shoes, it is not yet considered finished and is not מקבל טומאה. Similarly, a ring that is intended to be an ornament for a person is susceptible to טומאה; but if it is intended to be an ornament for an animal, it is not susceptible to טומאה. It is to this influence of a vessel's intended use that the principle stated in *Kelim* (25:9) relates: כל הכלים יורדין לידי טומאתן במחשבה ואינן עולין מידי טומאתן אלא בשנוי מעשה, שהמעשה מבטל מיד המעשה ומיד מחשבה, ומחשבה אינו מבטל לא מיד מעשה ולא מיד מחשבה. That is, מחשבה alone (designation for a certain purpose) suffices to render a vessel susceptible to טומאה; but once a vessel has been rendered susceptible to טומאה, and one now wishes to change its designation, it is necessary to express the change in designation by means of a physical change made in the vessel (see *Shabbos* 52b).

In *Chullin* 118a, the expression employed here in regard to כלי חרס, viz., טמאים יהיו **לכם**, and the similar expression used again in reference

לו אַךְ מַעְיָן וּבוֹר מִקְוֵה־מַיִם יִהְיֶה טָהוֹר וְנֹגֵעַ בְּנִבְלָתָם יִטְמָא׃

36 *But a spring and a cistern, a gathering of water, remains pure; however, anything that touches their carcass, even there, becomes impure.*

to זרעים, viz., טמא הוא **לכם** (v. 38), are expounded as follows: Vessels and foods are not only טמאים in themselves, but לכם — i.e., לכל שבצרכיכם; everything on them that is useful to man is fit to receive (להכניס), and even to convey (להוציא), טומאה. Hence, even the יד of a vessel or food — the handle or stalk by which it is held — is in this matter considered like the vessel or food itself; the יד, too, receives and conveys טומאה. Therefore, if טומאה comes in contact with ידות of כלים or אוכלים, the כלים or אוכלים become טמאים (=להכניס); and if the כלים or אוכלים are טמאים, and their ידות come in contact with another object, the object becomes טמא (=להוציא).

Obviously, in the case of a כלי חרס, the יד can only *convey* טומאה. For a כלי חרס can *receive* טומאה only מאוירו. Even if טומאה touches the outer surface of the vessel itself, the vessel does not become טמא; certainly, then, the vessel does not become טמא if טומאה touches only the יד of the vessel. (See תוספות, *Chullin* 24b, ד״ה וגבו טהור; see משנה למלך on הל׳ כלים, 17:1.)

36 **אך מעין ובור**. The word אך places the law of מעין ובור מקוה מים in contrast with the law of מים ומשקה בכל כלי of verse 34. This contrast relates to both of the *halachos* stated in verse 34 regarding משקים שאובים בכלים (liquids "drawn" in vessels) — namely, that (a) they are themselves susceptible to טומאה; and (b) they render אוכלים susceptible to טומאה. In contrast, it says here that מעין ובור מקוה מים יהיה טהור — i.e., springs and all waters similar to springs are not susceptible to טומאה and do not render other things susceptible to טומאה. This is the principle: All waters that are not drawn in a כלי, but, rather, are collected on the ground, מחוברים, without תפיסת ידי אדם, i.e., without being "held by man," are neither susceptible, nor render something else susceptible, to טומאה. (See תוספות, *Pesachim* 16a, ד״ה בשלמא, and ר״ש, *Machshirin* 4:5; *Toras Kohanim* to v. 34 says that מים שבבורות שיחין ומערות do not render other things

susceptible to טומאה because they are not מים שבכלי and are not תלושין מן הקרקע.)

Thus, initially we are told: if a dead שרץ falls into a vessel full of food or drink (vv. 33–35), the vessel and its contents become טמא. By contrast, if the שרץ falls into a מעין ובור מקוה מים, neither the cistern nor the water inside it becomes טמא. Nevertheless, ונגע בנבלתם יטמא — the dead שרץ in the מעין or מקוה has not lost its ability to render other things טמא. Although the water is not rendered טמא there, anything that touches the שרץ that is in the water becomes טמא.

Moreover, water in springs, and similarly water that is gathered in hollows in the earth without תפיסת ידי אדם, do not merely contrast with מים שאובים בכלי; they are contrary to it. Not only do they not receive, or render other things susceptible to, טומאה; they are also means to the restoration of טהרה. They are pure themselves, and they also purify others — just as טמא denotes not only a state of טומאה, but also the ability to render others טמא.

Elsewhere it is stated: ורחץ במים וטהר (below, 14:8); במים יובא וגו׳ וטהר (above, v. 32). From there we learn that man and vessels regain טהרה through immersion in water (see Commentary to v. 32). *Our* verse defines which are the waters that restore טהרה. Water does not effect טהרה unless it is similar to מעין ובור — i.e., collected in a hollow that is part of the earth, and not in a vessel such as a bathtub. Neither does water effect טהרה if it was drawn (שאובין) and subjected to תפיסת ידי אדם before reaching this hollow in the ground.

A further implication of the expression יהיה טהור is that הוייתן על ידי טהרה תהא — the water should not be conveyed to the מקוה by means of something that is susceptible to טומאה (*Zevachim* 25b). This halachah is not identical with the halachah of מים שאובים. On the one hand, waters received in a stone vessel are שאובים and פסולים for a מקוה — even though a כלי אבנים is not מקבל טומאה (see Commentary to vv. 32–33). On the other hand, a solid metal rail that is not hollowed out at all is unfit for leading water into the mikveh. Even though the rail has no בית קיבול, and the water on it does not become שאובים, the rail is מקבל טומאה in keeping with the law of פשוטי כלי מתכת (ibid.).

Water alone and no other liquid is fit for a mikveh (see *Chullin* 84a). The minimum amount of water in a valid mikveh is אמה על אמה ברום שלש אמות, one cubit square by three cubits deep — enough water to allow for the immersion of a person's entire body at one time. This

לז וְכִ֨י יִפֹּ֜ל מִנִּבְלָתָ֗ם עַל־כָּל־זֶ֥רַע זֵר֖וּעַ אֲשֶׁ֣ר יִזָּרֵ֑עַ טָה֖וֹר הֽוּא׃

37 *And if part of their carcass falls upon any sowing seed that is sown, it [the seed] remains pure.*

minimum amount of מים כשרים suffices to create the mikveh; it is then permissible to add as much מים שאובים as desired (see רמב״ם הל׳ מקואות, 4:1 and 6).

The water fit for immersion need not be spring water. מים חיים is required only in the case of a זב (below, 15:13). Our verse mentions ובור מקוה מים next to מעין; from this we learn that any water collected in cisterns or other cavities in the earth — e.g., rainwater — is fit for immersion, provided that the water meets the standards of the *halachos* stated above, and thus does not lose its elemental character.

There is only one difference between spring water and non-spring water: Non-spring water is fit only באשבורן, and not בזוחלין; that is, it is fit only when, as in a בור, it is standing in a closed-in place and not flowing. Spring water, however, is fit whether flowing or standing. Because of this difference it happens that at certain times and in certain conditions rivers, too, are unfit for immersion. For example: when rivers have swelled with winter's rain and melted snow, one must suspect that רבו נוטפין על הזוחלין, the flowing spring water in the river has been exceeded by the rainwater; and since rainwater is fit only באשבורן, the river is unfit for immersion (*Shabbos* 65b). According to another opinion (ibid.), however, נהרא מכיפיה מיברך — when the river is swollen by rain, the flow of spring water also increases; hence, זוחלין are always מרובין (see תוספות, ibid.).

37 **וכי יפל מנבלתם על כל זרע זרוע אשר יזרע**. In *Shabbos* (95b) the Gemara derives from here that what is planted in a perforated flower pot (עציץ נקוב) is treated as though it were attached to the ground (מחובר), so that it is not susceptible to הכשר טומאה. The Gemara says: ושאני לענין טומאה דהתורה ריבתה טהרה אצל זרעים שנאמר על כל זרע זרוע אשר יזרע. This can be construed to mean that the words זרע זרוע אשר יזרע refer to seeds that are attached to the ground (זרעים מחוברים); the repetition of the term זריעה (אשר יזרע) teaches that any planting — even in a perforated flower pot — gives a seed the status of being attached to the ground, so that it is not susceptible to הכשר.

Accordingly, the next verse — וכי יתן מים על זרע — refers to זרע אשר לא יזרע, i.e., detached seeds (זרעים תלושין), which are susceptible to הכשר.

The comments of *Toras Kohanim* to our verse can also be interpreted in this way — i.e., that the words אשר יזרע refer to seeds attached to the ground. For according to *Toras Kohanim*, the הכשר mentioned in verse 38 — i.e., that contact with water renders seeds susceptible to טומאה — applies only to מאכל אדם that is detached. Thus, the opposing case, in which contact with water does not render seeds susceptible to טומאה, is מאכל אדם that is attached — and that is the case of our verse (v. 37). (Perhaps the word זרוע is indicative of מאכל אדם, as in the verse: וְיִתְּנוּ־לָנוּ מִן־הַזֵּרֹעִים [*Daniyel* 1:12]. מאכל בהמה is thus excluded by obvious inference. The condition that water be put on the seed by man [בידי אדם], not by Heaven [בידי שמים], is alluded to in the wording, וכי יֻתַּן.)

In *Chullin* (117b, et seq.), however, the Gemara clearly understands the words זרע זרוע אשר יזרע to be referring to זרעים תלושין, seeds that are detached from the ground. In order to become susceptible to טומאה they require הכשר in the way described in the next verse.

The Gemara (ibid.) learns from the extra phrase, זרוע אשר יזרע, the following: The fruit's susceptibility to טומאה is not limited to where it was made ready for human consumption; rather, it is susceptible in the stage at which it is sown — together with its protective cover (שומר) and nipple (פיטמא). Moreover, the שומר is considered part of the fruit: its status is not merely like that of a יד (see Commentary to v. 35), contracting and conveying impurity, but it also combines (מצטרף) with the fruit towards the שיעור כביצה, the prescribed minimum for (contracting and) conveying טומאת אוכלין (see Commentary to v. 34). The Gemara says as follows: על כל זרע זרוע (אשר יזרע) - כדרך שבני אדם מוציאין לזריעה חטה בקליפתה ושעורה בקליפתה ועדשים בקליפתן — seed such as people take out to be sown: wheat in its husk, barley in its husk, lentils in their husks.

In accordance with this Gemara in *Chullin*, the Gemara in *Shabbos* (95b) cited above — התורה ריבתה טהרה אצל זרעים שנאמר על כל זרע זרוע אשר יזרע — is interpreted by רש״י to mean כדרך שאדם מוציא לזריעה למעוטי מחובר כל דהו. Clearly, the interpretation of רש״י should be explained as follows: הזרע אשר יזרע — seed that will, in the future, be sown, that has yet to be sown, remains טהור only for lack of being rendered fit by water (הכשר מים); but once it has been sown in any way — even if only in a perforated flower pot — it has the status of being attached to the ground, and is susceptible neither to הכשר nor to טומאה.

Nevertheless, it is possible that the words זרע זרוע אשר יזרע do actually refer to seeds already sown, and that the halachah stated in *Chullin* 117b — that the שומר is מצטרף toward the prescribed minimum for (contracting and) conveying טומאת אוכלין — is derived not from the additional words אשר יזרע but from the words זרע זרוע. The halachah, then, is derived as follows: זרע זרוע remains טהור, once it has been sown — i.e., once it has met the condition of אשר יזרע. But before it is sown, it is susceptible to טומאה in the זרע זרוע stage — i.e., כדרך שבני אדם מוציאין לזריעה חיטה בקליפתה וכו׳.

This interpretation — that our verse refers to seeds already sown — seems to us to be the correct one, and we have followed it in our translation; for *Toras Kohanim* derives from the words אשר יזרע טהור הוא that זרעים טמאים שנזרעו טהרו משהשרישו, seeds that are טמא regain their טהרה as soon as they are sown and have taken root. Thus, plants rooted in the ground are not susceptible to טומאה; moreover, even seeds that have become טמא become טהור again — once they are sown and have taken root.

In any case, we learn from verses 36 and 37 that anything that is מחובר to the ground — e.g., spring water and plants of the soil — is removed from the sphere of טומאה; moreover, השרשה בארץ and טבילה במים restore טהרה: הארץ מעלה את הטמאים מטומאתן והמקוה מעלה את הטמאים מטומאתן (*Toras Kohanim*). Hence, כלים שנעשו לקרקע ותשמישן עם הקרקע, things that are made to be permanently fixed to the ground and are to be used only while joined to the ground — e.g., a metal drainpipe (צינור) — are not susceptible to טומאה (see *Kelim* 11:2; ר״ש there). In some cases, the law is that תלוש ולבסוף חיברו, a detached object that is later attached to the ground, כחיבור דמי. In applying this law, however, one must distinguish between the various *halachos* (see *Chullin* 16a). Whether a vessel fixed to the ground is to be considered a כלי or not depends on whether חקקו ולבסוף קבעו or קבעו ולבסוף חקקו; that is, whether the material out of which the vessel is made — e.g., a piece of wood — was first fixed to the ground and then hollowed out to form a receptacle, or first possessed the form necessary for it to be a כלי and then was fixed to the ground (see *Bava Basra* 66a).

Included in the concept of זריעה is an additional halachah: Although אוכלין ומשקין have no טהרה במקוה, there is טהרה for water that has become טמא. A vessel full of such water is lowered into a mikveh, until the mikveh water is in contact with the water in the vessel. Through this

38 *But if water has been put on seed, and part of their carcass falls upon it, it is impure to you.*

לח וְכִ֤י יֻתַּן־מַ֙יִם֙ עַל־זֶ֔רַע וְנָפַ֥ל מִנִּבְלָתָ֖ם עָלָ֑יו טָמֵ֥א ה֖וּא לָכֶֽם׃ ס

השקה the טמא water regains its טהרה; it is as though the water is "sown" in the earth, and thereby regains its pure, elemental character (see *Pesachim* 34b; *Beitzah* 17b, רש״י, ad loc., ד״ה ושוין). According to the רא״ש (*Bava Kama* 67a) this is also the explanation of the halachah, mentioned above, that it is permissible to add מים שאובים to a mikveh of ארבעים סאה; for the זריעה frees the water of its שאובים character.

38 **וכי יתן וגו׳**. If Scripture had said here וכי יבוא מים על זרע — as in verse 34 — this would have indicated the absence of any intention; but it says כי יתן. Now, נתינה implies an intentional act. On the other hand, the verb appears here in the הפעל form, יֻתַּן, which denotes merely that an act was performed, but does not refer to the person by whose will the act was performed. יֻתַּן, then, indicates an intermediate case where both elements are present: the concept of נתינה which implies intention, and the הפעל form which denotes lack of intention.

Hence, the Sages expound: כי יותן דומיא דכי יתן, מה יתן דניחא ליה אף יותן דניחא ליה. That is to say, the act is not performed by man, but he is interested that it occur. An example is rain that wets fruit, and the owner is pleased that the fruit is washed (*Kiddushin* 59b). Even if he is not pleased about the wetting of the fruit, if he is pleased about the presence of מים תלושים the law of כי יותן applies. For example, הכופה קערה על הכותל בשביל שתודח, if one places a vessel out in the rain so that it be washed, and the rainwater splashes off the vessel and onto the fruit, even though he does not intend that the water reach the fruit, הרי זה בכי יותן (*Machshirin* 4:3; *Chullin* 16a). Hence the principle (*Machshirin* 1:1): כל משקה שתחילתו לרצון אף על פי שאין סופו לרצון, או שסופו לרצון אף על פי שאין תחלתו לרצון, הרי זה בכי יותן. Perhaps it can be said that this principle is indicated by the different expressions in verses 34 and 38. אוכל אשר יבוא עליו מים denotes that the fruit is wetted without one's intention; this is סופו שלא ברצון. By contrast, וכי יתן מים על זרע denotes that the water is put intentionally; this is תחילתו ברצון.

Liquid is not considered תחילתו ברצון unless a person needs it for the

39 *And if any animal that is fit for your consumption dies, he that touches its carcass shall be impure until evening.*	לט וְכִ֤י יָמוּת֙ מִן־הַבְּהֵמָ֔ה אֲשֶׁר־הִ֥יא לָכֶ֖ם לְאָכְלָ֑ה הַנֹּגֵ֥עַ בְּנִבְלָתָ֖הּ יִטְמָ֥א עַד־הָעָֽרֶב׃
40 *Whoever eats of its carcass must wash his garments and is impure until evening; even one who only carries its carcass must wash his garments and is impure until evening.*	מ וְהָֽאֹכֵל֙ מִנִּבְלָתָ֔הּ יְכַבֵּ֥ס בְּגָדָ֖יו וְטָמֵ֣א עַד־הָעָ֑רֶב וְהַנֹּשֵׂא֙ אֶת־נִבְלָתָ֔הּ יְכַבֵּ֥ס בְּגָדָ֖יו וְטָמֵ֥א עַד־הָעָֽרֶב׃

sake of a דבר תלוש (see *Toras Kohanim* to v. 34), as in the given example: לצורך הקערה. "תלוש" is defined, in this respect, in the widest sense of the term: even תלוש ולבסוף חיברו (see above) is considered תלוש — e.g., כותל בנין, a wall built of stones (see *Chullin* 16a).

The הכשר of אוכלין need occur only once; once they come in contact with משקין המכשירין (see Commentary to v. 34), they are מקבלין טומאה from then onward — even if the liquid upon them dries up (see *Bava Metzia* 22a).

טמא הוא לכם — see Commentary to verse 35.

39–40 These verses deal with טומאת נבלת בהמה טהורה and טומאת אבר מן החי. It does not say here וכי תמות בהמה וגו׳ הנוגע וגו׳, but, rather, וכי ימות מן הבהמה. *Chullin* 128b explains that this expression denotes a partial מיתה, where a limb of the living is severed and "dies" (אבר מן החי). At the same time, this expression limits the scope of הבהמה אשר היא לכם לאכלה: מקצת בהמה מטמאה ומקצת בהמה אינה מטמאה, ואיזו זו טרפה ששחטה. This means as follows:

The verses that deal with בהמה טמאה (24ff.) cite the term נבילה without any qualification. Accordingly, a forbidden animal that dies in any manner — even through שחיטה — is treated as a נבילה.

In the case of בהמה אשר היא לכם לאכלה it is different. Here, Scripture qualifies the law of נבילה with the condition וכי ימות; that is, an animal is not accorded the status of נבילה unless it suffers a מיתה that does not render it לכם לאכלה, fit for our consumption. Now, if Scripture had stated this condition absolutely, then even a שחיטה שאינה ראויה — a שחיטה that does not render the meat permissible to eat — would have been considered such a מיתה; and even a טריפה שנשחטה would have been accorded the status of נבילה, since its שחיטה did not render it permissible to eat. The word מן, however, limits the concept of such a מיתה: Only a מיתה that has no power to effect היתר אכילה results in נבילה; but שחיטה, which is *the* means of effecting היתר אכילה, precludes נבילה status. This is true of every שחיטה, even when the היתר אכילה is impeded for other reasons — provided that the animal is of the species אשר היא לכם לאכלה, and its שחיטה is meaningful as regards היתר אכילה. Hence, שחיטה מטהרת טריפה מטומאתה (see *Zevachim* 69b).

If, however, the act of שחיטה was not performed as prescribed; or if the animal's windpipe and esophagus, upon which the act of שחיטה is performed, were wounded, and as a result it is impossible to carry out שחיטה — in these cases the animal dies without שחיטה and contracts טומאת נבילה.

There are even cases of נבילה מחיים — e.g., נשברה מפרקת ורוב בשר עמה. Such an animal is considered dead even while it is still alive (*Chullin* 21a, 32b; ש״ך on יו״ד 33:3).

The concept of נבילה relates only to the muscles and nerves — not to the bones, horns, claws, etc. (*Chullin* 117b). Perhaps it can be said that the concept of נבל — the force that withers and dies — applies only to the active part of the body, to the part that is capable of sensing and moving. Bones, etc., comprise merely the passive frame of the body, which is set in motion and activated by the powers of the muscles and nerves. Death, therefore, manifests itself only in the muscles and nerves.

Previously, in our Commentary to 7:24–27, we explained the halachah that חלב נבילה and דם נבילה are not טמאים.

והאכל וגו׳ והנשא וגו׳. נבילה is מטמא במגע ובמשא, as explained above (vv. 24–28) in regard to נבלת בהמה טמאה (see Commentary there). Thus, the very moving (משא) of the נבילה is מטמא בגדים. It would have been superfluous, then, to repeat this in regard to אכילת נבילה, were it not that we thereby learn two additional things:

First, we learn that טומאה בלועה is not מטמא. An object can render the body טמא, only through external contact or external movement; but the presence of the object inside the body does not render the body טמא. For it says here that האוכל מנבלתה — and he could eat נבילה just

41 *And every creeping thing that creeps upon the earth is an abomination; it shall not be eaten.*

42 *Whatever goes upon the belly and whatever goes upon four legs or*

מא וְכָל־הַשֶּׁרֶץ הַשֹּׁרֵץ עַל־הָאָרֶץ שֶׁקֶץ הוּא לֹא יֵאָכֵל׃

מב כֹּל הוֹלֵךְ עַל־גָּחוֹן וְכֹל ׀ הוֹלֵךְ עַל־אַרְבַּע עַד כָּל־מַרְבֵּה רַגְלַיִם

before sunset (סמוך לשקיעת החמה) — can attain טהרה immediately, despite the fact that the נבילה is still present within him. (Even if one ate נבילה early in the day, he can become a טבול יום [a שני] immediately after the טבילה; but if טומאה בלועה were to convey טומאה, he would again become a ראשון at once. See *Chullin* 71a.)

Second, we learn that for מגע ומשא the prescribed minimum is the שיעור אכילה — namely, כזית: ליתן שיעור לנוגע ולנושא כאוכל מה אוכל בכזית אף נוגע ונושא בכזית (*Niddah* 42b).

41 **וכל השרץ וגו׳**. As we stated previously (in our Commentary to vv. 24–25), verse 41 is the direct continuation of verse 20, and it continues with the laws concerning prohibited creatures. השרץ השרץ על הארץ includes all wingless insects and worms, whether they were created on land, or were created in water and then left that element (see Commentary above, vv. 10–11). This includes all worms created במחובר — in fruit on the tree or in stalks. If they are created בתלוש, in things that are detached from the ground, they are classified as שרץ השורץ על הארץ only when they have left the element in which they were produced (see *Chullin* 67b).

Although כל היוצא מן הטמא טמא, and, hence, ביצי עופות טמאים אסורות (see Commentary above, v. 4), nevertheless, the איסור of שרץ begins only with the actual formation of the שרץ-form (ריקום): In the case of התליע בתלוש the איסור of שרץ begins only when the שרץ leaves the element in which it was produced, and ביצי שרץ are not included in the איסור (see תוספות, *Chullin* 64a, ד״ה שאם ריקמה ואכלה).

42 **לא תאכלום**. Scripture here repeats the prohibition against eating these creatures, and the Gemara (*Yevamos* 114a) derives from here that it is

לְכָל־הַשֶּׁרֶץ הַשֹּׁרֵץ עַל־הָאָרֶץ לֹא תֹאכְלוּם כִּי־שֶׁקֶץ הֵם:
וא"ו רבתי

more, of all creeping things that creep upon the earth — you shall not eat them because they are an abomination.

מג אַל־תְּשַׁקְּצוּ אֶת־נַפְשֹׁתֵיכֶם בְּכָל־הַשֶּׁרֶץ הַשֹּׁרֵץ וְלֹא תִטַּמְּאוּ בָּהֶם וְנִטְמֵתֶם בָּם:

43 *Do not make your souls abominable through all the creeping things that creep, and do not make yourselves impure through them; you would be completely ruined through them.*

prohibited to give forbidden food to minors: להזהיר הגדולים על הקטנים. *Toras Kohanim* derives this prohibition from the expression לא יֵאָכֵל (v. 41), לא יֵאָכְלוּ (v. 13): לחייב את המאכיל כאוכל — the מאכיל is liable for causing forbidden food to be eaten (see קרבן אהרן, v. 13).

43 **אל תשקצו את נפשתיכם וגו׳**. This warning concludes the laws of the forbidden שרצים. A similar warning is stated also in regard to the forbidden mammals and birds: ולא תשקצו את נפשתיכם בבהמה ובעוף וגו׳ (below, 20:25).

We have shown, in our Commentary on verses 10–11, that the term שקץ denotes the opposite of things moral. If, then, we are warned here not to allow our souls to become שקץ, the assumption must be that we are obligated to resemble a higher moral Being. That is to say, our nature must enable us to become like Him and to belong to Him. We are therefore warned not to bring ourselves into opposition to this Being; for, otherwise, He will not regard us as His intimates who are worthy of being associated with Him, but will reject us in disgust. We must maintain our resemblance to Him, so that we be worthy of His choice, His love, His longing, and His satisfaction. We must not make ourselves שקץ before Him, but merit that He dwell among us and not reject us (see below, 26:11). This higher Being is none other than God. He Himself points out — in verses 44–45 — the resemblance, as it were, between Himself and ourselves, and He stresses that this resemblance is the basis of our moral mission and the reason for our ability to accomplish it.

Our verse warns us of two effects of eating forbidden foods: שקץ (אל תשקצו את נפשתיכם) and טומאה (ולא תטמאו בהם). The objects affected by these two are not identical. ולא תטמאו relates to the entire personality; אל תשקצו relates to נפשתיכם. The נפש is none other than the will, which, in accepting or rejecting, manifests the essential power of life (see Commentary to *Bereshis* 1:20). שיקוץ נפש is the focusing of man's desires on aims that are antithetical to God's Torah — the Torah being the expression of God's Will. Thus, שיקוץ נפש is man desiring that which is abhorrent and detestable to God. The eating of מאכלות אסורות increases the desire for forbidden pleasures.

At the same time, the eating of מאכלות אסורות brings טומאה to the whole personality. We have already explained several times that טומאה signifies the lack of moral freedom (see Commentary above, 5:13 and 7:19–21). It signifies the paralysis of the free, moral will, which is charged with controlling the power of desire. Free will is a basic condition for קדושה, holiness, which is the ultimate purpose of moral perfection; and only he is holy who is ready to carry out — joyfully and unquestioningly — the dictates of the Divine Will. Free will must oppose base desire, which leads man on immoral paths; but the eating of מאכלות אסורות weakens this will.

Such eating, then, destroys our spiritual being in two respects: It leads to שיקוץ נפש, arousing and increasing immoral desires; and it leads to טומאה, paralyzing the free, moral will, which is charged with controlling these desires. It is also possible that the טומאה is the result of the שיקוץ. Now, where two destructive influences, one in the positive and the other in the negative, are unleashed, there is danger that finally —

ונטמתם בם. We noted previously (7:19–21) the phonetic relation of the root טמא to דמע and טמע. In Rabbinic Hebrew, דמע denotes mixture; טמע denotes complete absorption so that no trace remains, where something is nullified by a larger quantity of something different. We also mentioned there the root טמה, from which — in Rabbinic Hebrew — derives the word טמיון, meaning complete ruin. Here, ונטמתם derives from טמה and not from טמא. In our view טמא denotes the beginning, and טמה the completion, of the paralysis of the free moral faculty. טמה, then, denotes the last stage in the loss of moral freedom. Instead of being in control, man succumbs to physical compulsion. Man enters the first stage of טומאה by his own free will; hence תטמאו, in the reflexive form. The last

44 *For I,* God, *am your God; therefore sanctify yourselves, and then you will become holy, for I am holy, and do not make your souls impure through all the creeping things that move upon the earth.*

מד כִּ֣י אֲנִ֣י יְהֹוָה֮ אֱלֹֽהֵיכֶם֒
וְהִתְקַדִּשְׁתֶּם֙ וִהְיִיתֶ֣ם קְדֹשִׁ֔ים כִּ֥י
קָד֖וֹשׁ אָ֑נִי וְלֹ֤א תְטַמְּאוּ֙ אֶת־
נַפְשֹׁ֣תֵיכֶ֔ם בְּכָל־הַשֶּׁ֖רֶץ הָֽרֹמֵ֥שׂ
עַל הָאָֽרֶץ׃ מפטיר

stages, however, are automatic consequences. Man is merely passive in their regard; hence ונטמתם, in the passive form.

בכל השרץ השרץ — without the addition על הארץ — includes all the שרצים: שרץ העוף, שרץ המים, and שרץ הארץ.

44 **כי אני ה׳ אלקיכם** provides the reason for the preceding warning אל תשקצו and ולא תטמאו: I, ה׳, am your אלקים; that is to say, I, the One Who leads mankind to moral perfection in the future, and Who draws near to you now, in the present, in order to achieve this aim — I am the One to Whom you belong in your lives, your deeds, and your refraining from doing, and you are therefore obligated to guard your souls and to fulfill your destiny.

והתקדשתם, "sanctify yourselves"; focus all your energies upon yourselves — subjugate all opposing forces — in order to be ready to fulfill God's moral law.

והייתם קדשים, "then you will become holy" — you will have to struggle less and less, the opposition within you will gradually disappear. Finally, you will fulfill My moral law without struggle but with joy, and all that is low and corrupt will be loathsome in your sight.

כי קדוש אני: for this holiness, in its absolute and unfettered ideal state, is what characterizes My Being; this holiness is both the basis for your mission to become holy and the reason for your fitness to achieve it. Because קדוש אני, therefore והתקדשתם, and hence והייתם קדשים. *My holiness is the basis for* והתקדשתם: Because I am קדוש, those who are close to Me are obligated to become קדושים like Me. *And My holiness is the cause of* והייתם קדשים: Because I am קדוש, you *can* be קדושים. The Divine breath that I have breathed into you raises you above all physical compulsion, lets you participate in My holiness, and endows you with moral freedom. *Therefore, you must be as God:* you must rule over the microcosm of forces that I have placed under your control in your sensory nature, just as I, autonomous God, rule over all the forces in the macrocosm. Autonomous, personal God is the Guarantor of autonomous, personal man. Because I am holy, you *shall* and *can* be holy!

ולא תטמאו את נפשתיכם וגו׳. For the first stage, that of והתקדשתם, when the sensual desires still offer resistance, and one must overcome them through awareness of moral duty — for this stage we were warned (v. 43) אל תשקצו and ולא תטמאו, with אל תשקצו referring to sensual desire, and ולא תטמאו to moral awareness. Refrain from eating forbidden foods, so that base desire not be aroused through destructive enticements, and so that free, moral willpower not be paralyzed.

Now, when the stage of והייתם קדשים has been reached, the warning is repeated. For one should not imagine that these *halachos* are relevant only at the lower stage; that only he who is still torn and struggling to attain moral perfection is bound by the prohibition of מאכלות אסורות, but that once moral refinement is reached, and one is no longer torn, and the נפש — including its sensual desires — aspires only to what is holy, then the prohibition of מאכלות אסורות no longer applies. Hence, after the statement והייתם קדשים — after the נפש has already sanctified itself — the warning is repeated. It is now phrased: ולא תטמאו את נפשתיכם וגו׳. Even after you have attained the level of קדושים, be careful not to eat מאכלות אסורות, lest you make your souls טמא again, and lest they lose their joy in holiness! Such holiness can be maintained only by observing the same discipline through which the sanctity of sensual life was attained.

בכל השרץ הרמש על הארץ. From the change in expression — רומש instead of שורץ — *Toras Kohanim* (as interpreted by the רמב״ם in הל׳ מאכלות אסורות, 2:13) derives here that even שרצים that do not reproduce sexually (שאינם פרים ורבים) are prohibited. For the expression שרץ also implies multiplication by means of sexual reproduction; compare ושרצו בארץ ופרו ורבו על הארץ (*Bereshis* 8:17; cf. also *Bereshis* 9:7 and *Shemos* 1:7). רמש, by contrast, denotes merely movement by the feet, and — as opposed to שרץ — does not indicate the manner of creation.

45 *For I,* God, *am He Who leads you up out of the land of Egypt, to be your God; therefore be holy, for I am holy.*

מה כִּ֣י ׀ אֲנִ֣י יְהֹוָ֗ה הַֽמַּעֲלֶ֤ה אֶתְכֶם֙
מֵאֶ֣רֶץ מִצְרַ֔יִם לִהְיֹ֥ת לָכֶ֖ם
לֵאלֹהִ֑ים וִהְיִיתֶ֣ם קְדֹשִׁ֔ים כִּ֥י
קָד֖וֹשׁ אָֽנִי׃

46 *This is the teaching with regard to animals and birds and all living creatures that move in water, and for every creature that creeps upon the earth.*

מו זֹ֣את תּוֹרַ֤ת הַבְּהֵמָה֙ וְהָע֔וֹף וְכֹל֙
נֶ֣פֶשׁ הַֽחַיָּ֔ה הָֽרֹמֶ֖שֶׂת בַּמָּ֑יִם וּלְכָל־
נֶ֖פֶשׁ הַשֹּׁרֶ֥צֶת עַל־הָאָֽרֶץ׃

47 *To distinguish between the impure and the pure, and between the living creatures that may be eaten and the living creatures that shall not be eaten.*

מז לְהַבְדִּ֕יל בֵּ֥ין הַטָּמֵ֖א וּבֵ֣ין הַטָּהֹ֑ר
וּבֵ֤ין הַֽחַיָּה֙ הַֽנֶּאֱכֶ֔לֶת וּבֵין֙ הַֽחַיָּ֔ה
אֲשֶׁ֖ר לֹ֥א תֵאָכֵֽל׃ פפפ

45 **המעלה אתכם וגו׳**. The redemption from Egypt is to be an "elevation" from the moral decadence of Egypt. The introduction to פרשת עריות (below, chap. 18) also mentions this decadence and warns against it. The goal of this ascent which began with the exodus from Egypt is להיות לכם לאלקים, and the whole range of requirements stemming from this goal are capsulized in the mitzvah of והייתם קדשים כי קדוש אני (see Commentary to v. 44). Moral freedom is the purpose of national freedom; with the former, the latter stands or falls.

46–47 **זאת תורת וגו׳**. The laws which are summarized here are arranged above in a different order — namely, mammals, aquatic creatures, and birds. Here, however, עוף follows בהמה.

Above, they are arranged according to a formal didactic order: First, Scripture mentions those creatures whose legal status depends on סימנים — mammals and fish; only then does Scripture mention birds, which must be enumerated according to their various kinds.

Here, they are arranged in natural order, from higher to lower creatures. The earlier a creature is mentioned, the greater the intensity of its life. This greater or lesser degree of intensity of life is reflected also in the laws of שחיטה (see *Chullin* 27b): שחיטה of a בהמה requires cutting through two סימנים, the windpipe and the esophagus; שחיטה of an עוף requires cutting only one; and דגים require no שחיטה at all.

The summarizing statement זאת תורת interrelates all the forbidden creatures. The warning of the preceding verses — which is directed primarily at אכילת שרצים — applies, then, to all the creatures.

בין הטמא ובין הטהר: between בהמה and the שמונה שרצים, whose נבילה is מטמא, and עופות, דגים and שאר שרצים, whose נבילה is not מטמא; between טריפה שנשחטה and נבילה (v. 39). Also, as *Toras Kohanim* says here, one must maintain the fine boundary line that separates טמא from טהור and בין שנשחט רובו של קנה לנשחט חציו; וכמה היא בין רובו לחציו? מלא שערה :כשר.

Let us now summarize what the Torah says about the foods that it forbids: They are טמאות and are termed שקץ. Eating them leads to שיקוץ נפש, טומאה, and טמיון; conscientious observance of the prohibition against them leads to התקדשות. The point of view of the whole section — אני ה׳ אלקיכם, והייתם קדשים כי קדוש אני — occupies the whole moral pinnacle that is the purpose of the redemption from Egypt: המעלה אתכם וגו׳.

In light of all this it is clear, beyond any doubt, that the reason for these laws is not bodily health, but the *moral* integrity of our souls. All the things that are said about the "dietary regulations" of Mosaic law, in order to justify the assertion that these laws had importance only at a certain time and in certain places, are refuted by the words of the Torah itself. These laws are not intended to preserve the health of our bodies, but to ensure the spiritual and moral health of our souls. They guard the sensual aspects of our personality from unrestrained animalistic passion, and keep our moral and spiritual will from becoming dulled and unresponsive. They impress upon us the basic prerequisite for our ability to fulfill our mission: We must keep our physical bodies on the narrow path of living purity; *that* is what will enable the body to be the obedient servant of the nobler part of our being.

Previously, in חורב (chap. 68), we focused on this meaning of the dietary laws; we also mentioned that experience shows that food should be chosen based on consideration of moral values.

It is a demonstrated truth that the body exerts a great influence on the spirit and will. The lie of materialism is that it goes further to presume, on the basis of this truth, that the spirit and will are merely attributes of the material; the phenomena of spirit and will are merely the material products of material agencies and have no reality independent of the material.

In view of the basic truth that the body exerts a great influence on the spirit and will, how understandable, then, is the Torah's concern about the food we eat. The Torah does not identify power or spirit with the material; rather, the Torah views the material as an instrument that performs the work of the spirit. The spirit's *existence* transcends the material and material power, but the spirit's *activity* in our earthly lives depends upon them. How understandable, then, is the strict dietary regimen to which we are bound. For the spirit's "instrument" is constantly renewed by food materials. Hence, we must provide it only with those materials that sustain its ability to serve the spirit. We must make it easier for the spirit to control and use this instrument for the sake of fulfilling its mission (cf. our Commentary to *Bereshis* 1:27, 29, 30; 9:3–4; and chap. 17, on the dignity of the human body, on the dietary laws, and on the great importance Judaism attaches to the sanctity of the body).

This chapter (verses 11, 24–40, as well as the concluding verse 47) combines the teaching of טומאת מגע and the teaching of טומאת מאכלות אסורות; or, as they are called in *Toras Kohanim* according to our interpretation (above, v. 4): the teaching of טומאת קדושות and the teaching of טומאת גוויות. Both were given for one purpose: The laws of טומאת מגע symbolize what the laws of טומאת מאכלות אסורות help to actualize; and the laws of טומאת מאכלות אסורות preserve the ability to actualize what is symbolized by the laws of טומאת מגע.

To be sure, one does not become holy simply by observing the dietary laws; but one can achieve this more easily if he observes these laws. Moreover, he commits an offense against his own body, which belongs to God, and he denies the whole purpose of the redemption from Egypt, if he takes the dietary laws lightly. As the Sages say: חמורים שרצים שכל המודה במצות שרצים מודה ביציאת מצרים וכל הכופר במצות שרצים כופר ביציאת מצרים (*Toras Kohanim* according to the ילקוט; cf. ואנשי קדש וגו׳, *Shemos* 22:30, and our Commentary there).

The observance of the dietary laws merely gives one the ability to attain holiness, but one cannot actually attain holiness unless he is conscious of this ability and recognizes the task for which this ability has been given to him. The task is written in the Torah, and is expressed symbolically by מקדש וקדשיו. The laws of טומאת מגע constantly renew consciousness of the ability to attain holiness. We will now attempt to set these laws in order — to the extent in which they appear in this chapter; we will survey them and explain their meaning.

Every line in the laws of טומאת מגע testifies that טומאה is not a mystical, magical, noxious emanation — imperceptible but real — which is transmitted to persons and objects by contact with a corpse, a carcass, or an unwell individual. Rather, the subjects and relationships treated in these laws represent ideas and conceptions; it is they that are brought into focus by means of the laws of טומאת מגע.

Remember, for example, that not every כלי is מקבל טומאה; rather, it all depends on the material and shape of the כלי. כלי אבנים, כלי אדמה, and the like are טהורים. פשוטי כלי מתכות are טמאים, while פשוטי כלי עץ are טהורים. A כלי is מקבל טומאה only when its manufacture is completed so that it is fit for its intended purpose. But the intended purpose of a כלי depends entirely on the מחשבה, the intention of its owner: כל הכלים יורדין לידי טומאתן במחשבה (*Kelim* 25:9). When a כלי is damaged and rendered unfit for its intended use, it becomes טהור again. טומאת משא — where applicable — is more severe than טומאת מגע, even if the נושא causes the movement of the טומאה-conveying object when distant from it. From all this it is clear to us that טומאה is not something concrete that clings to the material, but is an idea, a notion, a conception. It is connected with relationships of people and things, and if these relationships cease or do not develop, טומאה, too, ceases or does not take effect.

Let us try, then, to identify the ideas that are expressed by the laws of טומאה appearing in this chapter. This chapter deals only with טומאת מגע — to the exclusion of טומאה היוצאת מגופו, which is discussed in the ensuing chapters.

The discussion here is of טומאת נבילה ושרץ. The prototype of all טומאה — and especially of טומאת נבילה ושרץ — is undoubtedly טומאת מת, the human corpse. All the laws stated here regarding טומאת נבילה and טומאת שרץ apply also to טומאת מת, whereas טומאת מת exceeds the former טומאות in that it entails טומאת שבעה, הזיית שלישי ושביעי, and טומאת אהל, and is subject to the principle that חרב הרי הוא כחלל, as explained in *Bemidbar*, chapter 19.

We have noted several times that the human corpse calls attention to a fact that is liable to foster the misconception that is called טומאה. For the fact is that, when a corpse lies before us, a human being has succumbed to the compelling physical forces of nature.

But the following is also true: The corpse we see before us is not the whole man, nor even his essence. For man's true being cannot be touched by the power of physical forces. It departed before the body was relinquished to the earthly forces of nature, as the body was merely its earthly garment.

Moreover, man, endowed with a godly nature, rules himself freely. As long as this free man was present in his body, which now succumbs to the forces of nature, the body, too, was freed from the coercive power of the physical and was uplifted — with all its capacities for action and also for pleasure — into the realm of moral freedom. Man, ruling his body in godlike freedom, fulfilled with his body the moral mission of his life. In short, death begins only with death. As long as there is life, man rules even his sensuous body, with all its powers, drives, and faculties. Free from all bodily coercion and compulsion, he directs his body in godlike freedom in order to fulfill the duties of the laws of morality.

These are the truths that must be impressed upon the mind of the living person who faces the phenomena of death. For whereas death brings to mind man's frailty and his submission to the forces of nature, man must stand tall in the midst of the physical world, proud of his vital freedom; he must immunize himself against the doctrine of materialism, which undermines all morality and draws its wisdom from post-mortem examinations.

Just as the human corpse gives rise to the notion of man's lack of freedom, so is this notion prompted by any body that resembles the human form and that has succumbed to death. Hence, טומאת נבילה applies to all the higher land mammals, whose bodies resemble the human body.

Only eight of the lower creatures (שרצים), however, are טמאים. Those among the שמונה שרצים that are known to us — the weasel, mouse, and mole — also belong to the class of mammals; and, as we noted in commenting on the text, all eight, apparently, are vertebrates. Thus, their bodies are not too dissimilar to that of man. Our theory is that the שמונה שרצים are those creatures that live in proximity to man. We are aware of their activity and are used to seeing them full of life. Hence, their carcasses embody for us, to a certain extent, the active force that has withered and died. The טומאה of שרצים is nevertheless lighter than that of נבילה, as they are מטמא only במגע but not במשא.

Creatures that do not live in the same element as man, i.e., on land, and are unlike him both in their bodily form and way of life do not remind us, even when they are dead, of a dead human body. Hence, fish and all aquatic creatures are excluded from טומאת נבילה. Birds, the inhabitants of the air, are also excluded — with the single exception of נבלת עוף טהור בבית הבליעה (see Commentary below, 17:15).

The law of a human corpse differs, though, from the law of an animal carcass. In the case of a human corpse, טומאה applies also to the bones, the passive part of the body. In the case of an animal carcass, however, טומאה applies only to the muscles and nerves, the active parts, whose vital activity has withered and died. We noted earlier that this halachah is indicated by the very term נבילה (see Commentary above, vv. 39–40). We also mentioned the halachah that דם and חלב are excluded from טומאת נבילה, and we noted the deep connection between this halachah and the entire teaching of טומאה and טהרה (see Commentary above, 7:26–27). In the case of the lower creatures (שרצים), which include cold-blooded amphibians such as the צב and לטאה, the blood is on the same level as the flesh, אין דמם חלוק מבשרם (see Commentary above, 11:29).

These are the things that are rendered טמא by contact with a נבילה: אדם, כלים, אוכלין ומשקין — i.e., man and those articles that characterize his personality in its appearance (clothing), aspirations (food and drink), and accomplishments (utensils). Once these have been rendered טמא by contact with a נבילה, they are to be excluded from מקדש וקדשיו. For the נבילה brings to mind the body's submission to the physical power of death; מקדש וקדשיו, by contrast, represent the moral mission of life. The meaning of the exclusion from מקדש וקדשיו is as follows: Life's mission, symbolized by מקדש וקדשיו, requires man's freedom from the compelling force of nature. Man — with all the aspects of his humanity, with all כליו אוכליו ומשקיו — must elevate himself to the lofty heights of moral freedom. The cornerstone of מקדש וקדשיו is man's freedom in his being, creativity, and enjoyment (cf. Commentary above, 5:13).

מגע. A person is rendered טמא only by contact with the outer parts of his body; מגע בית הסתרים is not מטמא (see Commentary above, 11:24). The whole parallel that is drawn between man and the body of an animal — and also between the living man and the dead one — is merely external and imaginary. This parallel gains a semblance of reality because man and animal exist on common ground; they "touch each other," as it were, on the earthly ground which is the basis of all earthly existence. This concept of belonging to the earth — that man and animal alike are dependent upon the earth for their worldly existence — is essential to the concept of טומאה. Hence, טומאה is not fully operative unless the טומאה-conveying object rests on the ground: ספק טומאה צפה טהור (see Commentary to vv. 29–31).

משא. If a person moves a נבילה directly or indirectly — even if he does not touch it — he contracts טומאת משא; for he comes in contact with it not with his mere being, but through his activity. More precisely, his activity comes in contact with the נבילה.

Hence, not only does the person become טמא, but so does every כלי (including a garment) that he touches and every garment that he wears when moving the נבילה. For, here, it is *active* man who relates to the נבילה. That is to say, it is man with the full force of his personality — with the clothes of his human appearance and with the tools of his human creativity — who is affected by the טומאה notion that is prompted by the נבילה. For this reason, even the clothes that are upon him, as well as any clothes or utensils that he touches when moving the נבילה, become טמא like himself on account of the נבילה, and like himself they become ראשון לטומאה.

Only אדם, another person, and כלי חרס are exempt from this טומאה בחיבורין; and it is likely — as we noted earlier on verses 24–25 — that אוכלין ומשקין are מדאורייתא exempt also. Clearly, a person is not a subordinate part of the personality of another, and does not represent him as "בגדיו." As for כלי חרס, together with אוכלין ומשקין they constitute the realm of man's *enjoyment*, a realm which is secondary for *active* man, who comes to the fore during משא.

כלים. Let us attempt to understand the difference between various objects in so far as their susceptibility or non-susceptibility to טומאה is concerned. Toward this end we must grasp an idea whose very opposite appears — at first glance — to be more credible.

Since the concept of טומאה is so disheartening and the concept of טהרה is so refreshing and uplifting, one would expect to find susceptibility to טומאה among the lower things, and immunity to טומאה among the higher things. And yet the opposite is the case:

Susceptibility to טומאה begins the moment an object belongs to the sphere of man's moral development, the sphere in which man's moral freedom must enable him to transcend a merely physical existence. The guiding principle of this free moral development is taken from מקדש וקדשיו. טומאה — the epitome of the lack of freedom — is antithetical to this sphere. Hence, any object that comes in contact with טומאה must be kept away from מקדש וקדשיו.

By contrast, an object that belongs to the sphere of purely physical existence; or that has not yet entered the sphere of man and hence does not represent man's moral freedom in being, aspiring and accomplishing; or that is not yet fit to represent this sphere — such an object belongs to the sphere of physical things, which by their very nature and purpose are subject to the force of physical compulsion. Accordingly, anything that is rooted to the ground, or that has not yet been detached from the ground, or even that is artificially attached to the ground, and so has become a part of it — e.g., plants rooted in the ground; water gathered in wells or cisterns; walls and houses and the like — is not susceptible to טומאה. The same applies to living animals, animal ornaments, and animal food. So, too, anything whose manufacture is not finished for human use, שלא נגמרה מלאכתו, is not susceptible to טומאה. None of these represent the sphere of man's free activity.

The foregoing also explains the reason susceptibility to טומאה is limited to certain types of vessels. For טומאה is not a physical condition which depends on the physical properties of material things. Rather, טומאה is an abstract concept to be negated in all aspects of human life. Utensils merely represent these aspects. A chest represents the aspect of possessions, a tool represents creative work, a pot represents preparation of food for nourishment and pleasure, etc. And since כלים merely symbolize certain aspects, טומאה does not apply to all כלים indiscriminately, but only to those כלים singled out as particularly representative of those aspects of human life that are reflected by the laws of טומאה.

This selectivity, this clear limitation of objects to which these laws apply, preserves the symbolic meaning of the halachah, as clarity and precision are prerequisites for all symbolic expression. So we find also in the case of the other symbolic *mitzvos*. For example:

ציצית serves as a reminder of the moral sanctification inherent in human clothing. The mitzvah applies primarily to garments of wool or linen, which are considered man's primary clothing (see Commentary to *Bemidbar* 15:37ff.).

מזוזה expresses the consecration of the home as the place where the Word of God is to attain its principal realization. The mitzvah does not apply to every dwelling place, but only to those places that can precisely represent the concept of a home — from the standpoint of spaciousness, height, and structure (see Commentary to *Devarim* 6:9).

Likewise, in the case of איסור מלאכה on שבת: the prohibition applies only to those activities that graphically demonstrate man's control over the world. Hence, מקלקל, שאין מתכוין, כלאחר יד, and the like are פטורים.

So it is also in the case of the איסור בשר בחלב: it applies only to בהמה טהורה — which is man's principal source of nourishment from the animal world — to the exclusion of חיה ועוף.

This selectivity ensures these *mitzvos* a symbolic character expressive of an idea. So, too, in the laws of טומאה, only a selection of the articles used by man is susceptible to טומאה: susceptibility to טומאה is limited to articles that most precisely represent the various activities that complement the human personality. Moreover, in each category selected, טומאה depends on the characteristic features of that category. Let us elaborate:

First, regarding materials: Not all כלים are susceptible to טומאה, but only כלי עץ, בגד, עור, מעשה עזים (שק), מתכות, and חרס — vessels made from wood, threads of animal or plant origin, the hair, skins, bones, horns, etc., of animals, metals, or baked clay. Thus, only the principal materials used in the manufacture of vessels are selected. This excludes materials derived from fish or other aquatic creatures, as well as from birds, unbaked clay, or stone.

The כלים that are susceptible to טומאה contract טומאה only in a fashion that is characteristic of their category and purpose: כלי עץ, עור, עזים, and בגד contract טומאה only if they are בני קיבול (able to contain something) or garments; פשוטיהם (flat pieces of these materials), however, are טהורים, unless they are ראויים למדרס (fit for one to lie, sit, ride, or stand on). In the case of כלי מתכות (metal vessels), even פשוטיהם contract טומאה. כלי חרס (earthenware vessels) are מקבלים טומאה only מאוירם (if the source of טומאה enters the inner space of the vessel), but not via external contact.

We have here, then, three categories of utensils:

(a) כלי עץ, בגד, עור, שק — utensils of plant or animal origin — are typically used as clothing for man, or as containers for his possessions. Hence, they are susceptible to טומאה only if they have a receptacle (בית קיבול). A further condition is that they be portable together with their contents (מיטלטלים מלא וריקן).

The meaning of this last condition is as follows: Man's possessions that are stored away for safe-keeping do not belong to the moral sphere. Dead-weight possessions are dead, and do not rise above the physical. Only if they are intended to be grasped and used by man do they come to life and participate in his personality, which is antithetical to the physical subjection represented by טומאה. Hence, handles of vessels (ידות הכלים) are considered integral parts of the vessels.

A further condition for susceptibility to טומאה is that the vessel be a כלי אשר יעשה מלאכה בו — i.e., it must have an independent use of its own. Vessel parts — e.g., vessel covers — are not מקבל טומאה by themselves.

This category represents man in his social appearance and in the activity of grasping and utilizing his possessions. (Utensils that are ראויים למדרס — in which case even פשוטיהם are susceptible to טומאה — will be discussed in chapter 15.)

(b) The outstanding feature of כלי מתכות, metal utensils, is that they are used as tools. Hence, even פשוטיהם — e.g., flat slabs or rods — are susceptible to טומאה. Their primary purpose is not to be a container; hence, the condition of מיטלטל מלא וריקן does not apply to them. They represent man in his creative activity.

(c) כלי חרס, earthenware utensils, are מקבל טומאה only מאווירם. This indicates that their whole significance lies solely in their inner space. Their purpose is accomplished by the objects present inside them. Proof is that they impart טומאה to the objects within their inner space, even if these are not touching the כלי.

They have the further peculiarity that אין להם טהרה במקוה ואינן נעשין אב הטומאה, their טהרה cannot be restored by immersion in a מקוה and they do not become אב הטומאה (see below). In these two respects כלי חרס differ from all other כלים; for all other כלים regain their טהרה via immersion in a מקוה, and they become אב הטומאה by contact with a corpse or by serving as משכב ומושב של זב. כלי חרס, then, are similar to אוכלין ומשקין, which also differ from כלים in these two respects (see below).

Hence, in our view, the significance of כלי חרס is this: They are intended for the preservation and preparation of the means of sustenance and enjoyment (in Scripture they are also called תנור וכירים). They represent man in the activity of seeking nourishment and enjoyment.

To summarize the ideas expressed by the laws of טומאת כלים. They exhort us in regard to our human and social relationships, our dealings with possessions, and our activities of work and pleasure. We must remove all these from the sphere of purely physical accomplishment; we must keep them from the impurity of physical subjection; and we must fulfill through them the life goals set for us by מקדש וקדשיו.

אוכלין ומשקין are self explanatory. They are man's means of nourishment and enjoyment. Here, too, we see the category of אוכלין limited to those materials that vividly represent the concept of food. This excludes pepper, saffron, and the like, as these are added to food only to improve its taste or appearance — דעביד לטעמא (*Niddah* 51b). The same is true of משקין: only seven liquids — water, milk, wine, etc. — are מקבל טומאה, and only these are considered representatives of this concept. Moreover, according to one opinion in the Talmud, the concept of food — as regards הלכות טומאה — is represented only by אוכלין, as they are a person's principal source of nourishment; משקין, however, מדאורייתא are not מקבל טומאה. Furthermore, we have seen that a vessel can be rendered susceptible to טומאה only by intention (מחשבה) and completion for its intended purpose; for only these remove it from the physical sphere and give it the character of a utensil for man's use. Similarly, food is not automatically susceptible to טומאה. Rather, its fitness to receive טומאה depends on an act of הכשר; and only this הכשר gives it the character of material destined for human consumption. The act of הכשר entails that food comes in contact with one of the seven liquids mentioned above, and this occurs with man's awareness.

The meaning of the act of הכשר is not easily explained. It is possible to interpret that only through the moistening of edible material is this material *designated* as food. For material dissolves only with the aid of liquid, and only thus does it become fit for human nourishment. Only when a solid has been reduced to liquid form can it be introduced into the blood stream as a nutrient to replenish the tissues that have been depleted by the body's metabolism. In this light we can understand the meaning of הכשר — provided that the wetting of the אוכלין requires intention or at least agreement. The רמב״ם (הל׳ טומאת אוכלין, chap. 12) apparently takes this to be the case, as he states throughout (ibid. 12:1–3): הניח בהן פירות ,נגיעת אוכלין ברצון, etc. (If the text of the רמב״ם has been transmitted to us faithfully, then the כסף משנה's comment on the ראב״ד's gloss is completely unfounded.)

According to all the other ראשונים, however, this interpretation of the meaning of הכשר — namely, that הכשר means designation of material as food — does not seem to fit. For in their view תחלתו לרצון אף על פי שאין סופו לרצון (*Machshirin* 1:1) means as follows: The wetting of the אוכלין (=סופו) need not be ברצון, provided that the water becomes תלוש (=תחילתו) intentionally or at least with agreement. (We mentioned this halachah earlier, in commenting on v. 33.) How is it possible to say, then — according to these ראשונים — that הכשר means designation of material as food? Nonetheless, perhaps this extraordinary halachah may be explained as follows: Material can be considered אוכל — as regards susceptibility to טומאה — only if מחשבה precedes the הכשר. The material must be designated as human food; or, given the definite nature of the material, this designation can be taken for granted (*Uktzin*, chap. 3). Now, since מחשבה has preceded, perhaps a moment of even unintentional wetting suffices for the material to be considered full-fledged food. וצע״ע.

אוכלין ומשקין have no טהרה במקוה. Neither do they become אב הטומאה. (As stated earlier, both these *halachos* apply also to כלי חרס.) By contrast, אדם וכלים are rendered אב הטומאה by contact with a corpse, and כלים are also rendered אב הטומאה by serving as משכב ומושב של זב. These two *halachos* are interconnected; so that the rule is: כל שאין לו טהרה במקוה אינו נעשה אב הטומאה (see *Chullin* 121a, רש״י ד״ה זרעים).

We shall now present what, in our view, is the reason behind these *halachos*, and the reason for the connection between them.

The difference between אב הטומאה and ולד הטומאה is that אב הטומאה by itself represents the idea of טומאה — e.g., נבילה, שרץ, etc. Hence, by touching it, אדם וכלים become טמא. ולד הטומאה, however, does not by itself call to mind the idea of טומאה, but is merely rendered טמא by contact with טומאה. Hence, it conveys טומאה only to אוכלין ומשקין but not to אדם וכלים.

Now, אב הטומאה — that which begets, and calls to mind, the idea of טומאה — can be one of two things: (a) נבילה or שרץ and the like, which by themselves represent a human corpse; or (b) an object that — in and of itself — belongs to the sphere of free man, but whose contact with a corpse calls to mind the antithetical idea of טומאה.

The primary representative of the free, human sphere is living man himself. Joining him are all those objects that are the products and means of his existence and creativity — which represent, then, his autonomous personality. These objects are כלים — vessels, tools, and clothes. They bear the stamp of man and of his creativity, and wherever they are found they automatically proclaim man's presence.

These objects, by coming in contact with a human corpse, have chanced upon a human being — whose sphere of activities they themselves represent — and lo, he has succumbed to the power of physical forces. Their whole purpose is to be pure — in moral freedom; but the fact of death, which they have now encountered, has shaken this purpose and is now reflected by them. In this respect, they resemble נבילה and שרץ. נבילה and שרץ are not themselves human corpses, but the resemblance of their bodies to the human body brings to mind the idea of the human corpse, and for this reason they are אבות הטומאה. The same is true of אדם וכלים שנגעו במת: they are not themselves akin to a מת, but the fact that they have touched a מת calls to mind the antithetical idea of death; hence, they become אבות הטומאה.

Moreover, כלים are so closely identified with the idea of the human personality that — according to the principle חרב הרי הוא כחלל (*Shabbos* 101b) — if they come in contact with a מת or a טמא מת, they identify completely with its טומאה character: they take from a מת the character of אבי אבות, and from a טמא מת the character of אב. For more details, see our Commentary to *Bemidbar* 19:16, et seq. (We have followed here the view of הר׳ יצחק מסימפונט, which is accepted also by the רמב״ם in הל׳ טומאת מת, 5:3. According to this view, the law of חרב הרי הוא כחלל applies to all כלים. According to רבינו תם and רש״י, however, it applies only to כלי מתכות. See ר״ש, *Ohalos* 1:2; רש״י, *Chullin* 3a, ד״ה חרב. Earlier, we explained that כלי מתכות are tools, and represent man in his creative activity. This helps us understand why the law of חרב הרי הוא כחלל might be limited to כלי מתכות. For tools — more so than clothes and other utensils — represent man who thinks and creates and who is free from blind physical compulsion.)

From all these standpoints אוכלין ומשקין are the exact opposite of כלים. They are the means of nourishment and enjoyment. They represent, then, that which man has in common with all other living creatures, which also must satisfy their bodily needs. Man, who requires nourishment and who is capable of sensual enjoyment, is connected with sensual, bodily nature. אוכלין ומשקין, then, in themselves, do not represent man's moral freedom, but his bodily subjection. This aspect is not so antithetical to a מת as is the aspect represented by כלים; hence, the contact of אוכלין ומשקין with a מת does not create a new אב הטומאה.

On the other hand, due to the sensuality represented by אוכלין ומשקין, man is in danger of forfeiting his moral freedom. Primarily, the main demands of מקדש וקדשיו are addressed to man in regard to his sensuality:

In satisfying the senses, he must free himself from subjection to the physical, and ascend to moral freedom; he must transform the very satisfaction of bodily needs into a moral act of serving God.

The sensuality represented by אוכלין ומשקין — precisely because it is distant from the uniquely human sphere — is the realm that is especially susceptible to moral טומאה; the weeds of moral טומאה thrive there. Paradoxically, the same factor that prevents אוכלין ומשקין from becoming אב הטומאה heightens their susceptibility to טומאה. While אדם וכלים are rendered טמאים only by an אב הטומאה, אוכלין ומשקין are rendered טמאים also by ראשון ושני; but their ability to convey טומאה is more restricted (see Commentary to v. 34).

For this very reason אדם וכלים differ from אוכלין ומשקין also in regard to טהרה במקוה. Only אדם וכלים have טהרה במקוה. For they intrinsically belong to the sphere of free and moral man; hence, טבילה במקוה restores to them their natural character of moral freedom. אוכלין ומשקין, by contrast, are purely physical products. In their purpose they represent the physical, sensual side of man. While morally free man is *obligated* to elevate them to the sphere of human freedom, physical subjection is their original character, and contact with טומאה restores to them their basic nature. Hence, טבילה במקוה is ineffective for them. Only זריעה — *actual* removal from the world of man, and restoration to the world of cosmic earth — can usher in a new existence marked by טהרה, and this applies only to מים and to זרעים (see Commentary to v. 37).

As we said earlier, כלי חרס represent the same aspect of man that is represented by אוכלין ומשקין, i.e., they represent man in the activity of seeking nourishment and enjoyment. We understand, then, why these same two *halachos* apply also to כלי חרס: אין להם טהרה במקוה and אינן נעשין אב הטומאה. Only in one respect are כלי חרס treated as כלים (since they, too, are the product of creative human intelligence) — they are not rendered טמא by a ולד הטומאה, but only by an אב הטומאה.

There is special significance to the halachah, mentioned earlier, that even מאכלות אסורות — which may be eaten only by non-Jews — are susceptible to טומאה. From this we learn that the Torah which issues forth from the Sanctuary of Israel, ממקדש וקדשיו, relates also to the partaking of food by a non-Jew. This Torah and its Sanctuary view every human being in the loftiness of his moral calling; and טומאת מאכליו — the debasement of his sensual enjoyment — is antithetical to this Torah, whose ultimate goal is the sanctification of all mankind.

In a special category of its own is the מפץ, the sleeping-mat. Since it is ראוי ומיוחד למשכב, it is מקבל טומאת מדרס; consequently, it is susceptible to other טומאות. For the rule is that כל המטמא מדרס מטמא טמא מת (*Niddah* 49a). Thus, it can become אב הטומאה as משכב ומושב, and yet it has no טהרה במקוה (see *Shabbos* 84b; רמב״ם הל׳ מקואות, 1:4; and our Commentary below, end of chap. 15).

טבילה. Earlier (v. 32), we noted the parallel that *Toras Kohanim* draws between the two factors upon which the restoration of טהרה depends: ביאה במים and ביאת שמש. The inner connection between these two factors is this: Both of them sever the connection between the טמא and the realm of טומאה. טבילה severs it in place, and הערב שמש in time.

Water that is collected in a hollow in the ground and that has not lost its elemental character (in accordance with the conditions mentioned in our Commentary to v. 36: not in a כלי, without תפיסת ידי אדם, not שאובים, and not על ידי דבר המקבל טומאה) is outside the realm of טומאה. As the Mishnah says (*Kelim* 17:13): כל שבים טהור — i.e., vessels made from aquatic creatures or materials cannot become טמא. The main realm of טומאה, then, is אדמה, land, the dwelling place of man (see Commentary to *Shemos* 29:4). When a person immerses his entire body in *such* water (viz., water that has not lost its elemental character), and sinks completely — בלי חציצה — into *this* element, all connection between him and the realm of טומאה is severed. He leaves the ground of man, and returns for a moment to the world of the elements, in order to begin a new life of טהרה. Symbolically, he is reborn.

And when afterwards the sun has set, and with it the day that saw him טמא has passed, then — as the Gemara says in *Berachos* 2b — טהר יומא, the day, too, has become טהור for him, and he has entered a fresh, pure day. At this point the connection between him and his state of טומאה has been severed in time as well, and his טהרה is complete.

Let us now picture to ourselves the laws of טומאה and טהרה in their full realization. True, these *halachos* are obligatory only as regards מקדש וקדשיו. A non-*Kohen* is permitted, in his ordinary life, to touch טומאה; it is not forbidden לגרום טומאה לחולין שבארץ ישראל (*Niddah* 6b), to make ordinary foodstuffs טמא. Nevertheless, all of Israel would set aside ביכורים, תרומה, חלה, מעשר שני — all of which must be kept בטהרה. Moreover, each individual is obligated לטהר את עצמו ברגל (*Rosh Hashanah* 16b). The national ascent to the Sanctuary three times a year laid the foundation from which the טומאה and טהרה laws spread throughout the life of the nation, as all things had to be safeguarded to maintain טהרה throughout the year, on account of the requirements of those great festive weeks.

We picture to ourselves the full life of the people — their work, creativity, and commerce; their national life and their home life — and we see that all is under the rule of the טומאה and טהרה laws. We then begin to appreciate the ennobling moral influence of these laws — upon the nation as a whole and upon the individual. The sanctification of man in moral freedom extends to all the works of his hands. Work and craftsmanship are put in the service of man's calling to become morally free and close to God. The chisel and the needle, the loom and the cooking pot all conform to the law of morality, which from the heights of Mount Moriah sanctifies all of life. The lowliest working people, men and women, are uplifted by the awareness that their labor is a moral act performed for a moral purpose, and that they are contributing to the fulfillment of man's mission, in the spirit of the Torah which is enthroned on Moriah. Under the rule of the laws of טומאה and טהרה, vulgarity and brutishness disappear, self-deprecation and degeneration vanish, and everyone stands tall to create for the Torah a holy nation of holy people.

So we find that at the dawn of our history the spiritual elite of the nation lived all of life in compliance with the טומאה and טהרה laws — which the Torah prescribes only in respect to the Sanctuary and its holy things: היו אוכלים חוליהן בטהרה, "they would eat their ordinary, unsanctified food in the purity of טהרה." They lived their whole life — even the life of the senses — as though they were in the environment of, and in the presence of, the Sanctuary. In all their dealings, in all their contacts with people and with things, they were living reminders of man's holy calling. As early as the time of Sha'ul and David (*Shemuel* I, 20:26; 21:6) we find even common soldiers observing laws of טהרה in their everyday lives. From the latter verse it is clear that they observed these *halachos* on the highest level of stringency: they ate their חולין not only על טהרת תרומה but even על טהרת הקודש. Hence, וַיִּהְיוּ כְלֵי־הַנְּעָרִים קֹדֶשׁ: all their equipment was טהור — not only from the standpoint of תרומה, but even from that of קודש (for the discussion there was about לחם קודש).

Those who strictly observed the laws of טומאה and טהרה even in everyday life were called in later times חברים. They formed a free, open society, whose membership was open to anyone who, in the presence of three חברים, undertook to observe דברי חברות, the duties of a חבר (see

Bechoros 30b). דברי חברות also entailed strict observance of the מעשר laws (see Commentary to *Bemidbar* 18:21, et seq.). But strict observance of the laws of טהרה and מעשר was only the symbol that characterized this society. From all Mishnaic and Talmudic sources it is clear that conscientious observance of *all* the laws of morality distinguished the character of a חבר. The חברים were a free society, open to all, and they considered their life's mission to be the study of Torah and its fulfillment.

We have seen that חברות was a widespread phenomenon even at the dawn of our history. If we are not mistaken in our approach, these were the people that, at all times, formed the core of the life of the nation. They were unassuming people who rose to the highest levels of morality. Historians of the dynasties do not mention them; only here and there do they allude to them. Personalities such as Elkanah and Channah, Shemuel and David, could have emerged only from their midst. The spirit of prophecy, which shone forth in the times of decline of the kingship, could have arisen only from among them. They are the answer to the riddle of the very existence of such personalities.

The חברים were also called פרושים, Pharisees — on account of their keeping apart (פרישות) from all טומאה (see *Chagigah* 18b). The פרושים themselves, more than anyone else, had scorn, contempt, and biting critique for all those who — with a mask of פרישות on their face and words of false piety on their lips — distorted true Pharisaism into hypocrisy. None were such sworn enemies of all pretense of piety as our פרושים, our Pharisees.

They transmitted to us sure signs of seven types of false Pharisees (see *Sotah* 22b). These seven — together with the חסיד שוטה, the foolish *Chassid*, the בתולה ציילנית ואלמנה שובבית, the maiden who is always at her devotions, the widow who is proud of her piety, and the קטן שלא כלו לו חדשיו, the self-appointed but immature exponent of the Torah — are all called מבלי עולם, ruiners of the world (ibid. 21b–22a).

The Gemara (ibid. 22b) concludes with a great saying: דמטמרא מטמרא, the concealed things are hidden from man, ודמגליא מגליא, and only what is revealed is known to him; בי דינא רבה ליתפרע מהני דחפו גונדי, but God's justice will exact punishment from those who wrap themselves in their *tallis* and pose as פרושים. אמר לה ינאי מלכא לדביתיה: אל תתיראי מן הפרושין ולא ממי שאינן פרושין, אלא מן הצבועין שדומין לפרושין, שמעשיהן כמעשה זמרי ומבקשין שכר כפנחס. "King Yannai said to his wife: Fear not the Pharisees, nor the non-Pharisees, but only the posers, who appear as Phar-

12 1 God *spoke to Moshe, saying:* יב א וַיְדַבֵּר יְהֹוָה אֶל־מֹשֶׁה לֵּאמֹר:

isees; they live like Zimri, and demand a reward like that of Pinchas" (ibid).

The first stage of אכילת חולין בטהרה has remained a regular practice in the daily regimen of the whole Jewish people, and is still the mark of the observant Jew. We are referring to נטילת ידים, the washing of the hands before meals. According to *Bechoros* 30b, the undertaking of נטילת ידים is a prerequisite for the undertaking of the other טהרות duties; and this first prerequisite for admittance into the טהרות society is called קבלה לכנפים. From רש״י (ibid.), the ערוך (ערך כנף), and the רמב״ם (הל׳ מטמאי משכב ומושב, 10:1–2) it is clear that קבלה לכנפים is קבלה לנטילת ידים; but *why* נטילת ידים is called כנפים (wings) remains to be explained. In our view, the likely explanation is as follows:

Any ascent to the lofty heights of טהרות depends on the practice of נטילת ידים. נטילת ידים confers wings upon the aspiring entrant to טהרות, lifting him to the very height of the practice of טהרות. The very term נטילת ידים is indicative of an uplifting. נטל is the Aramaic equivalent of נשא, and the literal meaning of נטילת ידים is the lifting of the hands. Even the vessel that is used especially for נטילת ידים is called נטלא, which literally means lifting. The meaning of נטילת ידים לסעודה is this: We must elevate our meal from the realm of bodily, sensual gratification and give it the character of a human, holy act. Indeed, the moral sanctification of every bodily act is the first prerequisite for the sanctification of Jewish life.

תזריע

CHAPTER 12

1 In the preceding chapter, two types of טומאה were discussed — טומאת גוויות and טומאת קדושות. טומאת גוויות relates to morality of the body, and is caused by eating food that defiles the purity of the body. טומאת קדושות relates to consciousness of moral freedom, which the Sanctuary requires and guarantees; and it is caused by contact with dead bodies, which suggests the idea of man's lack of freedom. These two types are, respectively, טומאת מאכלות אסורות and טומאת מגע נבילה ושרץ.

2 *Speak to the Children of Israel, saying: When a woman has matured a human seed and gives birth to a male, she shall be in a state of impurity for seven days, just as in the separation days of her [periodic] indisposition shall she be impure.*

ב דַּבֵּ֞ר אֶל־בְּנֵ֤י יִשְׂרָאֵל֙ לֵאמֹ֔ר אִשָּׁה֙ כִּ֣י תַזְרִ֔יעַ וְיָלְדָ֖ה זָכָ֑ר וְטָֽמְאָה֙ שִׁבְעַ֣ת יָמִ֔ים כִּימֵ֛י נִדַּ֥ת דְּוֹתָ֖הּ תִּטְמָֽא׃

This chapter and the chapters that follow it continue the teaching of טומאת קדושות. They discuss conditions that jeopardize — to an even greater degree — the consciousness of moral freedom. For these conditions represent the bodily submission of *living* man, טומאות היוצאות עליו מגופו. They show, as it were, the death of moral freedom in the midst of life itself; consequently, they require a special demonstration of the truth that contradicts this. They are יולדת and מצורע, נדה and זבה, בעל קרי and זב. Their טומאה lasts for a longer time (except in the case of בעל קרי) — not just יום אחד as in the case of טומאת נבילה ושרץ. Except for נדה and בעל קרי, they all require an offering — to express the teaching of moral freedom in a positive way as well. Thus, יולדת and מצורע, זב and זבה are called the ארבעה מחוסרי כפרה.

וידבר ה׳ אל משה לאמר — see Commentary to 13:1.

2 **דבר אל בני ישראל וגו׳.** בני ישראל excludes a non-Jewish woman; אשה includes a גיורת and a שפחה, as they, too, are part of Jewish society (see *Yevamos* 74b; *Kerisos* 7b).

כי תזריע. The primary meaning of זרע is "seed of a plant"; hence the expression עשב מזריע. הזריע זרע denotes the seed-forming process in plants for the continuation of the species. By extension, the term זרע is applied to human beings, and is the common expression for offspring, which propagate the human species.

The only other instance of the word תזריע is in *Bereshis* 1:11–12, where it denotes the process in plants for the continuation of the species. Scripture's use of this same expression here indicates that the mother's role in the formation of the child is likewise viewed as a purely physiological process. This one word, then, characterizes the whole concept of טומאה under discussion here. The highest and noblest task on which the whole future of the human race depends and in which the uniqueness of womankind finds its highest expression — the mother's effort and labor in producing a child — is merely a physical process. Man is formed, takes shape, and grows like a plant, and the most wonderful name that the human tongue can utter — the name "Mother" — reminds us, at the same time, of the purely physical process of our coming into being, which is not by our own free will.

For this reason the moral freedom of man, who is *brought into being*, must be stressed precisely here. For the mother — under the fresh impression of her passive and painful submission to the physical forces of nature while fulfilling her loftiest task as a woman — must now renew her consciousness of her moral stature. Only after this impression has receded should she return to the Sanctuary with an offering. With this offering, and in moral freedom, she is to rededicate herself to her calling — as a wife and mother — despite the painful moments.

תזריע וילדה זכר. Since the word תזריע is placed before וילדה, we infer that Scripture refers here not just to a full-term delivery, but to the early stages of pregnancy. On the other hand, the word זכר denotes a mature and completed stage. Moreover, from the next verse — וביום השמיני וגו׳ — we learn that the newborn is viable. From all this we learn that the halachah stated here applies also in the case of a נפל, a miscarriage. However, the halachah applies only if forty days have elapsed from the first formation of the fetus, and only if the נפל has the most salient features of a human being — יש בו מצורת אדם (the forehead, eyebrows, eyes, cheeks, and chin resemble those of a human being; see *Niddah* 23b) — and is ראוי לבריית נשמה (the deformity is not incompatible with the ability to sustain life). See *Toras Kohanim*; *Niddah* 30a and 21b, et seq.

כימי נדת דותה תטמא. Statements like this indicate that the entire Law was already known, before it was put down in writing; for our verse refers to a law that is treated in Scripture only later (15:19).

נדה derives from the root נדד. Every נודד moves away from his place or from a person with whom he is associated. נדה, then, is an appropriate expression for the condition that causes a temporary dissociation in marital life.

3 *And on the eighth day the flesh of his foreskin shall be circumcised.*	ג וּבַיּ֖וֹם הַשְּׁמִינִ֑י יִמּ֖וֹל בְּשַׂ֥ר עָרְלָתֽוֹ׃

דותה derives from the root דוה. Whereas חלה denotes the condition of illness from an objective, physiological standpoint (see Commentary to *Bereshis* 48:1), דוה denotes more the subjective feeling of the illness. Hence, דוה is frequently connected with לב, as in עַל־זֶה הָיָה דָוֶה לִבֵּנוּ (*Eichah* 5:17), לֵבָב דַּוָּי (*Yeshayahu* 1:5), and so forth. דוה denotes a periodic condition of not feeling well, of which נדה is the halachic result.

כימי נדת דותה תטמא: all the laws stated below (15:19–24) apply to her. The *halachos* of לידה are learned from the *halachos* of נדה. These two phenomena resemble and are related to each other — according to modern physiological opinion as well.

3 **וביום השמיני ימול בשר ערלתו**. Elsewhere (*Collected Writings*, vol. III), we explained the meaning of מצות מילה as the subordination of sensuality to God's Torah. Mastery over the body and its moral sanctification have already been prescribed as the basic code of the people of the God of Abraham (*Bereshis* 17). Scripture here repeats this mitzvah for two reasons: (a) to show the connection between מילה and טומאת לידה, which is discussed in the preceding verse and which was introduced only at the giving of the Torah; (b) to clarify that מילה performed at its proper time suspends the laws of שבת, and that מילה suspends the laws of צרעת, which are discussed in the next chapter. These *mitzvos* (שבת and צרעת), too, were introduced only at the giving of the Torah.

As regards the connection between מילה and טומאת לידה, this is the rule: כל שאמו טמאה לידה נימול לשמונה, וכל שאין אמו טמאה לידה אין נימול לשמונה (*Shabbos* 135a). In the above mentioned article (*Collected Writings*, vol. III, p. 96ff.) we discussed this rule as well. We noted there that seven days of טומאה conclude a period marked by a condition that must be overcome: A person ceases to be an unfree created being (symbolized by the number six) and becomes a human being endowed with freedom (symbolized by the number seven); and he attains this only through a covenant with God. On the eighth day he is reborn for the Jewish mission. This rebirth is on the basis of man's innate godly freedom, for the sake of a higher level of freedom, a higher calling. The eighth day is a repetition of the first day, the day of physical birth, on a higher level — the beginning of a higher "octave," as it were. The compelling force of nature — which is manifest in the mother and her son at the physical birth — brings the mother the seven days of טומאת לידה, and, as regards the son, requires in ordinary cases the passing of seven days before the fulfillment of מצות מילה.

By contrast, if the mother is not Jewish בשעת לידה and so does not contract טומאת לידה, it is the מילה — and not the birth — that connects the son to Judaism. Accordingly, the מילה by itself constitutes a new beginning of life, unconnected with what came before; the connection with the physical birth is no longer pronounced. Hence, there is no need for the passing of a seven-day cycle. In this light we can also understand the opinion of ר׳ אסי — which was not accepted as the halachah — that even a יוצא דופן is not נימול לשמונה. (See ibid. pp.108–109.)

We learn further from the words וביום השמיני וגו׳ the halachah of ביום ולא בלילה, which we explained in *Collected Writings* (vol. III, p. 86ff.) in the context of all the other *mitzvos* that must be performed during the day. This halachah relates the act of מילה to the calling of man, who is endowed with moral freedom; and it dispels the notion that מילה is a procedure to prevent disease, or is a heathen cultic rite (see ibid.).

And we learn further: וביום השמיני ואפילו בשבת (*Shabbos* 132a) — i.e., מילה בזמנה דוחה שבת. In *Collected Writings* (vol. III, p. 96ff.) we noted the deep connection between the meaning of the eighth day and Shabbos. We showed that Israel is the eighth work of creation, joining the seven works of the creation of the world. Moreover, Shabbos is a sign and reminder of the Creator, and Israel is the herald of Shabbos, bearing its message to all of mankind. Israel, as the "eighth," exists for the "seventh." The significance of Israel is essentially in its observance of Shabbos on the seventh day. Just as Israel, the "eighth," exists for the "seventh," so, too, the sole bearer of the message of Shabbos, the "seventh," is Israel, the "eighth." מילה that is performed on the eighth day exemplifies the covenant of Abraham — from the aspect of its mission on behalf of Shabbos. For Shabbos teaches that God is the Master of the world and of man; and מילה, performed on an infant boy of the House of Abraham, provides Shabbos with another fighter and keeper. מילה that is performed on the eighth day upholds the aspect of the

ד וּשְׁלֹשִׁ֣ים י֗וֹם וּשְׁלֹ֙שֶׁת֙ יָמִ֔ים תֵּשֵׁ֖ב
בִּדְמֵ֣י טָהֳרָ֑ה בְּכָל־קֹ֣דֶשׁ לֹֽא־
תִגָּ֗ע וְאֶל־הַמִּקְדָּשׁ֙ לֹ֣א תָבֹ֔א עַד־
מְלֹ֖את יְמֵ֥י טָהֳרָֽהּ׃

4 *And she shall remain in the blood of purification for thirty-three days; she shall touch no sanctified thing and not come into the Sanctuary until the days of her purification are complete.*

ה וְאִם־נְקֵבָ֣ה תֵלֵ֔ד וְטָמְאָ֥ה שְׁבֻעַ֖יִם
כְּנִדָּתָ֑הּ וְשִׁשִּׁ֥ים יוֹם֙ וְשֵׁ֣שֶׁת יָמִ֔ים
תֵּשֵׁ֖ב עַל־דְּמֵ֥י טָהֳרָֽה׃

5 *But if she gives birth to a female, she shall be in a state of impurity for two weeks, as during her periodic separation, and she shall remain in the blood of purification for sixty-six days.*

seventh. It is understandable, then, that מילה is to be performed even on Shabbos, if the eighth day falls on Shabbos (see *Shabbos* 133a). Although שבת is both a לא תעשה and an עשה, and the general rule is that an עשה is not דוחה לא תעשה ועשה, nevertheless, the עשה of מילה — שנכרתו עליה י״ג בריתות — does suspend the עשה and לא תעשה of שבת.

ימול בשר ערלתו: ואף על פי שיש שם בהרת יקוץ. The removal of a נגע צרעת is prohibited by a לא תעשה and an עשה — by a negative and a positive command, as it says: השמר בנגע הצרעת לשמר מאד ולעשות וגו׳ (*Devarim* 24:8). If, however, there is צרעת on the ערלה, מילה is nevertheless performed, ימול בשר ערלתו. As long as the מילה has not been performed, the בשר is regarded only as ערלה, and this is to be removed even if the נגע is removed with it (see *Shabbos* 132b).

(We should also mention that an עשה is not דוחה a לאו unless the עשה is fulfilled at the same moment [בעידנא] that the לאו is transgressed — as here in the case of מילה בצרעת, or in the case of כלאים בציצית. This excludes cases where the transgression of the לאו merely allows for the later fulfillment of the עשה [ibid]. Furthermore, an עשה is not דוחה a לאו unless it is impossible to fulfill the עשה [דלא אפשר לקיומיה לעשה] without transgressing the לאו [see *Kesubos* 40a].)

4–5 **ושלשים יום וגו׳ ואם נקבה תלד וגו׳**. טומאה היוצאת עליו מגופו — e.g., יולדת, זב, נדה, and מצורע — suggests the idea of man's lack of freedom. In such cases, this idea is not suggested by contact with a dead body that resembles the living human body, but is impressed upon man's consciousness by processes and conditions in his own body. And because he senses his own bodily submission, this idea strikes him as the truth.

Obviously, then, a longer lapse of time is required to overcome this impression, and one day does not suffice as it does in the case of מגע שרץ ונבילה. We find a similar phenomenon in the case of one who comes in contact with a מת: he remains טמא for a period of seven days. For the lack of freedom is demonstrated by the corpse of an actual human being — even though this is not a case of טומאה היוצאת עליו מגופו.

In cases of טומאות היוצאות עליו מגופו, however, it is reasonable to assume something further: The duration of the טומאה depends on the duration of the conditions that brought on the feeling of a lack of physical freedom. And just as *after* מגע מת one must complete a cycle of days before טהרה can be restored, so it is with these טומאות: *after* the bodily condition has passed, one must complete a cycle of days.

This is indeed the law in the case of מצורע (below, 14:8), זב (15:13), and זבה (15:28). It is reasonable to assume, then, that, in the case of יולדת as well, the cycle of טומאה and טהרה depends on the duration of the bodily aftereffects of childbirth. Also, there appears to be a difference in this respect — even physiologically — between the birth of a male and the birth of a female. The first טומאה cycle — of seven or fourteen days — is marked by the depressing aftereffects of childbirth. The bodily symptoms that appear with the eighth or fifteenth day are signs of the body's recovery process. Hence, they have the character of טָהֳרָה — not purity, but purification; the woman is undergoing purification, but is not yet טהורה. Only on the forty-second or eighty-second day does the body recover fully.

During the first seven or fourteen days the laws of נדה apply (see below, 15:19ff.). After these days have passed and the woman has immersed (ביומי וטבילה תלה רחמנא; see *Niddah* 35b), she is יושבת על דם טוהר: she is טהורה לבעלה ולמעשר שני, but she is still טמאה לתרומה ולקודש — like a טבול יום (see above, 11:24–25 and our Commentary there). Hence, until the end of the fortieth or eightieth day she is called טבולת יום ארוך (*Niddah* 71b). At nightfall of the forty-first or eighty-first day she becomes טהורה לתרומה but is still מחוסרת כפרה and so remains טמאה לקודש (see *Yevamos* 74b).

Thus, the prohibition בכל קדש לא תגע (v. 4) — which applies during ישיבתה על דם טוהר — relates also to תרומה: if she touches תרומה it becomes טמאה; if she eats תרומה she is liable to מיתה בידי שמים, just as she would be liable to כרת if she were to enter the מקדש.

מעשר שני is sanctification of sensual enjoyment; תרומה is sanctification of the spirit of the Torah and its bearers; קודש is a symbolic expression of the realization of the Torah ideal. The order of these holy things is clear: it is reflected by the greater or lesser degree to which they must be kept away from טומאה.

One further thought. The mitzvah of מילה (v. 3) is placed in the middle of the laws of טומאה (vv. 2–4), breaking their continuity. This indicates that מילה is deeply connected with these laws. Think about it: For seven days the mother is טמאה; on the eighth day, מילה is performed on the child; then, for thirty-three days she remains in the blood of purification, etc. The implication is that the seven days of טומאה of the mother are preliminary to the eighth day, the day of the מילה; the eighth day concludes the first stage of the mother's טומאה, and introduces the cycle of טהרה. The meaning of this is as follows:

The mitzvah of מילה is the fundamental condition of the covenantal relationship between God and Israel. מילה requires of man that he subordinate his body — in moral freedom — to God's Will and commandments. The fulfillment of this requirement is but the actualization of the potential for freedom, which the laws of טהרה are intended to preserve within us.

בשר ערלה — representing the undisciplined, unmastered body — is but the embodiment of the belief in man's lack of freedom, a belief that stems from the idea of טומאה. Thus, we find many *mitzvos* in which there is a correspondence between ערל and טמא: Both ערל and טמא are prohibited from eating תרומה and קדשים. Both ערל and טמא are exempt from the mitzvah of ראייה ברגל (see *Yevamos* 70a; *Chagigah* 4b); both are פסולים לעבודה (see *Zevachim* 22b); and ערל apparently is אסור בביאת מקדש, which is the law of a טמא (see לחם משנה on הל' חגיגה, 2:1). Moreover, ר' עקיבא so closely identifies ערלה with טומאה (דמרבי ליה לערל כטמא) that רבא (*Yevamos* 72b) expects there to be a tradition in the name of ר' עקיבא that an ערל — like a טמא — is מטמא by contact. When he finds no such tradition, he concludes that ר' עקיבא does not universally identify ערל with טמא.

From all of the above it appears that the day of מילה restores to our consciousness the teaching of moral purity. Hence, on this day the mother, too, enters the stage of returning טהרה. Moreover, on account of this day the טומאה and טהרה cycle of the יולדת is shortened by half.

In the case of a יולדת נקבה the period of טומאה and ימי טוהר is doubled; and the words שבעים כנדתה (v. 5) imply that this cycle is to be conceived of as a double cycle: one cycle in respect to the mother — similar to the cycle that is applicable following the birth of a male; and a second cycle in respect to the daughter, as the second cycle of seven and thirty-three days takes the place of what would have been מילה had the infant been a boy.

As we pointed out in the chapter on מילה (*Bereshis* 17:15ff.), one of the basic character traits of the Jewish woman, as a true daughter of Sarah, is her willingness to subordinate herself, of her own free will, to the "measure" of morality. By contrast, the male is bidden to acquire this virtue by the sign "די" of the מילה on his flesh (cf. Commentary to *Bereshis* 17:1, 17:10, 17:11; *Collected Writings*, vol. III, p. 80). Now, it appears that the טומאה and טהרה laws to be observed by women are to serve as equally forceful aids in training the woman for purity of character. Let us elaborate.

On the day of the מילה the father fulfills the first of the duties incumbent upon a father concerning his son. At this time the father resolves to prepare his son for the life that lies ahead: He must train him to walk before God, in complete adherence to the Torah (cf. *Bereshis* 17:1); and through his own conduct he must serve as a role model for his son to emulate on his future path.

So, too, following the birth of a daughter the mother's path to טהרה is twice as long as after the birth of a son. This should impress upon the mother the full solemnity and magnitude of her task — to be an example and role model for the Jewish woman of the future. Indeed, the mother's influence on the moral standards of her daughters is twice as great as her influence on the moral development of her sons. With sons, the crucial part of their education comes from the father, as the sons see in him a model for their own future male role. With daughters, however, the mother is both a role model and a molder of character. Hence, after the birth of each daughter she must doubly prepare herself — for her own sake and for the sake of her newborn daughter — to ascend the path of purity and morality to the lofty heights of the Sanctuary ideal.

6 *And when the days of her purification are completed, for a son or for a daughter, she shall bring a sheep in its first year for an ascent offering, and a young dove or a turtledove for an offering that clears of sin, to the entrance of the Tent of Appointed Meeting, to the priest.*	ו וּבִמְלֹ֣את ׀ יְמֵ֣י טָהֳרָ֗הּ לְבֵן֮ א֣וֹ לְבַת֒ תָּבִ֞יא כֶּ֤בֶשׂ בֶּן־שְׁנָתוֹ֙ לְעֹלָ֔ה וּבֶן־יוֹנָ֥ה אוֹ־תֹ֖ר לְחַטָּ֑את אֶל־פֶּ֥תַח אֹֽהֶל־מוֹעֵ֖ד אֶל־הַכֹּהֵֽן׃

6 **כבש בן שנתו**. בן שנתו, in *its* first year, without consideration of מנין עולם, the calendar year, but מעת לעת: the year is calculated from the day of birth — here, in קדשים, from the hour of birth — until the recurrence of the same day and hour. Within this period the כבש is כשר לקרבן. שעות פסולות בקדשים (*Zevachim* 25b) and also בבתי ערי חומה (below, 25:29; see *Arachin* 31a).

In other *halachos* — שתי שנים שבשדה אחוזה, שש שנים שבעבד עברי, וכן שבבן ושבבת (*Niddah*, 47b) — the years are calculated מיום ליום but not משעה לשעה (see תוספות, ibid.). So, too, in the calculation of years as regards obligation in *mitzvos*, twelve years for girls and thirteen for boys are calculated מיום ליום but not משעה לשעה. On the arrival of the twelfth or thirteenth birthday, even though the hour of birth has not yet arrived, the girl or boy becomes subject to *mitzvos* (see משנה למלך on הל' אישות, 2:21; או"ח 53:10, and מגן אברהם, there).

There are also *halachos* in which the year is calculated according to the calendar year. In the case of מעשר בהמה, ערלה, and נטע רבעי the second year begins on the first of Tishrei even if the animal was born as late as the last day of Elul, or the tree was planted as late as the fifteenth of Av (see *Rosh Hashanah* 2a).

לעלה. With "a sheep in its first year for an ascent offering" she should approach "the Shepherd of her life." She should vow before Him that she will follow His guidance and sustain the freshness of youth in mind and spirit. Then, freed from all depressing bodily influences, she should commit herself to God with all her strength. With renewed energy she should reach for the heights of her assigned task as a woman and as a

7 *He shall bring it near before* God *and effect atonement for her, and*	ז וְהִקְרִיבוֹ לִפְנֵי יְהֹוָה וְכִפֶּר עָלֶיהָ

mother. With her whole being she should perpetuate the fire of the Torah, to be a source of satisfaction before God.

ובן יונה או תר לחטאת. The vow expressed by the עולה is preceded by a חטאת עוף; for whenever both an עולה and a חטאת are offered, the חטאת is offered first. Before one dedicates his actions to God, he must first purge himself of carelessness and moral weakness. First he must wash his hands in purity; only then will his actions be acceptable. First סור מרע — and then עשה טוב. But עשה טוב is the goal, and that is why Scripture here mentions the עולה first. As the Gemara puts it: למקראה הקדימה הכתוב (*Zevachim* 90a). Particularly here, the עולה must be mentioned first (according to ה״ר חיים in תוספות there, the עולה must even be dedicated first — להקדישה); for advancement and ascent to the height of one's task in life — in consciousness and action — is the positive antithesis of passive submission to the compelling physical forces of nature.

Her חטאת, however, is חטאת העוף. For she just now experienced helpless suffering — which is represented by עוף (see Commentary above, 1:14, et seq.). Hence, she was in danger of losing all her טהרה. She was liable to lose sight of the challenge of moral freedom — viz., not to lose this freedom even in times of suffering. That is why she first brings a חטאת עוף and vows with her offering: The days of suffering that come with her life's calling will not break her moral strength. Rather, she will undertake and endure the suffering out of a sense of duty and for the sake of her exalted task. She will maintain her moral willpower so as to fulfill this task, and in this way transform the passiveness of suffering itself into active moral energy (see ibid.).

7 **והקריבו וגו׳ וכפר וגו׳ וטהרה**. The כפרה and the resultant טהרה depend only on the offering of the חטאת. Hence, the object of והקריבו is in the singular. With the offering of the חטאת her טהרה returns, and on this basis she brings the עולה — in order to ascend and advance toward a new and vital future.

וְטָהֲרָה מִמְּקֹר דָּמֶיהָ זֹאת תּוֹרַת
הַיֹּלֶדֶת לַזָּכָר אוֹ לַנְּקֵבָה׃

so she will be purified from the source of her blood. This is the teaching with regard to a woman who gives birth, be it to a male or to a female.

ח וְאִם־לֹא תִמְצָא יָדָהּ דֵּי שֶׂה
וְלָקְחָה שְׁתֵּי־תֹרִים אוֹ שְׁנֵי בְּנֵי
יוֹנָה אֶחָד לְעֹלָה וְאֶחָד לְחַטָּאת
וְכִפֶּר עָלֶיהָ הַכֹּהֵן וְטָהֵרָה׃ פ

8 *But if her means are not sufficient to defray [the cost of] a sheep, she shall take two turtledoves or two young doves, one for an ascent offering and one for an offering that clears of sin; the priest will effect atonement for her, and she will be purified.*

יג א וַיְדַבֵּר יְהוָה אֶל־מֹשֶׁה וְאֶל־אַהֲרֹן
לֵאמֹר׃

13 1 God *spoke to Moshe and to Aharon, saying:*

8 **ואם לא תמצא וגו׳**. In the case of a mother who is poor, her עולה, too, is an עוף. That is to say, as an "עוף" she approaches God — unrelated to the bodily weakness she experienced. The עוף represents her powerless condition, her lack of means, reflecting her general lot. As an "עוף" she draws near to God and to His Sanctuary and undertakes that, despite the many hardships of her situation — which are symbolized in the offering procedures of עולת עוף, she will not allow herself to be deprived of her self-respect and self-esteem. Even in her impoverished condition she will adhere to the heights of her godly calling as a Jewish woman and mother (see Commentary above, 1:14ff. and 5:8ff.).

CHAPTER 13

אל משה ואל אהרן. The mention of Aharon's name cannot be attributed to the role of the כהנים in ראיית נגעים. For פרשת מאכלות אסורות and פרשת זב ונדה also are addressed both to Moshe and to Aharon (above, 11:1; below, 15:1), even though no special role is played by the כהנים in these *mitzvos*. Furthermore, Aharon's name is not mentioned in the intro-

ב אָדָם כִּי־יִהְיֶה בְעוֹר־בְּשָׂרוֹ שְׂאֵת אוֹ־סַפַּחַת אוֹ בַהֶרֶת וְהָיָה בְעוֹר־בְּשָׂרוֹ לְנֶגַע צָרָעַת וְהוּבָא אֶל־אַהֲרֹן הַכֹּהֵן אוֹ אֶל־אַחַד מִבָּנָיו הַכֹּהֲנִים׃

2 *If a person has on the skin of his flesh a very white spot, or one that is nearly so, or one that is shiny white, and it forms a leprous mark in the skin of his flesh, then he shall be brought to Aharon, the priest, or to one of his sons, the priests.*

ductions to the whole סדר הקרבנות (above, chap. 1, et seq.), to קרבן יולדת (12:1), or to קרבן מצורע (14:1) — even though these פרשיות pertain especially to the כהנים and their function.

This, then, appears to be the reason for naming Aharon beside Moshe in the introduction to טומאת צרעת ,מאכלות אסורות וטומאת מגע and טומאת זב ונדה וזבה: Scripture seeks to emphasize the special importance of these laws — not only for theoretical understanding and practical fulfillment, which are represented by Moshe, but also for the training and education of all the individuals in Israel for such understanding and practice. (We noted this earlier, in our Commentary to 11:1.) The common idea of all these laws is טומאת גויות וטומאת קדושות (see chap. 11). Observance of these laws develops, nurtures, and trains holy people, educated for God's Torah.

2 **אדם כי יהיה וגו׳**. אדם — not only איש ואשה, adults, but even a תינוק בן יומו, a one day old child, is מטמא בנגעים (see *Niddah* 44a).

כי יהיה: if *henceforth* a נגע develops, מן הדיבור ואילך (*Horayos* 10a). These laws do not apply retroactively. Whoever was a מצורע when these laws were first given was unaffected by the laws of טומאה. The same is true of a נכרי ונתגייר or a קטן ונולד, if the נגע was present before his conversion or before birth (see *Toras Kohanim*).

שאת או ספחת או בהרת. According to *Shevuos* 5b, the נגעים mentioned here are white spots in four shades. The Gemara describes them in descending order of whiteness as עזה כשלג (white as snow), **כצמר לבן** (white as fleece), כסיד ההיכל (white as lime), and כקרום ביצה (white as egg-skin). בהרת is white as snow; **שאת** is white as fleece.

בהרת derives from בהר (related apparently to באר, clarify; בער, burn). Consider the verse בָּהִיר הוּא בַּשְּׁחָקִים וְרוּחַ עָבְרָה וַתְּטַהֲרֵם (*Iyov* 37:21): Though the light is hidden now, it is bright high above the clouds. If the wind comes and clears them, light shines forth white as snow.

שאת: אין שאת אלא גבוה (*Shevuos* 6b) — i.e., raised whiteness. For a dark color surrounding a bright color is perceived as covering the bright color — as though it were placed over it. The bright color appears to be deeper (כמראה חמה העמוקה מן הצל [ibid.]), while the surrounding dark color appears raised above it. The color of the שאת, too, is white, and in comparison with other colors it is also עמוק, deep. But it is darker than the בהרת — it appears raised and placed over it; thus it is called שאת. Similarly, in Scripture (*Yeshayahu* 2:14) we find the phrase הַגְּבָעוֹת הַנִּשָּׂאוֹת beside הֶהָרִים הָרָמִים. There (*Shevuos* 6b), too, נישא denotes only relative height — הינשאות — in contrast with רום, which denotes the absolute height of the mountains. שאת, a high white in contrast with deeper snow-white; or as we are accustomed to say: a darker white in contrast with a brighter shade. שאת is as white as the fleece of a newborn lamb (כצמר לבן) around which a protective covering has been tied to protect it from dirt — צמר נקי בן יומו שמכבנין למילת (ibid.).

ספחת is defined (ibid.) as טפילה, subsidiary, based on the verse: סְפָחֵנִי נָא (*Shemuel* I, 2:36). That is, ספחת is a subsidiary shade of white; it is a תולדה of both שאת and בהרת. בהרת and שאת — white as snow and white as fleece — are אבות, the two main shades of white. כסיד ההיכל, lime-white, is a תולדה of snow-white; it is subsidiary to בהרת. And כקרום ביצה, white as egg-skin, is a תולדה of fleece-white; it is subsidiary to שאת. Hence the statement in the Mishnah: מראות נגעים שנים שהן ארבעה (*Shevuos* 1:1). ספחת, then, denotes the shades of white just above and just below שאת.

והיה בעור בשרו לנגע צרעת. והיה, not והיו: מלמד שהם מצטרפין זה עם זה (*Toras Kohanim*). The singular form includes all four of the above mentioned shades and conceives of them as one category. From this we learn that a נגע the size of a גריס (= ½ bean = 9 lentils) is מטמא even if it consists of more than one מראה. According to the רמב״ם (הל׳ טומאת צרעת, 1:3), all four shades combine to form the minimum size; according to others, only the two אבות, or an אב with its תולדה (see ראב״ד, ibid.).

In the majority of cases where the word נגע occurs, it clearly refers not to an ordinary condition of disease, but to a disease that comes as a result of a special Divine decree. A person afflicted with a נגע is נגוע

— literally “touched” by the finger of God. נגע is a weaker form of נגף, which is the root of מגפה — a sudden stroke of death. נגע is commonly translated “disease”; and we, too, have translated it this way, for lack of a fitting word. But “disease” does not properly express the idea of נגע. “Plague” is not much better, for it denotes only the suffering of the afflicted, but does not capture the meaning of נגע from the standpoint of its origin. Thus the Gemara in *Horayos* 10a learns from the verse ונתתי נגע צרעת בבית וגו׳ (below, 14:34) that נגעי אדם, like נגעי בתים, are not מטמא unless they can be attributed to a special Divine decree, and not to other, pathological causes: פרט לנגעי רוחות פרט לנגעי כשפים.

צרעת derives from צרע (related to זרע, זרה, to throw away and remove; related also to סרה and to the Aramaic סרח, to rot). The term צרע denotes an inner rot that breaks out externally, whereas נגע denotes a plague that strikes from without, as a result of a special Divine decree, as we have stated. Thus, from the combined expression נגע צרעת we learn that צרעת is מטמאת only if it manifests itself as a נגע — as a special Divine decree; and a נגע is מטמא only if it is צרעת, an inner rot that breaks out and manifests itself externally on the skin.

According to *Toras Kohanim* here, נגע denotes also something painful and objectionable, מלמד שהוא מצטער ממנו; and here it denotes additionally that its proximity disturbs other people, too — אחרים מצטערים ממנו, as the ראב״ד (ad loc.) explains: מריחה, its odor is objectionable. This last connotation is indicated perhaps by the adjacent expression והובא, he is brought: *others* feel a need to bring him to the כהן.

לנגע צרעת. As we have stated, a נגע is מטמא only if it is at least the size of a גריס, half a broken bean — i.e., גריס הקלקי, apparently a Cilician bean (*Nega'im* 6:1). All the שיעורים, the prescribed measures and sizes for the various laws of the Torah, are הלכה למשה מסיני (see *Sukkah* 5b).

והובא אל אהרן הכהן או אל אחד מבניו הכהנים. By way of tradition we know that only the pronouncement “טמא” or “טהור” requires a כהן. The צרוע becomes טמא or טהור only if a כהן (any כהן — even a בעל מום — provided that he is not a חלל, who has forfeited his כהונה status) pronounces over him טהור or טמא. If, however, the כהן is not well versed in the law, anyone who knows the law can examine the נגע and diagnose it, and in accordance with his diagnosis the כהן then says טמא or טהור. Perhaps this halachah is indicated in our verse. והובא denotes the intervention of others, non-כהנים, who recognize that the נגע requires a כהן.

3 *The priest shall look at the mark in the skin of the flesh, and [if] the hair on the mark has turned white, and the color of the mark is deeper than the skin of his flesh, then it is a leprous mark; the priest must see it and declare him impure.*	ג וְרָאָה הַכֹּהֵן אֶת־הַנֶּגַע בְּעוֹר־הַבָּשָׂר וְשֵׂעָר בַּנֶּגַע הָפַךְ ׀ לָבָן וּמַרְאֵה הַנֶּגַע עָמֹק מֵעוֹר בְּשָׂרוֹ נֶגַע צָרַעַת הוּא וְרָאָהוּ הַכֹּהֵן וְטִמֵּא אֹתוֹ׃

אהרן denotes the אחד מבניו הכהנים .כהן בקי — as opposed to אהרן הכהן — denotes the כהן שאינו בקי: It suffices that he is a descendant of Aharon, provided that he is not a חלל.

In *Devarim* 21:5, Scripture groups together נגעים and civil litigations, as it says: ועל פיהם יהיה כל ריב וכל נגע. ר׳ מאיר (*Niddah* 50a) derives from this that just as ריבים are not to be judged by relatives, so are נגעים not to be examined by relatives — i.e., a כהן is disqualified from examining the נגעים of his relatives. On the other hand, נגעים do not require three כהנים; rather, one כהן suffices to examine the נגע, as it says: או אל אחד מבניו. (The halachah, however, follows the חכמים: Relatives are fit to examine נגעים — see רמב״ם הל׳ טומאת צרעת, 9:1.)

3 **וראה הכהן את הנגע וגו׳**: שיהיו עיניו בו בשעה שהוא רואה אותו (*Toras Kohanim*). He must focus his gaze on the נגע and compare it with עור הבשר, in accordance with the halachah of the חכמים that the נגע is to be compared with the tint of normal skin, בעור הבשר הבינוני (ibid.).

ושער בנגע הפך לבן: The normal hair found on the skin has lost its color — i.e., it has turned white. There must be at least two hairs, as מיעוט שיער שתי שערות: the term שיער implies at least two hairs. White hair is מטמא only if it turned white as a result of the נגע, but if it preceded the נגע (שיער לבן שקדם לבהרת) it is not מטמא. Moreover, even if one had a בהרת with שיער לבן and the בהרת disappeared, leaving שיער לבן in place, and then a new נגע formed about this שיער, the שיער is not מטמא. Such residual hair is called שער פקודה and is טהור. A נגע is rendered טמא by שיער לבן only if the נגע itself caused the bleaching of the שיער (see *Nega'im* 5:3).

ד וְאִם־בַּהֶ֨רֶת֩ לְבָנָ֜ה הִ֗וא בְּע֣וֹר
בְּשָׂר֔וֹ וְעָמֹק֙ אֵין־מַרְאֶ֣הָ מִן־
הָע֔וֹר וּשְׂעָרָ֖ה לֹא־הָפַ֣ךְ לָבָ֑ן
וְהִסְגִּ֧יר הַכֹּהֵ֛ן אֶת־הַנֶּ֖גַע שִׁבְעַ֥ת
יָמִֽים׃

4 *But if it is a shiny white spot in the skin of his flesh, even if its color is not so much deeper than the skin, and the hair has not turned white, then the priest shall have the [person with the] mark confined for seven days.*

ומראה הנגע עמק מעור בשרו: מראה הנגע עמוק אין ממשו עמוק (*Toras Kohanim*). The color of the נגע gives the illusion of depth, but actually there is no depression on the skin. See Commentary above, verse 2. The case here is that of a בהרת, which is white as snow, of the deepest white. However, the depth of whiteness does not effect the טומאה; rather, the שיער לבן effects it. Wessely in his *Commentary* speculates that שיער לבן generally develops only in a בהרת, and that is why it is mentioned in Scripture only in connection with the בהרת. Actually, though, שיער לבן is a סימן טומאה in the other three shades of נגעים as well.

וראהו הכהן וטמא אתו. וראהו implies כולו כאחת (*Toras Kohanim*); that is, the נגע — at least to the extent of a גריס — must be visible on one flat surface. This excludes fingertips and similar points on the body which lack a flat surface the size of a גריס. There are twenty-four such points that are not מטמא בנגעים (see *Nega'im* 6:7).

4 **ואם בהרת לבנה הִוא וגו׳**. Wessely's interpretation here is the best among the interpretations of this verse. In his opinion our verse is speaking of the lime-white נגע, the ספחת (subsidiary shade) of בהרת. Since it is slightly darker than the snow-white בהרת, our verse can say of it: ועמק אין מראה מן העור. It appears that this is also how the כסף משנה (הל׳ טומאת צרעת, 1:6) understands this sentence, of which רש״י says: לא ידעתי פירושו.

A difficulty remains, however, as the Gemara (*Shevuos* 6b) seems to take the case of our verse to be that of the intensely white בהרת. The Gemara expounds our verse as follows: ואם בהרת לבנה היא – היא לבנה ואין אחרת לבנה. This, apparently, is the reason רש״י refrained from interpreting our verse as referring to a weaker shade of בהרת.

This difficulty is resolved as follows. The Gemara (ibid.) does not say אין אחרת לבנה הימנה, but states broadly: אין אחרת לבנה. It appears, then, that the Gemara's statement refers to the entire category of בהרת — i.e., to בהרת and its תולדה. Both — snow-white and lime-white — belong to the category of pure white. It follows that בהרת, as the אב of this category, is עזה, the strongest white of all, snow-white. The other category — שאת ותולדתה, white as fleece and white as egg-skin — is not pure white, and is slightly blueish or yellowish. Thus, our verse speaks of the תולדה of בהרת, which is כסיד ההיכל. It, too, is white like the בהרת — only not as deep.

ושערה לא הפך לבן והסגיר וגו׳. This law, too, applies to all four מראות, but it is mentioned here only in the case of תולדת בהרת. For in the case of בהרת (the אב) הפיכת שיער לבן usually occurs (as mentioned above according to Wessely), and the בהרת is then טמא immediately, without הסגר.

והסגיר הכהן את הנגע וגו׳. There are two stages of טומאה in the case of the מצורע: הסגר and החלט. There are three symptoms (סימני טומאה) by which the נגוע is rendered a מצורע מוחלט: שיער לבן (v. 3), פשיון (vv. 7–8), and מחיה (vv. 10–11). If the נגע has the color of one of the four מראות, but has neither שיער לבן nor מחיה, the person becomes a מצורע מוסגר: he is isolated for seven days and is examined again on the seventh day. If one of three סימני טומאה has appeared, he is declared מוחלט. If the נגע has remained unchanged, a second הסגר of seven days is decreed upon him. The second הסגר begins on the last day of the first הסגר, so that altogether the number of days of the two הסגרים comes to thirteen. If by the end of the second הסגר one of the סימני טומאה has appeared, he is declared מוחלט; if not, he is פטור, declared free.

In the cases of שחין (v. 18, et seq.) and מכוה (v. 24, et seq.), there is only one period of הסגר, and מחיה is not a סימן טומאה.

Of the three סימני טומאה, שיער לבן and מחיה can be visible at the very first examination, in which case the מצורע is rendered מוחלט immediately; but פשיון applies only after הסגר. All three, however, result in החלט even לאחר פטור — i.e., even if they appear only after he has been declared free at the end of הסגר.

Thus we learn in the Mishnah (*Nega'im* 3:3–4): עור הבשר מיטמא בשני שבועות ובשלושה סימנין – בשער לבן ובמחיה ובפסיון, בשער לבן ובמחיה בתחלה ובסוף שבוע ראשון ובסוף שבוע שני לאחר הפטור, ובפסיון בסוף שבוע ראשון ובסוף שבוע שני לאחר הפטור, ומיטמא בשני שבועות שהן שלושה עשר יום. השחין והמכוה מיטמאין בשבוע

ה וְרָאָ֨הוּ הַכֹּהֵ֜ן בַּיּ֣וֹם הַשְּׁבִיעִי֮ וְהִנֵּ֣ה
הַנֶּ֗גַע עָמַ֣ד בְּעֵינָ֔יו לֹֽא־פָשָׂ֥ה
הַנֶּ֖גַע בָּע֑וֹר וְהִסְגִּיר֧וֹ הַכֹּהֵ֛ן שִׁבְעַ֥ת
יָמִ֖ים שֵׁנִֽית׃ שני

5 *And the priest shall look at him on the seventh day, and lo! the mark is still there, it has remained the same shade, and moreover, the mark has not spread in the skin, then the priest shall have him remain confined for another seven days.*

אחד ובשני סימנין – בשער לבן ובפסיון, בשער לבן בתחלה בסוף שבוע לאחר הפטור, ובפסיון בסוף שבוע לאחר הפטור, ומיטמאין בשבוע אחד שהוא שבעה ימים.

A מצורע מוסגר is treated the same as a מצורע מוחלט in respect to isolation (v. 46) and טומאה (see Commentary to vv. 6 and 46). They differ in two things only: (a) פריעה and פרימה (v. 45) do not apply during ימי הסגר; and (b) a טהור מתוך הסגר has no obligation of תגלחת וציפורים as does a טהור מתוך החלט (chap. 14; see *Megillah* 8b).

It appears that הסגר is not identical with שילוח מחנה. הסגר entails that, in addition to the מצורע's expulsion from מחנה ישראל, he must then be isolated (see רש״י below, 13:46). Furthermore, the Gemara (*Megillah* 8b) does not derive from the term והסגירו that a מצורע מוסגר requires שילוח. It has not been resolved whether הסגר means an actual confinement or merely a declaration of הסגר (see Commentary below, 14:38).

5 **וראהו הכהן ביום השביעי**. נגעים may be examined only by day — not in the dim light of early morning or late afternoon, nor in the blinding light of midday, but in the middle hours of morning and afternoon: בארבע בחמש בשמנה ובתשע (*Nega'im* 2:2).

והנה: He judges it strictly by its appearance on the seventh day. Any changes that may have occurred during the period of הסגר are of no consequence (ראב״ד on *Toras Kohanim*).

עמד בעיניו: even if it has not remained בעינו, exactly the same shade as before, so long as it is still בעיניו, within the range of the four מראות; for if it has become darker than קרום ביצה, it is בהק (v. 39) and טהור. According to the רמב״ן, בעיניו means: in his judgment.

ו וְרָאָה הַכֹּהֵן אֹתוֹ בַּיּוֹם הַשְּׁבִיעִי
שֵׁנִית וְהִנֵּה כֵּהָה הַנֶּגַע וְלֹא־פָשָׂה
הַנֶּגַע בָּעוֹר וְטִהֲרוֹ הַכֹּהֵן מִסְפַּחַת
הִוא וְכִבֶּס בְּגָדָיו וְטָהֵר׃

6 *And the priest shall look at him on the seventh day for a second time, and lo! the mark has become darker and the mark has not spread in the skin, then the priest must declare him pure; it is merely a mark resembling leprosy; he must wash his garments and he is then pure.*

והסגירו הכהן שבעת ימים שנית: Just as at the first הסגר, the day on which the הסגר is declared counts as one of the seven days, so, too, the seventh day of the first הסגר counts also as the first day of the second הסגר. Together, they total thirteen days (see *Toras Kohanim*).

6 **והנה כהה הנגע**: Even if the נגע has become darker, the טהרה still depends on the absence of פשיון. This holds true so long as the נגע has not become darker than קרום ביצה. פשיון, however, is מטמא even if the color remains unchanged (see רמב״ן). Wessely suggests that it is also possible that כהה relates not to the color but to the weakness of the נגע (as in וְלֹא כִהָה בָּם [*Shemuel* I, 3:13]). כהה, then, forms one idea with לא פשה: The נגע has stopped and has not spread.

מספחת הִוא — akin to ספחת (v. 2). It is not a real נגע, but only nearly a נגע. The designation מספחת supports the position of Wessely (see our Commentary to v. 4): Scripture here is discussing a phenomenon that is common not to a בהרת but to a ספחת of a בהרת.

וכבס בגדיו וטהר. From this we infer that until now he was טמא and מטמא. His טומאה was like that of a מצורע מוחלט: he was מטמא במגע ובמשא, מטמא משכב ומושב, and מטמא בביאה (see v. 46). For more on טומאת משכב ומושב see our Commentary below, 15:4ff. According to the רמב״ם (הל׳ טומאת צרעת, 10:11), the משכב ומושב of a מצורע — like that of a זב וזבה — is אב הטומאה. According to רש״י, תוספות, the ר״ש, and the ראב״ד, however, the משכב ומושב of a מצורע is only ולד הטומאה, and is מטמא only אוכלין ומשקין (see *Pesachim* 67b; משנה למלך to הל׳ טומאת צרעת, 10:11).

ז וְאִם־פָּשֹׂה תִפְשֶׂה הַמִּסְפַּחַת בָּעוֹר אַחֲרֵי הֵרָאֹתוֹ אֶל־הַכֹּהֵן לְטָהֳרָתוֹ וְנִרְאָה שֵׁנִית אֶל־הַכֹּהֵן׃

7 *But if the mark resembling leprosy spreads in the skin after it has been shown to the priest to be declared pure, it shall be shown to the priest again.*

ח וְרָאָה הַכֹּהֵן וְהִנֵּה פָּשְׂתָה הַמִּסְפַּחַת בָּעוֹר וְטִמְּאוֹ הַכֹּהֵן צָרַעַת הִוא׃ פ

8 *And the priest then looks, and lo! the mark resembling leprosy has spread in the skin, then the priest shall declare him impure; it is leprosy.*

ט נֶגַע צָרַעַת כִּי תִהְיֶה בְּאָדָם וְהוּבָא אֶל־הַכֹּהֵן׃

9 *If a leprous mark appears on a person, he shall be brought to the priest.*

י וְרָאָה הַכֹּהֵן וְהִנֵּה שְׂאֵת־לְבָנָה בָּעוֹר וְהִיא הָפְכָה שֵׂעָר לָבָן וּמִחְיַת בָּשָׂר חַי בַּשְׂאֵת׃

10 *And the priest then looks, and lo! it is a very white spot in the skin, and it has turned the hair white; and likewise if there is an area of healthy flesh in the very white [spot].*

7 **ונראה שנית אל הכהן**. As a rule, the כהן who examines it the first time examines it the second time (see *Toras Kohanim*). Indeed, only a כהן who saw it the first time can discern a subsequent פשיון הנגע.

9 **נגע צרעת וגו'**. This section deals with שאת. Its color is white as fleece, and it is the second major category among the shades of נגעים. In this section a third סימן טומאה is mentioned: מחיה. This סימן is apparently most common to שאת (Wessely), but like שיער לבן and פשיון applies to all of the four מראות.

10 **והיא הפכה שער לבן**. שיער לבן is a סימן טומאה only for the נגע that produces it. But if that נגע disappears, leaving only the bleached hair (שער פקודה), and then a new נגע forms about the bleached hair, the שיער לבן is not a סימן טומאה for this new נגע (see *Toras Kohanim*).

11 *Then it is an old leprosy in the skin of his flesh; the priest must declare him impure; he does not need to keep him confined, for he is impure.*

יא צָרַ֨עַת נוֹשֶׁ֤נֶת הִוא֙ בְּע֣וֹר בְּשָׂר֔וֹ וְטִמְּא֖וֹ הַכֹּהֵ֑ן לֹ֣א יַסְגִּרֶ֔נּוּ כִּ֥י טָמֵ֖א הֽוּא׃

ומחית בשר חי בשאת. It has already been stated in verse 3 that שיער לבן in and of itself is a סימן טומאה. Similarly, in verses 15 and 16 it is stated that מחיה in and of itself is a סימן טומאה. It must be, then, that the וי״ו החיבור in ומחית is not intended to join together the two סימנים, as though both need to be present in order for there to be טומאה. Rather, it is intended to equate the two סימנים — primarily in regard to size: מחיה is מטמאת only if it is at least the size of שתי שערות על שתי שערות. Furthermore, it says here that שיער לבן and מחיה can coexist in one נגע. From this we learn — regarding the minimum size of the נגע — that there must be room for both to exist side by side. Thus, there must be room in the נגע for two hairs beside the מחיה. Yet from the words ומחית בשר חי בשאת we learn that the מחיה is מטמאת only במבוצר, when it is surrounded on *all* sides by שאת — i.e., when there is room enough for שתי שערות on all sides of the מחיה. Thus, the minimum size of the whole נגע is six hairbreadths square — i.e., thirty-six square hairbreadths, which is the size of a גריס הקלקי (see *Toras Kohanim*).

In this, מחיה differs from שיער לבן. מחיה is מטמאת only במבוצר. שיער לבן, however, is מטמא even if it is at the very edge of the נגע — provided that it is still within the נגע; that is, it is מטמא במבוצר ושלא במבוצר (*Nega'im* 4:3). And there is another difference between them: שיער לבן is מטמא only in the case of הפוכה (=הפכה שיער לבן); hence, שיער לבן שקדמה לבהרת טהורה. מחיה, however, is מטמא הפוכה ושלא הפוכה; hence, מחיה שקדמה לבהרת טמאה (see ibid.).

11 **נושנת הִוא וגו׳**. The healthy flesh in the midst of the נגע is a sign of old צרעת: Either the healthy tissue had resisted the נגע for some time, and the נגע could only spread around it; or the נגע was displaced by the healthy flesh, which reappeared in its midst. Hence, מחיה מטמא הפוכה ושלא הפוכה (Wessely; see *Nega'im* 4:3).

יב וְאִם־פָּרוֹחַ תִּפְרַח הַצָּרַעַת בָּעוֹר
וְכִסְּתָה הַצָּרַעַת אֵת כָּל־עוֹר
הַנֶּגַע מֵרֹאשׁוֹ וְעַד־רַגְלָיו לְכָל־
מַרְאֵה עֵינֵי הַכֹּהֵן׃

12 *But if the leprosy then breaks out further in the skin, and the leprosy covers all the skin that is susceptible to the mark, from his head to his feet, as far as the eyes of the priest see.*

יג וְרָאָה הַכֹּהֵן וְהִנֵּה כִסְּתָה הַצָּרַעַת
אֶת־כָּל־בְּשָׂרוֹ וְטִהַר אֶת־הַנָּגַע
כֻּלּוֹ הָפַךְ לָבָן טָהוֹר הוּא׃

13 *And the priest looks, and lo! the leprosy has covered his whole body; then he must declare the mark pure. It has all turned white; therefore he is pure.*

12 **ואם פרוח תפרח**: even if it does not erupt all over him at once, but spreads gradually until it covers him entirely.

את כל עור הנגע: all those parts of the skin that are susceptible to נגעי עור בשר. This excludes, for example, areas affected by שחין המורדת ומכוה המורדת (see Commentary below, vv. 18 and 24).

מראשו ועד רגליו — this excludes תוך ראשו ותוך רגליו, the parts of the head covered with hair, and the soles of the feet (*Toras Kohanim*; see משנה למלך on הל׳ טומאת צרעת, 6:1).

לכל מראה עיני הכהן: פרט לבית הסתרים (*Toras Kohanim*); all that can be seen by the כהן when the person affected is standing in a natural position. This excludes places hidden by folds of the skin and by bending of the body. The legs are examined in the position of עודר, digging, and the arms are examined in the position of מוסק זיתים, plucking olives (*Nega'im* 2:4).

13 **כלו הפך לבן טהור הוא**: הפורח מן הטמא טהור מן הטהור טמא (ibid. 8:1). That is to say, if the נגע spreads over the whole body, it is טהור — providing that it does so from a condition of טומאה, whether הסגר or החלט. But if it does so from a condition of טהרה — whether at the beginning, at the first appearance of the נגע, or after it has been declared cured — then פריחה בכולו is a sign of טומאה. Hence, הבא כולו לבן יסגיר וכו׳ (ibid. 8:7): if

יד וּבְיוֹם הֵרָאוֹת בּוֹ בָּשָׂר חַי יִטְמָא׃

14 *But on the day that healthy flesh appears on him again, he becomes impure.*

טו וְרָאָה הַכֹּהֵן אֶת־הַבָּשָׂר הַחַי וְטִמְּאוֹ הַבָּשָׂר הַחַי טָמֵא הוּא צָרַעַת הוּא׃

15 *The priest shall look at the healthy flesh and must declare him impure. The healthy flesh is impure; it is leprosy.*

טז אוֹ כִי יָשׁוּב הַבָּשָׂר הַחַי וְנֶהְפַּךְ לְלָבָן וּבָא אֶל־הַכֹּהֵן׃

16 *Or if the healthy flesh turns white again, he shall come to the priest.*

the very first time he comes to the כהן he has turned white all over (כולו הפך לבן), he requires הסגר, he must be isolated. And in general, a בהרת גדולה בתחילה counts the same as a בהרת קטנה. Similarly, if he is declared טהור after the second הסגר (v. 6) and then כולו הפך לבן, he is מוחלט, just as in the case of a minor פסיון (v. 7).

14 **וביום הראות בו**. It does not say ובהראות בו but וביום הראות בו; from this we learn in *Mo'ed Katan* 7b that יש יום שאתה רואה בו ויש יום שאי אתה רואה בו, there are days on which one does not examine the נגע: חתן שנולד בו נגע נותנין לו שבעה ימי המשתה לו ולביתו ולכסותו וכן ברגל נותנין לו שבעת ימי הרגל, "If a נגע appears on a bridegroom, he is allowed to pass the seven days of rejoicing without being examined — neither himself, his house or his clothes (should a נגע appear on these). Similarly, no examinations are made on the seven days of a festival." The Gemara (ibid.) also mentions the law stated below (14:36): וצוה הכהן ופנו את הבית, the examination of a נגע on a house is deferred until all moveables are removed from the house, ולא יטמא כל אשר בבית, so that everything in the house will not become טמא. Thus, the examination is deferred even לדבר הרשות, for ordinary interests — and certainly לדבר מצוה. On שבת, too, ראיית נגעים is not performed, and if the seventh day of הסגר falls on a שבת the examination is deferred until the following day (*Nega'im* 1:4).

15–16 Only בשר חי brings back the טומאה, but not שיער לבן. Neither does the טומאה return on account of בוהק — i.e., if what appears is not healthy

17 *The priest looks at him, and lo! the mark has turned white, then the priest must pronounce the mark pure; he is pure.*

18 *And [as for] flesh on whose skin there is a boil and it has healed.*

יז וְרָאָהוּ֮ הַכֹּהֵן֒ וְהִנֵּ֛ה נֶהְפַּ֥ךְ הַנֶּ֖גַע לְלָבָ֑ן וְטִהַ֧ר הַכֹּהֵ֛ן אֶת־הַנֶּ֖גַע טָה֥וֹר הֽוּא׃ פ שלישי

יח וּבָשָׂ֕ר כִּֽי־יִהְיֶ֥ה בֽוֹ־בְעֹר֖וֹ שְׁחִ֑ין וְנִרְפָּֽא׃

flesh but a נגע-shade that is darker than the four מראות המטמאים (see v. 39, and see *Toras Kohanim*).

17 והנה נהפך הנגע ללבן: אפילו למראה בהק (*Toras Kohanim*).

טהור הוא: הוא טהור ואין הבא בכולו לבן בתחילה טהור אלא טמא (*Toras Kohanim*; see Commentary above, v. 13).

18 Elsewhere (Commentary to *Shemos* 9:8–10) we explained the meaning of שחין on the basis of words with similar roots. As an addendum we would mention also צחן (צַחֲנָתוֹ — *Yo'el* 2:20), which denotes the smell of rottenness. שחין denotes any skin inflammation that develops from within or results from a blow or external injury — with the exception of an inflammation that results from a fire burn. The latter is called מכוה (below, v. 24; see *Toras Kohanim*; *Chullin* 8a).

ונרפא. This does not mean that it heals completely; for later (v. 20) Scripture says: בשחין פרחה, from which we infer that the inflammation still exists. Rather, our verse here refers to the beginning of the healing process; as *Toras Kohanim* puts it: נרפא ולא נרפא. The skin had been broken by an inflammation, and it formed a new thin layer of skin, כקליפת השום. As long as this stage of healing has not begun, the inflammation is called מורדת, שחין מורד (apparently: ulcerating and festering), and no נגע טמא can form on it. Once the healing is complete and scar tissue (צלקת) has formed, this new skin counts as עור בשר and is subject to all the laws of נגעים discussed above: בשלושה סימנים ובשני שבועות. But if the healing has begun but is not complete, נרפא ולא נרפא, then the laws that follow here apply: A נגע appearing on the newly formed skin has only one week of הסגר and becomes מוחלט through only two סימנים: שיער

יט וְהָיָה בִמְקוֹם הַשְּׁחִין שְׂאֵת לְבָנָה
אוֹ בַהֶרֶת לְבָנָה אֲדַמְדָּמֶת וְנִרְאָה
אֶל־הַכֹּהֵן׃

19 *But there is on the place of the boil a very white or shiny white spot intermingled with red, it must be shown to the priest.*

כ וְרָאָה הַכֹּהֵן וְהִנֵּה מַרְאֶהָ שָׁפָל
מִן־הָעוֹר וּשְׂעָרָהּ הָפַךְ לָבָן
וְטִמְּאוֹ הַכֹּהֵן נֶגַע־צָרַעַת הִוא
בַּשְּׁחִין פָּרָחָה׃

20 *And the priest looks, and lo! its color is lower than the skin, and its hair has turned white; then the priest must declare him impure. It is a leprous mark that has broken out on the boil.*

כא וְאִם ׀ יִרְאֶנָּה הַכֹּהֵן וְהִנֵּה אֵין־בָּהּ
שֵׂעָר לָבָן וּשְׁפָלָה אֵינֶנָּה מִן־
הָעוֹר וְהִיא כֵהָה וְהִסְגִּירוֹ הַכֹּהֵן
שִׁבְעַת יָמִים׃

21 *But if the priest looks at it, and lo! there is no white hair upon it, and even if it is not so much lower than the skin, but is darker, then the priest must keep him confined for seven days.*

לבן ופשיון. מחיה does not apply. The same is true of מכוה (v. 24, et seq.; see *Nega'im* 3:4; 9:2).

19 **לבנה אדמדמת** — see Commentary below, verse 29. This shade of white tinged with red applies to all of the four מראות and also to נגעי עור בשר. In Halachah it is called פתוך, mixed (*Shevuos* 6a).

20 **בשחין פרחה**: אבל לא בעור הבשר (*Toras Kohanim*). One evaluates only the נגע as it is on the שחין. Manifestations on the adjoining skin are not taken into consideration.

21 **ושפלה איננה מן העור והיא כהה**. Verse 19 mentions only the two אבות — viz., שאת and בהרת. Our verse adds the two תולדות: ושפלה איננו מן העור — even if it is not "low" (i.e., bright) like the בהרת. והיא כהה — even if it is darker than the שאת (see Commentary above, v. 4).

כב וְאִם־פָּשֹׂה תִפְשֶׂה בָּעוֹר וְטִמֵּא
הַכֹּהֵן אֹתוֹ נֶגַע הִוא׃

22 *If it has then spread further in the skin, the priest must declare him impure; it is a [leprous] mark.*

כג וְאִם־תַּחְתֶּיהָ תַּעֲמֹד הַבַּהֶרֶת לֹא
פָשָׂתָה צָרֶבֶת הַשְּׁחִין הִוא וְטִהֲרוֹ
הַכֹּהֵן׃ ס רביעי (שני כשהן מחוברין)

23 *But if the shiny white spot has remained where it was, it has not spread, then it is a scar from the boil; the priest must declare him pure.*

22 **ואם פשה תפשה**: even if this פשיון appears only after the seventh day of הסגר (see *Toras Kohanim*).

23 **ואם תחתיה וגו׳ לא פשתה**. פשיון is מטמא only in the area of the שחין. Any spreading to עור בשר or to עור מכוה would not be מטמא (see *Toras Kohanim*).

צרבת השחין. According to *Toras Kohanim* on verse 18, צרבת השחין is the beginning of the healing, which is indicated by the formation of new skin. By contrast, צלקת appears at the end of the healing process.

In *Yechezkel* 21:3 it is written: וְנִצְרְבוּ־בָהּ כָּל־פָּנִים. The discussion there is of a spreading fire, whose mark is discernible upon the faces. Thus, clearly, the relation of צרב to שרף. In *Mishlei* 16:27 it is written: אִישׁ בְּלִיַּעַל כֹּרֶה רָעָה וְעַל־שְׂפָתוֹ כְּאֵשׁ צָרָבֶת. The expression על שפתו אש צרבת is beautifully explained by the sense of צרבת in our verse: Fire, poorly covered, is found continually upon his lips.

צרב is found also in Rabbinic language: משום דצריבן (*Beitzah* 7a). This word is used there to describe eggs that were laid — as opposed to eggs that were not laid. According to the *Aruch*, it means קשים וחזקים, hard and strong; thus the expression צורבא מרבנן: חוזק תלמידי חכמים — i.e., a sage whose learning is firmly in hand.

Let us remember the meaning of צרף in Rabbinic language: to strengthen and harden, as in מיחם שפינה וכו׳ מפני שמצרף (*Shabbos* 41b); כלי חרס וכו׳ משיצרפו בכבשן (*Beitzah* 32a; see רש״י, there). Let us also remember the common meaning of צרף in Rabbinic language: to join together and unite. We conclude that the basic meaning of צרף is to join together things of the same kind. The שורף breaks a thing down

24 *Or [as for] flesh in whose skin there is a burn caused by fire, and the spot where the burn has healed is shiny white intermingled with red, or pure white.*

כד אוֹ בָשָׂר כִּי־יִהְיֶה בְעֹרוֹ מִכְוַת־
אֵשׁ וְהָיְתָה מִחְיַת הַמִּכְוָה בַּהֶרֶת
לְבָנָה אֲדַמְדֶּמֶת אוֹ לְבָנָה׃

25 *And the priest looks at it, and lo! there is hair that has turned white in the shiny white [spot], and its color is deeper than the skin; then it is leprosy. It has broken out in the burn. The priest must declare him impure; it is leprosy.*

כה וְרָאָה אֹתָהּ הַכֹּהֵן וְהִנֵּה נֶהְפַּךְ
שֵׂעָר לָבָן בַּבַּהֶרֶת וּמַרְאֶהָ עָמֹק
מִן־הָעוֹר צָרַעַת הִוא בַּמִּכְוָה
פָּרָחָה וְטִמֵּא אֹתוֹ הַכֹּהֵן נֶגַע
צָרַעַת הִוא׃

26 *But if the priest looks at it, and lo! there is no white hair in the shiny white [spot], even if it is not so*

כו וְאִם | יִרְאֶנָּה הַכֹּהֵן וְהִנֵּה אֵין־
בַּבַּהֶרֶת שֵׂעָר לָבָן וּשְׁפָלָה אֵינֶנָּה

into its parts; the מצרף joins together things that are fit to be united. Thus the meaning of צרף: to refine. The dross interposes between the parts of pure metal, which are of one kind and are fit to be joined together. Upon the separation of the dross, they join together and become homogenous material. Thus also the meaning of צרף: to increase the cohesion, to compress the atoms of the material — to strengthen and harden.

Thus also סרב: to show opposition, as in סָרָבִים וְסַלּוֹנִים (*Yechezkel* 2:6) and in the common Rabbinic expression מסרב, to refuse. Its main meaning is to unite against someone or something.

צרבת, then, is the connective tissue that forms over an open sore. It is the beginning of the renewal of connecting skin, or the beginning of scar formation. As the Mishnah (*Nega'im* 9:2) says: עשו קרום כקליפת השום, זו היא צרבת השחין האמורה בתורה; חזרו וחיו, אע״פ שמקומן צלקת, נדונין כעור הבשר.

24 מחית המכוה is identical to צרבת המכוה (v. 28).

26 See Commentary above, verse 21.

much lower than the skin, but is darker, then the priest must keep him confined for seven days.

מִן־הָעוֹר וְהִוא כֵהָה וְהִסְגִּירוֹ
הַכֹּהֵן שִׁבְעַת יָמִים׃

27 *And the priest looks at him on the seventh day; if it has then spread further in the skin, the priest must declare him impure; it is a leprous mark.*

כז וְרָאָהוּ הַכֹּהֵן בַּיּוֹם הַשְּׁבִיעִי אִם־
פָּשֹׂה תִפְשֶׂה בָּעוֹר וְטִמֵּא הַכֹּהֵן
אֹתוֹ נֶגַע צָרַעַת הִוא׃

28 *But if the shiny white [spot] has remained where it was, it has not spread in the skin, and likewise if it is darker, then it is a very white [spot] due to the burn; the priest must declare him pure, for it is the scar of the burn.*

כח וְאִם־תַּחְתֶּיהָ תַעֲמֹד הַבַּהֶרֶת
לֹא־פָשְׂתָה בָעוֹר וְהִוא כֵהָה
שְׂאֵת הַמִּכְוָה הִוא וְטִהֲרוֹ הַכֹּהֵן
כִּי־צָרֶבֶת הַמִּכְוָה הִוא׃ פ חמישי

29 *And if a man or a woman has a mark on the head or beard.*

כט וְאִישׁ אוֹ אִשָּׁה כִּי־יִהְיֶה בוֹ נָגַע
בְּרֹאשׁ אוֹ בְזָקָן׃

---

28 וְהִוא כהה: and likewise if it is darker than בהרת and thus is שאת — as Scripture continues: שאת המכוה הִוא — then it is טהורה only if it has not spread. A change in the color — more intense or less intense — does not affect טומאה and טהרה, provided that it remains within the range of the four מראות and does not become darker than the ordinary color of the skin.

The laws of מכוה and שחין are identical. Scripture mentions them separately only to tell us that they cannot be combined one with the other: Half a גריס of שחין and half a גריס of מכוה do not combine to form the minimum size necessary to be regarded as a נגע (see *Nega'im* 9:2).

29 ואיש או אשה. Verses 29–37 and 40–43 deal with נגעי ראש וזקן. Verses 29–37 deal with נתק, while verses 40–43 deal with קרחת and גבחת. The symptoms that distinguish נתק from קרחת and גבחת is a subject of debate among the commentators.

30 *And the priest looks at the mark, and lo! its color is deeper than the skin and there is short, golden hair*	ל וְרָאָה הַכֹּהֵן אֶת־הַנֶּגַע וְהִנֵּה מַרְאֵהוּ עָמֹק מִן־הָעוֹר וּבוֹ שֵׂעָר

According to the ראב״ד on *Toras Kohanim* and according to the רמב״ן here, a נתק is an isolated spot that has become bald through the falling out of hair, a bald spot surrounded by hair (according to the ראב״ד apparently only if it is situated on the top of the head, between the front and back of the head, centrally); קרחת and גבחת are baldness starting from the back of the neck and upward, or from the forehead and upward.

According to the ר״ש (ibid. 10:10), however, the difference between נתק and קרחת וגבחת is not one of position and size, but of character. In the case of נתק the loss of hair is only temporary, while in קרחת and גבחת the loss is permanent, irreversible.

The רמב״ן here notes that the terms נתק and מריטה support the latter opinion. נתק — meaning to tear off — relates to the hair and does not indicate any permanent change in the skin. מרט, which is also the term for polishing metals, is indicative of permanent change of the skin.

נתק (the isolated or temporary bald spot) in and of itself is a נגע. According to most commentators it requires two periods of הסגר even if there is no skin discoloration. This is provided that it has the size of a גריס. It becomes מוחלט by שיער צהוב or פשיון, but the four מראות נגעים have no effect on a נתק spot.

By contrast, קרחת and גבחת in and of themselves are not a נגע. Rather, the bald scalp is regarded as עור בשר, which is affected by the ארבע מראות נגעים. It has two periods of הסגר and becomes מוחלט by פשיון or מחיה; but שיער לבן does not apply to it.

בראש או בזקן. זקן extends מן הפרק של לחי עד פיקה של גרגרת, from the joint of the jaw to the larynx.

30 **והנה מראהו עמק מן העור**. It is evident from what is stated below (vv. 31, 32, and 35 in conjunction with v. 34) that every נתק requires הסגר and becomes מוחלט by פשיון or שיער צהוב even if its color is not deeper than the skin. That is to say, a נתק is טמא even if its color is darker than קרום ביצה.

צָהֹ֖ב דָּ֑ק וְטִמֵּ֨א אֹת֤וֹ הַכֹּהֵן֙ נֶ֣תֶק
ה֔וּא צָרַ֧עַת הָרֹ֛אשׁ א֥וֹ הַזָּקָ֖ן הֽוּא׃

upon it, then the priest must declare him impure; it is an alopecia, a leprosy of the head or of the beard.

לא וְכִֽי־יִרְאֶ֨ה הַכֹּהֵ֜ן אֶת־נֶ֣גַע הַנֶּ֗תֶק
וְהִנֵּ֤ה אֵין־מַרְאֵ֙הוּ֙ עָמֹ֣ק מִן־הָע֔וֹר
וְשֵׂעָ֥ר שָׁחֹ֖ר אֵ֣ין בּ֑וֹ וְהִסְגִּ֧יר הַכֹּהֵ֛ן
אֶת־נֶ֥גַע הַנֶּ֖תֶק שִׁבְעַ֥ת יָמִֽים׃

31 *But if the priest looks at the alopecia mark, and lo! its color is not deeper than the skin and there is no black hair upon it, then the priest shall keep the [person with the] alopecia mark confined for seven days.*

לב וְרָאָ֨ה הַכֹּהֵ֥ן אֶת־הַנֶּ֘גַע֮ בַּיּ֣וֹם
הַשְּׁבִיעִי֒ וְהִנֵּה֙ לֹא־פָשָׂ֣ה הַנֶּ֔תֶק

32 *On the seventh day the priest shall look at the mark, and lo! [if] the*

This halachah offers an unforced explanation for the location of verses 38 and 39, which are situated between the law of נתק and the law of קרחת וגבחת. For these verses state that בוהק (which is darker than קרום ביצה) is טהור on עור בשר — as opposed to the preceding case of נתק.

Yet our verse states: והנה מראהו עמק מן העור. It appears, then, that the meaning of Scripture here is this: Even if the color of the נתק is מראה שאת or בהרת, the טומאה does not depend on שיער לבן but on שיער צהוב דק. *Toras Kohanim* derives further from the juxtaposition of מראה עמוק and נתק that just as מראה is בידי שמים, so, too, נתק is a נגע only if it is בידי שמים — but not if the hair is taken out בידי אדם.

שער צהב דק. שער: at least שתי שערות, as in the case of שיער לבן (v. 3). צהב: like gold in appearance. דק: according to ר׳ עקיבא, דק, in reference to hair, means short (see *Nega'im* 10:1).

ובו שער צהב דק: here it does not say הפך. Hence, שיער צהוב שקדם לנתק is טמא; it is מטמא הפוך ושלא הפוך (ibid. 10:2; see Commentary above, v. 3).

31 **ושער שחר אין בו**. Here, too, שיער means at least שתי שערות. If two black hairs remain within the נתק, it does not become טמא by פשיון or שיער

וְלֹא־הָיָה בוֹ שֵׂעָר צָהֹב וּמַרְאֵה
הַנֶּתֶק אֵין עָמֹק מִן־הָעוֹר׃

alopecia has not spread, and also no golden hair has grown upon it and the color of the alopecia is not deeper than the skin.

לג וְהִתְגַּלָּח וְאֶת־הַנֶּתֶק לֹא יְגַלֵּחַ
וְהִסְגִּיר הַכֹּהֵן אֶת־הַנֶּתֶק שִׁבְעַת
יָמִים שֵׁנִית׃
גִימ״ל רבתי

33 *Then he shall shave himself, but he shall not shave off the alopecia, and the priest shall keep the [person with the] alopecia confined again for seven days.*

לד וְרָאָה הַכֹּהֵן אֶת־הַנֶּתֶק בַּיּוֹם
הַשְּׁבִיעִי וְהִנֵּה לֹא־פָשָׂה הַנֶּתֶק
בָּעוֹר וּמַרְאֵהוּ אֵינֶנּוּ עָמֹק מִן־
הָעוֹר וְטִהַר אֹתוֹ הַכֹּהֵן וְכִבֶּס
בְּגָדָיו וְטָהֵר׃

34 *And the priest looks at the alopecia on the seventh day, and lo! the alopecia has not spread in the skin, and its color is not deeper than the skin, then the priest must declare him pure; he shall wash his garments and become pure.*

צהוב. According to *Toras Kohanim*, שחור is stated only as a contrast to צהוב. Any other color — except צהוב — is likewise מציל.

33 והתגלח: בכל אדם, by anybody (*Toras Kohanim*), whereas the גילוח prescribed in chapter 14 requires a כהן.

ואת הנתק לא יגלח. He must leave a circle of hair, two hairs deep, around the נתק in order to determine whether פשיון subsequently occurs (*Nega'im* 10:5). This supports the view, held by the majority of commentators, that a נתק needs no change in the skin; for otherwise there would be no need to leave a circle of hair to determine whether there has been any פשיון, just as there is no need to do so in the case of נגעי עור בשר (משנה למלך on הל׳ טומאת צרעת, 8:1).

34 וכבס בגדיו — see Commentary above, verse 6.

לה וְאִם־פָּשֹׂה יִפְשֶׂה הַנֶּתֶק בָּעוֹר
אַחֲרֵי טָהֳרָתוֹ׃

35 *But if the alopecia has spread in the skin even after it was declared pure.*

לו וְרָאָהוּ הַכֹּהֵן וְהִנֵּה פָּשָׂה הַנֶּתֶק
בָּעוֹר לֹא־יְבַקֵּר הַכֹּהֵן לַשֵּׂעָר
הַצָּהֹב טָמֵא הוּא׃

36 *And the priest looks at him, and lo! the alopecia has spread in the skin, then the priest need not look for golden hair; he is impure.*

36 **וראהו הכהן**. פשיון is מטמא without שיער צהוב, and שיער צהוב is מטמא without פשיון.

37 **ואם בעיניו עמד הנתק וגו'**. Above, in verse 5, it says: והנה הנגע עמד בעיניו, and the context there is after the first הסגר. The meaning of this statement is that the sign of טומאה that was present in the נגע at the beginning of the הסגר has remained. There, the only sign present was the skin color within the range of the four מראות.

Here, too, it says: ואם בעיניו עמד הנתק, but the context here is after פשיון or שיער צהוב that occurs following the פטור (= אחרי טהרתו). We are therefore inclined to say that בעיניו refers to these signs of טומאה, and the meaning of the statement here is as follows: Even if these signs of טומאה have remained in the נתק, but two black hairs have grown in it, נרפא הנתק טהור הוא, the נתק is cured and is טהור — in spite of the פשיון and the שיער צהוב.

Indeed, the halachah is so: הצומח מציל מיד השער צהוב ומיד הפשיון (*Nega'im* 10:3). And the Halachah distinguishes between שיער שחור הצומח (hair that grew after the נתק appeared) and המשואר (hair that had been in place and that remained in the נתק upon its appearance):

המשואר affords protection against טומאה only if it is מבוצר — i.e., if it is surrounded on all sides by the נתק and is at least two hairbreadths distant from the rest of the hair growth. The קרבן אהרן aptly observes here that for this reason it says (in v. 31) ושער שחר אין בו: black hair may well be there, but אין בו, its position is not as required, it is not completely within the נתק. By contrast, הצומח affords protection even שלא במבוצר — provided that it has grown anew on the bald patch: ושער שחר צמח בו.

However, *Toras Kohanim* says that בעיניו refers here to the כהן: "If in his judgment..."

37 *But if the appearance of the alopecia remained unchanged and black hair has grown upon it, then the alopecia has healed; he is pure and the priest shall declare him pure.*

לז וְאִם־בְּעֵינָיו עָמַד הַנֶּתֶק וְשֵׂעָר
שָׁחֹר צָמַח־בּוֹ נִרְפָּא הַנֶּתֶק טָהוֹר
הוּא וְטִהֲרוֹ הַכֹּהֵן: ס

38 *If a man or a woman has shiny spots on the skin of their flesh, [and] the spots are shiny white.*

לח וְאִישׁ אוֹ־אִשָּׁה כִּי־יִהְיֶה בְעוֹר־
בְּשָׂרָם בֶּהָרֹת בֶּהָרֹת לְבָנֹת:

39 *And the priest looks, and lo! there are shiny spots on the skin of their*

לט וְרָאָה הַכֹּהֵן וְהִנֵּה בְעוֹר־בְּשָׂרָם

נרפא הנתק טהור הוא: אע״פ שהלך לו שער שחור טהור, even if the black hair disappears and the שיער צהוב or the פשיון remains, the נתק is טהור, until other שיער צהוב grows or a new פשיון occurs (*Nega'im* 10:8; רמב״ם הל׳ טומאת צרעת, 8:8).

טהור הוא וטהרו הכהן: He does not become טהור until the כהן declares him טהור; and the כהן's declaration has no effect unless the declaration is in accordance with the laws of טהרה. A mistaken or intentionally false declaration of a כהן is invalid and of no consequence (see *Toras Kohanim*).

The same applies to טומאה: טמא הוא טמא יטמאנו הכהן (v. 44). He does not become טמא until the כהן declares him טמא; and the כהן's declaration has no effect unless the person's condition calls for a declaration of טומאה (see תוספתא *Nega'im*, end of chap. 1).

Thus, no power is given to the כהן. His words are subject to the scrutiny of anyone expert in the law.

39 **בהק הוא**: All white spots whose color is a darker white (כהות) than the darkest of the four מראות — i.e., darker than קרום ביצה — are termed בהק and are טהורים.

In Aramaic, בהק means to illuminate, to shine. Thus, apparently, the expression רבו המובהק — the teacher who has enlightened one's eyes with his Torah, from whom he has gained most of his knowledge, שרוב חכמתו ממנו.

בֶּהָרֹת כֵּהֹות לְבָנֹת בֹּהַק הוּא פָּרַח בָּעוֹר טָהוֹר הוּא: ס	*flesh but [they are] dull white, then it is only a shininess that has broken out on the skin; the person is pure.*
ששי (שלישי כשהן מחוברין)	
מ וְאִישׁ כִּי יִמָּרֵט רֹאשׁוֹ קֵרֵחַ הוּא טָהוֹר הוּא:	40 *And anyone whose head has become bald, it is [merely] an occipital baldness; he is pure.*
מא וְאִם מִפְּאַת פָּנָיו יִמָּרֵט רֹאשׁוֹ גִּבֵּחַ הוּא טָהוֹר הוּא:	41 *If his head becomes bald on the front side, it is [merely] a frontal baldness; he is pure.*

On the juxtaposition of the law of בוהק to that of נתק, see Commentary above, verse 30.

40ff. See Commentary above, verse 29.

40 טהור הוא — i.e., the קרח is not subject to the דין of נתק, to become טמא by שיער צהוב. Rather, the law of קרח is as explained in verses 42 and 43: The bald scalp is accorded the status of עור בשר; it is subject to the ארבע מראות and their *halachos.*

In *Nega'im* 10:9, the following halachah is stated: A נתק that has become מוחלט by שיער צהוב or by פשיון becomes טהור if the head then becomes completely bald, ניתק כל הראש. And the same applies to זקן: If the נתק was in the beard and then ניתק כל הזקן, the person is טהור. *Toras Kohanim* derives this halachah from our verse.

The law of פריחה בכולו in the case of נתק functions like the law of הפך כולו לבן in the case of נגעי עור בשר, with this difference: In the case of נתק the person is טהור even לאחר פטור (see Commentary, v. 13).

הבא בתחילה ניתק כל הראש או הזקן is treated as נתק, just as הפך כולו לבן בתחילה is treated as בהרת גדולה (ר״ש, ad loc., according to the תוספתא).

41 גבח. גבחת, baldness on the part of the head near the forehead. גבח is apparently related to גבה, גבע. As a result of the גבחת, the height (גובה) or extent of the forehead reaches up to the crown.

מב וְכִֽי־יִהְיֶ֣ה בַקָּרַ֗חַת א֚וֹ בַגַּבַּ֔חַת נֶ֖גַע לָבָ֣ן אֲדַמְדָּ֑ם צָרַ֤עַת פֹּרַ֙חַת֙ ה֔וּא בְּקָֽרַחְתּ֖וֹ א֥וֹ בְגַבַּחְתּֽוֹ׃

42 *But if a white mark intermingled with red appears on the occipital baldness or on the frontal baldness, then it is a leprosy breaking out on his occipital baldness or on his frontal baldness.*

מג וְרָאָ֨ה אֹת֜וֹ הַכֹּהֵ֗ן וְהִנֵּ֤ה שְׂאֵֽת־הַנֶּ֙גַע֙ לְבָנָ֣ה אֲדַמְדֶּ֔מֶת בְּקָרַחְתּ֖וֹ א֣וֹ בְגַבַּחְתּ֑וֹ כְּמַרְאֵ֥ה צָרַ֖עַת ע֥וֹר בָּשָֽׂר׃

43 *If the priest looks at him, and lo! the very white [color] of the mark is white intermingled with red, on his occipital baldness or on his frontal baldness, similar to the leprous color on the skin of the flesh.*

מד אִישׁ־צָר֥וּעַ ה֖וּא טָמֵ֣א ה֑וּא טַמֵּ֧א יְטַמְּאֶ֛נּוּ הַכֹּהֵ֖ן בְּרֹאשׁ֥וֹ נִגְעֽוֹ׃

44 *Then he is a leprous man, he is impure; the priest must declare him impure. His mark is on his head.*

---

43 כמראה צרעת עור בשר. קרחת וגבחת are מטמאות not only בפתוך (see Commentary above, v. 19), which is expressly mentioned in verses 42 and 43, but also by all of the four מראות, as in the case of עור בשר; and just as in the case of עור בשר, they are subject to two periods of הסגר. But they attain החלט only by two סימנים — viz., מחיה ופשיון, but not by שיער לבן (see *Nega'im* 10:10).

44 איש צרוע excludes a woman; והצרוע (v. 45) includes a woman. From this we learn that all the laws of מצורע apply to a woman, except that she is exempt from פריעה ופרימה (see *Sotah* 23).

טמא הוא — see Commentary above, v. 37. From the repetition of the word הוא we learn that טומאת צרעת alone — and not other טומאות — depends on the declaration of a כהן: זה טומאתו בכהן ואין שאר הטמאים טומאתן בכהן (*Toras Kohanim*).

45 *But every leper to whom the mark attaches, his garments shall be rent, his head shall remain unshorn, he shall cover himself down to his upper lip, and he shall call out: Impure! Impure!*	מה וְהַצָּר֜וּעַ אֲשֶׁר־בּ֣וֹ הַנֶּ֗גַע בְּגָדָ֞יו יִהְי֤וּ פְרֻמִים֙ וְרֹאשׁוֹ֙ יִהְיֶ֣ה פָר֔וּעַ וְעַל־שָׂפָ֖ם יַעְטֶ֑ה וְטָמֵ֥א ׀ טָמֵ֖א יִקְרָֽא׃
46 *All the days, as long as the mark is upon him, he shall be impure; he is impure. Isolated shall he remain, outside the camp shall his dwelling be.*	מו כָּל־יְמֵ֞י אֲשֶׁ֨ר הַנֶּ֥גַע בּ֛וֹ יִטְמָ֖א טָמֵ֣א ה֑וּא בָּדָ֣ד יֵשֵׁ֔ב מִח֥וּץ לַֽמַּחֲנֶ֖ה מוֹשָׁבֽוֹ׃ ס

45 **אשר בו הנגע**: מי שצרעתו תלויה בגופו. פריעה and פרימה apply only to a מוחלט, who attains טהרה only through bodily changes that heal the נגע. This excludes a מוסגר, שאין צרעתו תלויה בגופו אלא בימים; for at the end of the ימי הסגר he becomes טהור automatically if the נגע has remained unchanged (*Megillah* 8b).

פרמים — see Commentary above, 10:6.

פרוע: according to ר׳ עקיבא, the מצורע must also remain without his ordinary headcovering (see *Mo'ed Katan* 15a; תוספות ד״ה וראשו), although it says immediately afterward ועל שפם יעטה — from which we learn that the מצורע is obligated to cover his head, עטיפת הראש (ibid.). We find a similar phenomenon in *Kesubos* 72b: Lack of the usual headcovering in the case of a married woman is considered פריעת ראש — even where there is some other hair covering. וצ״ע דשם קלתה לא הוי אלא דת יהודית וכאן משמע דפרוע ראש מדאורייתא מקרי ואפשר דבכתובות הוי דלא כר״ע ומשום זה ג״כ לא מייתי הרמב״ם בחיבורו גבי מצורע דבעי ג״כ גלוי ראש וצ״ע.

ועל שפם יעטה: עד גובי דדיקנא (*Mo'ed Katan* 24a). One must draw the headcovering down over the mouth (see רש״י, ibid.); according to רבינו האי, only to the side whiskers (see טור יו״ד 386).

46 **כל ימי אשר הנגע בו**: Even if he cut off the בהרת in violation of the law, מן התורה he is טהור (see *Bechoros* 34b).

כל ימי וגו׳ — even during the ימי הסגר, although there is no פריעה ופרימה during that period. For in regard to טומאה and שילוח מחנה (בדד ישב), there is no difference between מוסגר and מוחלט: אין בין מצורע מוסגר למצורע מוחלט אלא פריעה ופרימה (*Megillah* 8b).

בדד ישב: שלא ישב טמא אחר עמו (*Zevachim* 117a). The מצורע is removed further than all other טמאים. Whereas טמא מת is excluded only from מחנה שכינה, and זב וזבה only from מחנה לויה, a מצורע is excluded even from מחנה ישראל (see Commentary, *Bemidbar* 5:2–3). However, only עיירות המוקפות חומה מימות יהושע בן נון, cities that were surrounded by walls when the land was first taken into possession, are considered מחנה ישראל (see Commentary below, 25:30; *Kelim* 1:7; ר״ש, there). In all other cities a מצורע is permitted to dwell among the population.

מושבו: מושבו טמא (*Toras Kohanim*); hence, הטמא עומד תחת האילן, והטהור עובר – טמא. הטהור עומד תחת האילן, והטמא עובר – טהור. אם עמד – טמא (*Nega'im* 13:7). That is, if a מצורע stands under a tree, and someone passes under the tree, that person becomes טמא; but if someone stands under a tree, and a מצורע passes under the tree, the person does not become טמא unless the מצורע stands still. Any place where a מצורע is at rest is considered מושבו, his resting place. If that place is roofed or under cover, anything that is there — whether standing or passing by — becomes טמא, unless there is a partition separating it from the מצורע. A partition at least ten טפחים high and four cubits wide affords the טהור protection against the טומאה (ibid. 13:12). The condition that the מצורע must be at rest applies only to a place that is not enclosed — e.g., under the branches of a tree. But in a house, even the passing through of a מצורע renders everything that is under the same roof with him טמא (*Yevamos* 103b, תוספות ד״ה כיון).

This טומאה of a מצורע is called ביאה: מצורע מטמא בביאה (*Kelim* 1:4). It is similar to the טומאת אהל of a מת, as noted in the ספרי (*Bemidbar* 12:12): אל נא תהי כמת – מה המת מטמא באהל אף מצורע מטמא בביאה, and as it says in *Yevamos* (103b): מוחלט איתקש למת. The main difference between the two טומאות is this: A מת — even if it merely passes through (עובר) — is מטמא everything in the אהל; and a מחיצת י׳ טפחים is not מציל in אהל המת. See ר״ש to *Kelim* 1:4.

Besides this טומאה בביאה which is unique to מצורע, a מצורע has the status of an אב הטומאה and is מטמא במגע ובמשא במשכב ובמושב. However, משכבו ומושבו of a מצורע become, apparently, only ולד הטומאה, whereas

47 *And [as for] the garment in which there is a leprous mark, in a woolen garment or in a linen garment.*

מז וְהַבֶּ֗גֶד כִּֽי־יִהְיֶ֥ה ב֖וֹ נֶ֣גַע צָרָ֑עַת
בְּבֶ֣גֶד צֶ֔מֶר א֖וֹ בְּבֶ֥גֶד פִּשְׁתִּֽים׃

48 *Whether it is in the warp or the woof, of flax or of wool, or on a skin or on anything made of skin.*

מח א֣וֹ בִשְׁתִ֔י א֣וֹ בְעֵ֔רֶב לַפִּשְׁתִּ֖ים
וְלַצָּ֑מֶר א֣וֹ בְע֔וֹר א֖וֹ בְּכָל־
מְלֶ֥אכֶת עֽוֹר׃

משכב ומושב of זב וזבה become אב הטומאה. We noted this earlier, in our Commentary to verse 6.

47 **והבגד וגו׳**. In *Nega'im* (11:1) we learn: כל הבגדים מיטמאין בנגעים חוץ משל נכרים. הלוקח בגדים מן הנכרים יראו בתחלה. Here we have a characteristic difference between נגעי בגדים and נגעי הגוף. נגעי הגוף that were upon a גר before he converted are not מטמאים (see Commentary above, v. 2); yet when a נגע-affected בגד of a נכרי comes into the possession of a Jew, it must be shown to a כהן, יראו בתחלה.

According to the ר״ש (*Nega'im* 3:1) they differ also in that בגדי גר תושב are susceptible to טומאת בגדים. From תוספות יום טוב (ibid.), however, it appears that this is merely a גזירה דרבנן.

As regards טומאה, a בגד מנוגע — whether מוסגר or מוחלט — has the same law as אדם. It is an אב הטומאה and is מטמא במגע ובמשא ובביאה. According to the רמב״ם (הל׳ טומאת צרעת, 13:13) it is מטמא also משכב ומושב, as in the case of אדם. See, however, ראב״ד and משנה למלך (ibid.).

As regards שילוח מחנה, בגדים המנוגעים are חמורים מאדם, as they must be sent out of all עיירות, even from those that were not מוקפות חומה in the days of יהושע בן נון (see רמב״ם ibid., 13:15; see Commentary, v. 46).

והבגד: not only an article of clothing, but also a curtain, the sail of a ship, and the like (*Nega'im* 11:11; see ר״ש, there).

48 **או בשתי או בערב**. שתי is the warp, the primary threads in the weaving process, the vertical threads. ערב is the woof, the horizontal threads that cross the warp. Scripture speaks here of the yet unwoven spun threads of the warp and the woof.

49 *And the mark is deep green or* מט וְהָיָה הַנֶּגַע יְרַקְרַק | אוֹ אֲדַמְדָּם

How remarkable is the term שתי, whose root (שתה) denotes drinking. Similarly, the root נסך denotes pouring, as well as the taut stretching of the warp threads in the web. Thus the words מַסֵּכָה and מַסֶּכֶת denote a web generally and a taut warp specifically. According to תרגום יונתן on *Shoftim* 16:13–14, מסכת denotes also the weaver's beam, to which the warp threads are attached. The identification of נסך and שתה with the web and the weaver's beam is clear there, as יונתן translates מסכת: משתיתא, and in verse 13 he translates תארגי: תשתין. The verse וַיֹּאמֶר אֵלֶיהָ אִם־תַּאַרְגִי אֶת־שֶׁבַע מַחְלְפוֹת רֹאשִׁי עִם־הַמַּסָּכֶת (*Shoftim* 16:13) is not speaking of the weaving of the woof threads, but means as follows: Tautly stretch out the locks like warp threads on the weaver's beam. The warp threads stretched tautly on the weaver's beam one beside the other appear as though they were being poured. Accordingly, it is no wonder that the attachment of the warp to the side of the weaver's beam is depicted as "drinking" (שתייה).

Compare the term for weaver's beam, מנור, as in כִּמְנוֹר אֹרְגִים (*Shemuel* I, 17:7). The warp is called נור, and the identical form נהר denotes flowing.

או בעור. According to the Halachah (*Nega'im* 11:1), only skins of land animals. Thus, the principle כל אשר בים טהור applies here also (see Commentary above, 11:32).

Woolen and linen yarn or material are מקבלים טומאת נגעים only if they are of a natural white color. Skins of any natural color are מקבלים טומאה; but if they are צבועים בידי אדם, it is not certain that they are מקבלים טומאה. See כסף משנה on הל' טומאת צרעת, 13:1.

או בעור. The עור must be similar to מלאכת עור: articles made from skin; i.e., they must be dressed skins ready for use, such as עורות אהלים (*Toras Kohanim*). In this, the law of עור differs from that of בגד. In the case of בגד, even simple spun thread — שתי or ערב — is מקבל טומאה. This explains, apparently, the expression לפשתים ולצמר: In the case of פשתים and צמר, simple spun thread is susceptible to טומאת נגעים; but in the case of עור, only when its manufacture is complete, and it is ready for use.

49 **ירקרק או אדמדם**: ירקרק שבירוקים ואדמדם שבאדומים (*Nega'im* 11:4), the greenest of greens (according to ר' אליעזר in the תוספתא, [also?] wax and

deep red, in the garment or on the skin, or in the warp or the woof, or on any utensil made of skin, then it is a leprous mark and must be shown to the priest.

בַּבֶּגֶד אוֹ בָעוֹר אוֹ־בַשְּׁתִי אוֹ־
בָעֵרֶב אוֹ בְכָל־כְּלִי־עוֹר נֶגַע
צָרַעַת הוּא וְהָרְאָה אֶת־הַכֹּהֵן׃

50 *If the priest sees the mark, he must keep [the article with] the mark confined for seven days.*

נ וְרָאָה הַכֹּהֵן אֶת־הַנָּגַע וְהִסְגִּיר
אֶת־הַנֶּגַע שִׁבְעַת יָמִים׃

51 *The priest shall look at the mark on the seventh day, [and if he sees] that the mark has spread in the garment, or in the warp or the woof, or on the skin, whatever the use for which the skin may have been manufactured, the mark is a malignant leprosy; it is impure.*

נא וְרָאָה אֶת־הַנֶּגַע בַּיּוֹם הַשְּׁבִיעִי
כִּי־פָשָׂה הַנֶּגַע בַּבֶּגֶד אוֹ־בַשְּׁתִי
אוֹ־בָעֵרֶב אוֹ בָעוֹר לְכֹל אֲשֶׁר־
יֵעָשֶׂה הָעוֹר לִמְלָאכָה צָרַעַת
מַמְאֶרֶת הַנֶּגַע טָמֵא הוּא׃

---

saffron yellow) and the reddest of reds. Accordingly, לבנה אדמדמת and לבן אדמדם of verses 19, 24, and 42 mean: white, shot with deep red (רמב״ם's commentary, *Nega'im* 11:4).

בבגד או בעור וגו׳. Scripture repeats each one of these materials at each new halachah — here, and in verses 51, 52, 53, 57, 58. This repetition is surely not without reason, and requires explanation.

51 **כי פשה הנגע בבגד וגו׳**. בבגד וגו׳ — anywhere in the garment, even if the פשיון is not בסמוך, but appears at a distance from the first spot.

ממארת: תן בו מארה ולא תהנה בו (*Toras Kohanim*); thus, from the word ממארת we learn that בגד המוחלט is אסור בהנאה.

The word ממאיר in *Yechezkel* 28:24 is an adjective modifying briers or thorns: סִלּוֹן מַמְאִיר. The derivation of the word is obscure. Perhaps מאר is related to מער, which is the root of מערה. If so, its original meaning is to bore through and hollow out, to dig under; thus the connotation of ruin and destruction.

נב וְשָׂרַף אֶת־הַבֶּגֶד אוֹ אֶת־הַשְּׁתִי ׀
אוֹ אֶת־הָעֵרֶב בַּצֶּמֶר אוֹ
בַפִּשְׁתִּים אוֹ אֶת־כָּל־כְּלִי הָעוֹר
אֲשֶׁר־יִהְיֶה בוֹ הַנָּגַע כִּי־צָרַעַת
מַמְאֶרֶת הִוא בָּאֵשׁ תִּשָּׂרֵף׃

52 *He shall burn the garment or the warp or woof, of wool or of flax, where the mark is, for it is a malignant leprosy; it shall be burned in fire.*

נג וְאִם יִרְאֶה הַכֹּהֵן וְהִנֵּה לֹא־פָשָׂה
הַנֶּגַע בַּבֶּגֶד אוֹ בַשְּׁתִי אוֹ בָעֵרֶב
אוֹ בְּכָל־כְּלִי־עוֹר׃

53 *But if the priest sees, and lo! the mark has not spread in the garment, or in the warp or woof or in any utensil of skin.*

נד וְצִוָּה הַכֹּהֵן וְכִבְּסוּ אֵת אֲשֶׁר־בּוֹ
הַנָּגַע וְהִסְגִּירוֹ שִׁבְעַת־יָמִים
שֵׁנִית׃ שביעי (רביעי כשהן מחוברין)

54 *Then the priest shall order that they wash the area that has the mark on it, and he shall keep [the article] confined for another seven days.*

בגד המוסגר, too, is אסור בהנאה, but becomes טהור and מותר בהנאה if it is cut up into pieces smaller than ג׳ על ג׳ אצבעות (*Nega'im* 11:12).

52 **ושרף את הבגד**: להוציא את האימריות (*Toras Kohanim*). Only the white part of the garment must be burned, but not the colored edges or hem.

53–54 **ואם יראה וגו׳ לא פשה**; that is to say, העומד בראשון יסגיר (*Nega'im* 11:5). If it remained unchanged during the first period of isolation, it must be isolated for a second period.

55 **לא הפך וגו׳**. It has not changed to a color other than ירקרק ואדמדם. If it changed from ירקרק to אדמדם or vice versa, this is not considered הפך, according to the חכמים (*Toras Kohanim*; *Nega'im* 11:4). Thus העומד בשני ישרף; in this, the law of בגדים differs from that of אדם (see above, v. 6).

פחתת הִוא — from the root פחת, a pit, a hollow. According to קרבן אהרן (on *Toras Kohanim* here), the color has not changed, has not heightened

55 *If the priest sees, after the mark was washed, and lo! the mark has not changed its color, and the mark has not spread; then it is impure. You shall burn it in fire. It is a deep-sunken mark, whether on a worn or on a fluffy place.*

נה וְרָאָה הַכֹּהֵן אַחֲרֵי | הֻכַּבֵּס אֶת־
הַנֶּגַע וְהִנֵּה לֹא־הָפַךְ הַנֶּגַע אֶת־
עֵינוֹ וְהַנֶּגַע לֹא־פָשָׂה טָמֵא הוּא
בָּאֵשׁ תִּשְׂרְפֶנּוּ פְּחֶתֶת הִוא
בְּקָרַחְתּוֹ אוֹ בְגַבַּחְתּוֹ׃

56 *But if the priest sees, and lo! the mark has become paler after it was washed, he shall tear it out from the garment, from the skin, or from the warp or woof.*

נו וְאִם רָאָה הַכֹּהֵן וְהִנֵּה כֵּהָה הַנֶּגַע
אַחֲרֵי הֻכַּבֵּס אֹתוֹ וְקָרַע אֹתוֹ מִן־
הַבֶּגֶד אוֹ מִן־הָעוֹר אוֹ מִן־הַשְּׁתִי
אוֹ מִן־הָעֵרֶב׃ מפטיר

57 *And if it appears again in the garment or in the warp or the woof or on any utensil of skin, it*

נז וְאִם־תֵּרָאֶה עוֹד בַּבֶּגֶד אוֹ־
בַשְּׁתִי אוֹ־בָעֵרֶב אוֹ בְכָל־כְּלִי־

---

or deepened; rather, the place has become sunken, the נגע has eaten into the material.

בקרחתו או בגבחתו. *Toras Kohanim* explains these terms as follows. בקרחתו: אלו השחקים, the worn out places which have become thread-bare; בגבחתו: אלו החדשים, the places that are still new, where the material is still fluffy (קרבן אהרן). According to the ראב״ד on *Toras Kohanim*, קרחת is generally the smooth (bald) reverse side of a garment, and גבחת is the wooly outer side; hence, a worn garment is called קרחת, and a still new garment is called גבחת.

56 **כהה**: still ירוק or אדום, but no longer ירקרק or אדמדם (קרבן אהרן).

וקרע: the place affected by the נגע is to be torn out, and a patch (מטלית) is to be inserted (see *Toras Kohanim*).

57 **ואם תראה עוד וגו׳** — on the מטלית or on the בגד. If it appears on the בגד, the מטלית is not burned (*Nega'im* 11:6).

עוֹר פֹּרַחַת הִוא בָּאֵשׁ תִּשְׂרְפֶנּוּ אֵת אֲשֶׁר־בּוֹ הַנָּגַע׃

is a recurrent [condition]; you shall burn in fire [the article] that has the mark on it.

נח וְהַבֶּגֶד אוֹ־הַשְּׁתִי אוֹ־הָעֵרֶב אוֹ־כָל־כְּלִי הָעוֹר אֲשֶׁר תְּכַבֵּס וְסָר מֵהֶם הַנָּגַע וְכֻבַּס שֵׁנִית וְטָהֵר׃

58 *But if the mark disappears when the garment, or the warp or woof, or the skin utensil is washed, the [article] shall be washed a second time and will be pure.*

נט זֹאת תּוֹרַת נֶגַע־צָרַעַת בֶּגֶד הַצֶּמֶר ׀ אוֹ הַפִּשְׁתִּים אוֹ הַשְּׁתִי אוֹ הָעֵרֶב אוֹ כָּל־כְּלִי־עוֹר לְטַהֲרוֹ אוֹ לְטַמְּאוֹ׃ פפפ

59 *This is the teaching with regard to the leprous mark of a wool or linen garment, of the warp or woof, or of any skin utensil, to declare it pure or to declare it impure.*

58 **אשר תכבס וגו' וכבס שנית וטהר**. The first כיבוס is intended to remove the נגע. It is an actual washing with שבעה סממנים in the order prescribed in the case of דם חטאת (*Zevachim* 95a; see Commentary above, 6:2). The second כיבוס, however, is טבילה for the sake of טהרה (see *Toras Kohanim*).

Thus, בגדים become טמאים through ירקרק and אדמדם, if these colors remain for two weeks, or if they spread after one week's הסגר: מיטמאין בשני שבועות ובשלשה סימנין, בירקרק ובאדמדם ובפשיון (*Negaim* 3:7). In *Zevachim* 49b we learn that פריחה בכולו in the case of בגדים is טהורה, as in the case of נתקים (see Commentary above, v. 40; see משנה למלך on הל' טומאת צרעת, 12:8).

59 **לטהרו או לטמאו**. The Mishnah (*Nazir* 65b) says: כל ספק נגעים בתחילה טהור עד שלא נזקק לטומאה; משנזקק לטומאה ספקו טמא. That is to say, one does not move from a state of טהרה to a state of טומאה unless the sign of טומאה is definite; in a case of doubt, he is טהור. According to ר' יהושע (ibid.), a case of doubt is declared טהור even where the חזקת הגוף was undermined — e.g., doubt whether בהרת קדמה לשער לבן או שער לבן קדם לבהרת (see above, v. 3), even though it appears that בהרת קדמה (see תוספות there and in *Niddah* 19a). Our verse is cited (*Nazir* 65b) as the source of this ruling: The verse states לטהרו first (before לטמאו), to teach us that cases of doubt

are to be ruled טהור. And although it is not certain that the halachah is in accordance with this ruling of ר׳ יהושע (see ר״ש on *Nega'im* 4:11; רמב״ם הל׳ טומאת צרעת, 2:9), the principle stands that כל ספק נגעים טהור — except for two cases (*Nega'im* 5:1).

What is more, the Mishnah (ibid. 5:4) says: If a person has two separate נגע spots, one the size of a גריס and the other the size of a סלע, and after the prescribed period of הסגר both are found to be the size of a סלע, but it is not known which one has spread, the case is ruled טהור — even though one of them has definitely spread and hence qualifies for החלט. For it is not sufficient that פשיון has occurred, if the place of the פשיון cannot be identified exactly.

Toras Kohanim, too, on verse 22, says: וטמא (הכהן) אותו – את הודאי הוא מטמא ואינו מטמא את הספק. This rule is one of the characteristic *halachos* of נגעים. It is crucial for an understanding of the whole reason behind the laws of נגעים.

נגעים

The laws of נגעים — more than all other parts of the Torah — have served as a source for the erroneous notions about the "sanitary purposes of Mosaic law." Indeed, at first glance there would appear to be support for such a notion. For, seemingly, the discussion here is of disease — a contagious disease. Those stricken with it must be quarantined. Why should that be done if not to prevent contagion? It is claimed that this is sufficient evidence to determine the character of these laws: Their whole purpose, as it were, is to protect the health of the people; and the כהנים, who minister in this realm, are merely expert physicians. And if, from the long list of human diseases, just this one disease, "leprosy," was singled out, and against it alone were these strict regulations adopted, then, it is claimed, the reason is that this was the one horrible disease from which the Jews suffered most of all. And then there must be some foundation to Tacitus' tall tale that the Jews were expelled from Egypt because they were carriers of leprosy!

Let us now examine the laws of נגעים — their principles and salient details — to determine whether there is justification for classing them as sanitary regulations.

True leprosy — שחין — in itself is not מטמא. שחין מצרים (*Devarim* 28:27), שחין רע אשר לא תוכל להרפא (ibid. 28:35), the "malignant" leprosy, the "incurable Egyptian leprosy," cannot possibly render a person טמא;

for it says in our chapter that a נגע טמא can arise only after the שחין has begun to heal (שחין ונרפא) and healthy skin has formed again over the affected area (see above, 13:18). If the "leprosy" covers a person's entire body מראשו ועד רגליו (vv. 12–13), he becomes טהור. The "health theorists" explain that if the disease erupts violently and covers the entire body, this is a sign of impending recovery. Yet precisely in the description of שחין מצרים, which has no cure (אשר לא תוכל להרפא), the disease is portrayed in its most horrible manifestation as extending מכף רגלך ועד קדקדך (*Devarim* 28:35). This simple fact should have been noticed and should have given these theorists pause.

Let us continue. In verses 10, 15, 16, and 17 we are told several times that the appearance of מחיה, healthy flesh, is a sign of טומאה; when the healthy flesh disappears, and the נגע takes its place, טהרה sets in again.

Verse 12 tells us that no careful examination is required of the body's creases, but only an examination לכל מראה עיני הכהן, of those parts of the body that are directly visible to the eye of the כהן.

In chapter 14, verse 36, the כהן is explicitly commanded to have everything removed from the house prior to the examination so that everything in the house not become טמא. Now, were the purpose of the isolation to prevent the spread of infection, would it not be a strange "sanitary" procedure to have all garments, beds, and household utensils — which might be carrying the infection — removed from the house, in order to spare the owner material loss?

Furthermore, from here (14:36) we learn, in the Oral Law, of the liberal consideration to be shown by these "public health physicians" in priestly garb. Now, if the declaration of טומאה and the isolation imposed in its wake had been intended to prevent the danger of infection, such consideration and leniency in dealing with so "dangerous" and "repulsive" a disease as "leprosy" would be utterly senseless.

When would such public health regulations and quarantine be more appropriate than at seasons when masses of people congregate in one place, in which case "lepers" mingling with the crowds could infect entire families and even the entire nation? Yet precisely at those seasons the כהנים were ordered to suspend their צרעת examinations. No such examinations were made during the seven days of rejoicing following a wedding (שבעת ימי המשתה); during the three pilgrimage festivals, when the entire nation streamed into the city of God's Sanctuary; and also never on any Shabbos or festival (see Commentary above, v. 14). (In Yerushalayim, of all places, leprous marks on houses are not מטמאים — see Commentary below, 14:34.)

We have cited (Commentary, v. 59) the rule that כל ספק בנגעים בתחילה טהור. This rule calls for greater leniency in הלכות נגעים than in other איסורים. Now, if the concern here were with diseases and their prevention, the applicable rule would be חמירא סכנתא מאיסורא (*Chullin* 10a), which would call for greater stringency in הלכות נגעים.

We have seen (Commentary, v. 59) that even in a case where it is known for certain that there exists a נגע with signs of טומאה, but there is doubt as to which of two marks is the נגע הטמא, the נגע is not pronounced טמא!

We also mentioned earlier (Commentary, v. 46) that a מצורע was expelled only from cities that were surrounded by a wall when the land was first taken into possession, but in other parts of the country — in all the open villages and in all the cities that were only later surrounded by a wall — the מצורע was allowed to move freely among the people. No quarantine was imposed to protect the people from the danger of becoming infected with leprosy. The only cases of leprosy that had to be removed from all inhabited places were those involving garments!

Consider also that the laws of נגעים applied only to the Jewish inhabitants of the land. A non-Jew was not rendered טמא by נגעים. His נגע did not require examination, and no isolation was imposed on him. Moreover, if before his conversion he had contracted a נגע, it is disregarded after his conversion (see Commentary, v. 2).

Similarly, the laws of נגעים did not apply to the house or clothing of a non-Jew while these were in his possession (see Commentary, v. 47).

These and similar considerations lead us to the clear conclusion that it is impossible to maintain that this chapter deals with the cure and prevention of disease. It is inconceivable that the כהנים served in the role of providing health care, for nowhere in this chapter do they take any remedial measures.

As a matter of fact, the symptoms described in this chapter have nothing at all in common with the skin diseases described in scientific medical writings under the heading "*Lepra*," leprosy. Whereas the latter start with an inflammatory swelling that destroys the skin and darkens its color, our נגעים consist solely of white patches on the skin; and *Toras*

Kohanim expressly says that there is no swelling of the skin. The ספורנו — who was a physician — in his commentary on the Torah, remarks on the difference between these נגעים and the dreadful diseases classified under the term "leprosy" in medical writings.

Accordingly, we have long been convinced that the laws of confinement and expulsion which the Torah imposes on the מצורע are in no way intended to prevent infection.

Just now we have received the *Report on Leprosy by the Royal College of Physicians* (reproduced in the journal *Ausland*, 1868, no. 14), filed by a commission appointed by the British Government to investigate the alarming increase in the number of cases of the quite common occurrence of leprosy in the British colonies. The investigation resulted in the finding that leprosy — even in its most terrible form — is *not at all infectious*. The report continues:

> The all-important question for the Government is whether this disease is contagious or not. There can be no doubt that the Jews considered it to be so, and that the strictest quarantine was imposed upon those who contracted it. Nevertheless, it seems probable from several indications that the Jews of old classed all skin diseases as leprous, and accordingly people who were affected by the contagious diseases of modern Europe, such as measles, scarlet fever or small-pox, were included in the laws of quarantine for leprosy. It is a remarkable fact, moreover, that present-day Jews seem to be less liable to the attacks of contagious illnesses than their European neighbors, which may be due to a trace which still remains from those ceremonious practices which exercised such great influence on the physical forces and energies of the ancient Jew. Be that as it may, *the practically unanimous conviction of our investigating reporters from all parts of the world is this: the disease is not infectious.*

We have seen above that the widely held view that the biblical laws of confinement are intended to prevent infection is totally mistaken.

The view that the laws of נגעים are sanitary regulations is, then, merely a figment of the imagination. Besides, the Torah itself leaves no room for doubt as to the meaning of these laws. In *Devarim* (24:8; see Commentary there), reference is made to the laws of נגעים in the midst of a long list of laws whose importance lies in the social sphere: they all promote preservation of the dignity of man and consideration for the happiness of the individual. The Torah there says as follows: השמר

בנגע הצרעת לשמר מאד ולעשות ככל אשר יורו אתכם הכהנים הלוים כאשר צויתם תשמרו לעשות. זכור את אשר עשה ה׳ אלקיך למרים בדרך בצאתכם ממצרים. "Take heed concerning leprous marks, to observe and to do according to all that the priests, the Levites, teach you; as I have commanded them, so shall you carefully observe to do. Remember what *God*, your God, did to Miriam on the way when you came out of Egypt." With those words, the observance of the laws stated in our chapter becomes a duty of conscience of every individual.

In particular, the Torah (ibid.) *prohibits* removal of the נגע by surgical or other means, even though מן התורה the טומאה ceases with the removal of the נגע, and there is no longer a need for any isolation (see above, v. 46). (The implication here, too, is that the obligation of isolation does not derive from considerations of health. For if that were the case, it would be desirable to remove the נגע, in order to eliminate the need for isolation.)

The Torah (*Devarim* 24:8) also demands observance of all the *positive* commands connected with the laws of נגעים: לשמר מאד ולעשות ככל אשר יורו וגו׳.

In regard to both — the prohibition of removing the נגע and the positive command — Scripture (ibid.) refers to an experience of Miriam the Prophetess, an experience that one must remember always. Clearly, the reference is to the account in *Bemidbar* 12: Miriam contracts leprosy because she has spoken לשון הרע, slander, about Moshe, and she is isolated outside the camp for seven days. Scripture (*Bemidbar* 12) explains that the leprosy and the isolation are a sign of God's anger at her words. For God's response to Moshe's prayer that his sister be cured is this: ואביה ירק ירק בפניה הלא תכלם שבעת ימים? תסגר שבעת ימים מחוץ למחנה ואחר תאסף. "If her father had spat before her, would she not have been ashamed for seven days? Let her be confined outside the camp for seven days, and afterwards she shall be taken in again" (ibid. v. 14). ואביה ירק ירק בפניה represents a father's anger that reaches even to contempt. That is how the צרעת sent by God is to be understood. This punishment is decreed as a consequence of a *social* sin, which is described (ibid.) as consisting of both *slander* and *arrogance*.

Henceforth, every נגע צרעת that strikes a member of the Jewish nation is to remind him of this experience of Miriam. This will lead him to careful observance of the relevant *halachos*. Every נגע צרעת, then, is to be regarded as a punishment for social wrongdoing; and the confinement מחוץ למחנה — outside the national area around the Sanctuary of the Torah — has no other purpose or reason than הִכָּלֵם: to instill in man the awareness of his unworthiness.

(Whereas בוש denotes disappointment regarding expectations for the future, and החפיר denotes disappointment regarding a misunderstood past, הִכָּלֵם denotes the feeling of sorrow that stems from a loss of worthiness in the present. כלם is related to גלם, which denotes formlessness. In Rabbinic Hebrew, גולם is used — in *Avos* 5:7 — also in the metaphorical sense: cultural and moral formlessness. This, then, is the meaning of הִכָּלֵם: One discovers himself to be a moral גולם; one is struck by the realization that, morally, he has lost the semblance of man.)

Isolation shows the מנוגע that the finger of God has "touched" (נגעה) him: he has forfeited the privilege of remaining in the *social* sphere of the Sanctuary.

Indeed, our Sages view נגעים as a Divinely decreed punishment — primarily for the sin of לשון הרע, but then also for the cardinal *social* sins, of which they enumerate seven (see below). Our Sages say: כל מי שיש בו אחד מארבעה נגעים הללו אינן אלא מזבח כפרה. "If a person is affected by one of these four מראות נגעים, it is none other than an altar of atonement" (*Berachos* 5b).

מה נשתנה מצורע שאמרה תורה בדד ישב מחוץ למחנה מושבו? הוא הבדיל בין איש לאשתו בין איש לרעהו, לפיכך אמרה תורה בדד ישב וגו׳; מה נשתנה מצורע שאמרה תורה יביא שתי ציפרים לטהרתו? אמר הקב״ה, הוא עשה מעשה פטיט, לפיכך אמרה תורה יביא קרבן פטיט. "Why just for the מצורע is it ordained, 'He shall dwell apart, outside the camp shall his dwelling be' (above 13:46)? He induced a rift between a man and his wife, between a man and his neighbor; therefore, he, too, is to be separated from everyone and remain alone outside the camp. Why just for the מצורע is it ordained that in his offering to regain טהרה he is to represent his personality by two birds? He sinned by chattering; therefore, he is to bring an offering of birds, which chatter" (*Arachin* 16b).

אמר ר׳ יהושע בן לוי, חמש תורות כתובות במצורע, זאת תורת נגע צרעת כו׳ זאת תהיה תורת המצורע – המוציא שם רע – ללמדך שכל האומר לשון הרע עובר על חמשה חומשי תורה (ויקרא רבה טז:ו). Phonetically, מצורע is expounded as an abbreviation of מוציא רע, a slanderer. So also in *Arachin* 15b: – זאת תהיה תורת המצורע זאת תהיה תורתו של מוציא שם רע.

In a wider sense, seven social sins are cited (*Arachin* 16a) as causes of נגעים: על שבעה דברים נגעים באין, על לשון הרע ועל שפיכות דמים ועל שבועת שוא

נגעים“ .ועל גילוי עריות ועל גסות הרוח ועל הגזל ועל צרות העין result from seven things: slander, the shedding of blood, perjury, sexual immorality, arrogance, robbery, and stinginess.”

In ויקרא רבה on פ׳ מצורע the social sins are reckoned as follows: עינים רמות, לשון שקר, וידים שופכות דם נקי, לב חורש מחשבות און, רגלים ממהרות לרוץ לרעה, יפיח כזבים עד שקר, ומשלח מדנים בין אחים. “Haughty eyes, a lying tongue, hands that shed innocent blood, a heart that devises thoughts of violence, feet that are quick to run to evil, a false witness who spreads lies, and one who incites conflict between brothers.” They are the same “six things that God hates, and seven that are an abomination to Him,” that are cited in *Mishlei* (6:17–19): שֶׁשׁ־הֵנָּה שָׂנֵא ה׳ וְשֶׁבַע תּוֹעֲבַת נַפְשׁוֹ (*Mishlei* 6:16). The division into six and seven is explained (in ויקרא רבה) as follows: ושבע? זו שביעית שקשה כנגד כולן. ואי זהו? זה משלח מדנים. “And seven” is a special reference to the seventh — viz., inciting conflict (לשון הרע) — which is worse than all the others put together. Indeed, slander — which dishonors a person in the eyes of his friends and kills him spiritually — includes all the other sins and negative qualities.

Notice that these sins and faults are not mentioned in the abstract, but are attributed to the organs of the body that are misused in practicing them; it does not say רום עינים, but עינים רמות. Thus, the eyes, the mouth, the hands, the heart, the feet — in short, the whole person is despised by God. For instead of using the organs and faculties that have been granted to him to conduct himself with humility and truth, to practice lovingkindness, justice, and good deeds, and to speak words of truth and peace, he has become the bearer of the opposite of all these. Hence, he is despised and abominated by God, Who sends a mark upon his body as a sign of His anger; thus He expels him from the social sphere of His Sanctuary — until הִכָּלֵם: so that he recognize his guilt and reflect on rectifying his character.

Just as in the case of Miriam it is said: ויחר אף ה׳ בם וילך והענן סר מעל האהל והנה מרים מצורעת כשלג (*Bemidbar* 12:9–10), so it is for all generations. If anyone sees a נגע on his body, on his garment, or on his house, this נגע is an indication to him that his social behavior provokes God's anger; God will not tolerate his presence and will not grant him His protection and blessing.

From this perspective — which is corroborated unequivocally in the Torah — we will now attempt to explain the laws of נגעים.

The opening phrase of our chapter reads: אדם כי יהיה וגו׳ (v. 2). We find such a phrase only in the introduction to two other sets of laws: אדם כי יקריב וגו׳ (above, 1:2) and אדם כי ימות באהל (*Bemidbar* 19:14). In both these cases — the laws of the offerings and the laws of טומאת אהל — the term אדם brings to mind man in the full glory of his destiny and dignity, and from this standpoint one should interpret these laws. In like manner one should interpret here, too, the phrase אדם כי יהיה בעור בשרו.

עור בשרו, which was struck by the נגע, should be considered in its relation to אדם. The נגע has struck עור בשר אדם. עור (the skin) is the servant of בשר האדם: It is ער — awake, sensitive — to impressions impacting upon it from the outside world (see Commentary, *Bereshis* 2:25), and in this role it serves the "herald" that was given to the "representative of God." For the mission of man (אדם) is to resemble (דמה) God, to be הדום רגליו on earth (see Commentary, ibid. 1:26); and the body's בשר was given to אדם as a מבשר, an agent that heralds and implements his high purpose (see Commentary, ibid. 2:21). He whose purpose is to be an אדם should see in the נגע the finger of God which נגעה, has "touched," עור בשרו. He who was created to fulfill God's Will, to resemble Him in nurturing truth and justice, is warned by the נגע which has struck him. For God's finger has struck his skin, which informs him of his standing in the world; he is thus warned of the total discrepancy between the life that he leads in the world and the life that he is called upon to lead.

God proclaims "white" spots — all of them עמוקים מעור בשר אדם בינוני, paler than ordinary human skin — as heralds of His anger; hence, He defines them precisely, to differentiate them from other skin diseases. Skin that has turned white may be indicative of a person's partial death: he is far removed from God, Who sustains every living thing — מצורע חשוב כמת (see *Bemidbar* 12:12 and our Commentary there; see *Nedarim* 64b); and skin that has turned white may also be indicative of הלבנת פנים and humiliation.

These spots have meaning only בגלוי, as it says: לכל מראה עיני הכהן, and only if they are visible in the prescribed size on one flat surface (vv. 2, 3, and 12); for the whole reason that they are sent is to be conspicuous.

Not in and of themselves, by their very presence on the body, do they render the afflicted person טמא, as do all other states of bodily טומאה (e.g., זב וזבה, and the like). Rather, only the declaration of a כהן,

a servant of the Sanctuary by birth, renders the person טמא. Through his declaration, the כהן excludes the person from the Sanctuary and its holy things, and excludes him also from the civilian society which forms around the Sanctuary — an exclusion that applies to no other טמא. נגעים are nothing but instructions to the כהן to declare in the name of the Sanctuary that the afflicted person is unworthy of the Sanctuary and its national circle (vv. 2–3). Only a מצורע is משתלח חוץ משלוש מחנות, expelled from the closed national circle. For God's sign upon his body shows him to be guilty of *social* sins.

We have seen that this expulsion is not intended to prevent infection. Nor is it intended to prevent the spread of טומאה; for we see that all other טמאים — who could spread טומאה just as easily — are allowed to remain in מחנה ישראל, and even the מצורע is expelled only from עיירות מוקפות חומה מימות יהושע בן נון, cities that have been considered מחנה ישראל since the conquest of the land (see Commentary on v. 46 and below, 25:29). It must be, then, that the expulsion is purely the consequence of the social wrongdoing to which the נגע attests.

This character of the expulsion is borne out clearly in these *halachos*. This, too, is why the כהן's declaration is treated as the verdict of a judge — מקיש נגעים לריבים — and a כהן קרוב is פסול לנגעים just as a דיין קרוב is פסול לדין (see Commentary, v. 2).

In this light it is understandable that there is no ראיית נגעים during a רגל and during the seven days of rejoicing for a wedding (Commentary, v. 14); for the כהן's examination and its consequences are moral means of punishment and rectification. When a person has a נגע that requires examination, he begins to think of his shortcomings; and he must search for these shortcomings in his previous social behavior. Festivals and holidays are days of intensified socialization among relatives and friends; and this offers him a suitable opportunity to examine and refine himself and his thoughts, his words and his deeds, in his contact with his fellow men. Refinement of his traits of character will bring about a change in the נגע, and he will then have nothing to fear from the כהן's examination.

There are two stages in the laws of the מצורע: (a) הסגר, the test stage, and (b) החלט, the confirmed stage. Whereas פריעה and פרימה (see Commentary above, 10:6) are prescribed only in the case of a מוחלט, and the laws of תגלחת וציפורים apply only to one who is healed from the החלט stage, טומאה and isolation apply at both stages (Commentary, v. 4); for the enforced loneliness of the הסגר weeks is liable to have a positive influence on the מוסגר. During the period of isolation he will contemplate changing his ways and will reconsider his past behavior. While apart from his fellow men he will examine his social conduct in thought, word, and deed. Thus he will come to a change in his attitudes and undertake to improve his character, and, as a result, he will emerge from the test stage in a pure state. Hence, we pay no heed to any changes that may occur in the נגע during this test period; the כהן must decide only on the basis of the condition that he sees at the end of the test period.

The כהן decrees הסגר — at the first examination — if the נגע is of the requisite size and color. He decrees החלט if he finds שיער לבן, מחיה, or פשיון. The first two symptoms, שיער לבן or מחיה, can be present at the first examination (בתחילה). If he finds one of them, he decrees החלט immediately. פשיון (spreading of the נגע), can, of course, be recognized only after the first or second week of הסגר (בסוף). See Commentary to verse 4. That פשיון indicates an intensification of the נגע-character is easily understood; why שיער לבן or מחיה should indicate such intensification is more difficult to understand. Perhaps there is some truth in the following explanation:

The skin is the body's sensory receiver; it receives impressions from the outside world and conveys them to the body. Now the finger of God strikes the skin and gives it a נגע צרעת, an external sign of an inner rot (see Commentary, v. 2); a sign that the afflicted person is unwell in his comprehension of the world around him. He no longer knows how to absorb from the world the impressions of truth, justice, and goodness; his conception of the world is, accordingly, neither true, just, or good.

Hair — from a physiological standpoint — is the opposite of skin. It is the protective covering of the skin, and does not receive impressions from the outside; it limits the sensitivity of the skin, thereby protecting it. Accordingly, the spreading of the נגע to the hair signifies — on the spiritual level — that not only are good and true impressions lacking, but bad impressions which should be rejected are being admitted. Be that as it may, just as פשיון is indicative of intensification in the strength of the נגע through its spreading on the surface of the skin, so is הפיכת שיער לבן a form of פשיון, but in another dimension: the bleaching reaches even into the hair. Hence, שיער לבן שקדם לבהרת and שער פקודה are טהורים (see Commentary, v. 3): the former, because it entails no advancement of the נגע; the latter, because it entails no advancement of the נגע under consideration.

Why מחיה should be a symptom that leads to החלט is more difficult to understand. מחיה is flesh that has remained healthy — or has become healthy again — in the center of the נגע; and yet precisely this healthy flesh is a sign of טומאה that leads to החלט! Verse 11 says of the מחיה: צרעת נושנת הִוא וגו׳ לא יסגרנו כי טמא הוא (שיער לבן was mentioned earlier as a סימן החלט, in v. 3, without this reasoning). The implication is apparently this: מחיה indicates that there had already been an attempt at moral influence — like the attempt that is generally made through הסגר, but this attempt did not succeed; hence, החלט must be decreed. Indeed, this is the meaning of מחיה מבוצר בתוך הנגע (see Commentary, v. 10): When the נגע first formed, the forces of good (מחיה) had already fought against the forces of moral death (נגע) — without any real success. Or, after the נגע had formed, the forces of good rallied and attempted in vain to overcome the evil. The good, the pure, stands "imprisoned," ineffectual, in the very midst of the rottenness.

Unlike the case of מחיה in a נגע, מחיה is not a symptom of טומאה in cases of שחין ומכוה. For in those cases, the מחיה is not a reaction against the נגע, but against the שחין or מכוה, which is in the process of healing (v. 24ff.).

A most unique phenomenon is the halachah that if the נגע spreads over the entire body, the declaration of טומאה is suspended: כלו הפך לבן טהור. But if such total spreading occurs during a condition of טהרה, the נגע is טמא and requires הסגר or החלט: הפורח מן הטמא טהור מן הטהור טמא (see Commentary, v. 13). From the standpoint of the moral purpose of נגעים, this halachah expresses the following idea:

Through הסגר and החלט, the person is excluded from the Sanctuary and from the society that surrounds it. The purpose of הסגר and החלט is to bring about repentance and refinement of character. But there is no hope that they can achieve this purpose unless moral good is still entrenched in the consciousness and is capable of combatting evil. With this concept of הסגר and החלט we can understand the different laws of פריחה בכולו depending on the circumstances of the spreading. If suddenly the person suffers a total deterioration (פרח בכולו) in the midst of his association with the Sanctuary and society, then if it is a new attack (בתחילה) he is מוסגר, and if it is a recurrence of a previous attack that had been declared cured (לאחר פטור) he is מוחלט. The idea of מקדש וקדשיו and of מחנה ישראל — from which he has been suddenly removed — accompany him to the place of his isolation, so that he may work on the refinement of his character. But if he suffers this פריחה בכולו *during* the isolation of הסגר or החלט, this signifies that the isolation has divested him of all moral feeling; hence, the isolation will not lead him to refinement of character. Hence, the טומאה declaration is suspended. He renews his association with מקדש וקדשיו and with the society of מחנה ישראל. The return of בשר החי signals the return also of moral feeling. Only then does he return to the החלט-isolation to work on the completion of his moral education (vv. 12–17).

The halachic modifications stated for נגעי ראש וזקן may be attributed, apparently, to the nature and significance of these parts of the body, and can be explained as we explained the laws of נגעי בשר.

The laws of נגעי בגדים are distinctive. In many respects they are stricter than the laws of נגעי אדם. For example:

(a) נגעי אדם apply only to ישראל. Even the נגע of a גר — a נגע that he had while still a נכרי — is disregarded. By contrast, a נכרי's garment that has symptoms of a נגע and that comes into Jewish possession requires examination by a כהן. What is more, the laws of נגעים might apply even to בגדי גר תושב (v. 47).

(b) בגד המנוגע — which, as regards הסגר, החלט, and טומאה, is treated in the same manner as אדם — is more חמור than אדם in regard to שילוח מחנה, as it is removed from all cities, even from those that are not מוקפות חומה מימות יהושע בן נון (see Commentary, v. 47).

(c) A person — whose נגע remains unchanged after the second הסגר — becomes טהור while the נגע is still upon him. A בגד, however, cannot become טהור while the נגע is still upon it: If it remains unchanged after the second הסגר, it must be burned (see Commentary, v. 55).

Also, the concept of בגד includes even simple spun thread — שתי וערב; and it includes every fabric woven from materials used especially for garments, צמר ופשתים, even if it is made into sails, and the like.

The point of view given in the Torah to explain the laws of נגעים sheds light also on these laws of נגעי בגדים. For נגעים appear on account of social sins. God sends a נגע upon a person, his clothes, or his house, to alert him to the gravity of these sins. Now, clothes are the main expression of the social character of man. This is especially true in Jewish thought, as we have noted several times. “Clothing” indicates character, and “clothing oneself” indicates the character one adopts. And if God sends a נגע upon a person’s clothing, He is rebuking him for social wrongdoing.

This explains why it is that precisely בגד המנוגע is banned absolutely from the entire social circle of the people; why the laws of נגעי בגדים may apply even to a גר תושב; and, in any case, why they apply also to בגד המנוגע that comes into Jewish possession. For, from a *social* standpoint, a גר תושב is an integral part of the nation; and *social* justice is an essential part of the Noachide laws which are binding also on a נכרי.

Thus, in נגעי בגדים, the meaning of the נגע is most clear; the נגע's warning about social uprightness is unmistakable. Hence, this warning is not limited to actual garments; rather, the concept of בגד includes even simple spun thread, and applies even where the garment material is made into some other article. That is why Scripture repeats in every sentence of the laws of נגעי בגדים the words בבגד או בשתי או בערב או בעור לכל אשר יעשה העור למלאכה. For the concept of בגד is mentioned at the beginning of the section dealing with נגעי בגדים: והבגד כי יהיה בו נגע צרעת (v. 47); and the extension of this concept to all materials used especially for garments — in any form — reflects the great importance of these laws of נגעי בגדים.

צמר ופשתים represent in the Torah the materials used especially for man's clothing. Hence, in their case, the concept of בגד begins even with simple spun thread. But the conception of "clothing" is extended here to עור as well, provided that its manufacture is complete, and it is ready for use.

פשתים and — in the vast majority of cases — צמר, too, are naturally white; they represent, then, through their original color, the "purity of character" with which a man should clothe himself: בְּכָל־עֵת יִהְיוּ בְגָדֶיךָ לְבָנִים (*Koheles* 9:8; see *Shabbos* 153a). Hence, נגעים are מטמאים only those linen or woolen garments that are of a natural white color. It is they that will warn man to remove every blemish from his social character.

Finally, in the case of נגעי אדם it is necessary to demonstrate their special relation to the social dimension. Hence, expulsion is limited to עיירות מוקפות חומה מימות יהושע בן נון. In the case of בגדים, however, their social dimension is self-evident in the very concept of a בגד. Hence, they require expulsion from all human habitations.

This interpretation of the laws of נגעים is given by the Torah itself, but it appears to be contradicted by the halachah that a תינוק בן יום אחד, a one day old child, is מטמא בנגעים (see Commentary, v. 2). For we would have thought that the moral warning — which is the whole purpose of the נגעים laws — would take effect only at the age of maturity.

However, children who have not yet reached maturity are part of their parents' personality. They are the tender shoots of humanity, and they grow up to be a likeness of God, nurtured by the home life and following the example of their parents. Just as a נגע on a garment or on a house is a sign of warning to its owner, so is a נגע on the forehead of an innocent child a shocking warning to his parents to examine their deeds and consider what picture of life they are presenting — through their social behavior — as an example to their child. The נגע-mark on their child's body and the declaration of טומאה with its consequences constitute a solemn warning to the parents: For your child's sake, improve your deeds; for the sake of your children's future, be decent and good! You are accountable for the moral stain that will cling to your children. Indeed, a נגע on the brow of their innocent child is a graver warning to the parents than a נגע that strikes their own bodies.

Let us now consider what impact the declaration of טומאה and its consequences have on the מנוגע.

Unlike נדה, זבה, זב, etc., whose טומאה יוצאת עליהן מגופן, the מנוגע does not automatically become טמא because of his physical condition. Rather, his טומאה depends on the declaration of the כהן. This indicates to the מנוגע that his טומאה derives not from his bodily condition, but from his moral behavior vis-à-vis the Torah, in whose Sanctuary the כהן serves. The נגע is like a Divine secret code, which must be deciphered by the כהן. The condition of the מנוגע is not to be equated with נבילה, זב, or מת; his bodily illness per se is not a phenomenon — like those just mentioned — that produces טומאה and its consequences. It entails more than these. For on account of his reprehensible social behavior, the servant of the Sanctuary declares upon him a status similar to that of נבילה and מת (cf. נְבָלָה and נְבֵלָה, and the saying: רשעים אפילו בחייהן קרויין מתים; see *Berachos* 18b). He is מטמא במגע ובמשא like a נבילה. What is more, he is מטמא משכב ומושב like — or at least similar to — a זב (see Commentary, v. 6, and Commentary, 15:4). Like a מת, he is מטמא בביאה; but a מחיצת עשרה טפחים affords protection from his טומאה, and this characterizes his טומאה as being socially significant. Unlike all other טמאים, he is isolated and expelled from society, as he requires הסגר and שילוח מחנה! Only if he repents can he expect a sign from God that the doors of society and the Sanctuary are to be reopened to him.

If we consider the נגעים laws in their totality, we will see them as a great institution of Divine providence over the individual. In God's

14 1 God *spoke to Moshe, saying:*	וַיְדַבֵּר יְהֹוָה אֶל־מֹשֶׁה לֵּאמֹר׃	יד א
2 *This shall be the teaching with regard to the leper on the day of his purification; he shall be brought to the priest.*	זֹאת תִּהְיֶה תּוֹרַת הַמְּצֹרָע בְּיוֹם טָהֳרָתוֹ וְהוּבָא אֶל־הַכֹּהֵן׃	ב

Jewish State there is punishment and correction even for those social sins — e.g., arrogance, falsehood, avarice, slander — that are beyond the jurisdiction of human tribunals. God Himself is the accuser and the witness for the prosecution, and He brings these sins out into the open. As *Toras Kohanim* (below, 14:35) says: – ובא אשר לו הבית והגיד לכהן לאמר לאמר, יאמר לו הכהן דברי כיבושין: בני, אין הנגעים באים אלא על לשון הרע וכו׳.

מצורע

CHAPTER 14

2 **זאת תהיה וגו׳**. From the word תהיה we learn that all of the *halachos* mentioned here, as well as the order in which they are to be performed, are מעכבות, indispensable. Thus, ארבעה מינין שבמצורע מעכבין זה את זה, each of the four kinds of objects prescribed in verse 4 is indispensable; if any one of them is missing, the whole ritual is invalid (*Menachos* 27a). Likewise, any deviation from the prescribed order of the procedures invalidates the whole ritual — e.g., הקדים שמן למתן דם וכו׳ מתן בהונות למתן שבע וכו׳, if the procedure described in verse 16 is performed before that of verse 14, or if that of verse 17 is performed before that of verse 16 (ibid. 5a).

תורת המצרע. We have already seen several times that the term תורת is a generalizing term (see above, 7:37). The same is true here: The laws stated here apply to every מצורע — בין גדול בין קטן — even to children; and the offerings mentioned from verse 10 onward, which render the מצורע ritually pure for the Sanctuary and its holy things, apply even to children who have no legal consent. Thus the principle: הכל צריכין דעת חוץ ממחוסרי כפרה. All offerings must be brought with legal consent of the

3 *The priest shall go out, outside the camp, and the priest shall look, and lo! the mark of leprosy is healed from the leper.*

ג וְיָצָא הַכֹּהֵן אֶל־מִחוּץ לַמַּחֲנֶה וְרָאָה הַכֹּהֵן וְהִנֵּה נִרְפָּא נֶגַע־הַצָּרַעַת מִן־הַצָּרוּעַ:

one who must bring the offering. Only the offerings that render זב וזבה יולדת ומצורע ritually pure for מקדש וקדשיו are valid even if brought without דעת בעלים, even if brought for another person without his consent; שהרי אדם מביא קרבן על בניו ועל בנותיו הקטנים (*Nedarim* 35b–36a).

The reason for this differentiation may be as follows: Let us remember that all the other offerings are meaningful only for the person who is obligated to bring them. It is his sin which must be atoned for, his actions and his life which must be brought near to God. By contrast, the effect of טומאה and טהרה extends beyond the person who is טמא or טהור. An object that he touches becomes טמא not only for himself, but for the entire Jewish community. And the טומאה idea arising from his condition must be addressed and rectified not only for himself, but for every person who is summoned to טהרה.

ביום טהרתו. The purification procedures of a מצורע are valid only during the day: כל היום כשר לטהרת מצורע (*Megillah* 20b). Thus, they leave the sphere of merely physical meaning and enter the sphere of human moral freedom (see Commentary above, 6:2).

ביום טהרתו והובא אל הכהן: שלא ישהא (*Toras Kohanim*). When the טומאה symptoms disappear, and it is possible to declare the מצורע as טהור, the declaration is not to be postponed. Whereas the transition from ימי הסגר to טהרה depends on the completion of the weeks, the cessation of the החלט condition is not dependent on the passing of time. If the signs of טומאה have disappeared, the מצורע מוחלט can become טהור: צרעתו תלויה בגופו. In the case of the מצורע מוסגר, however, אין צרעתו תלויה בגופו אלא בימים (*Megillah* 8b).

3 **ויצא הכהן**:כהן שאפשר לו ליכנס לפנים מן המחנה מטהר את המצורע, only a כהן who is permitted to be inside the מחנה is qualified for טהרת מצורע, but אין מצורע מטהר את המצורע (*Toras Kohanim*).

ד וְצִוָּה֙ הַכֹּהֵ֔ן וְלָקַ֧ח לַמִּטַּהֵ֛ר שְׁתֵּֽי־
צִפֳּרִ֥ים חַיּ֖וֹת טְהֹר֑וֹת וְעֵ֣ץ אֶ֔רֶז
וּשְׁנִ֥י תוֹלַ֖עַת וְאֵזֹֽב׃

4 *The priest shall then command to take for the one who is being purified two pure living birds and a piece of cedar wood and scarlet wool and hyssop.*

והנה נרפא וגו'. The נגע need not have completely disappeared, provided that it has lost the טומאה symptoms described in the previous chapter (see ibid.).

4 **ולקח למטהר**: לשם מיטהר בין איש בין אשה בין קטן וכו' (ibid.). The birds are to be designated for the sake of anyone to be purified, but need not be designated for a specific individual. They do not represent a specific personality, as do the offerings; hence, the law of שינוי בעלים does not apply to them.

שתי צפרים: מצוותן שיהו שוות במראה ובקומה ובדמים ולקיחתן כאחת, they should be alike in appearance, in size, and in value, and they should be bought at the same time (cf. below, 16:7). These *halachos*, however, are not מעכבות (*Nega'im* 14:5).

In *Toras Kohanim* on verse 53 (below) ר' יוסי הגלילי explains: ושלח את הצפור החיה אל מחוץ לעיר אל פני השדה – צפור שחיה חוץ לעיר ואיזו זו דרור. "This is a species of bird that lives outside of the city; it is the bird known as דרור." In the Gemara (*Shabbos* 106b) the צפור דרור is characterized further: שאינה מקבלת מרות, דתנא דבי רבי ישמעאל למה נקרא שמה צפור דרור – מפני שדרה בבית כבשדה. Its name indicates that "it lives in a house as in the fields" — i.e., it retains its freedom in the house as in the fields and does not submit to confinement and domestication. According to רש"י (*Beitzah* 24a), דרור derives from דור, "to live"; more likely, perhaps, is the view of the משנה למלך (הל' טומאת צרעת, 11:1) that it means "freedom," as in וקראתם דרור (below, 25:10). In *Chullin* 62a the bird that is fit for טהרת מצורע is called the סנונית, which is commonly said to be the swallow.

חיות טהרות. According to *Chullin* 139b, the term צפור always denotes a kosher bird. The additional word טהרות teaches that it must also be מותר באכילה, which excludes צפורי עיר הנדחת and the like; and the additional

ה וְצִוָּה הַכֹּהֵן וְשָׁחַט אֶת־הַצִּפּוֹר הָאֶחָת אֶל־כְּלִי־חֶרֶשׂ עַל־מַיִם חַיִּים׃

5 *The priest shall order to slaughter one of the birds in an earthen vessel over living water.*

word חיות teaches שחיין ראשי איברים שלהן — which excludes a bird lacking a limb (*Chullin* 140a).

ועץ ארז: a piece of cedar wood one cubit in length and whose thickness is "a quarter of the thickness of the leg of a bed," כרביע כרע המטה (*Nega'im* 14:6; *Toras Kohanim*). *Toras Kohanim* continues: ובראשה טרף, "and with cedar leaves at the top"; but in *Nega'im* 14:6 this latter halachah is not accepted. The ר״ש in *Nega'im* has a different version of the *Toras Kohanim*, but he cites this last halachah in the name of the תוספתא.

ושני תולעת: wool dyed with the fluid of a worm (commonly said to be crimson). The term לשון (*Nega'im* 14:1) indicates, apparently, that the wool is unspun. From *Menachos* 42b it appears that שני תולעת — like תכלת לציצית — must be dyed לשמה, i.e., for this purpose. Hence, טעימה פסולה — if one dyes a piece of wool merely for testing, it is פסול; and even טעמה פסלה, if one dips a piece of wool as a test into a pan of dye, all of the dye in the pan is unfit for שני תולעת.

ואזב: it must be the plant that is known simply as אזוב, and not one that has, in addition, a differentiating epithet: אזוב ולא אזוב יון וכו׳ ולא כל אזוב שיש לו שם לווי (*Toras Kohanim*).

5 **את הצפור האחת**: הברורה שבשתים (ibid.). That is to say, the better, the "most choice" of the two; or perhaps: the one that most clearly has the characteristic signs of the species.

אל כלי חרש על מים חיים: מה מים חיים שלא נעשתה בהן מלאכה אף כלי שלא נעשתה בו מלאכה (*Sotah* 15b). That is to say, the vessel must be as "fresh" as the water; it must not have been used. It must be a פיילי של חרס חדשה, a new earthenware basin (ibid.). מים חיים: שלעולם נובעים ולא פוסקים, waters that flow continually and never run dry (ר״ש, *Nega'im* 14:1).

6 *As for the living bird, he himself shall take it, and the piece of cedar wood with the scarlet wool and the hyssop, and shall dip them, together with the living bird, into the blood of the slaughtered bird over the living water.*

7 *He shall sprinkle [it] upon the person who is being purified from the leprosy, seven times, and shall let the living bird fly away into the open field.*

ו אֶת־הַצִּפֹּר הַחַיָּה יִקַּח אֹתָהּ
וְאֶת־עֵץ הָאֶרֶז וְאֶת־שְׁנִי
הַתּוֹלַעַת וְאֶת־הָאֵזֹב וְטָבַל אוֹתָם
וְאֵת | הַצִּפֹּר הַחַיָּה בְּדַם הַצִּפֹּר
הַשְּׁחֻטָה עַל הַמַּיִם הַחַיִּים:
ז וְהִזָּה עַל הַמִּטַּהֵר מִן־הַצָּרַעַת
שֶׁבַע פְּעָמִים וְטִהֲרוֹ וְשִׁלַּח אֶת־
הַצִּפֹּר הַחַיָּה עַל־פְּנֵי הַשָּׂדֶה:

After the bird is slaughtered, it is immediately buried, because it is אסורה בהנאה (see *Nega'im* 14:1).

6 **את הצפר החיה יקח אתה**: מלמד שהוא מפרישה לעצמה (*Toras Kohanim*). As we have stated (Commentary, v. 2), ארבעה מינין שבמצורע מעכבין זה את זה; thus, they combine to form one unit. Nevertheless, the bird remains by itself — and the other three items are tied together: נטל עץ ארז ואזוב ושני תולעת וכרכן בשירי לשון (*Nega'im* 14:1). That is to say, he places the three items together, and with the end of the wool — which hangs down and is longer than the cedar wood and the hyssop — he ties the three items together in one bunch. Thus, וטבל אותם ואת הצפר החיה וגו׳; at the dipping, he holds together the bird and the three tied items (see ibid.).

בדם וגו׳ על המים החיים. The proportion of the water to the blood must be such that both are recognizable in the mixture. Hence, the prescribed amount of water is a רביעית. For, thus, even if the bird is large, the water is still recognizable in the mixture; and even if the bird is small, its blood is still recognizable: אין לך גדולה שמדחת את המים ואין לך קטנה שנדחית מפני המים (*Sotah* 16b).

7 **והזה על המטהר**: לאחר ידו של מצורע ויש אומרים על מצחו (*Nega'im* 14:1). The sprinklings are administered to the back of the hand, or, according to another opinion, to the forehead.

ח וְכִבֶּס הַמִּטַּהֵר אֶת־בְּגָדָיו וְגִלַּח אֶת־כָּל־שְׂעָרוֹ וְרָחַץ בַּמַּיִם וְטָהֵר וְאַחַר יָבוֹא אֶל־הַמַּחֲנֶה וְיָשַׁב מִחוּץ לְאָהֳלוֹ שִׁבְעַת יָמִים׃

8 *The one who is being purified shall wash his garments, shave off all his hair, bathe in water and become pure, and after that he may come into the camp, but he must remain outside his tent for seven days.*

ושלח את הצפר וגו׳. In verse 53 it is written: ושלח את הצפר החיה אל מחוץ לעיר אל פני השדה. The Gemara in *Kiddushin* 57b explains: שדה – שלא יעמוד ביפו ויזרקנה לים, בגבת ויזרקנה למדבר, ושלא יעמוד חוץ לעיר ויזרקנה בתוך העיר; אלא כל שעומד בעיר ויזרקנה חוץ לחומה. Thus, the bird is sent out of the city toward a worked field — not toward the sea and not toward the desert. The preceding procedures, however, are performed outside the city. It must be, then, that the bird is first brought into the city — in order to be sent out of it (see תוספות, ibid.). שלחה וחזרה חוזר ומשלחה אפילו מאה פעמים; if the bird comes back into the city, he must send it away again and again (רמב״ם הל׳ טומאת צרעת, 11:1, based on the תוספתא).

Once the bird has been sent away, it may be eaten: כשדה מה שדה מותרת אף האי נמי מותרת. Or, as רבא says: לא אמרה תורה שלח לתקלה. Had the bird been אסור באכילה, the Torah would not have commanded us to set it free, for someone might then inadvertently eat it and thus violate a prohibition (*Kiddushin* 57b).

8 **וכבס וגו׳ וגלח וגו׳ ורחץ וגו׳**. בימי חלוטו — also called ימי גמרו — he was מטמא במגע ובמשא, משכב ומושב, ובביאה. He now exits ימי חלוטו and enters ימי ספרו. In this new stage he still is מטמא במגע, but the other טומאות do not apply to him. Hence, at the end of ימי גמרו his body and clothes require טבילה, to be purified of these טומאות (*Nega'im* 14:2 — וכבס בגדיו וטבל, טהור מלטמא בביאה והרי הוא מטמא כשרץ).

וגלח את כל שערו ורחץ וגו׳. Before the טבילה, all hair that is visible on the whole of his body must be shaved off with a razor: העביר תער על כל בשרו (ibid.). מגלח כדלעת — with the exception of שיער בית הסתרים, such as שיער בתוך החוטם (see Commentary below, v. 9; *Sotah* 16a–b).

וטהר: he is purified of טומאת משא מושב וביאה, but is still מטמא במגע כשרץ (see *Nega'im* 14:2).

ואחר יבוא אל המנחה: נכנס לפנים מן החומה (ibid.). Thus his exclusion from מחנה ישראל is ended; now he is permitted to enter the social sphere that surrounds the Sanctuary of the Torah. But the Sanctuary itself remains closed to him — until the passing of the seven days of ימי ספרו. Of these days it says in our verse: וישב מחוץ לאהלו שבעת ימים. In this stage יהא כמנודה ויהא אסור בתשמיש המטה; אהלו - אין אהלו אלא אשתו שנאמר שובו לכם לאהליכם (*Toras Kohanim*). בימי ספרו marital relations are forbidden to him. This prohibition did not apply in the earlier stages. In the case of an אשה מנוגעת, this prohibition is not imposed: מחוץ לאהלו - ולא מחוץ לאהלה (*Krisos* 8b).

Let us try to understand the meaning of the procedures described here in verses 2–8. They remove the מצורע from the isolation of ימי חלוטו and *restore him to the social community.* The ideas signified by these procedures undoubtedly relate to the idea of the *social* community. For only the *social* community is now open to him; he is now permitted to enter מחנה ישראל. But during ימי ספרו he is still excluded from מקדש וקדשיו; certain procedures must be performed (v. 9, et seq.) to permit his re-entry into the sphere of the Sanctuary. It follows, then, that the procedures described here in verses 2–8 reflect only those truths that are attendant upon his re-entry into *society.* From this perspective we should consider the objects and acts mentioned here.

First, let us note those objects and acts that have analogues in other *mitzvos* of the Torah:

The two birds, which למצוה should be שוות במראה בקומה ובדמים ולקיחתן כאחת (v. 4), remind us at once of the שני שעירים of יום הכיפורים (below, 16:5; see Commentary there). In the case of מצורע, as in the case of יום הכיפורים, one of the creatures is destined for שחיטה and the other for שילוח — which is the antithesis of שחיטה; only that, there the שילוח is המדברה, whereas here the שילוח is על פני השדה and not to the מדבר.

The nature of these birds — that they are not מקבלות מרות — is analogous to what is said of פרה אדומה: אשר לא עלה עליה על (*Bemidbar* 19:2), and is also analogous to what is said of עגלה ערופה: אשר לא עבד בה אשר לא משכה בעל (*Devarim* 21:3).

דם על מים חיים בכלי חרש is analogous to מים קדשים בכלי חרש of the סוטה (*Bemidbar* 5:17) and to אפר במים חיים אל כלי in the case of פרה אדומה (ibid.

19:17). Finally, עץ ארז ושני תולעת ואזוב are mentioned both here and in the case of שריפת הפרה (ibid. 19:6).

ציפרי הדרור symbolize an *unsociable* personality; for they cannot be tamed, and they live in the house with the same free wildness as in the fields — אין הן מקבלות מרות והן דרות בבית כבשדה. This quality is antithetical to the *social* values that are prerequisites for entrance into the social community of man. It exemplifies the contrast of the animal of the field to the man of the city.

This is the demand that is made of one who would enter the social community of man: ושחט את הצפור; that is, he must subordinate unbridled animality to the control of human will. However, this breaking of the animal nature in man does not entail the "killing of life." Rather, only דם הציפור השחוטה will attain אל כלי חרש על מים חיים. *Only if subordinated to the moral will of man can animality participate in his eternal life; for everlasting life is the lot of man — who is likened to a broken vessel.* (This is also the meaning of the ashes in the מים חיים of מי חטאת: *Although* man is אפר, he attains eternal life. And this is also the meaning of the עפר on the מים קדושים in the case of סוטה: Man derives from dust, and he is subject to all the urges of organic life; *nevertheless*, he is called to moral holiness. See Commentary, *Bemidbar* 5:17.)

עץ ארז and אזוב, cedar and hyssop — the highest and lowest manifestations of plant life — represent the entire range of flora (cf. *Melachim* I 5:13). Similarly, שני תולעת, wool dyed with worm blood — mammal and creeping thing, the highest and lowest of animal life — represents the entire range of fauna. (Perhaps that is why wherever שני תולעת is mentioned in conjunction with עץ ארז ואזוב Scripture mentions שני before תולעת: שני is parallel to ארז, and תולעת to אזוב. Otherwise, however, Scripture always says תולעת שני.) All three — cedar wood, wool, and hyssop — bound together with the red thread into one unit, represent the complete range of organic life, the flora and fauna of the open field (שדה), where the מנוגע is condemned to dwell because of his unsocial and inhumane character. To these is added the צפור החי — the living, free bird — to symbolize instinctual, unbridled animality, which is part of the organic nature of the plant and animal world.

Moral control over animal instincts leads man to everlasting life. This control is symbolized by דם הצפר השחטה על המים החיים, and is to be realized in the communal life of the moral human being. But a sevenfold gap separates unbridled animality from moral freedom. And the

הזיות שבע פעמים signify that he who was expelled from the community must bridge this gap and exert all his strength, seven times over, before he can part company with the plants and the animals and be pronounced pure and ready to rejoin the community of man.

These sprinklings — which remind him of the lofty heights of his calling — are performed לאחר ידו, on the back of his hand; according to another opinion, on his forehead. For hand and forehead are the most human parts of the human body. They are the outward manifestations of thought and action, which — more than anything else — characterize a human being. The halachah is in accordance with the opinion that the sprinklings are to be performed on the back of the hand; it is the wrongful actions toward his fellow men that was the cause of his exclusion from human society. Whereas לאחר ידו, the outstretched hand, represents action and deed, the palm — כף, the inner surface of the hand — represents possession, the man who has property.

ושלח את הצפר החיה על פני השדה, or more precisely: אל מחוץ לעיר אל פני השדה (v. 53). There are two points here: The lack of restraint that characterizes a life of following natural instinct — represented by the צפור דרור — is antithetical to the communal life of man. But it has justification and the right to exist in the life of the field and forest — in nature, which surrounds the city life of man. Hence, על פני השדה — and not to the desert, and not to the sea.

גילוח וטבילה. Through שחיטת הציפור and the הזיות, he has learned the conditions for renewal in the future. The next step for him is to sever all connection with the past. This is symbolized by טבילת בגדיו וגופו. But, in addition, he is liable also to גילוח — whose meaning we must now try to understand.

This גילוח, shaving the hair of the whole body with a razor (תער), is equal in importance to שחיטת הציפור and to the הזיות; for all three — שחיטת ציפרים והזיית דם ציפור ותגלחתו — must be performed ביום ובכהן, in daytime and by a כהן (*Toras Kohanim* on v. 1).

תגלחת של מצוה in respect to the hair of the whole body is found elsewhere only at the inauguration of the *Levi'im*, as it says: והעבירו תער על כל בשרם (*Bemidbar* 8:7).

The common denominator of these two cases appears to be that, in both instances, men are to be led away from a life of devotion to self, and led into a life of complete devotion to the community. This is true of the *Levi'im*: Until now, they led merely private lives, as was their right; but from now onward they must assume the service of the community, as expressed by סמיכה and תנופה (see Commentary, ibid. 8:10–11). And this is also true here of the מצורע: Until now, he lived only for himself — selfishly and antagonistic toward society; and this was his main sin. From now onward he must undertake the self-sacrifice of his duties toward the community.

In both cases, the meaning of תגלחת and העברת תער על כל בשרם is that man must cease living only for himself. Hair is intended to protect the body and shield it from the effects of the outside world; it is the material that insulates the body (cf. Commentary, end of chap. 13). Stripping a body of all hair exposes it to the effects of the outside world. For this reason תגלחת is well suited to awaken the heart to turn away from isolating selfishness.

Still, the תגלחת of the *Levi'im* is not identical to the תגלחת of the מצורע. For in the case of the *Levi'im*, it was their right until now to lead a private life. They now voluntarily give up that life. Hence, they themselves perform the תגלחת on their own body. The מצורע, however, led a selfish life, in violation of his duty. Hence, the כהן, who serves in the Sanctuary, must remind him of the obligation to give up his ways.

(Cf. *Yeshayahu* 7:20, where the king of Assyria is called תַּעַר הַשְּׂכִירָה, a "razor hired by God," a razor that shaves off all the hair; that is, he will deprive the Jewish national body of all protective elements.)

וישב מחוץ לאהלו וגו'. Even after he has been allowed to return to the social community, he is still barred from מקדש וקדשיו. For seven days he is considered אב הטומאה כשרץ; and during these ימי ספרו he is restricted also in his home life: he is אסור בתשמיש המטה — a prohibition that did not apply בימי הסגרו וחלוטו. While he was expelled from society because of his sin, he was allowed to maintain "his tent" outside. Now, however, he has been allowed to return to the society that surrounds the Sanctuary of the Torah, but he is still barred from the Sanctuary itself — because of his previous social sins. Hence, the Torah denies him the full enjoyment of his own home — as long as he is not cured from all his social sins, and as long as the Sanctuary is closed to him.

Does this not reflect a profound truth? Only he who acts justly toward *society* is entitled to enjoy his *own* home! He who undermines the harmony of his *neighbor*'s home will not settle tranquilly in his *own* home in the sphere of the Sanctuary. Only when the Sanctuary gates open to

9 *On the seventh day he shall shave off all his hair: [of] his head, his beard, his eyebrows; he shall shave off all his hair, and wash his garments, bathe his body in water and become pure.*	ט וְהָיָה בַיּוֹם הַשְּׁבִיעִ֗י יְגַלַּ֤ח אֶת־כָּל־שְׂעָרוֹ֙ אֶת־רֹאשׁ֤וֹ וְאֶת־זְקָנוֹ֙ וְאֵת֙ גַּבֹּ֣ת עֵינָ֔יו וְאֶת־כָּל־שְׂעָר֖וֹ יְגַלֵּ֑חַ וְכִבֶּ֣ס אֶת־בְּגָדָ֗יו וְרָחַ֧ץ אֶת־בְּשָׂר֛וֹ בַּמַּ֖יִם וְטָהֵֽר׃
10 *On the eighth day he shall take two sheep that are whole and a*	י וּבַיּ֣וֹם הַשְּׁמִינִ֗י יִקַּ֤ח שְׁנֵֽי־כְבָשִׂים֙

him does his "own tent" in the sphere of the Sanctuary open to him again: וישב מחוץ לאהלו – יהא כמנודה ויהא אסור בתשמיש המטה (*Toras Kohanim*).

9 **והיה ביום השביעי וגו׳**. Upon returning from unsocial animal standing to social human standing, he was obligated to shave off all his hair. This תגלחת taught him that he must devote himself to the community unreservedly (see Commentary, v. 8). This demand is now addressed to him again: Upon returning from the social human sphere to the sphere of the Jewish godly calling, he is liable to a repeated תגלחת, a תגלחת שניה. It teaches him to appreciate the moral ideal that is learned in the Sanctuary of the Torah — an ideal that far transcends the level of merely social man; and what he learns will lead him to the practice of self-development.

את ראשו ואת זקנו: Here we have the principle of עשה דוחה לא תעשה (see *Nazir* 41a; Commentary below, 19:27).

Our Sages say in *Sotah* 16b: יגלח כל שערו – ריבה. את ראשו וגו׳ – מיעט. ואת כל שערו יגלח – חזר וריבה. ריבה ומיעט וריבה – ריבה הכל; מאי ריבה? ריבה דכוליה גופיה, ומאי מיעט? מיעט שיער שבתוך החוטם. (For more on כלל ופרט and ריבה ומיעט see Commentary above, 11:9. See Commentary, v. 8.)

וטהר. After the טבילה he has the status of a טבול יום: he is מותר במעשר but אסור בתרומה. After הערב שמש he is מותר בתרומה, but being מחוסר כפרה he is still אסור בקדשים until he brings his offering on the following day.

10 **וביום השמיני** — see *Collected Writings*, vol. III, p. 96ff.

שני כבשים: שיהיו שניהן שוין, the two must be alike; but this is only למצוה and not לעכב (*Yoma* 62b; see Commentary below, v. 13).

שחיטת ציפור והזיית דם ציפור ותגלחתו accompany his return to human society. These teach him to be conscious of man's dignity and purpose. The fundamental condition for such consciousness is that man free himself of preoccupation with his own self. For egoism is the powerful stimulus of all non-human organic life, but is totally antithetical to the feeling of duty and brotherhood, which is the life principle of social man.

Thus far, he has attained rebirth only *as a man*; his rebirth *as a Jew*, however, is complete only ביום השמיני (see Commentary above, 9:1). The general feeling of duty is capable of creating man, but to this must be added the positive content of God's Will, which fashions one's life in accordance with what was revealed in the Torah. The rebirth of a Jew is complete only when he has renewed the bond of life with the Torah in the Sanctuary.

Only a renewal of the bond with the Torah assures one of a tranquil life in the future. That is what is expressed by the offering-ritual prescribed from here onward.

The שני כבשים mentioned here are אשם and עולה, and the כבשה אחת is a חטאת; and with each one of them a separate כפרה is stated (vv. 18, 19, 20). The מצורע's offering includes *all* the shades of dedication of actions: אשם, חטאת, and עולה. This is almost without parallel. (Only in the case of נזיר טמא [*Bemidbar* 6:10–12] do we find anything like it; but, there, the חטאת and the עולה are merely עופות.) All three of these offerings — even the אשם and the חטאת — are accompanied by נסכים (ושלשה עשרנים וגו'; see *Menachos* 90b and 91a), and this is without parallel.

The implication is that he must dedicate his actions as a כבש — i.e., from the standpoint of one who has been shepherded by God in his *lot* in life. For in his arrogance he forgot God; he imagined that his fate was in his own hands. This arrogance is the root of all social sin, and it was the cause of his expulsion from God's community. That is why, only here, also the אשם and the חטאת are accompanied by נסכים. For upon his full re-entry into God's community, he, more than anyone else, must remember that the "flour," "oil," and "wine" in his possession — his existence, prosperity, and joy in life — depend solely on his actions' faithfulness to duty. That is why אשם is his first offering; and why the distinctive procedures mentioned in verses 14–18 are concentrated around the אשם; and why, in the Halachah as well, the אשם is the decisive offering which settles his past. For if הביא ציפרים ונתנגע אין מביא אלא קרבן אחד: that is, if, *before* he has brought the אשם, he becomes afflicted with a נגע again, the two periods of צרעת are considered as *one*, and he brings only one offering for both. If, however, he becomes afflicted with a נגע *after* bringing the אשם, this counts as two periods of צרעת, for which one must atone with two separate offerings. Furthermore, the time of the bringing of the אשם determines whether he is to bring the offering of an עשיר or עני: לאקבועי בעניות ובעשירות לא מיקבע עד שיביא אשמו (*Kerisos* 9b).

We must recall that precisely אשם reflects the personality who is on the verge of *desolation* because of the sin of selfishness in the sphere of his control and interests (see Commentary above, 5:26). Then we can understand the prominence of the אשם in the מצורע's group of קרבנות.

In addition to the oil in the מנחה בלולה בשמן, he brings a separate לוג of oil. This, too, is without parallel. The לוג of oil is not intended for a sanctifying anointment; for after some of this oil is sprinkled, and applied to the body of the person to be purified (vv. 15–18), the remainder of the oil is consumed by זכרי כהונה in the עזרה (as in the case of שיירי מנחה), and its היתר אכילה is dependent on the preceding מתנות. According to ר׳ מאיר, the law of פיגול applies to the oil, as to all other שיריים (see *Zevachim* 44a; 91a), but the Halachah is in doubt on this point.

לוג שמן של מצורע, then, is similar in meaning to the שמן of מנחות. Nevertheless, there is a difference between them:

As we have stated previously (see Commentary above, 2:1), the oil that is added to the מנחה turns it into לחם שמן; thus, the concept of prosperity is added to that of plain sustenance. לוג שמן של מצורע, however, should be understood in light of the meaning of oil in its relation to the human body. This meaning becomes clear from Scriptural expressions such as וְכַשֶּׁמֶן בְּעַצְמוֹתָיו (*Tehillim* 109:18), וּבְשָׂרִי כָּחַשׁ מִשָּׁמֶן (ibid. v. 24), וְחֻבַּל עֹל מִפְּנֵי־שָׁמֶן (*Yeshayahu* 10:27), וּמִשְׁמַן בְּשָׂרוֹ יֵרָזֶה (ibid. 17:4), and כָּל־שָׁמֵן וְכָל־אִישׁ חָיִל (*Shoftim* 3:29). These verses show that the word שמן and its derivative forms denote bodily health. Now, the Divine decree upon the מנוגע took the form of a bodily disease, through which God expressed His anger at the moral and social behavior of this person. Clearly, there is a correspondence between this concept and the idea that is brought, through the לוג שמן, to the attention of the one to be *yearling ewe that is whole, and three tenths of fine flour, for an homage offering mixed with oil, and one* log *of oil.*

תְּמִימִ֔ם וְכַבְשָׂ֨ה אַחַ֥ת בַּת־שְׁנָתָ֖הּ
תְּמִימָ֑ה וּשְׁלֹשָׁ֣ה עֶשְׂרֹנִ֗ים סֹ֤לֶת
מִנְחָה֙ בְּלוּלָ֣ה בַשֶּׁ֔מֶן וְלֹ֥ג אֶחָ֖ד
שָֽׁמֶן׃

11 *And the priest who effects the purification shall place the one who is being purified and these things before* God, *in the entrance to the Tent of Appointed Meeting.*

יא וְהֶעֱמִ֞יד הַכֹּהֵ֣ן הַֽמְטַהֵ֗ר אֵ֛ת
הָאִ֥ישׁ הַמִּטַּהֵ֖ר וְאֹתָ֑ם לִפְנֵ֣י יְהֹוָ֔ה
פֶּ֖תַח אֹ֥הֶל מוֹעֵֽד׃

12 *The priest shall take one of the sheep and bring it near as a guilt offering, with the* log *of oil, and wave them as a wave [offering] before* God.

יב וְלָקַ֨ח הַכֹּהֵ֜ן אֶת־הַכֶּ֣בֶשׂ הָֽאֶחָ֗ד
וְהִקְרִ֥יב אֹת֛וֹ לְאָשָׁ֖ם וְאֶת־לֹ֣ג
הַשָּׁ֑מֶן וְהֵנִ֥יף אֹתָ֛ם תְּנוּפָ֖ה לִפְנֵ֥י
יְהֹוָֽה׃ שני

purified, who longs for health through renewal of his bond with the Torah.

11 **והעמיד הכהן המטהר וגו'**. לפני ה' — this is the entrance to the Sanctuary. In the Second Temple this was the Gate of Nikanor, שער ניקנור, on the eastern side (see *Toras Kohanim*), the gate that led from the עזרת נשים to the עזרת ישראל. With the עזרת ישראל begins the sanctified area, which מן התורה is forbidden to טמאים. The gateway itself was not sanctified; hence, the מצורע can stand in the gateway, even though he is still מחוסר כפרה and is forbidden to enter the Sanctuary (*Sotah* 7a; 8a). Thus he stands, in the east, facing the Holy of Holies; with him are the offerings, which will open for him the gate of the Sanctuary.

12 **והקריב אתו לאשם** — this והקריב is the dedication of the animal as an אשם.

והניף אתם וגו'. תנופה — which signifies dedication to God and to the community (תרומה and תנופה: see Commentary, *Shemos* 29:22–25) — is

יג וְשָׁחַ֣ט אֶת־הַכֶּ֗בֶשׂ בִּמְק֞וֹם אֲשֶׁ֨ר
יִשְׁחַ֧ט אֶת־הַֽחַטָּ֛את וְאֶת־הָעֹלָ֖ה
בִּמְק֣וֹם הַקֹּ֑דֶשׁ כִּ֡י כַּֽחַטָּ֩את
הָאָשָׁ֨ם הוּא֙ לַכֹּהֵ֔ן קֹ֥דֶשׁ קָֽדָשִׁ֖ים
הֽוּא׃

13 *And he shall slaughter the sheep in the place where he slaughters the offering that clears of sin and the ascent offering, in the holy place; for like the offering that clears of sin, the guilt offering, too, belongs to the priest; it is a holy of holies.*

found elsewhere only with שלמים and with מנחות. For these offerings relate to the offerer's fortunate position, and the תנופה signifies that the individual commits himself and all his worldly possessions to God and to the community.

Here, תנופה is found at the אשם מצורע. For the מצורע repents of the sin of selfishness, and the תנופה highlights that aspect of the אשם which is antithetical to selfishness. The name אשם denotes "a person who needs protection from the threat of desolation"; and the תנופה is performed immediately upon the dedication of the אשם. The meaning of תנופת האשם, then, is this: The offering that represents this person — together with the לוג of oil representing health — is to be dedicated to God and to the community (through תנופה and תרומה), facing the Holy of Holies of the Torah (לפני ה׳). In other words, the individual must commit his personality and his health to God and to the community by observing the *mitzvos* of the Torah.

13 **ושחט וגו׳**. It is already stated above (7:1–2) that אשם — like עולה and חטאת — is קודש קדשים and hence שחיטתו בצפון. Also stated there is that אשם resembles עולה as regards מתנות הדם, and resembles חטאת as regards הקטרת אימוריו ואכילת בשרו. Nevertheless, Scripture repeats here that the law of אשם מצורע is like the law of עולה and חטאת. This repetition is explained in *Zevachim* 49a in accordance with one of the hermeneutic rules by which the Torah is expounded: דבר שהיה בכלל ויצא לידון בדבר החדש אי אתה רשאי להחזירו לכללו עד שיחזירנו הכתוב לכללו בפירוש וכו׳ לפי שיצא אשם מצורע לידון בדבר החדש, בבוהן יד ובוהן רגל ואזן ימנית, יכול לא יהא טעון מתן דמים ואימורין לגבי מזבח ת״ל כחטאת האשם הוא וכו׳. Anything that was included in a general category, but was then singled out and made subject to something new (that contradicts that category — see תוספות there), is to be excluded from that category unless the Torah explicitly restores it to that category. Now, in the case of all other אשמות, the blood is applied entirely to the altar. Yet here, in the case of אשם מצורע, the Torah prescribes that the blood is to be applied to various parts of the body of the one being purified. Thus, had the Torah not repeated that אשם מצורע is similar to חטאת, we might have assumed that neither the דם nor the אימורים of אשם מצורע is presented at the altar.

Remember, now, what we learned in verse 10: כבש האשם and כבש העולה must, למצוה, be alike. It may well be, then, that the words העלה, החטאת, כחטאת of our verse refer especially to the חטאת and עולה of the מצורע himself and not just to the general offering of עולה and חטאת. This, then, is the idea expressed in our verse — according to the hermeneutic rule just cited:

The blood that is placed on the body of the offerer of the אשם underscores the unique meaning of אשם; for the אשם represents the person who progresses from desolation into life and health. Yet this personal aspiration — man's commitment to his own personality — *seems* to contradict the purpose of the altar and the commitment to the aims of the altar (= יכול לא יהא טעון מתן דמים ואימורין לגבי מזבח). To counteract this impression, Scripture here draws an equation — not merely a general equation between אשם and חטאת ועולה, but a particular equation between אשם מצורע and his חטאת ועולה. This teaches us a profound truth: Man's care for his own personality, his aspiration for life and health — these, too, are among the life aims that are sanctified by the altar. If they spring from the duty that is learned in the Sanctuary, they, too, become endeavors dedicated to God; they, too, become tasks sanctified by עולה and חטאת. Even the אשם of the מצורע is קודש קדשים — like his עולה and חטאת.

The Gemara (*Zevachim* 49a–b) says further: Scripture here, in teaching the law of צפון for אשם, likens אשם not only to עולה — which is the primary source of the law of צפון (see above, 1:11) — but also to חטאת, for which צפון is derived only via היקש to עולה. From this we learn that דבר הלמד בהיקש אינו חוזר ומלמד בהיקש; for we see here that a היקש to חטאת would not have sufficed. This rule — which limits the power of a היקש — and the rule that דבר הלמד בהיקש אינו חוזר ומלמד בגזרה שוה, and other rules like these, apply only to קדשים: בכל התורה כולה למידין למד מלמד חוץ מן הקדשים שאין דנין למד מלמד (ibid. 49b).

14 *Then the priest shall take up some of the blood of the guilt offering, and the priest shall put [it] upon the right ear cartilage of the person being purified, and upon the thumb of his right hand and upon the big toe of his right foot.*

יד וְלָקַ֣ח הַכֹּהֵן֮ מִדַּ֣ם הָֽאָשָׁם֒ וְנָתַן֙ הַכֹּהֵ֔ן עַל־תְּנ֛וּךְ אֹ֥זֶן הַמִּטַּהֵ֖ר הַיְמָנִ֑ית וְעַל־בֹּ֤הֶן יָדוֹ֙ הַיְמָנִ֔ית וְעַל־בֹּ֖הֶן רַגְל֥וֹ הַיְמָנִֽית׃

14 **ולקח הכהן** — this is the קבלה, the reception of the blood. Here, a double קבלה is performed. The first is the reception of the blood in a כלי for the altar. This resembles the קבלה that is performed at all the other offerings. It is performed by a כהן, who conveys the blood to the altar, to dash upon it the שתי מתנות שהן ארבע. The second קבלה is for the applications to the body of the מיטהר. It is done in the palm of a second כהן, who performs the מתנות to the body of the מצורע (*Yoma* 61b; *Nega'im* 14:8). According to the תוספתא (see ר״ש on *Nega'im* 14:8), the קבלה for the מזבח is to be done first.

In these respects, the קבלות and מתנות prescribed here differ, apparently, from those that were prescribed in the case of איל המילואים (*Shemos* 29:20). For, there, only one קבלה was prescribed — in a כלי; and the מתנות on the ear, hand, and foot preceded the מתנות על המזבח. In our case, the separate קבלות and the reversed order of the מתנות signify the following: The person nullified himself through שחיטה, and reawakened to seek a nobler life. Now he must conduct his life in two separate directions, two directions that complement each other. Having nullified his egocentric being, he belongs to the Sanctuary — and to the forces striving upward to the height of the altar (קבלה בכלי מקדש וזריקה למטה). At the same time, he reawakens to a new priestlike life — in his intellect, actions, and endeavors; and the כהן, clad in garments of the Sanctuary, exemplifies before him such a life (קבלה בכף הכהן ונתינה על תנוך אוזן, בוהן יד ובוהן רגל). Indeed, when a person uplifts himself to God and to His purposes, he attains also a lofty *life* of truth. Then…

טו וְלָקַח הַכֹּהֵן מִלֹּג הַשָּׁמֶן וְיָצַק עַל־כַּף הַכֹּהֵן הַשְּׂמָאלִית׃

15 *And the priest shall take some of the* log *of oil and pour it into the priest's left palm.*

טז וְטָבַל הַכֹּהֵן אֶת־אֶצְבָּעוֹ הַיְמָנִית מִן־הַשֶּׁמֶן אֲשֶׁר עַל־כַּפּוֹ הַשְּׂמָאלִית וְהִזָּה מִן־הַשֶּׁמֶן בְּאֶצְבָּעוֹ שֶׁבַע פְּעָמִים לִפְנֵי יְהוָה׃

16 *The priest shall dip his right index finger in the oil that is in his left palm and shall sprinkle some of the oil with his index finger seven times before* God.

15 **ולקח וגו׳ ויצק על כף הכהן השמאלית**. To life are added health and strength, represented by the לוג שמן. The כהן takes of the לוג השמן and pours it into his colleague's hand; but if he pours it into his own hand, it is כשר (*Nega'im* 14:10). It is repeatedly stressed that the oil is to be received in the *left* hand. This is not stipulated in the case of קבלת הדם; and, according to the רמב״ם (הל׳ מחוסרי כפרה, 4:2), קבלת הדם in the left hand would even be פסול.

Through its very reception in the hand of the כהן, the blood placed on the body of the מיטהר signifies a priestlike life of service. The hand of the כהן is to this blood as the vessel of the Sanctuary is to the דם שעל המזבח. Clearly, then, the blood must be received in the right hand. שמן, however, is different. Its connection to the mission of life indicated by God is established not by the hand of the כהן but by the הזיות toward the Holy of Holies (v. 16); only the שיריים come back to relate to the כהן. The hand of the כהן vis-à-vis the oil is merely a vehicle for הזיה. Hence, it follows that the oil should be received in the left hand, whereas קבלת השמן בימין would be פסול, as this would distort the meaning. Only the sprinklings toward the קודש הקדשים must be done with the right index finger.

16 **וטבל וגו׳ והזה וגו׳**: על כל הזיה טבילה (*Nega'im* 14:10). The finger must be dipped into the oil before each one of the seven הזיות.

לפני ה׳: כנגד בית קודש הקדשים (ibid.).

17 *And from the rest of the oil that is in his palm, the priest shall put [some] on the right ear cartilage of the one being purified, on the thumb of his right hand, and on the big toe of his right foot, on the blood of the guilt offering.*

יז וּמִיֶּתֶר הַשֶּׁמֶן אֲשֶׁר עַל־כַּפּוֹ יִתֵּן
הַכֹּהֵן עַל־תְּנוּךְ אֹזֶן הַמִּטַּהֵר
הַיְמָנִית וְעַל־בֹּהֶן יָדוֹ הַיְמָנִית
וְעַל־בֹּהֶן רַגְלוֹ הַיְמָנִית עַל דַּם
הָאָשָׁם׃

18 *The remainder of the oil that is in the priest's palm he shall put on the head of the one being purified,*

יח וְהַנּוֹתָר בַּשֶּׁמֶן אֲשֶׁר עַל־כַּף
הַכֹּהֵן יִתֵּן עַל־רֹאשׁ הַמִּטַּהֵר

17 **ומיתר וגו׳**. The location of the מתנות is exactly indicated by the words על דם האשם and על מקום דם האשם; nevertheless, Scripture again specifies (here and in v. 28): ועל בהן ידו וגו׳. From this we learn (in *Menachos* 9b–10a) that צדדין are כשרים, but צידי צדדין are not. That is, the blood and the oil may be placed on the upper surfaces of the thumb and big toe, and even on their sides; but they may not be placed on the under surfaces. These parts of the body are being considered here in their active state — when they are under the control of the extending muscles.

על דם האשם: The מתנות דם באוזן ובבהונות must be performed first, but it is not necessary that the blood still be there when the oil ritual is performed. For it says in verse 28: על מקום דם האשם, from which *Toras Kohanim* infers: מלמד שהמקום גורם (see also *Menachos* 10a).

During the מתנות of the blood and oil, the מצורע would stand in the Nikanor Gateway outside the עזרה. From there, he would extend his head, hand, and foot to the כהן in the עזרה. For if the דם האשם were to be taken outside the עזרה, it would become פסול ביוצא. In this regard the question is raised, in *Zevachim* 32b, whether ביאה במקצת — a טמא partially entering the Sanctuary, i.e., extending just a part of his body inside — שמה ביאה or not.

18 This is the order of the הזיות ומתנות of the oil: First, the כהן sprinkles of the oil seven הזיות toward the קודש הקדשים. Then, the כהן places of the oil on the ear, thumb, and big toe of the one to be purified. The כהן

and [thus] the priest will effect atonement for him before God.	וְכִפֶּ֥ר עָלָ֛יו הַכֹּהֵ֖ן לִפְנֵ֥י יְהוָֽה׃
19 *The priest shall then make the offering that clears of sin and effect atonement for the person being purified from his impurity; then he shall slaughter the ascent offering.*	יט וְעָשָׂ֤ה הַכֹּהֵן֙ אֶת־הַֽחַטָּ֔את וְכִפֶּ֕ר עַל־הַמִּטַּהֵ֖ר מִטֻּמְאָת֑וֹ וְאַחַ֖ר יִשְׁחַ֥ט אֶת־הָעֹלָֽה׃

then pours the remainder of the oil that is in his palm on the head of the one to be purified. The remainder of the לוג is consumed by the כהנים (*Toras Kohanim* on v. 13).

Through this whole procedure, a profound truth is conveyed to the one to be purified, who is about to be readmitted to the sphere of the Sanctuary: *His physical health depends solely on his spiritual and moral health.* He must devote to the Torah all the strength that he hopes to receive from God. With ever fresh, ever renewed energy (על כל הזיה טבילה), he must fully actualize (שבע הזיות) God's Torah, which rests in the קודש הקדשים. Toward this end he must devote first the *mind*, which absorbs ideas (as symbolized by his ear); the *deeds*, which implement (as symbolized by his thumb); and the *aspiration*, which seeks possessions and relationships (symbolized by his big toe). He must devote every thought and every action and every aspiration to the fulfillment of the Torah, so that this devotion takes hold of his *entire spirit* — at the root and source of all his thoughts, emotions, and actions (as symbolized by his head). Only if he behaves in this manner will he become hallowed in both body and spirit, a dedicated servant of God. And only if he becomes such a priestly individual may he hope to benefit happily from the strength and health he has attained (מתחלקת לכהנים).

18–20 **וכפר עליו הכהן לפני ה׳**. In the case of **חטאת** it says: **וכפר על המטהר מטמאתו** (v. 19); and in the case of **עולה**: **וכפר עליו הכהן וטהר** (v. 20). The **אשם**, the accompanying **לוג שמן**, and the procedures performed with these, atone for his social sins which had incurred him God's anger, as manifested by his **נגע**. This procedure seeks to impress upon him all those truths

20 *And the priest shall lift the ascent offering and the homage offering onto the altar; the priest will effect atonement for him, and he will become pure.*

כ וְהֶעֱלָ֧ה הַכֹּהֵ֛ן אֶת־הָעֹלָ֥ה וְאֶת־
הַמִּנְחָ֖ה הַמִּזְבֵּ֑חָה וְכִפֶּ֥ר עָלָ֛יו
הַכֹּהֵ֖ן וְטָהֵֽר׃ ס שלישי (חמישי
כשהן מחוברין)

21 *If, however, he is poor and his means are not sufficient, he shall take a sheep for a guilt offering to be waved, to effect atonement for him, and one tenth of fine flour mixed with oil for an homage offering, and one* log *of oil.*

כא וְאִם־דַּ֣ל ה֗וּא וְאֵ֣ין יָדוֹ֮ מַשֶּׂ֒גֶת֒
וְלָ֠קַח כֶּ֣בֶשׂ אֶחָ֥ד אָשָׁ֛ם לִתְנוּפָ֖ה
לְכַפֵּ֣ר עָלָ֑יו וְעִשָּׂר֨וֹן סֹ֜לֶת אֶחָ֨ד
בָּל֥וּל בַּשֶּׁ֛מֶן לְמִנְחָ֖ה וְלֹ֥ג שָֽׁמֶן׃

that form the basis of a life of social justice before God. With that, his past sins are erased. Henceforth, it all depends on him; it is within his power to act justly before God — in accordance with the dictates of God's Torah. Social justice, however, is only one aspect of the Jew's mission. Only if he adheres to the *whole* eminence of God's moral law (as symbolized by חטאת) and fulfills *all* the duties commanded by God (as symbolized by עולה) can he become a complete Jew. These are the root and stock of God's planting; *Jewish* social justice can flourish and flower only from this root. Jewish humanity and Jewish justice are merely a fragment of Judaism; a Judaism stripped of all its other values will never triumph in history.

The אשם of the מצורע must be supported by his חטאת and by his עולה. In offering the חטאת he must rid himself of טומאתו and keep far from the lack of moral freedom; and in offering the עולה he must vow to fulfill the good and devote himself to it in moral freedom. As a result, וטהר, he will attain purity and maintain purity. Never again shall a נגע appear upon him as a sign of God's anger; never again shall he be banished from the sphere of Jewish life, which forms around the Sanctuary of the Torah.

21–31 **ואם דל הוא וגו׳**. The אשם of the poor man is the same as that of the rich man. The duty of brotherhood and social justice is the same for rich and poor alike; a person's lot is not a factor when he is judged for

22 *And two turtledoves or two young doves, whichever he can afford, one to be an offering that clears of sin, and the other one an ascent offering.*

כב וּשְׁתֵּי תֹרִים אוֹ שְׁנֵי בְּנֵי יוֹנָה
אֲשֶׁר תַּשִּׂיג יָדוֹ וְהָיָה אֶחָד
חַטָּאת וְהָאֶחָד עֹלָה׃

23 *He shall bring them on the eighth day for his purification, to the priest, to the entrance of the Tent of Appointed Meeting, before* God.

כג וְהֵבִיא אֹתָם בַּיּוֹם הַשְּׁמִינִי
לְטָהֳרָתוֹ אֶל־הַכֹּהֵן אֶל־פֶּתַח
אֹהֶל־מוֹעֵד לִפְנֵי יְהוָה׃

4 *The priest shall take the sheep of the guilt offering and the* log *of oil, and the priest shall wave them as a wave [offering] before* God.

כד וְלָקַח הַכֹּהֵן אֶת־כֶּבֶשׂ הָאָשָׁם
וְאֶת־לֹג הַשָּׁמֶן וְהֵנִיף אֹתָם הַכֹּהֵן
תְּנוּפָה לִפְנֵי יְהוָה׃

25 *He shall slaughter the sheep of the guilt offering, and the priest shall take some of the blood of the guilt offering and put [it] on the right ear cartilege of the person being purified, on the thumb of his right hand, and on the big toe of his right foot.*

כה וְשָׁחַט אֶת־כֶּבֶשׂ הָאָשָׁם וְלָקַח
הַכֹּהֵן מִדַּם הָאָשָׁם וְנָתַן עַל־תְּנוּךְ
אֹזֶן־הַמִּטַּהֵר הַיְמָנִית וְעַל־בֹּהֶן
יָדוֹ הַיְמָנִית וְעַל־בֹּהֶן רַגְלוֹ
הַיְמָנִית׃

26 *The priest shall pour some of the oil into the priest's left palm.*

כו וּמִן־הַשֶּׁמֶן יִצֹק הַכֹּהֵן עַל־כַּף
הַכֹּהֵן הַשְּׂמָאלִית׃

---

social sins — for which the אשם מצורע is designed to atone. Only the tenor of life as a whole varies with the rich and the poor; different external conditions call for the testing of different aspects of moral strength. Hence, the אשם ולוג שמן are the same for rich and poor alike.

As regards the חטאת and the עולה, however, it is different. For these represent the sanctification of life in general. Hence, the עני brings a חטאת עוף and an עולת עוף — as in the case of קרבן עולה ויורד. See Commentary above, 1:14ff. and 5:7ff.

27 *With his right index finger, the priest shall sprinkle some of the oil that is in his left palm, seven times before* God.

כז וְהִזָּה הַכֹּהֵן בְּאֶצְבָּעוֹ הַיְמָנִית מִן־הַשֶּׁמֶן אֲשֶׁר עַל־כַּפּוֹ הַשְּׂמָאלִית שֶׁבַע פְּעָמִים לִפְנֵי יְהוָה׃

28 *The priest shall put some of the oil that is in his palm on the right ear cartilege of the one being purified, on the thumb of his right hand, and on the big toe of his right foot; in the [same] place [where he put] the blood of the guilt offering.*

כח וְנָתַן הַכֹּהֵן מִן־הַשֶּׁמֶן | אֲשֶׁר עַל־כַּפּוֹ עַל־תְּנוּךְ אֹזֶן הַמִּטַּהֵר הַיְמָנִית וְעַל־בֹּהֶן יָדוֹ הַיְמָנִית וְעַל־בֹּהֶן רַגְלוֹ הַיְמָנִית עַל־מְקוֹם דַּם הָאָשָׁם׃

29 *The remainder of the oil that is in the priest's palm he shall put on the head of the one being purified, in order to effect atonement for him before* God.

כט וְהַנּוֹתָר מִן־הַשֶּׁמֶן אֲשֶׁר עַל־כַּף הַכֹּהֵן יִתֵּן עַל־רֹאשׁ הַמִּטַּהֵר לְכַפֵּר עָלָיו לִפְנֵי יְהוָה׃

30 *He shall then offer one of the turtledoves or [one] of the young doves, of those that he can afford.*

ל וְעָשָׂה אֶת־הָאֶחָד מִן־הַתֹּרִים אוֹ מִן־בְּנֵי הַיּוֹנָה מֵאֲשֶׁר תַּשִּׂיג יָדוֹ׃

31 *Of those that he can afford, one shall be an offering that clears of sin, and the other an ascent offering along with the homage offering; and [thus] the priest shall effect atonement before* God *for the one being purified.*

לא אֵת אֲשֶׁר־תַּשִּׂיג יָדוֹ אֶת־הָאֶחָד חַטָּאת וְאֶת־הָאֶחָד עֹלָה עַל־הַמִּנְחָה וְכִפֶּר הַכֹּהֵן עַל הַמִּטַּהֵר לִפְנֵי יְהוָה׃

32 *This is the teaching with regard to one on whom there is a leprous mark, whose means do not suffice in his purification.*

לב זֹאת תּוֹרַת אֲשֶׁר־בּוֹ נֶגַע צָרָעַת אֲשֶׁר לֹא־תַשִּׂיג יָדוֹ בְּטָהֳרָתוֹ׃ פ

רביעי (ששי כשהן מחוברין)

33 God *spoke to Moshe and Aharon, saying:*	לג וַיְדַבֵּר יְהֹוָה אֶל־מֹשֶׁה וְאֶל־אַהֲרֹן לֵאמֹר׃
34 *When you come into the land of Canaan, which I give to you as a possession, and I shall cause a leprous mark to develop on a house of the land of your possession.*	לד כִּי תָבֹאוּ אֶל־אֶרֶץ כְּנַעַן אֲשֶׁר אֲנִי נֹתֵן לָכֶם לַאֲחֻזָּה וְנָתַתִּי נֶגַע צָרַעַת בְּבֵית אֶרֶץ אֲחֻזַּתְכֶם׃
35 *Then he who owns the house shall come and inform the priest,*	לה וּבָא אֲשֶׁר־לוֹ הַבַּיִת וְהִגִּיד לַכֹּהֵן

34 **כי תבאו וגו'**. נגעי בתים apply only in ארץ ישראל (which is apparently why they are dealt with in a separate section) and only after the Land has been divided into individual holdings, so that כל אחד מכיר את שלו. At such a time the Land will have become לאחוזה (v. 34), and the words אשר לו הבית (v. 35) — מי שמיוחד לו (*Yoma* 12a) — will have become a reality.

בית השותפים is מטמא בנגעים, as it has definite owners, though they be many. בית הכנסת is מטמא בנגעים only if יש בה בית דירה לחזן הכנסת, the supervisor of the בית הכנסת has a dwelling in it. On the other hand, houses in ירושלים are not מיטמאים בנגעים. For Yerushalayim was considered national property, לא נתחלקה לשבטים; hence, אין משכירין בתים בירושלים לפי שאינה שלהן: those who would go up to Yerushalayim for the festivals were entitled to free lodging. House owners were not allowed to charge rent, as they themselves were not considered full owners of their houses (ibid. 11b–12a).

Houses are מיטמאים בנגעים only if they are אחזתכם, Jewish property — which excludes בתי נכרים. Hence, הלוקח בתים מן הנכרים יראו בתחלה (*Nega'im* 12:1), as in the case of נגעי בגדים (see Commentary above, 13:47 and the discussion at the end of chapter 13).

35 **ובא אשר לו הבית**. The Gemara in *Yoma* 11b sees here an allusion to the social sin on account of which a house is afflicted with a נגע: **אשר לו הבית – מי שמייחד ביתו לו שאינו רוצה להשאיל כליו ואומר שאין לו, הקב"ה מפרסמו**

לֵאמֹ֑ר כְּנֶ֕גַע נִרְאָ֥ה לִ֖י בַּבָּֽיִת׃

saying: There appears to me to be [something] like a mark on [my] house.

לו וְצִוָּ֨ה הַכֹּהֵ֜ן וּפִנּ֣וּ אֶת־הַבַּ֗יִת
בְּטֶ֨רֶם יָבֹ֤א הַכֹּהֵן֙ לִרְא֣וֹת אֶת־
הַנֶּ֔גַע וְלֹ֥א יִטְמָ֖א כׇּל־אֲשֶׁ֣ר בַּבָּ֑יִת
וְאַ֥חַר כֵּ֛ן יָבֹ֥א הַכֹּהֵ֖ן לִרְא֥וֹת אֶת־
הַבָּֽיִת׃

36 *And the priest shall command that they empty the house before the priest comes to look at the mark, so that whatever is inside the house does not become impure, and [only] afterwards shall the priest come to look at the house.*

כשמפנה את ביתו. That is, a person thinks that his house is meant exclusively for himself; he does not want to lend his possessions, and says that he does not have the article requested. God exposes his lie by having the contents of his house emptied out into the street.

כנגע נראה לי בבית: אפילו תלמיד חכם ויודע שהוא נגע ודאי, לא יגזור ויאמר נגע נראה לי בבית, אלא כנגע נראה לי בבית (*Nega'im* 12:5). The Torah here teaches us proper conduct — that one must conduct himself with humility (רבינו אליהו מזרחי).

נראה לי: ולא לאורי, מכאן אמרו בית אפל אין פותחין בו חלונות לראות את נגעו (*Toras Kohanim*). A נגע is מטמא only if it is visible by daylight. If it can be seen only by the aid of artificial light or by cutting a window, it is not מטמא. And what applies to נגעי אדם applies also to נגעי בתים: נגעים בבית הסתרים — e.g., in a wall under the cover of panelling or wainscot, or under wallpaper — are not מטמא (תוספתא cited in ר״ש, *Nega'im* 13:1).

36 **וצוה וגו׳ ופנו וגו׳**. See Commentary above, end of chapter 13.

ולא יטמא כל אשר בבית. The question is raised whether even articles that, as a rule, are not מקבל טומאה — e.g., חבילי עצים וחבילי קנים — become טמא in a בית המנוגע (see משנה למלך on הל׳ טומאת צרעת, 14:4).

לראות את הבית. It does not say here לראות את הנגע, but לראות את הבית; for the build of the house must be examined also. Not every house is

37 *If he sees the mark, and lo! the mark on the walls of the house is a sunken-looking deep green or deep red that appears recessed from [the rest of] the wall.*

לז וְרָאָה אֶת־הַנֶּגַע וְהִנֵּה הַנֶּגַע בְּקִירֹת הַבַּיִת שְׁקַעֲרוּרֹת יְרַקְרַקֹּת אוֹ אֲדַמְדַּמֹּת וּמַרְאֵיהֶן שָׁפָל מִן־הַקִּיר׃

38 *Then the priest shall go out of the house to the entrance of the house*

לח וְיָצָא הַכֹּהֵן מִן־הַבַּיִת אֶל־פֶּתַח

susceptible to טומאת נגעים; rather, it depends on the shape and the type of build. A house is not מיטמא בנגעים unless it is four-sided, rests on the ground (מחובר בארץ), and is built of stone (not of bricks and not of marble), wood, and earth (according to *Toras Kohanim* not plaster and the like, but natural earth that is fit for building purposes; see קרבן אהרן). This is evident from the data supplied in the verses of this section (see *Nega'im* 12:1–2).

37 **וראה את הנגע והנה הנגע**. From this repetition we learn that the minimum size of נגעי בתים is twice that of an ordinary **נגע**. Thus, a house is rendered **מטא** only in the case of a **נגע** of two **גריסים** (*Toras Kohanim*).

שקערורת: שוקעות במראיהן (*Toras Kohanim*) — i.e., they appear as though they were recessed. The color of the **נגע** is deeper than the color of the wall (see above, 13:2, 3, and 20), but there is no actual depression in the wall. In our opinion, this interpretation of *Toras Kohanim* is not derived from the word שקערורת itself, but is evident from the end of the verse: ומראיהן שפל מן הקיר. As *Toras Kohanim* explains there: ומראיהן שפל מן הקיר ולא ממשן (cf. Commentary above, 13:3). The word **שקערורת** per se denotes a depression. For in our view the word derives from the root **קער** — just as **שלהבת** derives from the root **להב**. And **קער** — from which we get **קערה** (bowl) — undoubtedly denotes a depression (cf. the relation to **יאר**, **יער** — Commentary, *Bereshis* 41:1).

ירקרקת, אדמדמת: ירוק שבירוקים, אדום שבאדומים (*Toras Kohanim*).

38 **ויצא וגו׳ והסגיר וגו׳**. **ויצא**: he is to leave the house before declaring it **טמא**, but he is to go only **אל פתח הבית**, just outside the threshold: **עומד**

and declare the house closed up for seven days.

הַבָּיִת וְהִסְגִּיר אֶת־הַבַּיִת שִׁבְעַת יָמִים׃

39 *If the priest returns on the seventh day and looks, and lo! the mark has spread on the walls of the house.*

לט וְשָׁב הַכֹּהֵן בַּיּוֹם הַשְּׁבִיעִי וְרָאָה וְהִנֵּה פָּשָׂה הַנֶּגַע בְּקִירֹת הַבָּיִת׃

40 *Then the priest shall order that they remove the stones that have the mark on them and cast them outside the city in an impure place.*

מ וְצִוָּה הַכֹּהֵן וְחִלְּצוּ אֶת־הָאֲבָנִים אֲשֶׁר בָּהֵן הַנָּגַע וְהִשְׁלִיכוּ אֶתְהֶן אֶל־מִחוּץ לָעִיר אֶל־מָקוֹם טָמֵא׃

בצד המשקוף ומסגיר (*Toras Kohanim*). The Gemara in *Chullin* 10b cites our verse as the source of the principle אוקי מילתא אחזקיה — i.e., presume that the condition of an object remains as it was, until you ascertain that it has changed. That is what you find here: The כהן stands outside the house, in a position from where it is possible that he cannot see the נגע at all. Nevertheless, he declares the house closed up. He assumes, then, that the נגע has not changed and still bears the signs of טומאה.

והסגיר את הבית. It is not clear whether this הסגר (of the house — and similarly of the מצורע) means an actual locking up or merely a declaration of isolation. See משנה למלך on הל׳ טומאת צרעת, 14:5; and see Commentary above, 13:4.

40 **וצוה הכהן וחלצו**. From the plural form — וחלצו — we learn a halachah: If it is a common wall, between two houses, the neighbor is obligated to participate in this חליצה. מכאן אמרו אוי לרשע אוי לשכנו (*Nega'im* 12:6).

אל מקום טמא. Because of the stones that are thrown there, the place becomes טמא, since the stones are מטמאות במגע ובמשא ובביאה.

אתהן אל מחוץ לעיר. Whereas אדם is expelled only from cities that are מוקפות חומה מימות יהושע בן נון, stones are cast out of any city (see *Toras Kohanim*; cf. the law of בגדים, Commentary above, 13:47).

41 *And he shall have the house scraped off inside, all around, and the earth which they have scraped off they shall cast outside the city in an impure place.*	מא וְאֶת־הַבַּ֛יִת יַקְצִ֥עַ מִבַּ֖יִת סָבִ֑יב וְשָׁפְכ֗וּ אֶת־הֶֽעָפָר֙ אֲשֶׁ֣ר הִקְצ֔וּ אֶל־מִח֣וּץ לָעִ֔יר אֶל־מָק֖וֹם טָמֵֽא׃
42 *They shall then take other stones and bring them in the place of those stones, and he shall take other earth and plaster the house.*	מב וְלָֽקְחוּ֙ אֲבָנִ֣ים אֲחֵר֔וֹת וְהֵבִ֖יאוּ אֶל־תַּ֣חַת הָאֲבָנִ֑ים וְעָפָ֥ר אַחֵ֛ר יִקַּ֖ח וְטָ֥ח אֶת־הַבָּֽיִת׃
43 *If the mark comes again and breaks out on the house after he has removed the stones and after the house has been scraped and after it has been replastered.*	מג וְאִם־יָשׁ֤וּב הַנֶּ֙גַע֙ וּפָרַ֣ח בַּבַּ֔יִת אַחַ֖ר חִלֵּ֣ץ אֶת־הָאֲבָנִ֑ים וְאַחֲרֵ֛י הִקְצ֥וֹת אֶת־הַבַּ֖יִת וְאַחֲרֵ֥י הִטּֽוֹחַ׃

41 **ואת הבית וגו׳**. יקציע derives from the root קצע. Similarly, the following הקצו derives from the root קצה, from which we get the noun קצה, end. Phonetically related to both is גזע, a tree that was cut down. The basic meaning is undoubtedly to divide, to separate, to cut off; here it means to scrape off from the house. Perhaps the difference between קֶצַע and קָצֶה is that קֶצַע relates *exclusively* to an object *from which* something is taken, as in ואת הבית יקציע, and similarly the related גזע; קָצֶה, however, relates to both the object taken off and the object from which it is taken off. From the same root comes מקצוע, which apparently denotes a plane. Wessely infers from the expression מקצעת המשכן (*Shemos* 26:23) that he scrapes on both sides to form a right angle.

סביב: all around the נגע (*Toras Kohanim*).

42 **ולקחו וגו׳ ועפר אחר יקח וטח וגו׳**. His neighbor takes part, together with him, in removing the stones and bringing other stones, but he alone brings the earth and plasters the house (see *Toras Kohanim*; *Nega'im* 12:6).

43 **ואם ישוב**: at the end of a second week of הסגר, similar to what is said above: ושב הכהן ביום השביעי (v. 39; see *Toras Kohanim*).

44 *And the priest comes and looks, and lo! the mark has spread in the house, then this is a malignant mark on the house; it is impure.*	מד וּבָא֙ הַכֹּהֵ֔ן וְרָאָ֕ה וְהִנֵּ֛ה פָּשָׂ֥ה הַנֶּ֖גַע בַּבָּ֑יִת צָרַ֨עַת מַמְאֶ֥רֶת הִ֛וא בַּבַּ֖יִת טָמֵ֥א הֽוּא׃
45 *He shall demolish the house, its stones, its wood, and all the earth of the house, and shall take them*	מה וְנָתַ֣ץ אֶת־הַבַּ֗יִת אֶת־אֲבָנָיו֙ וְאֶת־עֵצָ֔יו וְאֵ֖ת כָּל־עֲפַ֣ר הַבָּ֑יִת

הִקְצוֹת: an irregular form. In the נפעל one would say: הִקָּצוֹת; in the הפעיל: הַקְצוֹת.

44 **ובא הכהן וראה והנה פשה וגו׳**. Since the same expression, צרעת ממארת, appears here as in the case of נגעי בגדים (13:51–52), *Toras Kohanim* draws an analogy: Just as in the case of בגדים, if the נגע returns — even without any increase in size (החוזר אע״פ שאינו פושה) — the garment must be burned, so, too, here in the cases of houses, if the נגע reappears after חלץ וקצה וטח, even if there is no פשיון, the house requires נתיצה. Thus, פשה here is synonymous with ופרח of verse 43. Wessely explains that the נגע returns to different stones, as the former stones have already been removed. Hence, the very return of the נגע entails פשיון. However, see below.

טמא הוא. Although it was already טמא as מוסגר, its טומאה is now intensified as מוחלט: בית המוסגר מטמא מתוכו, והמוחלט מתוכו ומאחוריו, זה וזה מטמאין בביאה (*Negaim* 13:4). According to our version in רש״י (*Yevamos* 103b, ד״ה מטמא מתוכו), the walls of a בית מוסגר impart טומאה to one who touches them on the inside — even if he does not enter the house; whereas the walls of a בית מוחלט impart טומאה even to one who touches them on the outside. However, this conception of the difference between בית מוסגר and בית מוחלט is not undisputed. See תוספות (ibid.) ד״ה מטמא מאחוריו and משנה למלך on הל׳ טומאת צרעת, 16:3.

45 **ונתץ את הבית את אבניו וגו׳**. Although the neighbor takes part in the חליצה, נתיצה is restricted to the בית המנוגע. The same applies to a two-storied house (בית ועליה על גביו): only the story affected by the נגע has to be demolished (*Nega'im* 13:2–3).

outside the city, to an impure place.

וְהוֹצִ֤יא אֶל־מִחוּץ֙ לָעִ֔יר אֶל־
מָק֖וֹם טָמֵֽא׃

46 *Whoever enters the house during the period that [the priest] has declared it closed up shall be impure until evening.*

מו וְהַבָּא֙ אֶל־הַבַּ֔יִת כָּל־יְמֵ֖י הִסְגִּ֣יר
אֹת֑וֹ יִטְמָ֖א עַד־הָעָֽרֶב׃

47 *But whoever lies down in the house must wash his garments, and whoever eats in the house must wash his garments.*

מז וְהַשֹּׁכֵ֣ב בַּבַּ֔יִת יְכַבֵּ֖ס אֶת־בְּגָדָ֑יו
וְהָאֹכֵ֣ל בַּבַּ֔יִת יְכַבֵּ֖ס אֶת־בְּגָדָֽיו׃

46–47 **כל ימי הסגיר אתו** — and certainly, then, בימי חלוטו.

והשכב וגו׳ והאכל וגו׳ — both of these are examples of remaining a while in the house (see below). והבא אל הבית (v. 46) is a momentary entry. As soon as one's head and the greater part of one's body, ראשו ורובו, have entered the house, he becomes טמא until nightfall, but he is not מטמא בגדים שעליו. בגדים and כלים that are brought into a בית המנוגע also become טמאים like a person — provided that they are brought in independently (that is, a person is not wearing them). If, however, they are serving as clothing for a person, they are not rendered טמאים by a momentary entry. Only if a person remains in a בית המנוגע are the בגדים שעליו rendered טמאים, as it says (v. 47): יכבס בגדיו.

The minimum period of time for such "remaining" is stated here by the words והאכל בבית. This period is set in *Nega'im* (13:9): שישהא כדי אכילת פרס פת חטין ולא פת שעורין מיסב ואוכלן בלפתן — i.e., the time it would take a person to eat half (פרס: to break and divide) a loaf of wheaten bread with jam or vegetables while he is seated comfortably at table. According to *Eruvin* 82b, a whole loaf is enough food for two meals (מזון שתי סעודות). Accordingly, a half loaf (פרס) is enough for one סעודה. That is the אכילה mentioned in our verse. For, by placing אכילה together with שכיבה in our verse, Scripture indicates that the אכילה denotes a meal and not merely a snack. And by placing שכיבה together with אכילה, Scripture indicates that the שכיבה denotes simply remaining in the house — for the duration (שיעור זמן) of אכילה אחת.

48 *But if the priest comes again and looks, and lo! the mark has not spread in the house after the house was replastered, then he must declare the house pure because the mark has healed.*

מח וְאִם־בֹּ֨א יָבֹ֜א הַכֹּהֵ֗ן וְרָאָה֙ וְהִנֵּ֗ה לֹֽא־פָשָׂ֤ה הַנֶּ֙גַע֙ בַּבַּ֔יִת אַחֲרֵ֖י הִטֹּ֣חַ אֶת־הַבָּ֑יִת וְטִהַ֤ר הַכֹּהֵן֙ אֶת־הַבַּ֔יִת כִּ֥י נִרְפָּ֖א הַנָּֽגַע׃

49 *In order to clear the house of sin, he shall take two birds and one piece of cedar wood, scarlet wool and hyssop.*

מט וְלָקַ֛ח לְחַטֵּ֥א אֶת־הַבַּ֖יִת שְׁתֵּ֣י צִפֳּרִ֑ים וְעֵ֣ץ אֶ֔רֶז וּשְׁנִ֥י תוֹלַ֖עַת וְאֵזֹֽב׃

50 *And he shall slaughter the one bird in an earthen vessel over living water.*

נ וְשָׁחַ֖ט אֶת־הַצִּפֹּ֣ר הָאֶחָ֑ת אֶל־כְּלִי־חֶ֖רֶשׂ עַל־מַ֥יִם חַיִּֽים׃

51 *He shall then take the piece of cedar wood, the hyssop and the scarlet wool and the living bird, dip them in the blood of the slaughtered bird and into the living water and sprinkle [it] toward the house seven times.*

נא וְלָקַ֣ח אֶת־עֵֽץ־הָ֠אֶרֶז וְאֶת־הָאֵזֹ֨ב וְאֵ֣ת ׀ שְׁנִ֣י הַתּוֹלַ֗עַת וְאֵת֙ הַצִּפֹּ֣ר הַחַיָּ֔ה וְטָבַ֣ל אֹתָ֗ם בְּדַם֙ הַצִּפֹּ֣ר הַשְּׁחוּטָ֔ה וּבַמַּ֖יִם הַחַיִּ֑ים וְהִזָּ֥ה אֶל־הַבַּ֖יִת שֶׁ֥בַע פְּעָמִֽים׃

Opinions differ as to the prescribed quantity of אכילת פרס (see *Eruvin* 83a). According to ר׳ יוחנן בן ברוקה, it is the quantity of ג׳ ביצים; this view is accepted by the רמב״ם and the רשב״א. According to ר׳ שמעון, however, it is the quantity of ד׳ ביצים; and this view is accepted by רש״י and תוספות. This view is also in accordance with the general rule that טומאת אוכלין בכביצה. See the בית יוסף on טור או״ח 612.

48 **ואם בא יבא וגו׳**. See below.

52 *He shall clear the house of sin with the blood of the bird and with the living water and with the living bird, the piece of cedar wood and the scarlet wool.*	נב וְחִטֵּא אֶת־הַבַּיִת בְּדַם הַצִּפּוֹר וּבַמַּיִם הַחַיִּים וּבַצִּפֹּר הַחַיָּה וּבְעֵץ הָאֶרֶז וּבָאֵזֹב וּבִשְׁנִי הַתּוֹלָעַת׃
53 *And he shall let the living bird fly out of the city into the open field; in this manner he effects atonement for the house, and it becomes pure.*	נג וְשִׁלַּח אֶת־הַצִּפֹּר הַחַיָּה אֶל־מִחוּץ לָעִיר אֶל־פְּנֵי הַשָּׂדֶה וְכִפֶּר עַל־הַבַּיִת וְטָהֵר׃ חמישי

52–53 The ציפרים ritual for a בית המנוגע is the same as for a מצורע, only that in the case of a person the הזיות are made onto the back of the hand (לאחר ידו), whereas in the case of a house they are made on the outer side of the lintel (על השקוף שבבית מבחוץ — *Nega'im* 14:1). In the case of a house, the object of these procedures is וחטא את הבית, וכפר על הבית. The purification from sin and the atonement — clearing away the past and opening a new future — are attained by means of the ציפרים procedures. In the case of a person, this attainment is connected with קרבנות — with אשם חטאת ועולה.

וחטא את הבית וגו': דם הציפור, etc., represents those truths that will free the house from sin *from now onward.* ושלח וגו' וכפר וגו': By contrast, sending the ציפור דרור out of the city to the freedom of the fields buries the unsocial past of the house and gives it the possibility of a pure future.

Let us analyze the laws of נגעי בתים stated in verses 37–57. Scripture discusses only one course of a נגע's development: After the first הסגר, the נגע has spread, פשיון לאחר הסגר ראשון (v. 39). After חליצה קיצה וטיחה and הסגר שני (vv. 40–42), either the נגע has returned, חזר (v. 43), and the house requires נתיצה (v. 45), or it has not returned, לא חזר (v. 48), and the house is declared טהור and requires ציפרים (v. 49ff.).

But this course of events discussed in Scripture presents a whole series of other possibilities. It is possible that instead of spreading, פשיון, the נגע remained unchanged, עמד; or decreased in intensity, כהה, and became a מראה כשרה; or disappeared altogether, הלך לו (or shrank below the minimum size, פחות מכשיעור, of two גריסין — a case that is treated the same as הלך לו).

The possibilities, then, are four: פשה, עמד, כהה, הלך — each of which could occur after הסגר ראשון or after הסגר שני; thus, these four cases become eight. To these must be added the two possibilities mentioned in Scripture, חזר or לא חזר after חליצה וטיחה. Altogether, then, there are ten possibilities, whose laws are set down in ten *halachos*: עשרה בתים הן: (א) הכהה בראשון; (ב) וההולך לו – קולפו והוא טהור; (ג) הכהה בשני; (ד) וההולך לו – קולפו והוא טעון צפרים. הפושה בראשון, חולץ וקוצה וטח ונותן לו שבוע; (ה) חזר – ינתץ; (ו) לא חזר – טעון צפרים. עמד בראשון ופשה בשני, חולץ וקוצה וטח ונותן לו שבוע; (ז) חזר – ינתץ; (ח) לא חזר – טעון צפרים. עמד בזה ובזה, חולץ וקוצה וטח ונותן לו שבוע; (ט) חזר – ינתץ; (י) לא חזר – טעון צפרים (*Negaim* 13.1). Thus, after the first הסגר: כהה או הלך – קולף וטהור. עמד – מסגיר. פשה – חולץ ומסגיר. After the second הסגר: כהה או הלך – קולף וטהור וטעון ציפרים. עמד או פשה – חולץ ומסגיר.

The difference, then, between the first and second הסגר is this: If the נגע has weakened or disappeared after the first הסגר, he scrapes off the site of the נגע, and without ציפרים the house becomes טהור. By contrast, if the נגע has weakened or disappeared after the second הסגר, ציפרים are required. Furthermore, if the נגע has remained unchanged after the first הסגר, it is מוסגר a second time, without חליצה; only if it has spread is חליצה required. By contrast, if the נגע has remained unchanged after the second הסגר, חליצה is required, as in the case of פשה. נתיצה is necessary only if the נגע reappears, חזר, after חליצה.

These *halachos* are alluded to in Scripture. In verse 44, the term פשה is used instead of פרח, even though פשיון is meaningful only after הסגר without חליצה. This is an allusion, then, to a case where פשה לאחר הסגר שני — i.e., where the כהן comes at the end of the first week and finds the נגע unchanged: שבא בסוף שבוע ראשון ומצאו עומד, ובא בסוף שבוע שני ומצאו פשה (for ובא הכהן of v. 44 is after a הסגר שני; see Commentary, v. 43). By גזירה שוה — ושב הכהן (v. 39) ובא הכהן (v. 44), זו היא שיבה זו היא ביאה — we learn: מה שיבה חולץ וקוצה וטח ונותן לו שבוע, אף ביאה חולץ וקוצה וטח ונותן לו שבוע (*Toras Kohanim*). That is, the law of פשיון after the second הסגר (alluded to by the verse ובא הכהן וגו׳) is like the law of פשיון after the first הסגר (which is spelled out in the verse ושב הכהן וגו׳). According to this interpretation, the words ובא הכהן וראה והנה פשה הנגע בבית should be understood as a parenthesis: "(the same applies if the כהן sees, only upon coming the second time, that the נגע has spread in the house)" — i.e., in this case as well, the procedure prescribed in vv. 40–43 must be followed.

Here we have a case of a גזירה שוה that is constructed not from two identical words — e.g., שיבה שיבה — but from two expressions that are identical in their meaning, שיבה and ביאה. In *Yoma* 2b — and in many other places — this case is cited as an example of the extension of the concept of גזירה שוה.

Again in verse 48, through the choice of the expression לא פשה instead of לא פרח, and through the repetition in ואם בא יבא, Scripture alludes to the case of עומד לאחר שתי ביאות — i.e., עומד בראשון ובשני. This halachah is supported by the parallel case in נגעי בגדים.

The laws of נגעי בתים — like the laws of נגעי אדם — have nothing whatsoever to do with sanitary precautions. Rather, the sole purpose of these נגעים is to serve as a warning of God's anger over man's moral failings. This is evident not only from the *halachos* they have in common with all the other נגעים, but also from the *halachos* unique to נגעי בתים.

Thus, first of all, the halachah that נגעי בתים apply only in ארץ ישראל — and even there, only after it has been divided into individual holdings; and they apply only to those buildings that can be defined as private dwellings. This halachah clearly shows that the נגע is not directed at the building per se, but, rather, addresses, as it were, the personality of the building owner. What is afflicted with the נגע is not the house, but the home. The life of the individual as distinct from the life of the community — that is what is represented here by the house, and that is what is afflicted with the נגע. For this reason a mark is regarded as a נגע only if it appears on the walls of the house, בקירות הבית, which close off the house against the outside; and even then, only if the mark appears on the central elements of the house — the stone, wood, and earth; and only on a house that is constructed in the normal manner, i.e., it must be a structure with four walls and must be made neither of brick nor of marble. All these specifications are intended to provide the clarity of definition desirable for any symbol: to divert the mind from all secondary matters and focus it on the one central concept. Here, that concept is the house as man's home, as the place of human domesticity.

Social sins produce נגעים — as a sign of God's anger. Our Sages single out one sin as particularly responsible for the advent of נגעי בתים: the selfishness that keeps a person from acting with kindness and makes him refuse to render services to his fellow man. אשר לו הבית (v. 35) — שמייחד ביתו לו. He acts as though his house were meant exclusively for himself. He follows מדת סדום, the principle of Sodom, conducting human relationships on the basis of strict rights. He says: שלי שלי ושלך שלך, "What I have is mine and what you have is yours" (see *Avos* 5:10). He forgets that to צדק (strict justice) must be added צדקה (charity) — to the exclusiveness of rights must be added the inclusiveness of love. Only thus will the society become a Jewish national society, and will the private existence of each household within it be justified.

In ארץ ישראל, which is the soil of the Torah, נגעים inveigh against such a barren, loveless conception of justice. נגעים begin this protest at the moment when the Land is divided among individual owners, for at that time the individual's right to landed property is sanctioned by the Torah.

In the spirit of these words of our Sages, how profound is the introduction to this section: כי תבאו אל ארץ כנען אשר אני נתן לכם לאחזה ונתתי נגע צרעת בבית ארץ אחזתכם ובא אשר לו הבית והגיד לכהן לאמר כנגע נראה לי בבית! That is to say: When you possess the Land that I have given you, I will send the touch of My finger upon the houses that you own; and he who reserves his house *for himself* will be forced to come to the כהן and say, "It seems to me that the finger of God has touched the house!"

The various possibilities of the נגע's development — remaining unchanged, weakening or spreading; reappearing or not reappearing; until finally the house is either demolished or pronounced pure — resemble those mentioned in the case of נגעים on people. They serve as admonitions and warnings, reprieves and periods of grace, designed to educate the owner of the house and lead him to repentance. The prescribed קליפה which must be performed on even the weakest level — that of כהה והלך לסוף הסגר ראשון — is designed to perpetuate the memory of the נגע-warning.

The blood of the slaughtered bird, together with the "living" water, are sprinkled seven times toward the threshold of the house. These sprinklings are performed with the live bird and with the bundle of cedar wood, hyssop, and scarlet wool. Then the live bird is sent into the free open country. Only after all these procedures does the household regain the right to a private existence in the midst of communal society.

The meaning of these procedures is like their meaning in the case of the מצורע who is readmitted into the social community. They reflect

54 *This is the teaching for all leprous marks and for alopecia.*

נד זֹ֣את הַתּוֹרָ֔ה לְכָל־נֶ֥גַע הַצָּרַ֖עַת וְלַנָּֽתֶק׃

the precondition for a person's future well-being: He must remember that selfishness is a justified motive only for organic life — for all stages of development in the *vegetable* and *animal* world. But *man*'s right to a social existence begins with self-sacrifice, through which he gains eternal life. And in his home, too — in his private life — he must strive with unfailing energy and without selfish motives to reach the moral ideal of devotion to duty. Only then can the walls carry a "roof" upon them; only then can the home life that is enclosed within four walls expect protection from above (cf. מזוזות ומשקוף in the case of קרבן פסח — Commentary, *Shemos* 12:7).

מקום טמא is cast into a אבן המנוגעת .מטמא במגע ומשא וביאה is בית המנוגע outside all the cities of Israel, and everyone avoids that place. Thus, the נגע on the house is transformed into a permanent warning, addressed to every Jew on the soil of the Torah, that he not fall also into unsocial behavior.

Entrance into such a house brings טומאה only to the person, but not to the בגדים שעליו; remaining in the house, שהייה בכדי אכילת פרס, brings טומאה to the person and also to his clothing. For he who enters merely "comes in contact" with the נגע; remaining, however, is an activity, and the whole personality participates. Entering is to remaining as מגע נבילה is to משא נבילה (see Commentary, end of chap. 11). And from the standpoint of the underlying theme of נגעים, entering is to remaining as עמידה בדרך חטאים is to ישיבה במושב ליצים (see *Tehillim* 1:1 and our Commentary there).

54–57 **זאת התורה וגו׳**. The order in which the נגעים are mentioned here can be explained as follows:

כל נגע צרעת and נתק are the two main categories which together include all the נגעים. נגע צרעת is a *positive* change in the color on the surface of things — on a person's skin, on fabric, or on the wall of a house. By contrast, נתק is the one form of נגע that depends on *negative* symptoms; it is consigned to הסגר by hair loss and to החלט by hair loss

55 *For the leprous marks of the garment and for the house.*	נה וּלְצָרַ֥עַת הַבֶּ֖גֶד וְלַבָּֽיִת׃
56 *For the very white and the near-white and for the shiny white [spots].*	נו וְלַשְׂאֵ֥ת וְלַסַּפַּ֖חַת וְלַבֶּהָֽרֶת׃
57 *So as to determine which is the day of impurity and which is the day of purity; this is the teaching with regard to leprosy.*	נז לְהוֹרֹ֕ת בְּי֥וֹם הַטָּמֵ֖א וּבְי֣וֹם הַטָּהֹ֑ר זֹ֥את תּוֹרַ֖ת הַצָּרָֽעַת׃ פ
15 1 God *spoke to Moshe and to Aharon, saying:*	**טו** א וַיְדַבֵּ֣ר יְהֹוָ֔ה אֶל־מֹשֶׁ֥ה וְאֶֽל־אַהֲרֹ֖ן לֵאמֹֽר׃

that is continued — פשיון — and שיער צהוב. See Commentary above, 13:29. Thus, זאת התורה לכל נגע הצרעת ולנתק is a general summation that encompasses all the types of נגעים — those with positive symptoms and those with negative symptoms.

Scripture then states: ולצרעת הבגד ולבית ולשאת וגו׳, listing the נגעים — from last to first — according to the various objects upon which they appear. Just as these נגעים differ in respect to the objects on which they appear, so do they differ in respect to their symptoms and laws. The list starts with בגד and continues with בית and אדם. Now, in this summary of the נגעים laws — from last to first — we would have expected the order to be בית, בגד, and אדם. But the list starts with בגד, as its טהרה is the simplest: ציפרים are not required. טהרת בית מנוגע, however, requires ציפרים וכו׳, and טהרת מצורע requires ציפרים and קרבן.

From the summation זאת התורה וגו׳ we learn further that all the נגעים laws form one unit; and only a כהן who is expert in the laws of all the נגעים is entitled to examine any one of them: כהן שבקי בנגעים אבל לא בנתקים וכו׳ וכו׳ לא יראה את הנגעים עד שיהא בקי בהם ובשמותיהם (*Toras Kohanim*).

ב דַּבְּרוּ אֶל־בְּנֵי יִשְׂרָאֵל וַאֲמַרְתֶּם אֲלֵהֶם אִישׁ אִישׁ כִּי יִהְיֶה זָב מִבְּשָׂרוֹ זוֹבוֹ טָמֵא הוּא:
ג וְזֹאת תִּהְיֶה טֻמְאָתוֹ בְּזוֹבוֹ רָר בְּשָׂרוֹ אֶת־זוֹבוֹ אוֹ־הֶחְתִּים בְּשָׂרוֹ מִזּוֹבוֹ טֻמְאָתוֹ הִוא:

2 *Speak to the Children of Israel and say to them: When any man has a discharge from his organ, his discharge is impure.*

3 *This shall be his state of impurity caused by his discharge — whether his organ runs with his discharge or his organ is closed up by his discharge, in any event, it renders him impure.*

CHAPTER 15

2 **דברו אל בני ישראל**: בני ישראל מטמאין בזיבה ואין עכו״ם מטמאין בזיבה (*Niddah* 34a).

כי יהיה: מן הדיבור ואילך. Even בני ישראל are מיטמאים בזיבה only if the זיבה occurred after these laws were given. A similar halachah exists also in the case of טומאת נגעים (*Toras Kohanim*).

מבשרו: ולא מחמת דבר אחר (*Toras Kohanim*); or as it says in *Kerisos* 8b and elsewhere: ולא מחמת אונסו. The זיבה is מטמאת only if it results from a local organic disorder of the male organ, but not if it is a secondary result of some other illness or bodily effect — e.g., over-eating or drinking, physical exertion, or excitation of the imagination and the like. Thus the halachah: בשבעה דרכים בודקין את הזב עד שלא נזקק לזיבה במאכל ובמשתה ובמשא ובקפיצה בחולי ובמראה ובהרהור (*Zavim* 2:2).

זובו טמא הוא: the discharged substance itself is מטמא במגע ובמשא. Even מגעו is מטמא בגדים, unlike נבילה which is מטמא בגדים only במשא but not במגע — i.e., חשוכי בגדים במגע (see *Kelim* 1:2–3; *Niddah* 55b).

3 **טמאתו בזובו**: טומאתו בזובו תלויה ואינה תלויה בימים. The טומאה depends solely on the ראיות (incidences) of the discharge. Two or three ראיות — even on the same day — add to the טומאה (see below and v. 13). In the case of זבה (v. 25), however, only separate ראיות on separate and consecutive days add to the טומאה (*Toras Kohanim*).

4 *Any bed on which a man who had a discharge reclines becomes impure, and any object on which he sits becomes impure.*	ד כָּל־הַמִּשְׁכָּב אֲשֶׁר יִשְׁכַּב עָלָיו הַזָּב יִטְמָא וְכָל־הַכְּלִי אֲשֶׁר־יֵשֵׁב עָלָיו יִטְמָא׃

רר בשרו וגו׳: whether the discharge flows and is plentiful — as רִיר (*Shemuel* I, 21:14) — or החתים בשרו וגו׳, the discharge is meager and remains in the orifice of the organ, so that the organ stops itself up with the discharge (see *Toras Kohanim*; רמב״ם הל׳ מחוסרי כפרה, 2:9; but see כסף משנה on הל׳ אבות הטומאות, 5:1). It appears that בשרו is the subject of רר בשרו את זובו, and apparently is also the subject of החתים; the following בשרו, however, is an object: the organ stops itself up with the discharge.

זב is mentioned twice in verse 2, and of this it says זב, זובו: טמא הוא. זוב is mentioned three times in verse 3, and of this it says טמא הוא. בזובו, את זובו, מזובו טומאתו היא: טומאתו היא. This is used as a support for the halachah (*Megillah* 8a) that טומאת זב is complete as regards מגע ומשא ומשכב ומושב ז׳ נקיים וביאת מים חיים after two ראיות, but the obligation of bringing the offerings mentioned in verse 14 takes effect only after three ראיות: מנה הכתוב שתים וקרא טמא, שלש וקרא טמא, הא כיצד שתים לטומאה ושלש לקרבן. A single ראייה leads only to a status like that described in verse 16 (see *Zavim* 1:1).

4 **כל המשכב אשר ישכב עליו וגו׳ וכל הכלי אשר ישב עליו וגו׳**. Not every object on which a זב has reclined or sat contracts the טומאה discussed here; rather, only an object that is *fit* for reclining or sitting, ראוי, and that is *designated* for such use, מיוחד לכך. Hence, it does not say here משכב אשר שכב, כלי אשר ישב, but אשר ישכב עליו, אשר ישב עליו — i.e., that is intended for such use. This excludes the case of כפה סאה וישב עליו וכו׳, where he overturns a measuring barrel or the like and sits on it, as such an object is intended for a different use. The proof that an object is intended for a different use is that, when the object is needed, he will be told: עמוד ונעשה מלאכתנו, "Get up, so that we may do our work with it" (*Toras Kohanim*; *Shabbos* 59a).

On the other hand, משכב and מושב are given here merely as examples. They include all vessels that are intended to be used by man as a support — whether for standing, sitting, reclining, hanging, or leaning: עומד

5 *Whoever touches his bed shall wash his garments and bathe in water and will remain impure until evening.*

ה וְאִ֕ישׁ אֲשֶׁ֥ר יִגַּ֖ע בְּמִשְׁכָּב֑וֹ יְכַבֵּ֧ס בְּגָדָ֛יו וְרָחַ֥ץ בַּמַּ֖יִם וְטָמֵ֥א עַד־הָעָֽרֶב׃

יושב שוכב נתלה נשען. Such vessels are rendered טמאים by the זב in any of these positions — i.e., even in the case of שוכב על המושב ,יושב על המשכב, etc. The term that includes all the vessels that are intended to support the body in these various positions is מדרס (see *Zavim* 2:4 and the רמב״ם's commentary there). However, a vessel is not susceptible to טומאת מדרס unless it is designed to support the body at rest, עשויה להנאת מדרס. This excludes a ladder, סולם, whose rungs are designed to support the body in motion, לירד בו ולעלות (תוספות, *Menachos* 31a, ד״ה שידה).

It is not necessary that the זב touch the article directly. Rather, a vessel that is susceptible to טומאת מדרס becomes טמא as soon as the זב's body rests on it, even if other כלים interpose between the vessel and the זב. This is so even if what interposes is a large, heavy stone, and the weight of the זב upon the vessel is negligible, considering the weight of the stone. This last case is called אבן מסמא (רמב״ם הל׳ מטמאי משכב ומושב, 6:5; כסף משנה, there; תוספות, *Niddah* 55a, ד״ה אבן).

The ר״ש on *Kelim* 1:3 defines the law of אבן מסמא as משא בלי היסט: the mere passive bearing of an object, without moving it, even if objects not susceptible to טומאה interpose between bearer and object borne. This is in contrast with all other טומאות, in which משא is identical with היסט (see Commentary above, 11:24–25).

The term אבן מסמא is explained (*Niddah* 69b) on the basis of the Scriptural phrase: וְשֻׂמַת עַל-פֻּם גֻּבָּא (*Daniyel* 6:18). The phrase refers to a large stone that can be moved only with great difficulty.

כלי אבנים ,כלי גללים ,כלי אדמה , as well as כלים made of marine materials or of bird bones are not susceptible to טומאת מדרס, just as they are not susceptible to other טומאות (see Commentary above, 11:32). However, כלי חרס, too, are excluded from טומאת מדרס (see *Shabbos* 84a).

5 **ואיש אשר יגע וגו׳.** משכב ומושב become אב הטומאה; they are מטמאים אדם במגע וכלים במגע ואדם במשא. And when they impart טומאה to אדם — even במגע — also בגדים שעליו become טמאים. That is to say, any כלים — except כלי

6 *One who sits on an object on which a man who had a discharge sat shall wash his garments and bathe in water and will remain impure until evening.*

ו וְהַיֹּשֵׁב֙ עַל־הַכְּלִ֔י אֲשֶׁר־יֵשֵׁ֥ב
עָלָ֖יו הַזָּ֑ב יְכַבֵּ֧ס בְּגָדָ֛יו וְרָחַ֥ץ
בַּמַּ֖יִם וְטָמֵ֥א עַד־הָעָֽרֶב׃

7 *One who touches the body of a man who had a discharge shall wash his garments and bathe in water and will remain impure until evening.*

ז וְהַנֹּגֵ֖עַ בִּבְשַׂ֣ר הַזָּ֑ב יְכַבֵּ֧ס בְּגָדָ֛יו
וְרָחַ֥ץ בַּמַּ֖יִם וְטָמֵ֥א עַד־הָעָֽרֶב׃

חרס — with which the person is in contact בשעת מגעו become ראשון לטומאה (cf. Commentary above, 11:24–25, vis-à-vis נבילה).

6 **והישב על הכלי**. We have seen (Commentary, v. 4) that a כלי מדרס becomes טמא not only by direct contact with the זב, but by simply being under the weight of the זב's body. Now, in the same way that such a כלי becomes טמא, so does it impart טומאה to a טהור person: not only by direct contact with the טהור person, but as soon as the weight of the person's body rests above the כלי — whether he is עומד, יושב, שוכב, נתלה, or נשען, even if many articles interpose between the כלי and the person, and even if he is upon an אבן מסמא: **עשרה מושבות זה על גבי זה ואפילו על גבי אבן מסמא** (*Toras Kohanim*).

7 **והנגע בבשר וגו'**: only one who touches his body, but not one who touches what is connected to his body — e.g., his ornaments and clothing. These are merely ראשון לטומאה, and אדם וכלים are מקבלים טומאה only from אב הטומאה. On the other hand, if the clothes are טמאי מדרס — e.g., the זב sat, reclined, or stood on them — they, too, impart טומאה to the one who touches them.

זב is more חמור than נבילה in that even מגעו — as stated earlier (Commentary, v. 5) — is מטמא בגדים שעליו.

8 *And even if a man who had a discharge spits on a person who is pure, that person shall wash his garments and bathe in water and will remain impure until evening.*

ח וְכִי־יָרֹק הַזָּב בַּטָּהוֹר וְכִבֶּס בְּגָדָיו וְרָחַץ בַּמַּיִם וְטָמֵא עַד־הָעָרֶב׃

9 *Any riding equipment on which a man who had a discharge rides becomes impure.*

ט וְכָל־הַמֶּרְכָּב אֲשֶׁר יִרְכַּב עָלָיו הַזָּב יִטְמָא׃

10 *And whoever touches anything that is under [the man who had*

י וְכָל־הַנֹּגֵעַ בְּכֹל אֲשֶׁר יִהְיֶה

8 **וכי ירק הזב וגו'**. רוקו and also כיחו וניעו ומי האף שלו are אב הטומאה, akin to זובו and the like (v. 2), and are מטמאים במגע ומשא (*Niddah* 55b). They are included in the general category of משקין של זב. Some of these משקין, e.g., זיעה (perspiration) and the like, are טהורים; others, e.g., דמעת עינו (tears) and the like, are not אב הטומאה. Those משקין של זב that are מטמאים טומאה חמורה are also called מעיינות הזב. Their defining characteristic is that, like spittle, they gather and then discharge, and when not discharged they can be retained: מתעגל ויוצא וחוזר ונבלע (ibid. 56a).

9 **וכל המרכב**. מרכב is equipment by which the body is held during riding, whereas the saddle itself is a מושב. So it says in *Eruvin* 27a: האוכף טמא מושב והתפוס טמא מרכב. *Kelim* 23:2 lists various parts of riding equipment — for riding camels and horses — which are accorded the status of מרכב.

On the other hand, the ברייתא דרבי ישמעאל on בנין אב מכתוב אחד explains the difference between מרכב and מושב as follows: משכב ומושב are עשויין לנוח אדם בלבד, intended only to bear people. מרכב, however, is עשוי לסבלן אחר, which, according to the ראב"ד, means: designated *also* for other burdens, פעמים לרכיבה פעמים למשא בשעה שאין שם רכיבה. It is difficult to reconcile these two explanations.

10 **וכל הנגע וגו'**. בכל אשר יהיה תחתיו refers to the מרכב mentioned in the previous verse. Through מגע it is מטמא only אדם, but not בגדים שעליו or

תַּחְתָּ֖יו יִטְמָ֣א עַד־הָעָ֑רֶב וְהַנּוֹשֵׂ֣א
אוֹתָ֗ם יְכַבֵּ֧ס בְּגָדָ֛יו וְרָחַ֥ץ בַּמַּ֖יִם
וְטָמֵ֥א עַד־הָעָֽרֶב׃
יא וְכֹ֨ל אֲשֶׁ֤ר יִגַּע־בּוֹ֙ הַזָּ֔ב וְיָדָ֖יו לֹא־

the discharge] will become impure until evening. But one who carries them shall wash his garments and bathe in water and will remain impure until evening.

11 *And whoever the man who had the discharge touches, when [the man] has not [yet] immersed his*

כלים שנוגע בהם בחיבורין. Therein lies the difference between מרכב and משכב ומושב. Of the נוגע במרכב it says here only that יטמא עד הערב — without כיבוס בגדים.

והנושא אותם וגו׳. By contrast, he who carries one of things mentioned above (they are all included in the word אותם: מרכב, מעינות, זב, מושב, and משכב) יכבס בגדיו וגו׳. So we learn in the Mishnah (*Kelim* 23:3): מה בין מרכב למושב? מרכב חלק מגעו ממשאו, ומושב לא חלק מגעו ממשאו.

The Gemara in *Niddah* 32b–33a derives from the words וכל הנגע בכל אשר יהיה תחתיו another law — namely, עליונו של זב. This law relates to an object that rests upon a זב, who is תחתיו — i.e., the זב is under it without necessarily touching it. עליונו של זב is ראשון לטומאה and is מטמא only אוכלין ומשקין, but not אדם וכלים. Therein lies the difference between עליונו של זב and תחתונו, which is אב הטומאה. This lesser טומאה of עליונו של זב is termed מדף — as in the Scriptural phrase קול עלה נדף (below, 26:36) — to indicate its weaker character (*Zavim* 4:6; *Niddah* 4b).

It is difficult to reconcile these two explanations (in מס׳ כלים and מס׳ נדה) of the word תחתיו (see תוספות, *Niddah* 32b, ד״ה עליונו). On this basis the כסף משנה (on הל׳ מטמאי משכב ומושב, 6:3) explains the רמב״ם's view that עליונו של זב — טומאת מדף — is only דרבנן. According to the ראב״ד, however, it is דאורייתא (ibid.); and the common statement that בועל נדה מטמא משכב תחתון כעליון (see Commentary below, v. 24) supports his view.

11 **וכל אשר יגע בו הזב וגו׳**. It has already been stated (vv. 5–8, 10) that the זב — and any object or person that has become טמא through a זב — can become טהור only through total immersion: ורחץ במים וגו׳. And of the זב in particular it is said that he can become טהור only by im-

mersing his entire body in living waters: ורחץ בשרו במים חיים וטהר (below, v. 13).

Hence, it is impossible to say that, according to our verse, he can become טהור merely by rinsing his hands — as implied by the words: וידיו לא שטף במים. Rather, שטיפת ידיו במים expresses only the effect of the immersion of the whole body — with respect to the hands, which are immersed with it. The immersion of the entire body removes the טומאה from the hands, too. It "washes away" the טומאה that comes to the hands via the טומאה of the whole body.

Why, though, does Scripture note, here, that the hands in particular are affected by טומאה, and require שטיפה for their purification? Why — precisely in the case of זב — does Scripture say that the טומאה of the hands comes to them via the טומאה of the whole body? And why does Scripture use the same term (שטף) in two adjacent verses: in regard to טומאה of the זב's hands (v. 11), and in regard to vessels that have been rendered טמא by him and that are able to be purified through טבילה (v. 12)?

It appears that the reasons are to be found in the Halachah and in the unique concept of טומאת הזב.

The Halachah says (*Niddah* 43a): וכל אשר יגע בו הזב וידיו לא שטף במים – זהו הסיטו של זב. That is to say, Scripture here is not discussing mere contact with the זב, which was already discussed above: והנגע בבשר הזב וגו׳ (v. 7). Rather, Scripture is discussing the *moving* of another person *by* the זב — the unique case of הסיטו של זב — שלא מצינו לו טומאה בכל התורה כולה (*Niddah* 43a); or, in the words of *Shabbos* 83b: שלא מצינו לו חבר בכל התורה כולה. For in all the other טומאות, היסט means the movement of the טומאה by the טהור. Previously, we have seen that this היסט is a secondary concept of משא, or, more precisely, is identical with it (see Commentary above, 11:24–25). It is not the body which comes in contact with the טומאה — as in טומאת מגע — but the person's power and activity; hence, the טומאה extends to the whole personality, and to כלים בחיבורין. But nowhere do we find that the טהור who is moved by the טומאה is rendered טמא by such היסט. That is true only of the זב — and of the נדה, זבה, and יולדת, who are similar to him.

Scripture, then, is speaking here of the power and activity which the זב brings to bear on a person or object. Thus, we understand why Scripture emphasizes here the ידים in particular, the limbs that are designed especially for the activity of moving things [and we also under-

hands in water, shall wash his garments and bathe in water and will remain impure until evening.	שָׁטַף בַּמַּיִם וְכִבֶּס בְּגָדָיו וְרָחַץ בַּמַּיִם וְטָמֵא עַד־הָעָרֶב׃
12 *An earthen vessel that the man who had the discharge touches shall be broken, and any wooden vessel shall be rinsed in water.*	יב וּכְלִי־חֶרֶשׂ אֲשֶׁר־יִגַּע־בּוֹ הַזָּב יִשָּׁבֵר וְכָל־כְּלִי־עֵץ יִשָּׁטֵף בַּמָּיִם׃

stand the connection between verses 11 and 12 as indicated by the use of the term שטף].

Later (Commentary, v. 33), we will attempt to grasp the meaning of טומאת הזב and those similar to him. We will see, then, that the idea of this טומאה relates not to human activity, to active man — like the idea of טומאת מצורע — but to the passive, physical aspect of man's personality. Conceptually, ידים (active man) are the antithesis to משכב ומושב (passive man). Hence, it is highly significant that טומאת ידים of the זב is described here as secondary טומאה, which comes to the hands via the טומאה of the whole body. A profound truth is expressed here: When טומאת הזב afflicts the passive aspect of physical man, it inevitably afflicts also the aspect of active man, which is represented by the ידים (see below).

The Halachah, however, continues (*Niddah* 43a): ואפקיה רחמנא בלשון נגיעה למימרא דהיסט ונגיעה כידיו, מה התם מאבראי אף הכא מאבראי. That is to say, הסיטו של זב is not called here משא — as it is called in the case of all the other טומאות; rather, Scripture calls it נגיעה and juxtaposes it to ידיו. From this we learn a halachah unique to this היסט: All היסט caused by a טהור is מטמא even if the היסט is done בבית הסתרים (unlike מגע). Hence, הנושא נבילה בקומטו טמא. הסיטו של זב, however, like his מגע, is restricted to his external body — such as ידיו (see ibid. 42b–43a).

12 וכלי חרש אשר יגע בו הזב וגו׳. Previously (11:33), it was stated that כלי חרס is מקבל טומאה only מאוירו. הסיטו של זב is the single case where כלי חרס becomes טמא also through its outer surface. That is why it does not say here בתוכו, but בו. For the נגיעה stated here, too, is היסט — like the נגיעה in the preceding verse (see *Toras Kohanim*).

יג וְכִֽי־יִטְהַ֤ר הַזָּב֙ מִזּוֹב֔וֹ וְסָ֨פַר ל֜וֹ שִׁבְעַ֥ת יָמִ֛ים לְטָהֳרָת֖וֹ וְכִבֶּ֣ס בְּגָדָ֑יו וְרָחַ֧ץ בְּשָׂר֛וֹ בְּמַ֥יִם חַיִּ֖ים וְטָהֵֽר׃

13 *And when the man who had the discharge is purified from his discharge, he shall count for himself seven days for his purification, and wash his garments. He shall bathe his body in living water and become pure.*

ישבר. See Commentary above, 11:33.

ישטף במים — like יכבס בגדיו — denotes טבילה.

13 **וכי יטהר הזב**. We mentioned earlier (Commentary, v. 3) that two ראיות complete the טומאה as regards ספירת ז׳ נקיים and טבילת מים חיים, but the obligation of bringing an offering applies only after three ראיות. As the Mishnah (*Megillah* 8a) states: אין בין זב הרואה שתי ראיות לרואה שלש אלא קרבן. Thus, the ספירת ז׳ נקיים and the טבילה במים חיים that are prescribed here apply even after two ראיות.

שבעת ימים לטהרתו. לטהרתו – שתהא טהרתו אחת (*Toras Kohanim*). The seven days of purification must form one unbroken period. He does not become טהור unless he counts seven consecutive clean days. A single טומאה-recurrence, even on the seventh day — even after the טבילה — nullifies the whole count retroactively (סותר למפרע), and he must start a new count of seven clean days. The same is said in verse 28 regarding ספירת שבעה נקיים of the זבה: ואחר תטהר – אחר אחר לכולן שלא תהא טומאה מפסקת ביניהן (*Niddah* 68b).

There is only one exception to this rule, and that is the case of היסט כלי חרס (v. 12), which applies only to a זב. In this case a טומאה-recurrence on the seventh day — after the טבילה — does not nullify the count *retroactively*: a כלי חרס שהיסט בין טבילה לראיה remains טהור (see *Megillah* 8b and רש״י ד״ה אלא).

וכבס בגדיו ורחץ בשרו במים: הקיש כיבוס בגדיו לרחיצת בשרו — both must be done בנקיות. All foreign matter must be removed before the טבילה, and the law of חציצה applies also to טבילת כלים (*Toras Kohanim*; see Commentary below, v. 16).

14 *On the eighth day he shall take for himself two turtledoves or two young doves, come before God to the entrance of the Tent of Appointed Meeting, and give them to the priest.*	יד וּבַיּ֣וֹם הַשְּׁמִינִ֗י יִֽקַּח־לוֹ֙ שְׁתֵּ֣י תֹרִ֔ים א֥וֹ שְׁנֵ֖י בְּנֵ֣י יוֹנָ֑ה וּבָ֣א ׀ לִפְנֵ֣י יְהוָ֗ה אֶל־פֶּ֙תַח֙ אֹ֣הֶל מוֹעֵ֔ד וּנְתָנָ֖ם אֶל־הַכֹּהֵֽן׃
15 *The priest offers them, one as an offering that clears of sin, the*	טו וְעָשָׂ֤ה אֹתָם֙ הַכֹּהֵ֔ן אֶחָ֣ד חַטָּ֔את

במים חיים. Among all the טמאים, זב is the only one who requires טבילה in מים חיים. For all the other טמאים — and even for כליו של זב — מי מקוה suffices (see *Toras Kohanim*; see Commentary above, 11:36).

וטהר. As we have noted, טבילה on the seventh day purifies the זב absolutely only as regards היסט כלי חרס. Otherwise, his purification depends on the seventh day remaining clean until nightfall.

14 **לפני ה׳ אל פתח אהל מועד**: in the Nikanor Gateway, as in the case of מצורע (see Commentary above, 14:11). שער ניקנור, which is the border between the עזרת נשים and the עזרת ישראל, is still part of מחנה לויה. For מחנה לויה begins at הר הבית and extends to עזרת ישראל, whereas מחנה שכינה begins at עזרת ישראל. See Commentary, *Bemidbar* 5:2–3.

Now, just as the מצורע is excluded even from מחנה ישראל, the זב וזבה are not allowed to enter מחנה לויה. It is not resolved whether מן התורה a טבול יום דזב is like a זב in this respect (see *Nazir* 44b, תוספות, there and *Zevachim* 32b; see also כסף משנה on הל׳ ביאת מקדש, 3:9, regarding מחוסר כפורים במחנה שכינה). If טבול יום דזב אסור מן התורה במחנה לויה, then the זב of whom our verse speaks, who stands in מחנה לויה, must have immersed on the seventh day before הערב שמש, so that with הערב שמש he ceased being a טבול יום.

15 **ועשה אתם הכהן אחד חטאת וגו׳**. These pairs of doves are called קינין, and each single dove of such a קן is called a פרידה.

Here (vv. 14–15) it says: יקח לו וגו׳ ונתנם אל הכהן ועשה אתם הכהן וגו׳; he gives the pair, as one, סתומין, to the כהן, and only at the time of the offering does the כהן determine which one is a חטאת and which is an *other as an ascent offering, and the priest will [thus] effect atonement for him, before* God, *for his discharge.*

וְהָאֶחָד עֹלָה וְכִפֶּר עָלָיו הַכֹּהֵן לִפְנֵי יְהוָה מִזּוֹבוֹ׃ ס ששי (שביעי כשהן מחוברין)

16 *And if a man has a discharge of semen, he shall bathe his whole body in the water and will remain impure until evening.*

טז וְאִישׁ כִּי־תֵצֵא מִמֶּנּוּ שִׁכְבַת־זָרַע וְרָחַץ בַּמַּיִם אֶת־כָּל־בְּשָׂרוֹ וְטָמֵא עַד־הָעָרֶב׃

עולה. Above (12:8), at the similar offering of the יולדת, it says: ולקחה שתי תרים וגו׳ אחד לעלה ואחד לחטאת וכפר וגו׳; the offerer, from the outset, takes one for an עולה and the other for a חטאת. Accordingly, the כהן receives them when they are מפורשין — i.e., when the designation of each one has already been determined; and he must offer them according to this designation. Thus, the halachah: אין הקינין מתפרשות אלא אי בלקיחת בעלים אי בעשיית כהן (*Nazir* 26b). The פרידות of the קן receive their designation in one of two ways only: through the owner, at the time of their selection; or through the כהן, at the time of the offering.

16 **ורחץ במים את כל בשרו**: שלא יהא דבר חוצץ בין בשרו למים (*Pesachim* 109a). His whole body must come in direct contact with the water; there should be nothing interposing between his flesh and the water.

במים: במי מקוה (ibid.). It does not say בְּמַיִם, "in water," but בַּמַּיִם, "in *the* water," in water that is in its natural, elemental state — מחוברין, not שאובין.

את כל בשרו: מים שכל גופו עולה בהן, "enough water to allow for the immersion of his entire body at one time." וכמה הן? אמה על אמה ברום שלש אמות, "And how much water is that? One cubit square by three cubits deep." ושיערו חכמים שיעור מי מקוה ארבעים סאה, the minimum amount of water in a valid mikveh is forty סאה (ibid. 109a–b; see Commentary above, 11:36).

את כל בשרו: את הטפל לבשרו וזהו שער (*Eruvin* 4b). The amplificatory word את (see Commentary, *Bereshis* 1:1) signals that "body" is to be taken in

יז וְכָל־בֶּגֶד וְכָל־עוֹר אֲשֶׁר־יִהְיֶה עָלָיו שִׁכְבַת־זָרַע וְכֻבַּס בַּמַּיִם וְטָמֵא עַד־הָעָרֶב׃

17 *And any garment or any hide that has semen on it shall be washed in water and will remain impure until evening.*

יח וְאִשָּׁה אֲשֶׁר יִשְׁכַּב אִישׁ אֹתָהּ שִׁכְבַת־זָרַע וְרָחֲצוּ בַמַּיִם וְטָמְאוּ עַד־הָעָרֶב׃ פ

18 *And a woman with whom a man has seminal relations — they shall [both] bathe in the water and will remain impure until evening.*

יט וְאִשָּׁה כִּי־תִהְיֶה זָבָה דָּם יִהְיֶה זֹבָהּ בִּבְשָׂרָהּ שִׁבְעַת יָמִים תִּהְיֶה בְנִדָּתָהּ וְכָל־הַנֹּגֵעַ בָּהּ יִטְמָא עַד־הָעָרֶב׃

19 *And if a woman has a flow, and her flow in her body is blood, she shall remain in her state of separation for seven days, and whoever touches her will become impure until evening.*

---

its widest sense — including the hair. The hair, too, must be completely immersed in the water, together with the body, and must have nothing חוצץ on it.

19 **בבשרה**. Here it does not say מבשרה, as it says מבשרו in verse 2. Hence, מחמת אונס is not excluded (see *Niddah* 36b; cf. Commentary, v. 2).

שבעת ימים תהיה בנדתה. In *Pesachim* 90b, these words are interpreted as follows: כל חייבי טבילות טבילתן ביום, נדה ויולדת טבילתן בלילה, דתניא יכול תהא טובלת מבעוד יום, תלמוד לומר שבעת ימים תהיה בנדתה, תהא בנדתה כל שבעה. She immerses only after the seven days have passed — on the night that follows them.

יטמא עד הערב: he is ראשון and not אב, the same as הנוגע בזב. And, like הנוגע בזב, he requires כיבוס בגדים; for even of הנוגע במשכבה it says (v. 21): יכבס בגדיו (see *Toras Kohanim*).

20 *Anything on which she reclines during her separation period becomes impure, and anything on which she sits becomes impure.*

כ וְכֹל֩ אֲשֶׁ֨ר תִּשְׁכַּ֥ב עָלָ֛יו בְּנִדָּתָ֖הּ
יִטְמָ֑א וְכֹ֛ל אֲשֶׁר־תֵּשֵׁ֥ב עָלָ֖יו
יִטְמָֽא׃

21 *Whoever touches her bed shall wash his garments and bathe in water and will remain impure until evening.*

כא וְכָל־הַנֹּגֵ֖עַ בְּמִשְׁכָּבָ֑הּ יְכַבֵּ֥ס בְּגָדָ֛יו
וְרָחַ֥ץ בַּמַּ֖יִם וְטָמֵ֥א עַד־הָעָֽרֶב׃

22 *Whoever touches any article on which she sits shall wash his garments and bathe in water and will remain impure until evening.*

כב וְכָל־הַנֹּגֵ֔עַ בְּכָל־כְּלִ֖י אֲשֶׁר־תֵּשֵׁ֣ב
עָלָ֑יו יְכַבֵּ֥ס בְּגָדָ֛יו וְרָחַ֥ץ בַּמַּ֖יִם
וְטָמֵ֥א עַד־הָעָֽרֶב׃

23 *And so, too, if he is on the bed or on the article on which she sits, if he only touches it, he becomes impure until evening.*

כג וְאִ֨ם עַֽל־הַמִּשְׁכָּ֜ב ה֗וּא א֛וֹ עַֽל־
הַכְּלִ֛י אֲשֶׁר־הִ֥וא יֹשֶֽׁבֶת־עָלָ֖יו
בְּנָגְעוֹ־ב֑וֹ יִטְמָ֖א עַד־הָעָֽרֶב׃

20–23 As regards טומאת משכב ומושב ומרכב והיסט ומעיינות — the law of נדה and זבה is like the law of זב.

ואם על המשכב הוא. In interpreting this verse (23) we encounter many difficulties. From the accentuation it appears that we are dealing with a case of נוגע במשכבה או במושבה; and this נוגע is טמא — according to what is stated here — only if הוא ישבת עליו בנגעו בו. However, it is clear from verses 20–22 that הנוגע במשכבה ובמושבה is טמא in all cases, even if the נדה is not on the משכב or מושב when he touches it; it is sufficient that the כלי is מיוחד לשכיבה או לישיבה, and she had used it as a support for her body while having the status of נדה — all as in the case of זב. Furthermore, in verses 20–22 it is stated that הנוגע במשכבה ובמושבה requires כיבוס בגדים, and yet here (v. 23) כיבוס בגדים is not mentioned. At any rate, the *halachos* of מגע משכבה have already been elaborated sufficiently in verses 20–22; hence, the words ואם על המשכב הוא must deal with a new case, which does not entail נגיעה במשכב.

Indeed, the *Toras Kohanim* to our verse says: The words ואם על המשכב

הוא refer to a case where the weight of the טהור person's body is above the underlying משכב or מושב. It is the case discussed in verse 6 in connection with a זב, i.e., a טהור who is supported above a משכב becomes טמא, even if he does not touch it in any way, even if many spreads interpose between them, and even if he is upon an אבן מסמא (see Commentary, v. 6). Here, an additional halachah is indicated by the word הוא. The טהור person becomes טמא, only if the whole weight of his body — or at least the greater part of it, which is considered the same as the whole (רובו ככולו) — rests above the משכב or מושב. The same applies to a זב who is supported above a משכב or מושב; he, too, is מטמא the משכב or מושב only on this condition: עד שינשא רובו עליו (*Toras Kohanim*).

Based on this *Toras Kohanim* and the following Gemara in *Pesachim* we can arrive at an interpretation of our verse that solves the difficulties.

The Gemara in *Pesachim* 3a teaches: תנא דבי רבי ישמעאל לעולם יספר אדם בלשון נקיה, שהרי בזב קראו מרכב ובאשה קראו מושב. "One should always use the cleanest possible expressions; for we find that the Torah uses the term מרכב when speaking of a זב, but changes it to מושב when speaking of a woman." According to רש״י (*Pesachim* 3a), the מרכב of a woman is derived in our verse from the entire expression על הכלי אשר הִוא יושבת עליו. This is unlike the view of תוספות (ibid.), based on *Toras Kohanim*, that the מרכב of a woman is derived only from the words על הכלי.

To the foregoing let us add (as noted above, on v. 10) that the difference between מרכב and מושב is this: Only in the case of מרכב do we say that חלוק מגעו ממשאו, i.e., he who carries the מרכב is טמא and requires כיבוס בגדים, whereas he who touches it is merely טמא עד הערב.

In light of the above it appears that the entire phrase הכלי אשר הִוא יושבת עליו בנגעו בו יטמא עד הערב is another way of saying מרכב: a כלי on which she sits, and which renders the one who touches it merely טמא until the evening — with no obligation of כיבוס בגדים. The added words יטמא עד הערב resolve the difficulty raised by תוספות (ibid.).

Thus, our verse is a continuation of the preceding verse. Verse 22 says that הנוגע במשכב ובמושב requires כיבוס בגדים. And verse 23 adds: The same applies if the weight of his body rests upon a משכב — or even upon a מרכב, even though הנוגע במרכב merely becomes טמא until the evening and does not require כיבוס בגדים.

The accent on the word בו, however, does not fit in with this interpretation.

כד וְאִ֨ם שָׁכֹ֜ב יִשְׁכַּ֥ב אִ֗ישׁ אֹתָהּ֙ וּתְהִ֤י
נִדָּתָהּ֙ עָלָ֔יו וְטָמֵ֖א שִׁבְעַ֣ת יָמִ֑ים
וְכָל־הַמִּשְׁכָּ֛ב אֲשֶׁר־יִשְׁכַּ֥ב עָלָ֖יו
יִטְמָֽא׃ ס

24 *And if a man cohabits with her, her state of separation comes upon him, and he becomes impure for seven days; any bed on which he reclines will become impure.*

כה וְאִשָּׁ֡ה כִּֽי־יָז֩וּב ז֨וֹב דָּמָ֜הּ יָמִ֣ים
רַבִּ֗ים בְּלֹא֙ עֶת־נִדָּתָ֔הּ א֥וֹ כִֽי־
תָז֖וּב עַל־נִדָּתָ֑הּ כָּל־יְמֵ֞י ז֣וֹב
טֻמְאָתָ֗הּ כִּימֵ֥י נִדָּתָ֛הּ תִּהְיֶ֖ה
טְמֵאָ֥ה הִֽוא׃

25 *And if a woman has a flow of her blood for many days, not within the [regular] period of her separation, or if she has a flow apart from that of her [regular period of] separation, [then] all the days of the flow of her impurity she shall be as during the days of her [regular] separation; she is in a state of impurity.*

24 **ותהי נדתה עליו**. Her state of separation comes upon him; he, too, becomes אב הטומאה like her and is מטמא אדם וכלים. But he is not עולה לרגלה (see *Toras Kohanim*); he does not assume her place in the נדה cycle. For example: If three נדה days had passed, she is טמאה for only four more days. He, however, is טמא שבעת ימים; he remains in a state of טומאה for seven days.

וכל המשכב אשר ישכב עליו יטמא. His משכב, though, contracts only טומאה קלה; it is only ראשון, and is מטמא only אוכלין ומשקין, but not אדם וכלים like יטמא טומאה קלה משמע, נתקו הכתוב מטומאה חמורה והביאו לידי טומאה: משכבו של זב קלה, לומר לך שאינו מטמא אלא אוכלין ומשקין (*Niddah* 33a). The טומאה קלה of the משכב בועל נדה is generally formulated as follows: מטמא משכב תחתון כעליון — i.e., כעליונו של זב, which is also only ראשון (see Commentary above, v. 10).

25 **ואשה כי יזוב זוב דמה וגו׳**. ימים רבים — at least three consecutive days. בלא עת נדתה: סמוך לנדתה — after the seven days of נדה have passed; that is, on the first, second, and third days after the seven days of נדה. או כי תזוב על נדתה: מופלג לנדתה — i.e., one day later (see *Niddah* 73a); that is, on the

26 *Any bed on which she reclines on any day of her [extra] flow shall be for her as the bed on which she reclines during her [regular period of] separation, and any article on which she sits will be impure like the impurity of her [regular period of] separation.*

כו כָּל־הַמִּשְׁכָּב אֲשֶׁר־תִּשְׁכַּב עָלָיו כָּל־יְמֵי זוֹבָהּ כְּמִשְׁכַּב נִדָּתָהּ יִהְיֶה־לָּהּ וְכָל־הַכְּלִי אֲשֶׁר תֵּשֵׁב עָלָיו טָמֵא יִהְיֶה כְּטֻמְאַת נִדָּתָהּ׃

second, third and fourth days after the seven days of נדה. In both of these cases, the halachah stated in verse 28 applies: She must count seven clean days (ז׳ נקיים) and bring a קרבן (v. 29); only then does she regain טהרה.

These days, which begin after the ימי נדה, are called ימי זיבה. In the first case (three ראיות immediately following the ימי נדה), the ימי זיבה last until the tenth day after ימי הנדה; in the second case (three ראיות beginning on the second day after ימי נדה), the ימי זיבה last until the eleventh day. The Halachah (*Niddah* 73a) says as follows: If there were three ראיות on three consecutive days during these י״א יום — even on the ninth, tenth, and eleventh days — she counts ז׳ נקיים and brings a קרבן; and only after ז׳ נקיים have passed can ימי הנדה start again. These eleven days are accordingly called the י״א יום שבין נדה לנדה (ibid. 72b).

כל ימי זוב טמאתה וגו׳. If she does not experience a flow on three consecutive days, she does not require ז׳ נקיים וקרבן. However, if, during these eleven days, she experiences a flow (זוב) even on only one day, or on two consecutive days, then כל ימי זוב טמאתה כימי נדתה תהיה וגו׳: she, too, is טמאה as with טומאת הנדה, with respect to טומאת משכב ומושב and לטמא את בועלה. Although she does not count ז׳ נקיים, she becomes טהורה only after one יום נקי. For this reason she is called שומרת יום כנגד יום.

If she experiences a flow on three consecutive days, she is called זבה גדולה; on one day, or on two consecutive days, she is called זבה קטנה.

The difference, then, between ימי נדה and ימי זיבה is this: During ימי נדה, multiple ראיות do not intensify the טומאה. A single ראיה on one day makes her טמאה for seven days; and many ראיות over many days do not make her liable to ז׳ נקיים and קרבן. During the eleven days that follow, however, she becomes either זבה קטנה or זבה גדולה and is subject to the law

27 *And whoever touches [these objects] will become impure; he shall wash his garments and bathe in water and will remain impure until evening.*

כז וְכָל־הַנֹּגֵעַ בָּם יִטְמָא וְכִבֶּס בְּגָדָיו וְרָחַץ בַּמַּיִם וְטָמֵא עַד־הָעָרֶב׃

28 *And when she is rid of her flow, she shall count for herself seven days, and after that she can be purified.*

כח וְאִם־טָהֲרָה מִזּוֹבָהּ וְסָפְרָה לָּהּ שִׁבְעַת יָמִים וְאַחַר תִּטְהָר׃ שביעי

29 *On the eighth day she shall take for herself two turtledoves or two young doves and bring them to the priest to the entrance of the Tent of Appointed Meeting.*

כט וּבַיּוֹם הַשְּׁמִינִי תִּקַּח־לָהּ שְׁתֵּי תֹרִים אוֹ שְׁנֵי בְּנֵי יוֹנָה וְהֵבִיאָה אוֹתָם אֶל־הַכֹּהֵן אֶל־פֶּתַח אֹהֶל מוֹעֵד׃

30 *The priest shall offer one as an offering that clears of sin and the other as an ascent offering, and [thus] the priest will effect atonement for her before* God *for her flow of impurity.*

ל וְעָשָׂה הַכֹּהֵן אֶת־הָאֶחָד חַטָּאת וְאֶת־הָאֶחָד עֹלָה וְכִפֶּר עָלֶיהָ הַכֹּהֵן לִפְנֵי יְהוָה מִזּוֹב טֻמְאָתָהּ׃ מפטיר

31 *Teach the Children of Israel to*

לא וְהִזַּרְתֶּם אֶת־בְּנֵי־יִשְׂרָאֵל

---

outlined above. (As regards the halachah stated below, 18:19, the universal practice is that she counts ז׳ נקיים in *all* cases: א״ר זירא בנות ישראל החמירו על עצמן שאפילו רואות טפת דם כחרדל יושבות עליה שבעה נקיים [*Niddah* 66a].)

28 **וספרה לה**: לעצמה (*Toras Kohanim*; see *Kesubos* 72a). תוספות in *Gittin* 2b (ד״ה עד אחד) cite this as an example of the law that עד אחד נאמן באיסורין (see Commentary, *Devarim* 17:6).

31 **והזרתם את בני ישראל וגו׳**. From the root נזר derives the term נֵזֶר, a circlet that distinguishes its wearer; a crown. Thus נָזִיר, one who is set

keep far from their impurity, so that they not die through their impurity by defiling My Dwelling Place which is in their midst.	מִטֻּמְאָתָם וְלֹא יָמֻתוּ בְּטֻמְאָתָם בְּטַמְּאָם אֶת־מִשְׁכָּנִי אֲשֶׁר בְּתוֹכָם׃

apart from the people, and who has sanctified himself with priestlike sanctity; see Commentary, *Bemidbar* 6:2. The primary meaning of this root, then, is "keeping far from," "separation" — not just spatially, but a separation that requires moral self-control. Thus הִנָּזֵר (*Zecharyah* 7:3), to fast.

Here, what is required is הינזרות, keeping far, from all טומאה — and especially "מטמאתם," from טומאה that stems from bodily conditions of man himself: טומאה היוצאת עליו מגופו. This הינזרות requires moral self-control. Its purpose — like the purpose of the טומאה laws in general — is the moral freedom that is manifest in self-control. Thus, the choice of this expression (והזרתם) is significant for the separation that is required here.

From a practical standpoint, we are commanded here to "make a fence" for הלכות טומאה. The people must be scrupulous in the careful observance of these *halachos*, by force of self-discipline. The mitzvah of הינזרות as regards the טומאה laws is similar to the duty of שמירה as regards the entire Torah: We are bidden to avoid not only טומאה that is present but also טומאה that is near — in time or place (see *Mo'ed Katan* 5a; *Niddah* 63b).

However, the command to keep far from טומאה is not addressed directly to the people. Scripture does not say here: וינזרו בני ישראל מטומאתם. The command is addressed, instead, to Moshe and Aharon (והזרתם), who are assigned the task of teaching and training the people to avoid all טומאה. For the whole mission of Moshe and Aharon — instilling theoretical knowledge and fostering practical observance — depends on the preservation of טהרה-consciousness. Hence, the reason for this command is given as: ולא ימתו בטמאתם בטמאם את משכני אשר בתוכם.

The observance of each one of the laws of טומאה places each member of the nation — from the first to the last — in relation to God's Dwelling Place (משכן ה'), through which His Presence is revealed. Each of the laws of טומאה says to every member of the nation: God does not dwell only

לב זֹ֣את תּוֹרַ֣ת הַזָּ֑ב וַאֲשֶׁ֨ר תֵּצֵ֥א

32 *This is the teaching with regard to a man who has a discharge and with regard to one who had a*

with "Moshe and Aharon" — with the intellectual and priestly elite. Rather, God dwells בתוך בני ישראל ,בתוכם; and freedom from the bonds of טומאה is the very first duty of *every* individual. For God established His Dwelling Place in the midst of the people, imposing upon them tasks that can be accomplished only on the basis of טהרה — i.e., on the basis of moral freedom.

These tasks do not presume a utopian, superhuman state of being that is not found among earth dwellers. Rather, as Scripture says in the next chapter (16:16): השכן אתם בתוך טמאתם; and as *Toras Kohanim* explains on our verse: בטמאם את משכני אשר בתוכם, אף על פי שהם טמאים שכינה ביניהם. God is aware of man's sensual nature and of all the stimuli that tempt him to give up his moral freedom. And precisely in considering this טומאה aspect of man's nature — and alongside of it (שכן, lit., "a neighbor") — He gave him the Torah, on which His שכינה depends. He did so in order that the Torah, with its blazing, life-giving flame, should awaken in man the Divine aspect that is within him. Through this Divine aspect, man can rule — in sovereignty and freedom — over all sensual compulsion and elevate even his sensual drives, so that he may serve God through them and fulfill His commandments.

Thus, *this* people is given a choice between two alternatives: Either it is trained for טהרה by the Torah and attains eternal life even in this world, or it perishes in its טומאה while violating the idea of purity, in contrast with "God's Dwelling Place, which is in its midst."

Not for naught is the penalty of כרת, pronounced elsewhere (17:16) for טומאת מקדש, expressed here by the term for ordinary מיתה. For, in the case of Israel, the flowering of ordinary earthly life depends on the accomplishment of the moral tasks assigned to Israel in the Sanctuary of the Torah.

32 **הזב**: בעל ראיה אחת. As stated earlier (Commentary, v. 3), his status is like that of a בעל קרי, discussed in verse 16. They both have only טומאת ערב and are not מטמא משכב ומושב.

מִמֶּנּוּ שִׁכְבַת־זֶרַע לְטָמְאָה־בָהּ׃

discharge of semen, by which he becomes impure.

לג וְהַדָּוָה בְּנִדָּתָהּ וְהַזָּב אֶת־זוֹבוֹ
לַזָּכָר וְלַנְּקֵבָה וּלְאִישׁ אֲשֶׁר
יִשְׁכַּב עִם־טְמֵאָה׃ פפפ

33 *With regard to the menstruating woman in her [period of] separation and with regard to one whose discharge flows, whether it be a male or a female, and for the man who cohabits with an impure woman.*

33 **והזב את זובו**. This is טומאת זיבה, which entails טומאת משכב ומושב — like נדה. Nevertheless, this טומאה differs for זכר and נקבה. לזכר: with two ראיות he is מטמא משכב ומושב ובעי ז׳ נקיים וטבילה במים חיים, but he is not liable to a קרבן; with three ראיות he is also liable to a קרבן. לנקבה: if she experiences a flow on one day, or on two consecutive days, she is מטמאת משכב ומושב, but she is merely a שומרת יום כנגד יום; if, however, she experiences a flow on three consecutive days, she counts ז׳ נקיים and brings a קרבן.

The bodily conditions that result in the טומאות discussed in this chapter have this in common: They all relate to the sexual aspect of man's nature and calling. Some of them are normal phenomena — e.g., verses 16, 18, and 19; and some are abnormal, as in verses 2 and 25. Only those who suffer abnormal conditions are מחוסרי כפרה.

As we noted earlier in connection with טומאת יולדת (Commentary, 12:2ff.), precisely the highest and noblest matters on which the whole future of man (and of the State, too) depends — marriage, the home, the family — are based on physiological processes, which are part of the unfree physical side of man. Therefore, it is imperative to bring these matters into the realm of moral freedom. One must beware, in these matters, of false notions that might lead to the denial of man's moral freedom. This concern clearly applies to childbirth, whose physiological nature is apparent; but it applies also to sexual matters in general. And the טומאות that take effect even as a result of normal processes are intended to make us aware that, although physiological compulsion cannot be denied, moral freedom is a fact attested to by the Sanctuary of God's Torah. Only he who acknowledges this freedom and actualizes it even in the sensual aspects of his life may enter the gates of the Sanctuary and draw near to God's holy things.

The abnormal phenomena, however, may attest to sexual sins — or to the need for a special warning against them. These phenomena are similar to נגעים, and their purpose is to warn and admonish. This accounts for the need for כפרה, and for the חטאת ועולת עוף, which permit re-entry into the Sanctuary.

Through חטאת העוף the person vows that, in spite of his recent experience of passively submitting to physical illness, he will pull himself up. With the energy of moral freedom he will *strive to rise upward*; he will try to attain the holiness of all of life, which beckons to him from the height of the altar.

Through עולת העוף he vows that he will elevate the passive, sensual aspect of his being, while *adhering* to the altar heights already attained.

In this light we can understand the different stages of זיבה קטנה and זיבה גדולה — ב׳ ראיות or ג׳ ראיות. These stages apply to the abnormal phenomena of זב וזבה; they correspond to the stages of warning and education in the case of מצורע מוסגר and מוחלט.

What distinguishes these טומאות is טומאת מדרס — משכב ומושב. It is unique to these טומאות. Although מצורע, too, is מטמא משכב ומושב, his משכב ומושב are only ראשון, whereas the משכב ומושב of זב וזבה נדה ויולדת are rendered אב הטומאה; and this very difference clarifies the meaning of these laws. Let us explain:

משכב ומושב are intended to support a person *who rests upon them with the weight of his body*. They represent, then, the passive, bodily aspect of man. Now, the conditions represented by זב וזבה וכו׳ are likewise connected with this sphere of sensual bodiliness. Thus, משכב ומושב של זב replicate, as it were, the זב; they, too, bring to mind the idea of sensual compulsion — like the זב himself. Hence, they become אב הטומאה (see Commentary, end of chap. 11). And when the טהור is supported by the משכב or מושב of the טמא, he, too, is rendered טמא. For, in such a case, this same sensual aspect is impressed upon the טהור.

(The foregoing explains the anomaly of מפץ, which we have already noted [ibid.]. For it appears that מפץ is a mattress designed especially for sleeping; see *Kesubos* 64b and *Bava Metzia* 113b. מפץ, then, represents man who sleeps, who to a great extent is subject to sensory compulsion. Hence, on the one hand, it is fit for משכב ומושב and becomes אב הטומאה. On the other hand, once it becomes טמא it has no טהרה במקוה; in this respect it is similar to אוכלין ומשקין וכלי חרס, and the reason for this halachah — in all these cases — is similar as well; see Commentary, סוף פ׳ שמיני.)

By contrast, the sphere of the מצורע relates to the opposite aspect — that of the active, social personality. Only secondarily, merely as ראשון לטומאה, do משכב and מושב apply also in the case of the מצורע, to teach us that the two spheres — social justice and personal morality — are intimately connected, and that when social justice is neglected, personal morality, as a rule, is endangered also.

But social conscientiousness itself depends to an even greater degree on moral purity. For this reason we find that היסטו של זב — which is mentioned in Scripture in terms of טומאת ידים — is not presented in a secondary way, but with full and equal force (see Commentary, v. 11). And perhaps for this reason we find in the case of זב — and in the case of his משכב and מושב, which represent him — that מגעם is not חלוק ממשאם, unlike the case of נבילה (see Commentary, v. 7). For touching a זב or his representatives (i.e., משכבו ומושבו) brings טומאה to the passive, bodily aspect of man, not to the active force; nevertheless, this טומאה spreads immediately to the whole personality, and even הנוגע בזב ובמשכבו ובמושבו requires כיבוס בגדים וכלים בחיבורין, which as a rule is required only in the case of משא. It appears that מרכב represents the זב to a lesser extent, which would explain why its טומאה is weaker in this regard. רכב does not represent purely passive bodiliness, as do שכב and ישב. However, the actual concept of מרכב has not been clarified sufficiently (see Commentary, v. 9).

The זב, the male in this class of טומאה that stems from abnormal phenomena, is the only טמא whose טהרה requires ביאת מים חיים. Perhaps the male in particular must be reminded of the meaning of purity in his sexual life. He must know that חיים and טהרה spring from one and the same source; that חיים is to be found only בדרך הטהרה — and what is more, that חיים and טהרה are identical; and that only when he is טהור will he be truly alive, חי.

Let us recall our commentary on וידיו לא שטף במים (v. 11): The ידים represent active man, whose purity depends on the morality of the *whole* man. In this light we can understand why our Sages attached to that verse the institution of טהרת הידים (see our discussion of נטילת ידים, at the very end of chap. 11). For this institution conveys the warning about moral purity to the whole of Jewish life. As ר׳ אלעזר בן ערך says in *Toras Kohanim* on that verse: מכאן סמכו חכמים לטהרת ידים מן התורה (see *Chullin* 106a).